Adobe® Acrobat® 6
PDF Bible

Adobe® Acrobat® 6 PDF Bible

Ted Padova

WILEY

Wiley Publishing, Inc.

Adobe® Acrobat® 6 PDF Bible

Published by
Wiley Publishing, Inc.
10475 Crosspoint Boulevard
Indianapolis, IN 46256
www.wiley.com

Copyright © 2003 by Wiley Publishing, Inc., Indianapolis, Indiana

Published by Wiley Publishing, Inc., Indianapolis, Indiana
Published simultaneously in Canada

Library of Congress Control Number: 2003105845

ISBN: 0-7645-4047-5

Manufactured in the United States of America

10 9 8 7 6 5 4 3 2

1O/SU/QZ/QT/IN

For general information on our other products and services or to obtain technical support, please contact our Customer Care Department within the U.S. at (800) 762-2974, outside the U.S. at (317) 572-3993 or fax (317) 572-4002.

Wiley also publishes its books in a variety of electronic formats. Some content that appears in print may not be available in electronic books.

WILEY is a trademark of Wiley Publishing, Inc.

About the Author

Ted Padova is the Chief Executive Officer and Managing Partner of The Image Source Digital Imaging and Photo Finishing Centers of Ventura and Thousand Oaks, California. He has been involved in digital imaging since founding a service bureau in 1990.

Ted has taught university and higher education classes over sixteen years in graphic design applications and digital prepress at the University of California, Santa Barbara and the University of California at Los Angeles. He has been and continues as a conference speaker nationally and internationally at PDF conferences.

Ted has written over a dozen computer books on Adobe Acrobat, Adobe Photoshop, and Adobe Illustrator. Recent books published by John Wiley and Sons include *Creating Adobe Acrobat PDF Forms, Teach Yourself Visually Acrobat 5, Adobe Acrobat 6.0 Complete Course*. He also co-authored *Adobe Illustrator Master Class — Illustrator Illuminated* for Peachpit Press. He is also host of the Total Training video series on Acrobat 6.0.

Credits

Acquisitions Editor
Michael Roney

Project Editor
Cricket Krengel

Technical Editor
Lori DeFurio

Copy Editor
Paula Lowell

Editorial Manager
Rev Mengle

Publisher
Barry Pruett

Permissions Editor
Laura Moss

Media Development Specialist
Travis Silvers

Project Coordinator
Kristie Rees

Graphics and Production Specialists
Beth Brooks
Amanda Carter
Jennifer Click
Joyce Haughey
Michael Kruzil
Lynsey Osborn

Quality Control Technicians
Susan Moritz
Angel Perez
Carl William Pierce

Proofreading
TECHBOOKS Production Services

Indexing
Joan Griffitts

Special Help
Adrienne Porter
Maureen Spears
Beth Taylor

Foreword

Ten years ago Adobe Acrobat 1.0 was publicly introduced at an event in New York City. John Warnock's brilliant yet simple vision for Acrobat was to solve the "document communication problem across operating systems and application environments." That is what Acrobat 1.0 did by introducing the Adobe Portable Document Format (PDF). Today Acrobat 6.0 greatly expands on that core vision and now is a solution for electronic review, approval, archiving, and publishing, supporting both PDF and XML. Ten years have made a big difference, and I'm privileged to have worked on making Acrobat since 1992.

In these 10 years we've seen the advent of the public internet, the replacement of the diskette by the CD-ROM for file sharing, and the adoption of e-mail as the most common form of electronic communication. During this time, more than 10 million copies of Adobe Acrobat have been sold, and over half a billion copies of Adobe Reader have been distributed. Today more than 20 million PDF files are posted on the public internet, PDF has been adopted by virtually every Global 500 company, and more than one and a half billion PDF tax forms have been downloaded from www.irs.gov alone. There are more than 50,000 PDF eBook titles available from about 300 commercial sites, and 35 magazine publishers are publishing 80 different PDF periodicals. Quite an achievement.

Acrobat 6.0 begins a new era in electronic communication. There are now three separate products, each targeted for different uses, to better specifically meet individual needs. In this book you will learn about the different products and their capabilities, guided by Mr. Padova's many years of using, testing, and working with us at Adobe. I hope you enjoy getting to know and use one or more of the Acrobat 6.0 family of products. Let us know what you think.

Sarah Rosenbaum
Director of Product Marketing, Adobe Acrobat
Adobe Systems Incorporated
July 2003

Acknowledgments

I would like to acknowledge some of the people who have contributed in one way or another to make this edition possible. Mike Roney, my Acquisitions Editor at Wiley and Sons; my Project Editor, Cricket Krengel; Copy Editor Paula Lowell; Permissions Editor Laura Moss; and Editorial Manager Rev Mengle; as well as all the Wiley and Sons crew who participated in the project.

A very special thank you to my technical Adobe PDF Evangelist, Lori DeFurio. Because of Lori's comments, suggestions, and assistance, this version of the Acrobat PDF Bible I believe is the best to date. Additionally I want to thank Steve Small and Brian Baxter for their assistance to Lori on the technical edits for the printing and prepress chapter.

Many thanks are extended for the contribution from Sarah Rosenbaum, who took time away from her work at Adobe Systems to write the foreword for the book.

I feel very fortunate in having so much support from many people at Adobe Systems who were continually available for comments, suggestions, and favors over a five-month period of time while Acrobat 6.0 was in development. The energy and enthusiasm of the engineering and marketing teams throughout the development period was evident from a group of people with passion and excitement for their work. Many thanks to:
Dave Stromfeld – Product manager
Rick Brown
Ray Brulotte
Penny Byron
Michael Chen
Christy Dunwoodie
Marc Eaman
Tricia Gellman
Gray Knowlton
Jonathan Knowles
Ron Mendoza
Kaari Peterson
Claudia Vo
Jeff Warnock
Michele Wohl
Christine Yarrow

Much appreciation goes to the people at Total Training Systems for assisting me in providing video work for the CD-ROM and support through a grueling filming series of Acrobat 6.0: Brian Maffitt, Dave Murcott, Darin Andersen, Scott Meinzen, Laura Perrotta, Barbara Ross, and Jenn Regnante.

Another special thank you goes to Jason Woliner who helped me in many ways including providing a sample video for the CD-ROM. Donny Bergthold and Fardad Farhat of DigitArch architects of Thousand Oaks, California, for sharing their AutoCAD files. Barbara Obermeier for her Photoshop album contributions, Tim Sullivan and Gina O'Reilly of activePDF; Carl Young, producer of the PDF Conference; and Dr. Lisle Gates for his golf photo contributions.

Thank yous are extended to my friends at Planet PDF, Karl DeAbrew, Kurt Foss, and Daniel Shea; Johanna Rivard of pdfZone; Jamie Shilliday of textHELP Systems, Ltd.; and Abbie Sommer of StarForce Technologies, Ltd.

Contents at a Glance

Contents

Part II: Converting Documents to PDF   167

Chapter 5: Converting to PDF from Adobe Acrobat 169

Chapter 6: Exporting to PDF from Authoring Applications 223

Part IV: PDF Interactivity   447

Introduction

This book is the third edition of the *Adobe Acrobat PDF Bible*. As a result of many users' feedback, this edition makes an effort to add a little more coverage in some topics missed in the last version or in areas where users asked for more amplification. As you will see by browsing the contents of the book or launching the new version of either Adobe Acrobat Standard or Adobe Acrobat Professional, there are many changes in the program. As such, an effort has been made to cover as much of the new version as is possible in this single, comprehensive book.

What Is Adobe Acrobat?

The reason some people first dismiss the thought of spending any energy on Acrobat is due to a lack of understanding of what Acrobat is and what it does. This, in part, is due to the fact that people jump on the World Wide Web and download the free Adobe Reader software. When acquiring Adobe Reader, many folks think the viewing of PDF documents with Acrobat Reader is the extent of Acrobat. Fortunately, we've come a long way in regard to dismissing the myths related to Acrobat, and many people using computers today realize that there's more to Acrobat than Adobe Acrobat Reader.

Note If you're familiar with the Acrobat family of products, you'll notice immediately the new reference to the Adobe Reader software. The product is still the same Acrobat Reader you used in earlier versions; however, Adobe has rebranded the product and now refers to the free download software as Adobe Reader. Future references to Acrobat Reader in this book shall henceforth be referred to as Adobe Reader.

For those who don't know the difference, I explain in Chapter 2 that Adobe Reader is only one small component of Acrobat. Other programs included in the suite of Acrobat software provide you with tools for creating, editing, viewing, navigating, and searching Portable Document Format (PDF) information.

Acrobat has evolved with many different changes both to the features it offers you and often to the names associated with the various components. In earlier versions of Acrobat names like Acrobat Professional, Acrobat Exchange, and then simply Acrobat were used to refer to the authoring application. Now in version 6.0 of Adobe Acrobat we are introduced to another name change. The high-end performance application is now referred to as Adobe Acrobat Professional. In release 6.0 there is also an Acrobat lighter version with many of the same features found in Acrobat 5.*x* called Adobe Acrobat Standard. This program has all the features you find available in Acrobat Professional with the exception of forms authoring, high-end printing and prepress, and a few minor differences in tools and menu commands. As you follow the pages in this book, you can apply most of what is contained herein to either Acrobat Standard or Acrobat Professional. With the exception of Chapters 25 through 27, where Acrobat PDF forms are covered, and parts of Chapter 23, where commercial printing is discussed, you'll find most of the remaining chapter contents covering topics that can be addressed in either viewer.

Another product you can purchase from Adobe Systems in the Acrobat family is Adobe Acrobat Elements. Elements is a low-cost PDF-creation tool designed for enterprises, and it requires purchasing a site license of a minimum of 1,000 copies. The Adobe Acrobat Reader software remains a free download from Adobe Systems and offers you even more features than found with previous versions of the Acrobat Reader software.

Nomenclature

The official name for the new release of Acrobat is Adobe® Acrobat® Professional. You'll notice the registered marks appearing in the name. For the sake of ease and clarity as you read through the book and see a reference to Acrobat, Adobe Acrobat, and Acrobat Professional (also called Acrobat Pro), please realize that the reference is to Adobe Acrobat Professional. For the other authoring application, the official name is Adobe® Acrobat® Standard. When referring to this product I may use terms such as Acrobat Standard or simply Standard. Where it makes sense I'll say it like it is supposed to be used; otherwise, I'll use an abbreviated name.

The official name for the light version is Adobe® Acrobat® Elements, and the free download-able software is Adobe® Reader. Again, for the purposes of communication and ease, I may refer to the applications as Elements or Reader. Please realize, however, that the official name should prevail when you communicate in writing about these products.

Why is this important? Adobe Systems, Inc. has spent much time, labor, and money on devel-oping branding for its products. With the different changes to product names and the different components of the software, some people using the products don't completely understand the differences or where the product came from. An Adobe Reader installer can appear on CD-ROMs distributed legitimately by users and some end-users may not know that it is a product available for upgrading at the Adobe Systems, Inc Web site. Therefore, using the formal name can help users understand a little bit more about the software.

And, there's a very good reason for helping Adobe Systems with the recognition and market-ing of these products. If the product doesn't do well in the marketplace, you might one day see it disappear. You won't want that to happen, because when your eyes gaze at your com-puter monitor and you see Acrobat Professional or Acrobat Standard version 6.0 for the first time, your reaction may be just like mine. In a word, it was "WOW!"

Adobe Systems and the Acrobat mission

Adobe Systems, Inc. began as a company serving the graphic design and imaging markets. With the release of PostScript, its first product, much development in the early years of its history was devoted to imaging programs, font libraries, and tools to help service graphic design professionals. When you speak to graphic designers and advertising people, they connect Adobe Systems with products such as Adobe Photoshop, Adobe Illustrator, Adobe InDesign, Adobe Premiere, and so on. With some of these flagship programs experiencing long histories and large installed user bases, some people may think that a product like Adobe Acrobat takes a back seat to the high-end graphics and multimedia programs.

Where does Acrobat fit into Adobe's mission and view of its product line? According to some interviews posted on the www.planetpdf.com Web site in late 2002, Adobe Chairman and CEO Bruce Chizen was quoted as saying that he expects the Acrobat family of products to weather economic storms in the software market. Acrobat is Adobe's fastest-growing product, experiencing between 40 to 60 percent growth in year-over-year sales. Chizen was also quoted as saying that more than 60 percent of Adobe's worldwide sales and marketing personnel were diverted to Acrobat-related products during the Acrobat 5 life cycle.

Adobe sees Acrobat as an integral part of its future and is investing much energy on Acrobat's growth. With more than 500,000,000 installed users of the Adobe Reader software, Acrobat and the PDF file format are among the most popular software products available today.

Acrobat has become a standard in many different industries. In the publishing market many large newspaper chains, publishing houses, and book and magazine publishers have standardized on the PDF format for printing and prepress. The prepress industry has long adopted PDF as a standard for commercial and quick print houses. Almost every software manufacturer includes last-minute notes, user manuals, and supporting information in PDF format on CD-ROM installer disks. The U.S. federal government, U.S. state and city governments, and U.S. government contractor organizations have standardized on PDF for everything from forms, applications, notices, and official documents to intraoffice document exchanges.

With the introduction of the Acrobat 6.0 product line, Adobe Systems is expanding existing markets and targeting new markets. New features in Acrobat Professional will appeal to all kinds of engineering professionals. With the support for layers and direct exports from programs like Microsoft Visio and Autodesk AutoCAD, engineers, planners, and architects will welcome the new additions to Acrobat. Enterprises in which document flows include different workgroups for almost any industry will welcome additions to the comment and review tools in Acrobat Professional. The already standardized prepress market will applaud new features for printing to high-end imaging devices without the use of third-party plug-ins. And new features have been added to support the eBook market, where Adobe expects to expand PDF as a standard for this industry. In short, Acrobat is a product that reaches just about every computer user today regardless of the kind of work he or she performs.

PDF workflows

The definition of a workflow can mean different things to different people. One of the nice features of working with Acrobat is the development of a workflow environment. Quite simply, workflow solutions are intended to get out of a computer what the computer was designed for: productivity in a more automated and efficient fashion. Editing page by page and running manual tasks to change or modify documents could hardly be called workflow solutions. Workflows enable office or production workers a method of automating common tasks for maximum efficiency. Batch-processing documents, running them through automated steps, and routing files through computer-assisted delivery systems are among workflow solutions.

The exchange and delivery of documents are part of any office workflow. By adding to the review and comment features, office workers will find many new additions in Acrobat to help workgroups exchange, comment in, review, revise, and publish documents. New editing tools will help people in workgroups modify, refine, and polish legacy files as well as newly created documents.

New Features in Adobe Acrobat Professional

As I mentioned earlier, when I first opened Acrobat Professional, my immediate reaction was "WOW!" The changes to Acrobat in version 6.0 represent a major software upgrade. Just about everything you could do in the last version is still available in version 6.0, but there have been many changes to where features are located and the names used to invoke a command. The user interface (UI) has had a complete overhaul as well. Before you tackle the chapters ahead, take a close look at the brief description of the many new features listed here. As you poke around the new release, don't get frustrated if you can't find a particular feature you're used to in Acrobat. Come back to this section and skim over the new features list or check the index or CD-ROM copy of this book to help you find what you think you may have lost.

All the features highlighted here and more are covered in the chapters ahead. This brief coverage gives you an idea for some of the new features found in Acrobat Professional. If you're an experienced Acrobat user, the reasons for upgrading to the newest version are obvious. If you're a new user, you'll find the current version of Acrobat an amazing program that offers you tools to help you with almost anything related to viewing, archiving, and sharing documents among your workgroup, clients, colleagues, and friends.

Application support

Acrobat Professional has a self-healing feature that automatically detects any problems that might have been created by missing or corrupt support files, implements a new plug-in finder, provides options for locking down preferences, and offers you methods for customizing the program before deployment (a feature that can help IT managers in charge of supporting site licenses).

Audio reading

A new feature has been added that reads PDF documents aloud through the speakers attached to your computer utilizing your operating system's Text to Speech engine. Vision- and motion-challenged users can use Acrobat for screen reading without the need for screen-reading devices. You can gather the family around the computer and have it read eBooks and PDFs aloud for family fun at holidays and special occasions. A new feature has been added for auto scrolling pages. You can instruct Acrobat to scroll pages of eBooks and PDFs automatically as you read them.

Authoring application support

One-click operations from authoring software to convert to PDF have been added for more applications and file formats. Microsoft Visio and AutoDesk AutoCAD can export directly to PDF as well as Microsoft Project and PDF creation from within Microsoft Internet Explorer and Microsoft Outlook Express.

Catalog

Acrobat Catalog has had many subtle changes. It offers the same options available with earlier versions of Acrobat, and now you can index Tags. The supporting file folders have been reduced from nine folders to a single subfolder containing index file structures. Acrobat Professional now enables you to index files that are encrypted with either 64-bit or 128-bit encryption.

Document repurposing

Much improvement has been added to PDF processing for repurposing, optimizing, and reducing file sizes of documents. Newer compression algorithms are now supported to improve compression for PDFs and file types you can export from Acrobat.

eBook support

Tremendous change has been implemented in handling eBooks in Acrobat 6.0. You can create an eBook library to store your volumes directly in Acrobat, change to an eBook viewing mode, set up a giving and lending program for your eBooks, and search Web directories.

Font diagnostics

Methods for embedding and unembedding fonts have been improved in this release of Acrobat. The methods for analyzing all the fonts embedded in a document have been improved as well.

Foreign-language support

This release has extended support for Eastern European, Middle Eastern, Japanese, Chinese, and Korean languages. Features like custom Japanese stamps have been added to Acrobat.

Headers and footers

You can add page headers and footers in Acrobat. Rather than writing JavaScripts to add numbers to pages in PDF documents, a simple dialog box offers you options for numbering pages, adding headers and footers, dates, and text for all pages or selected ranges of pages.

Help

To ease you through the transitions from earlier versions of Acrobat to the newest release, there's been an addition to the way you can get help for using the program and the tools, menus, and palettes. The new How To menu opens in the Acrobat window by default. In this palette you can search for a topic and Acrobat opens a help document, stopping on a page containing the searched words. You can also access help documents from buttons on dialog boxes.

JavaScript debugging

A new debugging feature has been added to the JavaScript console to help users find errors in JavaScript code. You'll find creating and editing JavaScripts much easier in the new release.

Layers

All of Adobe's imaging programs offer support for layers, and Acrobat joins this family of products. Now in Acrobat Professional you can take an AutoCAD drawing created with various layers, export it to PDF, and the layer data remains on separate layers. You can comment and mark up layer data and choose which layers you want to output to a printer.

Link management

Links can now be managed much like form fields for duplicating, copying, and pasting. This is a feature that has long been needed and has now arrived in Acrobat.

Multimedia enhancements

You can now embed video clips in a PDF file, capture Flash animation, and convert PowerPoint slides with motion objects all visible in the resultant PDF file. Acrobat Professional now supports newer file formats including MPEG3.

Object editing

You can manipulate more data on a document page by copying foreground or background data and pasting in front or back of selected objects all within Acrobat.

PDF creation

Creating PDF files has never been easier. Acrobat Professional extends the different file types you can open directly in Acrobat and convert to PDF. Want to convert a Microsoft Word document to PDF? Just drag the document on the Acrobat application icon or select a new menu command called Create PDF, and your Word document is converted to PDF. Multiple documents can be converted to PDF from within Acrobat and bound into a single file. New printing and prepress support offers creation of PDF/X files.

Prepress and printing

The printing and prepress industry will welcome the complete overhaul of the Print dialog box that now supports all the printing controls for printing color separations, large-format printing, and frequency and emulsion control all without the need for purchasing expensive third-party plug-ins. Within Acrobat Professional many new soft proofing tools have been added to expand the views for soft proofing colors, separations, and overprints. Now, amazingly, you can soft proof a color separation right in Acrobat without printing the file. Much-improved color management has also been added to Acrobat Professional as well as job ticketing. Support for PDF/X is also another feature that no longer requires use of third-party plug-ins. You can pre-flight PDF documents right in Acrobat Professional without the use of third-party plug-ins.

Review and comment

The Comment tools, the Comment tab, and many features associated with commenting have had dramatic changes. They are now referred to as Review and Comment. Many new tools have been added, such as an eraser for the Pencil tool, new drawing tools, lines with arrow-heads, callouts, a review tracker, comment and e-mail, easy creation of custom stamps, the ability to export comments into Word files, comment summaries in the Comment tab, and many more brand-new features.

Searching PDFs

You can now search collections of PDFs locally on hard drives and servers without the need for creating an index file. In addition, Acrobat provides you with a great new feature for searching the content of PDFs on the Internet.

Security and digital signature enhancements

Applying and validating digital signatures has been simplified and enhanced. Time frames for authenticity have been added as well as a method for creating a legally binding signature environment.

Snapshots

You can take a snapshot of a page or a portion of a page, copy it to the clipboard, and create a PDF from the clipboard data. When you copy information from any program, Acrobat can convert the clipboard data to a PDF. Snapshots can be managed with link actions, and they can be printed.

Transitions

In Acrobat Professional, transitions are no longer limited to Full Screen views. You can add page transitions while in Page view with tools and menus visible as page transitions take effect when scrolling pages.

User interface

The user interface builds on what was established in Acrobat 5. Toolbars can be undocked from the Command bar, which is now referred to as the Toolbar Well, and moved as floating palettes. Many icons and symbols representing tools have taken on a new look, and you'll find some toolbars handling options that were once acquired from dialog boxes and menu commands. Form tools and Review and Comment tools are some examples of the tools' rearrangement. You can also automatically dock toolbars scattered around the Document pane and choose an option to reset the toolbars to default positions.

Viewing and navigation

Some very nifty tools have been added to Acrobat Professional for viewing PDF files. If you've ever experienced long pauses for screen refreshes when zooming in on a document, you'll appreciate the new Loupe tool, the Pan and Zoom tool, and the Dynamic Zoom tool. Rulers have been added to Acrobat Professional, and, in addition to views you had in earlier versions for tiling and cascading windows, you can now view documents with a split view much like word processing and spreadsheet programs.

Watermarks and backgrounds

What you had to do with complex JavaScripts in earlier versions of Acrobat to add a watermark, overlay an image on existing pages, or even change the color and content of the background can all be performed with menu choices in Acrobat.

About This Book

This book is written for a cross-platform audience. Users of Microsoft Windows 98 Second Edition, Windows Millennium Edition, Windows NT 4.0 with Service Pack 6, Windows 2000 with Service Pack 2, Windows XP, and Apple Macintosh computers running OS X v10.2 and above will find references to these operating systems.

Now with Apple's introduction of System X, Macintosh users will find much more similarity with the same features found in the Windows edition. In earlier releases of Acrobat, some features provided to Windows were not available in Acrobat running on a Macintosh. In the current release for Acrobat 6.0 you'll find much more compatibility running Acrobat on either platform.

Most of the chapters in this book illustrate screenshots from Acrobat running under Windows. The user interface is closely matched between Windows and the Macintosh therefore Macintosh users will find the same options in dialog boxes and menu commands as found in the screenshots taken on a Windows machine. Where significant differences do occur, you'll find additional screenshots taken on a Macintosh to distinguish the differences.

How to read this book

I have to admit this publication is not a page turner that leaves you gasping for more time to finish up a chapter before retiring at night. After all, it's a computer book, and inasmuch as my editors at Wiley always strive to get me to add a little *drama* to the text, few people will pick up this Bible and read it cover to cover. This book should be thought of more as a reference where you can jump to an area and read over the contents to help simplify your work sessions in Acrobat Professional version 6.0.

Because Acrobat is such a behemoth program in its new version and can do so many things for almost any kind of work activity, most people won't use every feature the program provides. You may be interested in converting files to PDF and creating forms, or you may devote more attention to the area of prepress and printing, or perhaps it's accessibility or markup and review that's part of your work. Therefore, you may ignore some chapters and just want to jump to the area that interests you most.

Regardless of where you are in Acrobat experience, you should be able to gain much insight and skill at using the new version of Acrobat by studying in detail those areas that interest you most. However, don't completely ignore chapters that cover features you think you won't use. You can find many related concepts falling under headings that are not exclusively related to the general topic for each chapter. For example, you may not be interested in creating accessible PDFs for screen readers. However, what is covered in the Accessibility chapter (Chapter 18) also includes document structures and tagging, which will be important if you need to reflow PDFs on hand-held devices or get the content of a PDF back out to an authoring application.

Because many chapters may include features that will relate to the work you want to perform, studying over the most important features of interest to you and skimming over those chapters that appear to be less beneficial for your work is best.

To begin, I recommend you look closely at the section in this Introduction covering new features in Acrobat 6.0. No matter where you are in Acrobat skill, be certain to understand PDF navigation because many things have changed for moving around PDF files. Look closely at the help documents and the How To help features in Acrobat 6.0. Everyone should carefully look over the details covering PDF file creation, using Acrobat Search, and editing PDF documents. Then jump into your particular area of interest and read over the chapters that can help you get up to speed using this new release. As a final step, browse the remaining chapters to see what other features can help you in your workflow.

Throughout the book are sections called *Steps*. If you find the contents of a given series of steps interesting, follow the steps to see whether you can replicate what is covered in that section.

Icons

What would a John Wiley and Sons Bible book be without icons? The use of icons throughout the book offers you an at-a-glance hint of what content is being addressed. You can jump to the text adjacent to these symbols to get extra information, be warned of a potential problem, or amplify the concept being addressed in the text. In this book you'll find icons for the following.

Caution

A caution icon alerts you to a potential problem in using Acrobat Professional, any tools or menus, or any supporting application that may be the origination of a document to be converted to PDF. Pay close attention to these caution messages to avoid potential problems.

Engineering

Special attention to engineer professionals has been included in Acrobat 6.0. Support for PDF creation from CAD applications is a new feature, and there are tools to help you analyze drawings. For the engineers, I created some notes of specific interest.

Note

A note icon signifies a message that may add more clarity to a text passage or help you deal with a feature more effectively.

PDF workflow

Where workflow solutions are particularly applicable, you'll see an icon indicating that the text describes tasks or features that apply to workgroups and workflows. This icon will be an important signal for people in enterprises, government, and education where large workgroups with common tasks exist.

Prepress

Much support is offered in version 6.0 to the prepress and printing market. If you're a design professional or service bureau or print shop, take note of these icons for information related to prepress and printing.

Tip

Tips are handy shortcuts. They help to more quickly produce results or work through a series of steps to complete a task. Some tips provide you with information that may not be documented in the Help files accompanying Acrobat Professional.

Cross-Reference

The Cross-Reference icon indicates a cross-reference to another area in the book where more information can be found on a topic. Walking you through Acrobat in a linear fashion is almost impossible because it has so many interrelated features. Covering all aspects of a single feature in a contiguous section of the book just doesn't work. Therefore, some common features for a command, a tool, an action, or a task may be spread out and discussed in different chapters. When the information is divided between different sections of the book, you'll find a Cross-Reference icon that cross-references the current passage to another part of the book covering related information.

The silver platter

In the back of the book you'll find a CD-ROM. The CD is a hybrid that can be viewed by Windows or Macintosh users. The CD-ROM contains links to third-party manufacturer Web sites where you can find additional tools to help you work with Acrobat and PDF documents. You'll also find a PDF version of this book on the CD-ROM. You can open this file and employ a search to find something not found in the contents or index. You'll also find sample files and tutorial files to help you work through steps from all chapters.

As an additional learning tool you will find a video clip excerpt from my new video series on Acrobat 6.0 developed by Total Training Systems. If you want a personalized learning experience in video format, take a look at the CDs offered by total Training Systems covering Adobe Acrobat Professional.

The book contents

Almost all of what you can do with Acrobat is contained within the chapters that follow. I've made an effort to address many different uses for all types of users. This book covers Acrobat features and how to work with Adobe Acrobat Professional, Adobe Acrobat Standard, and companion products. Individual industries such as office occupations, digital prepress, engineering, enterprise workflows, and multimedia and Web publishing are covered. Regardless of what you do, you should be able to find some solutions for your particular kind of work. Whether you are an accounting clerk, a real estate salesperson, a digital prepress technician, an engineer, a Web designer, or a hobbyist who likes to archive information from Web sites, there's a reference to your needs, and Acrobat will provide a solution.

To simplify your journey through the new release, the book is broken up into six separate sections. A total of 27 chapters address Acrobat features and some individual purposes for using the software. The six sections include:

Part I: Welcome to Adobe Acrobat Professional. To start off, I offer some discussion on the PDF format and its new revision. Acrobat 6.0 has new help features that enable you to find help fast within the program. I cover tools, menus, and palettes to help you get an understanding of many Acrobat 6.0 features. Distinctions between different viewer types are covered in this section as well as navigation through PDFs and how to search PDF files. One of the marvelous new additions to the search capabilities is searching PDFs on the Internet, which ends the section.

Part II: Converting Documents to PDF. There are many different ways to create a PDF document, and all these methods are thoroughly covered in Part II. I begin by discussing the ease of creating simple PDF files that might be used by office workers and travel through to much more sophisticated PDF file creation for more demanding environments. In addition, I discuss how many application software manufacturers are supporting PDFs through direct exports from their programs. The advantages and disadvantages of using all these methods are discussed.

Part III: Editing PDFs. This section covers editing, modifying, and enhancing PDF files for many different purposes. Also covered are how to modify content and how to flow content between Acrobat and authoring programs. I also discuss scanning in Acrobat and converting scans to text with Optical Character Recognition (OCR). Document repurposing is covered in this section for users who want to modify files for different output mediums.

Part IV: PDF Interactivity: This section covers interactivity with PDF documents for work-groups through the use of review and markup tools, adding interactive elements such as multimedia, and all about links and buttons. I address the new layer feature in Acrobat Professional and include a chapter devoted to making PDF documents accessible.

Part V: PDF Publishing. This section covers distribution of PDF files in some of the more common means available today. I begin with security and authentication as your first step in document distribution and then move on to PDF workflows. Creating PDFs for different kinds of distribution such as presentations, a complete coverage of all the new printing and prepress features, and eBooks are also covered in Part V. Hosting your PDFs on the Web, sending them via e-mail, and writing collections of PDFs to CD-ROMs and DVDs are also covered in this section.

Part VI: Acrobat PDF Forms. This section covers PDF forms and data. Forms handling in Acrobat Professional has been revised. I cover all the changes and how to fill out and create Acrobat PDF forms. An introduction to JavaScript and writing simple JavaScript routines are also included in this section.

Appendixes

Appendix A describes the contents of the CD-ROM accompanying this book. It includes a description of the items on the CD and any special considerations for installing the files. Appendix B is useful listing of keyboard shortcuts.

Staying Connected

It seems like about every five minutes new products and new upgrades are distributed. If you purchase a software product, you can often find an updated revision soon after. Manufacturers rely more and more on Internet distribution and less on postal delivery. You should plan on making routine visits to Adobe's Web site and the Web sites of third-party product manufacturers. Any software vendor that has a Web site will offer a product revision for downloading or offer you details on acquiring the update.

Internet connection

At times I feel a *required* Internet connection is either a blessing or a curse. I have about six computers I use for different things. My laptop is a computer I just haul around to conferences, and I don't want an Internet connection on the computer I use to demonstrate software. Yet, at other times, on my computers I welcome an Internet connection that allows me to easily update a software product.

With newer releases of computer software, having an Internet connection is almost essential. Programs, including Acrobat, prompt you routinely to check for updates over the Internet. To optimize your performance with Acrobat, you should run the software on a computer that has an Internet connection.

Registration

Regardless of whether you purchase Acrobat Professional, Acrobat Standard, or Acrobat Elements, or download the free Adobe Reader software, Adobe Systems has made it possible to register the product. You can register on the World Wide Web or mail a registration form to

Adobe. If you develop PDF documents for distribution, Adobe likes to keep track of this information. You will find great advantage in being a registered user. First, update information will be sent to you, so you'll know when a product revision occurs. Secondly, information can be distributed to help you achieve the most out of using Acrobat. Who knows, some day you may be requested to provide samples of your work that might get you a hit from Adobe's Web site. By all means, complete the registration. It will be to your benefit.

Web sites to contact

Obviously, the first Web site to frequent is Adobe's Web site. Downloads for updates will be found when Acrobat and the Acrobat plug-ins are revised. You can also find tips, information, and problem solutions. Visit Adobe's Web site at www.adobe.com.

A Web ring is sponsored by PDFzone. Participants in the Web ring are individuals and companies that promote information and solutions for the PDF community. In addition, PDFzone publishes articles of interest and news and hosts an extensive list of third-party developers. You can find them at www.pdfzone.com.

Acrobat tips can be found on many Web sites, and all you need to do is search the World Wide Web for Acrobat information. The best source for information as well as a comprehensive collection of third-party plug-ins is available at Planet PDF. You can visit them at www.planetpdf.com.

If learning more about Acrobat is your interest, you can find regional conferences sponsored by DigiPub Solutions Corporation. If you want to meet and discuss PDF issues with some of the world's experts, look for a conference in your area. You can find information at www.pdfconference.com.

Another PDF conference program is offered by the American Graphics Institute. You can find out more information by logging on to www.AGItraining.com.

The Open Publish conference in Sydney, Australia, is an annual conference for design and creative professionals. It hosts many PDF-related seminars and workshops annually. Find it at www.openpublish.com.au/.

Yet another conference using a similar name is the Open Publish conference. Open Publish is a conference held in the U.S. covering printing and publishing. You can find it at www.open-publish.com. If video training helps complement your learning, you can purchase training CDs developed by Total Training Systems. Each video set covers specific areas of Acrobat 6.0 and comes with tutorial files to help you get up to speed fast in the new release. You can find a sample of the Total Training Acrobat 6.0 video series on this book's CD-ROM. For more information visit the Total Training Systems Web site at www.totaltraining.com/home.html.

Whatever you may desire is usually found on some Web site. New sites are developed continually, so be certain to make frequent searches. And now with Acrobat 6.0 you can narrow your searches to look for just PDF files on the Internet.

Contacting Me

If, after reviewing this publication, you feel some important information was overlooked or you have any questions concerning Acrobat, you can contact me and let me know your views, opinions, hoorahs, or complaints or provide information that might get included in the next revision. (If it's good enough, you might even get a credit line in the acknowledgments!) By all means, send me a note. E-mail inquiries can be sent to ted@west.net.

If you happen to have some problems with Acrobat, keep in mind I didn't engineer the program. Inquiries for technical support should be directed to the software manufacturer(s) of any products you use. This is one more good reason to complete your registration form.

There you have it — a short description of what follows. Don't wait. Turn the page and learn how Acrobat can help you gain more productivity with its amazing new features.

Welcome to Adobe Acrobat Professional

Getting to Know Adobe Acrobat

What Is Adobe Acrobat?

If, after perusing your local bookstore, you decided to lay down your money at the counter, carry away this ten-pound volume, and take it to bed with you tonight, you probably already know something about Adobe Acrobat. Why else would you buy this book? If you're at the bookstore shelf and you haven't bought it yet, then you're probably wondering how in the world anyone could write so many pages for such a simple application. After all, isn't Acrobat that little thingy you download from the Adobe Web site?

Assuming you know little about Adobe Acrobat, I start with a brief description of what Acrobat is and what it is not. As I explain to people who ask about the product, I usually define it as the most misunderstood application available today. Most of us are familiar with the Adobe Reader software, which is a product from Adobe Systems Incorporated that you can download for free from the Adobe Web site (www.adobe.com/acrobat). You can also acquire the Adobe Reader from all the installation CD-ROMs for other Adobe software. You can even acquire Adobe Reader from other users, as long as the Adobe licensing requirements are distributed with the installer program. The Adobe Reader, however, is *not* Adobe Acrobat. Adobe Reader is a component of a much larger product that has evolved through several iterations over more than a decade.

You're probably a little more sophisticated and realize there is a major difference between the applications noted previously and you may wonder why I even spend any time discussing the difference between Acrobat and Adobe Reader. Interestingly enough, I attended a PDF conference about six months before this book was written. The conference coincided with another technology conference and one of the speakers at the PDF conference took a video camera and microphone to the other conference and interviewed random attendees, asking questions like, "What is Adobe Acrobat?" and "What is PDF?" Surprisingly, most of the computer-savvy interviewees could not provide a correct response. Inasmuch as Acrobat has come a long way, many people still confuse what you purchase from Adobe Systems and what you can download free.

To add a little more confusion, this iteration of Acrobat includes three different kinds of viewer applications. The Adobe Reader software is still a free download from Adobe's Web site. The other two Acrobat viewers are software products you need to purchase from Adobe Systems or from software vendors. They include Adobe Acrobat Standard and Adobe Acrobat Professional. As I talk about Adobe Acrobat in this chapter, I'm referring to both Acrobat Standard and Acrobat Professional.

Note   There are distinctions between the Acrobat Standard product and the Acrobat Professional product in terms of tools and commands. Much of what can be accomplished in editing PDF documents can be handled by either viewer; however, Acrobat Professional does provide more editing features than Acrobat Standard. Throughout this book I delineate the differences and point out when an Acrobat Professional feature cannot be accomplished in Acrobat Standard.

Adobe Acrobat (either Standard or Professional) is the upgrade from Adobe Acrobat 5 and both viewers are the subject of the remaining chapters of this book. Acrobat is the authoring application that provides you tools and commands for a host of features outlined in the following chapters. If you haven't yet purchased a copy of Acrobat, either the Standard version or the Professional version, you might want to look over Chapter 2 and observe some of the comparisons between the viewers. If the fewer tools and features suit your purpose, you might find the Standard version satisfactory. Although there are some features that differ between the viewers, they both provide many features for editing, enhancing, printing, and working with PDF documents.

Acrobat is an authoring application, but it has one little distinction compared to almost any other authoring program. Rather than starting from scratch and creating a new document in Acrobat, your workflow usually involves converting a document, created in just about any program, to a Portable Document Format (PDF) file. Once the document is converted to PDF you use Acrobat to edit and refine the document, add bells and whistles, interactivity, or prepare it for professional printing. In addition to the Acrobat program, Acrobat Professional ships with companion programs such as Adobe Acrobat Distiller and Adobe Acrobat Catalog, and Acrobat Standard ships only with Acrobat Distiller. These companion products are used to convert PostScript files to PDF and create search indexes.

Cross-Reference   For information related to Acrobat Distiller, see Chapter 7. For more information on Acrobat Catalog, see Chapter 4.

Acrobat solutions are greatly extended with other supporting programs from Adobe Systems and many different third-party vendors. If Acrobat won't do the job, chances are you can find a plug-in or companion program to handle all you want to do with a PDF file.

Cross-Reference   For information related to Acrobat plug-ins and companion products, see Chapter 2.

What Is PDF?

PDF, short for *Portable Document Format*, was developed by Adobe Systems as a unique format to be viewed through Acrobat viewers. As the name implies, it is portable, which means the file you create on one computer can be viewed with an Acrobat viewer on other computers and on other platforms. For instance, you can create a page layout on a Macintosh computer and convert it to a PDF file. After the conversion, this PDF document can be viewed on a UNIX or Windows machine. Multi-platform compliance (to enable the exchange of files across different computers, for example) is one of the great values of PDF files.

So what's special about PDF and its multi-platform compliance? It's not so much an issue of viewing a page on one computer created from another computer that is impressive about PDF. After all, such popular programs as Microsoft Excel, Microsoft Word, Adobe Photoshop, Adobe InDesign, Adobe FrameMaker, and Adobe Illustrator all have counterparts for multi-platform usage. You can create a layout on one computer system and view the file on another system with the same software installed. For instance, if you have Adobe PageMaker installed on a Macintosh computer and you create a PageMaker document, that same file can be viewed on a PC with PageMaker running under Windows.

In a perfect world, you may think the capability to view documents across platforms is not so special. Viewing capability, however, is secondary to document integrity. The preservation of the contents of a page is what makes the PDF so extraordinary. To illustrate, suppose you have a PageMaker document created in Windows using fonts generic to Windows applications. After it's converted to PDF, the document, complete with graphics and fonts intact, can be displayed and printed on other computer platforms. And the other computer platforms don't need the fonts or graphics to print the file with complete integrity.

This level of document integrity can come in handy in business environments, where software purchases often reach quantum costs. PDF documents eliminate the need to install all applications used within a particular company on all the computers in that company. For example, art department employees can use a layout application to create display ads and then convert them to PDF so that other departments can use the free Adobe Reader software to view and print those ads for approval.

The benefits of PDF viewing were initially recognized by workgroups in local office environments for electronic paper exchanges. Today we have much more opportunity for global exchange of documents in many different ways. As you look at Acrobat Professional and discover some of the new features now available for document review and markup, comparing documents, support for layered files and preparing PDFs for screen readers, you'll see how Acrobat and PDF have evolved with new technologies.

Document repurposing

The evolution of the computer world has left extraordinary volumes of data on computer systems originally designed to be printed on paper. Going all the way back to UNIVAC, the number crunching was handled by the computer and the expression was the printed piece. Today, forms of expression have evolved to many different media. No longer do people want to confine themselves to printed material. Now, in addition to publishing information on paper, we use CD-ROMs, the Internet, and file exchanges between computers. Sometimes we use motion video, television, and satellite broadcasts. As high-speed access evolves, we'll see much larger bandwidths, so real-time communication will eventually become commonplace. And the world of tomorrow will introduce more communication media. Think of outputting to plasma, crystal, and holograms, and then think about having a font display or link problem with one of those systems!

Technology will advance, bringing many improvements to bandwidth, performance, and speed. To enable the public to access the mountains of digital data held on computer systems in a true information superhighway world, files will need to be converted to a common format. A common file format would also enable new documents to be more easily *repurposed*, to exploit the many forms of communication that we use today and expect to use tomorrow.

Acrobat Professional has added more tools for helping users repurpose documents. Tools for repairing problem files, downsizing file sizes, porting them to a range of different devices, and eliminating unnecessary data are part of the many features found in Acrobat Professional.

PDF and Adobe PostScript

The de facto standard of almost all printing in the graphics industry is Adobe PostScript. Ninety-nine percent of North America and about seventy-five percent of the rest of the world uses PostScript for all high-end output. Adobe developed this page description language to accurately display the design created on your computer screen to the printed page. If graphics and fonts are included in your files and you want to print the pages to high-end professional devices, then PostScript is the only show in town. The Adobe PostScript language was responsible for the rise of so many software and hardware manufacturers. If you stop and think about it, PostScript ranks up there with MS-DOS and Windows in terms of its installed user base.

Okay, so how does PostScript relate to PDF? In the initial release of Acrobat, all PDF conversion began with a file that was created as a PostScript file. Users selected the Print command in an authoring program and printed the file to disk — thus creating a PostScript file. This file was then opened in the Acrobat Distiller program and Distiller converted the PostScript to a PDF.

Distiller is still a part of Acrobat. In some cases, creating a PDF from a PostScript file rather than through any of the many other means available may be preferable. It could be that you have a problem with exporting to PDF from a program, such as fonts not appearing embedded, or you may need to create a PDF for a special purpose like printing and prepress. In such circumstances using Acrobat Distiller may be your best solution for generating a PDF document to properly suit the purpose.

Cross-Reference   For information related to printing PostScript files and using Acrobat Distiller, see Chapter 7.

Distiller's use is waning a bit because now so many programs support PDF creation through one-button clicks or using the Save As command. If a file export or other method creates *good* PDF files, then you can bypass Distiller and use the application's support for converting documents to PDF. Acrobat introduces more tools for converting files to PDF and there's more support from authoring programs for PDF creation.

PostScript can be a problem solver for you and you may have an occasional need to use it even if your workflow does not require its use all the time. The more you know about PostScript and Acrobat Distiller, the more often you might be able to rescue problem files that don't seem to properly convert to PDF. In addition, if you use certain export features in programs that support PDF creation, many of these programs use Acrobat Distiller in the background to create the PDF file. You may not see the Distiller window, but it is working away creating PDF files from some of your favorite programs. For these reasons, you should take a look at Chapter 7, where I explain PostScript and Distiller in detail.

PDF versions

Acrobat is now in version 6. The version number indicates the number of releases of the product. PDF is a file format and with it you'll also find a version number. The PDF version relates to the specifications of the file format, and for the end user it's usually not so important to understand all the specifications as much as it is to know what it does for you or what you can expect from it. If you create PDF documents for users of older Acrobat viewers and use the newer PDF format, your users may not be able to view your PDF files. Conversely, creating PDF files with the older version might prohibit you from using some newer features in the recent release.

With PDF file conversion you have choices for creating and saving PDF documents with your choice of version number. Depending on which version you select, you'll have different specifications assigned to the file. To give you an idea for how PDF format has changed, look over Table 1-1.

Table 1-1: PDF Version Compatibility Differences

Acrobat 3.0	*Acrobat 4.0*	*Acrobat 5.0*	*Acrobat Professional 6.0*
Supports PDF version 1.2	Supports PDF version 1.3	Supports PDF version 1.4	Supports PDF version 1.5
PDF files can be opened by Acrobat viewers 3.0 and later.	PDF files can be opened by Acrobat viewers 3.0 and later.	Minor viewing problems with earlier viewers may be experienced.	PDF files can be opened by Acrobat viewers 3.0 and later.
	Some viewing problems with earlier viewers may be experienced.	PDF files can be opened by Acrobat viewers 3.0 and later.	Some viewing problems with earlier viewers may be experienced.
Page size is limited to 45 inches × 45 inches.	Page size is available up to 200 inches × 200 inches.	Page size is available up to 200 inches × 200 inches.	Page size is available up to 200 inches × 200 inches.
Document conversion is limited to 32,768 pages.	Document length is limited only by RAM and hard drive space.	Document length is limited only by RAM and hard drive space.	Document length is limited only by RAM and hard drive space.
Color conversion supports CalRGB.	Color conversion supports sRGB.	Color conversion supports sRGB.	Color conversion supports sRGB.
ICC Profile embedding supported.	ICC Profile embedding supported.	ICC Profile embedding supported.	ICC Profile embedding supported.
DeviceN color space is converted to an alternate color space.	DeviceN color space is supported.	DeviceN color space is supported.	DeviceN color space with 32 colorants is supported.
Smooth shading is converted to images.	Smooth shading is supported.	Smooth shading is supported.	Smooth shading is supported.
Patterns display at 50% but print correctly.	Patterns display accurately and print correctly.	Patterns display accurately and print correctly.	Patterns display accurately and print correctly.

Continued

Table 1-1 *(continued)*

Acrobat 3.0	Acrobat 4.0	Acrobat 5.0	Acrobat Professional 6.0
Places halftone information in the PDF.	Will only place halftone information when the Preserve Halftone information is selected in the Color Job Options.	Will only place halftone information when the Preserve Halftone information is selected in the Color Job Options.	Will only place halftone information when the Preserve Halftone information is selected in the Color Job Options.
Preserve, remove, and apply Transfer functions are supported.	Preserve, remove but NOT apply Transfer functions	Preserve, remove, apply Transfer functions.	Preserve, remove, apply Transfer functions.
Masks do not display or print properly.	Masks are supported in viewing and printing.	Masks are supported in viewing and printing.	Masks are supported in viewing and printing.
Photoshop 6.0 layers and transparency not supported	Photoshop 6.0 layers and transparency not supported	Photoshop 6.0 layers and transparency supported in Saves as PDF from Photoshop only.	Photoshop 6.0 layers and transparency supported in Saves as PDF from Photoshop only.
Illustrator 9.0 transparency is supported.	Illustrator 9.0 transparency is supported.	Illustrator 9.0 transparency supported in Save as PDF from Illustrator only.	Illustrator 9.0 transparency supported in Save as PDF from Illustrator only.
Cannot embed double-byte fonts.	Can embed double-byte fonts.	Can embed double-byte fonts.	Can embed double-byte fonts.
TrueType fonts cannot be searched.	TrueType fonts can be searched.	TrueType fonts can be searched.	TrueType fonts can be searched.
Supports 40-bit encryption.	Supports 40-bit encryption.	Supports 40-bit encryption and 128-bit encryption.	Supports 40-bit encryption and 128-bit encryption.
			PDF X/1-A and PDF X/3 are supported.
			Support for Layers from certain authoring applications.

Table 1-1 lists a comparison of attributes of the different PDF versions and should not be confused with certain features you can employ in one release that may make the PDF unusable to users with earlier versions of Acrobat. For example, embedding movie clips in a PDF document or using a JavaScript that won't work in earlier versions is not a function of the PDF version. Rather, they are features added to the program and employed after the PDF has been created.

One of the nice new features of Acrobat Professional with the current PDF version is support for PDF/X files. If you work in the print industry, you'll welcome the addition of PDF/X support. However, PDF/X is not supported with Acrobat Standard.

Cross-Reference   For information related to PDF/X, see Chapter 23.

Acrobat Environment

Experienced Acrobat users will immediately notice a major change to the user interface (UI) when Acrobat Professional is first launched. As a matter of fact, it might look pretty darn crowded to you. There's a lot to absorb when looking at the Acrobat window and you'll need some initial help to understand all the changes. Fortunately you bought this book and, together with Adobe Systems and the new help features in all Acrobat viewers, I'll walk you through the many different items located in the Acrobat workplace.

Acrobat provides you with features such as menu commands, toolbars, and palettes to accomplish work for whatever purpose you hope to perform with PDF documents. When you launch the program you see many of these features in the Acrobat window. Just so you know what is being referred to when I discuss accessing a feature in Acrobat, take a look at Figure 1-1 to understand the names used to describe the various areas of the new Acrobat workplace.

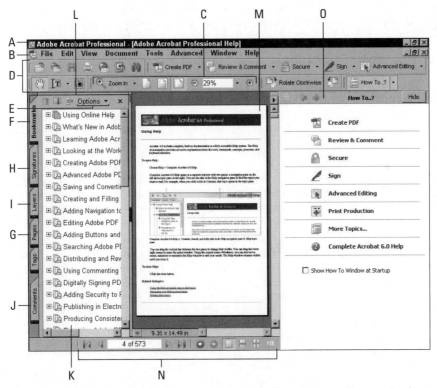

Figure 1-1: The Acrobat Professional workplace contains menus, toolbars, and palettes.

A Title Bar: By default the name of the file you open appears within parentheses in the Title Bar. The title appearing in the Title Bar can change according to an option for displaying the Document Title in the Open Options dialog box.

For information related to Open options and displaying document titles, see Chapter 3.

B Menu Bar: The Menu Bar contains all the top-level menu commands. These menu choices are also available from various actions associated with links and form fields when you choose the Execute Menu Item command in the Actions Properties dialog box for links, form fields, and other features that permit associating an action with a command.

For information related to link actions and the Execute Menu Item command action type, see Chapter 15. For more information on actions with form fields, see Part VI.

C Toolbar: A number of individual toolbars are nested below the Menu Bar. The toolbar noted in Figure 1-1 is the Zoom toolbar. Individual toolbars are marked with a vertical separator bar at the left side of the toolbar. This bar can be selected and dragged to move it out of the Toolbar Well.

For information related to working with toolbars, see the "Toolbars" section later in this chapter.

D Toolbar Well: The Toolbar Well is the well that houses the toolbars. You can drag toolbars away from the Toolbar Well or add other toolbars and expand the Toolbar Well to house your new additions.

E Palette Pull-Down menu: Individual tabs can be tucked away in the Navigation Pane (see Navigation Pane later in this list) or appear anywhere in the Acrobat window. Each palette contains its own menus accessible by clicking on the down-pointing arrow. These menus are referred to as palette pull-down menus in all subsequent chapters.

F Bookmarks tab: The first of the default tabs appearing in the Navigation Pane is the Bookmarks tab. If bookmarks are contained in the PDF document they will appear in the palette when the palette is open, as shown in Figure 1-1.

For information related to creating bookmarks, see Chapter 15.

G Pages tab: Users of previous versions of Acrobat will notice there is no tab for Thumbnails. The Thumbnails tab has been renamed to the Pages tab. When you open the Pages tab, you'll see thumbnail images of each page in your document and you'll find many page editing features available to you from the Pages tab palette pull-down menu.

For information related to using many options available in the Pages tab, see Chapter 10.

H Signatures tab: If digital signatures are included in your PDF document, they can be viewed in the Signatures tab.

Cross-Reference

For information related to digital signatures, see Chapter 19.

I Layers tab: Acrobat supports layers that have been created from some authoring applications and exported as a PDF file with layers intact. The Layers tab enables you to view or hide layers when they are present in the PDF.

Cross-Reference

For information related to working with Layers, see Chapter 17.

J Comments tab: A major overhaul has been made to the Comments tab. When you open the Comments tab, the display of comments and reviews are shown horizontally at the bottom of the Acrobat window.

Cross-Reference

To learn how to use the Comments tab options, see Chapter 14.

K Bookmarks: Figure 1-1 shows the Bookmarks tab opened with a display of bookmarks contained in the palette. Bookmarks enable you to jump to the page or view of the associated bookmark. In addition, you can assign attributes other than views to bookmarks with action items such as opening/closing files, running a menu command, invoking a JavaScript, and many other actions.

Cross-Reference

For information related to link actions associated with bookmarks, see Chapter 15.

L Navigation Pane: The Navigation Pane can be expanded or collapsed. The view in Figure 1-1 is an expanded view where the Bookmarks tab is the active palette. To open the Navigation Pane you can click on a tab to display the respective information associated with that tab in the expanded palette window. Clicking again on the tab collapses the view. You can also use the keyboard modifier F6 to expand and collapse the Navigation Pane.

M Document Pane: The Document Pane is the container for PDF files you see in Acrobat. When no file is open, the Document Pane is empty. When you open a PDF document, the document is viewed in the Document Pane.

N Status Bar: The Status Bar contains some viewing and navigation tools and displays information about your PDF document. You can see the page size and the number of pages in the open PDF at a glance in the Status Bar as shown in Figure 1-1 where page 2 of 620 is displayed. You can navigate pages in the status bar by clicking on a navigation tool, entering a number in the Status Bar, and pressing Enter/Return on your keyboard. You can change page views by selecting one of the three tools on the far right side of the Status Bar.

Cross-Reference

For information related to navigation with the Status Bar, see Chapter 3.

O **How To window:** The How To window is a new addition to Acrobat 6. The How To window enables you to perform searches and to obtain instant help with menu commands, tools, palette options, and many selected tasks you perform routinely.

For information on using the How To window, see the "Getting Help" section later in this chapter.

For more detail on specific menu commands, tools, and palettes, see the chapters associated with the different options available to you. Each of the items discussed here is explained in more depth in subsequent chapters.

Menus

As with any program operating on a computer system that supports a windows type of environment, you'll notice menu commands at the top level of the Acrobat window. For users of previous versions, you'll notice different menu commands have been relocated under different menu headings. If at first glance you don't see an option you used in Acrobat 5, poke around the menus. None of the Acrobat 5 features have been eliminated; they may just be in a different place or referred to by a different name. As you browse through the menus, you can see some changes in the UI where some menu commands now contain an icon adjacent to a menu name to help you easily access the desired command.

File menu

 The File menu is where you open/close documents, create PDF files, import and export certain data, access print commands, and use some other nifty new additions in Acrobat Professional. A distinction between the Mac and PC version is the location of recently viewed documents. On the Mac in OS X you'll find recently viewed documents located under the Open Recent File command. Accessing the command opens a submenu where recent documents can be accessed. On Windows, you'll find the recently viewed documents located at the bottom of the File menu as shown in Figure 1-2.

Upload for Browser-Based Review and Go Back Online is available only in Acrobat Professional. Export Comments to Word is available only in Acrobat Professional on Windows XP.

You'll note the Open as Adobe PDF command formerly used in Acrobat 5 is now named Create PDF. A submenu offers you choices for converting different file types to PDF. A new command titled Open My Bookshelf enables you to organize a library of eBooks and access them easily. Also notice there is a new command in the File menu for exporting comments to Word. Other new commands include saving a certified document, reviewing tracking, reducing file sizes, and printing online.

For information related to converting files to PDF, see Chapter 5. For information on eBook libraries, see Chapter 22. For more information on commenting and review tracking, see Chapter 14. For more information on reducing file sizes, see Chapter 13. For more information on online printing see Chapter 23.

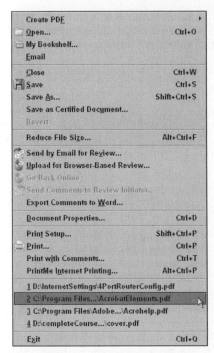

Figure 1-2: Recently opened files in Wi... appear listed at the bottom of the File menu. Macintosh users can display a list of recently viewed files by selecting the Open Recent File command under the Acrobat menu to the left of the File menu.

Edit menu

Edit The traditional Cut, Copy, and Paste commands are located in the Edit menu along with other familiar commands from Acrobat 5. One new command and a very nice feature in Acrobat is the Look Up Definition command. The menu option changes the word(s) within quote marks according to the last word you entered in the Search window. When you select the command, your Web browser is immediately launched and takes you to Dictionary.com (presuming you have an active Internet connection). Click the lookup button on the Web site and you can read the definition for the searched word. Very cool!

Note The default menu command is *Look Up Definition*. When a word is highlighted, the menu command changes to *Look Up "word,"* where *word* is the highlighted word. In Figure 1-3, I highlighted *ICC;* thus, the menu command reads: *Look Up ICC*. Preferences on the Macintosh are available from the Acrobat menu.

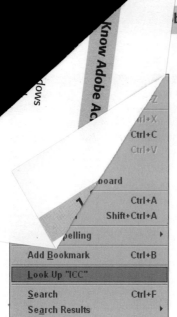

Figure 1-3: The Edit menu contains many of the same menu commands found in Acrobat 5. The new Look Up Definition command enables you to search a Web site for a word definition.

View menu

 The View menu, shown in Figure 1-4, contains all the commands you'll use for viewing PDF documents. If you are familiar with Acrobat 5, you can see many changes in the View menu for items introduced in Acrobat and some rearrangement for items you may have used previously. Additions to the View menu include items such as Task Buttons, Automatic Scrolling, Rulers, Comments List, and Review Tracking.

 Note Grids, Guides, and Rulers are only available in Acrobat Professional.

Cross-Reference For information related to Automatic Scrolling, see Chapter 18. For more information on Rulers, see Chapter 10. For more information on Comments and Review, see Chapter 14.

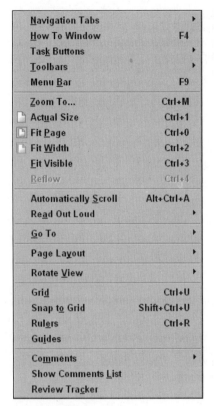

Figure 1-4: The View menu contains commands you'll use for viewing PDF documents and navigating through pages and different PDF files. The menu commands have many additions for new features appearing in Acrobat Professional.

Document menu

Document The Document menu, shown in Figure 1-5, contains a collection of commands specific to document handling. Many review and markup features are located as commands in the menu as well as some new features such as adding headers and footers, adding watermarks, and preflighting PDF files before sending them off to service centers for printing. You'll also find the Paper Capture command here and digital signature handling.

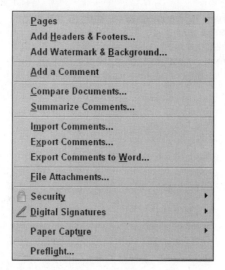

Figure 1-5: The Document menu contains commands for review and comment. New features such as adding headers and footers, adding watermarks, and preflighting PDFs are located in this menu.

Compare Comments and Preflight are available only in Acrobat Professional. Export Comments to Word is available only in Acrobat Professional running on Windows XP with Microsoft Office XP.

For information related to review and comment, see Chapter 14. For information related to adding headers, footers, and watermarks, see Chapter 10. For information on digital signatures, see Chapter 19. For information on preflighting PDFs, see Chapter 23.

Tools menu

Tools   The Tools menu in Acrobat logically places all your editing tools in a single convenient place (Figure 1-6). You can access certain tools from the Acrobat Toolbars (explained later in this chapter) or you can browse the submenus and access a command, and the respective toolbar appears in the Acrobat window. Users will immediately notice the default navigation tools are not all visible in the Acrobat Toolbar Well. If you want to see the Navigation tools you're familiar with, open the Tools menu and select Navigation tools from the submenu. From the menu options, select Show Navigation Toolbar. Each of the submenus contains similar commands all located at the bottom of each submenu. When you make the selection, the toolbar you chose opens in the Acrobat window. One of the new sets of tools in this menu is the Measuring tools set. Acrobat Professional offers you tools to measure distances, compound distances, and areas within a PDF document page.

Measuring tools are only available in Acrobat Professional.

For information related to the measuring tools, see Chapter 10. For more information on showing and hiding toolbars, see the "Toolbars" section later in this chapter.

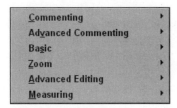

Figure 1-6: The Tools menu contains a collection of tools that can be accessed from submenus. Select a tool group from the menu options to open a submenu.

Advanced menu

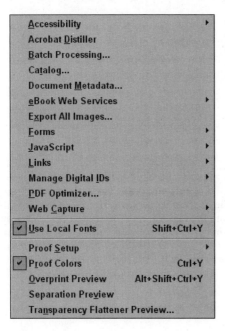

The Advanced menu in Figure 1-7 contains a collection of menu commands considered to be advanced Acrobat features. You won't find any of these tools in the Acrobat Standard software. You'll also notice many commands in this menu have been relocated from other menus in earlier versions of Acrobat. In the Advanced menu you'll find access to Distiller and Catalog, JavaScript commands, the Web capture tool, the PDF Optimizer, access to the Forms tools, and a host of view options for prepress and printing. You'll also notice more commands here for digital signatures. Because digital signature authentication is now handled by Adobe Reader and Acrobat Standard, some of the digital signature commands are contained in the basic tools area that shares these commands with the other viewers. For advanced operations only accessible to Acrobat Professional, these menu commands nest in the Advanced menu.

Figure 1-7: The Advanced menu offers menu commands related to advanced features that are only available to Acrobat Professional users.

Note   Batch Processing, Catalog, Forms, JavaScript, PDF Optimizer, Proof Setup, Proof Colors, Separation Preview, and Transparency Flattener Preview are only available in Acrobat Professional.

Cross-Reference   For information related to digital signatures, see Chapter 19.

Window menu

Window   The Window menu in Acrobat has been polished since Acrobat 5 and some of the menu commands from earlier versions of Acrobat have been eliminated from this menu, such as various palette accesses, toolbar access, and accessibility. The menu now deals primarily with window viewing options, and a new feature in Acrobat offers you a split window view like you might see in word processing and spreadsheet programs. All the open documents in the current Acrobat session are still found at the bottom of this menu as shown in Figure 1-8.

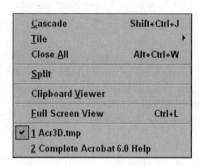

Figure 1-8: The Window menu handles all the window views such as tiling, cascading, and the new feature for displaying a split window.

Cross-Reference   For information related to Window views and the split window view, see Chapter 3.

Help menu

Help   The traditional help files added to your Acrobat folder at installation can be found in the Help menu, shown in Figure 1-9. But Acrobat contains a new help system with the addition of How To menus available in all Acrobat viewers. The How To menus can easily be accessed from the Help menu or when the How To window is open in the Document Pane. You also find online services from Adobe Systems in the menu and a new addition for examining your computer system.

Cross-Reference   For information related to Help and How To menus, see the "Help" section later in this chapter.

Figure 1-9: The Help menu gives you access to the Help PDF files installed with Acrobat and a new feature in Acrobat Professional enables you to search for a help topic instantly via the new How To menu commands.

Submenus

An extensive number of submenus are contained in each of the menus shown previously. A submenu is denoted in Acrobat by a right-pointing arrow on the right side of a given menu command. Select a command with one of these arrows adjacent to the command name, and a submenu opens. In a few cases you can find nested submenus where another right-pointing arrow may be visible in a given submenu command as shown in Figure 1-10. If you want to access the second submenu, move the cursor to the menu option containing a right-pointing arrow. To make a selection from a submenu command, move the cursor to the desired menu command. When the menu command highlights, click the mouse button to execute the command.

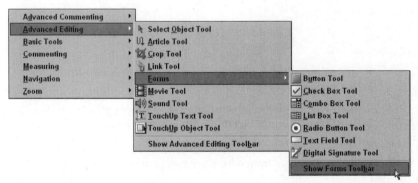

Figure 1-10: To access a submenu, move the cursor to the command containing a right-pointing arrow and slide the cursor over to the submenu options. Click on the desired command in the submenu to execute the command.

Context menus

Wherever you are in the Acrobat window—the toolbars, palettes, Document Pane, or the How To menus—you can gain quick access to menu items related to your task by opening a context menu. Context menus pop up in an area where you either click the right button on the mouse or use an appropriate key modifier. In Windows, right-click the mouse button to open a context menu. On a Macintosh, press the Control key and click the mouse button. Context menu options relate to the particular tool you have selected from a toolbar. By default the Hand tool is selected when you open Acrobat and open a PDF document. When you right-click the mouse button (Windows) or Control+click (Macintosh), a context menu pops up where you click the mouse as shown in Figure 1-11.

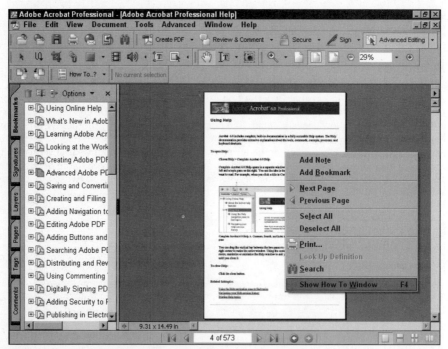

Figure 1-11: With the Hand tool selected, right-clicking (Windows) or Control-clicking (Macintosh) the mouse button opens a context menu. From the menu, scroll the list and select the desired menu command.

If you change tools in a toolbar and open a context menu, the menu options change to reflect choices with that particular tool. Likewise a context menu opened on a palette offers menu options respective to the palette, as shown in Figure 1-12.

Note   In order to open a context menu on a palette, the palette must be open in the Navigation Pane. Clicking on the tab for the palette name won't open a context menu.

You'll find context menus to be a great benefit during your Acrobat sessions and using them helps you work much faster. Throughout this book I often make references to the different choices you have in selecting a tool or command. In most references you find mention of context menus. Be certain you know how to open a context menu in Acrobat on your computer, because the fact that a menu option is contained in a context menu is mentioned without walking you through the steps to open the context menu.

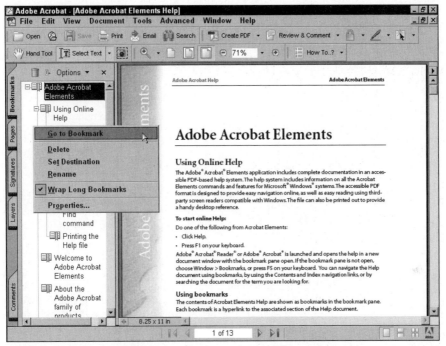

Figure 1-12: When a palette is open in the Navigation Pane and you open a context menu, the menu options reflect tasks you can perform respective to the palette.

Keyboard modifiers

Pressing one or more keys on your keyboard can also open menus and invoke different commands. When you become familiar with key modifiers that perform the same function as addressing a menu or context menu, you'll find yourself favoring this method for making different menu selections or grabbing a tool from a toolbar. Fortunately, you can learn as you work when it comes to memorizing keyboard shortcuts. As I'm certain you know, several key modifier combinations are noted in menu commands. You can learn these shortcuts when you frequently address a particular command. However, the keyboard modifiers you see in the menu commands are just a fraction of what is available in Acrobat for quick access to commands and tools. For a complete list of all keyboard modifiers, look over Appendix B. Mark the pages and use them as a reference when you want to learn more key combinations for work you frequently do in Acrobat Professional.

Note   Pressing a single key to access a tool requires you to have your Preferences set to accept single keystroke shortcuts. See the Steps for Setting Up the Acrobat Environment later in this chapter for proper preference settings.

Toolbars

Tools are grouped together in separate toolbars in the Toolbar Well below the Menu Bar. The default view when you launch Acrobat contains several toolbars visible in the Toolbar Well. You can remove various toolbars and *undock* (remove) them, move them around the Acrobat window, close them, and add different toolbars not visible when you open the default view. The Toolbar Well where the toolbars are contained can be collapsed and expanded according to the number of toolbars you add to it.

Default toolbars

When you launch Acrobat for the first time or you set the toolbars to default view, five different toolbars are docked in the Toolbar Well. The default toolbars include

✦ **File tools.** These tools shown in Figure 1-13 are used for general document handling. The File tools activate commands for Open, Open Web Page, Save, Print, and Search.

Figure 1-13: The File tools toolbar contains tools for document handling, such as opening PDF documents, saving documents, and printing files.

✦ **Task tools.** Task tools are used for editing tasks and document handling. The tools handle features such as Create PDF, Review and Comment, Security, Digital Signatures, and opening the Advanced Editing tools. All of these tools have toolbar pull-down menus. Notice in Figure 1-14 the down-pointing arrow appearing to the right of all the tools in this group indicating that they all have pull-down menus.

Figure 1-14: The Tasks tools contain tools used for file editing.

✦ **Basic tools.** Among the Basic tools are the Hand tool, text and graphics selection tools, and the Snapshot tool (Figure 1-15). Below the default Select Text tool you'll find other selection tools from the pull-down menu.

Figure 1-15: The Basic tools contain tools for selecting text and graphics. The default Hand tool is selected when you open Acrobat at the start of each session.

✦ **Zoom tools.** All the zooming in and out of the Document Pane can be handled in the Zoom tool group shown in Figure 1-16.

Figure 1-16: The Zoom tools handle zooming in and out of the current active document.

✦ **How To tool.** Help topics are readily available to you in Acrobat via the How To window shown in Figure 1-17. A list of How To items is contained in the pull-down menu as well as access to the complete Help document.

Figure 1-17: The How To tool enables you to obtain help for many common editing tasks in Acrobat.

✦ **Rotate tools.** These tools rotate document pages clockwise and counterclockwise in 90-degree rotations. The rotations you make with these tools are for temporary viewing purposes only. The views cannot be saved after rotating pages with these tools, shown in Figure 1-18.

Figure 1-18: The Rotate tools provide options for rotating pages clockwise or counterclockwise.

Managing default toolbars

As mentioned previously, toolbars can be moved, docked and undocked from the Toolbar Well. Here's a list of some of the things you can do with the default toolbars and any other toolbars you decide to view:

✦ **Undocking toolbars.** Toolbars can be relocated from within the Toolbar Well to another area within the Acrobat window. For example, you might find it more convenient to move a toolbar you frequently access during an editing session so it is positioned at the bottom of the Document Pane. If so, just place the cursor on top of the vertical line adjacent to the first tool in a toolbar and drag it away from the Toolbar Well as shown in Figure 1-19. This vertical line is the *hot spot* used to select the toolbar instead of a tool in the group. Clicking anywhere else in the toolbar selects a tool.

✦ **Docking toolbars.** To dock a toolbar back in the Toolbar Well after it has been removed, drag the toolbar, again by the vertical line adjacent to the first tool, on top of the Toolbar Well. The toolbar snaps to an available position in the toolbar. If you drop the toolbar between two other toolbars, the toolbar you relocate to the Toolbar Well snaps in position between the two docked toolbars.

Toolbars can also be docked vertically on the left and right sides of the Document Pane and at the bottom of the Acrobat window below the Status Bar. For example, if you drag a toolbar to the left of the Navigation Pane and release the mouse button, the toolbar snaps to a docking station and the tools display vertically.

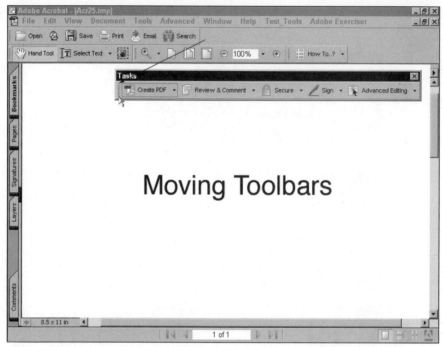

Figure 1-19: Move toolbars around the Acrobat window by selecting the vertical line adjacent to the first tool in the toolbar and dragging it away from the Toolbar Well.

You can dock a toolbar using a menu command instead of dragging the toolbar. Open a context menu on an undocked toolbar and select Dock in Toolbar Well. The toolbar docks back in the Toolbar Well.

Cross-Reference

For more information on docking toolbars vertically and below the Status Bar, see Chapter 3.

✦ **Resetting toolbars.** You can position toolbars all over the Acrobat window and return them to the default positions. This is particularly helpful if multiple users work on a single computer. Your view of where the toolbars are located may not be the desired view for another user. In such cases you can reset the toolbars to defaults. To set tool-bars to defaults, open a context menu from any toolbar by right-clicking (Control+click-ing in Macintosh) and selecting the menu item Reset Toolbars as shown in Figure 1-20.

Note

Only a single toolbar can be selected at a time. If the Toolbar Well is visible, opening a con-text menu from the Toolbar Well provides the same menu options as opening context menus from the toolbars. If all toolbars are removed from the Toolbar Well, the Toolbar Well disap-pears. If the Toolbar Well is not visible, you need to open a context menu on a toolbar to reset the toolbars to default views.

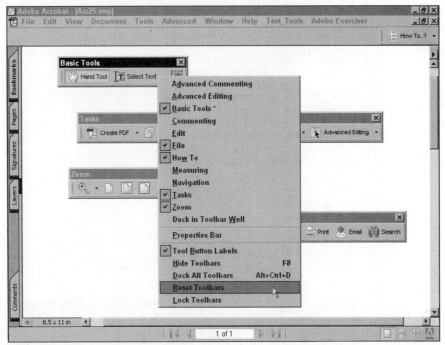

Figure 1-20: To return toolbars to the default view, open a context menu on any toolbar and select Reset Toolbars from the menu options.

✦ **Hiding all toolbars.** Toolbars can be hidden from view to offer you more room when editing a PDF document or browsing the contents of PDFs. If you master some of the keyboard shortcuts shown in Appendix B, you can move about PDF files in the Document Pane or perform many different editing tasks without the toolbars in view. To hide the toolbars from view, open a context menu on any toolbar and select Hide Toolbars. When toolbars are hidden you won't have access to a context menu to get the toolbars back in view. Press the F8 key on your keyboard and all toolbars reappear. The F8 key can also hide toolbars. It is to your benefit to remember to use the keyboard shortcut so you become familiar with turning the view back on.

✦ **Hiding a single toolbar.** You can hide a toolbar once it has been undocked from the Toolbar Well. Click on the X in the top-right corner of the toolbar to close and it disappears from view. From a context menu opened on any toolbar you can open the toolbar and display it in the Acrobat window again.

✦ **Locking toolbars.** The vertical line used to remove a toolbar from the Toolbar Well disappears when you select Lock Toolbars from a context menu. The toolbars cannot be inadvertently moved once you lock them. To unlock the toolbars, open a context menu and select Lock Toolbars again. The checkmark along side the menu command will be unchecked and show the toolbars unlocked in the Toolbar Well. If the toolbars are locked and you drag an undocked toolbar on top of the Toolbar Well, it won't dock. You need to first unlock the toolbars before you can redock them.

Note   You can also lock toolbars that are undocked outside of the Toolbar Well. The docking arm on the toolbar disappears on undocked toolbars the same as it does for toolbars docked in the Toolbar Well. However, locking undocked toolbars does not prevent you from moving them around the Acrobat window. You can grab the title bar for any undocked tool bar and move it to another location.

✦ **Setting new toolbar defaults.** If you decide to reposition your toolbars and want to keep them fixed as new defaults, Acrobat can do so for you automatically. Move the toolbars to the desired locations and go about your work. When you quit Acrobat and reopen the program, the toolbar positions remain as you last arranged them.

Understanding advanced toolbars

The default toolbars represent less than half of the tools available to you in Acrobat Professional. Many of the other toolbars remain hidden from view. The reason for this is obvious when you load all the toolbars in the Toolbar Well. You'll lose a lot of viewing real estate when all toolbars are docked in the Toolbar Well as shown in Figure 1-21. Unless you have a large display monitor or a second monitor, working on a file in the Document Pane when all toolbars are in view can be difficult. Fortunately, by managing the toolbars you can elect to show only the tools you want to work with and you can move them around the Acrobat window allowing for the best view.

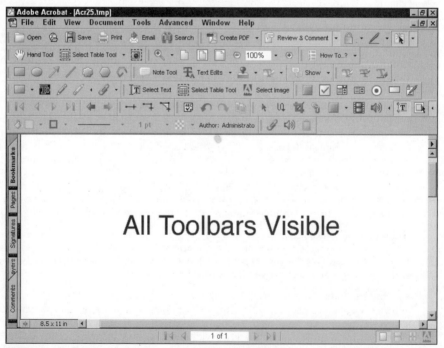

Figure 1-21: The first two rows contain the toolbars shown at the default view. The four rows following are toolbars added from menu commands.

You open toolbars from menu commands in the Tools menu or by opening a context menu. If you're a seasoned Acrobat user, your first encounter with Acrobat Professional might be a bit frustrating if you don't know how to access the tools you want to use. "Where is that Form tool?" you may ask. Don't worry; it's there. You just have to poke around and search for it, or better yet, look over the following descriptions to understand more about how these other tools are grouped into separate toolbars.

Acquiring advanced toolbars

For the purpose of discussion I'll refer to the non-default toolbars as advanced toolbars. Acrobat does not refer to all these tools as advanced tools. Some of the tools are noted in the menu commands by categories without the mention of being an advanced tool. For clarity though, consider all the following toolbars as advanced toolbars.

You can use two methods for displaying a toolbar not visible when you open Acrobat. You can visit the Tools menu where you find a list of tools with submenus. Select a menu item to display the toolbar outside the Toolbar Well as a floating toolbar. In some cases you can find nested submenus and may need to search around for a given toolbar. The other method for accessing these tools is to open a context menu. A number of toolbars appear as menu selections. When a checkmark is not displayed adjacent to the toolbar name, the toolbar is not visible in the Acrobat window.

Advanced Commenting tools

When you open either the View and Toolbars submenu menu or a context menu on the Toolbars Well, the first menu option is Advanced Commenting. Select the menu option and a submenu opens with Comment tools used for review and comment. If you select Show Advanced Commenting Toolbar at the bottom of the menu, the Advanced Comment tools open in their own toolbar as shown in Figure 1-22.

Figure 1-22: Choose Tools ⇨ Advanced Commenting ⇨ Show Advanced Commenting Toolbar or open a context menu on the Toolbar Well and select Advanced Commenting to open the Advanced Commenting toolbar.

Down arrows in the toolbar are noted where pull-down menus can be opened. Click on a pull-down menu and various other tools appear as additional choices. When you click the down arrow to open a pull-down menu adjacent to the Rectangle tool, the menu options show several new Drawing tools introduced in Acrobat.

The Arrow tools, the Cloud tool, and the Polygon tools are new additions to Acrobat. At the bottom of the menu you again have an option to show these tools in a separate Drawing toolbar as shown in Figure 1-23.

Note   The Cloud tool is available only in Acrobat Professional.

Figure 1-23: Selecting the Show Drawing Toolbar menu command opens another toolbar where the drawing tools are contained in their own group.

A down-pointing arrow appears to the right of the Pencil tool. When you click on the arrow a pull-down menu opens and the option at the bottom of the menu commands is Expand This Button. Instead of opening another toolbar, the Advanced Commenting toolbar expands and shows another new tool introduced with Acrobat. You can use the Pencil Eraser tool to erase lines or part of a line drawn with the Pencil tool.

The last pull-down menu opens the Attach toolbar where file and sound attachment tools are found, as shown in Figure 1-24. Another tool new to Acrobat appears in this toolbar. The Paste Clipboard Image tool on the far right side of the toolbar attaches the data you copy to the clipboard.

Figure 1-24: Expanding the Attach toolbar displays the Attach Sound and Paste Clipboard tools.

Notice the hierarchy of how these tools are positioned and how to open them. When you select a toolbar in the Tools menu or from a context menu, you don't immediately have access to the nested toolbars. You need to remember to open a toolbar and then open the pull-down menus to expose more toolbars.

Cross-Reference   To learn how to use each of the Advanced Commenting tools, see Chapter 14.

Commenting tools

The Commenting tools appear a little farther down the menu selections in the Tools menu and the Toolbars context menu. When you open the Commenting toolbar you'll see many of the Comment tools that were available in the last version of Acrobat. The familiar Note, Text Commenting, Stamp, and Highlighting tools are all found in the Commenting toolbar as shown in Figure 1-25.

Note   Text Edit tools are available only in Acrobat Professional running in Windows.

The Text Edit tools are new tools introduced in Acrobat Professional as you can see in Figure 1-25. The tools include: Insert Text at Cursor, Highlight Selected Text, Add Note to Selected Text, and Replace Selected Text. The tools are used to export comments to Microsoft Word files when using Office XP running in Windows XP. Changes have also been made to the Stamp tool where creating custom stamps has been simplified and managing stamp libraries has been changed. Various tool selections are all made from pull-down menus in the Commenting toolbar. The only subtoolbar that can be opened from the Commenting tools is the Highlight toolbar. When you select the pull-down menu for the Highlight tool on the far right side of the Commenting toolbar, a command exists to open the Highlighting toolbar. These tools are the same as the Highlight tools found in Acrobat 5.

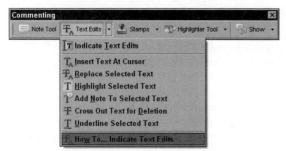

Figure 1-25: Selecting Commenting from the Tools menu or a context menu opens the Comment tools. Open the pull-down menu to view the Text Edit tools.

Cross-Reference

Using the Commenting tools is covered in Chapter 14.

Advanced Editing tools

Advanced Editing tools contain the TouchUp tools, Article tool, Crop tool, Link tool, Movie tool, and Sound tool. The behavior of these tools is similar to how they were used in Acrobat 5. The most radical change exists with the Form tools that are located within this toolbar. If you select the pull-down menu in the Advanced Editing toolbar adjacent to the Button tool, the remaining Form tools are exposed as shown in Figure 1-26. You can also break these tools away and display them in their own toolbar by selecting Show Forms Toolbar.

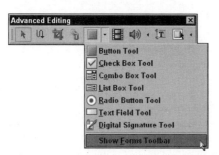

Figure 1-26: Open the Forms toolbar by selecting the pull-down menu adjacent to the Button tool and selecting Show Forms Toolbar.

The Form tools experienced the most obvious changes among the Advanced Editing tools. When you open the Forms toolbar or select a Form tool from the pull-down menu, you immediately have choices for what form field you want to create. No longer does the Field Properties dialog box open when a field is added to the page. For more options as you create fields you can open the Properties Bar by opening a context menu in the Toolbar Well and selecting Properties Bar. The Properties Bar, as shown in Figure 1-27, enables you to set some field properties such as field names, appearances, fonts, and point sizes. Additional properties are established by opening a context menu on the field you create and selecting Properties or clicking on the More button in the Properties Bar.

Cross-Reference

For complete descriptions of the Advanced Editing tools see Part IV. For information on using the Form tools, see Chapter 25.

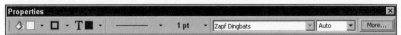

Figure 1-27: The Acrobat Professional Properties Bar enables you to set some field properties without opening the Field Properties dialog box.

Basic tools

The first of the Basic tools shown in the Basic Tools toolbar is the Hand tool followed by the Select Text tool as shown in Figure 1-28. A new tool added in Acrobat Professional is the Snapshot tool. When you select the Snapshot tool and click on a page in the Document Pane or click and drag to open a rectangle with a selection marquee, the area is copied to the clipboard and the tool takes a snapshot of the page or selection. From there you can create a new PDF file or a link to the snapshot.

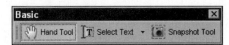

Figure 1-28: The Basic tools contain the Hand tool, Selection tools, and the Snapshot tool.

Selection tools

You can open another toolbar that contains the various selection tools by opening the pull-down menu and selecting Show Selection Toolbar. The toolbar opens with the Text Select, Select Table, and Select Image tools as shown in Figure 1-29. These tools are available to both Windows and Macintosh users.

Figure 1-29: The Selection toolbar contains tools for text, table, and image selections.

Cross-Reference   To understand how to use the Selection and Snapshot tools, see Part III.

Measuring tools

A new feature added to Acrobat with Acrobat Professional is the ability to measure distances on a document page. You have three different tools for measuring in the Measurement toolbar. When you select Measuring from the Tools menu or a context menu, the Measuring toolbar opens as shown in Figure 1-30.

Figure 1-30: The Measuring toolbar offers three tools to measure distances and areas on a PDF page.

The tools include the Distance tool for measuring linear distances, the Perimeter tool for measuring linear distances of angles and objects, and an Area tool for measuring the surface area of objects. Tools such as these might be used for examining measurements in engineering drawings.

For more information related to using the measuring tools, see Chapter 17.

Navigation tools

The most obvious change for previous users of Acrobat when they open any Acrobat 6.0 viewer with the default toolbars in view is the absence of the Navigation tools. These familiar tools are accessible in their own toolbar via the Tools menu or a context menu. Because so many different ways exist to page through PDF files, having the Navigation tools visible as a default isn't really necessary. The Status Bar contains all but the Go to Previous View and Go to Next View tools, and you can access these commands through keyboard shortcuts and other menu commands. If you want to use the navigation tools, shown in Figure 1-31, you can open the toolbar and click on the Navigation buttons.

Figure 1-31: The Navigation toolbar is not visible when Acrobat opens with default toolbars in view. To access the Navigation tools, select Show Navigation Toolbar from the Tools menu or a context menu.

For more information regarding navigating PDFs, see Chapter 3.

Zoom tools

The Zoom toolbar is a default toolbar that is also accessible from the Tools menu and a context menu. The familiar zoom and page views are contained in this toolbar as well as new additions to the way you can zoom in on documents in the Document Pane. Acrobat Professional offers you two more zoom tools that will be much appreciated by users who have experienced long waiting periods for screen refreshes.

When you open a pull-down menu adjacent to the Zoom tool, options for Dynamic Zoom, the Loupe tool, and the Pan and Zoom window are shown as menu options in addition to the familiar Zoom In and Zoom Out tools as shown in Figure 1-32. These new tools enable you to inspect smaller or larger portions of PDF pages without having to zoom in and out of the entire page. If your document pages take a long time to refresh the screen, you'll find these tools to be a big help in navigating through documents.

The Loupe tool and the Pan & Zoom Window are available only in Acrobat Professional.

For more information regarding the use of the new Zoom tools, see Chapter 3.

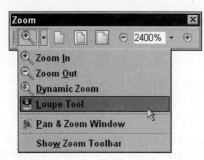

Figure 1-32: The new Zoom tools — Loupe, Dynamic Zoom, and Pan & Zoom — help you view PDF pages much faster.

Customizing the Acrobat workplace

Whether you're an Acrobat pro or a new Acrobat user, seeing all those toolbars scattered across the Toolbars Well the first time can be very intimidating. As you poke around and possibly feel a little frustration trying to identify the right tool icon to select the right tool for the task at hand, please realize that Acrobat is a multifaceted program serving a huge array of needs for different users. Not all the tools and features are intended for use in a single Acrobat session. You may be a PDF forms author and need only Basic tools, Navigation tools, and Form tools. In another session you may be a reviewer and only have need for the Review and Comment tools. You might be an eBook author and need to work with many new features for creating and viewing eBooks or you might want to edit PDF pages and post modified PDFs on your Web site.

When learning all the tools and commands contained in Acrobat Professional, be certain to look over all the chapters where tools are discussed. Learn how to access toolbars and organize them in the Toolbars Well. When you begin a new Acrobat session, set up your environment so you can easily select a tool from toolbars you dock in the Toolbar Well. Frequently return to Table 1-1 and look over the keyboard shortcuts to learn how to quickly access the tools you use most frequently.

As a starting point, you can configure Acrobat to provide you with immediate feedback related to tools selection and keyboard shortcuts. As you first start using Acrobat Professional, follow the steps in the next section to help you customize your environment for more efficient editing and less frustration. In this example, an environment for a PDF forms designer is set up. You can change the toolbars to meet needs in review and markup or PDF creation, or add tools for some other kind of work you do.

STEPS: Setting up the Acrobat environment

1. **Return to toolbar defaults.** If you moved toolbars around, added toolbars to the Toolbar Well, or changed the view from any defaults, start by resetting the toolbars. Position the cursor on any toolbar or an empty area in the Toolbar Well and right-click to open a context menu (Ctrl+click for Macintosh) and select Reset Toolbars.

2. **Show a toolbar.** Open the Tools menu and select the first toolbar you need to add to the Toolbar Well for easy access to the tools you intend to use. In this example, I select Tools ⇨ Advanced Editing ⇨ Forms ⇨ Show Forms Toolbar as shown in Figure 1-33.

3. **Dock the toolbar in the Toolbar Well.** Click the Title Bar of the toolbar floating in the Acrobat window and drag it toward the Toolbar Well. As you arrive at the bottom of the Toolbar Well, you should see a black horizontal line appear. When you see the line, release the mouse button. The toolbar is now docked in the Toolbar Well.

Note If at first you don't see a black horizontal line when the toolbar is moved to the bottom of the Toolbar Well, don't be concerned. If the toolbar you drag is moved anywhere on the Toolbar Well and you release the mouse button, the toolbar will dock.

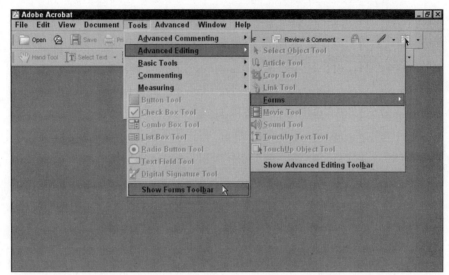

Figure 1-33: Open the Tools menu and select a toolbar to be viewed in the Acrobat window.

4. **Add toolbars for tools you intend to use.** If you need more tools, follow the previous steps and add just the toolbars containing the tools you expect to use in your editing session. In this example I open a context menu on a toolbar in the Toolbar Well and select the Properties Bar. The Properties Bar will be useful when I work with the Forms tools.

5. **Open the Preferences dialog box.** As a new user to Acrobat Professional, you want as much feedback from Acrobat as you can get in regard to the tool names and keyboard shortcuts. You learn as you frequently access a tool. In the Preferences dialog box, Acrobat offers different options for displaying Tool Tips and keyboard shortcuts. To open the Preferences dialog box press Ctrl+K in Windows or ⌘+K in Macintosh.

Note You can also access Preferences by opening the Edit menu and selecting Preferences in Windows or opening the Acrobat menu and selecting Preferences in Mac OS X.

6. **Set Viewing preferences.** Click General in the left pane of the Preferences dialog box. In the right pane open the pull-down menu for Show tool and property button labels and select All labels from the Menu options as shown in Figure 1-34. Check the box for Use single-key accelerators to access tools. Click OK to return to the Acrobat window.

Note When you select All labels, Acrobat displays each tool in the toolbars with an icon and a name. When you check the box for Use single-key accelerators to access tools, you can press a key on your keyboard to access a tool respective to the shortcut.

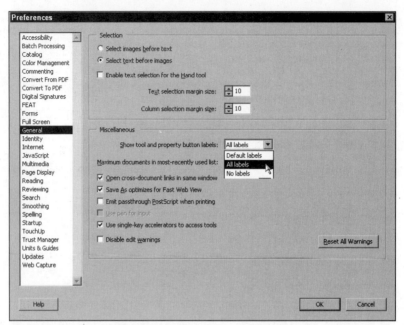

Figure 1-34: Open the Preferences dialog box by pressing Control+K in Windows or ⌘+K in Macintosh. Select the preference category in the left pane and make preferences choices in the right pane.

7. **Open a PDF document.** PDF files are opened via a menu command by clicking on the Open tool or by pressing keyboard shortcuts. You can choose File ➪ Open, click on the Open tool in the top-left corner of the Toolbar Well, or press Control+O for Windows or ⌘+O for Macintosh. Navigate to your hard drive in the Open dialog box and select the file to open. After selecting the file, click on the Open button. (You can also double-click on a filename in the Open dialog box to open the file.)

8. **Open a Tool Tip.** When you place the mouse cursor directly over a tool, a pop-up Tool Tip opens as shown in Figure 1-35. Note the Tool Tip displays the name of the tool and the keyboard shortcut that can be used to access the tool. In this example the cursor is placed over the Button tool. The keyboard shortcut to access a Form tool is F. When you press Shift+F the tool selections are cycled through the tools you see in the toolbar.

As you move the cursor over different tools, the Tool Tips change to reflect the description of the targeted tool and the keyboard shortcut that can be used to make the tool active. More Tool Tips are available to you in the form of Extended Tool Tips. An Extended Tool Tip opens when you keep the cursor over a given tool for approximately three or more seconds. The first Tool Tip is displayed, then after a few seconds more the Extended Tool Tip appears. Extended Tool Tips offer you a little more information about what the tool does.

As you become familiar with the tools, you can return to the Preferences dialog box and turn off the Show tool and property button labels by selecting No labels from the pull-down menu in the General Preferences dialog box. When No labels is active, your toolbars shrink and offer you more room in the Toolbar Well.

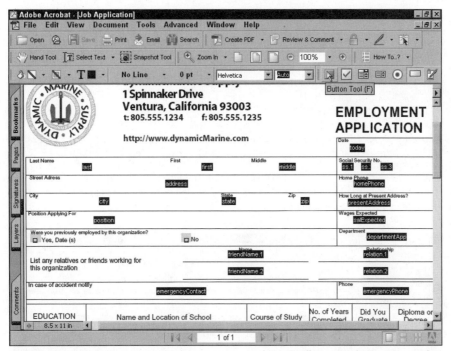

Figure 1-35: When you pause the cursor over a tool in a toolbar, a Tool Tip opens with a description of the tool beneath the cursor. When the preferences have been set to *Use single-key accelerators to access tools, display keyboard shortcuts,* the keyboard shortcut is noted within parentheses.

Palettes

Other tools available to you in all Acrobat viewers are palettes. Palettes are similar to tool-bars in that they can be docked to a docking station called the Navigation Pane; they can be undocked and floated around the Acrobat window much like toolbars; they contain pull-down menus for selecting more options; a series of default palettes appear docked in the Navigation Pane; and there are additional palettes you can view accessible from menu commands.

Some of the distinctions between toolbars and palettes are that palettes can be placeholders for information and tools can appear inside a palette. Whereas tools are used in the Document Pane, many palette operations can take place directly in the palette. Toolbars remain relatively fixed in size, but palettes can be sized and stretched along the Acrobat window to provide you with more room to work within the palette or view the information contained within the palette. In addition, some palettes contain their own tools where edits can be made in the palette and dynamically reflected on the document page. In Acrobat Professional, palettes help you organize content, view specific content across many pages, and provide some tools for global editing of PDF files.

Default palettes

Like toolbars, Acrobat Professional displays a series of palettes docked in a well when you first launch the program. Palettes are contained in the Navigation Pane along the left side of the Acrobat window. By default, the Navigation Pane is collapsed; however, PDF documents can be saved in such a manner where a palette can be expanded when a file is opened in any Acrobat viewer. These settings are document specific and can be toggled on or off for individual PDF documents.

Cross-Reference   For more information about setting various opening views for palette displays, see Chapter 3.

Bookmarks

The topmost default palette tab in the Navigation Pane is the Bookmark tab. PDF documents can be saved in a manner where the bookmarks are visible when the file opens in Acrobat. A good example of such a file is the Acrobat Help file. When you open the Acrobat Help file, bookmarks are visible in an open Navigation Pane as shown in Figure 1-36. You can open and close the Navigation Pane by pressing F6. You can also grab the vertical bar at the right edge of the Navigation Pane and move it left and right to size the pane.

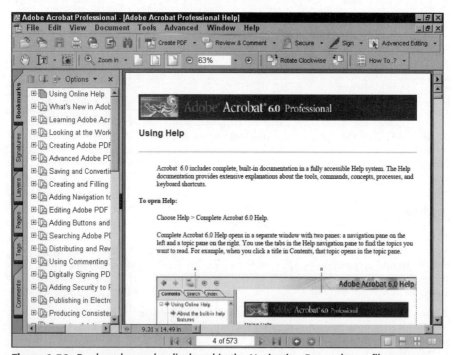

Figure 1-36: Bookmarks can be displayed in the Navigation Pane when a file opens.

Bookmarks are navigation buttons that can launch a page, a view, or one of many different Action types. Anyone familiar with Acrobat already knows much about bookmarks. In Acrobat Professional, features have been added for viewing bookmark names as well as expanding, collapsing, and creating bookmarks.

Cross-Reference For learning how to create and manage bookmarks, see Chapter 10. For learning more about actions associated with bookmarks, see Chapter 15.

Pages

Acrobat users have been familiar with the thumbnail view of each page since the early days of Acrobat. So, if you are familiar with Acrobat, you will immediately observe the absence of thumbnails when you see the Navigation Pane for the first time. Don't despair; you still have thumbnails in all Acrobat viewers, but they're not found in a palette called Thumbnails. The palette name has been changed to Pages. When the Pages tab is opened, the thumbnail views of each page are displayed in the palette window. The main change with Pages is the ability to size thumbnails to the same zoom levels as you can in the Document Pane. No longer do you need to squint your eyes to try to determine what's on a thumbnail page. In Acrobat Professional, you can zoom in to the thumbnail views as large or even larger than a page viewed in the Document Pane, as shown in Figure 1-37.

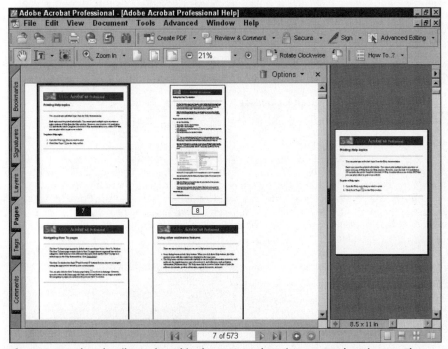

Figure 1-37: Thumbnails are found in the Pages palette in new Acrobat viewers. The thumbnail view of document pages can be sized larger or smaller than in previous Acrobat viewers.

Cross-Reference For a complete description for working with pages (thumbnails), see Chapter 10.

Signatures

The Signatures tab in the Navigation Pane has been repositioned to occupy the third tab spot from the top of the pane. Users of earlier versions of Acrobat will remember that Comments followed Thumbnails in Acrobat 5 viewers.

Digital signatures help you manage signed documents by displaying signatures in the Signature Pane, verifying signatures, clearing them, deleting them, and so on. All these editing tasks with signatures are still available in Acrobat Professional as well as signature validation, which is now available in other Acrobat viewers, too.

For a complete description of creating and managing digital signatures, see Chapter 19.

Layers

The new addition to the Navigation Pane in Acrobat is the Layers tab. Users of the many different Adobe imaging applications will appreciate the addition of support for layers in Acrobat Professional and will already understand terms such as flatten layers, merge layers, and so on, which are commands found in the Layers palette.

Flatten Layers and Merge Layers menu commands are only available in Acrobat Professional.

For a complete description for working with layers, see Chapter 17.

Comments

One of the most significant changes to the default Navigation Pane palettes is the Comments tab. You'll notice the palette is placed at the bottom of the Navigation Pane. Previously, it displayed the comments within a PDF document in a vertical window. The Comments palette now shows you comments in a horizontal window. When you open the Comments tab, you'll notice a number of pull-down menus signified by down-pointing arrows at the top of the pane, a list of comments that can be expanded and collapsed, and a host of tools within the palette as shown in Figure 1-38.

For a complete description for creating and managing comments, see Chapter 14.

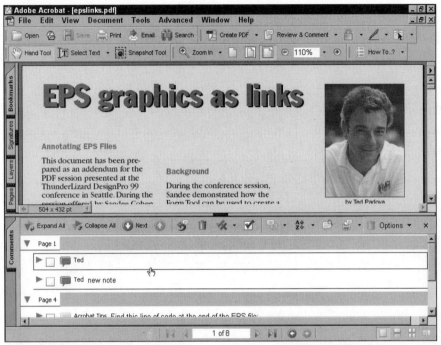

Figure 1-38: The Comments Pane has been radically changed in Acrobat Professional. Many more features have been added to the palette as well as tools used for review and markup.

Hidden palettes

Like toolbars, you can choose to view additional palettes through menu commands. A number of other palettes can be displayed in the Acrobat window and these palettes can also be docked in the Navigation Pane. To open a hidden palette, choose View ➪ Navigation Tabs. From the submenu, you'll find all the palettes available in Acrobat Professional. The list includes the default tabs. If you select a default tab, the Navigation Pane opens and the palette is selected. When you select a hidden palette, the palette opens in the Acrobat window as a floating window with one or more tabs contained in the window.

To dock a tab from a floating window to the Navigation Pane, select the tab to be docked and drag it away from the floating window. Move the tab on top of an expanded Navigation Pane or on top of one of the tabs in a collapsed Navigation Pane. When you release the mouse button the tab is docked in the Navigation Pane. If you dock a tab in the Navigation Pane and quit Acrobat, the tab will be in the same position when you launch Acrobat in your next session.

Articles

The first of the hidden palettes listed in the Navigation Tabs submenu is Articles. Choose View ⇨ Navigation Tabs ⇨ Articles to open a floating window. When you open the Articles palette, both the Articles tab and the Destinations tab appear in the window as shown in Figure 1-39.

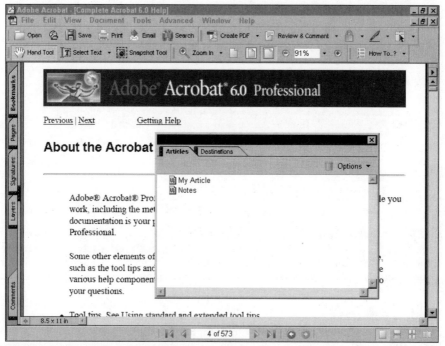

Figure 1-39: When you select Articles in the Navigation Tabs submenu, the Articles palette opens in a window with the Destinations palette.

Articles enable you to create article threads to help users follow passages of text in a logical reading order. No new features have been added to the Article tool since Acrobat 5.

Cross-Reference   For information on creating article threads and managing them, see Chapter 10.

Destinations

The Destinations palette is contained in the same window as the Articles palette. With options in the Destinations palette you can create links to views in documents much like bookmarks. Destinations have advantages over bookmarks. In Acrobat Professional, the menu commands are the same as those found in Acrobat 5.

Cross-Reference   For information on creating destinations and managing them, see Chapter 15.

Content

A new palette designed for managing the structural content of PDF documents is found in the Content tab. When you choose View ➪ Navigation Tabs ➪ Content, the Content palette opens in a floating window with the Fields and Tags palettes as shown in Figure 1-40. Content features help you reflow tagged PDF files and manipulate the structure of tagged documents.

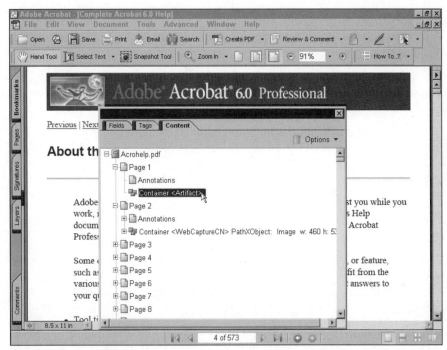

Figure 1-40: The Content palette opens in a floating window alongside the Fields and Tags palette tabs. The Content palette is a new feature in Acrobat Professional, enabling you to manipulate the structural content of PDF documents.

Cross-Reference   For information on working with the Content palette and tagged PDF documents, see Chapter 18.

Fields

The Fields palette enables you to manage form fields on Acrobat PDF forms. You can list all form fields in the palette and execute menu commands from the pull-down menu and context menu opened from within the palette. Inasmuch as there have been many changes to the way form fields are created in Acrobat Professional, only a few additions have been made to the palette options, as explained in Chapter 25.

Cross-Reference   For information related to Acrobat forms, see Part VI.

Tags

Tagged PDF files provide more editing capability with PDF documents and the files can be made accessible to adaptive devices such as screen readers. For adding, editing, and annotating tags in PDF documents, use the Tags palette. Together with the Content palette options, you now have much more control over document accessibility.

Cross-Reference

To understand accessibility and the advantages of creating tagged PDF documents, see Chapter 18.

Info

The Info palette displays the x,y position of the mouse cursor as you move it around the Document Pane. From this palette you can choose to display from among three different units of measure — inches, points, and millimeters. No changes have been made to the Info palette in Acrobat Professional.

Cross-Reference

For information on working with the Info palette, see Chapter 17.

Palette menus

Each of the palettes contains its own Palette menu. When a palette is open in the Navigation Pane or in a floating window, select the Options down-pointing arrow to open a pull-down menu as shown in Figure 1-41. Menu commands found in Palette menus may or may not be available from the top-level menu bar.

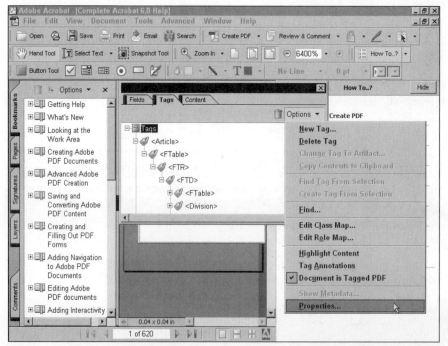

Figure 1-41: Each palette contains a pull-down menu made visible by clicking on the down-pointing arrow to the right side of Options appearing at the top of the palette.

Context menus

Context menus can display different options for palette choices depending on where you open a context menu. If you move the cursor to an empty area when all text and objects in a palette are deselected and open a context menu, the Menu options may be different than when you select text or an object in a palette. This is not always the case, because a few palettes provide you with the same options regardless of whether something is selected or not. In Figure 1-42 a context menu is opened within the Pages tab. No page is selected in the palette and you can see the context menu offers you few options.

Compare Figure 1-42 with Figure 1-43. In Figure 1-43 a page was selected in the Pages palette. When the context menu opens, you can see that many more options are available from the menu list than when all pages are deselected.

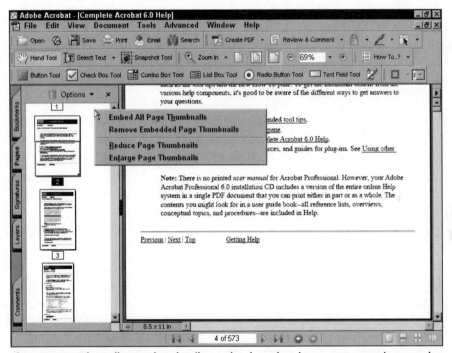

Figure 1-42: When all page thumbnails are deselected and a context menu is opened from within the Pages palette, only a few menu choices are shown in the open menu.

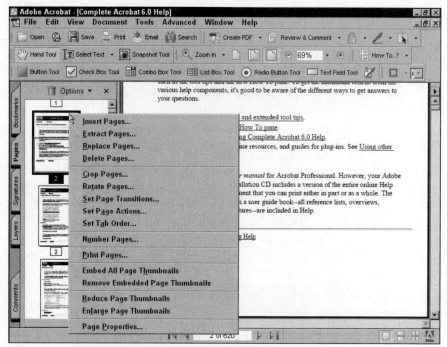

Figure 1-43: When a page is selected in the Pages palette and a context menu is opened, more menu choices are available than when no page is selected.

Accessing Help

You can see that the number of different commands and tools available in Acrobat Professional are extraordinary and that you haven't yet looked at all the submenu options or different preference options accessed from the top-level menu bar. With all these features available to you, your initial Acrobat Professional sessions can sometimes be overwhelming. Fortunately, the great engineers and program designers at Adobe Systems thought about you and they decided to provide some help.

Help with learning more about Acrobat Professional comes in several forms and you can choose from several help methods to find the one that works well in your workflow. This section covers different options for getting help in an Acrobat session.

How To menus

When you launch Acrobat Professional for the first time, you see a window on the right side of the Acrobat window. It occupies more than a third of the horizontal view and on smaller monitors, there won't be much room to work in the Document Pane.

The window is intended for you to toggle the view on and off as you need help in using Acrobat Professional on specific limited topics. To hide the menu, click the Hide button shown in Figure 1-44 or press the F4 key. To open the menu when it's not in view, choose Help ➪ How To or press the F4 key again. If you want the window to remain hidden from view when you launch Acrobat, uncheck the box at the bottom of the window.

Note　You can also open the How To menu from a menu command. Choose View ➪ How to Window and the window opens the same way as when you press the F4 key.

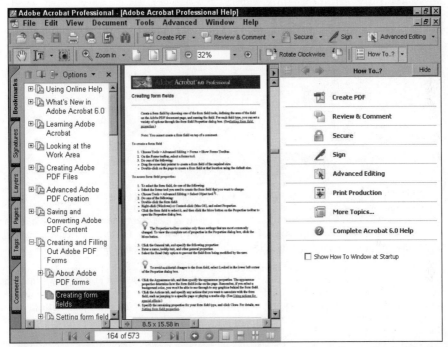

Figure 1-44: When the How To window is visible it occupies more than a third of the horizontal width of the Acrobat window. If you do not want the How To window to open when launching Acrobat, uncheck the box for Show How To Window at Startup.

When the How To window is open, several topics are listed with hot links that take you to definitions to the respective items. These items are a condensed version of a more comprehensive help document explained a little later in this chapter. Keep in mind that not all the Acrobat features are contained in the How To window.

Click on any blue text or the icons adjacent to the blue text to open a view inside the How To window that provides you with a topical listing to assist in refining your search. If you click on an item like Review and Comment, you can see a contents list for specific items related to help on working with comments as shown in Figure 1-45.

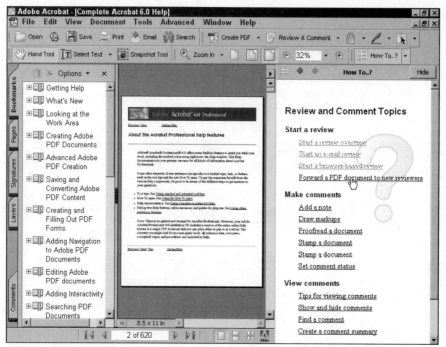

Figure 1-45: Click on a category in the How To window and the window information changes to reflect information about the topic. In most cases you'll see a contents list where specific information about a given category is listed to help you refine your search.

When you arrive at another page that lists the contents, as shown in Figure 1-45, click again on any text displayed in blue to link to information about the subtopic. Using the example of Review and Comments as a category, you could choose to click on Start an e-mail review. The window opens the page where you see a description for how to e-mail comments in a PDF file as shown in Figure 1-46.

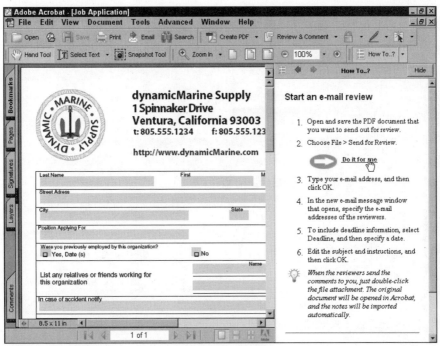

Figure 1-46: Click on an item in the contents page and you are linked to a page where a description appears that explains how to perform a task.

In some cases, you'll see a text description informing you how to go about archiving a result for the item you searched. In other cases you can find dynamic links that help you execute a task. For example, with regard to sending an e-mail with comments attached, there is a button in the How To window stating *Do it for me*. Click on this button and Acrobat invokes the command that permits you to e-mail a PDF attachment. With this particular task you are prompted in a dialog box to specify an e-mail address for the recipient of your data. The How To help item invokes the command for you and opens the dialog box where the e-mail address is typed as shown in Figure 1-47. Replace the default text with a legitimate e-mail address, click OK and the document is packaged and your e-mail program is launched with the PDF document attached to it.

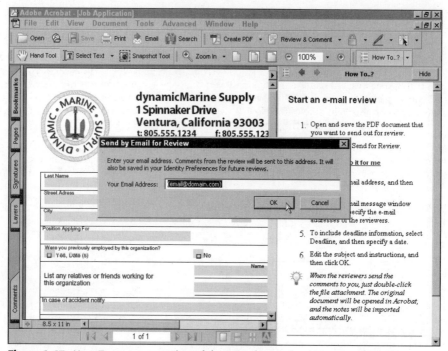

Figure 1-47: How To menus contain task buttons that perform aspects of a task you are learning. As an extension of providing you with help information, Acrobat walks you through steps in some tasks.

Some How To descriptions are text only and won't necessarily contain buttons to launch an action. In other cases you'll find this method of help to be of great assistance in executing some operation you're not familiar with. Task buttons in the How To window are actually executing some of the same commands you can find from using tools, menu items, pull-down menus, and palette tools.

Docking the window

The window is docked on the right side of the Acrobat window by default. You can move the window to the left side by opening a context menu on the title bar above the How To pages. When you open a context menu from the title bar, select the item Docked Left. The window moves to the left side of the Acrobat window and the Navigation Pane and Document Pane slide to the right.

The size of the How To window is fixed and you can't change the horizontal width. Be certain to remember the F4 shortcut to show/hide the window because there won't be much room to work in the Document Pane when the window is in view.

Navigating the How To window

You can return to the opening view of the How To window, called the *Homepage*, by clicking on the icon in the top-left corner of the window. The left and right arrows move to the previous and next window views, respectively. Clicking the arrow does not scroll pages. Rather, it helps you retrace your steps to go back and forth to the recent views. However, if you navigate through a series of pages and click on the Homepage button, it resets the viewing history and you won't be able to use the arrow buttons to retrace your last views. A vertical scrollbar is displayed on the right side of the How To window when the description is longer than can be viewed on your monitor. If the description is short, you won't see a scrollbar.

At the bottom of some descriptions you can find more related information on the topic you searched. Again with hot links, click on text or an icon to open another page offering you related information. If you want to return to the contents, click on another button, also visible at the bottom of a description page, indicating you will return to the topics.

If you want to open another topic without being on the Homepage, you can open the How To Tools menu in the Acrobat Toolbar Well. The down-pointing arrow opens a pull-down menu with the same topics as are listed on the How To Homepage.

Acrobat help

The How To window contains a select group of common Acrobat features where you can find help within the listed topics on the Homepage. You can also access more topics by clicking on the More Topics button on the Homepage. After you click More Topics, another list is displayed with more links to How To descriptions. However, Acrobat is a monster program with many features and listing all the methods for working in the program is not the intent for the How To help. To browse through a comprehensive help guide you need to access a different document. The comprehensive help guide contains more than 650 pages covering just about everything you want to know about Acrobat Professional. There are, in essence, two flavors of the Acrobat Help guide. You can access the Complete Acrobat 6.0 Help document from the Homepage in the How To window or you can open the Acrohelp.pdf file in Acrobat. These two documents are different in that one is part of the program's interface and the other is a PDF document. Depending on which one you open, you have some different methods for viewing and navigation.

Complete Acrobat 6.0 Help

The Complete Acrobat 6.0 Help is opened from the Homepage in the How To window. When you open this document without a PDF file open in the Document Pane you'll immediately notice you have no access to tools and menu commands. That's because the document you're looking at is not a PDF document. It appears similar to files you open in Acrobat with a Navigation Pane on the left side of the window and the page contents to the right. It can be sized and scrolled, but the file is not confined to the Document Pane like PDF files. It behaves more like a floating window on top of the Acrobat window.

To open the Complete Acrobat 6.0 Help file click on the Complete Acrobat 6.0 Help button on the Homepage in the How To menu. When the file opens you see a contents list on the left side and the page contents on the right side of the floating window as shown in Figure 1-48. You can size the Navigation Pane on the left side of the Help window to show more or less of the contents list by dragging the vertical bar left to size down and right to size up.

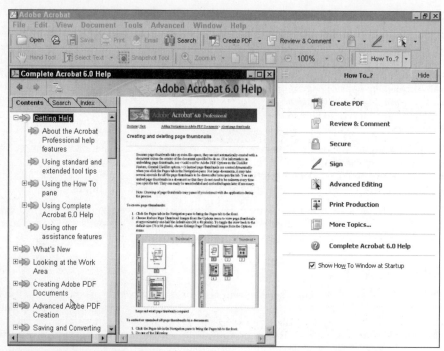

Figure 1-48: The Complete Acrobat 6.0 Help opens as a floating window. When no other file is open, all tools and menus are disabled.

The Complete Acrobat 6.0 Help document contains three tabs in the Navigation Pane and a Topic Pane where pages contain help information. The tabs enable you to list topics, search on keywords, and display an alphabetical index.

Contents tab

By default the Complete Acrobat 6.0 Help document opens with the Contents tab exposed as shown in Figure 1-48. In the Navigation Pane you'll find a table of contents for the document shown in a very similar manner to the way bookmarks are listed in a PDF document. To expand the parent item, click on the plus sign. Subtopics are listed when a parent topic is expanded. To collapse a parent item, click the minus sign adjacent to the parent item you expanded. Click on one of the parent or child topics listed in the Contents tab. The respective page appears in the Topic Pane.

Search tab

To find any word(s) in the help document you can search on words you type in the Search tab. Click the Search tab and the Navigation Pane changes to display a field box where you type your search criteria. Type one or more words in the field box and click Search. The results are then displayed in the Search tab. All text appearing in blue is linked to the page that opens in the Topic Pane as shown in Figure 1-49.

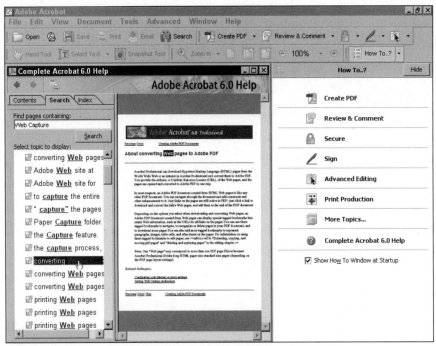

Figure 1-49: The Search tab enables you to search for words contained anywhere in the help document. The search results contain links to pages where the found words appear.

When performing a search in the Search tab you are limited to searching by words only in the search field. You cannot use operators or Boolean expressions. The Search tab works very similarly to the Find command in Acrobat. When you search multiple words, the search results are reported for all instances of all words.

Cross-Reference For more information on using expressions and Boolean operators when searching PDFs, see Chapter 4.

Index tab

The Index tab is similar to any index you find in a manual or book. When you click on the tab, a list of alpha characters (A to Z) appears in the Navigation Pane. The alpha characters are parent markers that can be expanded like the Contents items. Click on the plus sign and the category expands. Click on a child item in the expanded list and the page link opens in the Topic Pane as shown in Figure 1-50.

At the top of the Index tab is a pull-down menu where you can select any alpha character or select All to show the entire alpha list.

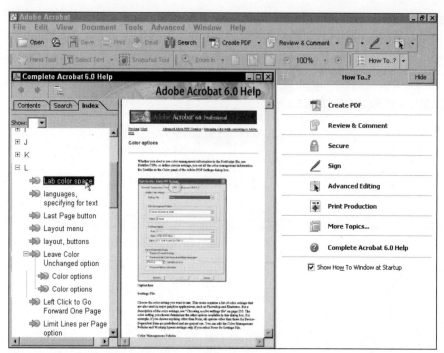

Figure 1-50: The Index tab displays an alpha list for index items. Click on the plus sign to expand an alpha list and click on a listed topic to display the corresponding page.

Navigating topics

The arrows at the top of the Navigation Pane enable you to move forward and back to the pages you view during your search. The review history remains in memory until you close the document. If you close the help file, the review history is flushed from memory and you need to begin again to find information on the same topics.

Printing topics

The Print tool located at the top of the Navigation Pane prints pages from the help document. Navigate to the page you want to print and click on the tool and print the respective page or select a range of pages to print in the Print dialog box.

Acrohelp.pdf

When you open the Complete Acrobat 6.0 Help from the How To window you access a document that can only be managed by the tools within the floating window. If you want to copy text, print multiple pages or the complete help document, make notes with Comment tools, or perform a sophisticated search with Boolean operators, the Complete Acrobat 6.0 Help file prohibits you from performing any of these tasks. Fortunately an identical file in terms of content is available in the Acrobat Help folder added as a PDF file when you install Acrobat. You can open this file and perform any tasks you normally do in Acrobat on any other PDF document.

When you open the Acrohelp.pdf file from the Help ⇨ ENU folder inside your Acrobat folder, the file opens like any other PDF as shown in Figure 1-51. The PDF document opens with bookmarks visible in the Bookmark tab in the Navigation Pane and these bookmarks contain similar descriptions as the contents do in the Complete Acrobat 6.0 Help file. You also have an index to help you search for topics from an alphabetical list.

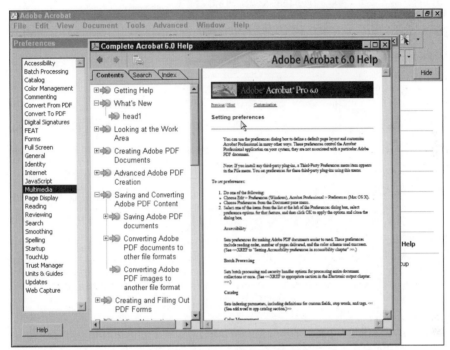

Figure 1-51: The Acrohelp.pdf document contains bookmarks and an index. You can use any of the Acrobat tools to view and print the document.

In addition to the use of tools and viewing the file like any other PDF document, you can search for information within the PDF file by entering your search criteria in the How To window. Type the word(s) to be searched and click on the Search button. The search results are reported in the How To window as shown in Figure 1-52. Click on any text shown in blue and the page containing your first search results opens in the Document Pane.

Advanced search is available to you using Acrobat Search. An index for the file has been created for you and is also installed with your Acrobat installation. You need to load the index before using more advanced search tools and then you can refine your search with many more search features.

Cross-Reference   There's a lot to know about Acrobat Search and you'll find it all covered in Chapter 4.

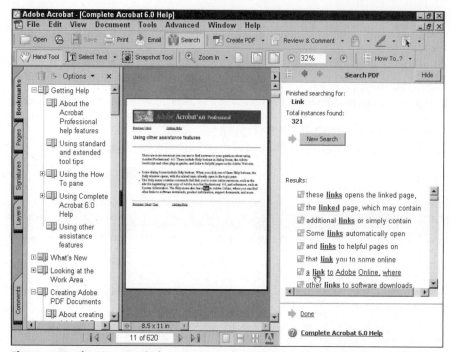

Figure 1-52: The How To window contains a field where search criteria are supplied. When you click on the Search button in the How To window, the search results are listed in a scrollable window below the Search button.

More help

In addition to the help file that covers working in Acrobat Professional, some other help PDF files are located in the Help folder inside your Acrobat folder. These help documents are specific to certain tasks like pdfmark and JavaScript. To view the help documents, open your Acrobat folder and open the Help:ENU folder. The files are PDF documents and can be opened in any viewer.

You will find some dialog boxes offering you help as you work in Acrobat. The discussion for acquiring help from dialog boxes will be addressed in subsequent chapters where help appears in dialog boxes opened while performing different tasks.

Online help is available to you as well from Adobe Systems. If you select the Help menu and choose the menu command Acrobat Online, your default Web browser launches and the Adobe Acrobat products page opens from Adobe's Web site. This Web page and links to the page are continually updated so be certain to make frequent visits to the Acrobat Online help Web pages.

Note   When accessing Adobe's Online Help, your Web browser opens in the foreground while Acrobat Professional remains open in the background. When you finish viewing Web pages and quit your Web browser, the Acrobat window returns to view.

Understanding Preferences

Preferences enable you to customize your work sessions in Acrobat. You can access a Preferences dialog box from within any Acrobat viewer and from within a Web browser when viewing PDFs as inline views. A huge number of preferences exist that all relate to specific tool groups or task categories, and it would not make as much sense to cover them here in the opening chapter as it would among all the chapters that relate to the preference choices. You had a glimpse of the Preference dialog box earlier in this chapter. The remaining preferences are covered in many of the chapters ahead.

Some general things you should know about preferences is that they are contained in a dialog box as shown in Figure 1-34. You make a topic selection in the list on the left side of the dialog box and the related preferences are shown to the right side of the list. You make choices for preferences by checking check boxes or making menu selections from pull-down menus. When you complete making your preference choices, click the OK button at the bottom of the dialog box.

Almost all the preferences you change in the Preferences dialog box are dynamic, which means you don't need to quit Acrobat and relaunch the program for a preference choice to take effect. Preferences remain in effect until you change them again. If you quit Acrobat and relaunch the program, the preferences you set are honored by Acrobat. However, if for some reason the program crashes and you don't shut it down properly, any new preference changes will not be recognized when the program is launched again.

If you find some operation in Acrobat not working as you think it should, first take a look at the Preferences dialog box. In many cases you'll find a check box or menu command not enabled to permit you to perform a task. As you become familiar with specific tool groups and menu commands, make a habit of routinely visiting the Preferences dialog box so you understand all the toggles and switches that affect tool and viewing behavior.

Summary

This chapter offers you a general introduction for working in Acrobat, both Acrobat Standard and Acrobat Professional, and helps you understand the environment, the user interface, and some of the many new features added to the commercial Acrobat products. At the very least, you should know how to go about finding help when you first start working in the program. Some of the more important points discussed in this chapter include the following:

✦ Adobe Acrobat is a multi-faceted program designed to provide solutions for many different business professionals. Several types of Acrobat viewers exist, ranging in features to suit different user needs. The most sophisticated of the three viewers is Acrobat Professional now in version 6. Acrobat Standard offers fewer tools and menu commands than Acrobat Professional.

✦ PDF, short for Portable Document Format, was developed by Adobe Systems and was designed to exchange documents between computers and across computer platforms while maintaining file integrity.

✦ The PDF language format has changed version numbers along with the Acrobat viewers. The current PDF version is 1.5.

✦ Acrobat Professional has introduced many new features and boasts a major upgrade and many new changes to the user interface.

✦ Tasks are performed through the use of menus, tools, and palettes that can be accessed through mouse selections and keyboard shortcuts.

✦ The extensive list of tools appears in an abbreviated form when you open Acrobat and view the default toolbars. You can open additional toolbars from menu commands. You can dock toolbars in the Toolbar Well or float them around the Acrobat window.

✦ Palettes are similar to toolbars in that they can be docked and undocked from a well called the Navigation Pane. Palettes contain pull-down menus, and some palettes contain tools.

✦ The Acrobat workplace can be customized to suit your work style through the use of different preference choices. When preferences, palettes, and toolbars are changed from their default views, the new views are saved when you quit your Acrobat session. They remain unchanged until you change them again or reset them to defaults.

✦ Acrobat Professional provides you extensive assistance through the use of help documents. You can gain immediate help on selected topics through choices in the How To window or by expanding your list of categories to seek help in the Complete Acrobat 6.0 Help window.

✦ A companion file identical to the Complete Acrobat 6.0 Help document is available in PDF form. The PDF file can be searched with Acrobat Search and printed in entirety.

✦   ✦   ✦

Using Acrobat Viewers

In Chapter 1 you got a feel for some of the tools and menu commands provided in Acrobat Standard and Acrobat Professional. If you're a PDF author and you use Acrobat Standard or Professional, knowing the capabilities of one viewer versus another is important. Knowing what capabilities exist with the free Adobe Reader software is equally important. You may be a forms designer and want your forms to reach a large audience. Therefore, you need to know what can be accomplished in Adobe Reader for a user to complete your form. You may be sending out a document for review and want to solicit comments. Therefore you need to know what viewer a user needs to send comments back to you.

Many of the chapters ahead give you an idea for distinctions between Acrobat Standard and Acrobat Professional and the tools accessible from one viewer over another. In this chapter you see some of the distinctions between these viewers, but more important, you see what can be accomplished with Adobe Reader.

Viewer Distinctions

The three Acrobat viewers and Adobe Acrobat Elements are designed to serve different users with different purposes. It should be obvious to you that Adobe Reader, as a free download from Adobe's Web site, is much more limited in features and performance than the products you purchase. It should also be obvious that because of the low cost of Acrobat Elements, it is much more limited in features than Acrobat Standard and Acrobat Professional.

For a general overview, take a look at the following descriptions of the Acrobat products.

Acrobat Elements

Acrobat Elements is available only for site license purchasing of 1,000 or more copies. The unit costs are very aggressive and are lowered with higher volume purchases. This product is intended to offer large companies and enterprises a means for employees to create PDF files. The primary features of Acrobat Elements include

✦ **Viewing and printing:** For viewing PDFs, the Adobe Reader software is used as the viewer. Elements in and of itself is not an Acrobat viewer.

✦ **PDF creation:** The PDF creation available from Elements is limited to creating PDF documents from Microsoft Office products, right clicking on the desktop, or printing files to the Adobe PDF printer.

Adobe Reader

Adobe Reader is available for download from Adobe's Web site free of charge. The Adobe Reader software is distributed for the purpose of viewing and printing PDF files created by users with the higher-end products. The major features of Adobe Reader include

✦ **Viewing and printing:** These features are common across all Acrobat viewers. You can view, navigate, and print PDF documents with Adobe Reader.

✦ **Forms completion and submission:** Adobe Reader enables you to complete forms but not save the form field data. Forms are submitted through the use of a Web browser or buttons created on forms for e-mailing or submitting data to Web servers.

✦ **Reader Extensions:** If a company uses the Adobe Document Server for Reader Extensions product available from Adobe Systems, the company's Adobe Reader users can digitally sign documents, save form data and add comments.

In addition to the preceding, Adobe Reader does provide support for eBook services, searching PDF documents, and extended support for working with accessible documents.

Acrobat Standard versus Acrobat Professional

Acrobat Standard is the lightweight of the authoring programs. However, Acrobat Standard still offers you many tools for PDF creation and authoring. Without going into every tool that differs between Acrobat Standard and Acrobat Professional, the major differences include the following limitations:

✦ **Form field authoring:** No form tools or form field authoring is available with Acrobat Standard. JavaScripts on form fields cannot be created in Acrobat Standard. Although, if a JavaScript is contained in an area accessible to Acrobat Standard, the JavaScript can be edited. You can write JavaScripts on Page Actions in Acrobat Standard.

For information on writing JavaScripts, see Chapter 27.

✦ **Professional Printing:** Acrobat Standard does not provide options for soft proofing color, preflighting jobs, or commercial printing using such features like color separations, frequency control, transparency flattening, and so on. All these print controls are contained only in Acrobat Professional.

For information on preflighting, soft proofing color and commercial printing, see Chapter 23.

✦ **Batch Processing:** Batch processing and running batch commands is not available in Acrobat Standard.

 For information on creating batch sequences, see Chapter 13.

✦ **Creating index files:** Acrobat Catalog is not part of Acrobat Standard. Index files are created only with Acrobat Professional.

For information on creating index files, see Chapter 4.

✦ **PDF Creation:** Acrobat Standard offers an impressive range of file types that can be converted to PDF. The limitations include producing PDFs from AutoCAD, Microsoft Visio, and Microsoft Project for creating layered PDF documents. Acrobat Standard does use Acrobat Distiller, but the Acrobat Standard Distiller does not support PDF/X compliance.

For information on using Acrobat Distiller, see Chapter 7.

✦ **Engineering Tools:** Acrobat Standard does not support tools used by engineers and technical illustrators such as the Measuring tools, certain drawing tools, and advanced features related to managing layers.

For information on using the Measuring tools and working with layers, see Chapter 17.

The preceding items are some of the major differences between the two commercial viewers. You will discover subtle differences as you work with the programs. For example, Acrobat Standard has fewer zoom tools, doesn't have support for drawing or measuring tools, doesn't support comparing documents, and so on.

If your mission is to recommend the product for purchase or make the decision for your own use, be aware that there are three primary distinctions between the products: Acrobat Standard does not support forms authoring, professional printing, or Engineering Tools. If your work is in one of these areas, you need to purchase Acrobat Professional.

Adobe Reader Tools

In addition to knowing the distinctions between Adobe Reader and other viewers, you should become familiar with the tools available to Reader users. These tools are related to the features a user can perform with Adobe Reader and it's helpful to know what the Reader user can do with tools if you intend to distribute documents to Reader users.

The tools available for readers have counterparts in Acrobat Standard and Acrobat Professional. Some of the Adobe Reader tools offer more limited features than the same tool used in the other viewers. The tools include

✦ **File tools:** The file tools include Open, Save a Copy, Print, Email, and Search. The Save a Copy tool saves a duplicate copy of the PDF document. You might use the tool for saving a PDF from an inline view in a Web browser. Saving a copy of files from Adobe Reader does not permit the Reader user to save form data.

✦ **Basic tools:** The basic tools include the Hand tool, Select Text tool, Select Image tool, and the Snapshot tool. The Select Text, Select Image, and Snapshot tools permit Reader users to copy data that can be pasted in other programs. No provision is available for converting the clipboard data to a PDF document. To view the Select Image tool, open the pull-down menu adjacent to the Select Text tool and select the tool or select Expand this Button from the pull-down menu.

✦ **Zoom tools:** The zoom tools include the Zoom In, Zoom Out, and Dynamic Zoom. The advanced zoom tools, such as the Loupe tool and the Pan and Zoom tool, are not available in Adobe Reader.

Rotate View tools: Rotate Clockwise and Rotate Counterclockwise provide temporary viewing rotations only. Rotated views cannot be saved.

Tasks buttons: The only task button available to Reader users is the eBook task button. All the features related to eBook reading and management found in the other viewers are available to Reader users.

Note   The Picture Tasks task button is made available only when certain file types are opened in Adobe Reader or other Acrobat viewers. By default the Picture Tasks button is not accessible. For more information on Picture Tasks, see "Using Picture Tasks" later in this chapter.

Cross-Reference   For information related to acquiring, viewing, and managing eBooks, see Chapter 22.

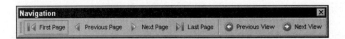

✦ **Navigation tools:** The First Page tool, Previous Page tool, Next Page tool, Last Page tool, Previous View tool, and Next View tool in the Navigation toolbar are made visible by choosing View ➪ Toolbars ➪ Navigation. This toolbar is not loaded by default.

✦ **Properties Bar:** Adobe Reader does have a Properties Bar; however, none of the default tools have options available in the Properties Bar. The Properties Bar is used with Reader Extensions when using the Adobe Document Server for Reader Extensions or other plug-ins that support using the Properties Bar or if you are filling out form fields that are set to Allow Rich Text Formatting.

Cross-Reference   For more information on plug-ins, see the related section at the end of this chapter. For more information on using the Properties Bar, see Chapter 15.

Tabs

Adobe Reader contains the same default tabs docked in the Navigation Pane as found in Acrobat Standard and Acrobat Professional, with the exception of the Comments tab. Commenting is not permitted in Adobe Reader unless you have an eBook created with Adobe DRM open or you've opened a PDF that is Reader-enabled. The Navigation tab not shown by default in the Navigation Pane is the Articles tab. To open the Articles tab, choose View ➪ Navigation Tabs ➪ Articles.

Cross-Reference   For more information on using the Articles tab, see Chapter 15.

Help

The How To Pane offers help topics similar to Acrobat Standard and Acrobat Professional. To view selected help topics, choose Help ➪ How To ➪ General Topics. The How To Pane opens with a list of topics. Click on a topic, and help for the respective topic is displayed in the Pane.

If you want to open the complete Adobe Reader Help document, choose Help ➪ Adobe Reader Help.

Cross-Reference   For more information on using the How To Pane and reviewing the Help documents, see Chapter 1.

Search

All the features available to you in Acrobat Standard and Acrobat Professional for searching information are contained in Adobe Reader. To open the Search Pane, click on the Search tool in the File toolbar. The How To Pane contains the Search Pane as shown in Figure 2-1.

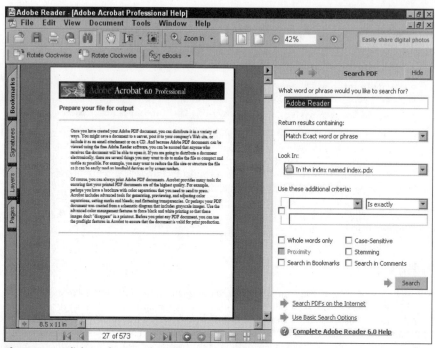

Figure 2-1: Click on the Search tool to open the Search Pane.

Cross-Reference   For information on searching PDF documents, see Chapter 4.

Using Picture Tasks

Picture Tasks is a feature available in all Acrobat viewers. It uses the Image Viewer plug-in, which is installed by default with Acrobat viewers, for the purpose of extracting images. If you look for the Picture Tasks tool in the Toolbar Well, you won't find it. Nor will you find the Picture Tasks tool listed among the toolbars in the View Í Toolbars or Task Buttons submenus. The Picture Tasks tool opens only in an Acrobat viewer Toolbar Well when certain file types are opened in the viewer. Files created from Photoshop Album, Photoshop Elements, JPEG file conversions to PDF, or when you create PDFs from a clipboard image from within Acrobat Standard or Acrobat Professional are the file types that support Picture Tasks.

Cross-Reference   For information on converting Adobe Photoshop Album files to PDF, see Chapter 16. For information on converting JPEG files to PDF, see Chapter 5.

Caution   When converting JPEG images to PDF that you later intend to use with Picture Tasks, don't compress the JPEG files with ZIP compression. ZIP-compressed files are not supported with Picture Tasks.

When one of the aforementioned file types opens in an Acrobat viewer, the Picture Tasks task button is loaded in the Toolbar Well. From the task button a pull-down menu offers you choices for handling the images contained in the open PDF document as shown in Figure 2-2.

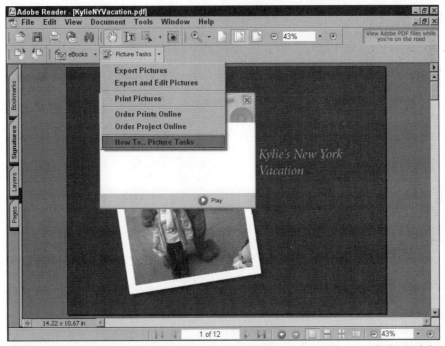

Figure 2-2: The Picture Tasks task button is installed in Acrobat viewers, including Adobe Reader when a file type permits using Picture Tasks operations.

When you open a file where Picture Tasks commands can be used, a dialog box opens as a help reminder that the file you see in the Document Pane has special features. If you click on the check box for Don't Show Again, the next time you open a similar file type, the dialog box shown in Figure 2-3 doesn't open. If you know Picture Tasks can be used with a file and the Picture Tasks task button is not visible in the Toolbar Well, choose View ➪ Task Buttons ➪ Picture Tasks. But remember, the task button in the submenu is only loaded when a file can take advantage of the Picture Tasks commands. Therefore, the task button won't be seen on other PDF files opened in the Document Pane.

Figure 2-3: When a file opens where Picture Tasks can be used, a dialog box opens, informing you that the file has special features. To eliminate the dialog box from opening each time similar files open, check the box for Don't Show Again.

Getting help

To help you understand more about using the Picture Tasks commands, some help information is available in the How To Pane. To open the How To Pane with Picture Tasks help, open the pull-down menu on the task button and select How To... Picture Tasks. The How To Pane opens with a list of the commands available for Picture Tasks and a brief description for each command as shown in Figure 2-4.

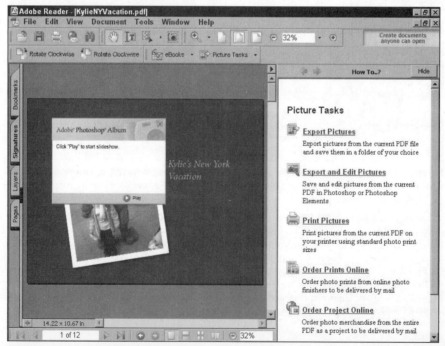

Figure 2-4: Select How To... Picture Tasks from the Picture Tasks pull-down menu and the How To Pane opens with a brief description for using the commands.

Exporting pictures

Adobe Reader, as well as the other viewers, can export images from a file compatible with Picture Tasks. If you want to export a single image, a group of images, or all images to save as separate JPEG images, select Export Pictures from the Picture Tasks pull-down menu or from the Export Pictures link in the How To Pane. Selecting either item opens the Export Pictures dialog box shown in Figure 2-5.

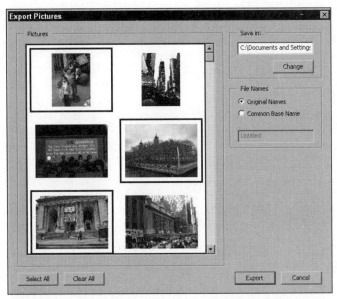

Figure 2-5: Select Export Pictures from either the pull-down menu or the How To Pane and a dialog box opens where you select the pictures to export.

Click on the Select All button to select all images. If you want to export a single image, select the image in the scrollable window. Make noncontiguous selections by holding down the Ctrl/⌘ key and clicking on the thumbnails in the Export Pictures dialog box.

Click on the Change button at the top of the dialog box to locate a folder where you want to save the exported images. In the Browse For Folder dialog box you navigate your hard drive to find the destination folder.

If you want the filenames to use a base name derived from your original filename, select Original Names. If you want to change the base name select Common Base Name and enter the name you want to use in the field box. The Acrobat viewer uses a base name plus 1, 2, 3, and so on plus a .jpg extension. All files are exported as JPEG images.

After making the selections and determining the destination and filenames, click on the Export button. If you make selections and decide to change your mind and want to start over selecting different images, click on Clear All. The images are not deleted from the file. Clear All simply deselects the images.

Exporting and editing pictures

When you select the second menu command for Export and Edit Pictures, you need to have a program installed that can open JPEG files. Ideally you would use an image editor to edit an image, but the export options extend beyond image editors. You can use programs such as Adobe Illustrator, CorelDraw, or Macromedia Freehand to open the files. Programs that import JPEG files (as opposed to *opening* them) are not supported. For example, you don't have an option for exporting from Picture Tasks to Adobe InDesign because it imports files as opposed to opening them.

The first dialog box you encounter when making the menu selection is the Export and Edit Pictures dialog box. Make selections in the dialog box like you do when exporting pictures. A button appears for Change in the Editing Application area of the dialog box. Click on Change and the Choose Image Editor dialog box opens. Navigate your hard drive and locate the image editor you want to use. Click on the Edit button in the Export and Edit Pictures dialog box and the selected image(s) opens in your image editor.

After making edits to images, you save the files from the image editor as new files. If you use a program such as Adobe Photoshop or Photoshop Elements or similar image editor, you can choose any file format supported by the program. When saving files, the original PDF document opened in the Acrobat viewer remains unchanged. This feature is much different than using image editors with PDF images when you select Edit Image from a context menu opened with the TouchUp Object tool. No dynamic updating in the PDF document occurs when using the Picture Tasks commands.

 For information on editing images using the Edit Image command in Acrobat, see Chapter 9.

Printing pictures

A marvelous way of printing PDF documents containing photos is to use the Picture Tasks command for Print Pictures. For photo albums and traditional photo prints that are obtained from photo finishing centers, the options with Picture Tasks offer you more layout flexibility than using the Print command in Acrobat viewers.

 For information on printing PDF files, see Chapter 23.

Select Print Pictures from the Picture Tasks task button or the How To Pane and the Select Pictures dialog box opens. Select the pictures you want to print and click on the Next button at the bottom of the dialog box. The Print Pictures dialog box shown in Figure 2-6 opens after clicking on the Next button. In this dialog box you make selections for the layout options you want for your prints. Among the choices are

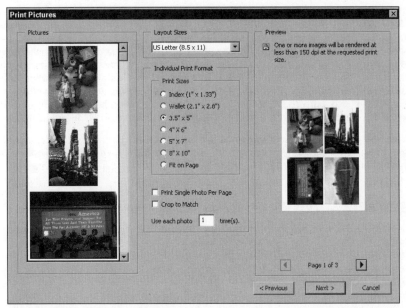

Figure 2-6: Select Print Pictures from either the pull-down menu or the How To Pane and a dialog box opens where you select the pictures to print and the layout options for the printed pages.

✦ **Layout Sizes:** Select a paper size from the pull-down menu.

✦ **Print Sizes:** Select the size of the prints. Notice the sizes match traditional photo finishing sizes. The Fit on Page item sizes the photo to the maximum size available for the selected page size.

✦ **Print Single Photo Per Page:** Photos are automatically positioned on pages according to size and the maximum number of images that can fit on the selected page size. If you want to limit the number of photos to a single image in each page, select this radio button.

✦ **Crop to Match:** The photo is sized to match the selected Print Size. This choice fills the Print Size as much as possible and eliminates any white borders that might otherwise print. Note, however, that the files need to be proportional to the Print Size to print borderless prints. If one side of the other does not fit the Print Size, you'll see a white border on that side.

✦ **Use each photo [ ] time(s):** For dupes, enter the number of duplicate images you want to print. If a single image is what you want, be certain to leave the default at one.

✦ **Arrows:** The left and right arrows below the thumbnail preview of the pages enable you to view a preview of each page by clicking on the next and previous arrows.

✦ **Next:** Click on Next and the Print dialog box opens. Make choices in the dialog box for the print attributes as described in Chapter 23 and click on Print.

Tip

The setup you create with Picture Tasks printing is not saved with the PDF document. If you want to take your PDF document to a photo finishing center to print photos on commercial photo print machines (something like a Fuji Frontier), you leave the Picture Tasks print attributes in the hands of technicians at the photo lab. To deliver a file ready to print and take away any room for error that might occur with others setting up the print attributes, print your file to disk as a PostScript file. In the Print dialog box, check the box for Print to file. Open the PostScript file in Acrobat Distiller and distill the PostScript. The file you create is print ready in a layout you created with the Picture Tasks print option. (Note: You need to have either Acrobat Standard or Acrobat Professional to distill PostScript files.)

Cross-Reference

For information on printing PostScript files and distilling files with Acrobat Distiller, see Chapter 7.

Using online services

The remaining menu commands for Picture Tasks relate to services you can order online. Select the menu option for Order Prints Online and the Select Pictures dialog box opens where you make choices for the prints you want to order. Click on the Next button and an online order service is opened in your default Web browser. Follow the instructions to place an order with a provider.

Select Order Project Online to place an order for your PDF file. Instead of selecting individual photos, the entire PDF is sent to the service provider. Follow instructions for placing the order and the merchandise you want to purchase.

At the introduction of Acrobat 6, the online services are minimal. As Acrobat matures, more service centers should appear in a list of online service providers and more products are likely to be offered. Be certain to update your online services if you see a dialog box prompting you for updates.

Using Plug-ins

All Acrobat viewers support a plug-in architecture. Plug-ins are installed during your Acrobat installation and many features you find by exercising commands and using tools are made possible by the use of plug-ins. To view the current plug-ins installed with the viewer you use, choose Help ⇨ About Adobe Plug-ins. The About Adobe Plug-Ins dialog box opens as shown in Figure 2-7.

The list of the left side of the dialog box lists the name of the installed plug-ins. Click on a name and you see a description for the plug-in including whether the plug-in is certified, the version number, creation date, text description, and dependencies. To examine different plug-ins, select them in the left pane and view the description on the right side of the dialog box.

Plug-ins can be developed by Adobe Systems or by third-party manufacturers. All Adobe plug-ins are *certified* plug-ins meeting standards set forth by Adobe Systems. All third-party plug-ins are not certified. For some features used in Acrobat, loading only certified plug-ins enables a given feature. Working with eBooks is one example where only certified plug-ins can be used.

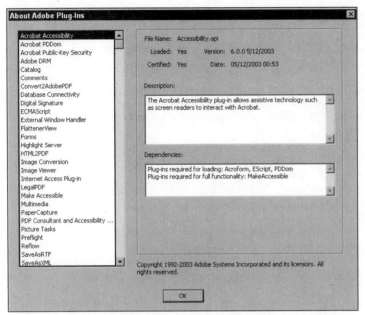

Figure 2-7: The About Adobe Plug-Ins dialog box lists all the plug-ins accessible to your viewer.

In order to instruct your Acrobat viewer to open with only certified plug-ins, open the Preferences dialog box by choosing Edit ➪ Preferences. Select Startup in the left pane and click on the Use only certified plug-ins check box as shown in Figure 2-8. When you quit your Acrobat viewer and relaunch the program, only certified plug-ins are loaded.

Plug-ins developed by third-party developers can also be loaded. The list of available resources for adding to Acrobat functionality in the form of add-ons and plug-ins is almost limitless. As you review all the chapters in this book and find that something you want to accomplish in your workflow is not covered, look for a plug-in developed by a third-party manufacturer. Chances are that you can find a product well suited to do the job.

Plug-ins for Acrobat are far too numerous to mention in this book. For a single source where you can view a list of plug-ins, download demonstration copies, and make purchases, visit the Planet PDF store at www.pdfstore.com. On the Planet PDF Web site you'll find product descriptions and workflow solutions with almost any third-party product designed to work with Acrobat. When you visit the Web site and review the products, be certain the product you purchase is upgraded to work with Acrobat 6.0 and the viewer you use. All products are listed with links to the manufacturer's Web sites, so you can find product descriptions, version numbers, and compatibility issues.

If you download a third-party plug-in you will need to disable using certified plug-ins. Return to the Preferences dialog box and disable the option if you experience problems accessing the features of the plug-in.

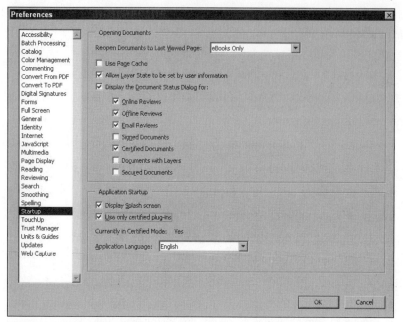

Figure 2-8: Select Use only certified plug-ins to open Acrobat, allowing only certified plug-ins to load.

At times you may find a plug-in conflict among several third-party products or a plug-in that may have a bug. If your Acrobat functionality is impaired and you can't launch the program, hold down the Shift key when opening your viewer. All plug-ins are disabled when you use the modifier key. Open the Preferences dialog box again and select Use only certified plug-ins. Quit and re-launch the program and the offending plug-in should be eliminated during startup.

If you find a plug-in creating a problem, you may need to use a process of elimination to diagnose the problem by opening your plug-ins folder and removing all plug-ins. Then add several plug-ins at a time back to the plug-ins folder and launch your viewer. Keep adding plug-ins back to the plug-ins folder until you discover which plug-in produces the error.

Summary

✦ Adobe Systems introduced four Acrobat products with the release of Acrobat 6.0. The viewers include Adobe Reader, Acrobat Standard, and Acrobat Professional. The Adobe PDF creators include Acrobat Elements, Acrobat Standard, and Acrobat Professional.

✦ Adobe Reader is a free download from Adobe's Web site. All other products require purchase. Acrobat Elements is available only in site license quantities of 1,000 or more.

✦ Adobe Reader does not support editing PDF documents, saving PDF form data, or any form of PDF creation.

✦ Picture Tasks are used with files that originated in Adobe Photoshop Album, Adobe Photoshop Elements, or JPEG files converted to PDF with Acrobat Standard or Professional.

✦ The Picture Tasks task button appears only in an Acrobat viewer Toolbar Well when opening one of the file types listed in the preceding bullet.

✦ Picture Tasks enable you to print, extract, and edit JPEG images. Online services provide a means of sending your photos and PDF creations to online services for printing and other packaging.

✦ Acrobat plug-ins are additions to Acrobat that offer features and tools for adding more functionality to Acrobat viewers. Plug-ins are installed with Acrobat from sources developed by Adobe Systems.

✦ Plug-ins are available from third-party software manufacturers. A complete list of plug-ins and demonstration products is available at the Planet PDF Store.

✦   ✦   ✦

Viewing and Navigation in Adobe Acrobat

Acrobat viewers provide you with many different kinds of tools to view pages and move around PDF documents. As a visitor to PDFs created by other PDF authors you can use many tools within the program to browse pages and find information quickly. As a PDF author you can create viewing options and links to views you know will help the end user explore your files. In this chapter I cover all viewing tools, pages, documents, and the different kinds of viewing options you have available in Acrobat viewers. I leave the authoring items and how-to methods to other chapters. For now, just realize this chapter is an abbreviated form of looking at a huge list of possibilities for viewing and navigation. The amplified explanations follow in several other chapters.

Many new features have been implemented in Acrobat and many changes have been made from earlier versions of the program. If you're an experienced user, don't pass this chapter by. There are new tools, many changes to names used to describe tools and commands, and a complete rearrangement of the menus and menu commands. I hope this chapter can help you save time finding something you know should still be in the program, but for the life of you, can't find it.

Setting Up the Work Environment

When viewing PDF documents you'll want to use tools that help you easily navigate pages and files. By default, navigation tools are not loaded in the Acrobat Toolbar Well. Open the View menu and select Toolbars ➪ Navigation. When the Navigation toolbar opens in Document Pane, open a context menu from the Toolbar Well and select Dock All Toolbars.

As is explained in this chapter, there are several tools and menu commands that provide a means for navigation pages and documents. When you're familiar with alternative methods, you can leave the Navigation toolbar hidden, especially if using other toolbars that occupy a lot of room in the Toolbar Well. If you're new to Acrobat, keep the Navigation toolbar open as you work through this chapter.

Navigating PDF Documents

Page navigation in an Acrobat viewer is handled by several means. You can scroll pages with tools, menus, and keystrokes; click hypertext links; and use dialog boxes to move through multiple documents and individual pages. Depending on how a PDF file is created and edited, you can also follow Web links and articles through different sections of a document or through multiple documents. All Acrobat viewers have many navigation controls and several ways to go about viewing and navigating PDF pages.

Navigation toolbar

Navigation tools are found in a toolbar and in the viewer Status bar. By default, the Navigation toolbar is hidden. If you want to open the toolbar and keep it around the Acrobat window in either the Toolbar Well or a comfortable place beside the Document Pane choose View ➪ Toolbars ➪ Navigation. The toolbar opens in the Acrobat window as shown in Figure 3-1.

As in many other applications, icons for these navigation tools resemble the buttons on VCRs, CD players, and tape recorders, which when clicked move you through the media. For the most part, the icons will be familiar if you've ever dealt with video frames in applications on your computer or worked a VCR. If you change your Preferences settings to show all labels for toolbar properties as I explain in Chapter 1, you won't need to rely on remembering what the icons represent. A text description explains what each tool does within the toolbar as shown in Figure 3-1.

Figure 3-1: The Navigation toolbar shows the icon and name for each tool when the Show All Labels menu selection is made in the Preferences dialog box.

The tools for navigation in Acrobat Professional and other Acrobat viewers include the following:

✦ **First Page:** In the current active document window, this tool returns you to the first page in the document.

✦ **Previous Page:** This moves you back one page at a time.

✦ **Next Page:** This tool scrolls forward through pages one page at a time.

✦ **Last Page:** This tool moves you to the last page in the document.

✦ **Go to Previous View:** This tool Returns you to the last view displayed on your screen. Whereas the four preceding tools are limited to navigation through a single open document, the Go to Previous View tool returns you to the previous view even if the last view was another file.

✦ **Go to Next View:** This tool behaves the same as the Go to Previous View tool, except it moves in a forward direction. Use of the Go to Previous View and Go to Next View tools can be especially helpful when navigating links that open and close documents. The

Next Page and Last Page tools confine you to the active document, whereas the Go to Previous View and Go to Next View tools retrace your navigation steps regardless of how many files you have viewed.

The Navigation toolbar can be docked horizontally in the Toolbar Well, vertically along either side of the Document Pane, or horizontally below the Status Bar. If you dock the toolbar vertically by dragging it to the right side of the Document Pane, the toolbar docks to the left side of the How To window. If you drag and dock to the left side when the Navigation Pane is open, the toolbar docks vertically to the left side of the Navigation Pane. Figure 3-2 shows the Navigation toolbar docked on the left side of the Navigation Pane and Figure 3-3 shows the Navigation Pane docked vertically along the left side of the How To window.

Cross-Reference   For docking toolbars below the Status Bar, see the discussion on the Status Bar later in this chapter.

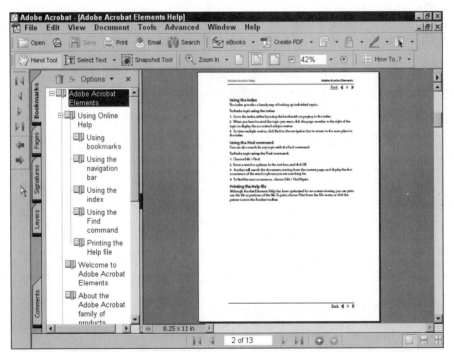

Figure 3-2: Dragging the Navigation toolbar to the left side of the Navigation Pane docks the toolbar vertically.

If the How To window is closed, the Navigation Pane docked on the right side appears on the far right side of the Document Pane.

Clicking on one of the tools in the toolbar invokes the action associated with the tool. If you want to move through pages left or right, click on the left or right arrows. If you want to go to the first or last page in the file, click on the respective tools described earlier.

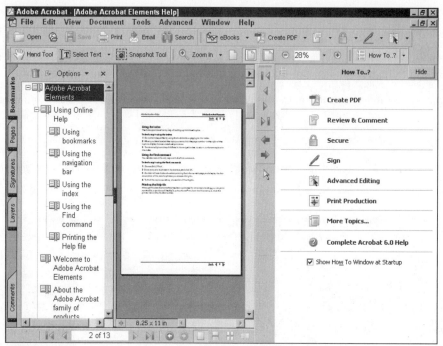

Figure 3-3: Dragging the toolbar to the right side of the Document Pane docks the toolbar vertically on the right side.

Context menus

Acrobat viewers make limited use of context menu commands for page navigation. This is a big change over previous versions of Acrobat, where you had many choices for page navigation and page viewing. In the new release of Acrobat, page navigation from a context menu is limited to moving between opening the next page and the previous page. To use a context menu for these navigation commands, select the Hand tool and open the context menu.

Navigation menu commands

The View menu contains all the page navigation commands formerly listed under the Document menu in Acrobat 5. You can use these commands to achieve the same results as using the Navigation tools when viewing pages in a PDF file. Notice that the View menu now more clearly describes viewing operations, and it should be less confusing for new users to find menu commands associated with views.

When you open the View menu you can select menu commands that perform the same operations as the Navigation toolbar does. However, many users would certainly opt for using the toolbar or keyboard modifiers to navigate pages because other methods for page navigation are much easier than returning to menu commands. The real value in the View menu is all the other viewing commands you have accessible in Acrobat viewers. In Figure 3-4 you can see the many commands for viewing not only pages, but also tools and tool buttons.

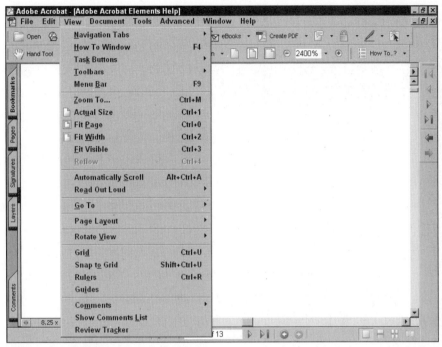

Figure 3-4: The View menu contains many different view commands for page viewing, tools, and tool buttons.

Those viewing commands apart from the same options you have for navigation with the Navigation toolbar include commands for viewing tools, for various page views, and alternatives to viewing such as reading and scrolling pages automatically. The tools that can be displayed in the View menu don't have anything to do with your page viewing and navigation, but I've included them here because many are listed in the View menu commands. Following is a list of what you can find in the View menu.

Task buttons

Task buttons don't have anything to do with PDF viewing; rather, they are used for PDF editing. However, the visibility of these tools is toggled on and off in the View menu. Unlike the other toolbars that contain several different tools in a single palette, the Task buttons are individual tools contained in the Task toolbar that can be toggled on and off. If you deselect a Task button, the tool disappears but the Task toolbar remains in view in the Toolbar Well or as a floating toolbar. From the View menu, open the Task buttons submenu as shown in Figure 3-5 and select the tools you want to view or hide.

Note You cannot pull a single Task button out of the Task toolbar and dock it or float it on the Acrobat window by itself. The tools are fixed to the Task toolbar, but they can be made visible or hidden from the Task toolbar by selecting the respective menu commands.

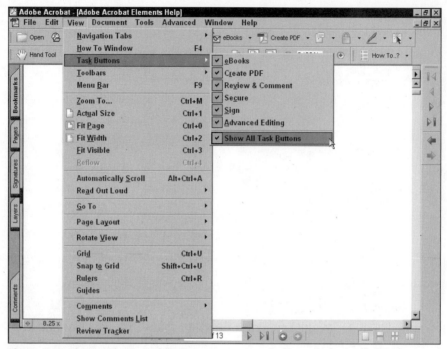

Figure 3-5: Choose View ⇨ Task Buttons to open a submenu where the Task buttons view can be toggled on/off.

The different Task buttons include:

 eBooks: Displays the eBooks button. Use this button to view your personal bookshelf library and to access a tool for getting eBooks online.

 For information related to displaying eBook libraries and getting online eBooks from within Acrobat viewers, see Chapter 22.

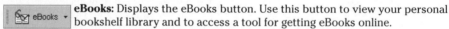 **Create PDF:** Displays the Create PDF toolbar button. Use the pull-down menu on this toolbar to select different file formats for PDF conversion within Acrobat Standard and Acrobat Professional.

For information related to how to use the Create PDF tool and PDF conversion from different file formats, see Chapter 5.

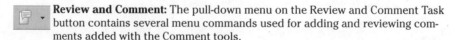 **Review and Comment:** The pull-down menu on the Review and Comment Task button contains several menu commands used for adding and reviewing comments added with the Comment tools.

 For information related to the use of the Review and Comment tools and menu commands, see Chapter 14.

Secure: Menu options from the Secure Task button enable you to encrypt your document; you can choose between Password Security and Certificate Security (formerly in Acrobat 5 known as Standard Security and Self-Sign Security). From a one-stop menu you can access all your security options.

 For information related to file encryption and security, see Chapter 19.

 Sign: Enables you to add a Digital Signature. Unlike previous versions of Acrobat, you don't access a Digital Signature tool. Signatures are added with menu selections from the pull-down menu options for this Task button.

 For information related to signing documents with digital signatures, see Chapter 19.

Advanced Editing: The Advanced Editing Task button has a single menu command for showing the Advanced Editing toolbar from the pull-down menu beside the Task Button icon. Use this option to open the Advanced Editing toolbar. When you open Acrobat in the default toolbar views, the many editing tools found in earlier versions of Acrobat, such as the Article tool, the Crop tool, the Link tool, the Form tool, the Movie tool, and so on, are hidden from view. These tools were always in view in earlier versions of Acrobat in the default toolbar views. In Acrobat 6 they are hidden from view by default. However, the tools are immediately available when you use the pull-down menu command from the Advanced Editing Task button.

About Screen Readers

The term *screen reader* as used here refers to hardware devices connected to computers that enable the reading aloud of computer files. Devices such as JAWS, Kurzwiel, and a host of other specialized software programs are sold to people with vision and motion challenges for the purpose of voice synthesizing and audio output. Many of these devices deliver audio output from proprietary formatted files or a select group of software applications. Some screen readers read raster image files saved in formats such as TIFF, perform an optical character recognition (OCR) on-the-fly, and read aloud text as it is interpreted from the image files. This method makes it easy to scan pages of books and papers and have the scanned images interpreted by the readers.

Because Acrobat has implemented many tools and features for working with accessible files for the vision and motion challenged, screen reader developers have been supporting PDF format for some time. When a PDF is delivered to a reader and you clear the box for Deliver data in pages when document exceeds ___ pages, the entire PDF file is sent to the reader before the first page is read. If you have long documents, you can choose to send the number of pages to the screen reader and break up the file into smaller pages. When the default of 10 pages is selected, ten pages are sent to the screen reader and the reading commences. After the pages are read, another ten pages are sent to the screen reader and read aloud, and so on.

Reflow

Reflowing documents has changed from using a tool in earlier versions of Acrobat to using a menu command in Acrobat 6; the command is accessed via the View menu. Document reflow enables users to view PDF documents on adaptive devices for the visually impaired and it is used when porting PDF files to handheld devices and tablets. When you reflow text onscreen or when using other devices, the text in the PDF wraps according to the zoom level of the page or the device viewing area. Therefore, when you zoom in on a paragraph of text and the text moves off the viewing area of your screen, as shown in Figure 3-6, you can access the Reflow command and the text automatically scrolls to your window size, as shown in Figure 3-7.

Cross-
Reference
                For more information on text reflow, see Chapter 18.

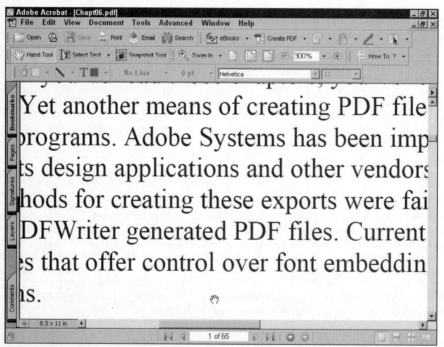

Figure 3-6: When zooming in on a page, the text disappears from the Document Pane without wrapping to conform to the screen size.

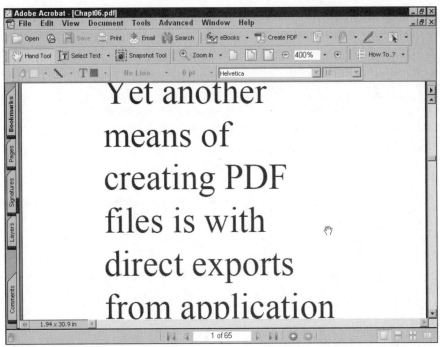

Figure 3-7: When you choose View ⇨ Reflow, the text wraps to conform to the zoom level and your monitor or device screen size.

Reflow works only with tagged PDF documents. When you choose View ⇨ Reflow you can immediately determine whether you are viewing a tagged PDF file. The Reflow tool is grayed out if the file is not a tagged PDF. To test the tool and view with Reflow, open the Acrohelp.pdf file in your Acrobat/Help/ENU folder. The file is a tagged PDF document and the Reflow tool is accessible when you open the file. Zoom in to a zoom level that clips the text on the left or right side of your screen; then choose View ⇨ Reflow.

Cross-Reference   To learn how to create tagged PDF files, see Chapter 6. To learn the benefits of using tagged PDF documents, see Chapters 12 and 18.

Automatically Scroll

Automatic scrolling scrolls pages in the open file at a user-defined speed. When you select the command, Acrobat automatically switches the Page Layout view to Continuous view, and the pages in the document scroll up, permitting you to read the text without using any keys or the mouse. Attribute changes for automatic scrolling include:

✦ **Changing scrolling speed:** To change the scrolling speed, press a number key from 1 (being the slowest) to 9 (being the fastest) on your keyboard.

✦ **Pausing:** To pause the scrolling, press the minus key.

✦ **Resuming:** To resume scrolling, press minus again.

✦ **Stopping:** To stop the scrolling, press the ESC key.

The Page Layout view automatically switches to Continuous when you select Automatically Scroll from the View menu. When you stop the scrolling, the Page Layout view remains in a Continuous view. If you want to return to Single Page view, use the Single Page tool or select the Single Page menu command.

For information related to page layout views, see the Page Layout section later in this chapter.

Read Out Loud

This command is a marvelous new addition to Acrobat. For accessibility, Acrobat PDF documents can be read aloud without the purchase of additional equipment such as hardware screen readers. If you want to turn your back on the computer while doing some other activity, you can have Acrobat read aloud any open document. For entertainment purposes you can gather the family around the computer and have an eBook read to you.

When you choose View ➪ Read Out Loud a submenu opens with four menu commands. The menu commands all have keyboard shortcuts associated with them, so you can use key shortcuts or the actual menu commands. For pausing and stopping the reading, you may want to remember these keyboard shortcuts. The commands include:

✦ **Read This Page Only** (Alt+CtrlV or Control+⌘+V)**:** The current page in view in the Document Pane is read aloud. Reading stops at the end of the target page.

✦ **Read To End of Document** (Alt+Ctrl+X or Control+⌘+X)**:** The reading starts on the page in view and reads to the end of the document. If you want to start at the beginning of your file, click the First Page tool before selecting the menu command.

✦ **Pause/Resume** (Alt+Control+Y or Control+⌘+Y)**:** After the reading begins, you see the Pause command in the submenu. Select Pause or press the keyboard shortcut keys and Resume appears in the menu. Use the same menu command or shortcut to pause and resume.

✦ **Stop** (Alt+Control+Z or Control+⌘+Z)**:** To stop the reading aloud, select the command or the keyboard shortcut.

Attribute settings for reading aloud are changed in the Preferences dialog box. To change the reading aloud attributes, choose Edit ➪ Preferences in Windows or Acrobat ➪ Preferences in Mac OS X or use the keyboard shortcut (Control+K or ⌘+K). In the left pane shown in Figure 3-8, Reading is selected. The Reading preferences are displayed in the right pane. Preference settings include:

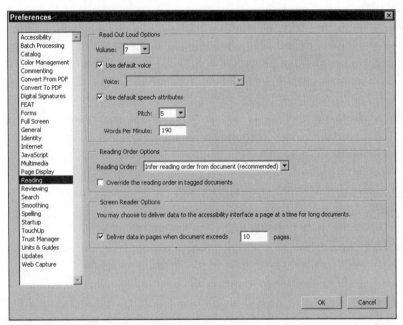

Figure 3-8: To open Reading preferences, select the Preferences command or press Ctrl+K or ⌘+K. Click on the Reading item in the list at the left side of the Preferences dialog box.

✦ **Volume:** Volume settings are adjusted in the pull-down menu. Choose from 0 (zero) to 10 to lower or raise the volume.

✦ **Use default voice:** By default the check box is enabled. If you want to change the voice deselect the check box and open the pull-down menu adjacent to Voice. The voice availability depends on voices installed with your operating system. Your text to speech default voice installed with your operating system is used. By default you may have only a single voice available. If you want additional voices, consult your operating system manual. If no additional voices are installed, you won't be able to change the voice. If you have multiple voices installed, select a voice from the pull-down menu as shown in Figure 3-9.

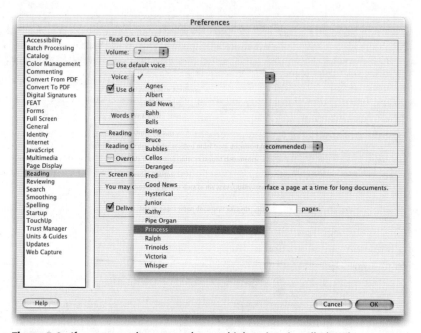

Figure 3-9: If your operating system has multiple voices installed and you want to change the default voice to another voice, deselect the Use default voice check box. From the Voice pull-down menu, choose the voice you want to use.

✦ **Use default speech attributes:** The speech attributes are settings for the pitch and the speed the voice reads your file. If you want to change the pitch and/or reading rate, deselect the check box. Pitch can be changed to a value between 1 and 10. To completely understand what's going on with the pitch settings, experiment a little and listen to the various pitch changes with the voice you select from the Voice pull-down menu. Words Per Minute enables you to slow down or speed up the reading. The default is 190 wpm. If you want to make a change, type a new value in the field box.

✦ **Reading Order:** Three choices are available from the pull-down menu. When in doubt, use the default setting to Infer reading order from document (recommended).

  • **Infer reading order from document (recommended):** With this choice Acrobat makes some guesses about the order for what items are read on the page. If you have multiple columns and the layout is not clearly set up as a page with no layout attributes, the reading order may need some finessing. Acrobat will do its best to deliver the reading in an order compliant to the page layout.

  • **Left-to-right, top-to-bottom reading order:** Reading order delivers the reading ignoring any columns or heads that may be divided across a page. This choice might be best used for a book designed as text only in a single column.

  • **Use reading order in raw print stream:** Delivers words in the document in the order recorded in the print stream.

✦ **Override the reading order in tagged documents:** Tagged PDF documents contain structural information and they are designed to be accessible with reading devices so the proper reading order conforms to the way one would visually read a file. Tagged PDF documents have a designated reading order based on the tree structure. If the PDF document is a tagged PDF with a reading structure defined and you want to ignore the order, deselect the check box. You might make this choice if the tagged PDF does not accurately support the proper reading order and the delivery is more problematic than delivering an untagged file.

✦ **Deliver data in pages when document exceeds ___ pages:** This setting is designed for use with screen readers that assist people with vision and motion challenges. The number of pages to be delivered to the reader can be set to a fixed value determined by the number you supply in the field box. Deselecting the check box sends the entire file to the screen reader.

Cross-Reference   For more information on screen readers, tagged PDF files, and accessibility, see Chapter 18.

Go To

The commands that are equal to the actions you perform with the Navigation tools are contained in the Go To submenu. You can choose any of the Navigation commands in this menu and the results are the same as using tools, the Status Bar, and keyboard shortcuts. You'll probably avoid using the Navigation commands since it will be so much easier to use any one of the other methods to scroll through pages. The exception is the Page command in this submenu. When you select Page or press Alt+Ctrl+N or Option+⌘+N, the Go To Page dialog box opens as shown in Figure 3-10.

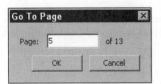

Figure 3-10: The Go To Page dialog box enables navigation to a page you type in the field box.

Enter a value for a page number and click OK. The page view opens a page respective to the number you typed in the dialog box.

Cross-Reference   See "Status Bar" later in this chapter for information on jumping to a page from a number typed in a field box.

Page layout

The page layout view can be any one of four different layout types. Choices for page layout are contained in a submenu in the View menu. Depending on the way a PDF file has been saved and depending on what preference choices are made for the Initial view, a PDF layout may appear different on different computers, depending on each user's Preference settings. Regardless of how you set your preferences, you can change the page layout view at any time.

Cross-Reference   For more information on setting Initial view preferences, see "Initial View" later in this chapter.

There are four page layout views as shown in Figure 3-11. They are

Single page: Single page views place an entire page in view when the zoom level is set to Fit Page. When you press the Page Down key or the down-arrow key to scroll pages, the next page snaps in view.

Continuous: Continuous page layout views show pages in a linear fashion, where you might see the bottom of one page and the top of another page in the Document Pane as you scroll down. The difference between this view and single page views is that the pages don't snap to a full page when viewed as continuous.

✦ **Facing:** A new Acrobat 6 addition is the facing pages view. This view shows two pages side by side — like looking at an open book. When the zoom level is set to Fit Page or lower, only two pages are in view in the Document Pane.

Continuous – Facing: This page layout view displays a combination of the preceding two options. When the zoom level is zoomed out, the view displays as many pages in the Document Pane as can be accommodated by the zoom level.

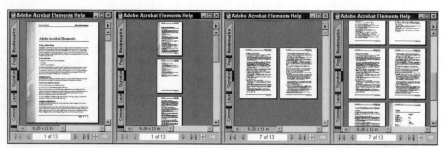

Figure 3-11: From left to right the four page layout views available in the View ⇨ Page Layout submenu include Single Page, Continuous, Facing, and Continuous – Facing.

Rotate view

If your PDF opens in Acrobat with a rotated view, you can rotate pages clockwise or counter-clockwise from two submenu commands. These commands are different from the command found in the Document menu for rotating pages. Rotate view rotates all pages in your PDF document and comes in handy if the PDF pages are rotated on the initial view or if you want to view PDFs on eBook readers, tablets, or laptop computers.

Grid

If you need to examine drawings where a grid can help analyze a document, you might choose to view your file displaying a grid. Grids can be useful when authoring PDF files, particularly PDF forms. For viewing purposes they can be useful where relationships to objects require some careful examination. To show a grid, choose View ➪ Grid. By default the grid is shown in the Document Pane as blue lines at fixed major and minor gridlines, as shown in Figure 3-12.

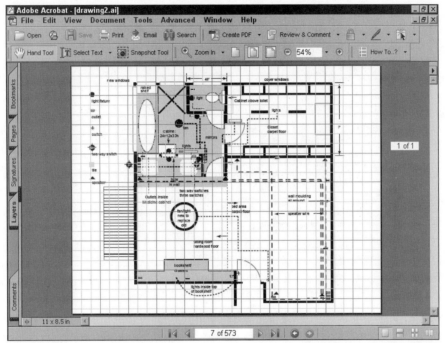

Figure 3-12: Access grids from the View menu or by pressing the Ctrl+U or ⌘+U modifier keys. You can change the grid lines for major and minor divisions in the Preferences dialog box.

If you want to change the distances for the major gridlines and the number of divisions for the minor gridlines, open the Preferences dialog box and select Units and Guides in the left pane. The preference settings enable you to change the units of measure and attributes for the grid layout as shown in Figure 3-13.

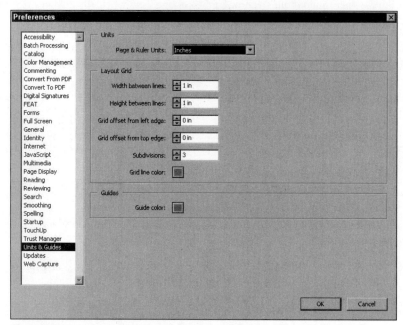

Figure 3-13: Preference choices for Units and Guides offer you options for changing the units of measure and the grid layout.

The Units and Guides preference settings are also used for changing attributes for the grid layout and rulers. The attribute choices include:

✦ **Page & Ruler Units:** Five choices are available from the pull-down menu. You can choose Points, Picas, Millimeters, Centimeters, or Inches. Whatever you choose here is reflected in the rulers when you display the rulers. Choices here also affect the units of measure found in the Info palette discussed in Chapter 1.

✦ **Width between lines:** The horizontal distance between the major gridlines is determined in the field box for this setting. You can click on the arrows, enter a number between 0 – 139 in the field, or press the up- or down-arrow keys to change the values.

Note   The limit of 139 relates to inches. If you change the units of measure, the limits are roughly the same as the 139-inch limit.

✦ **Height between lines:** The major gridlines appearing vertically are changed in this field. Use the same methods of changing the values here as for the lines for the Width option.

✦ **Grid offset from left edge:** Each grid has x and y coordinates indicating where the grid begins on a page. You set the x axis in this field.

✦ **Grid offset from top edge:** Use this field to set the starting point of the y axis.

✦ **Subdivisions:** The number of gridlines appearing between the major gridlines is determined in this field. The acceptable values range between 0 and 10,000.

✦ **Grid line color:** By default, the color for the gridlines is blue. You can change the grid color by clicking on the color swatch. When you click on the blue swatch for Grid Line color, a pop-up color palette opens as shown in Figure 3-14. Select a color from the preset color choices in the palette or click on Other Color. If you click Other Color, the system color palette opens, in which you can make custom color choices. The Windows and Macintosh system color palettes vary slightly as shown in Figures 3-15 and 3-16.

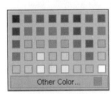

Figure 3-14: Click on the color swatch for the Grid line color and you can choose from a selection of preset colors or select Other Colors to open the system color palette.

✦ **Guide color:** Guides are created from ruler wells and can be manually positioned in the Document Pane. If you have ruler guides and a grid, you'll want to change one color to easily distinguish the guides from the grid. Both default to the same blue. To change the Guide Color, click on the Guide Color swatch and follow the same steps as described earlier for Grid line color.

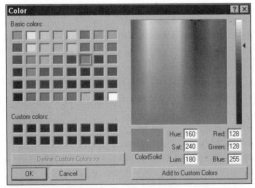

Figure 3-15: When you select Other Color on Windows, the Windows system color palette opens.

Figure 3-16: When you select Other Color on the Macintosh, the Macintosh system color palette opens. Inasmuch as the palettes differ in appearance, you can make the same custom color choices on both platforms.

Snap to Grid

When selected in the View menu, objects you draw snap to the major and minor gridlines. This feature can be particularly helpful with form designs and engineering drawings.

Cross-Reference   For more information on Snap to Grid, see Chapter 25.

Rulers

A long overdue feature in Acrobat is the ability to view rulers around the Document Pane. Fortunately, this version of Acrobat now supports rulers and turning them on is also found under the View menu or using the key modifiers Control/Command + R. When the menu selection is made, rulers appear on the top and left side of the Document Pane. Inside the top and left ruler is an inexhaustible supply of guidelines. To add a guideline on the document page, place the cursor within the top or left ruler, press the mouse button and drag away from the ruler to the Document Pane. Continue adding guidelines as you wish by returning to the ruler wells and dragging out more guidelines.

Tip   You can also add guidelines by double-clicking on a ruler. If you want guides positioned at 1-inch increments, as an example, move the mouse cursor to a ruler and double-click the mouse button on each 1-inch increment. Guidelines appear on the page in the Document Pane with each double-click of the mouse button. If you attempt to create a guideline outside the page area, Acrobat sounds a warning beep. Guides are not permitted outside the page area.

If you want to move a guideline after it has been placed in the Document Pane, select the Hand tool and place the cursor directly over the guideline to be moved. The cursor will change from a hand to a selection arrow. Press the mouse button and drag the line to the desired position.

Tip   If you have multiple guidelines to draw on a page at equal distances, use the Units and Guides preferences and set the major guides to the distance you want between the guides. Set the subdivision guidelines to zero. For example, if you want guidelines two inches apart, set the major Height and Width guides to 2 inches and enter **0** (zero) in the subdivisions. Click OK and you save yourself time over dragging guidelines from ruler wells.

To delete a guideline, click the line when you see the selection arrow described earlier and press the Delete key on your keyboard. You can also click and drag a guideline off the document page and back to the ruler well to delete it. If you want to delete all guides on a page, open a context menu (see Figure 3-17) on a ruler and select Clear Guides on Page. If you select Clear All Guides, all guides drawn throughout your document will be deleted.

Note   If for some reason you want to have a guideline appear off the PDF page but have it visible in the Document Pane outside the page area, you can place guidelines outside the page boundaries.

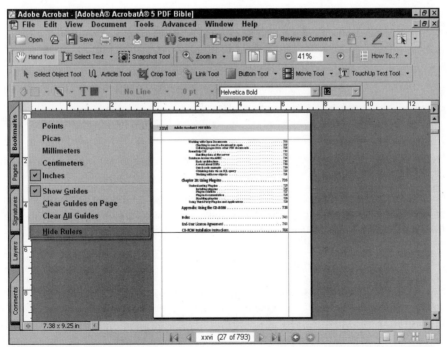

Figure 3-17: To clear guides on a page or throughout all pages, open a context menu on a ruler and make a choice for the desired task from the menu commands.

The context menu for rulers also enables you to hide the rulers, or you can use the shortcut keys Ctrl+R or ⌘+R or revisit the View menu. When rulers are hidden they don't affect the view of the guides that remain visible. Notice in the context menu that you also have choices for units of measure that makes changing units much handier than returning to the preference settings mentioned earlier. Guides can also be hidden from a menu selection in the context menu. To show and hide guides, return to the context menu and make the appropriate choice.

The last three menu selections in the View menu deal with Comments. For more information related to these commands and working with Comments, see Chapter 14.

Scrolling

Anyone familiar with window environments is no stranger to scrolling. Fortunately, scrollbars behave in a standard fashion among computer platforms and various computer programs. Page scrolling works the same in an Acrobat viewer as it does in Microsoft Word (or any other Microsoft product for that matter), or any illustration, layout, or host of other applications that you may be familiar with. Drag the elevator bar up and down or left to right to move the document within the active window. Click between the elevator bar at the top or bottom of the scrolling column to jump a page segment or full page. The arrow icons at the top, bottom, left and right sides allow you to move in smaller segments in the respective directions.

When dragging the elevator bar up or down in a multiple-page PDF file, a small pop-up Tool Tip displays a page number associated with the elevator bar position as well as the total number of pages in the document. The readout will be in the form of "*n* of *n* pages." The first number dynamically changes as the elevator bar is moved between pages. This behavior works only when you view a document in Continuous or Continuous Facing page layout mode.

For information on auto scrolling see the "Automatic Scrolling" section earlier in this chapter.

Status Bar

The Status Bar at the bottom of the Acrobat window provides you with navigation and viewing tools in all Acrobat viewers. The same tools for First Page, Previous Page, Next Page, and Last Page (reading left to right in the Status Bar) are identical to the tools you find in the Navigation toolbar. Additionally the Previous View and Next View tools appear on the right side of the other navigation tools.

The Go To menu command mentioned earlier enables you to jump to a specific page number. An easier method for navigating to a specific page is handled in the Status Bar. Click the cursor in the page numbers readout in the Status Bar and the numbers are highlighted. Type the page number you want to open and press the Enter/Return key. Acrobat opens the page you supplied in the Status Bar.

The Page Layout tools are located at the far right of the Status Bar. You can click on one of these tools to view your pages as Single Page, Continuous, Continuous — Facing, and Facing. Changing page layout views is much easier using the Status Bar than opening the View menu and Page Layout menu to access a different view.

Docking Toolbars Below the Status Bar

If it's easier for you to handle page navigation from tools at the bottom of your monitor and you want to keep the Navigation tools similar to the Status Bar tools all in one place, you can dock toolbars below the Status Bar. When toolbars are docked at the bottom of your screen and the How To window is open, the Status Bar slides over to make room for the How To window, but the toolbars remain below the How To window as shown here.

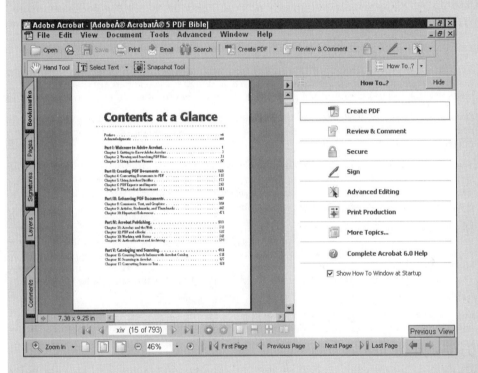

Like the toolbars docked in the Toolbar Well, where more rows can be added to the Well, tool-bars docked below the Status Bar can be docked in several rows. If viewing all tools below the Status Bar is more comfortable for you, Acrobat provides you with the ability to customize your environment as you like. If you decide to reset toolbars after docking them at the bottom of the Acrobat window, the toolbars are returned to the defaults from when you first launched Acrobat out of the shrink-wrap box.

When the How To window is open, the Document Pane shrinks and the Status Bar travels with it. Notice that when the How To window is open, the Page Layout tools slide to the left to make room for more viewing area in the How To window.

Zooming

Zooming in and out of document pages is a fact of life with many different programs. Even when you type text in a word processor, you often have a need to zoom in on text that is set in a style suited for printing, but views horribly at a 100% on your computer monitor. The same holds true for spreadsheets, all the imaging and layout programs, and any kind of program where page sizes grow beyond a standard letter-size page.

Because Acrobat accommodates a page size of up to 200×200 inches, PDF documents sporting large page sizes need some industrial-strength zoom tools. Such tools weren't available in previous versions of Acrobat, but in Acrobat6, anyone who sat and waited for screen refreshes while zooming in on a page will revel at the additions to the new zoom features.

Acrobat viewers provide you with the ability to zoom in and out of PDF pages using one of the Zoom tools. The Zoom tools permit views from 8.33 percent to 6,400 percent of a document page. Previous versions of Acrobat gave you a maximum zoom view of 1,600 percent.

Several tools are available for zooming. By default the Zoom In tool appears in a toolbar docked in the Toolbar Well. If you select the pull-down menu, you can select from one of five different Zoom tools.

You can also zoom by selecting the Zoom In or Zoom Out icons in the viewer toolbar (represented by a + and – symbol) or editing the zoom percentage field in the toolbar — just type a new value in the field box and press the Enter/Return key to zoom. When you click the down-pointing arrow, the preset pull-down menu opens.

Like many commands and features in Acrobat, you can choose from several alternatives for viewing at different zoom magnifications. A menu command also provides zooming in and out of your PDF document. After you choose View ➪ Zoom To, the Zoom To dialog box opens, enabling you to enter a zoom value or make any of the same choices available in the toolbar. You can press Ctrl+M or ⌘+M to open the dialog box and bypass the menu selection (see Figure 3-18).

Choices available to you in the Zoom To dialog box are the same preset choices found in the pull-down menu from the Zoom toolbar, with the addition of Reflow. Selecting Reflow from the Zoom To dialog box is the same as making this choice from the View menu as discussed earlier in this chapter.

Note   Reflowing documents only works with tagged PDF files.

Cross-Reference   For more information on creating tagged PDF files and using Reflow, see Chapter 18.

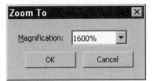

Figure 3-18: The Zoom To dialog box enables the user to specify magnification levels between 8.33 and 6,400 percent in 1 percent increments.

Zoom In tool

The Zoom In tool functions as you might expect when using a similar tool in other authoring applications. Select the tool in the Zoom toolbar and click on a page in the Document Pane. For temporary access to the Zoom In tool when another tool is selected, you can use the shortcut keys Ctrl+spacebar or Ô+spacebar. When you release the shortcut keys, you are returned to the selected tool. You can also temporarily access the Zoom Out tool when the Zoom In tool is selected by holding the Control/Ô key down and then adding the Alt/Option key and clicking the mouse button. The cursor inside the magnifying glass changes to a minus sign indicating the Zoom Out tool is selected.

When you click to zoom in or out, the page zoom follows the same zoom presets found in the pull-down menu from the Zoom toolbar. If you need zoom levels between the presets, type a number in the field box in the Zoom toolbar and press the Enter/Return key.

If you want to target a specific area to zoom in on, you can drag open a rectangle while the Zoom In tool is selected. The area you marquee zooms to view in the Document Pane when you release the mouse button. Zoom levels are also accessible from a context menu while a Zoom tool is selected. Open a context menu and you see the same preset zoom levels and page views found in the Zoom toolbar.

Zoom Out tool

The Zoom Out tool works exactly the same way as the Zoom In tool, only it zooms out rather than in. It also has the same options associated with it as are associated with the Zoom In tool. You can access the tool with modifier keys e Zoom In tool by adding the Alt/Option key. Be certain to first press the Control/⌘ key, and then add the Alt/Option key. The same presets, context menu, and ability to marquee an area are available with the Zoom Out tool.

Dynamic Zoom tool

When you first use the Dynamic Zoom tool it looks like you're watching a George Lucas sci-fi movie. It's downright mesmerizing. This new addition to zooming views in all Acrobat 6 viewers is much handier than drawing marquees with the Zoom In or Out tools.

To use dynamic zooming, select the tool from the Zoom toolbar pull-down menu adjacent to the Zoom In tool. Click and drag in any direction toward the page edge in the Document Pane to zoom in or toward the middle of the page to zoom out. As you move the cursor you see the page zoom dynamically. Stop at the desired zoom level by releasing the mouse button. Context menu options are the same as those found with the other zoom tools.

Loupe tool

 If you use other Adobe programs like Adobe Photoshop, Adobe Illustrator, or Adobe InDesign you know about the Navigator palette. In Acrobat Professional, the Loupe tool works similarly to the Navigator palette found in other Adobe programs with a little twist. Rather than show you a complete page in the Loupe tool window, you see just the zoom level while the page zoom remains static. This tool can be a great benefit when you work with files that take some time to refresh when you change screen views.

To use the Loupe tool, select the tool from the Zoom toolbar pull-down menu or press the Z key on your keyboard and then press Shift+Z until the Loupe tool comes in view in the toolbar. Move the cursor to an area on a page you want to zoom to and click the mouse button. The Loupe tool window opens and displays the zoomed area you selected, as shown in Figure 3-19.

Cross-Reference When using keyboard short cuts for accessing tools you need to enable the *Use single-key accelerators to access tools* preference setting. For more information on setting preferences for using keyboard shortcuts, see Chapter 1.

You can increase or decrease the magnification of the zoom area by adjusting the slider bar in the Loupe window or clicking on the minus or plus symbols in the window. Clicking on these symbols offers you smaller incremental changes than when using the same symbols in the Zoom toolbar. If you want the Loupe tool to show a larger portion, you can resize the Loupe Tool dialog box by grabbing a corner of the box and dragging.

When you click in the Document Pane with the Loupe tool, a rectangle appears around the area zoomed in to the Loupe window. You can place the cursor inside this rectangle and move it around the Document Pane to view different areas at the same zoom level. As you zoom in, the rectangle reduces in size. At some point it would be impractical to select the rectangle on the page. If you can't find it, zoom out a little in the Loupe tool window until you see the rectangle on the page. Click and drag it to a new position and you can adjust your zoom.

If you have oversized documents that take a long time to refresh, using the Loupe tool will speed up your PDF viewing. You can keep the document page in the Document Pane at a reduced view while using the Loupe tool to examine areas in detail, which won't necessitate screen refreshes.

Tip The Loupe window displays the zoom level on an open document and remains fixed to that document until you target a new area. When you have multiple documents open, you can zoom in on one document while that document is not visible in the Document Pane thereby observing a zoomed view on one page while actually viewing pages in a second document.

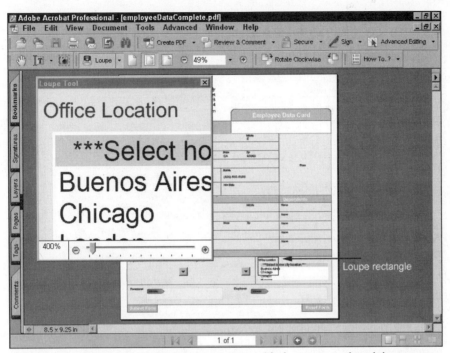

Figure 3-19: Click an area in the Document Pane with the Loupe tool, and the target area is viewed at a zoom level in the Loupe window.

Pan and Zoom tool

Where the Loupe tool displays the zoom view in its own window and the page in the Document Pane remains static, the Pan and Zoom tool works in the opposite manner. The zoom level changes on the page in the Document Pane while the complete page remains in view in the Pan and Zoom window. The zoom area is highlighted with a red rectangle in the Pan and Zoom tool window.

To use the Pan and Zoom Window, select the tool from the same pull-down menu where you selected the Loupe tool. The window displays a full page and the red rectangle showing the zoom area in the window. If you open the Pan and Zoom window when your PDF page is viewed as a Fit Page view, the page and the red rectangle are the same size.

To zoom a view in the Pan and Zoom window, select one of the four handles on a corner of the rectangle and resize the rectangle by dragging in or out to zoom in or out, respectively. The page thumbnail view in the Pan and Zoom window remains the same as the rectangle is sized, as shown in Figure 3-20.

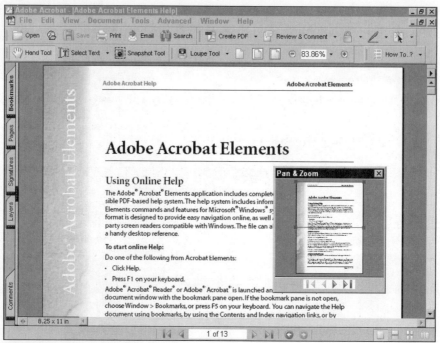

Figure 3-20: The Pan and Zoom window displays a thumbnail view of the entire document page. The rectangle in the window shows the zoom level corresponding to the page zoom view.

Also contained in the Pan and Zoom window are navigation buttons. You can establish a zoom view and then scroll pages in your document with the page tools in the window. As you do so, the page views hold the same zoom level you set in the Pan and Zoom window.

Zoom tool behaviors

There are a few specific differences between the Loupe tool and the Pan and Zoom tool that you should know. The Loupe tool targets an area on an open document and the zoom is fixed to that document while it remains open or until you target a new area. Regardless of the number of files you open, the Loupe tool window displaying your target view stays intact even if another document is brought to the front of the Document Pane. If you close a file where the Loupe tool was set to view a zoom, the Loupe tool window clears and displays no view.

The Pan and Zoom tool always shows a target view of the active document brought forward in the Document Pane. If you have multiple documents open, open the Pan and Zoom tool, then close a file, the page in view in the next file is viewed in the Pan and Zoom window. If you close all files, the Pan and Zoom window clears.

If you close a file during an Acrobat session, both the Loupe tool and the Pan and Zoom tool return you to the same views. The Pan and Zoom tool displays the opening page at the same zoom level as was last established in the window. The Loupe tool displays the same view last created with the tool. For example, if you zoom to 200% on page 25 of a file, close the file, and then reopen it, the Loupe tool window displays page 25 at 200% while the Document Pane displays the opening page.

Both tools can be used together to display different views in different documents as shown in Figure 3-21. If the page in view in the Loupe window is not the current active document brought forward in the Document Pane, you can still manage zooming on the hidden page. Use the slider of the minus/plus symbols to change zoom levels.

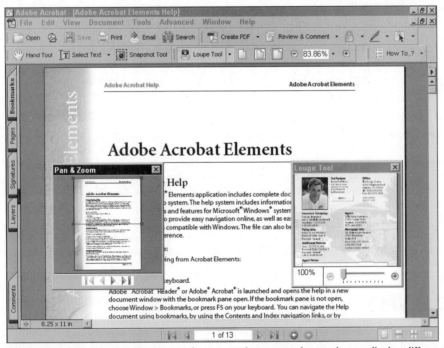

Figure 3-21: You can use the Pan and Zoom and Loupe tools together to display different views in different documents.

Page Views

The page views for Actual Size, Fit Page, and Fit Width are static views that you want to access frequently when navigating through a PDF document. Acrobat viewers provide several ways to change a page view. Three tools appear in the Zoom toolbar for toggling different page views, as shown in Figure 3-22. The different views include

 Actual Size: Displays the PDF page at actual size (a 100 percent view).

Fit Page: Displays the page at maximum size to fit within the viewer Document Pane. If the Acrobat viewer window is sized up or down, the Fit Page view conforms to the size of the Document Pane.

Fit Width: The data on a PDF page is displayed horizontally without clipping. If the page is large and data appears only in the center of the page, the page zooms to fit the data. The white space at the page edges is ignored.

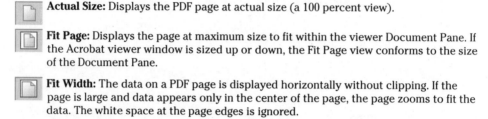

Figure 3-22: Page view icons for Actual Size, Fit Page, and Fit Width.

One of the keyboard shortcuts you'll want to remember is Ctrl+0/⌘+0 (zero). This enables you to view a page in a Fit Page view. As you browse pages in a PDF document, the page views are specific to the individual pages, not to the document. Therefore, scrolling PDF files with different page sizes may require you to frequently change views if you want to see the full page in the Document Pane. By using the keyboard shortcuts, you can reset page views much faster.

Page views can be established for the opening page and are user specified. Setting these attributes was referred to as Open Options in earlier versions of Acrobat. Now in Acrobat 6 they are referred to as Initial View. These and other kinds of page views available in Acrobat are covered in the following section on Initial View.

Initial View

Initial View is the page view you see when you first open a PDF document. You have several different attributes for an opening view and you can save your settings with the document. These views are document specific so they relate only to a document where you save the settings. When no settings have been saved with a file, you have a number of choices for how you want your default view to appear. Coincidently, even though previous versions of Acrobat provided you with tools to save an initial view, most PDF authors rarely use them. You can find thousands of PDF files on the Internet and most of them have no settings enabled for an opening view other than the program defaults. Hopefully by the time you finish this section, you can see some advantages for saving a particular initial view for the PDF documents you create and edit.

To set the attributes for the opening view, choose File ➪ Document Properties, or use the keyboard shortcut Ctrl+D/⌘+D. The Document Properties dialog box opens, displaying a list on the left side and the settings in a panel on the right much like the Preferences dialog box. Click on Initial View in the left pane as shown in Figure 3-23.

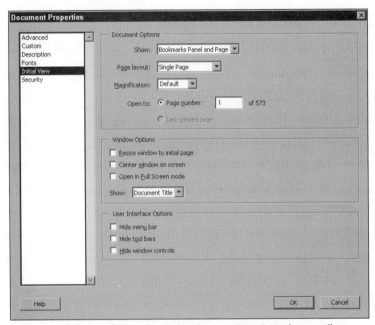

Figure 3-23: To set the attributes for the opening view, choose File ⇨ Document Properties and click on Initial View when the Document Properties dialog box opens.

Acrobat provides you with many different choices for controlling the initial view of a PDF when opened in any Acrobat viewer. Settings you make here can be saved with your document. When you establish settings other than defaults, the settings saved with the file override the user's default settings.

✦ **Document Options:** The default opening page is the first page of a PDF document. You can change the opening page to another page; you can also control the page layout views and magnification by selecting choices from the Document Options section. The choices include:

- **Show:** Four choices are available from the pull-down menu. Select *Page Only* to open the page with the Navigation Pane collapsed. Use *Bookmarks Panel and Page* to open the Bookmarks tab when the file opens. Use *Pages Panel and Page* to open the Pages tab where the thumbnails of pages are viewed. Use *Layers Panel and Page* to open the Layers tab when the file opens.

- **Page Layout:** The default for Page Layout is noted in the pull-down menu as Default. When you save a PDF file with the Default selection, the PDF opens according to the default value a user has set for page viewing on the user's computer. To override the user's default, you can set a page layout in the opening view from one of four choices. Choose *Single Page* to open the PDF in a single page layout. Choose *Continuous* to open in a continuous page view. Use *Facing* to open with facing pages or use *Continuous – Facing* to open in continuous facing pages view.

- **Magnification:** Choose from preset magnification views from the pull-down menu. If you want the PDF document to open in a fit in window view, select Fit Page. Choose from other magnification options of edit the field box for a custom zoom level.

- **Open to:** You can change the opening page to another page by entering a number in the field for Page Number. This setting might be used if you want a user to see a contents page instead of a title page.

- **Last-viewed page:** Another option for the opening page is the setting for Last-viewed page. When enabled, the most recently viewed page viewed opens. This setting is intended for eBooks where you might begin reading a novel and want to mark the page like a bookmark then later return to the page where you left off.

Cross-Reference

For more information on eBooks and marking the last-viewed page, see Chapter 22

✦ **Window Options:** The default window for Acrobat is a full screen where the viewing area is maximized to occupy your monitor surface area. You can change the window view to size down the window to the initial page size, center a smaller window onscreen, and open a file in Full Screen mode. If you enable all three check boxes, the Full Screen mode prevails.

- **Show:** From the pull-down menu choose either File Name or Document Title. If Filename is selected, the title bar at the top of the Acrobat window shows the file name. If Document Title is used, the information you supply in the Document Properties dialog box for Document Title is shown in the title bar.

Cross-Reference

Document titles are very important when archiving volumes of PDFs and creating search indexes. For information on creating Document titles and how they are used, see Chapter 4.

✦ **User Interface Options:** The Interface Options in the Initial View Document Properties dialog box have to do with user interface items in Acrobat viewers such as menu bars, toolbars, and scroll bars. You can elect to hide these items when the PDF document opens in any Acrobat viewer. You can hide any one or a combination of the three items listed under the User Interface Options. When all three are enabled, the PDF is viewed as shown in Figure 3-24. If you elect to save files without any of the user interface items in view, it's a good idea to create navigational buttons so users can move around your document.

Figure 3-24: When toolbars, the menu bar, and window controls are hidden, navigating pages requires keyboard shortcuts or navigational buttons on the pages.

The window controls you see in Figure 3-25 include the scroll bars, the Status Bar, and the Navigation Pane. If you hide the toolbars and menu bar but elect to leave the window controls visible, users can access tools for page navigation.

Caution If you elect to eliminate the toolbars and menu bar from view and later want to go back and edit your file, you need to use shortcut keys to get the menu bars and toolbars back. Be certain to remember the F8 and F9 keys — F8 shows/hides the toolbars and F9 shows/hides the menu bar.

Figure 3-25: If window controls are visible, users can access tools for page navigation.

Saving the Initial View

When you decide what view attributes you want assigned to your document you can choose between one of two save options. The first option updates the file. Click on the Save tool in the Acrobat File toolbar or choose File ➪ Save. Any edits you make in the Initial View properties activates the Save command. The Save command is inactive and grayed out by default until you make any changes to your file or reset any kind of preferences that can be saved with the document.

The second method for updating your file uses the Save As command. When you choose File ➪ Save As, the Save As dialog box opens as shown in Figure 3-26. The default file name is the same name as the file you opened. If you elect to save the file to the same folder where it resides, Acrobat prompts you with a warning dialog box asking whether you want to over-write the file. Click Yes and the file is rewritten. There are many times during your Acrobat sessions that using Save As will be a benefit. As you work on documents they retain more information than necessary to view and print the file. By using Save As and overwriting the file, you optimize it for a smaller file size. In some cases the differences between Save and Save As can be extraordinary in terms of the file sizes. As a matter of habit, try to use the Save As command after eight to ten different saves and completely rewrite the file. If you need a backup copy of a document you can also use Save As and supply a new name in the Save As dialog box. When you click Save, a copy of your PDF is written to disk with the new name.

Note After editing a file and using the Save command 10 times, Acrobat prompts you in a dialog box asking you if you want to use the Save As command to rewrite the file and optimize it.

Cross-Reference Saving in the PDF format is one of many options you have for different file formats when using the Save As command. For more information related to other file format options, see Chapter 12. For optimizing PDFs you have options in addition to the Save As command. For more information on PDF optimization, see Chapter 13.

Figure 3-26: Use the Save As dialog box and save a file with the same name to the same folder as the original file you opened to completely rewrite the file.

Viewing Files with the Window Menu

If you open a PDF file and then open a second PDF, the second file hides the first document. If several more PDFs are opened, the last opened document hides all the others. Fortunately, the Acrobat viewers have made it easy for you to choose a given document from a nest of open files.

When you load an Acrobat viewer with several open files, use tools to help you manage them. If a need exists to visually compare documents, manage multiple files by viewing them in the Document Pane. Fortunately, Acrobat viewers have many different tools to help you manage files when you need to have more than one at a time open in the Document Pane.

The Window menu contains options for helping you manage document views and, in particular, multiple documents. The options you find in the Window menu won't be found with tools or in the Status Bar, so you'll find yourself visiting this menu frequently if you work with multiple files open in Acrobat or if you need to create more than one view in the same document.

Cascade

If you have several files open and choose Window ➪ Cascade, the open files appear in a cascading view with the title bars visible as shown in Figure 3-27. You can see the name of each file and easily select from any one shown in the Document Pane. Click on a title bar to bring the document forward.

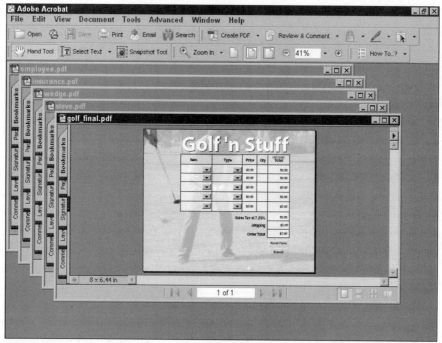

Figure 3-27: Cascaded views provide you with immediate access to any one of several files open in the Document Pane.

After bringing a file forward, if you want to see the title bars in a cascading view again, return to the menu command and select Cascade. The document currently selected in the foreground will appear first when you select Cascade again.

The Window menu also lists the open files by filename at the bottom of the window. When you have multiple files open, the files are numbered according to the order in which they were opened, with the filename appearing in the list as shown in Figure 3-28. Select any filename from the list in the Window menu and the file is brought forward in the Document Pane.

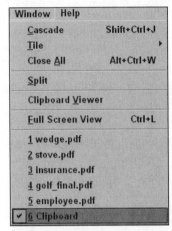

Figure 3-28: Acrobat lists all open files in the Window menu. To bring a document forward in the Document Pane, choose the name of the file you want to view from the Window menu.

Tile

Documents can be tiled horizontally and vertically from the Tile submenu in the Window menu. When you choose Window ⇨ Tile ⇨ Horizontally, the PDF files appear in individual windows stacked on top of each other, as shown in Figure 3-29. Choosing Window ⇨ Tile ⇨ Vertically displays the PDF files in individual windows placed side by side, as shown in Figure 3-30. If you have more than three documents open at one time, the display for Tile Horizontally and Tile Vertically will appear identical. With any number of documents displayed in tiled views, the Navigation Pane can be opened as shown in the following figures to help you navigate to individual pages in multiple documents.

Tiling documents can be helpful when you need to edit documents and exchange pages between two or more PDF files or when you need to compare documents for changes among them.

Cross-Reference For information related to editing files, see Chapter 10. For more information on comparing documents, see Chapter 14.

Figure 3-29: The files are tiled horizontally.

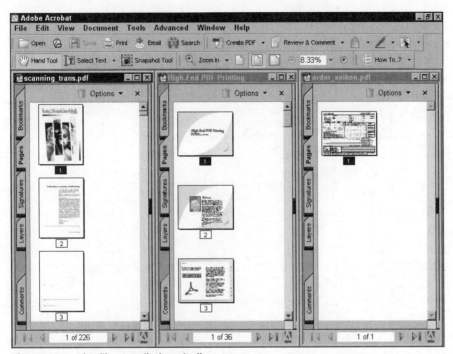

Figure 3-30: The files are tiled vertically.

Split

A new viewing option introduced in Acrobat is the Split view. When you choose Window ⇨ Split, the active document splits the Document Pane into two horizontal views similarly to the way you might see a split view in a word processing or spreadsheet program. The two views are independent of each other and offer you much flexibility. You can view the same page in two different zoom views as shown in Figure 3-31, or you can view two different pages at the same zoom level or different zoom views. You can view one pane in a single page layout and the other pane in Continuous, Facing, or Continuous-Facing page layout. You can also combine split and tiling to view two or more documents each with split views tiled horizontally or vertically. The horizontal bar can be moved up or down to adjust the window division showing a larger view in one pane and a smaller view in the other pane.

To toggle off the Split view, return to the Window menu and select Split. The view changes to a single view in the Document Pane.

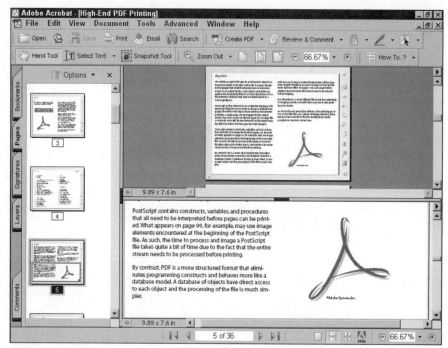

Figure 3-31: Split enables you to see two different views of the same document. Pages can be viewed in two separate panes with different zoom levels.

Full Screen

Another viewing option found in the Window menu is a command for Full Screen view. Full Screen displays your PDF document like a slide show and temporarily hides the menus, toolbars, and window controls. You can set up the Full Screen view for automatic page scrolling; walk away from the computer, and you'll have a self-running kiosk. You can give a presentation and automatically scroll pages or set preferences for pausing between slides.

Cross-Reference There's a lot to Full Screen viewing. To learn more about working with Full Screen views, see Chapter 21.

Links

For the purpose of discussion, links in Acrobat are *hot spots* where you click somewhere in the Acrobat window and some action takes place. With regard to viewing PDF documents, clicking the mouse button on a link takes you to another view. Links can be any one of a number of items including elements on a PDF page such as buttons, articles, fields, and so on, or they can be part of the user interface such as thumbnails and links you can create from options in palettes. In this chapter I stick to link behavior in Acrobat and where you can find links.

Navigation Pane

The Navigation Pane contains the default tabs discussed in Chapter 1 and most of these palettes have associated with them certain capabilities for linking to views and other kinds of actions that can be invoked with the click of a mouse button. In some cases a single click takes you to another view and in other cases a double-click takes you to another view. The palettes that contain some form of linking to views include:

To learn more about the Navigation tabs, see Chapter 1.

    ✦ **Bookmarks:** Any Bookmarks created in the PDF file are displayed in a list beside the Bookmarks tab. With a single click of the mouse button, a Bookmark may take you to another page, another view, or invoke an action.

For information on creating Bookmarks and setting link actions to them, see Chapter 10.

    ✦ **Signatures:** The Signatures palette contains a list of all digital signatures in a PDF document. You can open the Signatures palette and navigate to pages where signatures have been added to the file.

For information on creating digital signatures, see Chapter 19.

    ✦ **Layers:** The layers palette shows all Adobe PDF Layers contained in a document according to the layer names. If the palette is empty, no layers are contained in the file. You use the Layers palette to show and hide layers, set layer properties, and manage layers.

For more information on using Adobe PDF Layers, see Chapter 17.

    ✦ **Pages:** To view thumbnails of each page, click the Pages tab in the Navigation Pane. The page thumbnails are links to the respective pages. A single mouse click on a page thumbnail displays the respective page in the Document Pane.

For information on working with the Pages tab, see Chapter 10.

    ✦ **Comments:** The Comments palette contains any annotations added to the open file. You can navigate to any page where a comment has been added by double-clicking on a comment in the Comments palette.

For information on working with comments, see Chapter 14.

Navigation tabs

The additional palettes you can access from the Navigation Tabs submenu listed in the View menu described in Chapter 1 contain links to the content you create from various palette options. These palettes include

✦ **Articles:** Article threads are like link buttons. You can create article threads in a PDF file and the threads are listed in the Articles tab. Use the tab to open an article thread and click the mouse button inside the article to follow the thread.

Cross-Reference

For information on creating articles, see Chapter 10.

✦ **Content:** Document content can be displayed in the Content tab. When you open the tab and select individual items, you can highlight the respective item. In essence the Content tab is linked to the content appearing on the PDF pages according to the natural reading order of the PDF file.

Cross-Reference

For information on using the Content tab, see Chapter 18.

✦ **Destinations:** Destinations are similar to Bookmarks and are linked to a specific location in a PDF document. When you click on a destination, the view associated with the destination opens in the Document Pane.

Cross-Reference

For information on destinations, see Chapter 15.

✦ **Fields:** The Fields tab lists all fields created in the open document. Click on a field name in the tab and the field is highlighted in the Document Pane.

Cross-Reference

For information on creating Field buttons, see Chapter 26.

✦ **Info:** The Info tab offers pull-down menu choices for changing the units of measure in a document. Choose from Points, Inches, or Millimeters to change units. The information displayed in the Status Bar reports the page size in the units selected from the Info palette. As you move the cursor around the Document Pane, a read out in the info palette shows the cursor x,y position on the page. For example X: 3 and Y: 2 informs you the cursor is positioned 3 inches from the left side of the page and 2 inches up from the bottom of the page.

Cross-Reference

For information on using rulers, guides, and measuring tools according to units of measure, see Chapter 17.

✦ **Tags:** Tags list all the structural content in a PDF document. You can highlight an element from within the Tags tab. Whereas the Contents tab identifies all of the page content in any PDF file, the Tags tab shows only the structure and elements of tagged PDF files.

Cross-Reference

For information on using the Tags tab, see Chapter 18.

Hypertext links

In an Acrobat viewer, hypertext references enable you to move around the PDF or many PDFs much like surfing the Net. You've probably become so accustomed to clicking buttons on your desktop computer that link navigation is almost commonplace and needs little instruction. Invoking the action is nothing more than a click with the mouse. What the actions do in Acrobat is simply remarkable. To gain an understanding of how Acrobat has employed hyperlinks, the following sections describe all of the link actions as they can be created in Acrobat and executed in any viewer.

Buttons

Hypertext references, or *buttons,* are easily identified in a PDF document. As you move the mouse cursor around the document window, a Hand icon with the forefinger pointing is shown as the cursor is positioned over a button. You click, and presto — the link action is executed!

Link actions can be assigned to any one of several items in Acrobat. You can set a link action to links, fields, bookmarks, Page Actions, and page thumbnails. The link action types have changed considerably in Acrobat 6 compared to earlier versions of the program. The new action types now available in Acrobat Standard and Acrobat Professional include

Note

All the Link Action types are available with both Acrobat Standard and Acrobat Professional. Form fields can only be created with Acrobat Professional. Links Actions can be assigned to links, bookmarks and page actions in both Acrobat Standard and Acrobat Professional.

✦ **Go to a page in this document:** The go to a page action opens another view on the existing page, a view to another page in the same document, or a view to a named destination.

✦ **Go to a page in another document:** Cross linking takes you to pages in other PDF documents and is a new feature in Acrobat. It makes linking to multiple documents much easier than in previous versions of Acrobat.

✦ **Go to a snapshot view:** A snapshot of a page, text, or an object on a page can be made with the Snapshot tool. When you link to a Snapshot the link shows the last snapshot taken.

✦ **Open a file:** The open file link opens any kind of document. PDFs are opened in Acrobat. Other file types require having the authoring program installed on your computer. For example, if the link is to a Microsoft Word document, you need Word installed on your computer to open the link.

✦ **Read an article:** This navigates to the specified article in the open PDF document or another PDF document.

✦ **Execute a menu command:** This links to commands found in the Acrobat menus. For example, a button field or link can be created to execute the Save As command. The Save As dialog box would open from the link action just as it would from using the menu command.

✦ **Set layer visibility:** This shows all layers in the file in the Layers palette.

✦ **Show/hide a field:** With form fields, fields are hidden or made visible on a page.

✦ **Submit a form:** This is used for submitting data in user-prescribed formats to a specified URL (Uniform Resource Locator).

✦ **Reset a form:** All the fields or user-specified fields on a form are cleared of data.

✦ **Import form data:** Imports data exported from other forms into the active document where form field names match the form from where the data were exported.

✦ **Run a JavaScript:** Executes JavaScripts written in Acrobat.

JavaScripts can be created with links, bookmarks, and page actions in Acrobat Standard. The JavaScript Editor however, is not accessible from a menu command in Acrobat Standard. For information on using the JavaScript Editor in Acrobat Professional, see Chapter 27.

✦ **Play Media (Acrobat 5 Compatible):** Plays a movie file saved in formats compatible with Acrobat 5 and lower viewers.

✦ **Play a sound:** Plays a sound imported into the active PDF.

✦ **Play Media (Acrobat 6 Compatible):** Plays movie files saved in newer formats compatible with Acrobat 6 or movie clips embedded in Acrobat.

Embedding movie clips is a new feature in Acrobat 6. Older versions of Acrobat link to movie files stored locally, on a network, or on a Web server.

✦ **Open a Web link:** Opens a URL in your default Web browser.

The preceding list is a simplified brief description of action types that can be associated with tools that support link actions.

For more detail on how to create link actions and a host of attributes you can assign to them, see Part IV "PDF Interactivity" and Part VI "PDF Forms."

Cross-document links

A button linking one PDF document to another is a known as a *cross-document link*. When you click a button, or any tool where actions can be assigned that opens a second document, by default your original document closes and the second document opens. Whether a document closes when a link to another document is opened is determined in the Acrobat viewer preferences. By default a check box is selected for the General preferences item Open cross-document links in same window.

If you want to have all cross-linked documents opening in separate windows, you can change the default setting. Choose Edit ➪ Preferences. In the Preferences dialog box select General in the left pane. On the right side of the Preferences dialog box, clear the Open cross-document links in same window check box. Click OK. The next time you click a button that opens a cross-document link, the linked file opens in the Document Pane without closing any files.

For information on controlling cross document linking with links and form fields, see Chapter 15.

World Wide Web links

Talking about any kind of link without talking about the World Wide Web is almost impossible. After all, the Web *is* link mania. Therefore, it's no surprise that Acrobat has the additional capability to connect you to a Web site by the simple click of a button. When you encounter a Web link, Acrobat provides you some immediate feedback that a Web link will be executed before you click the mouse button. As the cursor is positioned over a Web link, a plus symbol appears inside the Hand icon and a Tool Tip displays a URL set to the link. After you click the mouse button on a Web link, Acrobat launches your Web browser and finds the URL associated with the link. Acrobat remains open in the background as the Web browser appears and the Web page in question is loaded.

Summary

This chapter offers you a brief overview of how to go about moving around PDF documents and viewing tools, palettes, and pages. As you can see, the list is long and there's quite a bit to understand in regard to viewing and navigation. Some of the more important points include the following:

✦ Page navigation tools are available in a toolbar not visible by default. You can place the toolbar in view and dock it left, right, top, or below the Document Pane for easy access to navigation tools.

✦ Task buttons can be hidden and viewed from menu commands in the View menu. Task buttons are contained in the Tasks toolbar. These tools offer you quick access to commonly used tasks.

✦ Document reflows are possible only from tagged PDF documents. Reflowing text is used with special adaptive equipment and porting PDF files to small devices such as hand-held PDAs and tablets.

✦ PDFs can be read aloud and pages can be auto scrolled without the need for any special equipment.

✦ PDF pages can be viewed in several different layout modes, with grids, guides, and rulers.

✦ The Status Bar contains tools for easy page navigation and changing page layout views.

✦ Acrobat Professional contains five tools used for zooming views. In addition to the Zoom In and Zoom Out tools found in earlier Acrobat viewers, the Loupe tool and the Pan and Zoom tool are new to Acrobat. The Loupe tool shows an exploded view of any document page regardless of the page in view in the Document Pane. The Pan and Zoom tool shows a thumbnail view of a page while the page zooms according to adjustments made in the Pan and Zoom window. Also new to Acrobat 6 is the Dynamic Zoom tool, where page zooms occur dynamically as the tool is dragged through the document.

✦ Initial Views of PDF documents can be displayed with pages and palettes, at different zoom levels, with or without menus, tools, and window controls. These settings are document specific and can be saved with different options for different documents. The settings are established in the Initial View document properties dialog box.

✦ Links are built into many different Acrobat tools and they can be assigned to items created in Acrobat. Different action types can be assigned to many tools and object elements.

✦ Links can be made to Web pages and URLs.

✦ ✦ ✦

Searching PDF Files

Abig change in Acrobat 6 as compared to earlier versions of Acrobat is related to finding words, phrases, and content through searches. The Find command is no longer present in Acrobat. It has been replaced with Search, which works similarly to the way the Find command did. Now it's more like Find on steroids.

The ability to find information contained in PDF documents is much more elaborate in Acrobat 6 and now it's extended to PDFs scattered around your hard drive and all over the Internet without the assistance of a search index. However, Acrobat Catalog and searching index files is still available to you for more sophisticated searches. In this chapter I cover all the tools and features available in Acrobat viewers for searching through PDF files and creating and searching index files.

Using the Search Pane

You perform searches by accessing a menu command, by choosing the Search tool in the File toolbar, or by using shortcut keys. To search from the menu, choose Edit ➪ Search. To use the toolbar, click on the Search tool, or open a context menu with the Hand tool, and select Search. To use the keyboard shortcut, press Ctrl/Ô+F. These all allow you to search for a word in an open document, in a collection of PDF files stored on your hard drive, or in any type of external media. When you invoke a search, the Search Pane opens on the right of your screen in the How To window. The Search Pane actually uses the How To window space and replaces the How To menu items with search-related options as shown in Figure 4-1.

At the top of the Search Pane are buttons that return you to the How To window. If you click on the Homepage icon, the How To window displays the contents page for the How To help items. The arrow keys take you back and forward through the How To pages, similar to using the Previous View and Next View navigation tools. If you click the Back arrow without searching for a word or phrase, the How To window opens the Homepage. When in the Search Pane, the items below the menu bar include search-related options.

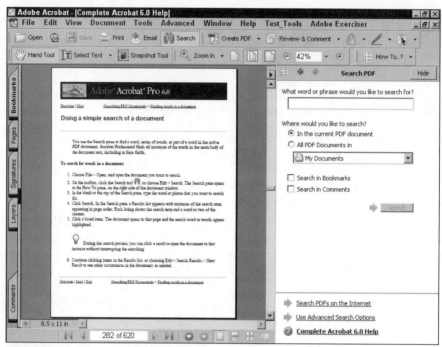

Figure 4-1: When you use the Search menu command or the Ctrl/⌘+F keyboard shortcut, the Search Pane opens in the How To window. All the options in the Pane change to search-related options.

Basic search options

When the Search Pane is in view, you type a word or words to be searched for in the field box that appears at the top of the Pane. You are limited to the actual word(s) you want to find when you perform a simple search. You cannot use Boolean (and, or, not) operators or any kind of search expressions if performing a simple search.

For more sophisticated searches where you can use Boolean operators, see "Advanced Searches" later in this chapter.

The area where you type words and phrases to be searched is in the field box following the text *"What word or phrase would you like to search for?"* in the Search Pane. Rather than describe this field box by name, the term *first field box* or *search field box* is used throughout this chapter. When you see such a reference, realize that it refers to the area where you type words and phrases to be searched for.

If you type more than one word in the search field box, the results are reported for all words typed in the field box regardless of whether both words appear together in a document. For example, if you search for *Adobe Acrobat Professional*, all the occurrences of Adobe, Acrobat, Professional, Adobe Acrobat, and Acrobat Professional are reported in the results list.

In the Search PDF Pane, you choose where you want to search and the options to narrow the search from the list following the first field box. There are several choices.

Where to search

The question presented to you is *Where would you like to search?* Two radio buttons appear where you choose whether to search the current open file or search locally on your hard drive, a network server, or a media storage device attached to your computer such as removable media or CD-ROMs. If you select the second radio button for *All PDF Documents in*, you can narrow the search to a directory, drive, or media device by opening the pull-down menu and choosing from the hierarchy of drives and folders appearing in the menu options.

Acrobat also permits you to search through Bookmarks and Comments. Check boxes appear below the pull-down menu for these items. If Bookmarks and Comments are to be part of your search, check the respective item(s). After you choose the options you want, click on the Search button.

The results appear in the Search Pane as shown in Figure 4-2. The total number of found instances for your search are noted at the top of the Pane and hot links appear in the scrollable list for the words found in the documents according to the search options you selected. Click on any text in blue and the respective document page opens in the Document Pane with the first occurrence of the searched word highlighted.

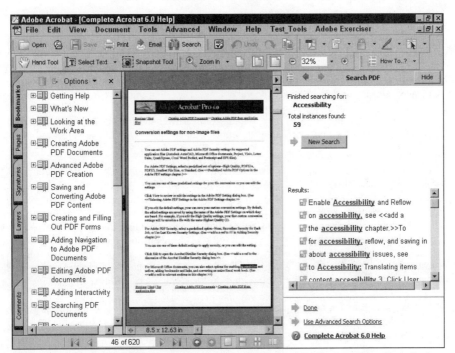

Figure 4-2: Search results are reported in a scrollable list for all occurrences in a single PDF or all occurrences in all documents searched. Click on any text appearing in blue to open a page where Search found words matching your criteria.

Navigating search results

As you browse the search results, you can move backward and forward to review last-viewed pages. The two arrows at the top of the Pane take you to the previous and next views. If you click the Back arrow and return to the Homepage in the How To menu, you can click on the Next arrow and it takes you back to your search results. However, if you click on the Homepage button in the Search Pane, all search results are cleared and you need to search again to see a list of results.

Menu commands are also available for navigating through search results. Choose Edit ⇨ Search Results to open a submenu where you find four menu commands used with searches. These menu items include:

✦ **Next Document.** (Ctrl/⌘+]). Click Next Document to bypass all found instances in the currently viewed file and open the next file listed in the Search results list.

✦ **Next Result.** (Ctrl/⌘+G). This command navigates to the next instance where a found word exists. If the next instance is within the current document, the page where the result is found opens in the Document Pane. If bookmarks or comments are searched and the next instance is within a bookmark or comment, that instance is highlighted and placed in view. If the next instance is on a hidden layer, Acrobat prompts you to make the layer visible. If the next instance is in another file, Acrobat opens the file and page, bookmark, comment, or layer where the result is found.

✦ **Previous Result.** (Shift+Ctrl/⌘+G). This command offers the opposite response as Next Result — it moves backward in the found instances.

✦ **Previous Document.** (Ctrl/⌘+[). This command offers the opposite response as Next Document — it moves backward through previously viewed documents.

Note Next Result and Next Document are not available until you first invoke a search. Next Document becomes active only when a search result exists in two or more documents. Previous Result and Previous Document become active only after you have visited a result in a document more than once, so as to retrace your steps backward to see previously viewed results.

Stopping a search

When you start a new search, a button appears in the Search Pane to Stop the search. Click Stop and the results found prior to stopping are listed in the scrollable list. After you click Stop, a button for Done appears at the bottom of the Search Pane. DO NOT CLICK DONE! If you click Done, Acrobat thinks you are finished searching and opens the How To Homepage. All your search results are flushed and you need to search again if you want to continue searching files. Only click Done when you want to return to edit mode in the Document Pane and you don't need to open any of the results found in the Search Pane.

Caution If you click the Hide button in the Search Pane, the Pane closes. Reopening the How To window by clicking on the How To tool or by clicking on the Search tool flushes all the search results.

Displaying results

The results list is neatly organized for you in the Search Pane. If you search the open document, the search results report found words beginning at the front of the document and list occurrences as they are found on following pages. If you search multiple documents, the occurrences are listed in groups according to the individual documents where the words were found. The hierarchy is similar to bookmarks. A plus symbol in Windows or a right-pointing arrow in Macintosh is shown for each document where results have been found. Click on the icon and the list expands the same way bookmarks and comments expand. The icon changes to a minus symbol in Windows or a down-pointing arrow in Macintosh when a list is expanded. Click on the icon again and the list collapses.

Cross-Reference   For information on displaying bookmarks, see Chapter 10. For information on displaying comments, see Chapter 14.

Below the search results list is a check box for Collapse file paths. By default the checkmark is collapsed. If you want to see the complete directory path for where a file is located, uncheck the check box. As you move the mouse cursor over a result in the scrollable list, a Tool Tip displays the complete directory path.

Sort orders

Also found below the results list is a pull-down menu for Sort by. There are four selections you can choose from the menu items. When you select one of the menu choices, the reporting is dynamic and you don't need to invoke another search when changing the sort order. The four choices Acrobat offers you are

✦ **Relative Ranking.** Files are sorted according to their ranking. Relative ranking has to do with the found words compared to the percentage of words contained in the document. Ten occurrences in a file with 20 words would have a higher ranking than 1,000 occurrences in a document with 10,000 words. The ten occurrences constitute 50 percent of the document whereas the 1,000 words constitute only 10 percent of found words compared to the total words in the documents.

✦ **Date Modified.** Files are sorted according the modification date. The dates are reported in ascending order, with the oldest file appearing first in the list.

✦ **Filename.** Results are reported in alphabetical order according to the name of the PDF file.

✦ **Location.** Files are sorted according to an alphabetized list of folders containing the documents with found words.

Searching files and folders

If you search through a large collection of PDF files, Search works away loading up the results window. Clicking on a link to open a page where results have been found won't interrupt your search. You can browse files while results continue to be reported. To search a hard disk, a media storage device, a network drive, or a folder in any of these locations, click on the radio button for All PDF documents in and open the pull-down menu.

The pull-down menu lists the drives and servers active on your system. If you want to search a particular folder, select the item denoted as Browse for Location. The Browse for Folder dialog box opens as shown in Figure 4-3. Navigate your hard drive like you would when searching for files to open. When you find the folder to be searched, click on the folder name and click OK.

After you click OK in the Browse for Folder dialog box, the Search Pane returns. The search does not begin until you click on the Search button. Before clicking Search, you can examine the name listed as the target folder. The folder identified in the Browse for Folder dialog box is displayed in the Search Pane by folder name. If all looks as you expect, click Search.

Figure 4-3: Select the folder to be searched in the Browse for Folder dialog box. Select the folder name and click OK to return to the Search Pane.

Search PDFs on the Internet

Below the search results scrollable list is a link to your default Web browser. The criteria you establish in the Search Pane are used to conduct a search on the Internet. By default, the Google (www.google.com) search engine opens and the search word(s) you typed in the search field box automatically copies to the Google search engine. When you click on the link to search for PDFs on the Internet, Acrobat is no longer in control. It is merely a means for launching your Web browser and searching for the words you typed in the Search Pane contained in PDF files on the Internet. If you are not in Acrobat, you can manually search for PDF content by adding **filetype:PDF** to your search criteria in a search engine in your Web browser. For example, you could type **Acrobat 6 filetype:PDF** in the Google search engine and the same results would occur as when clicking on the link in the Search Pane and searching for the same words.

> **Note**   You are not limited to using the Google Web site for searching PDF content. You can perform the same searches manually by opening search engines such as Yahoo! (www.yahoo.com), Lycos (www.lycos.com), and so on and adding the same criteria. The ability to search PDF content is dependent on the search engine support. Some search engines don't support searching for PDF content.

After clicking on the button for searching the Internet, you can change your criteria or continue with the search. The actual launching of the Web browser does not occur until you click the Search the Internet button that comes into view after you click on the link at the bottom of the Search Pane. When you click Search the Internet, the search results are reported in the Google Web site. Click on any link listed in the Google.com search results window and the linked PDF document opens in your Web browser as shown in Figure 4-4.

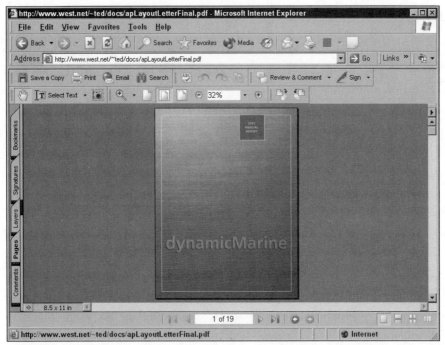

Figure 4-4: When you search the Internet for PDF content, the Google Web site opens with the search results from the criteria you supplied in the Acrobat Search Pane. Click on a link in the search results page and the linked PDF document opens in your Web browser.

The list you see in the Web search engine are links to only PDF documents containing the information you are searching. The searched words can appear on any page in the PDF file listed from the search results. The PDF opens as an inline view inside your Web browser. Within the Web browser window you have access to many different Acrobat tools, including the Search tool. When you click on the Search tool, you can search the PDF contained in the browser window using the same or different search criteria.

 For a better understanding of inline views in Web browsers, see Chapter 14 and Chapter 20.

Acrobat remains open in the background as you navigate a Web browser. When you quit your Web browser, the Acrobat window moves forward and you're ready to continue more searches or work on any other Acrobat-related tasks.

When you return to the Search Pane, the current search mode is set to search PDFs on the Internet. If you want to search an open PDF document or a folder of PDFs, click on the link at the bottom of the Search Pane where you see Search Across Local PDF Documents. You are then returned to the view where the radio buttons appear for selecting searches in open files or the pull-down menu for searching documents on hard drives and in folders.

Advanced searches

In all Acrobat viewers, you can now search PDF documents with selected criteria without the assistance of a search index. To take advantage of searching with advanced options, click the Use Advanced Search Options link at the bottom of the Search Pane. When you click the link, a series of advanced options appear in the Search Pane as shown in Figure 4-5.

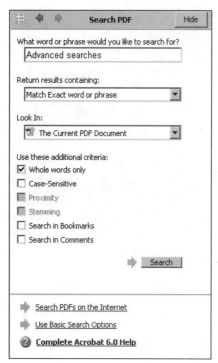

Figure 4-5: Click on Use Advanced Search Options to take advantage of more search options. When you select an open PDF file for the search, the options in this figure are available. If you search a collection of PDFs, the Advanced Search Options change.

Note   When you click on the link to show the advanced search options, the link at the bottom of the Search Pane changes to Use Basic Search Options. Click on this button or click the Back arrow at the top of the Pane to return to searching with the basic options.

Depending on whether you search an open PDF document or a collection of PDFs stored on drives and external devices, the Advanced Search Options change, offering you different options.

Searching the open PDF file with Advanced Search Options

When you select the Current PDF Document from the Look In pull-down menu, the search options shown in Figure 4-5 are available to you. These options include

✦ **Whole words only:** When checked, the search results return whole words. If you search for *forgiven*, the search ignores words like *for* and *give* that make up part of the whole word. If the check box is disabled, various stems and parts of a whole word are included with the search results.

✦ **Case-Sensitive:** Letter case is ignored if the check box is disabled. If enabled, then the search results return only words matching the precise letter case of the searched word.

✦ **Proximity:** Proximity is a powerful tool when performing searches. If you want to search for two independent words that may appear together in a given context — for example, *Acrobat* and *PostScript* — the proximity option finds the two words when they appear within 900 words of each other in a PDF.

✦ **Stemming:** If you want to search for all words stemming from a given word, enable this option. Words such as *header* and *heading* stem from the word *head* in the English language. If you type *head* in the first field box and select the Stemming option, all PDFs containing the search criteria from the word stem are listed.

✦ **Search in Bookmarks:** When bookmarks are checked the search results report the found instances in the bookmarks and the document pages.

✦ **Search in Comments:** Text in comment notes and text on document pages are returned when this option is checked.

When all the search criteria have been established, click on the Search button. The results are reported in the Search Pane, like the searches performed with the Basic Search Options.

Searching multiple PDFs with Advanced Search Options

When you change the search parameters to search through a collection of PDF documents, the Advanced Search Options change, offering you more options to help narrow down your search as shown in Figure 4-6. These options include

✦ **Return results containing:** Four options are available from a pull-down menu. These include:

• **Match Exact word or phrase:** If you search for something like *Human Resource Forms*, only these three words together in a PDF document are returned as results. The results report the precise order of the words.

• **Match Any of the words:** Using the same example, words like Human, Resource, Forms, Human Resource, Resource Forms, Human Forms, and Human Resource Forms would be reported in the results. Any one of the words or any combination of words in a phrase is reported.

• **Match All of the words:** In this case, all of the words need to be contained in the document, but not necessarily in the order described previously. You might see returns like *Forms Human Resource* returned from the search.

• **Boolean query:** You can search PDF collections using Boolean expressions without the assistance of a search index created with Acrobat Catalog. Note that Boolean queries are not available when you search an open document. You need to use the Advanced Search Options to search through a drive, external media, or a folder.

Cross-Reference For more detail on using Boolean queries, see the "Boolean queries" section later in this chapter.

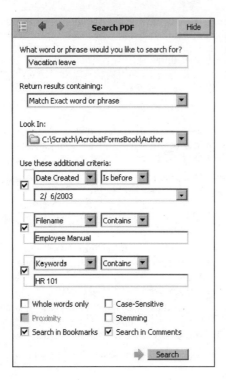

Figure 4-6: Advanced Search Options offer you additional criteria when searching through multiple PDF documents.

✦ **Use these additional criteria:** Three check boxes offer you one or a combination of several different options to help you refine your search. From the first pull-down menu you select the primary category. The second pull-down menu to the right of each primary category helps refine that particular category. The options for each of the three check box pull-down menus are the same. You might, for example, choose Date Created from the first check box option and define the date from the options contained in the adjacent pull-down menu. You then might add another criterion and ask for the Keywords option. Adjacent to Keywords, you might specify that the file does not contain certain words. In the field box you type any descriptions for the menu choices you make.

> **Note** All the preceding items require that you supply at least one character in *What word or phase would you like to search for?* The options that follow enable you to search for specific content related to the option of choice and you do not need to supply a word in the first field box in order to execute a search. When you move around adjusting criteria, the Search button will appear active or grayed out. If it is grayed out, know that you can't perform a search on the options you chose. In some cases, the missing option is a word or phrase that needs to be added to the first field box.

From the first pull-down menu, the choices available to you include

- **Date Created:** If you look for PDF documents that you know were created before or after a certain date, use the Date Created menu option. You have four choices for options associated with this category available in the second pull-down menu adjacent to the first menu choice. These options include Is exactly, Is before, Is after, and Is not. These four options are self-explanatory. When you make the choices from the two pull-down menus your next step is to type the date criteria in the field box appearing below the pull-down menus. If, for example, you select Date Created and Is not, you then add the date you want to exclude from the search. As an additional aid to you, Acrobat offers a calendar when you select the pull-down menu from the field box as shown in Figure 4-7. Make a date selection from the calendar and move to the option you want to change or click on the Search button.

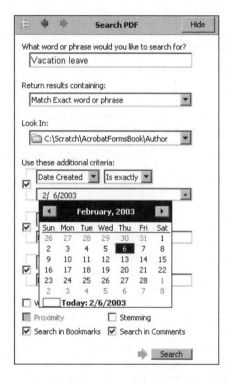

Figure 4-7: After making date selections from the pull-down menus, open the pull-down menu from the field box and a calendar opens to help you find the date parameters to be searched.

- **Date Modified:** The modified date searches for the date the PDF file was last modified. If you create a file on January 1, 2003 and then save some edits on July 1, 2003, the modified date is July 1, 2003. The manner in which you specify a date is handled the same as searching for the creation date.

- **Author:** The information is derived from the Document Properties in the Description Pane. Any data typed in the Author field is searched. This choice and the remaining options offer two menu options in the second pull-down menu. You can select from Contains or Does not contain. In essence your search includes or excludes the data you supply in the field box immediately following the pull-down menu choices.

Cross-Reference For information related to document descriptions, see the related section later in this chapter.

- **Title:** Same as the Author search where the Title field is used in the document description.

- **Subject:** Same as Author search where the Subject field is used in the document description.

- **Filename:** The name you provide for the PDF document is searched.

- **Keywords:** Same as the Author search where the Keywords field is used in the document description.

- **Bookmarks:** When you select this option, Acrobat searches for the words in the PDF document and the same words found in bookmarks. When the results are listed, the found words include both bookmarks and pages.

- **Comments:** Same as bookmarks, but the comment notes are searched. When the found words appear in comments, the results report the found words in comment notes.

- **JPEG Images:** Narrows the search for files meeting the search text criteria and where JPEG images are contained within the PDF.

- **XMP Metadata:** Searches for words or phrases contained in the document metadata.

 Cross-Reference   For more information on XMP metadata, see Searching XMP metadata later in this chapter.

Below the Use these additional criteria pull-down menus are additional options. These options are the same as those used for the advanced searches on open PDF documents. Jump several pages back in this book to review the descriptions for the items listed at the bottom of the Search Pane.

Searching dates

To help you target the precise date with the field box and the calendar, Acrobat offers you several options. To change the year, you can edit the field box and type the year for the date to be searched. In the field box you can change dates by clicking on the day, month, and year, then use the up or down arrow keys to scroll dates. The dates revolve like an odometer. Select a day, and then click the month to highlight the value and press the arrow keys again until you find the correct month. Move to the year and follow the same steps to select the correct year. You can also select any one of the three values and type new values you want to search when the text is selected. The text you type replaces all selected text. Acrobat only accepts a legitimate value, so if you type a value not permitted for a date search, for example, entering 33 in the day field, Acrobat will not accept it.

For changing dates with the calendar, click the down arrow in the pull-down menu adjacent to the date in the field box to open the calendar. For a month change, left-click in the title bar of the calendar on the month name. For example, if July appears listed in the title bar, click on July. Be careful not to left-click the mouse below the title bar because doing so selects a day and closes the calendar. When you left-click on the month name in the title bar, a pop-up menu displays the months of the year as shown in Figure 4-8. Move the cursor to the desired month and left-click again.

 Note   You can also change months by scrolling the calendar backward or forward. Click on the left arrow in the title bar to scroll backward or the right arrow to scroll forward. As you reach a year beginning or end, the next month in date order is opened. For example, scrolling backward from January 1996 opens December 1995.

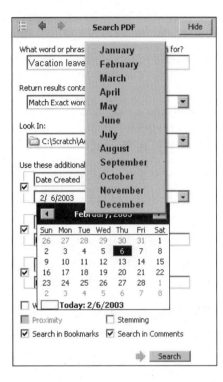

Figure 4-8: To open the pop-up menu for month selections, left-click on the calendar title bar. When the pop-up menu is visible, left-click on the desired month.

When you click to select the desired month, Acrobat leaves the calendar view where you can still make the year and day selections. To change the year in the calendar, left-click on the year in the title bar. The year becomes visible as editable text. You can edit the field or click on the up or down arrows adjacent to the year, as shown in Figure 4-9.

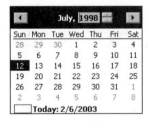

Figure 4-9: To change year in the calendar, left-click on the year in the title bar. Edit the text or click on the up or down arrows adjacent to the year field to change the date.

After the month and year have been selected, left click on the desired day from the calendar displayed below the title bar. Acrobat supplies the new date in the field box and closes the calendar.

Searching XMP metadata

The ability to search a document's metadata is a powerful tool in Acrobat. In order to use the tool, you need to know just a little bit about what *metadata* is.

Adobe Acrobat 5.0 and later contains metadata in XML (eXtensible Markup Language) format. The metadata of a file is information related to the document's structure, origination, content, interchange, and processing. Metadata might include, for example, the document author's name, the creation date, modified date, and the PDF producer. For example, suppose you created a document in a program like Adobe Persuasion and converted it to PDF a few years ago. You know the document is around somewhere, but you've forgotten the title and can't remember much of the content. Among your archive of many PDF files you want to search for this particular document. Therefore, because you know that the file was created in Adobe Persuasion, you can search the XMP data and enter Adobe Persuasion in the field box below the pull-down menu. If you happen to remember some of the content you can supply words to be searched for in addition to the XMP data. When you click Search, the search results report all files where Adobe Persuasion is contained in the various documents' metadata.

XMP (eXtensible Metadata Platform) is an XML framework that provides all Adobe programs a common language for communicating standards related to document creation and processing throughout publishing workflows. XMP is a format, and document metadata viewed in XML source code can be exported to XMP format. Once in XMP, it can be exchanged between documents.

To take a look at the XML source code of the XMP metadata, choose Advanced ➪ Document Metadata. The Document Metadata dialog box opens. Click on the Advanced item in the left Pane and the document metadata source code appears in a scrollable window in the right Pane, as shown in Figure 4-10.

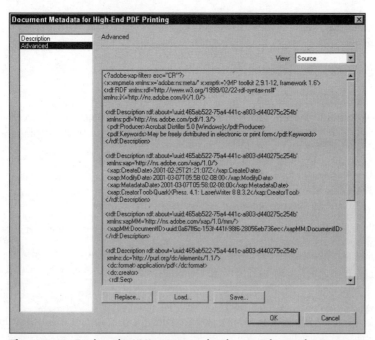

Figure 4-10: To view the XML source code, choose Advanced ➪ Document Metadata. Click on the Advanced tab in the left Pane to view the source code in a scrollable window on the right side of the dialog box.

To view the XMP formatted data, select Summary from the pull-down menu in the top-right corner of the dialog box. The XMP properties are shown in Figure 4-11.

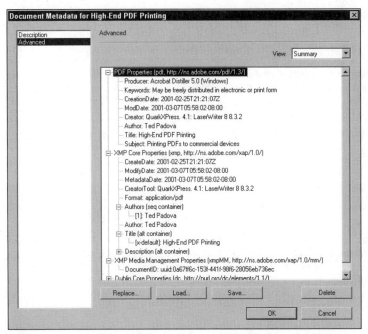

Figure 4-11: Choose Summary from the pull-down menu to view the XMP formatted data.

At the bottom of the dialog boxes are buttons used for importing and exporting XMP data that can be shared in workflows across many different file types. For the purposes of searching information, any of the text you see in the source code and the summary can be searched when you select XMP Metadata from the Additional criteria pull-down menus.

Tip

To gain experience in searching XMP data, open different PDF documents you have stored on your hard drive and browse the contents of the XML source code and XMP summaries. Try to look for information related to the file creator and associated tools that contributed to the PDF construction. Practice searching for the criteria you discovered in the Document Metadata. You don't need to be a programmer to make use of these tools that Acrobat offers you.

Searching layers

The search criteria discussed on the preceding pages works for documents containing layers. When you invoke a search in documents containing layers, Search automatically searches through all layers for the criteria you specify in the Search Pane. The results list contains items on any hidden layers as well as all visible layers. When you click on a result associated with a hidden layer, Acrobat prompts you in a dialog box, as shown in Figure 4-12, asking whether you want to make the layer visible.

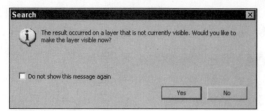

Figure 4-12: If searched words are found on hidden layers, Acrobat asks whether you want to make the hidden layer visible.

If you click Yes in the dialog box, the layer is made visible and the search stops at the found word. If you select No, the layer remains hidden and you are taken to the next search result.

Boolean queries

The *Return results containing* pull-down menu contains a menu option for searching with Boolean expressions. Boolean expressions include AND, OR, and NOT. You can use all the previously listed criteria when you want to use the Boolean expressions option.

✦ **AND operator:** You can select the Boolean query menu option. Acrobat recognizes Boolean operators AND, OR and NOT, such as when you invoke a search, for example, *Adobe AND Professional*, the search results report all found instances of the two words appearing together in a document. The AND operator is not really necessary, because you can produce the same results by using the Match All of the words menu command.

Note   When using Boolean operators, the text is not case sensitive. Uppercase letters for the Boolean expressions are used here to denote a Boolean operator as opposed to text. You can use lowercase letters and the results are reported the same as long as the Boolean query pull-down menu item is selected.

✦ **OR operator:** When you use OR, either word or phrase is returned in the search results. A search for *Acrobat OR JavaScript* returns all found instances of both terms.

✦ **NOT operator:** When NOT is used, words in a phrase that contain the NOT word are skipped. A search for *Adobe NOT Acrobat* returns all PDF documents where Adobe is found and those with Adobe Acrobat are not reported in the found list.

✦ **Multiple words:** Words appearing together like *Acrobat PDF* can be included in quotes. You would supply *"Acrobat PDF"* in the field box and all instances where these two words appear together are reported in the search results. If the words are not contained within quotes, the words *Acrobat, PDF,* and *Acrobat PDF* would all be returned in the search results. This behavior is similar to how you perform searches in Web browsers.

✦ **Searching and, or, not:** If you want to search for a term where these three words are part of the term, you can distinguish among words you search for and using operators. To search for something like *Ben and Jerry's* as a term, you would type *"Ben and Jerry's"* within the quote marks. If you want to search for two terms and a Boolean operator you might use *"Ben and Jerry's" AND "Ice Cream" NOT yogurt*. The results report back to you the documents where the words Ben and Jerry's and ice cream are contained in the files and the words Ben and Jerry's yogurt are not reported in the search results.

Search preferences

To open preference settings for Search, choose Edit ➪ Preferences. In the left Pane select Search. The preference options available to you are shown in Figure 4-13.

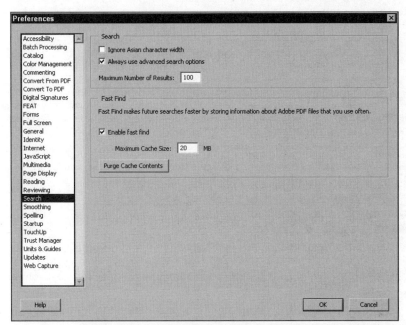

Figure 4-13: Choose Edit ➪ Preferences to open the Preferences dialog box. Click on Search in the list at the left to display preference settings for using Search.

The preference choices listed on the right side of the dialog box include

- ✦ **Ignore Asian character width:** This setting matches only Kana characters that match the text typed in the search field.

- ✦ **Always use advanced search options:** When the check box is enabled, you don't need to keep clicking on the Use Advanced Search Options button in the Search Pane. Enable this setting if you find yourself always using the advanced options.

Note   When you enable Always use advanced search options, the basic search options are inaccessible. The only way to return to basic search options is to disable the preference setting.

- ✦ **Enable fast find:** Searches are logged by Acrobat in a memory cache. After performing different searches, returning to search the same information is acquired from the cache that speeds up the search. You can edit the cache size by editing the field box for the number of megabytes on your hard drive you want to allocate to the cache. Be certain you have ample hard drive space when enabling the cache and raising the cache size.

- ✦ **Purge Cache Contents:** The cache occupies as much memory as available on your hard drive. If you want to clear the cache, click on the button and all the contents are erased.

After changing any settings in the Preferences dialog box, click OK. The changes you make are dynamically reflected in Acrobat and take effect the next time you perform a search.

Document Descriptions

Document descriptions are user-supplied data fields used to help you identify PDF files according to title, subject, author, and keywords. At the time you create a PDF document, you may have options for supplying a document description. In other cases, you may add descriptions in Acrobat either individually or with Acrobat's batch processing features.

Cross-Reference For learning how to create batch sequences, see Chapter 10.

After you add descriptions and save your files, the data added to these fields are searchable when you perform advanced searches and when searching index files. Developing an organized workflow with specific guidelines for users to follow regarding document descriptions significantly helps all your colleagues search PDFs much more efficiently.

To add a document description, choose File ➪ Document Properties. When the Document Properties dialog box opens, click on Description in the left Pane as shown in Figure 4-14.

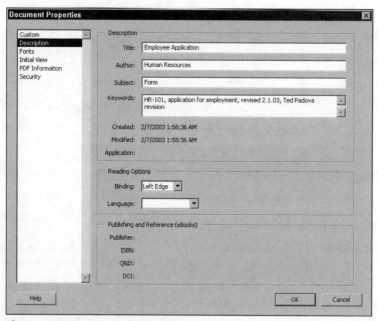

Figure 4-14: Document descriptions are added to the Descriptions Pane in the Document Properties dialog box.

The four fields for document descriptions include

✦ **Title:** The Title field in this example contains a description of a form. Other forms in a company using a similar schema might include Title fields using titles such as W-2 Form, Travel Expense, Employee Leave, and so on.

✦ **Author:** In the example, the Author field contains the department authoring the form. Notice that an employee name is not used for the Author field. Rather than use employee names, departments are a much better choice. A company typically turns over employees more often than they rename departments.

✦ **Subject:** In the example, the Subject field contains Form. The subject here might be used to distinguish a form from Policy, Procedure, Memo, Directive, and so on.

✦ **Keywords:** The first entry in the Keywords field is the form number used by the company to identify the form. Other words in the Keywords field are descriptors related to the form contents. If you want to add an employee author name, add it to the Keywords field.

Note Users of earlier versions of Acrobat will notice the rearrangement of the description fields where the Author and Subject fields have swapped positions. This is no more than a UI change and won't have any effect on descriptions you added to PDFs in earlier versions of Acrobat.

The reason the field information is important for any organization using a PDF workflow is that document description information can be used when a user searches a collection of PDF files. Each field is searchable by the summary title and the words contained in the fields. Therefore, a user can search for all PDF files where the Title field contains the word *Purchase* and the Subject field contains the word *Form*. The search results display all PDF documents where the Title and Subject fields have these words contained in the document description.

As a comparison, imagine searching for the words *Purchase Order*. The search would return all PDFs where these words appear in either the document summary or the text in the PDF files. Purchase Order might be used in memos, policies, procedures, and forms. The user might have to search through many PDFs in order to find the Purchase Order form, thus spending much more time trying to locate the right document.

Searching document descriptions

To search for document descriptions, you need to use either the advanced search or an index file search. Click on the Search tool in an Acrobat viewer and click on Use Advanced Search Options. Select a folder to search from the Look In pull-down menu.

Cross-Reference For searching index files, see the section on searching index files later in this chapter.

Under Use these additional criteria select one of the descriptions items from the first pull-down menu (Title, Author, Subject, or Keywords). Select either Contains or Does not contain from the pull-down menu adjacent to the first menu. Type the words to be searched in the field box below the pull-down menus. Continue adding additional description fields as desired. In Figure 4-15 two description fields are marked for the search.

Note that no criteria need to be supplied in the first field box for specific words to be searched in the document. If you click Search in the Search Pane with the descriptions shown in Figure 4-15, all PDF files in the designated folder with the words Purchase Order in the Title field and Forms in the Subject field are returned in the results list for files matching the criteria.

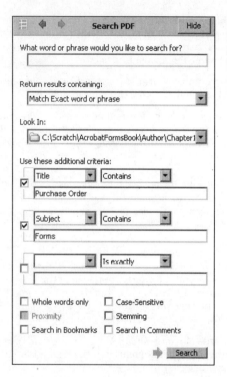

Figure 4-15: Two descriptions fields are identified. When you click the Search button, Acrobat searches the document descriptions for matches.

Document descriptions and Boolean queries

You can add Boolean queries when searching document descriptions. You might know some content in PDF files as well as information contained in the document descriptions. In this case you address the additional criteria items in the same manner and add the Boolean query as discussed earlier in this chapter. In Figure 4-16, document descriptions are added to a Boolean query.

When you click the Search button, the number of results returned in the Search Pane is significantly reduced compared to searching for individual words — especially when common words are contained in many PDF documents. What the document descriptions offer you is a method for targeting the exact file you're looking for as fast as possible. If you have 100 PDF documents in the search results list, looking through the list and finding the file you want will take some time. Compare that to two or three files listed. Obviously the time savings will help you browse around PDFs from among very large collections.

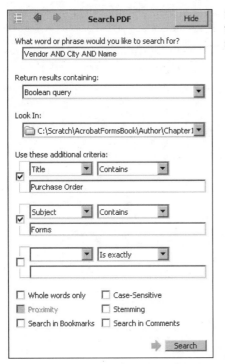

Figure 4-16: Boolean queries can be added to searches with additional criteria selections such as document descriptions.

Full Text versus Index Searches

This is a pivotal point for this chapter. All of what has been covered so far is information about finding content in PDF documents with a very elaborate *find* feature in Acrobat. The name used in Acrobat to refer to what has been discussed so far is *Search*. Users of earlier versions of Acrobat may take this to mean using Acrobat Search as it was used in Acrobat viewers earlier than version 6.0. What has been covered thus far, however, is not Acrobat Search in a traditional sense. Understanding the difference between the preceding pages and what follows requires a little explanation.

When you click on the Search tool in Acrobat, you open the Search Pane in the How To window. Searches are performed without the assistance of a search index file when you search the current open document or you select a location and search through a folder of PDF documents.

From the Look In pull-down menu you'll see an option for Select Index and another option for Currently Selected Indexes. When these items are chosen you begin to experience behavior similar to searches you used to perform with Acrobat Search in earlier versions of Acrobat; that is, the use of an index file and searching index files created with Acrobat Catalog.

At first blush, you may wonder why you would go through the trouble of creating an index file and loading indexes to search for the same information you can search for without the use of an index file. If that question comes to mind, then a few clarifications need to be made here before moving along.

The most important distinction between searching PDF documents with advanced searches compared to searching an index file is speed. When you open the Search Pane and select a folder to be searched and execute the search, Acrobat reads through each PDF document, looking for matches to your search criteria. This would be analogous to your reading every PDF document in a collection to find a citation or topic you wanted to research.

When you create an index file, the file contains a word list with a marker to the document and page where the word can be found. When Acrobat finds a searched word, the document is listed in a results list where you can click and view the document associated with the found word(s). This behavior is the same as looking at an index at the back of a book. You see a page number, then open the page and begin reading—obviously a much faster method than reading through all pages. By the same token, Acrobat finds information much faster when scanning an index file compared to searching through PDF documents.

When would you use an index file? Quite simply it all depends on your workflow and for what reasons you use Acrobat. If your PDF usage is limited to working locally on your own hard drive and preparing PDF documents for your own use, then you might just want to skip the rest of this chapter and move on to something else. On the other hand, if you work in a company where large collections of PDFs reside on a server, you prepare PDF files for distribution on CD-ROM or DVDs, or your personal collection of PDF documents is huge, then working with search indexes will be of interest to you.

Search Index Procedures

I explain the details for working with search indexes in the remaining pages in this chapter. To provide you with an overall summary for how index file creation and management is dealt with in Acrobat, I give you a short summary of the procedures here.

Using index files to perform searches begins with using a current index file or creating a new one. For users who have been working with index files, make sure that all your previous indexes are updated for compatibility with Acrobat 6.0 viewers.

Index files are created and updated with Acrobat Catalog. Catalog is available from a menu selection in the Advanced menu. You open Catalog and make a decision for creating a new index or opening an existing index file for rebuilding or editing in the Catalog dialog box.

After an index file is created or updated, you load the index file into the Search Pane. Multiple index files can be loaded and searched. When you search index files, the results are reported in the Search Pane like all the searches discussed earlier in this chapter.

Earlier releases of Acrobat offered you options for various menu selections related to managing indexes and loading new index files. Earlier releases of Acrobat also offered you dialog boxes where results were reported and information about an index file could be obtained. In Acrobat 6.0 viewers, you handle all your index file management in the Search Pane. Menu commands are limited to viewing search results as described earlier in this chapter.

If you edit PDF documents, delete them, or add new documents to folders that have been indexed, you need to rebuild index files periodically. You can purge old data and re-index files in Acrobat Catalog. Index files can be copied to different hard drive locations, across servers, and to external media. When copying files, you need to copy all files/folders associated with the index file. Failure to copy all the files renders the index inoperable.

Creating Search Indexes

In order to search an index file, you must have one present on your computer, network server, or some media storage device. When you install an Acrobat viewer, a help index file is included during your installation. You can use this file to search for words contained in any of the help documents. If you want to search your own files, you need to create an index. To create an index file you use Acrobat Catalog.

Note   Acrobat Catalog is available only in Acrobat Professional. Search indexes can be used by all Acrobat viewers including Adobe Reader.

To launch Acrobat Catalog from within Acrobat Professional, choose Tools ➪ Catalog. Catalog is robust and provides many options for creating and modifying indexes. After a search index is created, any user can access the search index in all Acrobat viewers to find words using the Search Pane. However, before you begin to work with Acrobat Catalog, you need to take some preliminary steps to be certain all your files are properly prepared and ready to be indexed.

Preparing PDFs for indexing

Preparation involves creating PDFs with all the necessary information to facilitate searches. All searchable document description information needs to be supplied in the PDF documents at the time of PDF creation or by modifying PDFs in Acrobat before you begin working with Catalog. For workgroups and multiple user access to search indexes, this information needs to be clear and consistent. Other factors, such as naming conventions, location of files, and optimizing performance should all be thought out and planned prior to creating an index file.

Note   Adding document descriptions is not a requirement for creating search indexes. You can index files without any information in the document description fields. Adding document descriptions merely adds more relevant information to your PDF documents and aids users in finding search results faster.

Document descriptions

Document description information should be supplied in all PDF files to be searched. As discussed earlier in this chapter, all document description data are searchable. Spending time creating document descriptions and defining the field types for consistent organization will facilitate searches performed by multiple users.

The first of the planning steps is to develop a flow chart or outline of company information and the documents to be categorized. This organization may or may not be implemented where you intend to develop a PDF workflow. If your information flow is already in place, you may need to make some modifications to coordinate nomenclature and document identity with the document summary items in Acrobat.

Document summaries contained in the Title, Subject, Author, and Keywords fields should be consistent and intuitive. They should also follow a hierarchy consistent with the company's organizational structure and workflow. The document summary items should be mapped out and defined. When preparing files for indexing, consider the following:

✦ **Title:** Title information might be thought of as the root of an outline — the parent statement, if you will. Descriptive titles should be used to help users narrow searches within specific categories. The Title field can also be used to display the title name at the top of the Acrobat window when you select viewing titles in the Initial View properties.

Cross-Reference

For information on how to set document title attributes in the Initial View dialog box, see Chapter 1.

✦ **Author:** Avoid using proper names for the Author field. Personnel change in companies and roles among employees change. Identify the author of PDF documents according to departments, work groups, facilities, and so on.

✦ **Subject:** If the Title field is the parent item in an outline format, the Subject would be a child item nested directly below the title. Subjects might be considered subsets of titles. When creating document summaries, be consistent. Don't use subject and title or subject and keyword information back and forth with different documents. If an item, such as employee grievances, is listed as a subject in some PDFs and then listed as titles in other documents, the end users will become confused with the order and searches will become unnecessarily complicated.

✦ **Keywords:** If you have a forms identification system in place, be certain to use form numbers and identity as part of the Keywords field. You might start the Keywords field with a form number and then add additional keywords to help narrow searches. Be consistent and always start the Keywords field with forms or document numbers. If you need to have PDF author names, add them here in the Keywords fields. If employees change roles or leave the company, the Author fields still provide the information relative to a department.

To illustrate some examples, take a look at Table 4-1.

Table 4-1: Document Summary Examples

Title	Author	Subject	Keywords
Descriptive Titles.	Department Names.	Subsection of Title.	Document Numbers and random identifiers.
Titles may be considered specific to workgroup tasks.	Don't use employee names in organizations; employees change, departments usually remain.	Subjects may be thought of as child outline items nested below the parent Title items — a subset of the Titles.	Forms ID numbers, internal filing numbers, and so on can be supplied in the Keyword fields. If employee names are a MUST for your company, add employee names in the Keywords field box. List any related words to help find the topic.
Employee Policies	Human Resources	Vacation Leave	D-101, HR32A, H. Jones, policy, employee regulations

Title	Author	Subject	Keywords
FDA Compliance	Quality Assurance	Software Validation	SOP-114, QA-182, J. Wilson, regulations, citations, eye implant device
Curriculum	English Department	American Literature	Plan 2010, Martha Evans, senior English, Emerson High, 11th grade
Receivables	Accounting	Collection Policy	F-8102, M-5433, Finance, collections, payments
eCommerce	Marketing	Products	M-1051, e-117A, golf clubs, sports, leisure

Tip

Legacy PDF files used in an organization may have been created without a document description or you may reorganize PDFs and want to change document summaries. You can create a batch sequence to change multiple PDF files and run the sequence. Organize PDFs in a folder where the document summaries are to be edited. In the Edit Sequence dialog box, select the items to change and edit each document summary item. Run the sequence and an entire folder of PDFs can be updated.

Cross-Reference

For more information on creating batch sequences, see Chapter 10.

File structure

The content, filenames, and location of PDFs to be cataloged contribute to file structure items. All the issues related to file structure must be thought out and appropriately designed for the audience that you intend to support. Among the important considerations are

✦ **Filenaming conventions:** Names provided for the PDF files are critical for distributing documents among users. If filenames get truncated, then either Acrobat Search or the end user will have difficulty finding a document when performing a search. This is of special concern to Macintosh users who want to distribute documents across platforms. As a matter of safeguard, the best precaution to take is always use standard DOS filenaming conventions. The standard eight-character maximum filename with no more than three-character file extensions (`filename.ext`) will always work regardless of platform.

✦ **Folder names:** Folder names should follow the same conventions as filenames. Macintosh users who want to keep filenames longer than standard DOS names must limit folder names to eight characters and no more than a three-character file extension for cross-platform compliance.

✦ **File and folder name identity:** Avoid using ASCII characters from 133 to 159 for any filename or folder name. Acrobat Catalog does support some extended characters in this range, but you may experience problems when using files across platforms. (Figure 4-17 lists the characters to avoid.)

133	à	139	ï	144	É	149	ò	154	Û
134	å	140	î	145	æ	150	û	156	Ł
135	ç	141	ì	146	Æ	151	ù	157	¥
136	é	142	Ä	147	ô	152	_	158	
137	è	143	Å	148	ö	153	Ö	159	ƒ
138	ê								

Figure 4-17: When providing names for files and folders to be cataloged, avoid using extended characters from ASCII 133 to ASCII 159. Although some of the characters are supported in Acrobat Catalog, you may have problems when copying files across platforms.

✦ **Folder organization:** Folders to be cataloged should have a logical hierarchy. Copy all files to be cataloged to a single folder or a single folder with nested folders in the same path. When nesting folders, be certain to keep the number of nested folders to a minimum. Deeply nested folders slow down searches, and path names longer than 256 characters create problems.

✦ **Folder locations:** For Windows users, location of folders must be contained on a local hard drive or a network server volume. Although Macintosh users can catalog information across computer workstations, creating separate indexes for files contained on separate drives would be advisable. Any files moved to different locations make searches inoperable.

✦ **PDF structure:** File and foldernaming should be handled before creating links and attaching files. If filenames are changed after the PDF structure has been developed, many links become inoperable. Be certain to complete all editing in the PDF documents before cataloging files.

Optimizing performance

Searches can be performed very fast if you take a little time in creating the proper structure and organization. If you don't avoid some pitfalls with the way that you organize files, then searches perform much slower. A few considerations to be made include the following:

✦ **Optimize PDF files:** Optimization should be performed on all PDF files as one of the last steps in your workflow. Use the Save As optimizes for Fast Web View found in the General category in the Preferences dialog box and run the PDF Optimizer located in the Advanced menu. Optimization is especially important for searches to be performed from CD-ROM files.

Cross-Reference

For information on PDF Optimizer, see Chapter 13.

✦ **Break up long PDF files:** Books, reports, essays, and other documents that contain many pages should be broken up into multiple PDF files. If you have books to be cataloged, break up the books into separate chapters. Acrobat Search runs much faster when finding information from several small files. It slows down when searching through long documents.

Managing Multiple PDF Documents

Books, reports, and manuals can be broken up into separate files and structured in a way that still appears to the end user as a single document. Assuming a user reads through a file in a linear fashion, you can create links to open and close pages without user intervention. Create navigational buttons to move forward and back through document pages. On the last page of each chapter, use the navigation button to open the next chapter. Also on the last page of each chapter, create a Page action that closes the current document when the page is closed. (See Chapter 10 for creating links and Page actions.) If the end user disables Open cross-document links in same window in the General category in the Preferences dialog box, the open file still closes after the last page is closed. All the chapters can be linked from a table of contents where any chapter can be opened. If you give your design some thought, browsing the contents of books will appear to the end user no different from reading a book in the analog world.

Cross-Reference

For more information on PDF interactivity and creating link buttons to open and close files, see Chapter 15 and Chapter 27.

Creating search help

You can have multiple indexes for various uses and different workgroups. Personnel may use one index for department matters, another for company-wide information, and perhaps another for a research library. When searching information, all relevant keywords will appear from indexes loaded in the Index Selection dialog box. When using multiple indexes, employees may forget the structure of document summaries and knowing what index would be needed for a given search.

Readme files and index help files can be created where key information about what search words can be used to find document summaries is stored. You can create a single PDF file, text files, or multiple files that serve as help. Figure 4-18 shows an example of a PDF help file that might be used to find documents related to a company's personnel policies, procedures, and forms.

In the top-right corner of Figure 4-18, the document summary for the help file is listed. The Title fields for this company are broken into categories for policies, procedures, forms, and charts. The Subject fields break down the title categories into specific personnel items, and the Author fields contain the department that authored the documents. Form numbers appear for all Keywords fields.

Tip

When creating help files that guide a user for searching document information, use a common identifier in the Subject, Author, and Keywords fields reserved for only finding help files. In Figure 4-18, the identifier is *Table*. Whenever a user searches for the word *table* in the Author field, the only returns in the Search Results dialog box will be help files. When using the Title and Author field together, a user can find a specific help file for a given department. In the previous example, the Title is *HR* and the Author is *Table*. When these words are searched for the document information, the help file for the HR department will be returned in the Search Results. If you reserve keywords for the document Summary fields, any employee can easily find information by remembering only a few keywords.

Widget Company
Human Resources Index Description

Title: HR
Subject: Table
Author: Table
Keywords: Table

Title	Subject	Author	Keywords
Policy	PTO	HR	HR 501
Policy	Maternity	HR	HR 521
Procedure	Maternity	HR	HR 520
Form	Payroll	Accounting	FM 261
Policy	Bonus	Accounting	AC 245
Policy	Manual	Admin	AD 109
Procedure	Grievance	HR	HR 546
Policy	EAP	HR	HR 593
Policy	Hiring	HR	HR 506
Form	ID	HR	FM 505
Chart	HR	Admin	AD 117
Form	Leave	HR	FM 531
Procedure	Pay deduction	Accounting	AC 228
Policy	Benefits	Table	Table
Procedure	Extended Leave	HR	HR 564
Policy	Education Leave	HR	HR 568
Form	Insurance	HR	FM 533
Form	Dental	HR	FM 512
Policy	401K	HR	HR 555

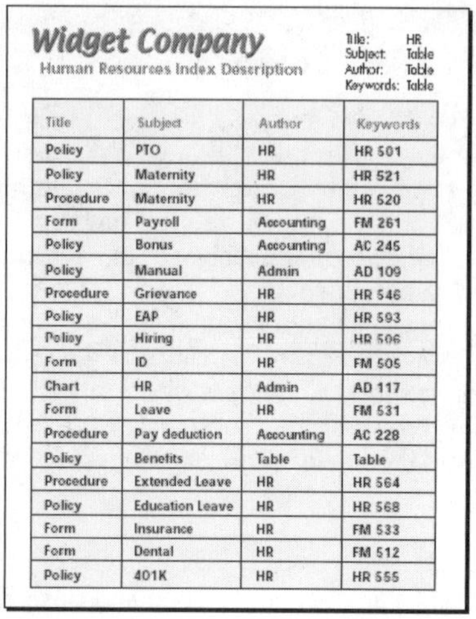

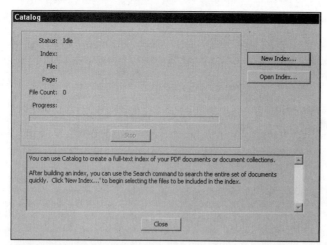

Figure 4-18: A PDF help file can assist users in knowing what keywords need to be used for the Title, Subject, Author, and Keywords fields.

Creating a new index file

After your files are optimized and saved in final form, it's time to create the search index. Choose Advanced ➪ Catalog to open the Catalog dialog box as shown in Figure 4-19. In the dialog box you make choices for creating a new index file or opening an existing index file. Click on the New Index button to create a new index file.

Figure 4-19: Click on the New Index button in the Catalog dialog box to create an index file.

The New Index Definition dialog box shown in Figure 4-20 opens where you set specific attributes for your index and determine what folder(s) are to be indexed.

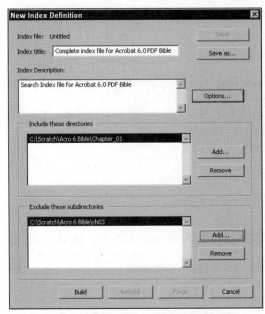

Figure 4-20: Attributes for your new index file are set in the New Index Definition dialog box.

Index title

The title that you place in this field is a title for the index, but not necessarily the name of the file you ultimately save. The name you enter here does not need to conform to any naming conventions because in most cases it won't be the saved filename. When you open an index file, you search your hard drive, server, or external media for a filename that ends with a .pdx extension. When you visit the Search Pane and select the menu option for Select Index, the Index Selection dialog box opens as shown in Figure 4-21. What appears in the Index Selection dialog box is a list of indexes appearing according to the Index Title names. These names are derived from what you type in the Index Title field in Acrobat Catalog.

Note When you get ready to build a file, Acrobat prompts you for the index filename. By default the text you type in the Index Title field is listed in the File name field in the Save Index File dialog box. This dialog box opens when you click on the Build button in the Catalog dialog box (see the section "Building the index" later in this chapter). In most cases where you supply a name as a description in the Index Title, you'll want to change the filename to a name consistent with standard DOS conventions (that is, eight-character maximum with a three-character maximum extension). Make this change when you are prompted to save the file.

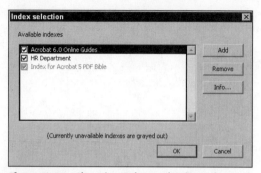

Figure 4-21: Choosing Select Index from the Look
In pull-down menu in the Search Pane opens the
Index selection dialog box. All loaded indexes are
listed according to the index title supplied in
Acrobat Catalog at the time the index was created.

Index description

You can supply as many as 256 characters in the Index Description field. Descriptive names
and keywords should be provided so that the end user knows what each index contains.
Index descriptions should be thought of as adding more information to the items mentioned
earlier in this chapter regarding document descriptions. Index descriptions can help users
find the index file that addresses their needs.

When an index is loaded, the index title appears in the Select Indexes dialog box. To get more
information about an index file, click on the Info button shown in Figure 4-21. The Index information dialog box opens as shown in Figure 4-22. The Index information dialog box shows
you the title from the Index Title field and the description added in Acrobat Catalog in the
Index Description field.

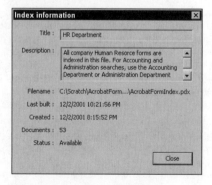

Figure 4-22: The Index Description is contained
in the Index information dialog box. Users can
click on the Info button in the Index selection
dialog box to see the description added in the
Index Description field box in Acrobat Catalog.

Include these directories

If you add nothing in this field, Catalog won't build an index because it won't know where to
look for the PDF files to be included in the index. Adding the directory path(s) is essential
before you begin to build the index. Notice the first Add button on the right side of the dialog
box in Figure 4-20. After you click Add, a navigation dialog box opens, enabling you to identify

the directory where the PDFs to be indexed are located. Many directories can be added to the Include these directories list. These directories can be in different locations on your hard drive. When a given directory is selected, all subfolders will also be indexed for all directory locations unless you choose to exclude certain folders. When the directories have been identified, the directory path and folder name will appear in the Include these directories field.

Exclude these subdirectories

If you have files in a subdirectory within the directory you are indexing and want to exclude the subdirectory, you can do so in the Exclude these subdirectories field. The folder names and directory paths of excluded directories appear in the Exclude these subdirectories field as shown in Figure 4-20.

Remove

If you decide to remove a directory from either the Include these directories or Exclude these subdirectories lists, select an item in the list and click on the Remove button. You can add or delete directories in either list prior to building an index or when modifying an index.

Saving index definitions

Two buttons appear at the top-right corner of the Catalog dialog box for saving a definition. If you begin to develop an index file and supply the index title and a description and want to come back to Catalog later, you can save what you type in the Index Definition dialog box using the Save As button. The Save button does not appear active until you have saved a file with the Save As option or you're working on a file that has been built. Saving the file only saves the definition for the index. It does not create an index file. The Save As option enables you to prepare files for indexing and interrupt your session if you need to return later. For example, suppose you add an index title and you write an index description. If you need to quit Acrobat at this point, click Save As and save the definition to disk. You can then return later and resume creating the index by adding the directories to be cataloged and building the index.

After you have saved a file you can update the file with the Save button. After a definition is saved, when you return to Acrobat Catalog, you can click on the Open button in the Catalog dialog box and resume editing the definition file. When all the options for your search index have been determined, you click on the Build button to actually create the index file.

Using Save As or Save is not required to create an index file. If you set all your attributes for the index and click on the Build button, Acrobat Catalog prompts you in the Save Index File dialog box to supply a name for the index and save the definition. Essentially, Catalog is invoking the Save As command for you.

If at any time you click on the Cancel button in the lower-right corner of the Index Definition dialog box, all edits are lost for the current session. If you add definition items without saving you'll need to start over when you open the Index Definition dialog box again. If you start to work on a saved file and click Cancel without saving new edits, your file reverts to the last saved version.

Options

To the right of the Index Description field is a button labeled Options. Click this button and the Options dialog box appears, allowing you to choose from a number of different attributes for your index file as shown in Figure 4-23. Some of these options are similar to Preference settings for Acrobat Catalog made in the Preferences dialog box. Any edits you make here supersede preference settings.

Cross-Reference   For information on setting catalog preferences, see "Setting preferences" later in this chapter.

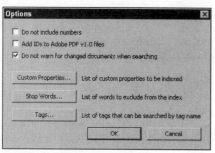

Figure 4-23: Clicking the Options button adjacent to the Index Description field opens the Options dialog box. Here you can assign further attributes to the index file.

Do not include numbers

The first item in the Options dialog box is a check box for excluding numbers. By selecting the Do not include numbers option, you can reduce the file size, especially if data containing many numbers is part of the PDF file(s) to be indexed. Keep in mind, though, that if numbers are excluded, Search won't find numeric values.

Add IDs to Acrobat 1.0 PDF files

Because Acrobat is now in version 6.0, it may be rare to find old PDF 1.0 files that need to be updated with IDs for Acrobat 1.0 files. If you do have legacy files saved as PDF 1.0 format, it would be best to batch process the older PDFs by saving them out of Acrobat 6.0. As software changes, many previous formats may not be supported with recent updates. To ensure against obsolescence, update older documents to newer file formats.

Cross-Reference   For more information on batch processing, see Chapter 10.

If you have legacy files that haven't been updated and you want to include them in your search index, check the box. If you're not certain whether the PDFs were created with Acrobat 1.0 compatibility, check it anyway just to be safe.

Do not warn for changed documents when searching

If you create an index file, then return to the index in Acrobat Catalog and perform some maintenance functions, save the index, and start searching the index, Acrobat notifies you in a dialog box that changes have been made and asks whether you want to proceed. To sidestep the opening of the warning dialog box, check the Do not warn for changed documents when searching option.

Custom Properties

The Custom Properties button opens a dialog box as shown in Figure 4-24. Custom Properties are used when customizing Acrobat with the Acrobat Software Development Kit (SDK). This item is intended for programmers who want to add special features to Acrobat.

To add a Custom Property to be indexed, you should have knowledge in programming and the PDF format.

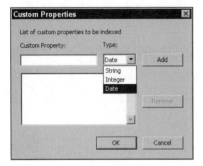

Figure 4-24: You can add custom data fields to Acrobat with the Acrobat Software Development Kit.

Custom Properties are added to the field box and a selection from the pull-down menu is made for the type of property to be indexed. You type the property values in the field box, identify the type, and click the Add button. The property is then listed in the window below the Custom Property field box.

The types available from the pull-down menu include

✦ **String:** This is any text string. If numbers are included with this option they are treated as text.

✦ **Integer:** The integer field can accept values between 0 and 65,535.

✦ **Date:** This is a date value.

Support for programmers writing extensions, plug-ins, and working with the SDK is provided by Adobe Systems. For developers who want to use the support program, you need to become a member of the Adobe Solutions Network (ASN) Developer Program. For more information about ASN and SDK, log on to the Adobe Web site at http://partners.adobe.com/asn/developer.

Stop words

To optimize an index file that produces faster search results, you can add stop words. You may have words, such as *the*, *a*, *an*, *of*, and so on that would typically not be used in a search. You can choose to exclude such words by typing the word in the Word field box and clicking the Add button in the Stop Words dialog box. Click on Stop Words in the options dialog box to open the Stop Words dialog box shown in Figure 4-25. To eliminate a word after it has been added, select the word and click the Remove button. Keep in mind every time you *add* a word, you are actually adding it to a list of words to be excluded.

Tip　You can create an elaborate list of stop words and may want to apply the list to several index files, but Acrobat (as of this writing) does not include an ability to import or swap a list of words to be excluded from an index file. For a workaround, you can open any existing Index Definition field and change all attributes except the stop words. Add a new index title, a new index description, and select a new directory for indexing. Save the definition to a new filename and click on the Build button. A new index is built using stop words created in another index. In workgroups you can save an index definition file without adding directories and use it as a template so all index files have consistent settings for the stop words.

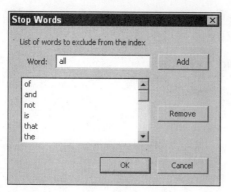

Figure 4-25: You can eliminate words from an index file by adding words in the Stop Words dialog box. When a word is added to the list, the word is excluded from the index file.

Tags

If you have a Tagged PDF you can search document tags when the tags are included in the search index. Click on Tags in the Options dialog box to open the Tags dialog box shown in Figure 4-26. Tagged PDFs with a tagged root and elements can have any item in the tagged logical tree marked for searching. To observe the tags in a PDF file open the Tags palette and expand the tree. All the tags nest like a bookmark list. When you want to mark tags for searching, type the tag name in the Tags dialog box and click the Add button. You remove tags from the list window by selecting a tag and clicking the Remove button.

Cross-Reference   For more information on tagged PDF documents and using the Tags palette, see Chapter 18.

Figure 4-26: You can mark tags for searches in index files by adding tag names in the Tags dialog box.

Building the index

After all the attributes for the index definition have been set, the index file is ready to be created. Clicking the Build button in the New Index Definition dialog box creates indexes. When you click this button, Acrobat Catalog opens the Save Index File dialog box where you supply a filename and target a destination on your hard drive. The default file extension is .pdx. Do not modify the file extension name. Acrobat recognizes these files when loading search indexes.

The Structure of Index Files

Users who have created index files in all earlier versions of Acrobat are no doubt familiar with the end product of creating a search index. As you may recall, the index file with a .pdx extension and nine subfolders containing all associated files were produced by Acrobat Catalog for every new index. The relationship between the index file and subfolders in terms of directory paths needed to be preserved in order for the index to work properly. When you copied an index file to another directory or source, you needed to copy all the files together and keep the same relative path between the files.

When you produce an index file in Acrobat Professional, you won't find the same nine folders created during the index build. The new version of Catalog creates a single folder where files with an .idx and .info extensions reside. The relative directory path is still a factor in relocating files, but now in Acrobat 6.0 you need only copy an index file and a single folder to relocate your index and keep it functional.

The .pdx file you load as your search index file is a small file that creates the information in the .idx and .info files. The .idx files contain the actual index entries the end user accesses during a search. When you build an index, rebuild an index, or purge data from an index, the maintenance operation may or may not affect the .pdx file and/or .idx files depending on which option you choose. For specific information related to how these files are affected during index creation and maintenance, see the following pages for building, rebuilding, and purging index files.

The location where you instruct Catalog to save your index file can be any location on your hard drive regardless of where the files being indexed reside. You can choose to save the index file inside or outside the folder that Catalog created during the indexing. Therefore you have an index file and a folder containing index resources. The relationship between the index file and resource folder locations is critical to the usability of the index. If you move the index file to a different location without moving the supporting folder, the index is rendered unusable. To avoid problems, try to create a folder either when you are in the Save Index File dialog box or before you open Catalog and save your index file to your new folder. Make the name descriptive and keep the index file together in this folder. When you want to move the index to another directory, another computer, or to an external media cartridge, or CD-ROM, copy the folder containing the index and supporting files.

Click the Save button in the Save Index File dialog box, and Catalog closes the Index Definition dialog box, returns you to the Catalog dialog box, and begins to process all the files in the target folder(s). Depending on how many files are indexed, the time to complete the build may be considerable. Don't interrupt the processing if you want to complete the index generation. When Catalog finishes the progress bar stops and the last line of text in the Catalog dialog box reads "Index build successful." If for some reason the build is not successful, you can scroll the window in the Catalog dialog box and view errors reported in the list.

Stopping builds

If you want to interrupt a build, you can click on the Stop button while a build is in progress. When building an index, Catalog opens a file where all the words and markers to the PDF pages are written. When you click on the Stop button, Catalog saves the open file to disk and closes it with the indexed items up to the point you stopped the build. Therefore, the index is usable after stopping a build and you can search for words in the partial index. When you want to resume, you can open the file in Catalog and click on the Rebuild button in Catalog.

Building existing indexes

When files are deleted from indexed folders and new files are added to the indexed folders, you'll want to maintain the index file and update to reflect any changes. You can open an index file and click on Build for a quick update. New files are scanned and added to the index, but the deleted files are marked for deletion without actually deleting the data. To delete data no longer valid, you need to use the Purge button. Purging can take a considerable amount of time even on small index files. Therefore, your routine maintenance might be to consistently build a file and only periodically purge data.

Building legacy index files

When you open an index file created with an Acrobat Catalog version earlier than version 6.0, a dialog box opens, as shown in Figure 4-27, informing you the index is not compatible with the current version of Acrobat. In the dialog box you have three options: Create copy, Overwrite old index, and Cancel. Click on the Create copy button to make a copy of the index file. A new index file is created leaving the original index file undisturbed. You can click on the Overwrite old index button and the file rewrites, replacing the old index. If you choose this option your new index file won't be compatible with Acrobat viewers earlier than version 6.0. Clicking on Cancel in the dialog box returns you to the Index Selection dialog box, leaving the index file undisturbed.

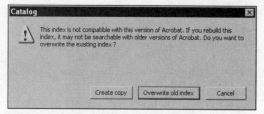

Figure 4-27: When you open an index file created with Acrobat Catalog version earlier than 6.0, a dialog box opens, informing you the index won't work with Acrobat 6.0.

If you know some users won't be working with the new Acrobat viewers, then be certain to make copies of your index files. Until all users have upgraded to a viewer 6.0 or higher, you may need to organize your indexes according to viewer versions.

Tip

If you work in an organization where many users have different versions of Acrobat viewers, then keeping a complete installation of Acrobat 5.05 installed on a separate computer on your network is to your advantage. If you inadvertently overwrite index files or need to perform some task specifically related to Acrobat versions less than 6.0, you can use the older version to keep compatibility with other users. In addition, you can test many new files you edit in version 6.0 or higher to ensure they work with viewer versions less than 6.0. Ideally, all your colleagues, co-workers, and clients should upgrade to Acrobat 6.0. However, in the real world, we know some users are reluctant to let go of the familiar, and convincing all users that upgrading Acrobat is the best solution may take some time.

Building index files from secure documents

In all earlier versions of Acrobat you could not create index files from secure PDFs encrypted with either Acrobat Standard Security or Acrobat Self-Sign Security. Now in version 6.0 of Acrobat you have complete access to secure files with Acrobat Catalog. Any form of encrypted file using the Acrobat-supported security features can be included in your index files. Creating an index does not compromise your security and won't affect the permissions you set forth when the files were saved.

If you have legacy files that have been secured, you can index them like other files saved in earlier PDF format compatibilities. These files, and any other files you create with Acrobat Professional, can only be used by Acrobat viewers 6.0 and later.

Cross-Reference For more information on encryption and security, see Chapter 19.

Rebuilding an index

Rebuilding index files completely recreates a new index. You can open an Acrobat 6.0-compatible index file and click on Rebuild. The file rewrites the file you opened much like you would use a Save As menu command to rewrite a PDF document. If a substantial number of PDF documents have been deleted and new files added to the indexed folders, rebuilding the index could take less time than purging data.

Purging data

As indexes are maintained and rebuilt, you will need to perform periodic maintenance and purge old data. A purge does not delete the index file, nor does it completely rewrite the file; it simply recovers the space used in the index for outdated information. Purging is particularly useful when you remove PDF files from a folder and the search items are no longer needed. If you have built a file several times, each build marks words for deletion. A purge eliminates the marked data and reduces the file size. With a significant number of words marked for deletion, a purge will improve the speed when using Search. This operation might be scheduled routinely in environments where many changes occur within the indexed folders.

Tip When changing options for eliminating words and numbers from indexes or adding tags and custom properties in the Options dialog box, first open the index.pdx file in Catalog and purge the data. Set your new criteria in the Options dialog box and rebuild the index. Any items deleted will now be added to the index, or any items you want to eliminate will subsequently be eliminated from the index.

Setting preferences

Preference settings are contained in the Preferences dialog box. Choose Edit ➪ Preferences and click on the Catalog item in the left Pane as shown in Figure 4-28. Notice that the Index Defaults items use the same settings as found in the Options dialog box from the New Index Selection dialog box. The top three options under Indexing in Catalog preferences are obtained only here in these preference settings.

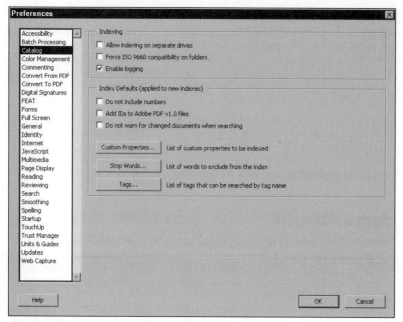

Figure 4-28: Open the Preferences dialog box and click on Catalog in the left Pane to observe options settings for Acrobat Catalog.

Indexing

The three options found in the Indexing section of the Catalog preferences include

✦ **Allow indexing on separate drives:** When creating index files where you want to include folders on network servers and/or computers on your network, select this item in the Catalog preferences. The indexing option only includes indexing files on local networks. Unfortunately, you can't index files on Web servers and use indexes from within Web browsers.

✦ **Force ISO 9660 compatibility on folders:** This setting is a flag that tells Catalog to look for any folders that are not compliant with standard DOS conventions (eight-character maximum with three-character maximum extensions) for folder/directory names. If Catalog encounters a folder name that is not acceptable, the processing stops and an error is reported in the Catalog dialog box. Folder names and directory paths are listed for all incompatible names. You can review the list and manually rename folders. After changing folder names, try to create the index again.

✦ **Enable logging:** A log file is created during an index build that describes the processing for each file indexed. The file is ASCII text and can be opened in any text editor or word processor. Any errors occurring during the build are noted in the log file. All documents and directory paths are also contained in the log file. If you don't want to have a log file created at the time of indexing, deselect the check box and logging is disabled. When you disable logging, you are prevented from analyzing problems when you close the Catalog dialog box.

Index Defaults

The options listed in the Index Defaults area of the Catalog preferences are identical to the options you have available in the New Index Description Options dialog box described earlier in this chapter. These default/options settings exist in two locations for different reasons.

When you set the options in the Preferences dialog box, the options are used for all index files you create. When you elect to use the options from the New Index Selection Options dialog box, the settings are specific to the index file you create. When you create a new index file, the options return to defaults.

If you set a preference in the Catalog preferences and disable the option in the New Index Selection Options dialog box, the latter supercedes the former. That is to say, the New Index Selection Options dialog box settings always prevail.

Using Index Files

As I stated earlier, the main reason you create index files is for speed. When you search hundreds or thousands of pages, the amount of time to return found instances for searched words is a matter of seconds compared to using the Search tool in the Search Pane.

Loading index files

To search using an index file, you need to first load the index in the Search Pane. From the Look In pull-down menu, choose the Select Index menu option as shown in Figure 4-29.

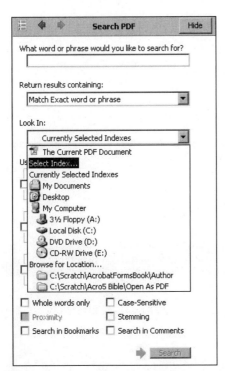

Figure 4-29: Your first step in using indexes is to load the index file(s) by choosing the Select Index menu option from the Look In menu in the Search Pane.

The Index Selection dialog box opens after making the menu selection. Click on the Add button and the Open Index File dialog box opens as shown in Figure 4-30. In this dialog box, navigate your hard drive to find the folder where your index file is located. Click on the index filename and click on the Open button.

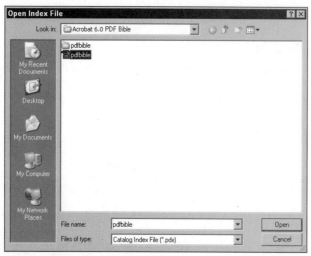

Figure 4-30: Select an index to load and click on the Open button in the Open Index File dialog box.

After selecting the index to load, you are returned to the Index Selection dialog box. A list of all loaded indexes appears in the dialog box. To the left of each filename is a check box. When a check mark is in view, the index file is active and can be searched. Those check boxes that are disabled have the index file loaded, but the file remains inactive. Search will not return results from the inactive index files. If an index file is grayed out as shown in Figure 4-31, the file path has been disrupted and Acrobat can't find the index file or the support files associated with the index. If you see a filename grayed out, select the file in the list and click on the Remove button. Click on the Add button and relocate the index. If the support files are not found, an error is reported in a dialog box indicating the index file could not be opened.

If you can't open a file, you need to return to the Catalog dialog box and click on the Open button. Find the index file that you want to make active and rebuild the index. After rebuilding, you need to return to the Index selection dialog box and reload it.

Note

If you load an index file from a CD-ROM and the CD is not inserted in your CD-ROM drive, the index file name is grayed out in the Index Selection dialog box. After inserting the CD-ROM containing the index, the index file name becomes active. If you know index files are loaded from CDs, don't delete them from the Index Selection dialog box. Doing so requires you to reload the index file each time you insert a CD.

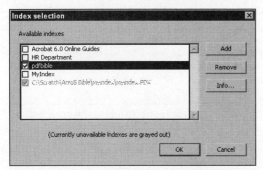

Figure 4-31: Loaded index files are active when a check mark appears adjacent to the index filename. If a file is grayed out, the index is not accessible and may need to be rebuilt.

Disabling indexes

If an index is to be eliminated from searches, you can deactivate the index by disabling its check box. In a later Acrobat session, you can go back and enable indexes listed in the Index Selection dialog box. You should always use this method rather than deleting an index if you intend to use it again in a later Acrobat session. However, at times you may want to delete an index file. If the index will no longer be used, or you relocate your index to another drive or server, you may want to completely remove the old index. If this is the case, select the index file to be deleted and click the Remove button. Indexes may be enabled or disabled before you select Remove. In either case, the index file is removed without warning.

If you inadvertently delete an index, you can always reload the index can always by clicking the Add button. Placing index files in a directory where you can easily access them is a good idea. To avoid confusion, try to keep indexes in a common directory or a directory together with the indexed PDF files. Acrobat doesn't care where the index file is located on your hard drive or server — it just needs to know where the file is located and the file needs to keep the relative path with the support files. If you move the index file to a different directory, be certain to reestablish the connection in the Index Selection dialog box.

Index information

When a number of index files are installed on a computer or server, the names for the files may not be descriptive enough to determine which index you want to search. If more detailed information is desired, the information provided by the Index Information dialog box may help identify the index needed for a given search.

Index information may be particularly helpful in office environments where several people in different departments create PDFs and indexes are all placed on a common server. What may be intuitive to the author of an index file in terms of index name may not be as intuitive to other users. Index information offers the capability for adding more descriptive information that can be understood by many users.

Fortunately, you can explore more descriptive information about an index file by clicking the Info button in the Index Selection dialog box. When you click the Info button, the Index Information dialog box opens, displaying information about the index file as shown in Figure 4-32. Some of the information displayed requires user entry at the time the index is built. Acrobat Catalog automatically creates other information in the dialog box when the index is built. The Index information dialog box provides a description of the following:

✦ **Title:** The user supplies title information at the time the index is created. Titles usually consist of several words describing the index contents. Titles can be searched, as detailed earlier in this chapter, so the title keywords should reflect the index content.

✦ **Description:** Description can be a few words or several sentences containing information about the index. (In Figure 4-32, the description was supplied in Acrobat Catalog when the index was created.)

✦ **Filename:** The directory path for the index file's location on a drive or server is displayed with the last item appearing as the index filename.

✦ **Last built:** If the index file is updated, the date of the last build is supplied here. If no updates have occurred, the date will be the same as the created date.

✦ **Created:** This date reflects the time and date the index file was originally created, and is therefore a fixed date.

✦ **Documents:** Indexes are created from one or more PDF documents. The total number of PDF files from which the index file was created appears here.

✦ **Status:** If the index file has been identified and added to the list in the Index Selection dialog box, it will be Available. Unavailable indexes appear grayed out in the list and are described as Unavailable.

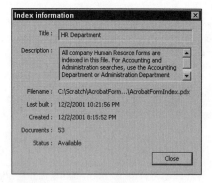

Figure 4-32: The Index information dialog box appears when you select the Info button in the Index selection dialog box.

Searching an index

After your index file(s) is prepared and loaded in the Index selection dialog box it is ready for use. You search index files in the Advanced Search Pane just as you search multiple files explained earlier in this chapter. From the Look In pull-down menu select Currently Selected Indexes as shown in Figure 4-33.

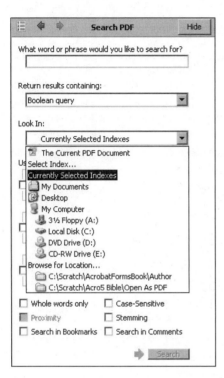

Figure 4-33: To search all active index files, select Currently Selected Indexes in the Look In pull-down menu.

All the options discussed earlier for advanced searches are available to you. Select from the Return results containing pull-down menu, enter your search criteria, and select the options you want. Click on the Search button and you'll find the search results reported much faster than using other search methods.

Index files can be created from PDF collections contained on external media where the index file can remain on your computer without the need for copying the PDF documents to your hard drive. When you insert a media disk like a CD-ROM, your search index is ready to use to search the media. To understand a little more about creating search indexes and using them with external media, follow these steps.

STEPS: Creating index files from media storage

The book's CD-ROM contains several PDF documents and a PDF version of this book. The PDF version of the book is password protected and the remaining files are open with no security. These steps walk you through creating a search index for all files contained on the book's CD-ROM. Insert the CD-ROM accompanying this book and open Acrobat Professional without opening any file.

1. **Set preferences.** Choose Edit ➪ Preferences. Click on Catalog in the left Pane. Check Allow indexing on separate drives. In order to create an index file from a device other than your local hard drive(s), this preference setting must be enabled. Click OK to exit the Preferences dialog box.

2. **Open Catalog.** Choose Advanced ➪ Catalog.

3. **Open the New Index Definition dialog box.** Click on New Index in the Catalog dialog box and the New Index Definition dialog box opens in the foreground.

4. **Add an Index title.** Click in the first field box and type a title for your index file. The example in Figure 4-34 uses "Acrobat 6.0 PDF Bible" for the title.

5. **Add an Index Description.** Type a description for the index. You can use any text you want to help remind you later what this index file is used for. An example description appears in Figure 4-34.

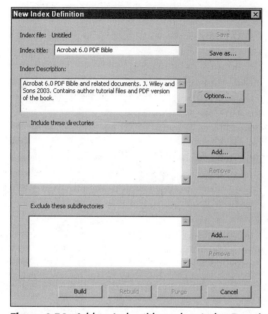

Figure 4-34: Add an Index title and an Index Description.

6. **Change Options.** Click on the Options button to open the Options dialog box, as shown in Figure 4-35, where you can make options choices. Check Do not warn for changed documents when searching. Click OK.

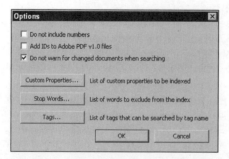

Figure 4-35: Check the box for Do not warn for changed documents when searching. When the check box is enabled Acrobat won't open any unnecessary warning dialog boxes.

7. **Add the CD to the Include these directories list.** Click the first Add button adjacent to the list for Include these directories. The Browse For Folder dialog box opens as shown

in Figure 4-36. Click on the CD drive where you inserted the book's CD-ROM to select it. Click OK in the Browse for Folder dialog box.

Figure 4-36: Select the CD drive where you inserted the book's CD-ROM and click OK.

8. **Build the Index.** Click on the Build button in the Catalog dialog box. Acrobat prompts you with the Save Index File dialog box for the location to save your index file. Select the location on your hard drive where you want to save your file. Type a name in the File name field. Use a short name for the file. In this example, the file is named pdfBible. The extension defaults to .pdx. Leave the default extension and click the Save button.

Acrobat Professional reads all the files on the CD-ROM and writes the Index file. Let your computer continue writing the index until it finishes the build.

9. **Examine the Build results.** When Acrobat completes the build, the Catalog dialog box reports the results of the build. The last line in the results list reports the Index build as successful as shown in Figure 4-37.

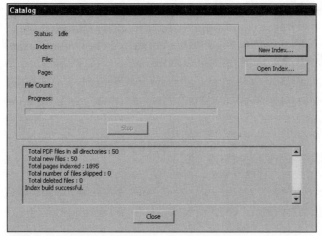

Figure 4-37: After Acrobat completes the build, examine the results to verify that the build was successful.

10. **Quit Catalog.** Click on the Close button to quit Catalog.

11. **Load the index file.** Click on the Search button in the Acrobat File toolbar or press Ctrl/⌘+F and select Use Advanced Search Options. Open the Look In pull-down menu and click on Select Index. The Index selection dialog box opens. Deselect any active index files by clicking on the check boxes to remove the checkmark adjacent to the index names in the list. Click on the Add button and select your new index in the Open Index File dialog box. Click OK to return to the Index selection dialog box. Verify your new index is listed and the check box is enabled as shown in Figure 4-38.

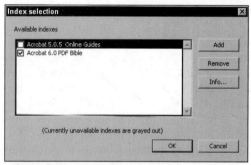

Figure 4-38: Deselect all active index files and be certain your new index file is loaded and enabled before clicking OK.

12. **Review the index information.** Select the index file in the Index selection dialog box. Click on the Info button to open the Index information dialog box as shown in Figure 4-39. Review the contents and notice the description appears as you added it in the Index Description dialog box. Click Close to return to the Index selection dialog box. Click OK in the Index selection dialog box to return to the Acrobat Document Pane.

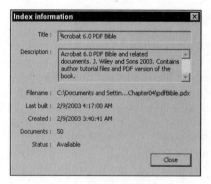

Figure 4-39: Examine the Index information. When you load this index file in the future, you can return to the information if you forget about some of the contents of the index file.

13. **Search the new index file.** The index file is loaded and active. Be certain the menu option for Currently Selected Indexes is active in the Look In pull-down menu. Enter **Search AND Index Description** in the first field box. Select Boolean query from the Return results containing pull-down menu. Click on Search in Bookmarks at the bottom of the Search Pane as shown in Figure 4-40.

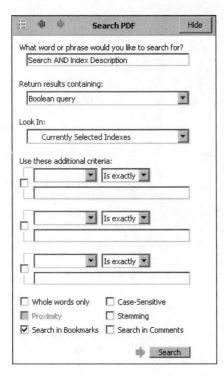

Figure 4-40: Type the word(s) to be searched for and select the options you want to use in the Search Pane. Click Search when finished making options selections.

14. **Invoke the Search.** Click on the Search button at the bottom of the Search Pane. The results are reported in the list within the Search Pane. Click on any text highlighted in blue to open the file and page where the results are found. Figure 4-41 shows a page and bookmarks in the Acrobat PDF Bible matching the search criteria.

Practice searching your new index file using different options and search criteria. To compare the difference between using a search index file and using the advanced search options, you can choose the Browse for Location menu item and search the CD-ROM for the same criteria. Go back and forth to see the differences between searching folders and searching an index file.

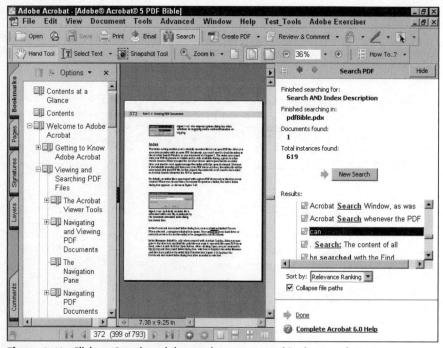

Figure 4-41: Click on Search and the results are reported in the Search Pane.

Searching external devices

A computer network server, another computer on your network, a CD-ROM, DVD-ROM, external hard drive, or removable media cartridge are considered external to your local computer hard drive(s). Any of these devices can be indexed and the index file can be located on any of the devices you index. If you want to save an index file on a device different from where the PDF collection is stored, you need to be certain to open the Preferences dialog box for the Catalog preferences and enable the check box for Allow indexing on separate drives. This preference setting enables you to index across media devices.

Note   When you want to write index files to read only media such as CD-ROMs and DVDs, you need to create the index file from PDFs stored on your hard drive. After the index file is created, copy the index file, the supporting files, and the PDFs to your media and burn the disk.

When you want to search an index, you can activate the index in the Index selection dialog box and invoke a search whether your external media is mounted and accessible or not. The search index returns results from the index .pdx file and the .idx files without looking at the PDFs that were indexed. You can examine the results of the search in the Search Pane and find the files where the search criteria match the PDF documents in the index collection.

If you want to open the link to the PDF document where a result is reported, you need to have the media mounted and accessible. If a network server or other computer contains the related files, the server/computer must be shared with appropriate permissions and visible on your desktop. If you use external media storage devices, the media must be mounted and visible on your desktop in order to view the PDFs linked to the search results. If you attempt to view a document when the device is not mounted, Acrobat opens an error dialog box as shown in Figure 4-42.

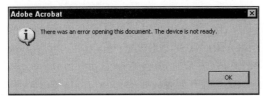

Figure 4-42: When you click on a search result to find the linked PDF document and your media is not accessible (or mounted) from your computer, an error dialog box informs you the device is not ready.

If you see an error dialog box like the one shown in Figure 4-42, click OK in the dialog box and insert your media, connect an external hard drive, or access a computer or network server. You don't need to quit Acrobat to make your device accessible. Wait until the media is mounted and click on a search result. Acrobat opens the linked page and you're ready to continue your search.

A search index file created on one computer can be moved or copied to another computer. To copy an index file to another computer, be certain you copy the index file (.pdx) and all supporting files in the folder created by Catalog. Be certain you maintain the same relative directory path for the index file and the supporting files. If an index file appears in a root folder and the supporting files appear in a nested folder, copy the root folder to other media. If you place the index file in the same folder as the supporting files, copy the single folder containing all files to your media.

You can load the index file and external media on another computer and perform the same searches as were performed where the index file was created. When distributing CD-ROMs and DVDs you can copy these index files to your media and all users can access the index files. If you access an index file on a network server and the PDF collection is stored on an external device such as a CD-ROM, you cannot open files from another computer unless the CD-ROM is mounted. You may see your network server, but the associated devices with the server need to be individually mounted in order to open PDF files remotely.

Summary

✦ Searching PDF files occurs in the Search Pane. When a search is requested, the Search Pane appears in the How To window.

✦ The Search Pane enables basic and advanced searches.

✦ Basic searches are used to search open PDF files just as the Find command was used in Acrobat versions lower than 6.0.

✦ Advanced searches enable searching multiple PDFs locally, on external media and across networks with the use of a search index file.

✦ Acrobat viewers 6.0 and greater support searching content of bookmarks and comments through advanced searches and index file searches.

✦ Searches for PDFs on the Internet can be accessed from within Acrobat with a one-click operation that launches a Web browser and searches the Google (www.google.com) Web site for PDF files.

✦ Searches can be made with a variety of options, including Boolean queries, without the use of an index file.

✦ Search index files are created in Acrobat Catalog. Searching index files returns results much faster than basic and advanced searches.

✦ Document descriptions can be searched with advanced searches and via index file searches.

✦ Index files can be built, rebuilt, and purged with Acrobat Catalog. Old index files created with PDF formats earlier than version 6.0 need to be rebuilt with Acrobat Catalog.

✦ Tags and XML data can be searched with advanced searches and from index searches.

✦ Index files can be copied to other computers, network servers and external media storage units. When copying search indexes, all supporting files and the relative directory path(s) need to be duplicated on the destination units.

✦   ✦   ✦

Converting
Documents
to PDF

Converting to PDF from Adobe Acrobat

Unlike almost every other computer program, Acrobat does not contain a menu option for creating a new file. Acrobat was never intended for use as an original authoring program. Where Acrobat begins is with file conversion to the PDF format. Users start with a document authored in another program and the resulting document is converted to PDF using tools either from within Acrobat or from tools or commands within programs that support PDF conversion from native documents.

With Acrobat Standard and Acrobat Professional, the number of methods you can employ for converting documents to PDF is enormous. Any program file can be converted to PDF through a number of different methods offered by Acrobat, operating systems, and many different authoring applications. The method you use to convert a document to PDF and the purpose for which the PDF is intended requires you to become familiar with a number of different options at your disposal for PDF file conversion. This chapter begins a new section entirely devoted to PDF creation. In this chapter you learn basic PDF conversion methods available in Acrobat Professional and Acrobat Standard. The following chapters in this section cover more advanced PDF creation methods.

Setting Up the PDF Creation Environment

Creating PDF documents from within Acrobat is handled with default tools and with menu commands. To regain the default toolbars, open a context menu on the Toolbar Well and select Reset Toolbars from the menu commands.

If you intend to edit documents after PDF creation, you need to open toolbars specific to your editing session. Depending on the type of edits you anticipate, open toolbars as needed after you finish converting files to PDF.

Understanding How PDFs Are Created

You can use Acrobat Professional or Acrobat Standard to open various file formats in the viewer and the files are immediately converted to PDF. You can also print a file to the Adobe PDF printer, installed with your viewer, from just about any authoring program and the native document is converted to PDF. It all sounds like simple stuff, but there are two very important distinctions between these methods of conversion that you need to understand before you start converting files to PDF. Quite simply, opening a file in Acrobat Professional or Acrobat Standard does not involve any intervention from companion programs. On the other hand, using the Adobe PDF printer gets some help from the Acrobat Distiller software. Understanding the fundamentals of document conversion requires you to know a little bit about Acrobat Distiller.

Cross-Reference   Acrobat Distiller is thoroughly covered in Chapter 7, where you'll find information on setting all the options Distiller offers you.

Acrobat Distiller accepts either a PostScript file or an Encapsulated PostScript file that it processes to produce a PDF document. Through the processing mechanism, Distiller applies different options during conversion. These options can include image sampling, font handling, color control, PDF format compatibility assignment, document encryption, and a host of other settings. Each of the settings is designed to produce PDF files for different purposes. Because so many different options can be applied to PDF conversion via the Distiller software, Distiller provides you the capability to save an assortment of specific settings to individual Adobe PDF Settings files. When the files are saved to a specific location on your hard drive, they are made accessible from a pull-down menu in Acrobat Distiller or from within authoring programs where Adobe PDF Settings are used.

Note   Adobe PDF Settings was referred to as Job Options in earlier versions of Acrobat.

In addition to custom settings you can save to Adobe PDF Settings files, Acrobat Distiller, when installed with Acrobat Professional and Acrobat Standard, has five different preset settings. When you create a PDF file that calls upon Distiller to produce the PDF document, the default Adobe PDF Settings last used by Distiller control the options for your resulting PDF document. The danger here is that if you intend to have a file created for printing, for example, and the settings are optimized for screen viewing, you wind up with a PDF document that won't be usable for printing. Therefore, it is imperative that you know what settings are applied to PDFs created with the Acrobat Distiller software.

Prior to the conversion process you'll have an opportunity to make a choice for the Adobe PDF Settings that are applied during distillation. These choices may or may not be available depending on the type of files you convert to PDF. If access to the Adobe PDF settings is not made available when you convert to PDF, the default settings in Acrobat Distiller are used. You need to be certain you open Acrobat Distiller and change defaults when conversion of a particular file type does not open Acrobat Distiller where Adobe PDF settings are selected. Regardless of where you access the settings choices, the same options are always available. Without having saved any custom settings, the defaults appear as shown in Figure 5-1.

Cross-Reference   For a complete description of the Adobe PDF Settings, see Chapter 7.

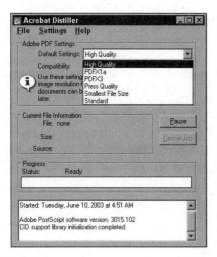

Figure 5-1: The default Adobe PDF Settings are selectable from a pull-down menu in the Acrobat Distiller window.

In this chapter you look at using the Press Quality, Smallest File Size, and Standard settings. Without an elaborate definition of these settings, for the purposes of this chapter, think of Press Quality as suited for commercial printing. Smallest File Size is suited for Web hosting and screen viewing, and the Standard settings are used for everything else.

Converting Native Documents to PDF

Many authoring programs offer you methods for converting to PDF, such as exporting or saving to PDF directly, or using a macro utility installed with Acrobat that supports certain authoring programs. However, when these methods are not available you can use the Print command in your authoring program to produce a PDF document. Virtually any document created in an authoring program that allows printing can be converted to PDF through the use of the Adobe PDF printer (Windows and Mac OS X.2 and higher).

You access the Adobe PDF printer in the application Print dialog box. Rather than print a file to a printer, you print your file to disk. During this process the file is temporarily saved as a PostScript file and the PostScript is distilled in Acrobat Distiller. The Adobe PDF Settings assigned to Distiller control the attributes of the resulting PDF file. The process is relatively the same on both Windows and Macintosh platforms, but initial printer selection and dialog box selections vary a little.

Adobe PDF Printer (Windows)

When you install Acrobat Professional or Acrobat Standard, the Adobe PDF Printer is installed in your Printers folder. As a printer driver, the file is accessible from any program capable of printing, including your computer accessories and utilities. Like any other printer you install on Windows 2000, NT, or XP, you can set the Adobe PDF Printer as the default printer. Once you have set it as the default printer, you don't need to make a printer selection each time you want to create a PDF document.

Note   You may also have the Acrobat Distiller Printer installed in your Printer's folder. The features associated with the Adobe PDF Printer and the Acrobat Distiller Printer are identical.

To convert any application document to PDF, choose File ➪ Print or access the Print dialog box with the command from menu options in your authoring program. Some dedicated vertical market programs, such as accounting and other office programs, may have print commands located in menus other than the File menu. When you arrive at the Print dialog box, the various printer drivers installed on your computer are shown. Select the Adobe PDF Printer in the Select Printer window as shown in Figure 5-2.

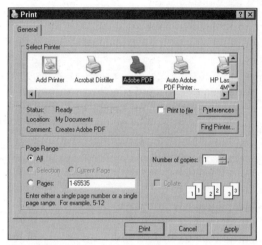

Figure 5-2: From any authoring program, select the Print command and click on the Adobe PDF printer to convert the open document to a PDF file.

Before printing to the Adobe PDF Printer, check your output options by clicking on the Preferences button. In Windows 2000 and earlier, you will see Properties appear in the Print dialog box. If you see Properties, click on the Properties button. The Printing Preferences/ Properties dialog box opens as shown in Figure 5-3. In this dialog box you choose options for the resulting PDF document. Click on the Adobe PDF Settings tab to choose the PDF options.

Choices you can make about the PDF file and handling the PDF conversion are contained in the Adobe PDF Settings window. Items you'll want to control include

✦ **Adobe PDF Page Size:** A pull-down menu offers an extensive list of page sizes derived from the printer driver and not the PPD (PostScript Printer Description file) for your printer. If you don't have a custom size that matches your document page, click on the Add Custom Page button adjacent to the pull-down menu. The Add Custom Page Size dialog box opens where you make choices for the page size to add a new custom page option in the pull-down menu as shown in Figure 5-4.

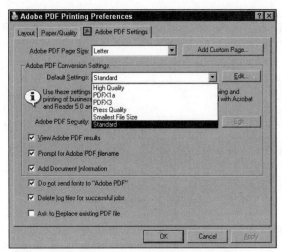

Figure 5-3: You choose PDF options in the Printing Preferences dialog box in the Adobe PDF Settings window.

Figure 5-4: The Add Custom Paper Size dialog box enables you to create a page size up to 200 × 200 inches.

Acrobat accepts sizes up to 200 × 200 inches (5080 × 5080 millimeters/14,400 × 14,400 points). Enter your new custom page size in the units of measure desired and click on the Add/Modify button. Your new page size is added to the Adobe PDF Page Size pull-down menu and selected for you after you click on the Add/Modify button. If you want to delete a page after it has been created, click on Add Custom Page in the Printing Preferences dialog box and select the page you want to delete from the Add Custom Paper Size dialog box. Click the Delete button and the page is deleted from both pull-down menus. Clicking Cancel (or pressing the Esc key) in the dialog box returns you to the Printing Preferences dialog box without affecting any changes.

✦ **Adobe PDF Conversion Settings:** This item relates to the discussion earlier in this chapter concerning the Acrobat Distiller Adobe PDF Settings. The choices you have from the pull-down menu are the same six preset choices provided to you with your

Acrobat installation and any custom settings if you've created them. It's important to make the proper choice for the options you want. When you print to the Adobe PDF Printer, Acrobat Distiller is used in the background and applies the settings you specify in this dialog box.

For a better understanding of Adobe PDF Settings, see Chapter 7.

✦ **Adobe PDF Security:** If you want to password protect your document, you can apply security settings at the time the PDF is created. Choose the security options from the menu choices in the pull-down menu. The default choice for None results in PDF documents created without any password protection.

To learn how to apply password protection to PDF documents, see Chapter 19.

✦ **View Adobe PDF Results:** When the check box is enabled, the resulting PDF document is opened in the Acrobat Document Pane. If Acrobat is not open, the program launches after the PDF is created.

✦ **Prompt for Adobe PDF filename:** By default, the name of your document is appended with a .pdf extension. For example, if you have a text document open in a text editor and the filename is myTextFile, the name of the PDF document will be myTextFile.pdf. If the check box is disabled, the default name is used for the PDF filename. If the check box is enabled, the default filename is placed in a Save PDF File As dialog box in the Filename field. The conversion process pauses where you can click Save and use the default name or edit the name and click Save to create the PDF file.

✦ **Add Document Information:** If the check box is enabled, a dialog box opens where you are prompted for a Document Description. You add data for the Title, Author, Subject, and Keywords fields in the dialog box. This information is added to the Document Description at the time the PDF is created. If you don't want to add a Document Description, disable the check box and the PDF file is created with the Title field containing the filename of your authoring document and the Author field contains the name derived from your log on name when you sign on to your computer.

For more information on document descriptions, see Chapter 4.

✦ **Do not send fonts to "Adobe PDF":** When enabled, the fonts used in the current document are sent to Distiller for font embedding. If the Adobe PDF Settings are established for font embedding, the fonts are embedded from the fonts sent to the Adobe PDF Printer. If the check box is disabled, the fonts are not sent to the printer. As a matter of default, you can disable this check box. If fonts are to be embedded, Distiller has its own means of font management and sending the fonts to Distiller from the Adobe PDF Printer is not necessary. If the Adobe PDF Settings are disabled for font management, the fonts are not embedded regardless of whether they are sent or not.

For more information on font management and font embedding, see Chapter 7.

✦ **Delete log files for successful jobs:** During PDF creation the processing information is written to a log file in the form of ASCII text. You can open the log file in any text editor and review the steps used to produce the PDF. Each time a PDF is successfully created, the log file is deleted. In the event you want to review the PDF creation process logged in the text file, disable the check box and open the file in a text editor.

✦ **Ask to Replace existing PDF file:** If you elect to not have Acrobat prompt you for a file-name, the PDF file is created using the authoring document filename. If you make changes in the document and want to create a new PDF document, the second creation overwrites the first file if the check box is disabled. If you're creating different versions of PDF files and want to have them all saved to disk, be certain to enable the check box.

When all the options in the Printing Preferences dialog box have been reviewed, click OK. You are returned to the Print dialog box and are ready to create the PDF document. Click Print in the dialog box, and the PDF is produced with the options you chose in the Adobe PDF Settings dialog box. If the check box was enabled for View Adobe PDF results, the PDF opens in Acrobat.

Because this method of PDF creation uses a printer driver, you can create a PDF document from virtually any application program. The only requirement is that the program is capable of printing. If you use programs such as Microsoft Office, other Adobe Programs, certain CAD drawing programs, high-end imaging programs, or a host of other applications, you may have other methods for creating PDF documents depending on the level of PDF support for the program. It is important to understand when to use the Adobe PDF Printer and other methods available to you from different applications. Before you integrate using the Adobe PDF Printer into your workflow, be certain to review the next two chapters because they discuss other options for creating PDF documents.

Adobe PDF (Macintosh OS X)

Mac OS X and Adobe PDF are married at the operating system level and you can find several ways to convert your authoring files to the PDF format. The Acrobat supported method is the same type of printer driver you find on Windows. From any authoring program, select the Print command (most commonly accessed by choosing File ➪ Print). When the Print dialog box opens, select Adobe PDF from the printer pull-down menu. From the default selection for Copies and Pages, open the pull-down menu and select PDF Options as shown in Figure 5-5.

Note
Mac OS users earlier than version X can create PDF files with the Create Adobe PDF printer driver in earlier versions of Acrobat. You can find specific details on using Create Adobe PDF in the Acrobat documentation. Support for operating systems lower than Mac OS X is dying away and newer applications support only Mac OS X. Acrobat 6.0 is no exception. Because Acrobat is released for use with Mac OS X.2 and above, all the references in this book are strictly to Mac OS X.

The dialog box changes so that you can access Job Options from a pull-down menu. The default selection is Use Default. If you leave this option active, the most recent settings selected in the Distiller application are used to produce the PDF file. The remaining options are the same as those discussed for Windows users. In Figure 5-6 an additional item, Standard(1), is a custom setting I added to the Distiller PDF Settings. You'll notice that as you add new custom settings they appear in the Job Options pull-down menus from the Print dialog boxes on Windows and Macintosh operating systems.

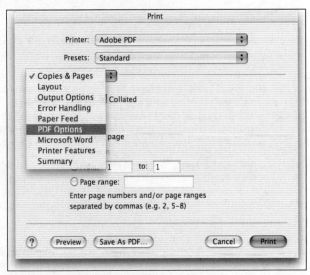

Figure 5-5: PDF Options settings are available after you select the PDF Options pull-down menu command.

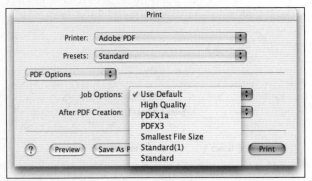

Figure 5-6: Select the Adobe PDF Settings from the Job Options pull-down menu. All the presets and custom settings are listed in the menu options.

Another setting for viewing the PDF file appears from the pull-down menu: After PDF Creation. You can choose to view your PDF in the default Acrobat viewer or leave the default at Launch Nothing, which allows you to go about your work and view the PDFs later. After you choose the settings, click on the Print button to convert the file to PDF using the Adobe PDF Settings you selected from the menu choices.

You'll also notice a button for Save as PDF in the Print dialog box. Clicking this button also creates a PDF file, but the PDF creation is not an Adobe-based PDF creation method per se. This button appears in a generic installation of Mac OS X and it is supported by the operating system without the use of Acrobat Distiller. When you use Save As PDF, the PDF is created from the profile for the active printer selected in the Mac OS X Print Center. If you have a non-PostScript color printer selected as your default printer, the PDF created with Save As PDF could present problems if you want to print the file on PostScript devices. Settings like page sizes and margins can vary greatly between PostScript and non-Postscript devices.

 Cross-Reference For more information on PostScript and creating PostScript files, see Chapter 7.

Save As PDF was designed by Apple to provide users with screen-optimized PDF creation, for sending a PDF version of a document to people across the Internet for screen viewing and low-resolution printing. As a matter of practice, using the Adobe PDF Printer is your best choice for creating more PDFs suited for purposes other than screen displays.

Creating PDFs from Files

Acrobat 5.0 introduced a menu command called Open as Adobe PDF. The menu option enabled you to open files from certain file formats within Acrobat and convert the document to PDF on-the-fly. In Acrobat the Open as Adobe PDF command has been replaced with the Create PDF tool appearing in the Tasks toolbar or through the File menu by selecting Create PDF. In addition, you can use another menu command to achieve similar results for file conversion from within Acrobat. Click on the Open tool or choose File ➪ Open and you can open files saved in a variety of formats. Using any of these tools opens the file in Acrobat and converts it to PDF. The documents open as untitled documents and need to be saved from Acrobat if you want to keep them around and PDFs.

The Create PDF tool offers several different options for PDF creation when you open the pull-down menu for the task button as shown in Figure 5-7. You use the first two menu options, From File and From Multiple Files, to convert files saved from authoring documents to the PDF format. Converting to PDF with either of these commands requires you to access files supported by Acrobat's Create PDF option. Although the number of file formats supported by Acrobat through the internal conversion process is greatly expanded in version 6.0, not all files can be converted with the tools or menu option.

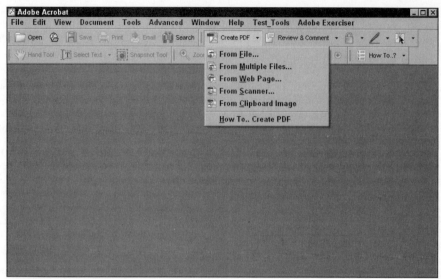

Figure 5-7: The Create PDF task button offers several different options for PDF file creation from within Acrobat.

Supported file formats

To convert files to PDF from within Acrobat you first need to understand all the formats that are supported. You can try to convert any file format to PDF with the Convert PDF tool. If the file format is supported, it is converted to PDF and opens in Acrobat. If the format is not supported, a dialog box opens, informing you the format is not supported. It won't hurt to try, but it's better to know ahead of time what formats are supported.

Each file format that is acceptable to Acrobat can also have conversion settings defined by you. Options for the conversion settings are the same as you have available with the Adobe PDF printer, as discussed earlier in this chapter, and they're accessible in the Preferences dialog box. Before you begin converting files to PDF with the Convert PDF tool, be certain to choose Edit ➪ Preferences (Ctrl/⌘+K) and click on the Convert to PDF item in the left pane. On the right side of the Preferences dialog box you'll see a list of supported file formats as shown in Figure 5-8.

The file formats that are supported by Acrobat include

- ✦ **AutoCAD:** AutoDesk's AutoCAD files can be opened in Acrobat directly. Layered files are preserved and opened with data on different layers when layer data are created in the AutoCAD file. AutoCAD is also supported with the PDF Maker macro, which installs Acrobat tools and menu options in the authoring application at the time you install Acrobat.

- ✦ **BMP:** Bitmap is a file format that can be saved from Adobe Photoshop in the bitmap format. Bitmap is also commonly referred to as a color mode in Photoshop. As a color mode, the file can be saved in other file formats. For example, a 1-bit bitmap image can be saved as a TIFF formatted file. In regard to Acrobat, the bitmap file format that is capable of rendering images in 1-bit, 4-bit, 8-bit, and 24-bit color depths can be opened as PDF. Furthermore a bitmap color mode saved as any of the compatible formats listed here can also be opened as a PDF.

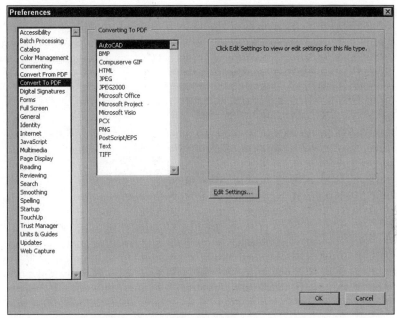

Figure 5-8: PDF Settings assigned to different file formats when you are using the Create PDF tool are established in the Convert to PDF preferences.

✦ **Compuserve GIF:** CompuServe's Graphic Interchange Format (GIF) was developed years ago to port image files to and from mainframes and microcomputers. It remains a popular format for Web graphics, and the later version of GIF89a supports interlacing. If using Photoshop, you can either save in the CompuServe GIF87 format or use Photoshop's Save for Web command and choose the GIF89a format. Regardless of what format is used, Acrobat can import either as a PDF.

✦ **HTML:** HyperText Markup Language files are documents written in HTML for Web pages. You can open any HTML file and the file and file links convert to PDF. Clicking on an HTML link in a converted file in Acrobat appends the linked file to the open document.

✦ **JPEG:** Joint Photographic Expert Group (JPEG) images are also used for Web graphics and file exchanges on the Internet. JPEG compression is a lossy compression scheme that can degrade images rapidly when compressed at high levels. These files are already compressed. Adding further compression with the PDF conversion options won't compress files smaller than the original compression. Inasmuch as the Settings button is active in the Open dialog box, you can't actually get more compression out of the file when converting to PDF.

✦ **JPEG2000:** JPEG2000 is a newer compression scheme that also offers a lossless option for compressing images. You can use JPEG2000 with lossless compression for the most discriminating quality required in high-end printing.

✦ **Microsoft Office:** Microsoft Office files from the office programs of Word, Excel, and PowerPoint. These programs also include installation of the PDF Maker macro, which installs tools and menu options in the authoring applications at the time you install Acrobat, as mentioned in the AutoCAD bullet.

✦ **Microsoft Visio and Microsoft Project:** These programs also use the PDF Maker macro. Microsoft Visio files with layers can be converted to PDF with the layers intact.

✦ **PCX:** PCX files are native to the PC and were commonly used as an extension for PC Paintbrush. Adobe Photoshop can export in PCX format, but today it is rarely used for any kind of image representation. The advantage you have in opening PCX files in Acrobat is when converting legacy files saved in this format. Rather than a two-step operation of opening a PCX file in an image editor and saving in a more common format for file conversions, Acrobat can import the files directly.

✦ **PICT (Macintosh only):** The Apple Macintosh equivalent to PCX (preceding bullet) is the PICT (Picture) format native to the Macintosh. Photoshop supports PICT file exchanges in both opening and saving. However, Acrobat only supports the format for conversion to PDF via the From File or From Multiple Files commands. On Windows the format can be seen when in the Open dialog box, but attempting to open the file in Acrobat under Windows fails.

✦ **PNG:** Portable Network Graphics (PNG — pronounced ping) is a format enabling you to save 24-bit color images without compression. The format was designed for Web use and is becoming more popular among Web designers. Older Web browsers need a special plug-in in order to view the images, which has slowed PNG's wide acceptance. Interestingly enough, PNG images are saved from image editors without compression, yet Acrobat can apply image compression when converting to PDF. You can use all the compression options in the Conversion Options dialog box with PNG images to reduce file sizes.

✦ **PostScript/EPS:** PostScript and EPS files were formerly only converted with Acrobat Distiller. In Acrobat 6 you can open the files in Acrobat using the Create PDF tool and Distiller works in the background handling the conversion to PDF.

✦ **Text:** Text listed in the Convert to PDF preferences relates to plain text files. Unformatted text from word processors, text editors, and any file saved in a text-only format can be opened in Acrobat.

✦ **TIFF:** Tagged Image File Format (TIFF) is by far the most popular format among the print people regardless of platform. TIFF files originate from image editors and scans. When scanning text you can save as a TIFF format and import the file in Acrobat; then proceed to convert the image file to rich text with Paper Capture.

For more information on the Paper Capture feature, see Chapter 11.

Applying settings

Many of the file formats supported by Acrobat can have PDF Options or other settings applied during conversion. These settings are available to all formats except HTML, Text, GIF, and JPEG2000. Depending on the file type to be created, you can apply some different options. By default, Acrobat enables a series of settings to all the file types except HTML, Text, GIF, and JPEG2000. You can edit the settings where different options are selected for different file types. You edit settings by selecting a file type from those listed in the Preferences dialog box shown in Figure 5-8 and clicking on the Edit Settings button. If the settings cannot be adjusted, the Edit Settings button is grayed out.

✦ **AutoCAD, PostScript/EPS, MS Project, and MS Visio:** The same settings are available for AutoCAD files, PostScript/EPS, MS Project files, and MS Visio files. Click on the Edit

Settings button after selecting a file type and the Adobe PDF Settings dialog box shown in Figure 5-9 opens.

Figure 5-9: Options for the AutoCAD, PostScript/ EPS, MS Project, and MS Visio file formats are editable in the Adobe PDF Settings dialog box accessed by clicking on the Edit Settings button in the Preferences dialog box.

The Adobe PDF Settings enable you to make selections for the settings applied to Distiller during PDF file creation. These settings are the same as those you can access with the Adobe PDF Printer discussed earlier in this chapter. Adjacent to the pull-down menu for the Adobe PDF Settings is the Edit button. Clicking on this button opens the Adobe PDF Settings dialog box where you can edit custom settings and save them as a new setting preference. The options in this dialog box are the same as you find when editing settings in Acrobat Distiller. Users of earlier versions of Acrobat can think of the Edit button as a way to open the Job Options dialog box.

Cross-Reference For information on adjusting the Adobe PDF Settings, see Chapter 7.

The Adobe PDF Security pull-down menu offers options for adding password protection at the time the PDF file is created. By default, no security is added to PDFs converted from these file types. You have choices for using *None* for adding no security, *Reconfirm Security for each PDF* that opens a confirmation dialog box after each file is converted to PDF, and a third option for *Use the last known security settings* which uses the current default Adobe PDF settings for each file converted. Adjacent to the pull-down menu is the Edit button. Clicking on this button opens the Acrobat Distiller – Security dialog box where security options can be further edited. Be aware that the first Edit button specifically handles the Adobe PDF Settings and the second Edit button handles the security options.

When you click OK in the Adobe PDF Settings dialog box, any new settings you added become new defaults. Every time you open one of these file formats in Acrobat, the same settings are applied until you edit them again.

✦ **BMP/JPEG/PCX/PNG/PICT (Macintosh only)/TIFF:** These file formats all use identical settings. Whereas many other file formats use the Acrobat Distiller application in the background and has Adobe PDF Settings applied during file conversion, these image file formats don't use Distiller and no Adobe PDF Settings are applied during file conversion. Different conversion settings can be applied from the same options lists to each of the file types individually. Therefore, a BMP file, for example, can be converted with one level of image compression and a TIFF file can be converted with another level of compression.

All of these file formats are image formats and the types of settings you apply to them relate to image options, such as file compression and color management. The same set of options available from pull-down menus exists for all the different color modes listed in the Adobe PDF Settings dialog box shown in Figure 5-10.

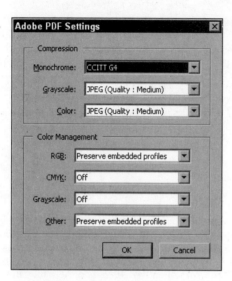

Figure 5-10: Adobe PDF Settings for image files are available for file compression and color management.

Note   Inasmuch as the Adobe PDF Settings dialog box appears the same for all image formats, some options may be grayed out depending on the type of file to be converted. For example, TIFF images can have compression applied during conversion, while JPEG images cannot have compression applied during PDF conversion. Therefore, the compression options for JPEG images are grayed out.

The top of the Adobe PDF Settings dialog box offers you options for file compression for monochrome (black and white line art), grayscale, and color images. The compression options you can select for each of these color modes include

- **CCITT G4:** CCITT Group 4 compression is only available for monochrome images. This compression scheme is similar to the same compression used by fax machines and works best for black-and-white images and results in smaller file sizes without data loss.

- **JBIG2 (Lossless):** JBIG2 is a newer compression scheme for bi-level (black-and-white) images. It offers as much as three to five times the compression as Group 4 compression and is supported in earlier versions of Acrobat Reader and all viewers 6.0 and greater. The compression algorithm is lossless and stores images with no perceptible loss of image clarity even when magnified more than 15×.

- **JBIG2 (Lossy):** This compression scheme also offers higher compression than Group 4 and JBIG2 Lossless. As a Lossy compression, scheme data loss does occur and artifacts can be noticed when zooming in on PDF files in higher zoom levels.

- **JPEG (Quality: Low/Medium/High/Maximum):** For grayscale and color images you can select from several options for the amount of data loss according to the compression options available. Medium is sufficient for almost any kind of desktop printing and low-end output. High and Maximum are more suited for high-end printing and digital prepress. Use JPEG for files that need to be exchanged with users of earlier versions of Acrobat.

- **JPEG2000 (Quality: Minimum/Low/Medium/High/Maximum):** JBIG2000 is a newer compression scheme that offers much better compression and image quality than JPEG. For the amount of compression to be applied, select from the Quality settings for Minimum, Low, Medium, High, and Maximum. High and Maximum settings result in very little data loss that can be visibly seen in printed documents and high magnification levels onscreen. Medium is sufficient for any kind of desktop printing and the minimum and low compression levels are more suited to screen displays. Use JPEG2000 compression when exchanging files with users of Acrobat 6.0 and later.

- **JPEG2000 (Quality: Lossless):** JBIG2000 lossless offers the most compression without data loss for grayscale and color images.

- **Zip:** Zip compression is a lossless compression scheme. It works best where you have large areas of a common color. For example, a background with one color and a few foreground images with different colors.

The lower section of the Adobe PDF Settings dialog box handles Color Management. You have choices for three color modes: RGB, CMYK, and Grayscale. The Other option at the bottom of the dialog box handles special color considerations such as spot colors you might find in duotones, tritones, and quadtones.

For more information on color management and understanding different color modes, see Chapter 23.

The color-management polices you can apply to each color mode are identical and they all include options from one of three choices:

- **Preserve embedded profiles:** If you work with images that have been assigned a color profile, choosing this option preserves the profile embedded in the document. Theoretically, no color changes occur when porting the files across platforms and devices.

- **Off:** If a color profile is embedded in an image, the profile is discarded.

- **Ask when opening:** If you select this option, Acrobat prompts you in a dialog box to use the embedded profile or discard it. You can make individual selections as you open files.

✦ **JBIG2000:** These image files are already compressed. When you convert to PDF the files maintain the compression at the time they were saved. When you open a compressed file, you have options regarding color management as discussed above. The same options are available to you as found in the other image formats for managing color.

✦ **Microsoft Office:** The Microsoft Office options contain the same option choices you have for Adobe PDF Settings and Adobe PDF Security as found with the AutoCAD, PostScript/EPS, Microsoft Project and Mirosoft Visio settings listed earlier. In addition you have options for enabling accessibility, adding bookmarks from style sheets, and converting an Excel workbook as shown in Figure 5-11. These options apply to Microsoft Office applications, Microsoft Project, and Microsoft Visio files.

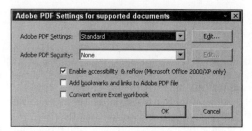

Figure 5-11: Settings for Microsoft Office applications include options for enabling accessibility and converting heads and styles to bookmarks.

Cross-Reference

Specific uses for enabling accessibility and adding bookmarks and links to PDFs from Microsoft Office applications are covered in Chapter 6 and Chapter 18.

After making choices for the options you want to use for file conversions, click the OK button in the Preferences dialog box. All the settings are set as new defaults until you change them. These settings are applied to documents you import from a file, from multiple files, and when you use the Open command in Acrobat.

Importing files

The pull-down menu for the Create PDF task button or menu command File ➪ Create PDF contains submenu commands for importing a single file or multiple files in Acrobat. If you want to open one file, use the From File command. You can also Open Multiple Files from the same menu command and have each file converted to PDF in separate documents. When you select From Files, Acrobat concatenates all files into a single PDF document. Either command enables you to import files saved in any of the formats acceptable to the Create PDF command. Therefore you could, for example, import a TIF, BMP, and PDF document (which are the file formats listed on the preceding pages) with either command. When From File is used, the TIF and BMP files are converted to PDF in separate windows and the PDF file opens as it would open with the Open menu command. When using the From Multiple Files command, the TIF, BMP, and PDF files are opened in a single PDF document. In essence, the TIF and BMP files are converted to PDF and appended to the PDF document.

Converting to PDF from file

To convert files to PDF, select the menu option from the pull-down menu in the Create PDF task button, choose File ➪ Create PDF ➪ From File, or choose File ➪ Create PDF ➪ From File. Either of these commands enables you to convert the acceptable file format to PDF. Acrobat opens the Open dialog box where you select the directory and file to be imported. You can make several choices from the Files of type (Windows) or Show (Macintosh) pull-down menu for file type. If you select All Files (*.*) (Windows) or All Files (Macintosh), all files within a directory are displayed in the list in the Open dialog box shown in Figure 5-12. You can select one or more files to open, but be certain that the file types are supported by Acrobat.

If you want to open a single file and you know the file type, you have an advantage when you select the file format from the Files of type pull-down menu. If, for example, you want to open a TIFF file, select TIFF (*.tif, .tiff) from the menu options. When the file format is selected, the Settings button becomes active. If you want to override the preferences you set for file conversion options, you can access the settings from the Open dialog box. When you select All Files (.*), the Settings button is grayed out.

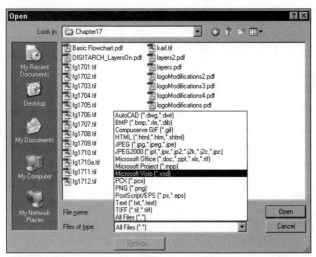

Figure 5-12: From the File of type pull-down menu, select the file type to be imported or select All Files (*.*) to view all files within a directory.

For multiple file selection when using the From File command, click on a filename in the Open dialog box, hold down the Shift key and click on the next file to be converted. All files between the selected two in a contiguous group are selected. If you want to select files at random in a non-contiguous group, click to select the first file and Ctrl/⌘+click to select subsequent files.

Click the Open button and Acrobat converts the files you selected in the Open dialog box. The files are opened as separate documents in the Document Pane. If you want to toggle trough the views of the documents, select the Window menu and the file you want to bring forward.

If a PDF file is opened and you close the file without editing, the file is treated like any other PDF document you open with the File ⇨ Open command or by clicking on the Open tool in the File toolbar. Acrobat converts all other file types to PDF, but they are not yet saved. When you close a file after converting to PDF, Acrobat prompts you to save the file. If you elect to not save the file, the file remains in its original format undisturbed. If you save the file, you can save as PDF or as a new file, choosing from many other file formats supported by Acrobat and again leaving the original file undisturbed.

Converting to PDF from multiple files

Select From Multiple Files from the menu commands in either the Create PDF pull-down menu or the File ⇨ Create PDF submenu and the Create PDF from Multiple Documents dialog box opens as shown in Figure 5-13. Files are added to the list in the Files to Combine window. The order displayed in the window is the same order in which the files are concatenated into a single document. The top file in the list is added at the front of the PDF and the following files are added in successive order. To add a file to the list, click on the Browse button. You can browse your hard drive or network to add files to the list. Files can be collected from multiple directories, hard drives, external media, networked servers, and workstations.

If you want to remove a file from the list, select the file in the list and click on the Remove button. Reorder files by selecting them in the list and clicking on the Move Up and Move Down buttons.

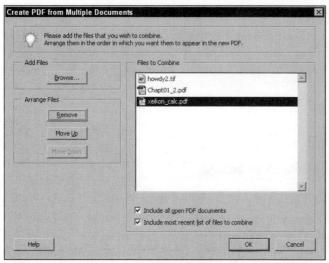

Figure 5-13: The Create PDF from Multiple Documents dialog box offers options for selecting and organizing files to be converted to PDF.

At the bottom of the Create PDF from Multiple Files dialog box you'll find two check boxes. The Include all open PDF documents item adds any open files in Acrobat to the list in the Files to Combine window. When the check box is enabled, all open files appear in the list. If you want to remove some files, but keep some open files active in the list, select the files to be eliminated and click on the Remove button. If no open files are to be added to the new file, deselect the check box.

The second check box lists the most recent files you viewed in your Acrobat session. If you want to include any recently viewed files, enable the check box. Again, you can also selectively remove files by clicking on a file in the list window and clicking on the Remove button for each file to be discarded. When all selections are made, click on the OK button and the files are concatenated into a new PDF file. If you have an open file in the Document Pane that's part of the group, your original file is left undisturbed and a copy of it is included in the new file appearing in the Document Pane.

Tip   If you've previously worked with the Insert Pages command to combine PDF documents in Acrobat, you no doubt experienced much frustration over the fact that the PDF pages were imported in a different order than you viewed in your folder containing the files. Rather than use the Insert Pages command, now in Acrobat 6.0, select From Files from the Create PDF task button pull-down menu and organize the PDF documents in the Files to Combine window. Click OK and the PDFs are ordered as you specify in the Create PDF from Multiple Documents dialog box.

Drag and drop

If using the menu commands doesn't suit you, Acrobat enables you to convert all acceptable file types to PDF via drag and drop actions. Select one or more files and drag them to the open Acrobat Document Pane, to the Status Bar when Acrobat is minimized, or to the program icon when the program is either launched or closed. Files are converted to PDF as when using the From File command where each file is opened in a separate window.

Converting Web Pages to PDF

Earlier versions of Acrobat had a tool for converting Web pages to PDF called the Web Capture tool. The tool has been replaced by the From Web Page menu command, also appearing in the Create PDF pull-down menu, from the File ➪ Create PDF submenu, or from the Create PDF from Web Page tool. From Web Page enables you to convert Web pages hosted on Web servers to PDF. This command is different from converting HTML documents to PDF that are stored locally on hard drives, but the settings and the means for conversion are quite similar.

 Note   The nomenclature has changed in Acrobat 6 over previous versions of Acrobat from using Web Capture to converting to PDF from a Web page. For clarity I'll refer to the process of converting to PDF from Web pages as Web Capture, capturing Web pages, or converting Web pages to PDF. When you see these terms described in this chapter, think of them all having the same meaning.

With a complex set of preferences and tools, Web Capture provides different options for converting Web pages, a Web site, or multiple sites to PDF. A captured Web site converts HTML, text files, and images to PDF, and each Web page is appended to the converted document. Conversion to PDF from Web sites can provide many opportunities for archiving information, analyzing data, creating search indexes, and many more uses where information needs to reside locally on computers.

Now available in Acrobat 6, Web pages containing animation such as Flash animation can be converted to PDF. When animated pages are captured, the animation effects are viewed in the PDF file in any Acrobat viewer.

Web site structure

To understand how to capture a Web site and convert the documents to PDF, you need a fundamental understanding of a Web page and the structure of a site. A Web page is a file created with the Hypertext Markup Language (HTML). There is nothing specific to the length of a Web page. A page may be a screen the size of 640×480 pixels or a length equivalent to several hundred letter-sized pages. Size, in terms of linear length, is usually determined by the page content and amount of space needed to display the page. PDF files, on the other hand, have fixed lengths up to 200×200 inches. You can determine the fixed size of the PDF page prior to converting the Web site from HTML to PDF. After the PDF page size is determined, any Web pages captured adheres to the fixed size. If a Web page is larger than the established PDF page, the overflow automatically creates additional PDF pages. Hence, a single Web page converted may result in several PDF pages.

When Web sites are designed, they typically follow a hierarchical order. The home page rests at the topmost level, where direct links from this page occupy a second level. Subsequently, links from the second level refer to pages at a third level, and so forth.

When pages are captured with Acrobat, the user can specify the number of levels to convert. Be forewarned, though, that even two levels of a Web site can occupy many Web pages. The number of pages and the speed of your Internet connection determine the amount of time needed to capture a site.

Captured pages structure

One or more levels can be captured from a Web site. You decide the number of levels to convert in the Create from Web Page dialog box. PDF pages are converted and placed in a new

PDF file or appended to an existing PDF file. One nice feature with Create From Web Page is it can seek out and append only new pages that have not yet been downloaded.

After pages are converted to PDF they can be viewed in Acrobat or linked directly to a Web browser for viewing on the Internet. Among the file types that can be converted to PDF include the following:

✦ **Adobe PDF Format:** Although not converted to PDF because they already appear in the format, PDF pages can be downloaded with Create From Web Page.

✦ **FDF:** Form Data Format files can be captured and converted to PDF. An FDF file might be from data exported from a PDF form.

✦ **GIF Image Format (Graphics Interchange Format):** GIF images, as well as the last image in an animated GIF, can be captured when converting a Web site. GIFs, like JPEGs within the HTML file, can also appear on separate PDF pages.

✦ **HTML documents:** HTML files can be converted to PDF. The hypertext links from the original HTML file are active in the PDF document as long as the destination documents and URLs have also been converted.

✦ **JPEG (Joint Photographic Expert Group) Image Format:** Images used in the HTML documents are also captured and converted to PDF. JPEGs may be part of the converted HTML page. When captured, they can be part of a captured HTML page and can also appear individually on PDF pages.

✦ **Plain Text:** Any text-only documents contained on a Web site, such as an ASCII text document, can be converted to PDF. When capturing text-only files, you have the opportunity to control many text attributes and page formats.

✦ **PNG Image Format:** Portable Network Graphics (PNG) contained in Web pages can be converted to PDF like GIF and JPEG images.

✦ **XDP:** Forms can be saved in XDP (XML Data Package) that can be understood by an XFA plug-in. The plug-in is used with high-end forms solutions.

✦ **XFDF:** XML-based FDF files typically exported from PDF forms can be converted to PDF.

✦ **Image maps:** Image maps created in HTML are converted to PDF. The links associated with the map are active in the PDF as long as the link destinations are also converted.

✦ **Password-secure areas:** A password-secure area of a Web site can also be converted to PDF. In order to access a secure site, however, you need the password(s).

Accepted file types and links

If a Web page link to another Web page or URL exists, it is preserved in the converted PDF document. Links to pages, sites, and various actions work similarly to the way they do directly on the Web site. However, if a PDF document contains a link to another PDF document, the converted file doesn't preserve the link. When the site is converted, the captured pages reside in a single PDF document. In order to maintain PDF links that open other PDF documents, the destination documents need to be captured as individual pages or extracted and saved from the converted pages.

Links to other levels are also inactive if they have not been converted during the capture. You can append individual linked pages to the converted PDF document by viewing Web links and opening a dialog box. Selections for converting individual links can be made available. One or more links can then be appended to the converted document. Specifics on how to accomplish this task are explained in Appending Pages a little later in this chapter.

For executed animation, such as an animation from a GIF file or other programming application, the download only contains the last image in the sequence. A mouseover effect that changes an image is preserved in the converted PDF document as long as both the original image and the image associated with the mouseover are downloaded. In addition, sounds contained in documents can be captured.

Form fields can be converted to PDF and field types like radio buttons, check boxes, list boxes, and combo boxes often convert with the data intact. You might want to convert a form that has a list of countries and use the form field in your own PDF forms. The Acrobat implementation of JavaScript varies considerably from JavaScript written for Web pages, so many JavaScripts do not work in converted Web pages.

Cross-Reference   For more information on form field types, see Chapters 25 and 26.

For Web pages that contain non-English characters, you need to have the appropriate resources loaded in order to download and convert the files. Japanese characters, for example, require installation of the Far East language files and additional system files. Using non-English characters requires you to additionally make settings choices for Language Scripts. The options are available in the HTML Conversion Settings dialog box in the Fonts and Encoding tab. For making adjustments in the HTML Conversion Settings dialog box, see the section Conversion Settings later in this chapter.

Bookmarks in converted pages

After a Web site has been converted to PDF, you can edit the document in Acrobat like you would any other PDF. Links to pages become editable links — that is, their properties can be changed and modified. When a site has been converted to PDF, all the PDF pages contain bookmarks linked to the respective pages, as shown in Figure 5-14. The first bookmark is a regular (unstructured) bookmark that contains the name of the server from which the site was captured. All bookmarks appearing below the server name are structured bookmarks linked to the converted pages. With the exception of specific Web applications, these bookmarks can be edited and modified like any other bookmarks created in Acrobat. In addition, structured bookmarks can be used for page editing by moving and deleting the bookmarks and associated pages.

Cross-Reference   For more information on bookmarks, see Chapter 10.

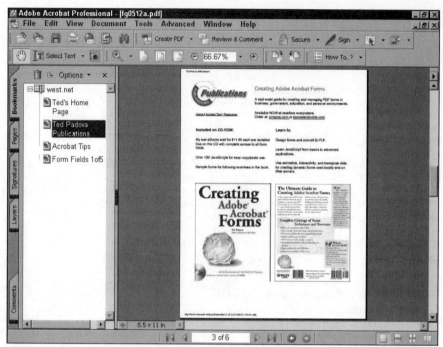

Figure 5-14: A captured Web site converted to PDF displays the Web server name as a normal bookmark at the top of the list. All bookmarks below the server name are structured bookmarks linked to the converted pages. The bookmark names refer to HTML filenames, PDF document names, and URLs.

Capturing Web pages

To begin capturing Web pages, select From Web Page in the pull-down menu for the Create PDF task button, click on the Create PDF from Web Page tool, or choose File ⇨ Create PDF ⇨ From Web Page. The Create PDF from Web Page dialog box opens as shown in Figure 5-15.

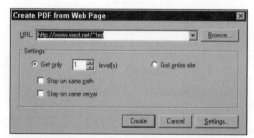

Figure 5-15: When you select the From Web Page command, the Create PDF from Web Page dialog box opens.

In the Create PDF from Web Page dialog box, various settings determine many different attributes for how a Web page is converted to PDF and how it appears in the Acrobat Document Pane. The first level of controls is handled in the Create PDF from Web Page dialog box. Additional buttons in this dialog box open other dialog boxes where many more settings are applied. If this is your first attempt at capturing a Web page, leave the default values in the dialog box as shown in Figure 5-15 and supply a URL in the URL field box. Click on the Create button and watch the page appear in Acrobat.

Caution   Be certain the Levels field box is set to 1 on your first attempt. Entering any other value may keep you waiting, depending on how many pages download from additional levels.

Depending on the site, the number of different links from the site to other URLs, and the structure of the HTML pages, there is often a need to wade through the maze of dialog boxes that control settings for the PDF conversion from the HTML files. You don't need to memorize all of these, but just use the following as a reference when capturing Web pages.

Settings in the Create PDF from Web Page dialog box

The controls available to you in the Open Web Page dialog box begin with the URL you supplied in the Create PDF from Web Page dialog box when downloading the first Web page. This URL determines the site where the pages, which are converted, are hosted. After the URL is entered, the remaining selections include

✦ **Get only *x* levels:** Appended pages can contain more than one level. The URL link may go to another site hosted on another server or stay on the same server. Select the levels to be downloaded by clicking the up or down arrows, or entering a numeric value in the field box.

Caution   A Web site can have two levels of extraordinary size. If the Home page is on the first level and many links are contained on the Home page, all the associated links are at the second level. If you're downloading with a slow connection, the time needed to capture the site can take quite a long time.

✦ **Get Entire Site:** When you select this radio button, all levels on the Web site are downloaded.

✦ **Stay on Same Path:** When this option is enabled, all documents are confined to the directory path under the selected URL.

✦ **Stay on Same Server:** If links are made to other servers, they are not downloaded when this option is enabled.

✦ **Create:** When ready to convert Web pages from the site identified in the URL field box, click on the Create button.

✦ **Browse:** Selecting this button enables you to capture a Web site residing on your computer or network server. Click on Browse and a navigation dialog box opens where you can find the directory where HTML pages are stored and captures the pages.

Although it may not be entirely practical, Web designers who are more comfortable with WYSIWYG HTML editors than layout applications may find it beneficial to create layout assemblies in their favorite editor. You can't get control over image sampling, but you can achieve a layout for screen display. Create the layout in a program such as Adobe GoLive, Microsoft Front Page, or Macromedia DreamWeaver. When finished with the pages, launch Acrobat and select Create PDF from Web Page. Click the Browse button in the Create PDF from Web Page dialog box and navigate to your HTML files. Click on the Create button and your pages are converted to PDF. These pages can be sent as an e-mail attachment to a colleague or printed to your desktop printer. It may sound a little crazy, but some people just don't like to leave familiar ground.

Caution   Even though you may Browse to a folder on your hard drive and convert a local Web site to PDF, any external links launch your Internet connection and capture pages on another site. If you want only local pages converted, be certain to click on the Stay on Same Server button in the Create PDF from Web Page dialog box.

Tip   An alternative to using the Create from Web Page dialog box for a single Web page stored locally on your computer is through drag and drop. Select the HTML document to convert to PDF and drag it to the top of the Acrobat window or program icon. If you have multiple HTML files to convert, you can also use the Create From Multiple Files menu command.

Cross-Reference   Web pages can also be created from tools installed by Acrobat in Microsoft Internet Explorer in Windows only. For information related to converting Web pages to PDF from within Microsoft Internet Explorer, see Chapter 20.

Conversion settings

Clicking on the Settings button in the Create PDF from Web Page dialog box opens a second dialog box. Two tabs are visible in the Web Page Conversion Settings dialog box where you can supply file conversion attributes and page layout settings. The General tab deals with the file attribute settings as shown in Figure 5-16.

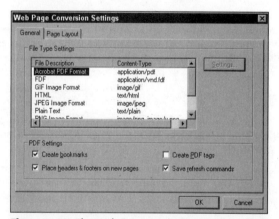

Figure 5-16: The Web Page Conversion Settings dialog box offers controls for file types and how they will be converted to PDF.

Under the File Description heading, the file types are listed for those file types discussed in the section related to Captured Pages Structure earlier in this chapter. Each file type can be selected in the list. Only the file types for HTML and Text offer more options, which you access by selecting the Settings button on the right side of the dialog box. If a file type other than HTML or Plain Text is selected, the Settings button is grayed out. At the bottom of the dialog box, four General Settings for Generated PDF include check boxes for

✦ **Create bookmarks:** When enabled, pages converted to PDF have structured bookmarks created for each page captured. The page's title is used as the bookmark name. If the page has no title, Acrobat supplies the URL as the bookmark name.

✦ **Place headers & footers on new pages:** A header and footer are placed on all converted pages if this option is enabled. A header in the HTML file consists of the page title appearing with the <HEAD> tag. The footer retrieves the page's URL, the page name, and a date stamp for the date and time the page was downloaded.

✦ **Create PDF tags:** The structure of the converted PDF matches that of the original HTML file. Items such as list elements, table cells, and similar HTML tags are preserved. The PDF document contains structured bookmarks for each of the structured items. A tagged bookmark then links to a table, list, or other HTML element.

✦ **Save refresh commands:** When enabled, a list of all URLs in the converted PDF document is saved. When the capture is refreshed, these URLs are revisited and new PDF pages are converted for any new pages added to the site. If appending new pages to the PDF, this item must be enabled for Acrobat to update the file.

Returning to the top of the dialog box, the two items where additional settings can be edited include HTML and Plain Text files. When HTML is selected in the File Description list and the Settings button clicked, a dialog box opens for HTML Conversion Settings as shown in Figure 5-17.

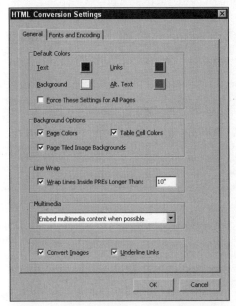

Figure 5-17: When HTML is selected in the File Description list and you click on the Settings button, the HTML Conversion Settings dialog box opens.

The two tabs in the HTML Conversion Settings dialog box are the General tab and the Fonts and Encoding tab. The first group of settings handles the general attributes assigned to the page layout. These include

✦ **Default Colors:** Assigns new default colors for Text, Background color, Links, and Alt Text with user-specified colors. A set of preset colors, as well as an option for custom colors, is selected from a palette that opens after you click on the swatch.

✦ **Force These Settings for All Pages:** HTML pages may or may not have assigned color values. When no color is assigned for one of these items, the Default Colors define unassigned elements with the colors. If this check box is enabled, all colors, including HTML assigned colors are changed to the Default Colors.

✦ **Background Options:** These include settings for the background colors used on the Web page, tiled image backgrounds, and table cells. When these check boxes are enabled, the original design is preserved in the PDF document.

Tip

If table cells, background colors, and tiled background images are distracting when you're reading Web pages either in a browser or converted to PDF, disable the Background Options check boxes before converting to PDF. The original design is changed, but the files are easily legible for both screen reading and when printed.

✦ **Line Wrap:** Enables you to choose a maximum distance for word-wrapping the text in an HTML file. When the `<PRE>` tag is used in HTML, the text is preformatted to preserve line breaks and indents. The field box for this option enables controlling the maximum length for text lines in inches.

✦ **Multimedia:** A new feature in Acrobat 6 enables you to set options for handling multimedia clips. From the pull-down menu you can choose from three options:

 • **Disable multimedia capture:** Movie and sound clips are ignored. Only the Web pages are converted to PDF and no links to the media are included in the capture.

 • **Embed multimedia content when possible:** Acrobat 6 enables you to embed multimedia clips in the PDF document. Selecting this option captures the Web page and embeds any multimedia files that meet the compatibility requirements of Acrobat. Be aware that embedded multimedia files are only available to Acrobat viewers 6.0 or later.

 • **Reference multimedia content by URL:** The captured Web page contains a link to the URL where the multimedia files are hosted.

Cross-Reference

For more understanding of the new features for handling multimedia in PDF documents, see Chapter 16.

✦ **Convert Images:** Converts images contained in the HTML as separate PDF pages. If the option is disabled, the JPEG, GIF, and PNG images are not converted to separate PDF pages, but appear on the HTML converted page. You may wish to modify Web pages from your own site and want to capture images separately to make your revisions. Therefore, capturing the image files may come in handy if you don't have access to the original files used to create your Web site.

Tip

To produce faster downloads, disable the Convert Images check box. The number of pages to be converted is significantly reduced thereby reducing the amount of time to capture a Web site.

✦ **Underline Links:** Displays the text used in an `<A HREF...>` tag with an underline. This option can be helpful if the text for a link is not a different color than the body copy.

After you choose the General settings, click on the Fonts and Encoding tab to open the Fonts and Encoding portion of the HTML Conversion Settings dialog box. The display appears as shown in Figure 5-18.

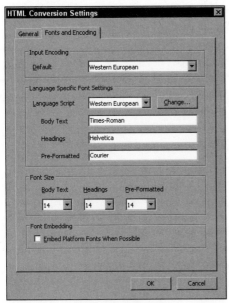

Figure 5-18: When you select the Fonts and Encoding tab in the HTML Conversion Settings dialog box, Acrobat offers options for font handling.

Options for font handling include

+ **Input Encoding:** This sets the encoding for the Web page text encoding for body text, heads, and preformatted text. The default is consistent with the language you install. Other supported languages include Chinese, Japanese, Korean and Unicode characters.

+ **Body Text, Headings, and Pre-Formatted text:** The items appearing under the Language Specific Font Settings section contain editable fields for changing the text encoding and fonts used for the respective items. Global changes are made by clicking the Change button, which opens a dialog box for font selections as shown in Figure 5-19. Fonts are chosen from all the fonts installed in your system. A pull-down menu is available for body text, headings, and preformatted text. Fonts can be individually assigned to each item.

+ **Font Size:** You choose font sizes for each of the three text items from pull-down menus or by editing the field boxes.

+ **Embed Platform Fonts When Possible:** Fonts used to view the pages are embedded when the check box is enabled. File sizes are larger with embedded fonts, but file integrity is preserved and eliminates the need for font substitution. Embedded fonts ensure the display and print of the PDF documents precisely as seen in the Web browser.

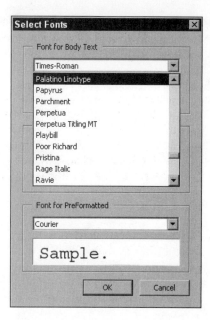

Figure 5-19: When you click the Change button, a dialog box opens where you can select a system font and point size. The chosen font appears as the new default for text from font sets listed in pull-down menus for body text, headings, and preformatted text.

After choosing all the settings for how HTML files are converted, click on the OK button in the HTML Conversion Settings dialog box. The dialog box disappears and returns you to the Conversion Settings dialog box. The other file format where settings are applied is for Plain Text files. Select Plain Text in the File Description list and click on the Settings button. (Refer to Figure 5-16). The Text Conversion Settings dialog box opens as shown in Figure 5-20.

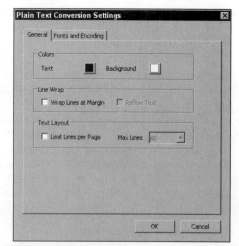

Figure 5-20: In the HTML Conversion Settings dialog box, select Plain Text in the File Description list and click on the Settings button. The Plain Text Conversion Settings dialog box opens where you apply settings for ASCII text file conversion to PDF.

Choices in this dialog box are similar to the choices available in the HTML Conversion dialog box for the Color, Font, and Line Wrap items, which were just discussed. Line Wrap behaves similarly to the Pre-Formatted text discussed earlier in the chapter. One item has been added to this dialog box:

✦ **Text Layout:** For large bodies of text, the number of lines on the page can be user defined. Depending on point size, the standard number of lines on an 8.5×11 letter-size page is 66. The default in Acrobat is 60 when the check box is enabled. You can make a choice for the number of lines by editing the field box only after selecting the Limit Lines per Page check box.

You can also make font choices for plain text files. Click on the Fonts and Encoding tab to reveal more options in the Plain Text Conversion dialog box as shown in Figure 5-21.

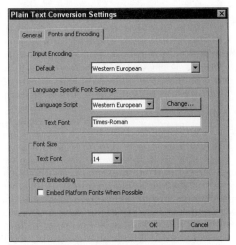

Figure 5-21: Select the Fonts and Encoding tab to apply font options for plain text conversions.

Options available in the Fonts and Encoding tab are similar to the font options you have with HTML page conversions. Make choices in this dialog box for text encoding, text font, and whether the fonts are to be embedded in the resulting PDF. After making changes in the Page Layout dialog box for Plain Text documents, click on the OK button. Once again you return to the Conversion Settings dialog box.

Page Layout conversion settings

All the settings discussed on the previous few pages were related to the General Conversion Settings. In the Conversion Settings dialog box another option is available. Page layout offers you options for describing the physical size and orientation of converted pages. Click on the Page Layout tab and the Web Page Conversion Settings dialog box opens as shown in Figure 5-22.

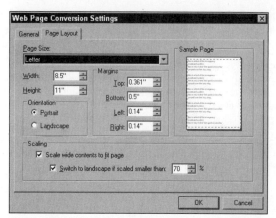

Figure 5-22: The Page Layout options are available from the Web Page Conversion Settings dialog box when you select the Page Layout tab.

Page layout attributes enable you to force long HTML pages into more standard page sizes for viewing or printing. If an HTML page spans several letter-sized pages, you can determine where the page breaks occur and the orientation of the converted pages. Many options are available in the Page Layout section of the Web Page Conversion Settings dialog box, and they include

✦ **Page Size:** A pull-down menu with default page sizes provides selections for a variety of different sizes. Acrobat supports page sizes from 1-inch square to 200-inches square. You can supply any value between the minimum and maximum page sizes in the Width and Height field boxes below the pull-down menu to override the fixed sizes available from the pull-down menu. To make changes in the field boxes, edit the text, click on the up and down arrows in the dialog box, or click in a field box and press the up and down arrow keys on your keyboard. Press Tab and Shift+Tab to toggle between the field boxes.

✦ **Margins:** The amount of space on all four sides of the PDF page before any data appears can be set in the four Margins field boxes. Changes for the margins sizes are made by using the same methods described in the preceding bullet.

✦ **Sample Page:** The thumbnail at the right side of the dialog box displays a view of how the converted page appears when sizes are established for the Width, Height, and Margin settings.

✦ **Orientation:** You choose portrait or landscape orientation from the radio button options. If a site contains all Web pages that conform to screen sizes such as 640 × 480, you might want to change the orientation to landscape.

✦ **Scale wide contents to fit page:** Once again, because HTML documents don't follow standard page sizes, images and text can be easily clipped when converting to a standard size. When this option is enabled, the page contents are reduced to fit within the page margins.

✦ **Switch to landscape if scaled smaller than:** The percentage value is user definable. When the page contents appear on a portrait page within the limit specified in the field box, the PDF document is automatically converted to a landscape orientation. The default is 70%. If the default value is used, any vertical page scaled lower than 70% is auto-switched to landscape as long as the orientation is selected for Portrait.

If your workflow is dependent on capturing Web pages routinely, then you'll want to use the same conversion settings for your Web captures. Educational facilities, government agencies, research institutes, and large corporate offices, may have repeated needs for archiving research information found on the Web.

Unfortunately, Acrobat makes no provision for saving and loading Web Capture settings established in the dialog boxes discussed in the preceding pages. To develop a workflow suited to organizations or workgroups, your alternative may be setting up a single computer dedicated to the task of capturing data from the Web. The computer needs to be licensed for Acrobat, but using a single computer ensures all Web captures are performed with the same conversion settings. The PDF files that are captured can be retrieved across a network or intranet by users with any Acrobat viewer.

Download status

After you choose all settings and options in all the dialog boxes pertaining to converting Web sites to PDF, you can revisit the Create PDF from Web Page command from any one of the three methods discussed earlier. As pages are downloaded and converted to PDF, a dialog box opens displaying the download status. After the first page downloads, the dialog box shown in Figure 5-23 moves to the background behind the converted Web pages.

Web Capture places the converted PDF in memory and uses your hard drive space as an extension of RAM. The PDF is not saved to disk until you perform a Save or Save As operation. If your computer crashes or you quit without saving, the file is lost and you'll need to capture the site again.

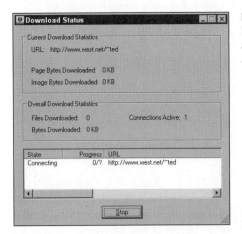

Figure 5-23: The Download Status dialog box appears momentarily, then disappears as Acrobat continues to download pages and convert them to PDF.

The dialog box actually remains open, but hides behind the PDF pages being converted as the download continues. If you want to bring the Download Status dialog box to the foreground, choose Advanced ➪ Web Capture ➪ Bring Status Dialogs to Foreground. The dialog box opens in the foreground while Acrobat continues to convert pages. It continues to show the progress of the download as shown in Figure 5-24.

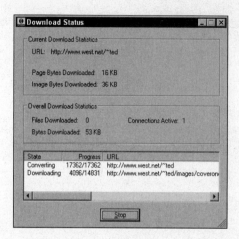

Figure 5-24: The Download Status dialog box can be brought into the foreground at anytime during the download.

Appending pages

When a PDF file is open in the Document Pane, you can append pages from URL links by choosing Advanced ⇨ Web Capture and then selecting the appropriate choice from the submenu commands. Pages are also appended by opening a context-sensitive menu. To open a context-sensitive menu, the cursor must be positioned over a structured bookmark when you right-click (Control+click on the Macintosh) the mouse button. The context menu in Figure 5-25 includes options for appending Web pages and commands for handling pages. The submenu options from the Advanced ⇨ Web Capture menu shown in Figure 5-26 relate to Web Capture features.

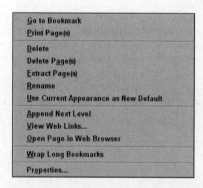

Figure 5-25: A context menu opened on a structured bookmark offers options for appending pages and page-editing commands.

Figure 5-26: When you choose Advanced ⇨ Web Capture, the submenu displays options for treatment of Web captures.

To append pages to the open PDF, make choices from the following selections in the submenu command:

✦ **Append Web Page:** Selecting this option opens the Add to PDF from Web Page dialog box where you make attribute choices. The dialog box offers the same choices as originally displayed in the Open Web Page dialog box. When appending pages, you can change the attribute choices for all conversion options such as the URL, number of levels to be downloaded, settings, and so on.

✦ **Append All Links on Page:** When you select this submenu option, no dialog box opens before the download commences. All Web links to other HTML pages are converted and appended to the PDF. Conversion settings are used from the last options choices made in the Create from Web Page dialog box. If the conversion settings need to be changed for links to other pages, you can use the View Web Links dialog box.

✦ **View Web Links:** The Select Page Links to Download dialog box opens when you select this menu command. In the dialog box all Web links are listed according to URL, as shown in Figure 5-27.

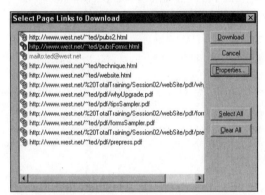

Figure 5-27: When you select View Web Links in the Web Capture submenu, the Select Page Links to Download dialog box opens where a list of all Web links in the PDF appears.

The list contains an icon displayed at the far left of the URL list informing you a link exists to the URL. Each of the items in the list can be selected. After you select a link, the Properties button on the right side of the dialog box becomes active. Click on the Properties button and another dialog box opens. You'll notice in the next dialog box the options for conversion settings appear within three tabs. These options are the same as those described when using the From Web Page command.

✦ **Page Info:** A dialog box opens displaying information about the current page viewed in the PDF file. As you scroll through pages the Page info changes according to the page viewed. The information supplied in the dialog box as shown in Figure 5-28 includes the original URL, title of the page, creation date, a description of the content, and the preferred zoom level for viewing.

When a context menu is opened from a structured bookmark, the menu options appear as shown in Figure 5-26. The two choices from the menu commands for appending pages to the PDF include Append Next Level and View Web Links.

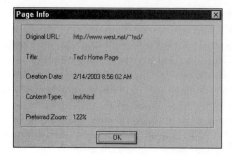

Figure 5-28: Page Info is dependent on the page viewed in the PDF. As you scroll pages the dialog box reflects the information on the respective page.

Tip   You can also append Web pages by clicking on a link in the PDF page. If the link destination is not contained in the PDF, the URL is contacted and the page appended to the PDF. When the cursor is positioned over a link, the cursor displays a hand icon and index finger pointing upward. If a link has not yet been converted, the icon displays a plus (+) symbol inside the hand and a ToolTip shows the URL where the link can be found. If the link has been converted to PDF, no plus (+) symbol and no URL are shown.

Refreshing Web pages

You use the Refresh pages command to update a previously captured site. If content has changed, the updated pages are downloaded. Any pages remaining constant without changes are ignored. To update a PDF file created with Web Capture, choose Advanced ⇨ Web Capture ⇨ Refresh Pages. The Refresh Pages dialog box opens as shown in Figure 5-29. In order to update pages with the Refresh Pages command, the Conversion Settings in the original Web Page Conversion Settings dialog box must have the Save refresh commands check box enabled as shown in Figure 5-16 earlier in the chapter.

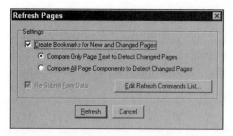

Figure 5-29: The Refresh Pages dialog box offers options for updating pages in the open PDF file.

Updates occur according to options selected in the Refresh Pages dialog box. You have two choices for comparing the page to be downloaded with a page in the PDF document:

✦ **Compare Only Page Text to Detect Changed Pages:** If you are interested in only changes made to the text on Web pages, then click on this radio button. Acrobat ignores new graphics, colors, backgrounds, and other non-text elements.

✦ **Compare All Page Components to Detect Changed Pages:** When enabled, this option downloads and converts pages where any changes have occurred.

If you want to selectively update different page links, click on the Edit Refresh Commands List button in the Refresh Pages dialog box. Another dialog box opens similar to the one used with the View Web Links command, which is discussed in the "Appending pages" section of this chapter. When the Refresh Commands List dialog box opens, all links are selected by default. Options in this dialog box are similar to those found in the View Web Links dialog box.

If you want all links to be updated, leave the default alone and proceed with the download. If selected links are to be updated, click on the desired link to update. For multiple links hold down the Shift key as you select the links. For non-contiguous selections in the list, hold down the Control key (⌘ key on Macintosh) and click on links to be included in the update. Click OK and exit the Refresh Pages dialog box. The download commences and the Download Status dialog box disappears. To view the status dialog box, bring it to the front by choosing Advanced ➪ Web Capture ➪ Bring Status Dialogs to Foreground.

Tip   To compare Web pages for obvious changes prior to refreshing the page, visit the Web page in your browser. In Acrobat, choose Edit ➪ Preferences ➪ Web Capture. In the Web Capture Preferences, select In Web Browser from the Open Web links pop-up menu. Click OK and click on the URL link in the PDF file. The Web page opens in your Web browser. Compare this page to the PDF page to determine any discrepancies before downloading the pages.

Locate Web addresses

If you have a PDF file that has been converted from a document that contains text formatted as a URL, Acrobat can convert the text to a Web link. The text must have the complete URL listing including *http://*. After the Web link is converted, you can click on the link and append pages by using Web Capture. PDF authors may also create Web links for end users when distributing files to others.

To create Web links on pages containing URLs, choose Advanced ➪ Links ➪ Create from URLs in Document. A dialog box opens as shown in Figure 5-30.

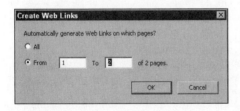

Figure 5-30: The Create Web Links dialog box enables you to create Web links from text for user-defined page ranges in the open PDF file.

In the Create Web Links dialog box you specify page ranges for where Acrobat should create the links. Acrobat performs this task quickly and creates all links where the proper syntax has been used to describe the URL. If you want to delete links from a PDF document, open the Remove Web Links dialog box by choosing Advanced ➪ Links ➪ Remove All Links from Document. The Remove Web Links dialog box opens where page ranges are user supplied for eliminating Web links.

Preferences for Web Capture

To access the Web Capture preferences choose Edit ➪ Preferences. In the left pane click on Web Capture, and the preference settings shown in Figure 5-31 appear. You can set the additional attributes for Web Link behavior as well as options for converting Web pages to PDF.

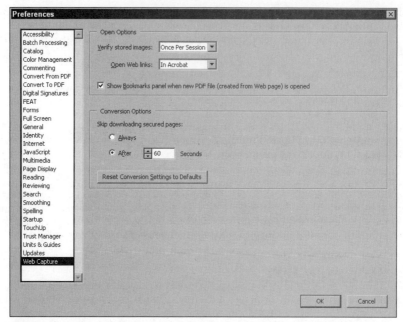

Figure 5-31: The Web Capture Preferences dialog box opens when you choose
Edit ➪ Preferences and click on Web Capture in the list in the left pane.

The options available in the Web Capture Preferences dialog box include

✦ **Verify stored images:** From the pull-down menu, options are available for verifying
   images stored on a captured Web site Once Per Session, Always, or Never. When you
   select the default setting, Once Per Session, Acrobat checks the Web site to see
   whether stored images have changed on the site. If changes have occurred, new pages
   are converted.

✦ **Open Web links:** You can elect to open Web links in either Acrobat or your default Web
   browser. When you choose the browser option, clicking a Web link in the converted
   PDF document launches your browser and opens the URL for the associated link.
   Regardless of whether links are a result of captured pages or authored PDF files, the
   view appears in the Web browser.

Tip   Regardless of which option you elect to use for opening Web links, you can use the alternate
          method by pressing the Shift key and clicking on the link. For example, if the preference set-
          ting is used to display the link in the Web browser, Shift+click displays the link in Acrobat and
          vice versa.

✦ **Show Bookmarks panel when new PDF file (created from Web page) is opened:**
   When this option is enabled, the converted PDF file is viewed with the Navigation Pane
   open and the structured bookmarks listed in the Bookmarks tab. When this option is
   disabled, the Navigation Pane is closed, but the bookmarks are still created.

✦ **Skip downloading secured pages:** Secured areas of a Web site can be downloaded, but
   you must have permission to access the password-protected areas and supply all passwords to gain access to the site. To avoid inadvertently attempting to download a

secure area, you can elect to always skip secured pages or skip secured pages at specified intervals ranging between 1 and 9999 seconds.

✦ **Reset Conversion Settings to Defaults:** Clicking this button resets all options in the Conversion Settings dialog boxes back to the default settings established when Acrobat was first installed.

Capturing a Web site

The number of options available for converting Web pages and controlling the behavior of Web links may seem overwhelming when you first attempt to capture a site. There is no substitute for practice. The more you use the tools and options discussed earlier in this chapter, the more proficient you'll become at converting Web sites to PDF documents. To help simplify the process, take a look at some steps for converting Web pages.

STEPS: Capturing a Web site

1. **Set the Web Capture preferences.** Before attempting to capture a site, review all the preference settings. To open Web Capture Preferences, choose Edit ➪ Preferences and click on Web Capture in the left pane when the Preferences dialog box opens. Click the Reset Conversion Settings to Defaults button. Click OK after making the changes.

2. **Open the pull-down menu from the Create PDF task button.** Select From Web Page from the menu options to open the Create PDF from Web Page dialog box.

3. **Enter the URL for the site to be captured in the Create PDF from Web Page dialog box.** You can use any site on the World Wide Web. If you have a company Web site, use the URL for your site. If not, pick another site. The URL must be complete, so verify the address before proceeding.

4. **Enter the number of levels to capture.** If working with a modem connection, you should first attempt to capture only a single level, especially if you are not familiar with the site structure. If you have a faster connection, try capturing two levels. Enable the check box for Stay on same path, which downloads files under the same path for both levels.

5. **Stay on the same server.** In the Create PDF from Web Page dialog box, enable the check box for Stay on same server. The settings made in the Create from Web Page dialog box should appear as shown in Figure 5-32.

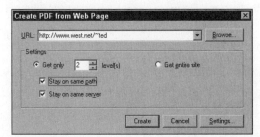

Figure 5-32: The Create PDF from Web Page dialog box displays 2 levels to be captured, and the check boxes for Stay on same path and Stay on same server are enabled.

6. **Click the Settings button in the Create from Web Page dialog box.** You can elect to use Acrobat's default settings or make some choices for bookmark attributes and how the HTML and plain text files are converted. When the Settings button is clicked, the Web Page Conversion Settings dialog box opens.

7. **Create PDF Tags.** In the Conversion Settings dialog box, three of the four check boxes at the bottom are enabled by default. Add to the enabled check boxes Create PDF Tags and place a check mark in the box. With tags you can add new structured bookmarks that link to the page content. Click OK in the Web Page Conversion Settings dialog box to return to the Create PDF from Web Page dialog box.

8. **Capture the site.** You could navigate to the other options for Conversion Settings, but at this point you'll just look at capturing the Web site with the remaining conversion options at the default values. Click the Create button to begin downloading the site.

9. **View the download progress.** If your connection is slow, and it appears as though the computer is sluggish, files are continuing to download. You can easily determine whether files are downloading by showing a status dialog box. To display a status dialog box, choose Advanced ➪ Web Capture ➪ Bring Status Dialogs to Foreground.

10. **Stop the progress.** If an inordinate amount of time passes and you want to stop the download, click the Stop button in the Download Status dialog box. Acrobat displays all PDFs converted from Web pages before the Stop was invoked.

11. **View the PDF file.** Examine the number of pages and scroll through the document. Open the Navigation Pane and view the bookmarks.

Regardless of whether you downloaded the entire site or stopped the download progress, you'll end up with converted pages appearing in Acrobat. The PDF document can be edited or saved for further use. If you save the file, appending Web pages can be accomplished in other Acrobat sessions at a later time. If you performed the preceding steps, save the file to use it later for working through some editing steps.

Converting Clipboard Images to PDF

If you're an author, a technical writer, an IT manager, or you create help documents for users of computer software, you'll absolutely love the addition of the Create PDF From Clipboard Image feature. Anyone who needs a screen shot of a dialog box, an image file, a document page, or a desktop can capture the screen data and instantly convert the captured image to PDF format. If you copy a file to the system clipboard, you can convert the clipboard data from any program to a PDF document. You no longer need any kind of third-party utility for screen captures nor do you have to be concerned about compatible file formats when exchanging data.

Due to differences in operating systems and methods used to copy data to the system clipboard, you'll find the means to be different between Windows and Mac OS X. The result of converting the clipboard data to PDF, however, is the same.

Convert clipboard image (Windows)

Suppose you have a map contained as part of a layout and you want to clip out the map and send it off to a friend for directions to an event, or perhaps you want to take a screen shot of an ftp client application to show log-on instructions, or maybe you want to clarify the use of a dialog box in Acrobat or another application. All of these examples and many more are excellent candidates for screen captures.

To capture a screen shot of the entire monitor screen in Windows, press Shift+PrtScrn (Print Screen) or PrtSc keys. The keystrokes copy the current view of your monitor to the clipboard. You can launch Acrobat or maximize it and select From Clipboard Image from the Create PDF task button pull-down menu. The clipboard data opens as a PDF document in the Acrobat Document Pane. If you have a menu or dialog box open, the screen capture includes the foreground items in the capture like the screen shot shown in Figure 5-33. Screens captured on Windows through these methods create 96 ppi images.

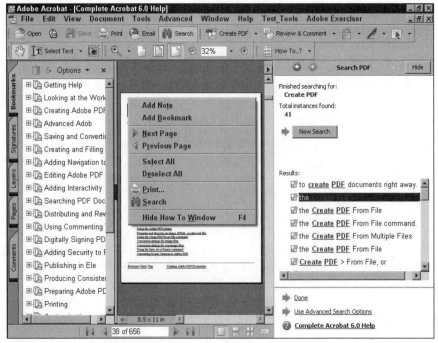

Figure 5-33: Open a dialog box or menu and press Shift+PrtScrn to capture the foreground elements and the background.

If you want to capture a dialog box without the background, use Alt+PrtScrn (or PrtSc). The dialog box screen shots in this book were all taken by using these key modifiers.

Note   Copying a screen shot to the clipboard works with any program or at the operating system level when capturing desktop or folder views, accessories, or virtually any view you see on your computer monitor. Once data are on the clipboard, you can open Acrobat and convert the clipboard data to a PDF document.

Convert clipboard image (Macintosh)

Macintosh OS X.2 and later offers you many different options for converting clipboard data to PDF and creating PDFs from screen shots through built-in methods of the operating system. On the Mac you won't find the From Clipboard Image menu command in the Create PDF pull-down menu. The Mac travels along its own path for these tasks.

PDF files can be created from screen shots taken with a Mac OS X utility or through the use of modifier keys. The result of either method is an image capture at 72 ppi (pixels per inch). If you use the Mac's utility, the screen shot can be opened in the Acrobat Document Pane. Using modifier keys saves the file to disk in PDF format.

Using Grab

You use the Mac utility Grab for taking a screen shot either from the entire screen, a selection, or a timed delay. You access the application by choosing Acrobat ➪ Services and then choosing Screen, Selection, or Timed Screen from a submenu. If you use other applications, the submenu item may not be accessible. To access Grab, you often need to launch the program from the Utilities folder or click on the program icon if it's aliased in the Dock.

To get a feel for capturing a screen shot with Grab and importing the screen in Acrobat, first launch Acrobat. Choose Acrobat ➪ Services ➪ Grab and make one of the following selections from the submenu choices:

✦ **Screen:** This option captures the entire screen. A dialog box opens informing you that the screen capture requires you to click the mouse button outside the dialog box. The dialog box providing the information is not included in the screen capture. Click outside the dialog box and the full screen view is converted to PDF in Acrobat.

✦ **Selection:** The Selection Grab dialog box opens informing you to marquee a selection in the area you want to capture. Screen coordinates are displayed in a readout aside the cursor to assist you if you want to capture a specific size—for example, a 300×200-pixel selection. Drag the marquee around the area to be captured and a rectangle box shows you the selection as you draw it. Release the mouse button and the selection is converted to PDF in Acrobat.

✦ **Timed Screen:** Timed screen enables you to capture the cursor, menus, and actions on the screen. The timer is delayed 10 seconds. When you're ready to start the capture, click the Start Timer button in the Timed Screen Grab dialog box.

Using one of these methods captures the screen according to the choice made for Grab and the screen shot is opened in Acrobat. The file then needs to be saved to disk if you want to keep it.

Tip   The Grab utility via the Adobe ➪ Services menu command operates a little slower than using it from its own menu selections. In addition, keyboard shortcuts are not available for Grab when you access the utility through Acrobat. You can launch Grab from the Utilities folder inside your Mac OS X Applications folder and press ⌘+Z for capturing a screen, ⌘+Shift+A to capture a selection, and ⌘+Shift+Z for a timed screen. The captured results are opened in a Grab window where you can save the file as a TIFF image. Use the Create PDF From Files command in Acrobat when you finish capturing all your screens, and the images are converted to PDF.

Using keyboard shortcuts

Directly from the operating system, you can use keyboard modifiers to capture screens, selections, and dialog boxes. All the captures you make with keystrokes are instantly saved as PDF files. Even if a user doesn't have Acrobat installed on a computer, the files are saved in PDF. When the operating system saves a PDF file from a screen capture the files are automatically numbered as either Untitled 1, Untitled 2, and so on or Picture 1, Picture 2, and so on. The types of screen shots available to you from the operating system include

✦ **Capturing the screen (⌘+Shift+3).** Using the keystrokes shortcut, the entire screen is captured and saved as PDF to your Desktop.

✦ **Capturing a selection (⌘+Shift+4).** The cursor changes to a target with crosshairs. Drag a rectangle marquee and the selection is saved as a PDF document to the Desktop when you release the mouse button.

✦ **Capturing a snapshot (⌘+Shift+4 then Spacebar).** This is a very neat little feature in Mac OS X.2 and later. If you want to capture a dialog box, a menu, a program icon, the Dock (see Figure 5-34), a folder, or any kind of single element on screen, press ⌘+Shift+4 and then press the Spacebar. The cursor changes to a camera. As you move the camera around the screen, the Mac OS shows you a selection for the capture. You are alerted to what is being captured when the object changes color as you move the cursor to different items. Click the mouse button and the screen capture is saved as PDF to the Desktop.

Figure 5-34: To capture a dialog box, a menu, an icon, or any kind of window, press ⌘+Shift+4; then press the Spacebar. Move the cursor to the item to be captured and click the mouse button. Any item, including the Dock, can be captured and saved as PDF.

Taking Snapshots

A new tool introduced in Acrobat 6.0 is the Snapshot tool. In the default Basic toolbar, select the Snapshot tool and click on a page. The entire page is copied to the clipboard. You can then create a PDF file From Clipboard as described in the previous section. The page you create, however, is a raster image when you convert it to PDF. You lose all text attributes when copying a page in this manner. A better solution for converting an entire page is to use the Extract Pages command.

Cross-Reference

For information on extracting pages, see Chapter 10.

The advantage of using the Snapshot tool is when taking a snapshot of a partial page in Acrobat. You can select the Snapshot tool and drag a marquee in an area you want to copy. When you release the mouse button, the selected area is copied to the clipboard. Choose Create PDF ⇨ From Clipboard Image from the Create PDF task button and the selection is converted to PDF. Again, you lose all type attributes, but you can use this method if retaining text is not an issue or if you want to crop an image. Using the Crop tool doesn't reduce the page size or file size of a PDF document. Using the Snapshot tool results in smaller file sizes when copying smaller sections of a PDF page.

Snapshots cannot be taken in password-protected files. If a file is encrypted you need to eliminate the file encryption before using the Snapshot tool.

Cross-Reference

For information on using the Crop tool, see Chapter 10. For linking to snapshots, see Chapter 15. For information on file encryption, see Chapter 19.

Saving and Exporting PDF Files

If you use any of the methods for PDF creation discussed in this chapter, or if you edit a PDF document, eventually you'll want to update or save your file. Like most programs, Acrobat offers you a Save and Save As command in the File menu. You'll also find the Save tool in the Acrobat File toolbar.

By default, saving a file is written in PDF format. However, Acrobat offers you many different save options and formats for saving files. If you need to update a file or export data from PDF files, choose File ⇨ Save As and choose a file format from the Save as type (Format on Macintosh) pull-down menu as shown in Figure 5-35.

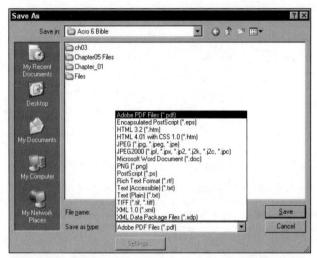

Figure 5-35: Choose File ⇨ Save As and choose the file format to be saved from the Save as type pull-down menu.

Selecting all but the Adobe PDF Files (*.pdf), Text (Accessible) (*.txt), and XML Data Package Files (*.xdp) formats provides user-definable options in the Settings dialog box for the respective file type. When you select any of the formats other than the preceding three, the Settings button becomes active. Click Settings and the Save As Settings dialog box opens. The various options change according to the file format selected from the Save as type pull-down menu in the Save As dialog box.

Adobe PDF files (*.pdf)

By default the Acrobat PDF Files (*.pdf) format is selected in the Save as type pull-down menu. Saving as PDF without changing the filename overwrites the existing PDF when saved to the same directory as where the open file resides. As you edit a PDF document and choose Save from the File menu or click the Save tool, the document can consume more memory than needed to update the file Redundant data are saved with a file during periodic saves. To optimize a file for smaller sizes, select Save As, choose the PDF format, and overwrite the file on your hard drive. The document is completely rewritten and often results in a smaller file size. Some files can be significantly reduced when using Save As and overwriting the file.

Note
The default PDF format is one of the many nice little changes you'll notice between Acrobat 6 and earlier versions of Acrobat. In earlier versions the default file format was the last file format you selected in the Save as type pull-down menu. If you forgot that the last time you saved a file was in RTF format and you opened a new file in Acrobat, made some edits, and saved the file without checking the format option, you probably said, "oh darn" as you waited for a useless save to finish. In Acrobat 6 the default always returns to PDF as the file format. Never again do you have to worry about rechecking the format option before saving to PDF.

Encapsulated PostScript (*.eps) and PostScript (*.ps)

EPS files are saved as single page files. When multiple page PDFs are saved to EPS, each page is saved as a new EPS document. PostScript files save the PDF to disk like you would print a file to disk as PostScript. PostScript files can then be distilled in Acrobat Distiller to convert to PDF. PostScript files can also be downloaded to PostScript printers through the use of a downloading utility or a hot folder, used for sending files directly to the printer.

Many of the options for creating either an EPS file or a PostScript file are identical. There are some differences as you travel through the many options found in the Save As Settings dialog box. Select either Encapsulated PostScript (*.eps) or PostScript (*.ps) from the Files of type (Format on Macintosh) pull-down menu and click on the Settings button. The options appear in the Save As Settings dialog box. Shown in Figure 5-36 is the EPS Save As Settings dialog box.

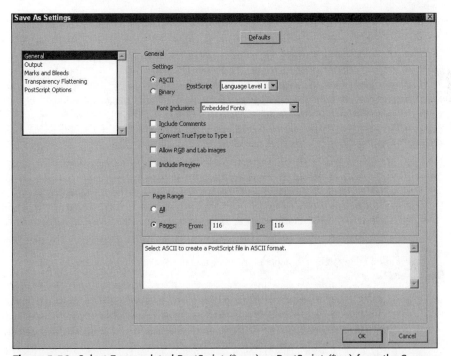

Figure 5-36: Select Encapsulated PostScript (*.eps) or PostScript (*.ps) from the Save as type (Format on Macintosh) pull-down menu. Click on the Settings button to open the Save As Settings dialog box. In this figure, Save as EPS was selected.

General settings

On the left side of the Save As Settings dialog box are several categories for choices you make on the right side of the dialog box. The first of the categories is the General settings where you set some general attributes for the way an EPS or PostScript file is saved. These settings include

✦ **PostScript Description File (PostScript only):** A PostScript Printer Description (PPD) file selection can be made from choices available in the pull-down menu. Use Device Independent for composite printing and Acrobat 6 Defaults for separations.

✦ **Defaults:** The Defaults button at the top of the dialog box returns all settings to the original defaults. This button can be accessed at any time you travel through the various option categories in the list at the left side of the dialog box.

✦ **ASCII:** PostScript files are encoded as ASCII (American Standard Code for Information Interchange). ASCII files are larger than the binary that you see as the second option for encoding selections. If you want to place an EPS file in another program for color separating, use the ASCII settings.

For information on color separating EPS files and Acrobat PDF, see Chapter 23.

✦ **Binary:** Binary files are much smaller than ASCII files. Use binary encoding when the PostScript language level is 2 or 3.

✦ **PostScript:** Select the language levels from the pull-down menu choices. For ASCII encoding use Language Level 1 from the menu. For exporting EPS files to Adobe InDesign, you can use Language Level 2. If using language Level 2 or 3, use binary encoding. Use PostScript 3 only when the output devices use PostScript 3 RIPs.

Users of previous versions of Acrobat had to either export PDF files to EPS, place PDFs in separating programs, or use third-party plug-ins to print color separations and to high-end devices. These workarounds are all a part of the past. Acrobat Professional affords you almost all the printing controls you need for high-end printing. Forget about exporting EPS files if your only need is to print color separations or composites to high-end devices.

✦ **Font Inclusion:** You have three choices for font inclusion. Choose None to not embed fonts. Choose Embedded Fonts to keep the same fonts embedded in the PDF in the exported EPS file. Choose Embedded and Referenced Fonts to keep the PDF embedded fonts and fonts referenced from fonts loaded in your system. If using a font that is not embedded in the PDF document but loaded as a system font, the font is embedded in the resulting PDF.

For more information about font embedding and understanding font embedding limitations, see Chapter 7.

✦ **Include Comments:** When the check box is enabled, any comment notes are included in the resulting EPS or PostScript document. When the PostScript document is distilled in Acrobat Distiller the comment notes are retained in the resulting PDF document.

✦ **Convert TrueType to Type 1:** Check the box to convert TrueType fonts to Type 1 fonts.

For more information on TrueType and Type 1 fonts, see Chapter 7.

✦ **Allow RGB and Lab images (EPS only):** If you choose Language Level 1, this check box should be enabled; otherwise, any RGB or Lab images won't be converted in the EPS file.

✦ **Include Preview (EPS only):** The preview is a screen view of the EPS file. If the check box is not enabled, the EPS file appears as a gray box when you place the file in another program. The data are all there, but you won't be able to see the EPS image. When the check box is enabled, a preview is embedded in the EPS file. Preview image formats are TIFF on Windows and PICT on the Macintosh.

✦ **Page Range:** You can export all pages by selecting the All radio button or enter the page numbers for a range of pages to be exported. EPS files are exported as individual files for each page and automatically numbered by Acrobat.

✦ **Comments:** At the bottom of the dialog box is a comment box offering you help descriptions of each item you select. If uncertain about an option, select a radio button or a pull-down menu command and look at the comment box. Dynamic help is available for all the options.

Output

Click on the Output item in the list on the left side of the Save As Settings dialog box and the options change as shown in Figure 5-37.

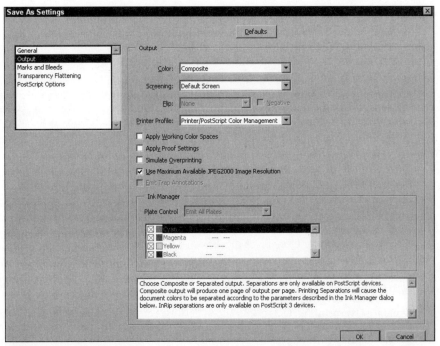

Figure 5-37: Select Output and the options change to attribute settings designed for printing and prepress.

Output options enable you to control prepress output attributes that include

✦ **Color:** The four choices for handling color in resulting EPS and PostScript file(s) are

- **Composite:** The file is exported as a composite image. If the file is a four-color image, you can still import an EPS file in a separating program and print separations. The intent for Composite is for use with composite color printing and printing separations to non-Adobe PostScript devices. For PostScript files, composites can be downloaded directly to PostScript 2 and 3 devices.

- **Composite Gray:** If the files are grayscale, use Composite Gray.

- **Separations:** This option creates a DCS (Desktop Color Separation) file, and each color as well as a composite is exported as separate files. If pre-separating the EPS file(s), be certain you use a program like Adobe InDesign that supports DCS files or you can directly download each plate to your RIP. For PostScript files, the file is separated. When downloading the PostScript file all colors print on separate plates.

Cross-Reference   For more information about DCS files and color separations and RIPs, see Chapter 23.

- **In-RIP Separations:** This option only works on Adobe PostScript 3 RIPs. A composite color image is printed to the RIP and the RIP color separates the composite file.

✦ **Screening:** Make choices for screening from the pull-down menu. Unless you have some special need for embedding half-tone frequencies in the EPS file, leave the Screening set to Default Screen and handle all your frequency control at the RIP. For PostScript files, set the screening as desired before downloading the file.

✦ **Flip:** The single limitation in Acrobat for prepress and printing is the lack of emulsion control for composite prints. Flip and Negative are only available for Separations or In-RIP Separations. If you want to save the EPS as Emulsion Down and Negative, check Flip and the Negative box. For PostScript files, set the output to Emulsion Down and Negative only when using service centers controlling emulsion through authoring applications. Many centers want Positive, Emulsion Up files because the emulsion control is handled at the RIP.

✦ **Printer Profile:** You can embed a printer profile in the EPS file(s) from the available choices in the pull-down menu. If you want to eliminate color management, select the option at the top of the menu choices for Save As Source (No Color Management).

✦ **Apply Working Color Spaces:** If you want to embed a CMYK working profile in the EPS for uncalibrated color files, check this box.

✦ **Apply Proof Settings:** Proof settings enable you to soft-proof color across multiple devices. Check the box to apply proof settings that can be viewed onscreen for soft proofing color.

✦ **Simulate Overprinting:** Overprints and knockouts can be soft-proofed onscreen for color-separated devices. The check box is grayed out unless you choose one of the separation items in the Color pull-down menu.

✦ **Use Maximum Available JPEG2000 Image Resolution:** For any raster images contained in the EPS file export, the file compression uses JPEG2000 at the maximum setting when the check box is enabled. If disabled, the original compression level at the time the PDF was created is used.

✦ **Emit Trap Annotations:** The check box is grayed out unless you save the file with one of the color separations options from the Color pull-down menu. If trapping annotations are to be eliminated, check the box.

✦ **Plate Control:** Unchecking the box on the far left of each color plate eliminates the plate for separated files. Scroll the box to see any spot colors and you can select spot colors for conversion to CMYK color.

Marks and Bleeds

Select the Marks and Bleeds item in the list at the left of the Save As Settings dialog box and the options for adding printer's marks appear, as shown in Figure 5-38.

The options include

✦ **Marks:** You can select from Emit Printer Marks and All Marks in the first two check boxes. Selecting All Marks checks all the boxes below the Marks Style pull-down menu.

✦ **Marks Style:** You have choices for the style of printer's marks that appear on the exported EPS/PS file. Western-style is used by U.S. and European printers, and Eastern-style is used by printers in Japan and far Eastern countries.

✦ **Marks:** The check boxes below the pull-down menu for Crop Marks, Trim Marks, and so on, should be self-explanatory. You can include the marks desired by checking boxes individually. Only the checked items appear on the exported file.

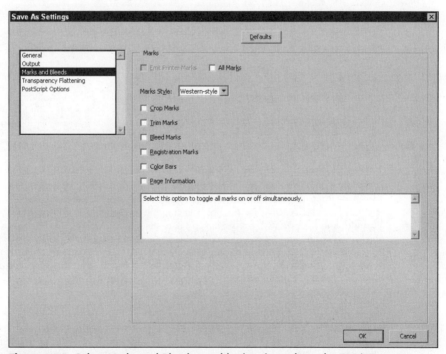

Figure 5-38: Select Marks and Bleeds to add printer's marks to the EPS/PS export.

Transparency Flattening

For anyone who's experienced difficulty with printing transparency on PostScript RIPs, you can now choose to rasterize vector objects in EPS and PostScript files to eliminate printing problems on PostScript Level 2 devices and some PostScript 3 devices. Click on Transparency Flattening in the Save As Settings dialog box and the options for controlling rasterization and flattening appear as shown in Figure 5-39.

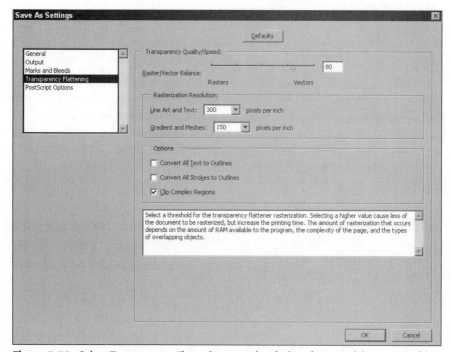

Figure 5-39: Select Transparency Flattening to make choices for rasterizing vector objects.

Note   Raster objects are pixel based. Photos and scans you might edit in image-editing programs like Adobe Photoshop are known as raster images. Vector objects are constructed with mathematical formulas describing the paths and contents of the objects in programs like Adobe Illustrator and CorelDraw. The pixel-based raster objects are much easier than vector-based objects to print on PostScript and non-PostScript devices. Vector-based objects are more difficult to print than raster objects and can sometimes fail to print properly on non-PostScript devices. The process of converting vector objects to raster data is known as *rasterization*.

The Transparency Flattening options include

✦ **Transparency Quality/Speed:** The slider enables you to flatten vector objects where the true transparency in vector objects is rasterized and results in simulated transparency. The level of rasterization is determined by moving the slider left or right. Moving left rasterizes and flattens transparent objects. Moving right reduces rasterization and preserves more vector objects.

✦ **Rasterization Resolution:** Vector-based objects are device dependent and carry with them no resolution values. Resolution is dependent on the machine's resolution where the vector data are printed. Raster objects are device independent and a fixed resolution is embedded in the raster data. When rasterizing vector data, you assign the resolution to the resulting raster images. For type, you'll want much higher resolution on most printing devices. You can often gain acceptable results with lower resolutions for gradient objects. The options here let you assign resolutions individually for type and gradients when rasterized.

✦ **Convert All Text to Outlines:** All text in the EPS/PS is converted to outlines. As a standard operating procedure, you should avoid converting type to outlines. Converting type to outlines makes printing these files on PostScript RIPs more difficult. If you have a stubborn font that doesn't want to print you can use this option as a last resort.

✦ **Convert All Strokes to Outlines:** If stroke weights present problems with transparent objects, you can convert the strokes to outlines and simplify the transparency. The results, however, can be unpredictable and often you'll find the stroke weights thicker in the EPS/PS export than the original design.

✦ **Clip Complex Regions:** Depending on where you set the slider for Transparency Quality/Speed, you'll have distinct boundaries between raster and vector objects. When part of an object is rasterized and another part is a vector object, artifacts along the boundaries can appear. Checking this box reduces the stitching artifacts produced when flattening and rasterizing vector objects.

PostScript options

Click on the last item in the list for EPS/PS exports and the options shown in Figure 5-40 appear. The PostScript options offer you settings for embedded PostScript attributes in the EPS/PS file.

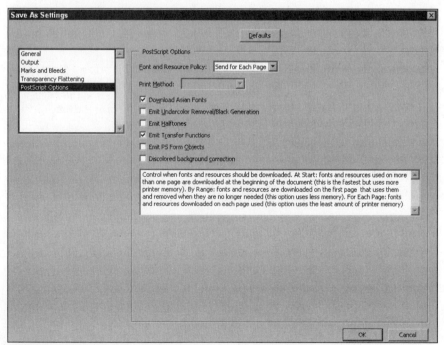

Figure 5-40: Select PostScript Options to add various PostScript printing attributes to the EPS/PostScript file(s).

The PostScript options include

✦ **Font and Resource Policy:** How fonts download to a printer's RIP is determined from three choices in the pull-down menu. The three options are

- **Send at Start:** The entire font sets for all pages are downloaded to the printer's RIP. The file prints faster than any of the other methods, but puts a memory burden on the printing device to hold all the font matrices in memory during printing.

- **Send by Range:** Fonts are downloaded from the first page where the fonts are used and stays in memory until the job is printed. The font downloading occurs as each font is found on a page that uses them. The job prints a little slower than when using the Send at Start option, but uses less memory initially as the job is printed.

- **Send for Each Page:** Fonts encountered on a page are downloaded to the RIP; then they are flushed as the next page is printed. The second page's fonts are then downloaded and flushed after printing, and so on. This method requires the least memory. Files print slower than when using either of the other two methods.

✦ **Print Method:** Choose from the PostScript Language Levels from the pull-down menu options. Use PostScript Language Level 3 for PostScript 3 devices.

✦ **Download Asian Fonts:** Check this box if Asian fonts are in the document and not available on the RIP nor embedded in the document. If the fonts are embedded, you need not be concerned about checking this option.

✦ **Emit Undercolor Removal/Black Generation:** GCR/UCR removal is only necessary if the original document contained assignments in the PostScript file converted to PDF. If you want to remove any embedded settings for handling the amount of black or compensating for black generation with different inks check the box. If you don't know what any of this means, checking the box or not won't have an effect on your own personal documents.

✦ **Emit Halftones:** If a halftone frequency was embedded in the original file, you can eliminate it in the exported document. Unless you want to use embedded frequencies, leave the box checked in case you accidentally preserved a frequency in the original file for EPS files. For PostScript files you'll want to assign frequencies at the time the PostScript file is created when printing to high-end devices.

✦ **Emit Transfer Functions:** The same criteria as the preceding bullet apply to transfer functions. If you intend to use embedded transfer functions, leave the check box disabled. Otherwise, keep it checked as a default.

✦ **Emit PS Form Objects:** This option relates to PS Form XObjects. XObjects are used to create a description of multiple smaller objects repeated several times like patterns, brushes, backgrounds, and so on. Emitting the XObjects reduces the size of the print job; however, more memory is needed to RIP the file(s).

✦ **Discolored background correction:** If white backgrounds assume a discolored appearance like a yellow or gray tint, select this radio button to correct the discoloration.

Click OK in the Save As Settings dialog box and click Save in the Save As dialog box. The PDF is exported in EPS or PostScript format, containing all the attributes you described for all the options listed earlier.

Because printing in Acrobat Professional takes care of all the print controls you need, exporting EPS files for printing is a task you won't need to perform unless there's some strange problem that needs to be resolved in a file that won't print. A more practical use for exporting EPS files from Acrobat is if you need to import a PDF file in another program that does not support PDF, but does support EPS. In such cases you'll find it helpful to understand all the options you have available for EPS exports.

You have many advantages in creating PostScript files from Acrobat. Files can be re-distilled in Acrobat Distiller with PDF/X formats for printing and prepress, sometimes as a workaround for repurposing documents, and for downloading directly to PostScript Level 2 devices (PostScript 3 devices accept PDFs directly).

Cross-Reference   For more information about PDF/X files, see Chapters 7 and 23.

HTML 3.2 (*.htm), HTML 4.01 with CSS 1.0 (*.htm), XML 1.0 (*.xml), and Text (Plain) (*.txt)

Options available for exporting PDFs to HTML files, HTML files with Cascading Style Sheets, Plain Text, and XML files all use the same attribute settings. Text is exported according to the encoding method you select and images are exported according to the format option you select. These settings are available when you select any one of the three file formats from the Save as type (Format on Macintosh) pull-down menu. Select a format and click on the Settings button. The Save As Settings dialog box opens as shown in Figure 5-41.

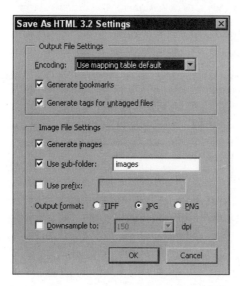

Figure 5-41: To set attributes for file exports for HTML, XML, or TXT files, select one of three file formats in the Save as type (Format on Macintosh) pull-down menu and click on Settings.

✦ **Encoding:** Choose the encoding method from options for Unicode settings (UTF-8, UTF-16, or UCS-4), ISO-Latin-1, HTML/ASCII, or the default setting of Use mapping table default.

✦ **Generate bookmarks:** Generates bookmark links to content for HTML or XML documents. Links are placed at the beginning of the resulting HTML or XML document.

✦ **Generate tags for untagged files:** Tags are temporarily created for file conversion for untagged documents. You need to select the check box for legacy untagged files or with files created with Acrobat 4 or in order to complete the conversion. The tags are temporary for the conversion to work and are not added to the PDF. If you do not select this for legacy PDFs, you will not get the conversion.

✦ **Generate images:** Enable the check box for images to be exported as separate files.

✦ **Use sub-folder:** Images are saved to a subfolder below the directory where the HTML files are created. The default name for the folder is *images*. In the field box you can change the folder name by editing the line of text.

✦ **Use prefix:** Prefixes are added to image filenames. Check the box and supply the prefix text in the field box.

✦ **Output format:** Three options buttons enable you to determine the file format for the saved images. Choose from TIFF, JPG, or PNG.

✦ **Downsample to:** Images are downsampled to the setting selected from the pull-down menu. The settings are fixed with choices for 72, 96, 150, and 300 pixels per inch (ppi).

JPEG (*.jpg, .jpeg, .jpe), JPEG2000 (.jpf, *.ipx, *.jp2, *.j2k, *.j2c, .jpc), PNG (.png), and TIFF (*.tif, *.tiff)

The PDF document can be exported as any one of the preceding image file formats. The entire page including text and images is exported as a single image file. From the settings dialog box you choose options for image compression and color management. The options settings for exporting image file formats are the same as the options used when importing images in Acrobat with the Create PDF From File or From Multiple Files commands discussed earlier in this chapter.

Caution   When exporting PDF documents containing images, you cannot achieve a better resolution than the resolution in the source file. If you have, for example, a PDF document with a TIFF image where the image was originally sampled at 72 ppi, you cannot gain any resolution by saving the file from Acrobat as a TIFF file with 300-ppi resolution. The file is saved with the resolution you specify in the Save As Settings dialog box, but image resolutions higher than source files are upsized with image interpolation. The results are often unusable and produce poor quality images. If you need image resolutions higher than the source images, you need to return to your scanner and scan images at higher resolutions. Recreate the original document and convert to PDF.

Cross-Reference   For a better understanding of image resolutions required for printing, see Chapter 23.

Microsoft Word document (*.doc) and Rich Text Format (*.rtf)

PDF files can be exported to Microsoft Word format and Rich Text Format files (RTF). The conversion settings include choices for image handling and sampling. Unlike HTML and XML files, exports to Word and RTF embed the images in the exported text files when you choose to export images. Acrobat does not offer an option for exporting images apart from the text data.

Be aware that although you can export PDF documents directly to MS Word format, the integrity of your file all depends on how well you created the PDF. If the PDF was created without tags and through less desirable PDF-creation methods, the ultimate file you produce in Word or RTF format may not be suitable for editing and converting back to PDF. Inasmuch as tags are added during conversion to PDF, the tagged structure is not retained in the resulting file.

Cross-Reference

For more information on programs supporting exports to PDF as structured and tagged files, see Chapter 6.

As a general rule you should keep native documents archived and return to them to perform any major editing tasks. As a workaround, you can use the export to Word and RTF formats for legacy files where no original documents are available. In some cases you'll need to perform some extensive editing in either your Word processor or page layout program.

Clicking on Settings in the Save As dialog box for exports to MS Word or RTF opens the Save As Settings dialog box. The settings are the same for RTF as for Word-formatted file exports (shown in Figure 5-42).

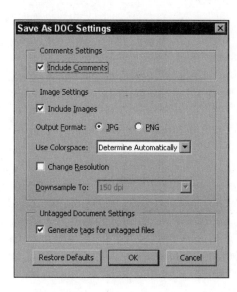

Figure 5-42: Select either MS Word or RTF for the file export and click on the Settings button. The options in both dialog boxes are identical.

Settings for exporting to MS Word or RTF formats include:

✦ **Include Comments:** Like EPS and PostScript files discussed earlier, Comment notes can be exported to Word or with RTF files. Check the box for Include Comments and the Comment notes are exported.

✦ **Include Images:** Image files can be extracted from the PDF and embedded in the .doc or .rtf file in either of two formats. Select JPG or PNG for the image file format.

✦ **Use Colorspace:** You have choices for colorspaces from a pull-down menu. See the section earlier in this chapter on Applying Settings for a definition of the options choices for Colorspace.

✦ **Change Resolution:** Downsampling and resolution issues are the same as those noted when exporting PDF documents to image formats. Look at the section earlier in this chapter on Applying Settings to review the resolution options and resampling problems encountered when upsizing images.

✦ **Generate tags for untagged files:** If you attempt to save an untagged document as either a .doc or .rtf file with the Generate tags for untagged file check box disabled, Acrobat prompts you in an alert dialog box to set the preference option. This check box must be enabled in order to export the file.

Text (Accessible) (*.txt)

Files are saved as text. For tagged PDF documents made accessible, all alternative text used to describe items such as images and form fields that are contained in the document tags are converted to text. The alternate tags can be viewed in the tags palette in Acrobat but won't necessarily appear in the document page. When you export PDFs as Accessible Text, the text is generated in the body of the document.

XML Data Package Files (*.xdp)

XDP files can be understood by the XFA plug-in. The XFA plug-in is used with high-end forms systems for data exchanges between documents that comply with the XFA Forms Architecture. As an alternative to exporting FDF data to database applications, the XDP files can be easily ported to systems using the plug-in.

XDP contains not only the XML form data, but can contain the PDF file, Style Sheets, XSL transformations, and XML template data. The benefit (or use) of exporting to XDP is that XML standard industry tools can process the form data.

Summary

✦ Acrobat is a program that uses documents converted to PDF from files originating in other programs.

✦ PDF Documents can be created with the Adobe PDF printer. The Adobe PDF printer can have a variety of Adobe PDF Settings applied to the PDF conversion. Adobe PDF Settings are used by Acrobat Distiller and the Adobe PDF Printer.

✦ A variety of different native file formats can be converted to PDF by Acrobat using the Create PDF From a File command. Multiple files can be converted to PDF and concatenated into a single document.

✦ Web pages can be downloaded by Acrobat and converted to PDF. Web pages residing locally on hard drives can be converted to PDF. All Web page conversions preserve page and URL links.

✦ Data copied to the system clipboard can be converted to PDF. Screen shots copied to the clipboard from both Windows and Macintosh can be converted to PDF.

✦ Acrobat can save PDFs in a variety of different formats. Many formats have an elaborate number of options settings to set attributes for the saved files.

✦   ✦   ✦

Exporting to PDF from Authoring Applications

The last chapter covered PDF file creation using built-in features in Acrobat. If you read the chapter, you know that Acrobat 6 offers many more PDF creation methods than earlier versions. Some of the PDF creation options you have from within Acrobat are also available directly from the authoring programs. In other cases, you'll find PDF creation a feature in a program where support is not available from within Acrobat. Adobe Systems has been implementing PDF support for some time in many of its design applications, and other vendors are continually providing support for direct export to PDF.

It stands to reason that the software manufacturer that has implemented the best PDF integration with other programs is Adobe Systems. With programs such as Adobe Illustrator, Adobe InDesign, Adobe FrameMaker, and Adobe Photoshop PDF integration and the use of core PDF technology has grown with each new release of Adobe's imaging applications.

Other software manufacturers are also adding more support with every program upgrade. Manufacturers such as Corel Corporation, Macromedia, and Quark, Inc., also implement PDF support in their recent program releases. And now in Acrobat 6 there's support for more programs, including Microsoft Visio and AutoDesk AutoCAD, and Internet applications such as Microsoft Internet Explorer and Microsoft Outlook Express.

In this chapter I give an overview of different programs capable of exporting to PDF and throw in a few programming options using pdfmark annotations.

For information about using Internet applications, see Chapter 20.

Setting Up the Environment

This chapter is concerned with creating PDFs and adding annotations to PDFs with the pdfmark in programs other than Acrobat. Therefore, no toolbars need to be loaded in the Toolbar Well. You can leave your toolbars in Acrobat set to the default view to follow what's covered in this chapter.

Acrobat and Adobe Photoshop

Adobe Photoshop version 4 introduced support for exports and imports of PDF documents. You could save a Photoshop image directly in PDF format and open the file in an Acrobat viewer. Importing PDF files, however, was limited to only those files that were originally saved from Photoshop. If a PDF was created from another application through PostScript, Acrobat Distiller, or an export to PDF, Photoshop couldn't open it. Version 5.5 of Adobe Photoshop included much better support for PDF and permitted opening multiple-page PDFs as well as files from any PDF producer. When Photoshop 6 was released, PDF exports handled preserving vector art and type. For an imaging program that is suited to working with PDF documents, you'll find Adobe Photoshop the best source for handling raster data while preserving vector objects.

 Note Raster data is comprised of pixels. Scanned images are one form of raster-based images. Vector objects are created in illustration and layout programs where the objects are not represented by pixels, but rather by math equations. In Photoshop you can open a scanned image (raster) and add type (vector) and objects. When you save the image as a PDF file, the vector type and objects are preserved.

Exporting to PDF from Photoshop

Creating a PDF file from Photoshop is nothing more than choosing the PDF format from the Save dialog box. Photoshop supports many different file formats for opening and saving documents. In versions prior to Photoshop 6.0, you had to flatten all layers before you could save a document as a PDF file. In versions 6.0 and 7.0, you can preserve layers and vector art. When you save a layered file from Photoshop 7.0 as a PDF and open it again in Photoshop, all layers are retained. Type and vector art work the same way. You can create type without rasterizing it and save the file as a PDF. Later, if you want to edit the file, you can reopen it and edit the type. What's more, you can search and edit the type in Acrobat when you save the file as PDF from Photoshop.0

To save a multilayered Photoshop image, Photoshop document, or flattened image, you use the Save As command. In Photoshop 7.0 choose File ➪ Save As. The Save As dialog box (see Figure 6-1) provides many options for preserving the Photoshop file integrity while saving in PDF format that include

- ✦ **File name:** As when saving any file you supply the filename and destination in the Save (or Save As) dialog box. Note Save In at the top of the dialog box and the File name field (stpete.pdf) in Figure 6-1.

- ✦ **Format:** From the pull-down menu you can choose many formats for layered documents and documents containing vector art. However, preserving both can only be achieved with either Photoshop's native format or the Photoshop PDF format.

- ✦ **As a Copy:** If you use the Save As command, the file you save is a copy of the original document presuming you use a different filename than the original. If you open a PDF file and select Save As, you can click on the As a Copy check box to duplicate the file. The filename is automatically extended to include the word *copy* after the filename and before the extension.

- ✦ **Alpha Channels:** The PDF format also retains all Alpha Channel data. Use of Alpha Channels is restricted to Photoshop when you reopen the file in Photoshop. In Acrobat, the use of Alpha Channel data isn't useful.

✦ **Layers:** Saving as a Photoshop PDF also preserves all layers. When you reopen the file in Photoshop, you have access to all layer data.

✦ **Annotations:** You can add text notes and audio comments in Photoshop much like when using Comment tools in Acrobat. When you add a comment to the file, it is preserved in the PDF file. If you open the PDF in Acrobat, you can edit or delete text notes and audio comments.

✦ **Spot Colors:** If a Spot Color is included in the Photoshop file, Spot Colors are preserved when you save the file as a PDF.

✦ **Use Proof Setup:** Proof viewing can accommodate different viewing options for color separations. Saving as a PDF displays the document in Acrobat with the Proof Setup enabled.

For information on using Proof Setup in Acrobat, see Chapter 23.

✦ **ICC Profile:** You can embed the current profile used for the respective color mode in the PDF file.

✦ **Thumbnail:** Thumbnails are created for Photoshop format images. No Thumbnail preview is embedded in the resulting PDF document.

✦ **Use Lower Case Extension:** Filenames default with an extension. PDF files automatically have a .pdf extension added to the filename. When the check box is enabled, the extension appears in lowercase.

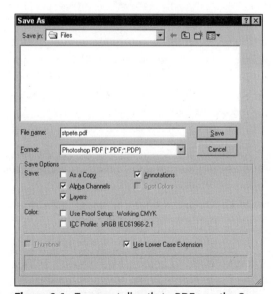

Figure 6-1: To export directly to PDF, use the Save or Save As dialog box in Photoshop. Layers are saved in the PDF document, but they do not appear as layers in the PDF file.

After enabling all check boxes for the file attributes and then clicking on Save, Photoshop opens a second dialog box where you handle settings for the compression, font, and security. Figure 6-2 shows the PDF Options dialog box.

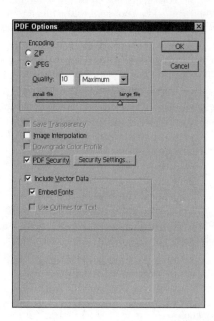

Figure 6-2: After you click on the Save button in the Save As dialog box, the PDF Options dialog box opens.

The first of two choices available to you is the encoding method.

✦ **ZIP:** ZIP compression is lossless. Files will not be compressed as much as you have available from JPEG, but the data integrity will be optimal. ZIP compression is usually preferred for images with large amounts of a single color.

Note   Acrobat 5.0 eliminated use of LZW compression in favor of the more efficient ZIP compression. No access to LZW compression exists in either Photoshop 6.0 or Acrobat 5.0.

✦ **JPEG:** JPEG compression in this dialog box corresponds to the compression amounts you observed in Chapter 5. Depending on your output, the compression amount corresponds to the examples discussed in Chapter 5.

✦ **Save Transparency:** A single-layer image may have transparency on the layer. If you select Save transparency, the PDF viewed in Acrobat appears with the transparent area white — regardless of the background color you used in Photoshop.

✦ **Downgrade Color Profile:** If you selected an ICC (International Color Consortium) Profile (Windows) or Embed Color Profile (Macintosh) for a version 4 profile, checking this option downgrades the profile to version 2. The option is available only when a profile has been saved with version 4 and, you need to use it only when an application doesn't support version 4 profiles.

✦ **PDF Security:** When files are saved from Photoshop to the PDF format, you can secure the files with either 40-bit or 128-bit security. The same options available in Acrobat for securing files are also available when you click on the Security Settings button adjacent to the check box.

Cross-Reference

For more information on securing PDF files, see Chapter 19.

✦ **Image Interpolation:** Anti-aliasing is applied to lower resolution images. If you use higher compression on files, you can somewhat improve appearances by using interpolation.

✦ **Include Vector Data:** Vector data may be in the form of vector objects or type. When either is used, the data are not rasterized. Vector data and type is preserved in the PDF and recognized by Acrobat and Photoshop.

✦ **Embed Fonts:** Font embedding will occur much as it does with Distiller. If you create a Photoshop file and preserve the type layer, embedding the font will eliminate another user from needing the font if the file is opened in Acrobat.

✦ **Use Outlines for Text:** Text is converted to outlines (or paths) when the check box is enabled.

Note

Many designers have resolved themselves to always converting type to outlines regardless of the program or fonts used. This habit has developed due to many continuing font problems found when using imaging service centers. Converting type to outlines is not a panacea for resolving all the problems. Fonts converted to outlines put undue burden on RIPs and imaging equipment, not to mention your desktop printers. Avoid converting to outlines whenever possible and reserve the procedure for only those fonts where a known problem exists.

PDF and color modes

Photoshop provides a number of choices for the color mode used to express your image. You can open files from different color modes, convert color modes in Photoshop, and save among different formats available for a given color mode. File formats are dependent on color modes, and some format options are not available if the image data are defined in a mode not acceptable to the format.

Tip

See Table 6-1 later in this section for Photoshop PDF exports supported by the Photoshop color modes and relative uses for each mode.

Color mode choices in Photoshop include the following:

✦ **Bitmap:** The image is expressed in two colors: black and white. In Photoshop terms, images in the bitmap mode are referred to as line art. In Acrobat terms, this color mode is called monochrome bitmap. Bitmap images are usually about one-eighth the size of a grayscale file. The bitmap format can be used with Acrobat Capture for converting the image data to rich text.

✦ **Grayscale:** This is your anchor mode in Photoshop. Grayscale is like a black-and-white photo, a halftone, or a Charlie Chaplin movie. You see grayscale images everywhere, including the pages in this book. I refer to this as an anchor mode because you can convert to any of the other modes from grayscale. RGB files cannot be converted directly to bitmaps or duotones. You first need to convert RGB to grayscale, and then to either of the other two modes. From grayscale, although the color is not regained, you can also convert back to any of the other color modes. Grayscale images significantly reduce file sizes — they're approximately one-third the size of an RGB file, but larger than the bitmaps.

✦ **RGB:** For screen views, multimedia, and Web graphics, RGB is the most commonly used mode. It has a color gamut much larger than CMYK and is best suited for display on computer monitors. There are a few printing devices that take advantage of RGB — for example, film recorders, large inkjet printers, and some desktop color printers. In most cases, however, this mode is not used when printing files to commercial output devices, especially when color separating and using high-end digital prepress.

✦ **CMYK:** The process colors of Cyan, Magenta, Yellow, and black are used in offset printing and most commercial output devices. The color gamut is much narrower than RGB; and when you convert an image from RGB to CMYK using Photoshop's mode conversion command, you usually see some noticeable dilution of color appearing on your monitor. When exporting files to PDF directly from Photoshop or when opening files in other applications and then distilling them, you should always make your color conversions first in Photoshop.

✦ **Lab:** Lab color, in theory, encompasses all the color from both the RGB and CMYK color spaces. This color mode is based on a mathematical model to describe all perceptible color within the human universe. In practicality, its color space is limited to approximately 6 million colors, about 10+ million less than RGB color. Lab color is device-independent color, which theoretically means the color is true regardless of the device on which your image is edited and printed. Lab mode is commonly preferred by high-end color editing professionals when printing color separations on PostScript Level 2 and PostScript 3 devices. Earlier versions of PDFs saved from Lab color images had problems printing four-color separations. Now with Acrobat 6 you can print Lab images to process separations.

Cross-Reference

For more information on printing color separations, see Chapter 23.

✦ **Multichannel:** If you convert any of the other color modes to Multichannel mode, all the individual channels used to define the image color are converted to grayscale. The resulting document is a grayscale image with multiple channels. With regard to exporting to PDF, you likely won't use this mode.

✦ **Duotone:** The Duotone mode can actually support one of four individual color modes. Monotone is selectable from the Duotone mode, which holds a single color value in the image, like a tint. Duotone defines the image in two color values, Tritone in three, and Quadtone in four. When you export to PDF from Photoshop, all of these modes are supported.

✦ **Indexed Color:** Whereas the other color modes such as RGB, Lab, and CMYK define an image with a wide color gamut (up to millions of colors), the Indexed Color mode limits the total colors to a maximum of 256. Color reduction in images is ideal for Web graphics where the fewer colors significantly reduce the file sizes. You can export indexed color images directly to PDF format from Photoshop.

Table 6-1: Photoshop Color Modes

Color Mode	Export to PDF	Screen View	Print Composite	Print Separations
Bitmap	Yes	Yes	Yes	No
Grayscale	Yes	Yes	Yes	No
RGB	Yes	Yes	Yes*	No
CMYK	Yes	No	Yes	Yes

Color Mode	Export to PDF	Screen View	Print Composite	Print Separations
Lab	Yes	Yes	Yes	Yes
Multichannel	Yes	No	No	No
Duotone	Yes	Yes	No	Yes
Indexed	Yes	Yes	No	No
Spot Color (DCS 2.0)	No	No	No	No
16-bit	No	No	No	No

* When working with high-end commercial devices, CMYK is preferred.

Compression and color modes

When you choose File ➪ Save or File ➪ Save As and choose PDF as the format, the PDF Options dialog box opens after click Save. Choose a level of compression and make other choices as desired in the PDF Options dialog box and click OK. The file is saved as a PDF and can be opened in Acrobat.

Because Photoshop does not have an automatic choice for compression types, you should know that different compression choices are available depending on the color mode of the Photoshop image. Table 6-2 includes the compression types available according to the color mode of the image to be exported.

Table 6-2: Compression Methods According to Color Mode

Color Mode	Export to PDF	Compression Type
Bitmap	Yes	No compression option
Grayscale	Yes	JPEG/ZIP
RGB	Yes	JPEG/ZIP
CMYK	Yes	JPEG/ZIP
Lab	Yes	JPEG/ZIP
Duotone	Yes	JPEG/ZIP
Indexed	Yes	ZIP only
Multichannel	No	N/A

Acquiring PDF files in Photoshop

PDF documents may be composed of many different elements depending on the design of the original file. If you design a page in a layout program for which you create text, import Photoshop images, and also import EPS illustrations, the different elements retain their characteristics when converted to PDF. Text, for example, remains as text, raster images such as Photoshop files remain as raster images, and EPS illustrations remain as EPS vector objects. Although the images, text, and line art may be compressed when distilled in Acrobat Distiller, all the text and line art remain as vector elements. In Photoshop, if you open an illustration or text created in any program other than Photoshop, the document elements are rasterized and lose their vector-based attributes. Photoshop rasterizes PDF documents much as it does with any EPS file.

In Photoshop, you have several methods of handling PDF imports. PDF documents opened in Photoshop are handled with the File ➪ Open command, File ➪ Place command, File ➪ Import command, and through a File ➪ Automate command. Each of the methods offers different options, so let's take the methods individually.

Opening PDF files in Photoshop

When you choose File ➪ Open, the Open dialog box will permit you to choose from formats in a pull-down menu for Files of type. The three file formats listed that specifically reference PDF documents are

✦ **Generic PDF:** Any PDF file from any producer application can be opened in Photoshop. Files other than those saved from Photoshop are rasterized by Photoshop's Generic Rasterizer.

✦ **Photoshop PDF:** PDFs originating from Photoshop and those containing layers where vector art and/or type are preserved and appear on different layers when opened. If the PDF was not produced from Photoshop and this file type is selected, Photoshop automatically switches to Generic PDF and prompts you for rasterizing attributes.

✦ **Acrobat TouchUp Image:** When working on a PDF in Acrobat, you have an opportunity to edit a raster- or vector-based object in Photoshop or an illustration program. Using the Select Object tool, hold down the Ctrl key (Option Key on Macintosh) and double-click on the object or open a context menu and select Edit Image. The respective image opens in one of the supporting applications. The object you open is saved as a TouchUp Image. If you save the file and reopen it in Photoshop, this format is recognized by Photoshop as a file exported from a PDF file.

Cross-Reference   For information on dynamically editing objects and images from PDF documents, see Chapters 8 and 9.

Placing PDF files in Photoshop

Instead of opening a PDF file through the File ➪ Open command, you can use File ➪ Place to add a PDF within an open Photoshop document. Placing PDFs also requires rasterization. The advantage of using Place instead of Open is the placed PDF won't fully rasterize until you finish scaling it. When you select File ➪ Place, the Place dialog box opens. Locate the file to place in Photoshop and click Place. The file appears within a rectangle containing handles in each corner. Click and drag a handle to resize the placed image. You can size the image up or down in the Photoshop document window. When finished scaling, press the Enter (Windows) or Return (Macintosh) key. Pressing the key lets Photoshop know you have accepted the size. At that point the image is rasterized. The disadvantage of using Place over the Open command is you have no control over resolution and color mode. The PDF is rasterized at the same resolution and mode where the document is placed.

Importing PDFs in Photoshop

When you choose the File ➪ Import ➪ PDF Image command and select a PDF file to open, is the PDF Import Image dialog box opens. The file you import, however, won't be a PDF document. Photoshop searches for images contained in the PDF file and permits you to selectively import a single image or all images found in the document. You can navigate thumbnail views before electing to import an image and see a thumbnail in the PDF Image Import dialog by clicking on the up and down arrows or dragging the elevator bar as shown in Figure 6-3.

Figure 6-3: The PDF Image Import dialog box displays thumbnails of each image contained in a PDF file. To navigate, scroll with the elevator bar or click on the up and down arrows.

When you select the Import All button, all the images contained in the PDF are imported at the original size, resolution, and color mode they were when the PDF was created. Because the images are already raster images, Photoshop's rasterizer isn't used.

Multi-page PDF imports

The File ⇨ Automate ⇨ Multi-page PDF to PSD command is similar to a Photoshop Action in that it automatically opens PDF files, rasterizes them in Photoshop, and saves the files to a destination directory specified by the user. When you select this command in Photoshop, a dialog box opens, enabling you to determine the same rasterizing characteristics as used with the Open command. When you select the menu command, the dialog box shown in Figure 6-4 opens.

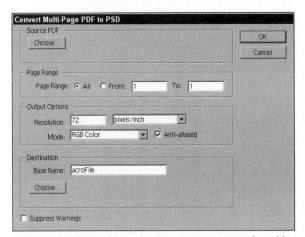

Figure 6-4: The Multi-Page PDF to PSD command enables conversion of several pages within a PDF file to be rasterized in Photoshop.

The dialog box offers several choices for automating the sequence that include

✦ **Choose:** Select the source PDF file by clicking the Choose button at the top left of the dialog box, as shown in Figure 6-4. Photoshop can't use multiple PDF files as a source. You are limited to opening a single PDF document. The document, of course, can have multiple pages.

✦ **Page Range:** You can select all pages in the PDF or a range of pages. The page range choices require you to know ahead of time the number of pages in the PDF file to be converted. If you select pages by clicking the From radio button and choose a range outside the PDF page range, a warning dialog box opens indicating the problem. For example, if you attempt to select pages 21 to 22 in a 20-page PDF file, pages 21 and 22 are out of range. Photoshop opens a warning dialog box to inform you the first page it attempts to convert is out of range. If you attempt to convert pages 18 to 22 in the same example, Photoshop converts pages 18 through 20 and then opens another dialog box, informing you that not all pages within the specified range exist in the PDF document.

✦ **Output Options:** These options are the same as those for single-page conversions. You can choose the resolution, color mode, and whether anti-aliasing is used. One option you do not have available in the dialog box is the capability to choose size and proportions. If you want to size the PSD files, you can set up a Photoshop Action to open the saved files and resize them with values used in creating the Action.

✦ **Base Name:** The base name you specify appears in the filename for the saved PSD files. If you use a name like *acroFile*, Photoshop saves the PSD files as acroFile0001.psd, acroFile0002.psd, acroFile0003.psd, and so on. Photoshop adds the 000*n* and .psd extension to the filename you supply as the base name.

✦ **Choose (Destination):** The second Choose button is used for the destination folder or directory. You can highlight a directory name in the hierarchy list and click the Select button, or you can open a directory in the hierarchy list and click the Select button.

Rasterizing PDF files

For those conversion methods that require rasterization, such as the Open command discussed in the "Opening PDF files in Photoshop" section, Photoshop opens a dialog box where user-defined rasterization attributes are supplied. If you have a multipage document and you use the Open command, the first dialog box that appears is the PDF Page Selector dialog box. Select a page to open and click OK. The second dialog box that opens is the Rasterize Generic PDF Format dialog box shown in Figure 6-5.

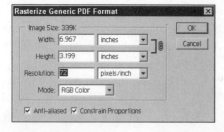

Figure 6-5: The Rasterize Generic PDF Format dialog box enables you to define the rasterization attributes.

If a single-page PDF file is opened, the PDF Page Selector dialog box does not open. Regardless of whether you select a page within a range of pages or a document with only one page, Photoshop wants some information before it rasterizes the PDF page. The rasterization attributes you can control in the Rasterize Generic PDF Format dialog box include

✦ **Width/Height:** You can determine the physical size of the final Photoshop image by changing the width and/or height of the rasterized image. The default size of the original PDF document is shown when the dialog box first opens.

✦ **Resolution:** The default resolution regardless of the size is 72 ppi. You can choose to supply a user-defined resolution in this dialog box. If the original raster images were at a resolution different from the amount supplied in this dialog box, the images are resampled. Text and line art will be rasterized according to the amount you define in the dialog box without interpolation.

Image resampling is a method for tossing away pixels (downsampling) or manufacturing new pixels (upsampling). Either way the process is referred to as interpolation where Photoshop makes some guesses as to what pixels to toss or what pixels to create.

✦ **Mode:** The color mode is selected from the pull-down menu that includes choices for Grayscale, RGB, CMYK, and Lab color.

✦ **Anti-Aliased:** This option is used to smooth edges of text, line art, and images that are interpolated through resampling. If you disable this option, text appears with jagged edges. Text in PDF files rasterized in Photoshop looks best when anti-aliased and when the display is more consistent with the original font used when the PDF was created.

✦ **Constrain Proportions:** If you change a value in either the Width or the Height field and the Constrain Proportions option is enabled, the value in the other field (Height or Width) is automatically calculated by Photoshop to preserve proportional sizing. When the check box is disabled, both the Width and Height are independent values — that is, they have no effect on each other. If you don't preserve proportions, the rasterized file is likely to be distorted.

One problem you may encounter when rasterizing PDF documents in Photoshop is maintaining font integrity. Photoshop displays a warning dialog box when it encounters a font that is not installed on your system, which presents problems when you attempt to rasterize the font. If such a problem exists, the font can be eliminated from the document or changed after you open the file in Photoshop and edit the type layer.

When files are password protected, users are prevented from opening a PDF file in Photoshop or any other application. If you attempt to open a secure document, an alert dialog box opens. The dialog box indicates the PDF file can't be parsed. If you encounter such a dialog box, open it in an Acrobat viewer and check the security settings.

For information about Acrobat security, see Chapter 19.

If you want to convert catalogs and lengthy documents to HTML-supported files, the PDF to PSD conversion can be useful. You can set up Actions in Photoshop to downsample images, convert color modes, and save copies of the converted files in HTML-supported formats.

Comments and Photoshop

Photoshop supports use of Comment tools. You can create a note or sound attachment in Photoshop much like you do in Acrobat. The comment is an object and won't be rasterized with any other Photoshop data. You can delete the annotation at any time by selecting the Note icon or Attach Sound icon and pressing the Backspace (Windows) or Delete (Macintosh) key.

Comments from PDF files can also be imported into Photoshop. You must use the Comment Note or tool because Photoshop does not support the other comment types available in Acrobat. If a Note is contained in a PDF document and you want to import the Note into Photoshop, select File ➪ Import ➪ Annotations. Photoshop can import an annotation only from PDF formatted files.

In addition, Photoshop can import Form Data Format files. Data exported from Acrobat in FDF format can be chosen as another import format from the File ⇨ Import ⇨ Annotations command. Data from FDF files are imported in a comment or a note comment window.

Cross-Reference   For more information about comment notes and sound attachments, see Chapter 14.

Acrobat and Microsoft Office Applications

On Windows and Macintosh, Microsoft Word, Excel, and PowerPoint accommodate a macro developed by Adobe Systems called PDFMaker. When the PDFMaker macro is installed in Office applications in Office 97 and higher, the PDFMaker macro appears in the toolbar for all three applications. When installing Acrobat and the Office products, be certain to first install the Office applications. The Acrobat installer automatically detects the Office applications and installs the PDFMaker macro.

The PDFMaker macro is used to convert Office files, Microsoft Visio Files (Windows), Microsoft Project files (Windows), AutoDesk AutoCAD files (Windows), and Internet Explorer (Windows) files to PDF. Depending on the authoring program you have different options for assigning attributes to the resulting PDF documents.

All the aforementioned files can also be printed to PostScript and converted to PDF with the Acrobat Distiller software. However, you have many more advantages using the PDFMaker macro, and as a matter of practice, you should use this option over using Acrobat Distiller. Among the most important advantages is the ability to produce structured and tagged PDF files, thereby making them accessible and having more options for editing the content.

Cross-Reference   For more information on using Acrobat Distiller, see Chapter 7. For more information on working with accessible and tagged PDF documents, see Chapter 18.

Microsoft Word

Of all the Office applications, Microsoft Word gives you great support for PDF file creation. Microsoft Word is the only word-processing application that provides access to the structural data of the document. The structural data of the Word document such as titles, heads, tables, paragraphs, figure captions, and so on can be converted to tagged Bookmarks. Tagged Bookmarks give you much more control over the PDF content. You can navigate to the element structures, and move, copy, extract, and delete pages through menu commands in the Bookmarks tab.

PDFMaker offers several tools to control PDF file creation from within Microsoft Word. After you install Acrobat and later open Word, three Acrobat icons appear on the far left side of the toolbar.

The first of these three icons is the Convert to Adobe PDF macro. Clicking on this icon opens a dialog box where you supply the filename and destination. Enter a name and choose a destination, then click on the Save button to create the PDF.

Note   Three tool icons are installed in Windows. Two tool icons are installed on the Macintosh.

The second icon is Convert to Adobe PDF and Email. This tool performs the same function as the Convert to Adobe PDF tool and then adds the resulting PDF as an e-mail attachment. The user-defined default e-mail application is automatically launched and the PDF is attached to the message you send. Figure 6-6 shows an e-mail attachment created from the Convert to Adobe PDF and Email tool.

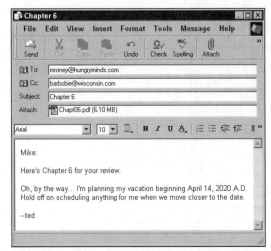

Figure 6-6: After you click on the Convert to Adobe PDF and Email tool in Microsoft Word, the PDF is created and automatically placed as an e-mail attachment in your default email application.

The third tool installed in Microsoft Office Applications is Convert to PDF and Send for Review (Windows only). When you click on the tool, the Word document is converted to PDF with the PDFMaker macro, your default e-mail program is launched, and the resulting PDF is attached to the e-mail message for commencing a review process. In Figure 6-7 you can see the default e-mail message prepared by Acrobat with instructions to recipients for beginning the review.

Cross-Reference   For more information concerning e-mail reviews, see Chapter 14.

In addition to tools, two menus (Windows only) are also installed with the PDFMaker macro. The first menu is the Adobe PDF menu. The second menu is the Acrobat Comments menu.

You have the same menu selections in the Adobe PDF menu as you have available for the tools (Convert to Adobe PDF, Convert to Adobe PDF and Email, Convert to Adobe PDF and Send for Review). In addition, a fourth menu command controls the PDF settings where attribute assignments are made for the PDF conversion. Conversion options from the Acrobat PDF Maker dialog box enable you to adjust the attributes for the PDF conversion process. As a matter of practice, you should visit the conversion settings each time you launch Word and prepare to convert documents to PDF to understand what attribute assignments are applied to the resultant PDF documents.

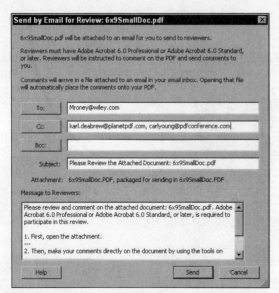

Figure 6-7: After you click on the Convert to Adobe PDF and Send for Review tool in Microsoft Word, the PDF is created and automatically placed as an e-mail attachment in your default e-mail application, with instructions for recipients to participate in the review.

Changing conversion settings (Macintosh)

Windows users have an elaborate set of conversion settings they can address in menu commands when the PDFMaker macro is installed on Windows. Macintosh users may look for the menus I mention, but they won't find them in OS X or any other flavor of the Macintosh operating system. Conversion settings for Macintosh users are much more limited than their Windows cousins and you need to choose your conversion options, as much as can be done, in the Distiller Adobe PDF settings. To learn how to change the Adobe PDF settings, see Chapter 7.

Changing conversion settings (Windows)

PDFMaker prints Word documents to disk and then converts them through Distiller's Adobe PDF Settings. However, the Adobe PDF Settings used in Acrobat Distiller are only part of the attributes assigned to the conversion process. The other assignments are made in Word before the file gets to Distiller. When you choose Acrobat ➪ Change Conversion Settings, the Adobe PDFMaker dialog box opens. In the dialog box, four tabs offer attribute choices for how the PDF is ultimately created. The tabs are Settings, Security, Word, and Bookmarks.

Cross-Reference   Acrobat Distiller is covered in Chapter 7. All subsequent references to Distiller in this chapter are explained in more detail in Chapter 7.

Settings

The Settings tab is the first of the four tabs where you select options. At the top of the Settings tab is a pull-down menu for Conversion Settings. When you open the pull-down menu, you make a choice for the settings used in Distiller to convert the file to a PDF. If you want to edit the settings or create a new Adobe PDF Setting, click on the Advanced Settings button shown in Figure 6-8.

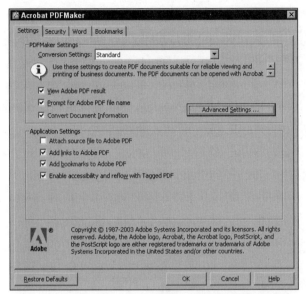

Figure 6-8: The Settings tab offers you choices for selecting the Adobe PDF Settings used by Acrobat Distiller to convert the file.

Options in the Settings tab include

✦ **View Adobe PDF result:** When the PDF is created, the document opens in Acrobat if the check box is enabled. If disabled, the PDF is created and the Word file remains in view.

✦ **Prompt for Adobe PDF file name:** If the check box is enabled, you won't inadvertently overwrite a file with the same name. Leaving this check box enabled is a good idea.

✦ **Convert Document Information:** Document information created in Word is added to the PDF Document Properties.

✦ **Attach source file to Adobe PDF:** If you want to attach the Word file from which the PDF was created, enable the check box.

✦ **Add links to Adobe PDF:** Links created in Word are converted to links in the PDF document.

✦ **Add bookmarks to Adobe PDF:** Bookmarks are created from Word style sheets. Check the box here to convert styles and headings to Bookmarks. Make selections for what styles and headings are converted to Bookmarks in the Bookmarks tab.

✦ **Enable accessibility and reflow with Tagged PDF:** Document structure tags are created. Accessibility meeting Microsoft accessibility standards for visually challenged and developmentally disabled that are contained in the Word document are preserved in the PDF. Reflowing text enables the Acrobat user to use the Reflow text tool. As a matter of default, leave this check box enabled. Tagged PDF documents also help you export the PDF text back out to a word processor with more data integrity than when exporting files without tags.

Note   If you enable accessibility and reflow, the file sizes of your PDF documents result in larger sizes compared to exporting to PDF without accessibility and tags. If you need to produce the smallest file sizes for specific purposes where you know accessibility and preserving structure are not needed, disable the checkbox.

Security

Click on the Security tab to open options for security settings. Security options for permissions are only available for High-Bit encryption (128-bit). If you choose to add security from the Word options, the PDF document is compatible with Acrobat 5.0 viewers and greater.

Cross-Reference   For specific definitions of the security options, see Chapter 19.

Word

Click on the Word tab to choose options for Word content as shown in Figure 6-9.

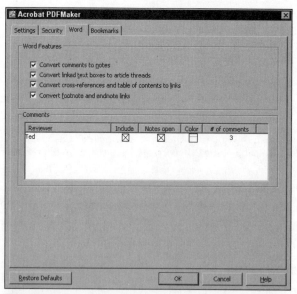

Figure 6-9: The Word tab contains items specific to some of the content in Word that can be converted in the resulting PDF document.

Options on the Word tab include

✦ **Convert comments to notes:** Notes can be converted to annotation comments that will appear in a text note in the PDF file.

✦ **Convert linked text boxes to article threads:** Text body copy defined with a style can be converted to an article thread. When different styles are used, the article threads are unique to each style.

✦ **Convert cross-references and table of contents to links:** Any cross-references, such as Table of Contents and indexes, will have links to their respective destinations. These links are preserved in the PDF file.

✦ **Convert footnote and endnote links:** Bookmark links are added for all footnotes and endnotes.

✦ **Comments:** The lower window lists all comments in the file. If you check the box in the Include column, the comments are converted to Acrobat comments. The Notes open column enables you to set the default for note comments with open note popup windows.

Bookmarks

In the Bookmarks dialog box shown in Figure 6-10 are two items that can determine what Bookmarks will be created in the PDF file. These are

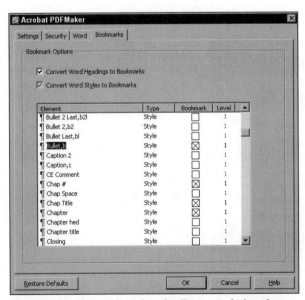

Figure 6-10: The Bookmarks tab offers two choices for determining what Bookmarks are created in the PDF file.

✦ **Convert Word Headings to Bookmarks:** Word headings can be converted to Bookmarks. In the box below the check boxes, a list of all headings and styles contained in the Word document appears. Click on the box under the Bookmark column to determine what heads are converted to Bookmarks.

✦ **Convert Word Styles to Bookmarks:** Style sheets that are user defined can be selected for conversion to Bookmarks. Scroll the list of elements and place a check mark for the styles you want to convert.

After you select the options in the Adobe PDF maker dialog box, you can click on the Convert to PDF tool or select the menu option to convert the file.

Working with comments (Windows)

The other menu installed with the PDFMaker is the Acrobat Comments menu. The commands in the menu address handling comments in Word and exchanging comments with PDF documents. The menu items are

✦ **Import Comments from Acrobat:** The file from which you import comments must have been created with the PDFMaker from Word 2002/XP. When you select the menu item, the Import Comments from Adobe Acrobat help window opens. Read the helpful tips on how to import comments and click on the Yes button to proceed. The next dialog box that opens is Import Comments from Adobe Acrobat, as shown in Figure 6-11. In the dialog box, you make choices for what files to select, what comments to import, and whether you want to filter the comments.

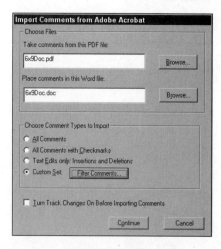

Figure 6-11: The Import Comments from Adobe Acrobat dialog box offers choices for file selection and the comment types to import into the Word document.

✦ **Continue Integration Process:** This continues the integration of PDF comments in the Word document for text edits such as inserts and deletions. If review tracking is on, you can merge tracked changes.

✦ **Accept All Changes in Document:** After the comment integration, select this menu command to accept the comments. Comments such as text marked for deletion are deleted; text marked with insertion adds the inserted comments, etc.

✦ **Delete All Comments in Document:** All comments imported from the PDF document are deleted from the Word file.

✦ **Reviewing Toolbar:** Comment tools like those you have in Acrobat for comment navigation, review tracking, accepting/rejecting comments, and so on are added to the Word Toolbar Well as shown in Figure 6-12. To hide the tools, uncheck the command by selecting it in the menu.

✦ **Show Instructions:** The dialog box that opens when you choose the Import Comments from Acrobat command (see the first bullet in this list) also opens when you choose the Show Instructions menu command. See Figure 6-13.

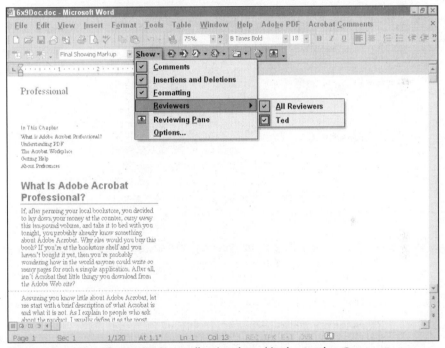

Figure 6-12: When the Reviewing Toolbar is selected in the Acrobat Comments menu, the comment and review tools are made visible in the Microsoft Word Toolbar Well.

Working with custom page sizes (Windows)

The many different options available for PDF conversion from Microsoft Word require that you practice a little and become familiar with the settings that work best in your workflow. There's no substitute for spending some quality time studying the settings and observing the results. Many of the options discussed earlier in this chapter are intuitive and should be easily understood. A less intuitive task is creating PDF documents from custom page sizes in Word. To create PDFs from non-standard page sizes requires a little configuration. To understand how to create a PDF document from a Word file with a non-standard page size, follow these steps.

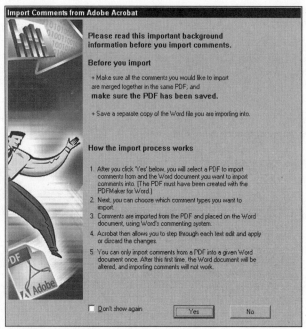

Figure 6-13: You can access the instructions at any time by selecting Show Instructions. In the dialog box, you see steps to follow for importing comments from Acrobat into a Word file.

STEPS: Creating PDFs from Word files using non-standard page sizes

1. **Open the Adobe PDF Printer.** When you create a Word document with a non-standard page size, you need to add the same page size in the Adobe PDF Printer. The first step is to open the Adobe PDF printer from the Start menu by choosing Settings ➪ Printers and Faxes ➪ Adobe PDF.

2. **Open the printer properties.** In the Adobe PDF Printer dialog box, choose Printer ➪ Properties as shown in Figure 6-14. The Adobe PDF Properties dialog box opens.

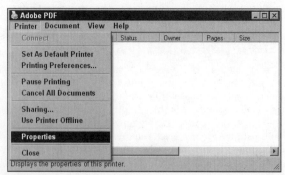

Figure 6-14: Open the Properties dialog box by choosing Printer ➪ Properties.

3. **Open the Printing Preferences.** In the Adobe PDF Properties dialog box, shown in Figure 6-15, click on the Printing Preferences button.

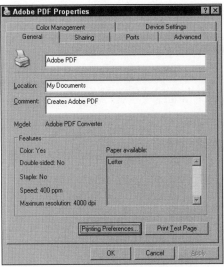

Figure 6-15: In the Adobe PDF Properties dialog box, click on the Printing Preferences button to open the Adobe PDF Printing Preferences dialog box.

4. **Add a custom page.** In the Adobe PDF Printing Preferences dialog box, you'll see a button titled Add Custom Page. Click on the button to open the Add Custom Paper Size dialog box, where the page sizes are defined.

5. **Set the paper size attributes.** In the Add Custom Paper Size dialog box, supply a name in the Paper Names field. It is important to add a new name because overwriting fixed paper sizes is not permitted. Add the values for the Width and Height. In Figure 6-16 I created a custom page size for 6 × 9 inches.

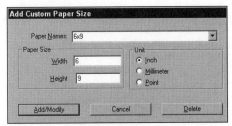

Figure 6-16: Add a name for the new paper size, enter the page size values, and click on the Add/Modify button.

6. **Return to MS Word.** Click on the Add/Modify button in the Add Custom Paper Size dialog box and click OK through the dialog boxes until you arrive at the original Adobe PDF printer dialog box. Close the window and open Word.

7. **Select the new page size.** In Word, choose File ➪ Page Setup. From the pull-down menu for Paper size, select the new paper size you added to the Adobe PDF Printer. In Figure 6-17 you can see the 6 × 9 page I added to my Adobe PDF printer. You can begin a new document or open an existing document and reform the pages to the new page size.

8. **Convert to Adobe PDF.** Click on the Convert to Adobe PDF tool in the Word Toolbar Well. If you enabled View Adobe PDF result in the Adobe PDFMaker Settings tab, the resulting PDF opens in Acrobat.

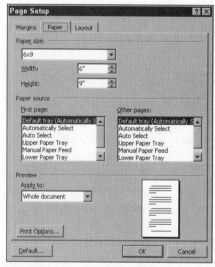

Figure 6-17: In Microsoft Word, choose File ➪ Page Setup and choose the new paper size in the Paper size pull-down menu.

Note   Creating custom page sizes is particularly important for programs like Microsoft Visio, Microsoft Project, and AutoDesk AutoCAD where non-standard sizes are commonly used. Acrobat supports a page size of up to 200 inches square. Make certain you have the proper page size defined for the Adobe PDF printer before attempting to Convert to Adobe PDF.

Microsoft Excel

The PDFMaker can also be used with Microsoft Excel. Options for conversion settings are common between the programs with a few exceptions. Excel Bookmarks are created from different sheets in an Excel Workbook. Spreadsheets and charts are converted with the PDFMaker macro and the menu options for the Adobe PDF menu are the same in Excel as in Word. Excel doesn't support the Adobe Comments menu, but you can convert Excel files to PDF and send them for an e-mail review.

Cross-Reference Microsoft PowerPoint also uses the PDFMaker for conversion to PDF. For information concerning PowerPoint conversions to PDF, see Chapter 21.

Microsoft Publisher

Microsoft Publisher began as a simple product designed to produce newsletters, fliers, brochures, and pamphlets on desktop printers. Some people in the user community began to take their Publisher files to service centers for output to film and commercial printing. Most service center technicians will tell you their greatest nightmares have often been from attempting to print Publisher files.

When Microsoft Publisher 2000 was introduced, Microsoft made several efforts to accommodate professional printing. The newest incarnation of Publisher supports all the controls needed to output to image setters and on-demand printing devices. Color separations, crop and registration marks, and halftone frequencies are all supported in Publisher's print dialog box.

PDFMaker isn't available in the Publisher toolbar; therefore, the way to produce PDF files is to first print the file to disk as PostScript, and then distill it in Acrobat Distiller. If all the print controls are correctly selected through Publisher's print dialog box, you should have no problem producing files for high-end output. As many service centers are Macintosh based, the best way to get Publisher files to them is by delivering PDFs.

Acrobat and Illustration Programs

Illustration programs, at least the most popular ones, are vector-based applications. You can import raster data such as Photoshop images; however, all you create with tools in an illustration program is object-oriented (vector) art. Programs such as Adobe Illustrator, Macromedia FreeHand, and CorelDraw are among the most popular, and they all have the capability to save files in EPS format as well as export directly to PDF.

With programs such as Adobe Photoshop and Adobe Acrobat, little significant competition exists among manufacturers for market share. Photoshop clearly dominates the market in photo-imaging applications, and Acrobat has no worthy counterpart. Illustration programs, on the other hand, have some pretty fierce competition. CorelDraw has a tremendous share of the PC user market, and it clearly overshadows Illustrator and FreeHand. On the Mac side, most of Corel's attempts have seen failure, which leaves the major market first to Adobe, then to Macromedia. Because these three companies are battling to keep current market share and gobble up more, the advances in feature-rich applications have been aggressive.

The competitive nature of the manufacturers of these products can present some problems for all of the end users. With each revision of illustration software, it appears as though the manufacturers are attempting to make the programs all things to all people. Each of these three illustration programs uses a different dialect when exporting files in PostScript, which may impact your output for distillation in Acrobat Distiller. Add to this the difference in the way the PostScript coding is handled, and the addition of new whiz-bang features, and some additional printing or distillation problems can occur. On the other hand, these programs all export to PDF and if the PDFs are created properly, they are often printed successfully at the print shop.

Macromedia FreeHand

Whereas Adobe Illustrator has a weak set of print controls, FreeHand has always excelled at printing files either as composites or color separations. FreeHand has great control over bleeds, too. FreeHand documents can be printed to disk as PostScript files and distilled in Acrobat Distiller or exported directly from FreeHand to PDF. When using Distiller you have much more control over the attributes assigned for professional printing.

FreeHand does permit user-defined compression control and font embedding, which makes it suitable for many PDF document purposes. To export a FreeHand document to PDF, choose File ➪ Export ➪ PDF. The Export Document dialog box opens. Click on the Options button where you choose options for the PDF. All the PDF attributes are assigned in the Options dialog box.

In the Image Compression settings are two pull-down menus where you set the color and grayscale image compression. The amount of compression from the available choices is the same amount available with the Adobe PDF settings. FreeHand supports color conversion as a choice from a pull-down menu below the compression settings. You have three choices that include RGB, CMYK, and RGB & CMYK. Depending on your output needs be certain to make the correct choice.

Tip   If you want screen images for CD-ROM replication, Web graphics, or file exchanges with other users, be certain to choose the Export command for creating PDFs rather than using Acrobat Distiller. Files printed to PostScript from FreeHand and later distilled from RGB colors don't retain the original color values as well as exporting to PDF from FreeHand.

CorelDraw

Whereas Adobe Illustrator is the purest of the PostScript-compliant applications, CorelDraw has commonly been the most deviant. Some nuances with PostScript code have at times been a little problematic, but Corel has had a lot of experience in imaging and is developing as a strong contender in the Illustration application software market. Hence, it comes as no surprise that Corel 11 offers one of the most sophisticated PDF exports available from almost any application.

You won't find the Corel export buried among the Save formats or nested in a list of Export options. Corel has placed a separate menu item dedicated to PDF under the File menu. When you choose File ➪ Publish to PDF, the first of many dialog boxes opens. The Publish to PDF dialog box contains several tabs, much like Distiller's Adobe PDF Settings, where you select file attributes.

Without going into the elaborate number of dialog boxes for adding Job Tickets and many other attributes assigned when you select Publish to PDF, there is one new item in CorelDraw 11 worth mentioning. CorelDraw is the first of the illustration programs to support PDF/X exports. When you open the Publish to PDF dialog box shown in Figure 6-18, select PDF/X-1 from the Compatibility pull-down menu.

Cross-Reference   If you don't know what a PDF/X file is or anything about the various versions of PDF/X, look over Chapter 23 where all the PDF/X information is contained.

The caveat in using Corel's PDF/X format is that it doesn't support newer PDF/X versions that are available with Acrobat 6.0 Distiller Adobe PDF settings. Although it may be tempting, distilling PostScript files is preferred over PDF/X exports from CorelDraw for commercial printing. For other purposes, you can use the Publish to PDF command and make choices from the many dialog box options for how the PDF conversion is processed.

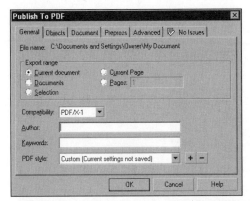

Figure 6-18: CorelDraw supports exporting PDF/X complaint documents. Select either PDF/X from the Compatibility pull-down menu and click OK to save the file as PDF/X.

Adobe Illustrator

Adobe Illustrator, like other Adobe programs, is built on core PDF technology. As a matter of fact, the PDF specification in the past was developed by the Adobe Illustrator development team. It should be apparent then that one of the best applications supporting direct export to PDF is Adobe Illustrator.

Illustrator has evolved to a sophisticated integration with PDF and supports through direct export the following: transparency, edibility, layers, blending modes, text, and filters. Further integration with the program in non-PDF workflows embraces exports for Web design where its current iteration now supports one-step optimization for formats such as GIF, JPEG, PNG, SWF, and SVG.

Saving PDFs from Adobe Illustrator

To export PDF files from Adobe Illustrator, you use the File ⇨ Save command. The format options available to you include the native Illustrator format, Illustrator EPS, SVG, SVG Compressed, and Adobe PDF. In Illustrator, choose File ⇨ Save from a new document window. A Save dialog box opens that enables you to name the file, choose the destination, and select one of the formats just noted. When you select Acrobat PDF and click the Save button, the Adobe PDF Format Options dialog box opens where various PDF options appear as shown in Figure 6-19.

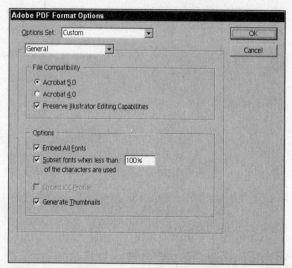

Figure 6-19: When you select the PDF format and click the Save button in the Save dialog box, a new dialog box opens, enabling you to select PDF export options.

These options include

✦ **PDF Options Set:** Three choices are available for PDF options from the pull-down menu. You can choose from Default, Screen Optimized, or Custom. Choices you make here change the downsampling and compression options according to the output requirements.

   • **Default:** When you select this option, the Preserve Illustrator Editing Capabilities check box is enabled and compression settings are switched to Zip compression. Default is intended for print graphics, although you probably want to view options individually and select custom choices for various printing output.

   • **Screen Optimized:** When you select Screen Optimized all compression defaults to screen resolutions and the compression method changes to JPEG compression. File sizes are larger when the Illustrator editing capabilities are preserved, so this check box is disabled for screen graphics.

   • **Custom:** Custom doesn't necessarily hold a set of preset values. It is designed to accommodate custom options you determine necessary for your output needs. If you make any changes in either the options or the compression settings, Illustrator automatically selects the Custom options in the Options Set pull-down menu to inform you that a change from one of the presets has been made.

✦ **General:** The pull-down menu below the Options Set menu offers two choices. By default General is selected. After making the choices in this dialog box, click on the pull-down menu and select Compression to advance to compression choices (see the last bullet in this section).

✦ **File Compatibility:** Three choices are available in the File Compatibility section of the options dialog box. Here you can set the file compatibility and determine whether the PDF will retain the Illustrator editing capabilities.

- **Acrobat 5.0:** Unless you have special needs for exchanging files with users of earlier versions of Acrobat, the version 5.0 compatibility should be your default. Transparency created in Illustrator 9.0 or 10 is preserved with only the Acrobat 5.0 compatibility.

- **Acrobat 4.0:** For the rare circumstances where version 4.0 compatibility is needed, the choice can be made here. Be aware that any objects created with transparency flatten the artwork and convert the type to outlines.

- **Preserve Illustrator Editing Capabilities:** For those who have attempted to edit PDF files in Illustrator, you know there have been many problems with nested grouped objects, masking, and handling text. With this option, PDF files are preserved in terms of their editing capabilities once they are saved as PDF and reopened in Illustrator. For all but screen and Web graphics, enabling this check box should be your default.

✦ **Options:** The Options section of the dialog box includes choices for font handling and color management.

- **Embed All Fonts:** Font Embedding is available with Illustrator's direct save to PDF. Some fonts, such as protected Japanese fonts, can't be embedded in the PDF.

- **Subset fonts when less than [ ]:** Font subsetting is handled the same way here as it is handled in Acrobat Distiller. One thing you'll notice with Illustrator is the font subset defaults to 100% when you select the Screen Optimized Option Set. This default is the same as Distiller; however, you may want to change the value when saving PDFs for the Web. Using lower values helps economize space, especially when hosting long text documents like newsletters or product catalogs.

> **Cross-Reference**
> For more information on font embedding, subsetting, and font permissions, see Chapter 7.

- **Embed ICC Profile:** In order for the check box to be active, you must have an ICC profile identified and available for embedding. If no color management is used in the Illustrator file, the check box remains grayed out. To select color profiles open the Edit ⇨ Color Settings menu. After determining your color management policies, save the PDF with the selected profiles embedded. Color management must be assigned before you attempt to save the file. If you need to embed a profile and the option is grayed out, cancel out of the dialog box and choose your profile. Return to the Save as Acrobat PDF dialog box and then select the color management options.

- **Generate Thumbnails:** Because creating thumbnails increases file size, the Screen Optimized Options Set disables the check box. If using the Default Option Set, Generate Thumbnails is enabled. For most output needs, you'll want to create PDFs without thumbnails. If print is your intended output and you select the Default options, disable this check box.

✦ **Compression:** Compression settings, like font subsetting, change from the defaults associated with the choices you make in the PDF Options Set. If you want to use a different level of compression or manually set the compression type, you make those changes here. Also, the downsampling amounts are established in this dialog box. While the Compression options are in view, you change the PDF Options Set and make your choices according to the attributes of the PDF file to be created.

When you click OK in the PDF Export Options dialog box from either the settings for General or Compression, the document is saved in PDF format. From Illustrator, the file is converted to PDF directly, and Distiller isn't introduced in the background.

Note   Notice there are no options for viewing the PDF and no opportunity to supply document information in the PDF Export Options dialog box within Adobe Illustrator.

Converting EPS files to PDF

Any one of the illustration and layout programs mentioned in this chapter in one way or another can create an EPS file. In years past, EPS files had their place and distilling EPS was at times preferred as a workaround for resolving printing problems. With the introduction of Acrobat 6, you have many different means for preparing files for suitable output on commercial printing equipment.

With Acrobat 6 there is seldom a need to either print to PostScript or export to EPS from Adobe Illustrator. Through the options available in Acrobat Professional for preflighting PDF documents and creating PDF/X files from application exports to PDF, you have all the tools necessary for successfully printing files. Although EPS files can be converted to PDF with the Acrobat Distiller software, don't bother with saving your Illustrator files to EPS and distilling them.

Illustration programs and layers

As you can see in the PDF Options dialog box in Adobe Illustrator (refer to Figure 6-19), the file format compatibility options include Acrobat 4 and Acrobat 5. The dialog box illustrated was from Adobe Illustrator 10, a predecessor to Adobe Acrobat 6. Likewise CorelDraw 11 and Macromedia FreeHand 10 were developed before the introduction of Adobe Acrobat 6 and the release of the PDF 1.5 specification. Therefore, although each of the programs discussed supports creating and saving layer files, none of the versions support direct export to PDF with Acrobat 6 Compatibility. If using one of these programs, don't waste time on struggling to preserve layers in a PDF export.

Cross-Reference   For more information on creating layered PDF documents and understanding the requirements for producing files with visible layers in Acrobat, see Chapter 17.

Acrobat and Layout Programs

Contenders in the high-end imaging arena with regard to layout applications are Adobe Systems and Quark, Inc. Adobe markets PageMaker, FrameMaker, and InDesign. Quark's flagship program is QuarkXPress. Although Microsoft Publisher is a favorite among Microsoft Office users, it hasn't had much impact within the professional design market. See my discussion of Publisher earlier in the chapter in the section "Microsoft Publisher." The remaining layout programs are all suited for handling PDFs, so let's look at them individually.

With all the layout programs listed here you have options for both exporting and importing PDFs. With InDesign, the export and import features are built into the application. With PageMaker and QuarkXPress you need a plug-in or XTension, respectively.

Exporting to PDF from Adobe InDesign

To begin this discussion on InDesign I want to offer a confession and perhaps some personal opinion. For years I favored either Aldus/Adobe PageMaker or QuarkXPress. I grabbed one or the other routinely to produce all the files seen at my conference sessions, hosted on my Web site, and any other document with multiple pages that was ultimately converted to PDF.

Frankly, when Adobe InDesign was first introduced, I was disappointed and experienced problems with printing files on commercial printing equipment as well as just adapting to the new user interface in InDesign.

All that changed with the introduction of System X on the Macintosh and InDesign's support for running native in Apple's new operating system. Since that time and since the introduction of Acrobat 6, I find Adobe InDesign to be one of the best applications to work with Acrobat. As a personal choice, InDesign is my favorite program for page layouts and seamless support for producing PDF documents.

With InDesign, you create PDFs via the File ⇨ Export menu. Before you begin, be certain to select the Adobe PDF Printer. When the Export command is executed, the Export dialog box opens asking for the destination and filename. Advancing to the Export PDF dialog box is where you make choices for all the document attributes for links, bookmarks, compression, printer's marks, security, and document information. Click on the Export button and the InDesign file is converted to PDF.

For prepress and commercial printing, when using InDesign 2.x you have two choices. Either create a PDF file and handle conversion to PDF/X in Acrobat, or print the file to disk as PostScript and use Acrobat Distiller to produce a PDF/X file. The best method is one you need to discover for your personal print requirements.

If your output is not intended for commercial printing, use the Export to Adobe PDF command from InDesign. When exporting to PDF from InDesign you can create accessible files with structure and tags.

Cross-Reference   For more information on using tags and creating accessible documents, see Chapter 18.

Exporting to PDF from PageMaker

Adobe PageMaker has an export command that permits export to PDF first by printing the file to PostScript, and then automatically launching Distiller in the background. With PageMaker you have a choice of holding off on the distillation by creating PostScript files that can be distilled later.

In order to export a PDF from PageMaker in versions earlier than 7.0, you must have the Export PDF plug-in properly installed on your computer. This plug-in is available free for downloading from Adobe's Web site. After you install the plug-in choose File ⇨ Export. The option available is Adobe PDF. This command only appears when the plug-in is available. If you don't see it, then the plug-in is not properly installed in the PageMaker plug-in folder. For users of PageMaker 7.x, support for export to PDF is built into the application. Just choose File ⇨ Export to export a PageMaker 7 document to PDF.

I know many users of PageMaker exist who have not switched to newer layout applications. We all tend to like the programs we know and dislike the programs we don't understand. Unfortunately, PageMaker's development has not been aggressive and support for native operation in Apple's System X is not available, nor are any of the newer compatibility formats for Acrobat PDFs available. If you decide to continue using PageMaker, your best option for producing PDFs for commercial printing is to print PostScript and let Distiller apply newer Adobe PDF settings during distillation.

Like InDesign, if your output is intended for anything but commercial printing, use the Adobe PDF Export command. In PageMaker 7 you can create accessible and tagged PDF documents like those produced from InDesign exports.

Exporting to PDF from QuarkXPress

QuarkXPress has been the premier choice of layout applications for design professionals on Macintosh computers. Quark, Inc., has paved its own road and traveled the digital highway in its own way. What has been accomplished in page layout for high-end design profession-als has been magnificent, and one only needs to look at the incredible number of Quark XTensions to see the pinnacle of success accomplished by a company that has survived on a single product in a fiercely competitive world. For all intent and purposes, the company has literally maintained its dominance in page layout software prior to version 4.0 without a major revision for almost a six-year period. No other off-the-shelf product can claim such success.

On the Windows side QuarkXPress has taken a backseat to Adobe PageMaker. More high-end professionals working in Windows tend to prefer PageMaker to QuarkXPress. Both programs are completely cross-platform and you'll find little difference between the two running on either platform.

Like PageMaker, QuarkXPress uses an addition in the form of a Quark XTension to export directly to PDF. For versions earlier than QuarkXPress 6.0, you need to an XTension from Quark's Web site. In QuarkXPress 6 and above, support for the PDF format is installed with the program. You can export to PDF and import PDFs in a Quark layout. QuarkXPress uses settings from the Adobe PDF Settings assigned in Acrobat Distiller. You can change the Adobe PDF set-tings from within Quark XPress and choose the options best suited for your output needs.

 Cross-Reference For more information on changing Adobe PDF Settings, see Chapter 7.

Exporting to PDF from Adobe FrameMaker

Adobe FrameMaker has been the choice for technical documents and publications produced by many publication designers and companies. The user guides you see shipping with all the Adobe software are created in Adobe FrameMaker. Adobe's award-winning publications such as the *Classroom in a Book* series are all printed from FrameMaker files. FrameMaker doesn't have the installed user base to match PageMaker or QuarkXPress, but the product does have significance among those who produce substantial publications and technical documents.

FrameMaker handles both an export to PDF, in which case Distiller is introduced in the pro-cess, and importing PDFs. FrameMaker combines many of the features from Microsoft Word, Adobe PageMaker, and QuarkXPress all into a single PDF producer that rivals most other application programs. If in the market for a software program needed for creating long docu-ments, technical manuals, books, or briefs, you can find none better than the easy-to-use, fea-ture-rich application of Adobe FrameMaker. The FrameMaker user is well advised to export documents to PDF for digital imaging and portability. Because FrameMaker exists more often in the commercial publications market, average consumer use is quite limited.

FrameMaker appears to be a simple program when you first look at the user interface, but it offers a robust set of tools that enable you to deliver HTML content, XML tags, and PDF struc-ture to the PDF files exported.

Engineering Applications (Windows)

Engineers, technical professionals, and architects are among the many users of programs such as Microsoft Project, Microsoft Visio, and AutoDesk AutoCAD. Each of these programs uses the Adobe PDFMaker macro to produce PDF documents. Inasmuch as you can either print PostScript or save as EPS from one or the other and distill the files in Acrobat Distiller, using PDFMaker is a much better choice.

With Microsoft Project you convert files the same way you do other Office files. Only the current view of the Project worksheet can be converted to PDF. From the desktop you can also convert Project files to PDF by right-clicking on the document icon and selecting Convert to Adobe PDF.

With AutoCAD and Visio you have options for converting the AutoCAD and Visio layers to PDF layers. It is critical to be certain that the Adobe PDF settings are enabled for converting layers with either program.

From either program, open the Adobe PDF menu and select Change Conversion Settings. The Adobe PDFMaker dialog box opens like when using Convert to Adobe PDF from Microsoft Office applications. In Figure 6-20, notice the check box disabled for Always flatten layers in Adobe PDF. Be certain to disable the check box if you want layers converted to Adobe PDF layers. If you want the PDF opened in Acrobat with the Layers tab open, check the Open Layers Pane when viewed in Acrobat box.

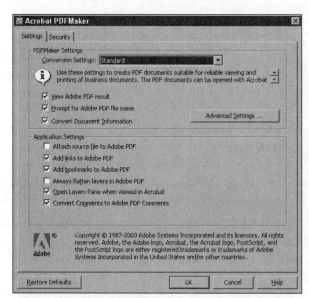

Figure 6-20: When converting AutoCAD and Visio files, disable the check box for flattening layers if you want the layers converted to Adobe PDF layers.

Caution   Adobe PDF Layers are only supported in Acrobat 6 or greater and when creating Acrobat 6 compatible files. Before you attempt to create a PDF file with layers, be certain to click on the Advanced button in the Adobe PDFMaker dialog box to open the Adobe PDF Settings dialog box. Select the General tab and verify that Acrobat 6.0 (PDF 1.5) is selected from the pull-down menu for Compatibility. If you use another compatibility setting, the PDF won't contain layers.

Other options are similar to the attributes used with Adobe PDFMaker in Office applications. After setting the options in the Acrobat PDFMaker dialog box, click OK and click on the Convert to Adobe PDF tool in the AutoCAD or Visio toolbar. The same tools are installed in AutoCAD and Visio as they are in the Office applications. As with Microsoft Office, be certain you install Acrobat after installing the other programs.

If you select View Adobe PDF result in the Acrobat PDFMaker dialog box, the PDF file is opened in Acrobat. In Figure 6-21 you see layers opened for a converted Visio file. In Figure 6-22 an AutoCAD file is converted to PDF.

Cross-Reference   For information on working with layers in Acrobat, see Chapter 17.

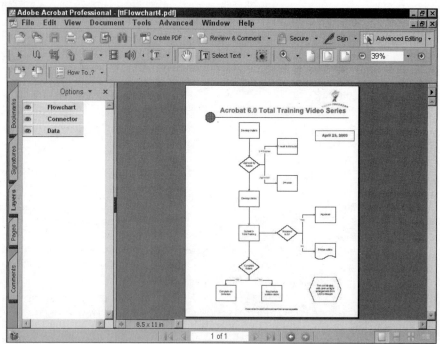

Figure 6-21: A Microsoft Visio file is converted to PDF with the Layers tab opened and the individual layers visible.

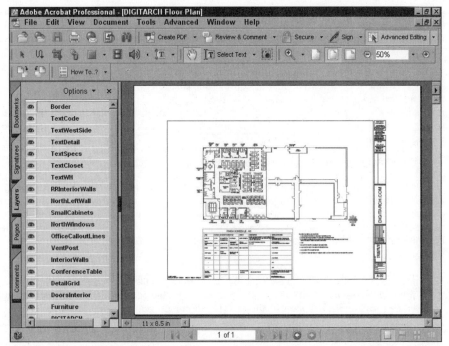

Figure 6-22: An AutoDesk AutoCAD file is converted to PDF with the Layers tab opened and the individual layers visible.

pdfmark

All of what was discussed with regard to layout programs is fine if you are willing to learn one of the applications. In a perfect world, you would all be up to speed on the tools needed to produce documents with ease and clarity. Unfortunately, you don't live in a perfect world, and some programs don't support the many features available with InDesign, PageMaker, QuarkXPress, or FrameMaker. So what do you do if you're not willing to take advantage of PDF export controls from the major layout applications? Fortunately, there is an option for you. It may not be easy, and you may need to poke around with some programming steps, but just about anything you can do to a PostScript file from programs supporting PostScript can also be accomplished by using a pdfmark annotation.

If you stop and think about it, anything you see as a graphic image on your screen could be created in a text editor using PostScript programming code. You certainly wouldn't want to create graphics by code. It takes many pages of raw text in PostScript code just to create a page with a single word and graphic. Imagine what you might have to do just to draw an object, let alone an entire layout?

Fortunately, you don't have to begin editing a PostScript file by starting from scratch. You can make edits to PostScript code in the form of annotations known as *pdfmark annotations*. A pdfmark operator can be used to identify a TOC entry, add a note to a PDF file, add a Bookmark, create a transition, or add almost any kind of element you desire. You add pdfmark annotations in one of two ways. You write the code in a text editor and concatenate (combine) two PostScript files; or you create an EPS file that is placed on a page to create elements and effects you want to appear in the PDF file. The EPS file you place contains the pdfmark annotations needed to produce the desired effect.

Technical information on pdfmark annotations is provided in the Help files contained on your Acrobat Installer CD. When you install Acrobat and include all the Help files in the installation, the Pdfmark.pdf document is added to the Help folder. This document is the pdfmark Reference Manual provided by the Adobe developer team, and it explains how to use pdfmark annotations. For a complete review of pdfmark and the syntax used for adding notes, bookmarks, links, and many other features in PDF files, refer to the technical manual.

To help understand how to annotate PostScript code, take a look at adding a note to a PDF document during distillation. When you work with Adobe PageMaker as an example, you can add a note to the first page of the PDF when you use the Export to Adobe PDF command. The note appears in the PDF in a fixed position on the first page. However, you cannot use this command to change the note position on page 1 or to have a note or several notes appear on pages other than page 1. Furthermore, when using programs such as QuarkXPress, Microsoft Publisher, or other applications, you don't have options to create notes at the point of conversion to PDF.

In a PDF workflow environment, you may want to set up files that can automatically create notes when distilling PostScript files with Acrobat Distiller. Whereas document information is limited to some description of the PDF file, notes provide you opportunities for adding descriptions to individual document pages. Furthermore, notes can be customized to display different colors and titles that can be set up to be unique for each individual PDF author. In a workflow environment, you can exercise control over who's adding note information and easily identify the contributors.

After you create a PDF file from a program such as Adobe PageMaker, QuarkXPress, Microsoft Word, or any other application capable of generating multiple pages, you may want to have a note or several notes added to the PDF file. Notes can be added in Acrobat; but, in order to do so, you need to individually open each PDF document in Acrobat and add the notes manually. By using pdfmark, you can create a separate PostScript file with the note contents and note color, and specify the document pages on which you want the notes to appear and use the routine for adding notes to multiple documents. When you open the PDF in an Acrobat viewer, the note(s) appear as you defined them.

Note attributes

To add a note with pdfmark, you need to be precise about coding the information in the PostScript file that you write, which ultimately is concatenated with the PostScript file created from the document. There are several note attributes to be addressed. Some of these attributes are required and others are optional. Table 6-3 describes the note attributes available for definition with pdfmark. In Table 6-3 several *types* are associated with the attributes:

✦ **string:** An alphanumeric string of characters. Typically, strings include text, for example, the contents of the notes.

✦ **array:** A mathematical expression consisting of numeric values. A quadrant would be composed of four numeric values in an array to define the x, y coordinates of the opposite diagonal corners.

✦ **integer:** Always a whole number.

✦ **Boolean:** A conditional item. May be a switch such as on or off; expressed as `true` for on and `false` for off.

✦ **name:** A specific reference to a procedure or call. Must be expressed as `/Name`. For example, Page `/Next` would proceed to the next page in a PDF document.

✦ **Required:** Not among the types already listed. You will find a reference to Required in relation to pdfmark semantics in the technical manual. When Required is indicated, a value for the procedure must be included.

✦ **Optional:** The opposite of Required. If an Optional reference is made, you don't need to include the procedure for the key in question.

Table 6-3: Note Attributes

Key	Type	Options	Syntax/Semantics
`Rect`	array	Required	Rect is an array describing the note boundaries beginning from the bottom-left corner to the top-right corner. Measurement is in points, with the page boundary at the lower-left corner defined as 0, 0 for the x, y coordinates. Syntax for the `/Rect` key is something like `[ /Rect 117 195 365 387 ]`. In this example, the lower-left corner of the note is 117 points to the right of the left side of the page and 195 points up from the bottom. The top-right corner of the note is 365 points from the left side and 387 points up from the bottom. The array data must be contained within brackets as shown in the syntax example.
`Contents`	string	Required	The contents string is what you want to appear as the note message. The maximum number of characters you can include in the note is 65,535. The text string will scroll within the note boundaries. If you want to add paragraph returns, enter `\r` where the return should appear. An example of the syntax for the contents is `/Contents (This is my first note with examples in using pdfmark annotations.)` Notice the text is contained within parentheses.
`SrcPg`	integer	Optional	By default, notes will appear on the first page in the PDF file. Eliminate the `SrcPg` key, and the note will appear as you define using the `Rect` and `Contents` keys. If you have multiple pages, you can choose to place a note on any page in the document. An example of the syntax for `SrcPg` is `/SrcPg 2`, which specifies the note is to appear on page 2. When identifying a page in a PDF file, you should be aware all pages begin with page 1. Do not use page 0 as the first page when counting the pages.
`Open`	Boolean	Optional	By default, all notes will appear open. If you want to have a note appear collapsed, you can use the `Open` key to do so. The syntax for closing a note is `/Open false`.

Continued

Table 6-3 *(continued)*

Key	Type	Options	Syntax/Semantics
Color	array	Optional	Note colors can be determined prior to conversion to PDF. A three-character array is used with the acceptable values of 1 and 0 (zero). There are eight total permutations for color choices. An example of the syntax for the color array is /Color [1 0 0]. Notice the array values must be contained within brackets.
Title	string	Optional	The title string will appear in the title bar for the note. You can add any text up to 65,535 characters. If you want to be practical, you would limit the number of characters to display a short descriptive title. An example of the syntax for the Title key is /Title (My Personal Note). Notice the text string is included within parentheses.
ModDate	string	Optional	The date can be described in terms of the month, day, year, hour, minute, and second. Any one or all of the above can be included. Unless you have a need for time stamping, use only the year, month, and day dates. Syntax is either yymmdd or yyyymmdd — for example, /ModDate (20100101) would be used to specify January 1, 2010. Notice the date field is contained within parentheses and no spaces are entered between year, month, and day. When you view the note in an Acrobat viewer, the date stamp will not appear. You need to summarize the notes in the PDF in order to view the date.
SubType	name	Optional	A subtype will commonly not be used with notes. A subtype for something like a link might look like /View [/xyz n n n], where the contents within the bracket is an array describing the view magnification. Another example is /View /Next, which specifies the next page will be viewed when the link button is selected.

Creating a pdfmark annotation

The keys and syntax described in Table 6-3 must be saved in a text file to be distilled by Acrobat Distiller. You can create a pdfmark annotation with a text editor or word processor. If using a word processor, be certain to save the file as text only. You can then combine the text file with the application document that is printed to disk as a PostScript file — just use the RunDirEx.txt file, discussed in Chapter 7, to concatenate the two files. To see how all this is accomplished, take a look at the steps to produce a note on page 2 in a two-page document.

Cross-Reference   For information on using RunDirEx.txt, see Chapter 7.

STEPS: Using pdfmark to add a note to a PDF file

1. **Print a document to disk.** Create a two-page layout in an application such as a layout program or a word processor. After creating the layout, print the file to disk. If using PageMaker and the Export Adobe PDF command, be certain to select the option

Prepare PostScript for distilling separately and not the option Distill now. If using QuarkXPress, Microsoft Word, Publisher, or other application, print the file to disk as a PostScript file and save the file for later use.

2. **Add a comment.** Open a text editor and supply a comment line for your file. All comments begin with %. In my example, I used these three comment lines:

```
% Custom Note pdfmark annotation
% Created by Ted Padova
% Places note on page 2
```

Comments are optional. You don't need the comment line, but it will be helpful if you create many different files for pdfmark annotations. Try to use a comment line so you can return to the file later and know what to expect after distillation.

3. **Define the note boundary.** Your first attempt to create a note and locate it precisely on a page may be awkward. If the coordinates are not supplied properly, your notes may not appear where you expect them. To aid you in the process, try to use a program such as Adobe Illustrator that can provide you with information about coordinate values for an element created on a page. In my example, I used Illustrator to determine where I wanted the note to appear and recorded the coordinates.

Note

When recording coordinate values, do not use a rectangle boundary as your assessment device. The top-right corner of the rectangle will be the coordinates from lower left to upper right for the rectangle and not the page. You need to record coordinate values for the lower-left and upper-right corners respective to the page. To determine these values, use rulers and guides in your application program and read the coordinates from an info palette.

When I drew the guidelines in Illustrator, I used the Info palette to determine the coordinates for each x and y position. In Figure 6-23, the x, y position for the lower-left corner of the note can be read in the Info palette.

4. **Enter the coordinates in the text file.** After you determine the coordinates for the note position, enter those values for your first line of code. In my example, I entered the following:

```
[ /Rect 108 200 360 360 ]
```

You must include all the data within brackets [ ].

5. **Enter the note contents.** The next line of code will be the note content you want to appear when the note is open. Add text as you desire. In my example, I added the following line:

```
/Contents (This document was created by Ted Padova
The document was originally a multiple
page QuarkXPress file and
the note was added to page 2.)
```

Note

All carriage returns used in coding the PostScript file will be retained in the note text.

6. **Identify the source page.** If you have only a single-page PDF, or you want to use the default placement of the note on page 1, you don't need to use the SrcPg value key. In my example, I decided to place the note on page 2, so I added the following line:

```
/SrcPg 2
```

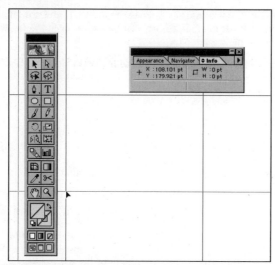

Figure 6-23: When assessing x, y coordinates, do not use elements as a measuring tool; use rulers and guidelines. The x position is measured from the left side of the page, and the y position is measured from the bottom of the page. Here, the x, y position is measured for the first x, y values.

7. **Opening and closing notes.** If you want to collapse the note, use the Open key value and enter false. If you want to have the note appear open, you use the Open key and enter true. In my example, I used the Open key, as shown here, and entered true so the note opens when the page is viewed:

```
/Open true
```

8. **Enter a title for the note.** The Title value key allows you to specify a string of text to appear in the note title bar. In my example, I included the following line:

```
/Title (PDFMark Note)
```

Be certain all the text to appear in the note title is included within the parentheses.

9. **Enter a color value for the note color.** The note adheres to the defaults set up in the Acrobat viewer unless you make changes, such as choosing another color for the note. To examine the colors available for the note, you can change the array values for the three data fields, by toggling 1s and 0s, and then distill each change. I wanted to change the note color for my example, so I included the following line:

```
/Color [ 1 0 0 ]
```

These values produced a red note.

10. **Date stamp the note.** Enter a date for a creation date for the note. The date can be viewed when you summarize notes in Acrobat. In my example, I included the following line:

```
/ModDate (20030704)
```

When the note is viewed as a summary, the date reads as July 4, 2003 (07/04/03).

11. **Save the file as text only.** The file must be saved in text format and not as a native word processor file. In my example, I saved my file as note.ps (see Figure 6-24).

```
% Custom Note pdfmark annotation
% Created by Ted Padova
% A note will be placed on the second page in the PDF file

[ /Rect [ 108 200 360 360 ]
  /Contents (This document was created by Ted Padova
  The document was originally a multiple
  page QuarkXPress file and
  the note was added to page 2.)
  /SrcPg 2
  /Open true
  /Title (PDFMark Note)
  /Color [1 0 0]
  /ModDate (20001104)
  /ANN
pdfmark

%%EOF
```

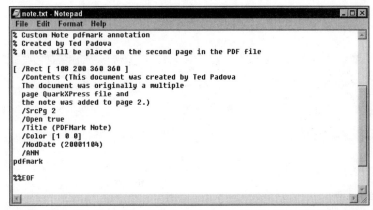

Figure 6-24: The final file was saved as a text-only file from Windows NotePad.

12. **Edit the RunDirEx.txt file.** Open the RunDirEx.txt file from the Adobe Acrobat installer CD and edit it to include the directory path for the files to be distilled in Acrobat Distiller. In my example, I edited the file for the directory path where both my .ps files were saved and left the name at the default — remember, if you name this file with a .ps extension, it is distilled and adds another page to the PDF file. To avoid distilling the RunDirEx.txt file, always use an extension that is different from the extensions of the files you are distilling. Figure 6-25 shows the code I supplied for my directory path and files to be distilled.

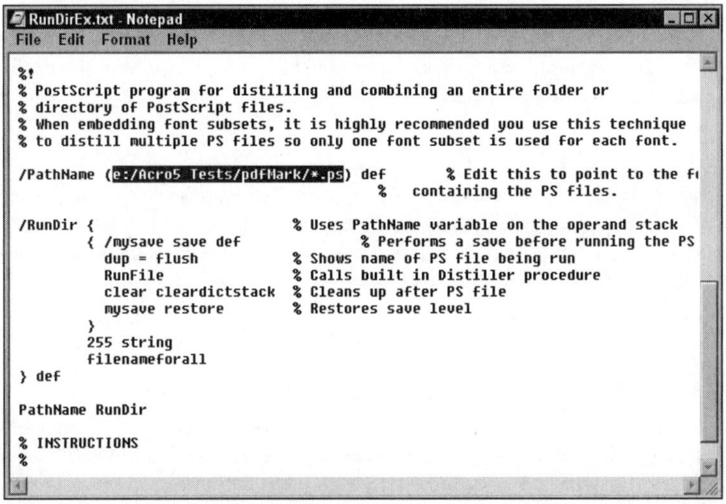

```
%!
% PostScript program for distilling and combining an entire folder or
% directory of PostScript files.
% When embedding font subsets, it is highly recommended you use this technique
% to distill multiple PS files so only one font subset is used for each font.

/PathName (e:/Acro5 Tests/pdfMark/*.ps) def       % Edit this to point to the f
                                         %   containing the PS files.

/RunDir {                           % Uses PathName variable on the operand stack
        { /mysave save def                  % Performs a save before running the PS
          dup = flush               % Shows name of PS file being run
          RunFile                   % Calls built in Distiller procedure
          clear cleardictstack      % Cleans up after PS file
          mysave restore            % Restores save level
        }
        255 string
        filenameforall
} def

PathName RunDir

% INSTRUCTIONS
%
```

Figure 6-25: I included the directory path of the folder where my PostScript files were saved and used the name RunDirEx.txt.

13. **Distill the RunDirEx.txt file.** Open the new RunDirEx.txt file in Acrobat Distiller and save the PDF to a directory of your choice. In my example, I opened RunDirEx.txt in Acrobat Distiller.

14. **View the PDF in an Acrobat viewer.** In an Acrobat viewer, verify that the note appears on the page where you expect it (see Figure 6-26).

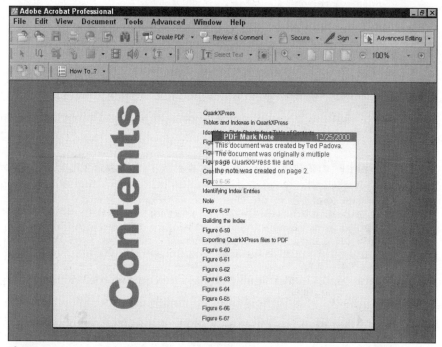

Figure 6-26: I opened my PDF file and navigated to page 2, where the note was successfully added to the page.

Tip   One excellent use of adding a pdfmark annotation to create a note is when producing many different PDF files for distribution. If you want to have identifying information included in all your PDFs such as name, address, phone, fax, e-mail address, and so on, adding the annotation will save much time in your workflow. After the code has been written and saved to disk, it can be reused an infinite number of times without re-editing.

Summary

✦ Adobe Photoshop can export directly to PDF. Photoshop can open single and multiple PDF documents created by any producer and preserve text and vector art when exporting to PDF.

✦ Microsoft Office applications such as Word, Excel, and PowerPoint export directly to PDF with the assistance of the PDFMaker macro. Office applications retain document structure and convert structured elements to Bookmarks and links in exported PDFs when Adobe PDFMaker is used.

✦ Illustration programs such as Adobe Illustrator, Macromedia FreeHand, and CorelDraw support direct export to PDF. Adobe Illustrator 9.0 and later preserves transparency with native data.

✦ PageMaker supports PDF export and import through a plug-in available free from Adobe's Web site.

✦ QuarkXPress offers PDF support for importing and exporting PDFs through a free downloadable Quark XTension from its Web site.

✦ Adobe FrameMaker offers a robust set of controls for exporting and importing PDF files.

✦ Programs such as Microsoft Visio and AutoDesk AutoCAD export to PDF with native layers converted to Adobe PDF layers. The PDFMaker macro is available to Visio and AutoCAD when Acrobat is installed after these programs.

✦ RunDirEx.txt and RunFilEx.txt can be used to concatenate a PostScript file containing pdfmark annotations and multiple application document PostScript files.

✦ You can develop pdfmark annotations in independent text files and have them contained within a PostScript or EPS file or save them as an EPS graphic and placed in an application document. The annotations add many different features to a PDF document when those features are not supported in authoring applications.

✦   ✦   ✦

Using Acrobat Distiller

Because PDF file creation has been much simplified in Acrobat 6, you may bypass thoughts of learning what Acrobat Distiller does and how PDF documents are converted with the Distiller application. If you remember the PDF conversion steps discussed in the previous two chapters, the Adobe PDF Settings were mentioned many times. These settings apply to Acrobat Distiller, and also the conversion of documents for many options from within Acrobat and via exports from authoring programs. They all use Distiller's Job Options, now referred to as the Adobe PDF Settings.

In order to successfully produce quality PDF documents, you need to have a basic understanding of how Acrobat Distiller works and what the settings control in regard to converting files to PDF. In some cases Distiller works in the background using Adobe PDF Settings you assign to the distillation process. Therefore, knowing how to change settings and understanding what options are available to you is essential. In this chapter I cover some advantages for using Acrobat Distiller and discuss how to change the Adobe PDF Settings.

Setting Up the Work Environment

You can access Acrobat Distiller in several ways. You can open Distiller from the Advanced menu command in Acrobat Standard and Acrobat Professional, you can launch Distiller from the desktop, or you can drag and drop files to the Distiller program application. None of these methods require loading special tools.

Cross-Reference For a detailed description of the various ways to access Acrobat Distiller, see the section "Accessing Distiller" at the end of this chapter.

When you convert files to PDF you typically create a PostScript file in other applications and convert the PostScript to PDF in Distiller. Therefore, the default view of the toolbars is all you need to follow the instructions throughout this chapter.

Understanding PostScript

Adobe PostScript is a *page description language* — that is, it describes the text and images on your monitor screen in a language. A raster image processor (RIP) interprets this language. Whereas PostScript is the language, the RIP behaves like a compiler. The RIP interprets the file and converts the text and images you see on your monitor to a bitmap image in dots that are plotted on a printing device. In the office environment, you won't see a RIP independent of a PostScript laser printer you use — but it exists. It's built into the printer. With high-end devices such as imagesetters, platesetters, large-format inkjet printers, on-demand printing systems, high-end composite color devices, and film recorders, the RIP is often a separate component that may be either a hardware device or software operating on a dedicated computer.

One of the reasons PostScript has grown to its present popularity is its device independence. When you draw a Bézier curve, rectangle, oval, or other geometric object in a vector art authoring application, the resolution displayed by your monitor is 72 pixels per inch (ppi). This image can be printed to a 300 dots per inch (dpi) laser printer or a 3,600 dpi imagesetter. Through the device independence of PostScript, essentially the computer "says" to the printer, "Give me all you can." The printer responds by imaging the page at the resolution it is capable of handling. When the file is ripped, the laser printer RIP creates a 300-dpi bitmap, whereas the imagesetter RIP creates a 3,600-dpi bitmap.

With all its popularity and dominance in the market, PostScript does have problems. It comes in many different dialects and is known as a *streamed* language. If you have a QuarkXPress file, for example, and import an Adobe Illustrator EPS file and a Macromedia EPS file, you'll wind up with three different flavors of PostScript — each according to the way the individual manufacturer handles their coding. If the same font is used by each of the three components, the font description resides in three separate areas of the PostScript file when printed to disk. PostScript is notorious for redundancy, especially with fonts.

As a streamed language, PostScript requires the entire code to be processed by the interpreter before the image bitmap is created. Ever wonder why you need to wait while the RIP is churning for an endless amount of time only to eventually end up with a PostScript error or RIP crash? PostScript can't begin plotting the bitmap image until the entire PostScript stream has been interpreted.

About Imaging Devices

Imagesetters are high-end devices ranging from $10,000 to over a $100,000 and are usually found in computer service bureaus and commercial print shops. Imagesetters use laser beams to plot the raster image on either sheet-fed or roll-fed paper or film. The paper is resin coated, and both paper and film require chemical processing through a developer, fix, and wash much like a photographic print. The material is used by a commercial printer to make plates that are wrapped around cylinders on a printing press. These prepress materials are an integral part of offset printing, and much of the printing performed today is handled from a form of digital output to material that is used to create plates for presses.

Direct-to-plate and direct-to-press systems bypass the prepress materials and expose images on plates that are used on print cylinders or directly to the press blankets where the impression receives the ink.

On-demand printing is a term describing machines that bypass the prepress process by taking the digital file from a computer directly to the press. Depending on the engineering of the output device, the consumable materials may consist of toner (as used in copy machines) or ink (as used on printing presses).

PDF, on the other hand, is like a database file—it has a database structure. PDF eliminates redundancy with file resources. Fonts, for example, only appear once, no matter how many occurrences are used in imported EPS files. In addition, PDF takes all the dialectical differences of PostScript and converts them to a single dialect. Whereas a PostScript file containing many pages requires the entire file to be downloaded to the RIP and ultimately printed, a PDF file is page independent in that each individual page is imaged before proceeding to the next page. In short, PDF is much more efficient than PostScript for printing purposes.

Creating PostScript files

In some ways a PostScript file is very similar to a PDF file. If, for example, you create a layout in Adobe PageMaker, Adobe InDesign, Adobe FrameMaker, or QuarkXPress with images and type fonts, the document page can be printed to disk as a PostScript file. In doing so, you can embed all graphic images and fonts in the file. If you take your file to a service center, the file can be downloaded to a printing device. Assuming you created the PostScript file properly, the file prints with complete integrity.

On desktop printers, printing to a PostScript file is just like printing to a device. On printers in commercial imaging centers, many different requirements need to be considered that are not typically found on a desktop printer. Some of the considerations that need to be understood when printing PostScript files for high-end devices include the following:

The following items address PDF creation for the purpose of printing files on commercial printing equipment. For more information on commercial printing, see Chapter 23.

✦ **PPD device selection:** In past years it was essential for you to use a device PostScript Printer Description (PPD) file. Today your PPD selection can be either a device PPD, an Acrobat Distiller PPD, or the Adobe PDF printer that doesn't offer you a separate PPD choice. In some cases you'll find more success in using a Distiller PPD or the Adobe PDF printer than using a device PPD, especially with PostScript clones and older printing devices.

✦ **Page size:** With desktop printers, you often have only one or two page sizes. With printers that have multiple trays or interchangeable trays, you select the appropriate page size for the tray used. With imaging equipment, you need to be certain the page size is properly selected to include all image data and printer's marks. Assume for a moment a document is created in the standard page size for a letter (8.5 × 11 inches) page. However, to accommodate printer's marks (registration and color bars), it turns out that the page area needs to be defined larger than a letter page. In the Paper Size area of the dialog box shown in Figure 7-1, the word Custom appears, indicating the page is a custom size. The thumbnail on the right in Figure 7-1 shows how the page fits within the defined size. In this example, all data and printer's marks print within the defined page. If your page is too small, some clipping of the data occurs when printed or when a PDF file is generated.

✦ **Font inclusion:** You may need to specifically tell the host application to include fonts in the PostScript file. If the file is printed at a service center, you definitely need to include the fonts in the file you submit for output. If you distill the file in Acrobat Distiller, the fonts need to be loaded on your system in order to embed the fonts in the PDF file. When you have options in Print dialog boxes for font inclusion, always choose to embed the fonts.

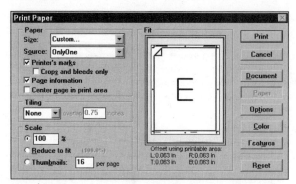

Figure 7-1: The page size was defined as a Custom size to include the printer's marks and page information.

✦ **Screening:** Halftone frequencies, or *line screens,* can be printed at different settings. With desktop printers the maximum line screen available for the device is often the default. 600-dpi laser printers, for example, most commonly use a maximum line screen of 85 lines per inch (lpi). With imaging equipment, you need to first know the requirements of the commercial printer and take his/her advice depending on the paper, press, and prepress material. Therefore, if your file is ultimately printed at 133 lpi, this value must be entered in the Print dialog box for the application creating the PostScript file.

Setting the halftone frequency is an important issue only if the PostScript file is downloaded to an imaging device where the default screens are not overridden by a technician. For files printed from Acrobat directly to printing devices, the technician who prints the file also sets the frequency in the Acrobat Advanced Printing dialog box.

Screening can also be a particular type relative to the printing device and RIP. Stochastic screening, Crystal Raster, AGFA Balanced Screens, and others are available from a PPD selection for a particular device. For these settings you need to contact your service center for the precise screening options needed and use a device PPD.

✦ **Color:** If separations are to be printed, you must make certain all identified colors are properly named in the host document. There is often an option in a Print dialog box to select separations. As you view a color list of potential separations, it is imperative to verify all colors appearing are those you specified in the document. If a spot color is in the current document, the color doesn't print unless it is an identified color in the Print dialog box. Fortunately, in Acrobat 6 a method is available for previewing separations. Before sending files off to a service center, make a habit of previewing files for printing in Acrobat.

Cross-Reference

For information regarding separation previews and soft-proofing color, see Chapter 23.

Encoding

Encoding comes in two flavors: Binary and ASCII. Binary encoding results in smaller files and prints faster on PostScript Level 2 and PostScript 3 devices. As a default you'll want to use binary encoding if you see options in the Print dialog box to choose between ASCII and Binary. If no option is available for choosing between ASCII and Binary when you print a PostScript file, the file encoding defaults to Binary.

PostScript levels

PostScript originated sometime in 1976, and later it was updated to a version called Interpress at the Xerox Palo Alto Research Center (PARC). Interpress was designed for output to early laser printers. Xerox abandoned the project, and two of the staff at Xerox PARC decided to take it forth and develop it. In 1981, John Warnock and Chuck Geschke formed Adobe Systems Incorporated, and PostScript was their first product.

On March 21, 1985, the digital print revolution was founded when Apple Computer, Aldus Corporation, Adobe Systems, and Linotype collaborated on an open architecture system for electronic typesetting. Later that year Apple Computer introduced the LaserWriter printer that came with a whopping 13 fonts fried into the printer's ROM chips and a price tag of $6,500. If you were outputting to a PostScript device in 1987, when Adobe Illustrator first appeared, you may still be waiting for that 12K Illustrator file to spit out of your laser printer. PostScript Level 1 was a major technological advance, but by today's standards it was painfully slow. Many in the imaging world remember all too well still waiting at 3:00 a.m. for the final file to print after ripping over eight hours.

In 1990, Adobe Systems introduced PostScript Level 2, which was a more robust version of PostScript and a screamer compared to the first release. In addition to speed, PostScript Level 2 provided these features:

✦ **Color separation:** In earlier days, color was preseparated on Level 1 devices. PostScript Level 2 enabled imaging specialists to separate a composite color file into the four process colors, Cyan, Magenta, Yellow, and Black. Also, there was support for spot color in PostScript Level 2.

✦ **Improved font handling:** In the early days of PostScript imaging, there were more font nightmares than you can imagine. Font encoding for PostScript fonts only handled a maximum of 256 characters. Other font sets such as Japanese have thousands of individual characters. PostScript Level 2 introduced a composite font technology that handled many different foreign character sets.

✦ **Compression:** Getting the large files across a 10-Base-T network was also a burden in the Level 1 days. PostScript Level 2 introduced data compression and supported such compression schemes as JPEG, LZW, and RLE. The files are transmitted compressed, which means they get to the RIP faster, and then decompressed at the RIP. In a large imaging center, the compression greatly improved network traffic and workflows.

In 1996, Adobe introduced PostScript 3 (note *Level* was dropped from the name). Perhaps one of the more remarkable and technologically advanced features of PostScript 3 is the inclusion of Web publishing with direct support for HTML, PDF, and Web content. PostScript 3 also provides the ability to create In-Rip separations. When you send a PDF file to an imaging center using PostScript 3 RIPs you can deliver composite color files that are sent directly to the RIP where they are separated at the imaging device.

Using Acrobat Distiller Preferences

Acrobat Distiller is launched from within Adobe Acrobat Standard or Adobe Acrobat Professional. As a separate executable application, Acrobat Distiller can also be launched from a desktop shortcut or alias or by double-clicking on the program icon contained in the Distiller folder inside the Acrobat 6.0 folder.

When you first launch Acrobat Distiller, it looks like a fairly simple application. Examining the menus immediately tells you there's not much to do in the File menu. This menu is limited to opening a file, addressing preferences, and quitting the program. Distiller's real power is contained in the second menu item — the Settings menu. The commands listed in this menu offer all the control for determining how PostScript files are converted to PDF.

Before making choices in the Settings menu, look over the options in the Preferences menu. When you choose File ⇨ Preferences on the Distiller Window (Windows) or the top-level Acrobat ⇨ Preferences (Macintosh) a dialog box opens. The options available are listed among three groups (Windows) that include Startup Alerts, Output Options, and Log Files as shown in Figure 7-2. On the Macintosh, five choices appear as check boxes and radio buttons as shown in Figure 7-3.

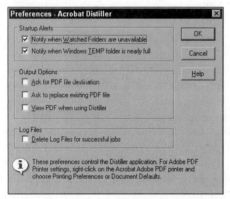

Figure 7-2: Access Acrobat Distiller Preferences by choosing File ⇨ Preferences. Preferences enable you to customize startup and output options.

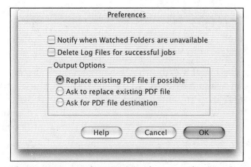

Figure 7-3: On the Macintosh, you select Preferences from the Acrobat top-level menu.

Startup Alerts

The two items listed in the Startup Alerts section of the Distiller Preferences dialog box have to do with your initial startup upon launching the Distiller application:

✦ **Notify when watched folders are unavailable:** This command enables Distiller to monitor a folder or directory on your computer or network server to automatically distill PostScript files placed in watched folders. In an office environment, you can have different users create PostScript files and send them to a server for automatic distillation.

For more information on working with watched folders, see the "Creating watched folders" section later in this chapter.

✦ **Notify when Windows TEMP folder is nearly full (Windows only):** Distiller needs temporary disk space to convert the PostScript files to PDF documents. If the available hard disk space on your startup volume becomes less than 1 megabyte, Distiller prompts you with a warning dialog box. Leaving this preference setting enabled is always a good idea. The amount of temporary space required by Distiller is approximately twice the size of the PostScript file being distilled.

Output Options

Output options relate to what you intend to do with the PDF both in terms of where it is saved and what to do after conversion.

✦ **Ask for PDF file destination:** When enabled this option prompts you for the location of the saved file.

✦ **Ask to replace existing PDF file:** Selecting this option warns you if a PDF of the same name exists in the folder where the new PDF is saved. If you want to use different Adobe PDF Settings and create two PDF files, you may forget that you have a PDF with a filename the same as the new one you are creating. With this option, you are warned if Distiller attempts to overwrite your existing file.

✦ **View PDF when using Distiller (Windows only).** After the PDF has been created the default Acrobat viewer launches and the PDF opens in the Document Pane.

If you are running Adobe Reader and Adobe Acrobat Standard or Professional on the same computer, open the viewer you want to designate as the default viewer. When prompted to set the viewer as the default, click Yes in the dialog box. All subsequent PDF files are opened in the default viewer.

✦ **Notify when Watched Folders are unavailable (Macintosh only):** If you set up a watched folder and delete it, the folder is unavailable. If Distiller is monitoring folders, a warning dialog box opens informing you that the watched folder is no longer available.

Log Files

The Log Files section describes the sequence of steps used to produce the PDF file. This section offers a choice on what to do with the log file.

✦ **Delete Log Files for successful jobs:** A log file is an ASCII text file detailing the distillation process. If an error is produced during distillation, the log file records the error even though the PDF is not created. Viewing the log file can be helpful in debugging problems with files not successfully being converted to PDF. If the PDF is successfully created, there would be no need to keep the log file on your computer. By default, you'll want to enable this check box to eliminate the clutter.

Editing Adobe PDF Settings

In earlier versions of Acrobat, the Adobe PDF Settings were referred to as Distiller Job Options. The various options you have available through several tabs in the Adobe PDF Settings dialog box control how PDFs are produced with Distiller and what attributes are assigned to the files.

When you launch Distiller, a pull-down menu appears for Default Settings, shown in Figure 7-4, for the preset options installed with Acrobat. There are six separate settings presets designed to produce PDF files for different purposes. When you distill a PostScript file in Acrobat Distiller, or use Adobe PDF Settings when accessing the Create PDF From File menu commands that addresses different settings, the currently selected setting is used to convert the file. From the pull-down menu you select one of the menu options to produce the PDF suited for your needs. If you want to create a different setting, you select Settings ⇨ Edit Adobe PDF Settings in Distiller where you can create and save custom settings.

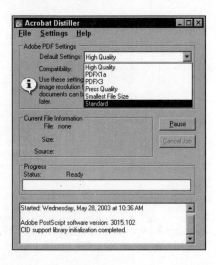

Figure 7-4: The Default Settings pull-down menu lists all currently available settings for converting PostScript files to PDF. By default, six different preset settings are listed in the menu.

Preset Adobe PDF Settings

The Default choices for Adobe PDF Settings when you install Acrobat include

✦ **High Quality:** The preset settings associated with this option are established for the highest-quality images for high-end digital prepress and printing. The lowest levels of compression and downsampling are used to preserve image quality.

✦ **PDF/X-1a:** For prepress and printing, PDF/X files are streamlined for print output. PDF/X is an ISO standard developed by a committee outside Adobe Systems. Although Adobe participates in the standards committee, the format is a collaborative effort between members of the ISO standards committee. PDF/X files result in PDF documents that eliminate data not essential for printing. It does not mean the file sizes are necessarily smaller, but they are optimized for printing and produce fewer problems than non-PDF/X files. The PDF/X-1a format supports process (CMYK) and spot color.

✦ **PDF/X-3:** Like PDF/X1a, the file format is a subset of the PDF format. PDF/X-3 files support ICC profile embedding. If working in a color-managed workflow, use this flavor of PDF/X.

✦ **Press Quality:** These settings are virtually identical to the settings for High Quality (see first bullet). The difference between the two is that when using the High Quality settings, any fonts not available for embedding during distillation are noted in the log file but the PDF is produced without the embedded fonts. When using Press Quality, the job cancels at the first encounter of a font not available for embedding and the PDF is not produced.

✦ **Smallest File Size:** The intent for this option is to produce files for Web hosting, e-mailing, and screen views. The name implies that the file sizes are very small, but in reality, you can create smaller file sizes by editing the downsampling of the images. The sampling resolution only downsamples files above 150 pixels per inch (ppi) to 100 ppi. You can create a new set for smaller file sizes and downsample all images to 72 ppi for Web hosting when the images don't need to be displayed above a 100% view.

✦ **Standard:** The general-purpose settings and quite often the default when accessing settings the first time in Acrobat is the Standard choice. For office desktop color printers, laser printers, photocopiers, and general-purpose printing, the settings create PDF files with no lower than 150 ppi resolutions and embed fonts when necessary.

If one of these preset conditions comes close to producing the type of PDF you want to create, but it doesn't exactly meet your needs, go ahead and select that preset option and then choose Settings ⇨ Edit Adobe PDF Settings to open a dialog box where you can make changes. When you finish editing the settings to your satisfaction, you have an opportunity to save your own custom preset file that you can access at a later time. There are six tabs where you can choose to change the settings. They are General, Images, Fonts, Color, Advanced, and PDF/X.

General settings

If you need to make any changes in the Adobe PDF Settings from one of the preset options, or you need to create a new setting, choose Settings ⇨ Edit Adobe PDF Settings to open the Adobe PDF Settings dialog box as shown in Figure 7-5. The first of six tabs appear, labeled General, which covers some general controls:

✦ **Description:** A field box at the top of the General tab is editable and enables you to add a message description about the new settings you create. Place the cursor in the field box, highlight any existing text and delete it. Type your new description in the field box. When you save the new setting, the description is saved along with your chosen options.

✦ **Compatibility:** You have choices for Acrobat 3.0, 4.0, 5.0, and 6.0 compatibilities. Using earlier compatibility versions may affect the visibility of PDFs with earlier viewers. If you work in an enterprise where a large installed user base is using a particular version of Acrobat, create files for the compatibility version consistent with the site license of the Acrobat version. If you're creating files for mass distribution, think about forgetting Acrobat 3 and 4 compatibilities and focus on versions 5 and 6. Be aware that if you create Acrobat 6-compatible files and use new features like embedding media clips, users of earlier versions won't be able to view your files. It's always a tradeoff, and you need to clearly think about whom you want to target when distributing content. The different compatibility settings and what features are supported are listed in Table 7-1.

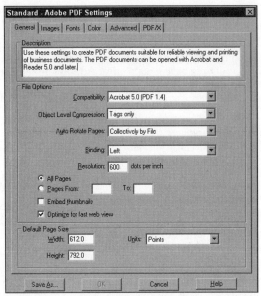

Figure 7-5: The first Adobe PDF Settings that appear when you select Settings ⇨ Edit Adobe PDF Settings are those under the General tab.

Table 7-1: Acrobat Compatibility Differences

Acrobat 3.0	Acrobat 4.0	Acrobat 5.0	Acrobat 6.0
Supports PDF version 1.2	Supports PDF version 1.3	Supports PDF version 1.4	Supports PDF version 1.5
PDF files can be opened by Acrobat viewers 3.0 and later.	PDF files can be opened by Acrobat viewers 3.0 and later.	PDF files can be opened by Acrobat viewers 3.0 and later.	PDF files can be opened by Acrobat viewers 4.0 and later.
	Minor viewing problems with earlier viewers may be experienced.	Some viewing problems with earlier viewers may be experienced.	Using newer features may be problematic with older viewers.
Page size is limited to 45 inches × 45 inches.	Page size is available up to 200 inches × 200 inches.	Page size is available up to 200 inches × 200 inches.	Page size is available up to 200 inches × 200 inches.
Document conversion is limited to 32,768 pages.	Document length is limited only by RAM and hard drive space.	Document length is limited only by RAM and hard drive space.	Document length is limited only by RAM and hard drive space.
Color conversion supports CalRGB.	Color conversion supports sRGB.	Color conversion supports sRGB.	Color conversion supports sRGB.

Acrobat 3.0	Acrobat 4.0	Acrobat 5.0	Acrobat 6.0
ICC Profile embedding supported.	ICC Profile embedding supported.	ICC Profile embedding supported.	ICC Profile embedding supported.
DeviceN color space is converted to an alternate color space.	DeviceN color space is supported.	DeviceN color space is supported.	DeviceN color space is supported with 32 colorants.
Smooth shading is converted to images.	Smooth shading is supported.	Smooth shading is supported.	Smooth shading is supported.
Patterns display at 50% but print correctly. correctly.	Patterns display accurately and print correctly.	Patterns display accurately and print correctly.	Patterns display accurately and print
Places halftone information in the PDF.	Only preserves halftone information when Preserve Halftone information is selected in the Color Job Options.	Only preserves halftone information when Preserve Halftone information is selected in the Color Job Options.	Only preserves halftone information when Preserve Halftone information is selected in the Color Adobe PDF Settings.
Transfer Functions are supported.	Transfer Functions are not supported.	Transfer Functions are supported.	Transfer Functions are supported.
Masks do not display or print properly.	Masks are supported in viewing and printing.	Masks are supported in viewing and printing.	Masks are supported in viewing and printing.
Photoshop 6/7 layers and transparency not supported.	Photoshop 6/7 layers and transparency not supported.	Photoshop 6/7 layers and transparency supported in Saves as PDF from Photoshop only.*	Photoshop 6.0 layers and transparency supported in Saves as PDF from Photoshop only.*
Illustrator 9/10 transparency is supported.	Illustrator 9/10 transparency is supported.	Illustrator 9/10 transparency supported in Saves as PDF from Illustrator only.*	Illustrator 9/10 transparency supported in Saves as PDF from Illustrator only.*
Cannot embed double-byte fonts.	Can embed double-bytefonts.	Can embed double-bytefonts.	Can embed double-byte fonts.
TrueType fonts cannot be searched.	TrueType fonts can be searched.	TrueType fonts can be searched.	TrueType fonts can be searched.
Supports 40-bit encryption.	Supports 40-bit encryption.	Supports 40-bit encryption and 128-bit encryption.	Supports 40-bit encryption and 128-bit encryption.
Adobe PDF layers not supported.	Adobe PDF layers not supported.	Adobe PDF layers not supported.	Supports Adobe PDF layers.

*Distilling files from Photoshop and Illustrator does not support transparency.

✦ **Object Level Compression:** Non-compressed objects are consolidated into streams for more efficient compression. You have choices for applying no compression (Off), or using Tags Only. You can reduce file sizes by selecting Tags only for Object Level Compression.

✦ **Auto-rotate Pages:** You can have pages automatically or individually rotated during distillation. Choices from the pull-down menu include turning off rotation, rotating collectively by file, and rotating individually. When Collectively by File is selected, Acrobat analyzes the text in the file and rotates pages based on the orientation of the majority of the text in the entire file. When Individually is chosen, each page is rotated based on the majority of text on a given page. Selecting Off results in no page rotation. Figure 7-6 shows a page where the layout was designed with the text rotated in the design. When distilled in Acrobat without auto-rotation, the page is viewed as it was designed. Figure 7-7 displays the same layout converted to PDF with Collectively by File selected.

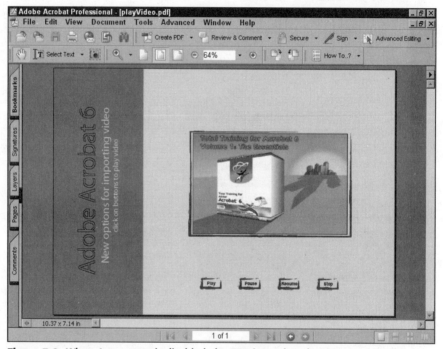

Figure 7-6: When Auto-rotate is disabled, the PDF is produced as it was originally designed without rotation regardless of the orientation of the text.

Tip

Users of Acrobat 4 can control auto-rotation even though the Job Options in this version do not support it. The Job Options files are ASCII text files and can be opened in a simple text editor or word processor (see Figure 7-8). Open a joboptions file in WordPad (Windows) or Simple Text (Macintosh) from the Distiller/Settings (Windows) or Distiller:Settings (Macintosh) directory. Find the line of code beginning with `/AutoRotatePages` / `PageByPage`. Change this line from `/PageByPage` to `/None` to disable auto-rotation. To enable page rotation, change `/None` to `/PageByPage`. Save the file under a new name with the .joboptions extension to the Settings folder. The next time you open Acrobat Distiller, the new Job Options appear in the pull-down menu.

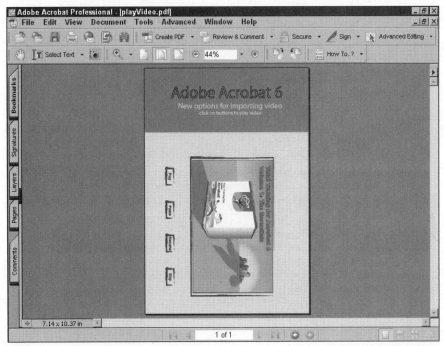

Figure 7-7: When Auto-rotate is used, the text on the pages or in the file is analyzed for orientation. If the predominant text orientation is rotated, the PDF is rotated during distillation.

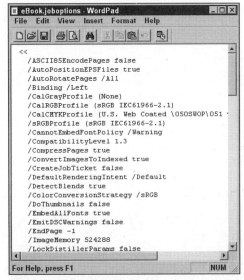

Figure 7-8: Acrobat 4.0 does not have auto-rotation control among the Job Options. Auto-rotation can be enabled or dis-abled by editing a .joboptions file in the Distiller ⇨ Settings folder.

✦ **Binding:** This setting relates to viewing pages in an Acrobat viewer with Continuous — Facing or Facing page layouts and with thumbnails when viewed aside each other. In addition the binding can affect other items like the direction of scrolling text across the screen and certain animated effects you add. By default, the binding is left-sided.

✦ **Resolution:** Settings for Resolution affect only vector objects and type in EPS files. The settings range between 72 and 4000 dpi. A handy Tool Tip appears when you click in the field box that shows the upper and lower limits of acceptable values. Lower resolution settings may create banding with gradients when files are printed. In practicality you'll notice no visual difference if you change the resolution about the default of 600. Setting the resolution to 2400 adds less than 3K to your file size.

✦ **All Pages/Pages From:** You can choose to create a PDF within a specified range of pages from a PostScript file that has been printed to disk from a document containing many pages. If one page is having trouble converting to PDF, you can eliminate it from distillation by choosing a specified page range. The default All Pages distills all pages in the PostScript file.

✦ **Embed thumbnails:** Thumbnails add about 3K per page to your PDF file. Thumbnails are helpful when editing PDF files in Acrobat or when browsing PDF files onscreen. However, because they create larger files, you'll want to eliminate thumbnails when producing PDF files for Web use or sending your PDF files across the Internet for output to printing devices. If using Acrobat viewers 5.0 and greater, thumbnails are displayed on-the-fly regardless of whether they have been embedded. Any legacy PDFs created with older PDF formats are also displayed with thumbnails without embedding when viewed in later viewers.

✦ **Optimize for fast web view:** An optimized PDF file is smaller than one created without optimization. All files intended to be used for screen views, CD-ROM replication, and Web usage should all be optimized. Generally, almost any printing device also accepts optimized files. As a default, keep this option on. Acrobat optimizes files by eliminating repeating elements and supplying pointers to where the first occurrence of an object is found in the file. Optimization also prepares files for page-at-a-time downloading from Web servers. If byte-serving capability exists on a server, the optimized files download pages as they are viewed.

✦ **Default Page Size:** Setting page sizes in these field boxes only applies to distillation of EPS and PostScript files where page boundaries are not specified. Whatever you enter in the field boxes when distilling PostScript files is ignored if the page boundary is included in the file. If you want to trim a page size or create a larger page size for an EPS file, you can establish the dimensions in the field boxes for width and height. The Units pull-down menu enables you to choose from four different units of measure.

Images

Compression and sampling of images is managed better with Acrobat Distiller than some other methods used to create PDFs. With Create PDF from File, for example, there are more limited sampling options than exist with Distiller. You have much control over how much compression are used and what methods of downsampling are used in the Images tab. Compression and sampling choices are available for three different image types: Color images, Grayscale, and Monochrome images.

Color images

The first category handles color images used in your original file. You have choices for the sampling method and the amount of compression you want to apply. These include

✦ **Downsample:** The Downsample pull-down menu offers choices for no sampling or three different sampling methods that include:

- **Off:** This turns off all compression for color images.

- **Bicubic Downsampling to:** A pull-down menu and two field boxes appear as your first choices in the Color Image section. Bicubic Downsampling is the default setting for all preset Adobe PDF Settings. Bicubic downsampling uses a weighted average to determine the resampled pixel color. The algorithm is much more mathematically intensive, and as a result this method takes the longest time to complete distillation when files are downsampled. The upside is it produces the best image quality for continuous tone images. With this method as well as the other two choices for resampling images there are two field boxes where the amount of sampling is user defined. The values range between 9 and 2400 ppi. The *for images above* field box enables you to choose when an image is resampled. For example, in Figure 7-9, only images above 225 dpi are affected when distilled with this setting.

- **Average Downsampling to:** From the pull-down menu the item following the Off selection is Average Downsampling to. When you resample an image by downsampling, the average pixel value of a sample area is replaced with a pixel of the averaged color. The field boxes to the right of the sampling method are for user-determined sampling amounts, used in the same way as the preceding Bicubic method.

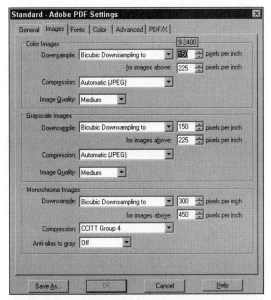

Figure 7-9: Distiller provides many more compression controls than some other PDF creators. In this dialog box, you make choices for the type of sampling and the amount of compression applied to images.

- **Subsampling to:** When Subsampling is specified, a pixel within the center of the sample area is chosen as the value applied to the sample area. Thus, downsampling noted previously replaces pixels from averaged color values, whereas the subsampling replaces pixels from a given color value. Of the two methods, subsampling significantly reduces the amount of time to resample the image. Because all that averaging is taking place with downsampling, the calculations are more extensive, thereby increasing the distillation time. Subsampling, however, may result in more problems in the printed PDF file. Unless you have a large single-color background, you are better off choosing Bicubic downsampling when printing to hard copy.

✦ **Compression:** The pull-down menu enables you to select from Automatic (JPEG), JPEG, ZIP, or Off. When Automatic is selected, Distiller examines each image and automatically determines which compression to use (that is, either ZIP or JPEG). If an image has large amounts of a common color value, ZIP compression is used. If an image consists of smooth transitions of color, such as a continuous tone photograph, JPEG compression is used. If you want to apply the same compression to all images, you can select either the JPEG or ZIP options. Doing so eliminates any decision making by Distiller about the type of compression to be applied. When you select Off, no compression is applied. You might want to downsample images as noted earlier with one of the downsampling options, but not want to apply compression to the images.

✦ **Image Quality:** After the compression type is selected, you have one of five choices for the amount of compression applied. Maximum relates to less compression, whereas Minimum relates to high compression. For high-end prepress, use the Maximum or High choice from the pull-down menu. For desktop color printers, use Medium quality; and for Web, screen, or CD-ROM replication, use Low quality. The Minimum setting might be used in some cases with screen or Web graphics, but continuous tone photographs often appear visibly degraded. You might use this setting to transfer files quickly across the Internet for client approvals and then later use a higher setting for the final production documents.

Grayscale

All the choices you have for color images are identical for grayscale images. You can use different settings for color and grayscale images by toggling through all the options. When the final PDF is produced, the sampling and compression for your images are respectively applied from choices made for each image type.

Monochrome images

Monochrome images include only two color values — black and white. Photoshop line art is a monochrome image. This is not to be confused with line art as we define it with vector art applications. The sampling methods available to you for monochrome images are identical to those described for color images. Compression settings, however, are much different. In addition to Off for applying no compression, the options include

✦ **CCITT Group 3:** The International Coordinating Committee for Telephony and Telegraphy (CCITT) Group 3 compression is used by fax machines. The images are compressed in horizontal rows, one row at a time.

✦ **CCITT Group 4:** CCITT Group 4 is a general-purpose compression method that produces good compression for most types of bitmap images. This compression method is the default and typically the best method for bitmap images.

✦ **ZIP:** ZIP compression is more efficient than earlier versions of Acrobat that used LZW compression. ZIP achieves approximately 20 percent more compression. It should be used when large areas of a single color appear in an image.

✦ **Run Length :** The Run Length format is a lossless compression scheme particularly favorable to bitmap monochrome images. You can run tests yourself for the compression method that works best for you. Typically CCITT Group 4 handles most of your needs when compressing these images.

✦ **Anti-Alias to gray:** Bitmap images may appear pixelated onscreen or, in some cases, when printed. By using anti-aliasing images are rendered with a smoother appearance. The amount of anti-aliasing can be selected from the pull-down menu. Choices are for 2, 4, and 8 bits that produce 4, 16, and 256 levels of gray, respectively. If you use anti-aliasing with scanned type, small point sizes may appear blurry, especially with higher gray levels.

Guidelines for sampling images

Acrobat handles sampling appropriate for your output needs as long as image sampling is equal to or greater than the requirements for the output. If image resolution is lower than the output needs, then Distiller isn't able to upsample images to provide the necessary resolution. Even though Distiller can effectively downsample images, you should observe a few rules.

First, the resolution for all images in a layout or design should be sampled at the highest output requirement. For example, if prepress and commercial printing is to be used, then the image sample needs a resolution to support commercial printing. In this regard, you want to sample images in Photoshop at the required resolution. Don't rely on Distiller to downsample images during distillation. The time you save can add up if you're converting many files with high-resolution images. When you open the Adobe PDF Settings and select the Images tab, select Off for the sampling items.

The second rule is to be used when repurposing images. If you have a PostScript file that has been printed for a higher order of output, like the commercial printing discussed earlier in this chapter, then you don't need to create a second PostScript file for another output destination. Use the same PostScript file and select the sampling options appropriate for the output. Using this same example, if you now want to create a PDF for screen views, select Bicubic Downsampling to and set the resolution to 72 dpi.

Tip   If you don't distill files in Acrobat Distiller to produce PDFs and you want to repurpose several documents, you can create Batch Sequences and use the PDF Optimizer to run a sequence on a collection of PDF documents. For more information on using the PDF Optimizer and creating Batch Sequences, see Chapter 13.

Fonts

The distinctive advantage of using the Portable Document Format is that it maintains file integrity across computers and across platforms. One of the greatest problems with file integrity is the handling of fonts. Fortunately, Distiller provides the ability to embed fonts within the PDF so the end user won't need font installations to view and print PDF files. The Fonts tab shown in Figure 7-10 offers options for setting font-embedding attributes during distillation.

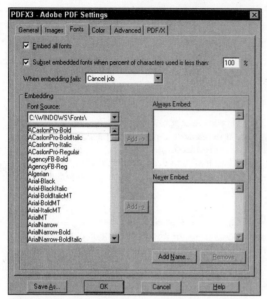

Figure 7-10: The Fonts tab in Adobe PDF Settings displays the control over font embedding available to you during distillation.

Options on the Fonts tab include

✦ **Embed All Fonts:** Unless you have a specific reason to not embed fonts, this option should always be enabled for file exchanges and printing. Circumstances for when not to embed fonts might be for where you want to reduce file sizes to the smallest possible size for Web hosting.

Many different font manufacturers exist, and the permissions for use of fonts from these manufacturers vary considerably. To legally include font embedding in a PDF file, you need to know whether the manufacturer provides the permission for inclusion. Adobe original fonts that are owned by Linotype-Hell, International Typeface Corporation, AGFA, AlphaOmega, Bigelow & Holmes, Fundicion Typografica Neufville, and Monotype Typography, Ltd., as well as those in the Adobe library, can be used for font embedding without written releases. Fonts with licensing restrictions often appear with an explanation of the limitations of use. If in doubt, you'll need to check with the manufacturer or distributor to inquire as to whether you can legally distribute PDF files that include certain fonts. Failure to do so may result in a copyright violation.

✦ **Subset embedded fonts when percent of characters used is less than [ ].** Some PDF producers provide you an opportunity to subset both PostScript and TrueType fonts. The difference between the subsetting in Distiller as opposed to other producers is your ability to determine when a font is subset. With Distiller, you can specify when you want subsetting to occur. The subsetting percentage has to do with the percentage of *glyphs* (special renderings) in the font. If 100% is selected, Distiller includes all information necessary to draw all the glyphs in the font. Lower percentages determine what characters among the set are embedded. Type 3, TrueType, and CID fonts are always embedded regardless of what value is supplied. (For font format descriptions see Table 7-2 later in this chapter.)

When two or more PostScript files are converted to PDF with Acrobat Distiller using font subsetting, Distiller gives the resulting PDF only one font subset. The result is a more efficient PDF document and produces smaller file sizes, especially when combining several PostScript files to produce a single PDF.

Note

For information on concatenating PostScript files, see the section "Concatenating PostScript Files" at the end of this chapter.

✦ **When Embedding Fails:** This pull-down menu offers three choices. Choose Ignore to ignore a failed font being embedded, in which case distillation continues. The Warn and Continue option displays a warning and then continues distillation. Choose Cancel to cancel the distillation if a font embedding error occurs. When sending files off to service centers for imaging or when font substitution is not desired, use this latter option as your default. If the PDF is not produced, you won't inadvertently forget there was a problem with font embedding.

✦ **Embedding:** The left side of the dialog box lists all fonts available for embedding. From the pull-down menu you select from the different folders Distiller monitors for fonts. Distiller can monitor font locations on your computer. If you want to view the font list from another monitored folder, click the pull-down menu and select the folder. Regardless of what is listed in the Embedding list, Distiller can also embed fonts that were included in the PostScript file or all the folders listed for monitoring. The fonts to be embedded must be present in either the PostScript file or a monitored folder.

Note

Fonts that have license restrictions are shown in the Font Source list with a padlock icon. If you select the font, the restriction attributes are displayed in the Fonts tab. Locked fonts cannot be moved to the Always Embed list.

Cross-Reference

For information related to monitoring font folders, see the section "Identifying Font Locations" later in this chapter.

✦ **Always Embed:** A list of fonts for always embedding appears to the right of the Embedding list. You add fonts to this list by selecting them from the Embedding list and clicking the right-pointing chevron (double arrows). You can select multiple fonts by pressing the Ctrl (Windows) key or ⌘ (Macintosh) key and clicking all the fonts to be included. If the fonts are listed in a contiguous display, press Shift+click. After selecting the font(s), click the right-pointing chevron. A good use for the Always Embed list might be for a font that appears in your company logo. Regardless of the type of document you create, you may want to always include your corporate font set in all your documents to avoid any font substitution.

Note

The design of TrueType fonts enables the type designer the ability to prevent font embedding. These fonts can be moved to the Always Embed list, but if designed without embedding permissions, they fail to embed in PDFs. Font embedding errors are reported in the log file that can be viewed in a text editor. If a PDF is produced, you can choose File ⇨ Document Properties ⇨ Fonts to determine whether the font was embedded.

✦ **Never Embed:** This list operates the same way as the Always Embed list. You select fonts to be eliminated from the set of monitored fonts or fonts contained in a PostScript file. One use for this list might be to eliminate Courier, Times, Helvetica, and Symbol (the Base 13 fonts). Because they are usually burned into ROM chips on most PostScript devices, you rarely have a problem either viewing them or printing documents containing these fonts.

Note The Base 14 fonts are sometimes referred to as the Base 13 + 1 fonts. The Base 13 fonts consist of Courier, Helvetica, Times, and Symbol. Courier, Helvetica, and Times include Roman, bold, italic, and bold italic, thus resulting in four fonts for each family. The extra font added to the base set is Zapf Dingbats. The fonts shipped with Acrobat 6 are no longer the Base 14 fonts that were shipped with earlier versions of Acrobat. Acrobat 6 ships with a new set of Base Fonts that include: AdobePiStd (a replacement for Zapf Dingbats), Courier, Symbol, AdobeSansMM, and Adobe SerifMM). Acrobat Distiller 6 does not embed the Base Fonts.

✦ **Add Name:** You can add fonts to the Always Embed list or the Never Embed list by entering the font name in a separate dialog box. To add a font name, you must type the name in the dialog box precisely as the font is identified. When you click the Add Name button in the Fonts tab, a dialog box opens where you add the name. In the Add Font name dialog box, you type the name in the field box. Two radio buttons exist for determining where the font is added. Select either the Always Embed list or Never Embed list as needed. Click Done, and the font appears in the appropriate list.

✦ **Remove:** If you add a font name to either the Always Embed list or the Never Embed list, and you want to delete that name, select the font name to be deleted and click Remove. Fonts can't be removed from the Embedding list. The only time Remove is enabled is when you select a font name in either the Always Embed list or Never Embed list.

Note The priority used by Distiller to decide whether to embed a font in the PDF follows an order to resolve ambiguity. The Never Embed list is viewed by Distiller as having the highest order of priority. If a font is placed in the Never Embed list it is not to be embedded even though the same font may be added to the Always Embed list.

Font types

Any PDF author will tell you the continuing problem with file displays and printing as well as producing PDFs is in regard to font handling. People swear at times that they have enabled all the appropriate controls for font embedding and PDF file creation, yet the resulting PDF either displays or prints with font substitution. Gathering as much knowledge as you can with regard to font evolution, design, engineering, and proper use helps you understand how to overcome problems and provide solutions for your workflow. To gain a little more understanding, look at the font types, formats, and their characteristics:

✦ **Type 0:** Type 0 (zero) is a high-level composite font format that references multiple font descendents. Type 0 fonts use an OCF (Original Composite Font) format that was Adobe's first effort in attempting to implement a format for handling fonts with large character sets. A good example of a font using a large character set is Asian Language font types. Today, the OCF format is not supported.

✦ **Type 1:** By far the most popular PostScript font today is the Type 1 font. These are single-byte fonts handled well by Adobe Type Manager (Windows and Macintosh OS X) and all PostScript printers. Type 1 fonts use a specialized subset of the PostScript language, which is optimized for performance. For reliability, use of Type 1 fonts presents the fewest problems when embedding and printing to PostScript devices.

Note The one problem with Type 1 fonts is there isn't a means for flagging the font for *don't embed*. As a result, the end user can't determine font permissions for embedding Type 1 fonts. As of this writing Adobe is converting all Type 1 fonts to Open Type fonts. Open Type fonts always have an extra bit to determine embedding rights. For more information on Open Type fonts, see "Open Type Font Format" later in this section.

✦ **Type 2:** Type 2 fonts offer compact character description procedures for outline fonts. They were designed to be used with the Compact Font Format (CFF). The CFF format is designed for font embedding and substitution with Acrobat PDFs.

✦ **Type 3:** Type 3 fonts are PostScript fonts that have often been used with some type-stylizing applications. These fonts can have special design attributes applied to the font such as shading, patterns, exploding 3-D displays, and so on. The fonts can't be used with ATM (Adobe Type Manager) and they often present problems when you're printing to PostScript devices. They should not be used when creating PDF files.

✦ **Type 4:** Type 4 was designed to create font characters from printer font cartridges for permanent storage on a printer's hard drive (usually attached by a SCSI port to the printer). PostScript Level 2 provided the same capability for Type 1 fonts and eventually made these font types obsolete.

✦ **Type 5:** This font type is similar to the Type 4 fonts but used the printer's ROM instead of the hard drive. PostScript Level 2 again made this format obsolete.

✦ **Type 32:** Type 32 fonts are used for downloading bitmap fonts to a PostScript interpreter's font cache. By downloading directly to the printer cache, space is saved in the printer's memory.

✦ **Type 42:** Type 42 fonts are generated from the printer driver for TrueType fonts. A PostScript wrapper is created for the font making the rasterization and interpretation more efficient and accurate. Type 42 fonts work well with PDFs and printing to PostScript printers.

✦ **OpenType Font Format:** OpenType is a recent joint effort by Adobe Systems and Microsoft to provide a new generation of type font technology. OpenType makes no distinction between Type 1 and TrueType fonts. It acts as a *container* for both Type 1 and TrueType. OpenType doesn't care whether the font is Type 1 or TrueType, it uses the font inside the OpenType container accordingly. Font developers have a much easier way of porting font designs to a single format in production and mastering as well as across platforms. The OpenType format is supported with font embedding and distillation. Fonts eventually produced with this technology are as reliable as you find with Type 1 and Type 42 fonts. In addition OpenType offers a means for flagging the fonts for embedding permissions.

✦ **Compact Font Format:** CFF is similar to the Type 1 format but offers much more compact encoding and optimization. It was designed to support Type 2 fonts but can be used with other types. CFF can be embedded in PDFs with the PDF version 1.2 format and Acrobat 3.0 compatibility. Fonts supporting this format are converted by Distiller during distillation to CFF/Type 2 fonts and embedded in the PDF. When viewed onscreen or printed, they are converted back to Type 1, which provides support for ATM and printing with integrity.

✦ **CID-keyed Fonts:** This format was developed to take advantage of large character sets particularly the Asian CJK (Chinese, Japanese, and Korean) fonts. The format is an extension of the Type 1 format and supports ATM and PostScript printing. Kerning and spacing for these character sets are better handled in the OpenType format. On the Macintosh a utility called Make CID can be found in the Distiller: Xtras folder. For Asian TrueType or Type 1 OCF formats, use the utility to convert the fonts to CID-keyed fonts. The first time Distiller is launched with the Asian character set installed, you are prompted to convert any of these fonts found in monitored folders. If you want to manually convert the fonts you can double-click on the application icon. On Windows, the Make CID application isn't available. Converted fonts can be copied across platforms, and Distiller running under Windows processes PostScript files created under Mac OS that have references to the character widths.

When distilling PostScript with Acrobat Distiller, font embedding and substitution are allowed as described in Table 7-2.

Table 7-2: Distiller Handling of Font Embedding and Subsetting According to Type Format

Font	Never Embed	Always Embed	Subset
Type 1	Yes	Yes	Yes
Type 2	No — Always embedded		No — Always subsetted
TrueType			
Type 42	Yes	Yes	No — Always subsetted
CIDFontType0	Yes	Yes	No — Always subsetted
CIDFontType1	No — Always embedded		No — Always subsetted
CIDFontType2	Yes	Yes	No — Always subsetted
OpenType*	Yes	Yes	No — Always subsetted

*OpenType is supported only with Distiller 5.0 and greater.

Color

Adobe has been working on developing standard color viewing and file tagging for color spaces for some time. Releases of the latest software products continue to support sophisticated color-handling methods. Latest releases of products such as Adobe Illustrator and Adobe Photoshop have color control options consistent with the new color-handling features initially introduced in Acrobat 5. When making choices for color handling, your first decision to make is whether to convert color. After your conversion choice, you move on to working spaces and profile assumptions. If you tag a file for conversion, what profiles do you want to embed in the document? Under the Color Management Policies settings, you choose control for many conditions for prepress operations as well as onscreen viewing. As you view the Color tab in the Adobe PDF Settings, examine each of the controls available for color handling (see Figure 7-11).

Adobe color settings

Working with a color management system requires you to make some decisions about how the color is viewed on your computer monitor and on the final output medium. In some cases the monitor view and output medium view are the same, such as Acrobat viewer files onscreen and Web files. You make the first of your color decisions from among the choices in the pull-down menu for Settings File. The choices available to you include

✦ **Settings:** When you select None from the pull-down menu, you can custom edit the Color Management Policies and Working Spaces choices. If you choose an option other than None, the Color Management Policies and Working Spaces options are grayed out. Other choices for Settings include prepress defaults, Photoshop emulation, defaults for Web graphics, and turning color management off. When color management and profile embedding is controlled by other programs such as Photoshop, leave the setting to None and turn off all color management for the choices discussed next.

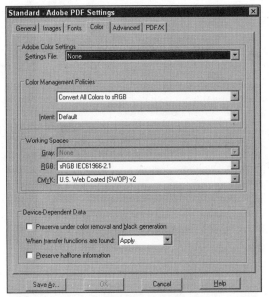

Figure 7-11: Manage color profiles in the Color tab.

Color management policies

If you select None from the Settings drop-down menu, the options for Color Management Policies and Intent are active. If you make any other choice from the menu, these items are grayed out. Choices for the Color Management Policies are different depending on what compatibility choice you select in the General tab of the Adobe PDF Settings dialog box. Acrobat 3.0 compatibility offers different options than the 4.0, 5.0, and 6.0 compatibility. As you look at the following policy choices, keep in mind the settings change according to the compatibility selection made:

✦ **Leave Color Unchanged:** This menu item should be enabled if you presume all color handling in the PostScript file is defined for your specific needs. No color conversion occurs and device-dependent colors remain unchanged. When you send files to color-calibrated devices, you should use this option. The presumption is the device specifies all color handling and the file is not to be tagged for color management.

✦ **Tag Everything for Color Management:** When you choose Acrobat 3.0 compatibility or above, a color profile selected in the Working Spaces section is used to Tag Everything for Color Management, which embeds an ICC profile for the images, artwork, and text. The printed PDF file maintains the integrity of any documents containing embedded profiles; however, the view on your monitor screen assumes the color viewing space of the assumed profile selected respective to choices made in Working Spaces. When you choose Acrobat 3.0 compatibility, the option changes to Convert Everything for Color Management and no ICC profiles are embedded. Device-dependent color spaces for all color modes are converted to device-independent color spaces of CalRGB, CalGray, and Lab.

✦ **Tag Only Images for Color Management:** The same holds true as noted in the preceding entry except only raster images are tagged for color management according to the same compatibility options selected in the General tab. Text and vector objects remain unaffected.

✦ **Convert All Colors to sRGB:** Selecting this option converts all colors to sRGB. The RGB and CMYK color images are converted. When using Acrobat 3.0 compatibility, the RGB and CMYK images are converted to CalRGB (Calibrated RGB). Converting colors to sRGB is best used for screen and Web images. The file sizes are smaller and screen redraws appear faster. Grayscale images are unaffected by choices made for color tagging and conversion.

Below the first pull-down menu is another pull-down menu used for the Intent for how color will be mapped between color spaces. Choices for Intent include

✦ **Default:** The first of the Intent choices is Default. Default involves no color compensation.

✦ **Perceptual:** Perceptual (Images) has to do with the mapping of pixels from one gamut to another. When you select this item, the image is mapped from the original pixels to the color gamut of the printer profile. All the out-of-gamut colors are remapped.

✦ **Saturation:** Saturation (Graphics) maintains relative saturation values. If a pixel is saturated and out of the color gamut of the printer, it is remapped preserving saturation but mapped to the closest color within the printer's gamut.

✦ **Absolute Colormetric:** This disables the white point matching when colors are converted. With no white point reference, you will notice a change in brightness values of all the remapped colors.

✦ **Relative Colormetric:** This preserves all color values within the printer's gamut. Out-of-gamut colors are converted to the same lightness values of colors within the printable gamut.

Working spaces

Profile management for working spaces involves your decisions for embedding profiles for the color space while viewing your images onscreen. If a color space is defined for a given image and viewed on one monitor, theoretically it can be viewed the same on other monitors if the color profile is embedded in the image. Working space definitions are applied only to images tagged for color management. Either of the two tagging options, Tag Everything for Color Management or Tag Only Images for Color Management, must be selected in order for a working space to be defined:

✦ **Gray:** Selecting None from this menu prevents grayscale images from being converted. The Dot Gain choices affect the overall brightness of grayscale images. Lower values lighten the image whereas values above 20% display grayscale images darker. Gray Gamma choices might be used for images viewed between computer platforms. A Gray Gamma of 1.8 is suited for Macintosh viewing while the higher 2.2 Gamma is better suited for Windows.

✦ **RGB:** If you use a color calibration system or monitor profile, you can select the respective profile from this pull-down menu. Choices available to you depend on profiles installed on your computer. If you have created custom profiles from Adobe Photoshop and saved them, they are listed as menu options. Default RGB profiles from Photoshop appear here after Photoshop is installed on your computer. The default option is sRGB IEC61966-2.1. If in doubt, use this option. It is becoming an industry standard and generally good for matching color between display and color output devices.

✦ **CMYK:** CMYK profiles also appear according to those stored in the respective folder according to platform as mentioned in the preceding bullet. Profile tagging is uniquely applied to images according to the color mode of the image. Thus, the Gray options only apply to grayscale images. RGB choices are applied to only RGB images whereas the CMYK choices tag only CMYK images. When using CMYK output for prepress you may have a profile embedded in the CMYK images. You can select None for this setting while changing the Gray and RGB working spaces, which preserves the color for output while enabling you to tag the other color modes for screen views. It would be unlikely that you would use RGB and CMYK images together for prepress, but you could set up the Adobe PDF Settings for consistent display of files regardless of the color mode used.

Device-Dependent Data

All options available under the Device Dependent Data section are applied to images intended for prepress and printing. Whatever choices you make here have no effect on screen views:

✦ **Preserve under color removal and black generation:** If you made changes to under-color removal or black generation settings in Photoshop, these changes are preserved when the file is distilled. Disabling the check box eliminates any settings made in Photoshop.

✦ **When transfer functions are found:** If you embed transfer functions in Adobe Photoshop, you can preserve them by selecting Apply from the pull-down menu. If transfer functions have not been saved with your Photoshop file, it won't matter if Apply is used. Use Apply when you intentionally set them up in a Photoshop image and you have the settings confirmed by your printer. You can eliminate transfer functions set in a file by selecting Remove from the pull-down menu. As a matter of default, if you don't use transfer functions or know what they are, select Remove from the pull-down menu. If you inadvertently save a Photoshop file as EPS and embed transfer functions, they are removed when the file gets distilled.

✦ **Preserve halftone information:** Preserving the halftone information does not disturb halftone frequencies embedded in documents, as well as custom angles, spot shapes, and functions specified. Depending on the service center you use, they may want to have you set halftone information in the PostScript file and preserve them in the PDF. For PostScript 3 devices, PDFs can be sent straight to the imagesetter and printed at the halftone frequency preserved in the file. Service centers using PostScript Level 2 RIPs won't care if the halftone frequency is preserved or not. They'll have to manually print the PDFs using the Print and Advanced Print Setup dialog boxes.

Advanced

Advanced settings enable you to make choices for other miscellaneous attributes. The controls listed in this dialog box greatly distinguish Acrobat Distiller from other PDF producers. When you select the Advanced tab in Adobe PDF Settings, the settings shown in Figure 7-12 appear.

Advanced settings contain a variety of options for job ticketing, document structure, and other items not found in the previous tabs. These include

✦ **Allow PostScript file to override Adobe PDF settings:** If you are certain the PostScript file you printed to disk has all the settings handled properly for output, enabling this option allows the PostScript file to supersede any changes you make in Adobe PDF Settings. Disabling the check box allows all Options specifications settings to take precedence.

✦ **Allow PostScript XObjects:** A PostScript XObject stores common information in a document, such as backgrounds, headers, footers, and so on. When PostScript XObjects are used, printing is faster, but requires more memory. If you disable the check box, XObjects won't be used and the memory burden is reduced.

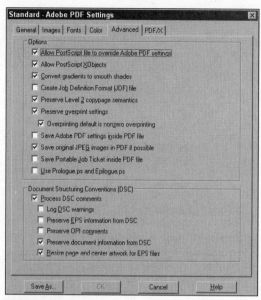

Figure 7-12: The Advanced Adobe PDF Settings offer a group of miscellaneous settings often not available with other PDF producers.

✦ **Convert gradients to smooth shades:** This feature only works with Acrobat 4.0 compatibility and greater. Gradients are converted to smooth shades and appear much smoother when rendered on PostScript 3 devices. The appearance of the gradients is unaffected when viewed onscreen, but has noticeable differences when printing some files with more gray levels.

✦ **Create Job Definition Format (JDF) file:** This option creates a job ticket in XML. The job ticket contains information related to the file for use by print shops. For information about the contents of job tickets, see the "Save Portable Job Ticket inside PDF file" bullet later in this list.

✦ **Preserve Level 2 copypage Semantics:** This setting has to do with semantic differences between PostScript Level 2 and PostScript 3. If you are imaging to PostScript Level 2 devices, enable this option. If you're printing to PostScript 3 devices, disable this option. If you are sending files to an imaging center, ask the technicians which level of PostScript is used on their devices.

✦ **Preserve overprint settings:** Overprints manually applied in applications, such as illustration and layout programs, are preserved when you enable this option. Overprinting only has an effect when your files are color separated or possibly when you print composite color to proofing machines that display trapping problems from files printed as separations. If your workflow is consistent and you don't deviate between creating overprints and relying on a service center to perform them, then you could leave this item as a default for your high-end output needs. Enabling the check box has no effect on images where overprints are not present.

✦ **Overprinting default is nonzero overprinting:** When enabled this option prevents objects with no color values specified as CMYK from knocking out other CMYK colors.

✦ **Save Adobe PDF settings inside PDF file:** This option embeds the Adobe PDF Settings used to produce the PDF inside the PDF document as a file attachment. Print shops can review the settings to diagnose problems that may have been produced during distillation. Choose Document ⇨ File Attachments to see the embedded file.

✦ **Save original JPEG images in PDF if possible:** Distiller decompresses JPEG files during distillation. If you select this option, the decompressed JPEG files are not recompressed by Distiller.

✦ **Save Portable Job Ticket inside PDF file:** Job tickets contain information about the original PostScript file and not the content of the PDF file. Information related to page sizes, page orientation, resolution, halftone frequencies, trapping information, and so on is some of what is contained in job tickets. When printing PDF files, enable this option. If you produce PDF files for screen, Web, or CD-ROM, you can eliminate job ticket information.

✦ **Use Prologue.ps and Epilogue.ps:** There are two files, named prologue.ps and epilogue.ps, located in the Documents and Settings\All Users\Documents\Adobe PDF 6.0\ Data folder (Windows) or Users\Shared\Adobe PDF 6.0\Data folder (Macintosh) when you install Acrobat. In order to use the files, they must be moved to the same folder as the Acrobat Distiller application and both files must reside together in this location. The files contain PostScript code appended to a PDF file when it is created with Distiller. By default the files do not contain any data that affect distillation. They serve more as templates where you can write code to append data to the PDF. The prologue.ps file can be used to append information to the PDF such as a note, cover page, or job ticket information. The epilogue.ps file is used to resolve PostScript procedure problems.

Note

Both of these files can be edited; however, you need to be familiar with the PostScript language to effectively change the files. When relocating the files, be certain to place a copy in the Distiller folder and leave the original in the Data folder, especially if you decide to edit either file. You can also use the files with watched folders, as explained a little later in this chapter. When using watched folders, place the prologue.ps and epilogue.ps files at the same directory level as the In and Out folders.

✦ **Process DSC comments:** Document structuring comments (DSC) contain information about a PDF file. Items such as originating application, creation date, modification date, page orientation, and so on are all document-structuring comments. To maintain the DSC, enable this option. Because some important information such as page orientation and beginning and ending statements for the prologue.ps file are part of the document structure, you'll want to keep this item enabled as a default.

✦ **Log DSC warnings:** During distillation, if the processing of the document-structuring comments encounters an error, the error is noted in a log file. When you enable this check box, a log file is created. You can open the log file in a word processor or text editor to determine where the error occurred. Enable this option whenever document-structuring comments are processed.

✦ **Preserve EPS information from DSC:** This item is similar to the Process DSC comments option. If your file is an EPS file, enabling this check box preserves document-structuring comments.

✦ **Preserve OPI comments:** Open Press Interface (OPI) is a management tool used by many high-end imaging centers to control production. An OPI comment might include the replacement of high-resolution images for low-resolution FPO (for position only) files used in a layout program. OPI comments can include many different issues related to digital prepress such as image position on a page, crop area, sampling resolution, color bit depth, colors (in other words, CMYK, spot, and so on), overprint instructions, and more. If you're outputting to high-end imaging devices at service centers using OPI management, enable this option.

✦ **Preserve document information from DSC:** Document information items, discussed later in this book, include such things as title, subject, author, and keywords. Enabling this option preserves document information.

✦ **Resize page and center artwork for EPS files:** In earlier versions of Acrobat, distillation of a single-page EPS file, created from programs such as Adobe Illustrator, Macromedia FreeHand, or CorelDraw, used the EPS bounding box for the final page size. Many problems occurred when distilling EPS files directly as opposed to printed PostScript files. At times, a user would experience clipping and lose part of an image. With this option you have a choice between creating a PDF with the page dimensions equal to the artwork and having the artwork appear on the size of the original page you defined in your host application. When the check box is enabled, the page size is reduced to the size of the artwork, and the artwork is centered on the page. When the check box is disabled, the entire page appears consistent with the page size used in the host application.

Many of the controls available in the Advanced tab are explained when I discuss prepress and printing in Chapter 23. At this time, it is important to realize that Acrobat Distiller provides you with many more controls for setting attributes for PDF document creation and permits flexibility in designing PDF files for specific purposes. With all these toggles and check boxes, becoming confused and feeling overwhelmed is easy. Fortunately, Acrobat can help make this job a little easier for you. If you work in an office environment where a network administrator sets up all the controls for your PDF workflow, you can load preset custom Adobe PDF Settings. If you are the responsible party for creating the Adobe PDF Settings, you can create different custom settings, save them, and later load them from a menu option in Acrobat Distiller. Either way, you won't have to go back and reread this chapter every time you want to distill a file for another purpose.

PDF/X

As explained earlier, PDF/X is a subset of the PDF format developed by an ISO (International Organization for Standardization) standards committee outside Adobe Systems. Adobe is a participant on the committee and supports the development and advances in PDF/X standards.

PDF/X has gained much acceptance among commercial printing companies for the purposes of creating files suitable for printing. PDF is a reliable format for any kind of electronic file exchanges. However, files developed for viewing in Acrobat viewers, Acrobat PDF forms, Web-hosted documents, and so on carry a lot of overhead not necessary for printing on commercial printing devices. The PDF/X compliance standard was developed to streamline documents by eliminating unnecessary data and optimizing files for print. The process of tailoring a PDF document for print by creating a PDF/X-compliant file does not necessarily reduce file size. In many cases, file sizes grow from a standard PDF to a PDF/X file.

The PDF/X options available to you in Acrobat Distiller are producing either a PDF/X-1a- or PDF/X-3-compliant file. These file types are different versions of the PDF/X format. PDF/X-1a is designed to work well with both process and spot color, but no support is provided for color management or profile embedding. PDF/X-3 supports process and spot color and does support color-managed workflows and ICC (International Color Consortium) profile embedding.

The PDF/X tab appears only in Acrobat Professional and is not available to Acrobat Standard users.

When you use PDF/X during distillation you are checking the file for PDF/X compliance. If the file does not meet the PDF/X standard you select (that is, PDF/X-1a or PDF/X-3), you can halt the distillation process much like halting distillation when fonts don't embed properly. If a file meets PDF/X compliance, you have much greater assurance that your PDF document will print on almost any kind of commercial printing device.

You create PDF/X-compliant files with Acrobat Distiller or an authoring program that specifically addresses PDF/X compliance when exporting to PDF. Other PDF producers such as the PDFMaker used with Microsoft Office applications, Microsoft Project, Microsoft Visio, and AutoDesk AutoCAD do not support PDF/X. If you want to print any of these files on commercial printing devices, print PostScript files and distill them with Acrobat Distiller and PDF/X enabled.

The options you have in the PDF/X tab in Acrobat Professional, shown in Figure 7-13, include the following:

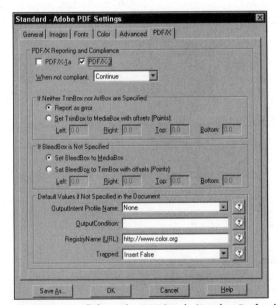

Figure 7-13: Click on the PDF/X tab (Acrobat Professional only) and the PDF/X options choices are accessible.

A thorough coverage of color management is a complex subject and beyond the scope of this book. If you are confused about many issues discussed in this chapter or you want to work on developing a color-managed workflow, open any Acrobat viewer. Click on the Search tool and click on Search PDFs on the Internet. Add *color management* for the search criteria and select Match Exact word or phrase from the pull-down menu. Click on the Search the Internet button. Many PDF documents are available on the Internet that define color management and discuss how to setup color-managed workflows. You can build a library of articles and essays on the subject and keep them readily available on your local computer.

✦ **PDF/X Reporting and Compliance:** Use these two check boxes to check for PDF/X compliance. You can check both check boxes for assessing the file for compliance with both PDF/X versions. The results of the analysis are reported in a log file. If problems were encountered during distillation, the problems are reported in the log file. A single log file is created if you check both boxes. If neither check box is enabled, no PDF/X compliance is assessed and all options below the check boxes are grayed out.

✦ **When not compliant:** Two menu choices are available from the pull-down menu. Select Continue to create the PDF file if the file does not meet PDF/X compliance. The PDF file is created and a log file is generated reporting problems. If you select Cancel Job the PDF is not created and assures you of only producing files that meet the PDF/X standards.

✦ **Report as error:** Enabling the radio button reports the file noncompliant if one or both of the PDF/X Reporting and Compliance check boxes are checked and trim box or media box are missing on any page in the document.

✦ **Set TrimBox to MediaBox with offset (Points):** The (Points) item is the default. The unit of measure is determined by the units set in the General tab. If you change the units, the name in the title field changes to the same units selected in the General tab. When the radio button is enabled, the trim box is calculated against the media box for offset distances if neither is specified in the PostScript file. The trim box is always equal to or smaller than the media box. Edit the field boxes for determining the offset amounts that are analyzed.

✦ **Set BleedBox to MediaBox:** Uses the media box values for the bleed box if no bleeds are specified in the PostScript file. In many layout authoring programs you have options for specifying bleed areas. If no bleeds are defined in the print dialog boxes, the media box values are used.

✦ **Set BleedBox to TrimBox with offsets (Points):** Again the unit of measure is determined from the General tab Units selection. If the bleed box is not defined, the values specified in the field boxes are computed against the trim box.

✦ **OutputIntent Profile Name:** If the file does not specify an output intent, such as SWOP coated for example, Distiller uses the intent you select from the pull-down menu. The field box is editable and you can type an output intent in the field box. If you don't require an output intent for the devices you use, select None. When the file is distilled and no intent was used when the PostScript file was printed, selecting None forces the job to fail compliance.

✦ **OutputCondition:** This field box is where you supply the intended output condition. The field value is not assessed for compliance. It is used by the service center for information purposes. If you leave the field blank, it has no effect on whether the job meets compliance.

✦ **RegistryName (URL):** This item is also informational. The default URL is http://www.color.org where more information is obtained regarding sets of characterization data for standard printing processes.

✦ **Trapped:** Three options are available from the pull-down menu. PDF/X compliance requires that the Trapped state be analyzed for True or False. If you select Undefined, you are checking the file against trapping. If it does not specify a trapping state the file fails PDF/X compliance. Insert True checks for a trapped state. If no trapping was added to the file, the file fails compliance. Insert False checks for no trapping. If trapping is applied to the file, the file fails compliance when this item is selected.

✦ **Help:** The four icons with question marks to the right of the items in the Default Values if Not Specified in the Document area of the PDF/X tab offer help information. Click on one of the icons and a pop-up menu opens with a definition for the respective option.

✦ **Save As:** The Save As button captures all the settings you make for the Adobe PDF Settings and opens a dialog box that defaults to the Settings folder. If you change any item in one of the preset options and click OK in the Adobe PDF Settings dialog box, the Save As dialog box opens automatically to prompt you to save the new options choices to a new file. Provide a filename and click the Save button to create a new settings file. In Figure 7-14, I named a new set myJobOptions.joboptions.

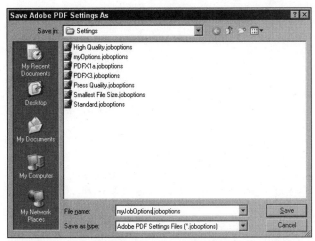

Figure 7-14: When you click the Save As button, a navigation dialog box opens enabling you to supply a name and find a location for the new settings to be saved. By default, the new file is saved to the Settings folder. The files must reside in this folder in order to appear in the Distiller window in the Default Settings pull-down menu.

Identifying Font Locations

Font embedding as described earlier in this chapter occurs when Adobe PDF Settings is enabled for font embedding and a font is contained in the PostScript file or loaded in the system with a utility such as Adobe Type Manager, Extensis Suitcase, or the system folder where fonts are accessed. If fonts reside neither in the PostScript file nor are loaded in your system, Distiller offers another method for locating fonts. Open the Settings menu and select Font Locations. The Acrobat Distiller–Font Locations dialog box opens as shown in Figure 7-15.

In this dialog box you add folders of fonts that Distiller looks in when a font is neither contained in the PostScript file nor loaded in the system memory. Monitored font folders are listed in the window shown in Figure 7-15. To add a new folder, click on the Add button. To remove a folder, select it in the list and click on the Remove button.

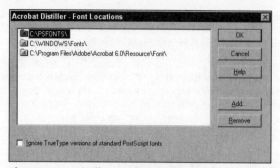

Figure 7-15: Distiller monitors fonts installed on your hard drive when the fonts appear in a list in the Acrobat Distiller– Font Locations dialog box.

A check box at the bottom of the dialog box enables you to resolve some problems that may occur when a TrueType font has the same name as a PostScript font. To eliminate embedding TrueType fonts with the same names as PostScript fonts, check the box at the bottom of the dialog box.

Creating Watched Folders

Watched folders enable you to automate distillation of PostScript files in a business or production environment. You can easily develop a PDF workflow by hosting a server on a network where Acrobat Distiller is continually running in the background and watching a folder or many folders for the introduction of new PostScript files. When Distiller encounters a new PostScript file, the file is distilled in the background while foreground applications are running. The resulting PDF files are automatically moved to another folder or directory, and the PostScript files are either preserved or deleted automatically.

Licensing restrictions

Before moving on to working with watched folders, please look over this section carefully and try to understand the proper use and authorization of working with watched folders on networks. Adobe Systems grants you license for working on a single computer when installing Acrobat. When you create PDFs on your computer you can distribute them to anyone who uses an Acrobat viewer. Therefore, the PDFs you create can legitimately be distributed to anyone who acquires the free Adobe Reader software.

Creating PDFs, whether locally or on a network, assumes you have complied with the proper licensing agreements for use of the Acrobat Distiller application. Ambiguity arises when using the Distiller application on networks with watched folders. If you set up a watched folder on a network where multiple users access the watched folders, you need a site license to use the Acrobat Distiller application, you need to have a licensed copy of Acrobat Standard or Professional for each user, or you can purchase Acrobat Distiller Server. Because Distiller is used by multiple users in this example, site licensing or individual purchases of the product is required.

Therefore, the licensing policies in this regard are related not to distribution, but rather, how the PDFs are created. As I move through the discussion on watched folders, keep in mind that when I make mention of using watched folders on networks, I'm assuming you are compliant with the proper licensing agreements.

Creating watched folders (Acrobat Professional only)

Watched folders can be individual folders, hard drive partitions, or dedicated hard drives. When you choose Settings ➪ Watched Folders, the Watched Folders dialog box opens, enabling you to establish preferences for the watched folders and distillation attributes.

The options available in the Watched Folders dialog box include the following:

✦ **Path:** The list window displays all folders identified as watched folders. The name of the watched folder appears in the list as well as the directory path. In Figure 7-16, notice the directory path is shown.

Figure 7-16: Watched folder preferences are established in the Acrobat Distiller–Watched Folders dialog box. When you open the Acrobat Distiller–Watched Folders dialog box a reminder for the licensing restrictions appears at the bottom of the dialog box.

✦ **Check Watched Folders every [ ] seconds:** This user-definable field accepts values between 1 and 9999 seconds. When Distiller monitors a watched folder, the folder is monitored according to the value entered in this field box.

✦ **PostScript file is:** Distiller automatically treats the PostScript file according to the options available in this pull-down menu. You can select the Deleted menu item, which deletes the PostScript file after distillation, or select Moved to "Out" folder, which moves the PostScript file to a folder entitled Out. If you intend to repurpose files for different uses, be certain to keep the PostScript file.

✦ **Delete output files older than [ ] days:** If you elect to keep the PostScript files in the Out folder, they can be deleted after the time interval specified in this field box. The acceptable range is between 1 and 999 days.

✦ **Add Folder:** To create a watched folder or add to the current list of watched folders, click the Add Folder button. A navigation dialog box opens. To add a folder to the watched folders list, the folder must first be created before you click on the Add Folder button. Folders as well as partitions and drives can be added to your list. On a network, remote folders, partitions, and drives can also be added to the list. If you want to select a folder, browse your hard drive and select the folder name after clicking on the Add Folder button. If you want to have the entire hard drive watched, select the drive designation (C:\, D:\, E:\, and so on in Windows or Macintosh HD, Hard Drive, and so on with a Macintosh) and click the OK button in the Browse For Folder dialog box.

✦ **Remove:** To delete watched folders, select the folder name in the watched folders list and click the Remove Folder button. If a folder is moved or deleted from your hard drive, the next time you launch Distiller, a warning dialog box opens notifying you that Distiller cannot find the watched folder(s). Removal of watched folders must occur in the Acrobat Distiller–Watched Folder dialog box. If you inadvertently deleted a watched folder on the desktop, you need to delete the folder name in the watched folders list. Return to your desktop and create a new folder; then return to the dialog box and add the new folder to the list.

✦ **Edit Security:** Security can be applied to PDF files during distillation. Adding security during distillation is handy for multiple files created in PDF workflow environments. If the Acrobat 3.0 or 4.0 compatibility option is selected in the current General tab, the security level is limited to 40-bit encryption. If Acrobat 5.0 compatibility is selected in the General tab, 128-bit encryption is used. If Acrobat 6.0 compatibility is selected, 128-bit encryption and the new additions to Acrobat security are available.

Cross-Reference

For more information on applying security to PDF documents, see Chapter 19.

✦ **Clear Security:** Select any one or all of the watched folders in the list and click on Clear Security. The Security is removed from the folders.

✦ **Edit Settings:** The Edit Settings button becomes active when you select a watched folder name in the watched folders list. With a folder name selected in the list, click the Edit Settings button to open the Adobe PDF Settings dialog box. You can apply different settings to different watched folders. If, for example, you print PostScript files to disk and have them distilled for high-end output and Web page design, you will want compression and color modes distinctive for the output sources. You can set up two watched folders and have the same PostScript file distilled with the different settings. Editing settings here overrides Distiller's defaults and applies new options to the specific watched folder where the attributes are established.

✦ **Load Settings:** All the settings contained in the Settings folder are available for loading and applying to watched folders listed in the window. Click on Load Settings and the Settings folder opens.

✦ **Clear Settings:** Any settings applied to a watched folder are removed. If you leave the watched folder listed with no specific settings assigned to the watched folder, the current default Adobe PDF Settings are used.

PDF Workflow

Watched folders greatly help your PDF workflow and assist you in automating the smallest office environment to large offices with multiple networks and servers. When you install a site-licensed copy of Acrobat Distiller on a server, the burden of PDF creation is dedicated to the server and relieves individual workstations.

In identifying watched folders, you need only have the directory or folder created on a hard drive. After you identify the watched folder, Distiller automatically creates the other folders needed to execute distillation from watched folder files. The In folder created by Distiller is monitored. When a PostScript file is placed or written to the In folder, the distillation commences according to the interval you establish in the Watched Folder settings dialog box. Files can be placed into the In folder, or you can print to PostScript directly to the In folder from within an application.

Watched folders work well in cross-platform environments, too. In order to use a watched folder from one platform and have the distillation performed on another platform, you need to have the computers networked and have software installed that enables you to communicate between two or more computers on your network.

Working with Non-Roman Text

Acrobat provides great support for text created from character sets foreign to U.S. English and other Roman text alphabets. Eastern languages such as Russian, Ukrainian, and similar languages based on forms of Cyrillic characters require proper configuration for font access and keyboard layouts. After configuration and you use the fonts in a layout application, be certain to embed the fonts in the PostScript file or have Distiller monitor the font's folder of the character set used. As is the case with any font embedded in the PDF, the document is displayed without font substitution. In Figure 7-17, I used a Cyrillic font in Microsoft Word. The file was printed to disk as PostScript and font embedding was used in Distiller's Adobe PDF Settings.

Figure 7-17: When fonts are properly configured from character sets foreign to Roman characters, the fonts can be embedded and viewed without font substitution.

Eastern language support is provided by Acrobat but requires much more in regard to configuration and proper installation of the Asian Language Support option (Windows) or the Asian Language Kit (Macintosh). As long as the language support respective to your platform is installed with the Acrobat installer, files can be printed as PostScript and embedded in the PDFs. Viewing PDFs with embedded Asian languages such as Traditional Chinese, Simplified Chinese, Japanese, and Korean (CJK) are displayed without font substitution.

When installing Acrobat for use with these languages, you need to use the custom installation and include the language support with the other Acrobat components. After the support is installed, font problems need to be resolved when you print to PostScript. PostScript fonts have fewer problems being embedded. TrueType fonts require special handling depending on the platform and type of fonts used. Special documentation for managing PostScript and

TrueType fonts is included in the Acrobat documentation. For specific handling of Eastern Language support and TrueType fonts, review the documentation thoroughly before attempting to convert PostScript files to PDF.

Accessing Distiller

After all the controls have been established in the Adobe PDF Settings dialog boxes you're ready to use the Distiller application. Files used with Distiller need to be PostScript files printed to disk or EPS files. You can access the Distiller application several ways. These include:

✦ **Open from Distiller:** Find the Distiller application on your hard drive and double-click the application icon to launch Distiller. When the Distiller application window opens, choose File ⇨ Open. Navigate to the file you want to convert to PDF and select it in the Acrobat Distiller–Open PostScript File dialog box. Select multiple files by using the Shift key to select a contiguous group of files or Ctrl/⌘ to select a non-contiguous group. If the Preferences have been set up to ask for a filename or ask to replace a PDF, a navigation dialog box opens where you supply filename and destination.

✦ **Drag and drop to the application icon:** Either the application icon or a shortcut (alias in the Dock on Macintosh OS X) of the application can be used for drag-and-drop distillation. In this regard you can drag multiple PostScript files, EPS files, or a combination of both to either icon. Release the mouse button when the files are placed over the icon and Distiller launches and subsequently converts the file(s) to PDF.

✦ **Drag to the application window:** You can drag and drop a single file or multiple files on the Distiller application window. Launch Distiller to open the application window. Select a single file or multiple files and release the mouse button. All files are converted as individual PDFs.

✦ **Launch Distiller from within Acrobat:** To open Distiller from within Acrobat choose Advanced ⇨ Acrobat Distiller. The Distiller application launches and opens in the foreground in front of the Acrobat window. Choose File ⇨ Open or use the drag-and-drop method to open the file.

✦ **Print to Adobe PDF printer:** From any authoring program, open the Print dialog box and select Adobe PDF. Execute the Print command and the file is distilled with the current default Adobe PDF Settings.

✦ **Use the Run command (Windows):** You can create PDFs with Distiller by accessing the Run command from the Windows status bar. Select Run and supply the directory path first for Distiller, then the path for the files to be converted. Syntax must be exact. Pathnames need to be contained within quotation marks and a space needs to separate the pathname for Distiller and the pathname for the file(s) to be converted. Filenames having spaces need to be contained within quotation marks. To distill multiple files enter the pathname and filename, and separate each file with commas. Inasmuch as Acrobat offers you this capability, you'll often find drag-and-drop methods much easier.

✦ **Exporting to PDF:** From many application programs, such as Microsoft Office, and illustration and layout programs as discussed in Chapters 5 and 6, Distiller is used to produce PDFs. When distillation is complete, the user is returned to the application document window.

✦ **Watched folders:** As described earlier in this chapter, copying a PostScript or EPS file to the In folder inside a watched folder prompts distillation at the interval specified in the Acrobat Distiller–Watched Folders dialog box. Distiller must be launched before distillation of files from watched folders occurs.

When Distiller is used in all the preceding circumstances other than the use of watched folders, the current Adobe PDF Settings selected in Distiller are used to produce the PDF. That is to say, if Distiller is launched and the Standard settings appear in the pull-down menu, the Standard settings are used to create the PDF. When using watched folders, the settings associated with the watched folder are used to produce the PDF. If no settings are assigned to the watched folder, the current default settings are used.

Concatenating PostScript Files

Suppose you have several documents that you want to convert to a single PDF file. All these documents can be of a single application type — for example, a group of Microsoft Excel spreadsheets. Or the documents may come from many different applications — for example, PageMaker, Microsoft Word, Microsoft Excel, QuarkXPress, and Photoshop. In either case, if you want to create a single PDF document from all those separate files, there are two ways to handle the task. You can use the Create Adobe PDF From Multiple Files command and select the various file types for conversion, or you can choose to let Distiller combine the files into a single PDF document.

Acrobat Distiller reads PostScript code and as such, Distiller can begin its job by looking at a PostScript file that includes instructions to concatenate, or join together, all PostScript files in a given directory. If you attempt to write this code from scratch, you'll need to be fluent in PostScript. For those of us with much more limited skills, Adobe has made performing the task easier.

When Acrobat is installed, a folder entitled Example Files includes two files with PostScript code that are used for concatenating distilled files into a single PDF file. The PostScript code is generic and needs to be edited in a text editor. You need to edit these files for the directory path and filenames or file directory for the files you want to distill.

Note The path for the two files is the same path where the epilogue.ps and prologue.ps files are found: Documents and Settings\All Users\Documents\Adobe PDF 6.0\Example Files folder (Windows) or Users\Shared\Adobe PDF 6.0\Example Files folder (Macintosh).

The RunFilEx.ps and RunDirEx.txt files installed in the Example Files folder inside your Adobe PDF 6.0 folder concatenates PostScript files — RunFilEx.ps concatenates individual files, and RunDirEx.txt combines all the files in a specified directory whose names include a common extension. These two files need to be edited individually.

Note RunFilEx.ps and RundDirEx.txt have two different extensions. The idea is that the RunFilEX.ps file is distilled and only produces the PDF from the files listed in the code. When RunDirEx.txt is distilled, it also produces a PDF with files in the code. But if it has a .ps extension, the RunDirExt file is also distilled creating a blank page.

Combining files by name

The *Fil* in RunFilEx.ps is your first clue that this file is used for concatenating PostScript files by filename, each of which you identify in the PostScript code. When using this file, you must tell Distiller specifically which files (by exact name) are to be distilled. To edit the file name for distillation, open the RunFilEx.ps document in a text editor, as shown in Figure 7-18. If using a Macintosh, you can edit this file in TextEdit. In Windows, use Windows Notepad or WordPad.

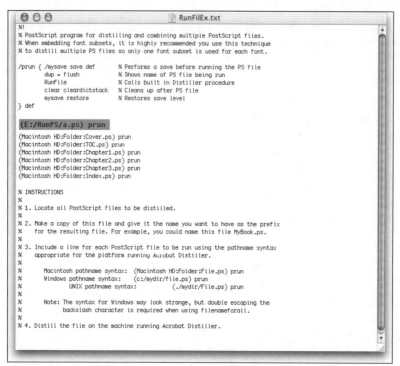

```
○ ○ ○                    📄 RunFilEx.txt
%!
% PostScript program for distilling and combining multiple PostScript files.
% When embedding font subsets, it is highly recommended you use this technique
% to distill multiple PS files so only one font subset is used for each font.

/prun { /mysave save def      % Performs a save before running the PS file
        dup = flush           % Shows name of PS file being run
        RunFile               % Calls built in Distiller procedure
        clear cleardictstack   % Cleans up after PS file
        mysave restore        % Restores save level
} def

(E:/RunPS/a.ps) prun
(Macintosh HD:Folder:Cover.ps) prun
(Macintosh HD:Folder:TOC.ps) prun
(Macintosh HD:Folder:Chapter1.ps) prun
(Macintosh HD:Folder:Chapter2.ps) prun
(Macintosh HD:Folder:Chapter3.ps) prun
(Macintosh HD:Folder:Index.ps) prun

% INSTRUCTIONS
%
% 1. Locate all PostScript files to be distilled.
%
% 2. Make a copy of this file and give it the name you want to have as the prefix
%    for the resulting file. For example, you could name this file MyBook.ps.
%
% 3. Include a line for each PostScript file to be run using the pathname syntax
%    appropriate for the platform running Acrobat Distiller.
%
%       Macintosh pathname syntax:  (Macintosh HD:Folder:File.ps) prun
%       Windows pathname syntax:    (c:/mydir/file.ps) prun
%            UNIX pathname syntax:          (./mydir/File.ps) prun
%
%       Note: The syntax for Windows may look strange, but double escaping the
%             backslash character is required when using filenameforall.
%
% 4. Distill the file on the machine running Acrobat Distiller.
```

Figure 7-18: Open the file RunFilEx.ps in a text editor such as Windows NotePad or WordPad (EditText on the Macintosh) to supply filenames for distilling in Acrobat Distiller.

When you open RunFilEx.ps, the PostScript code containing instructions for concatenating files from user-supplied names appears. All lines of code beginning with a % symbol are comment lines that do not supply instructions to Distiller. These comments are provided to explain the procedures.

Tip   If you double-click on the file on the desktop, it may open in Adobe Illustrator or Acrobat Distiller. To avoid problems when launching the file, to open it in a text editor, change the file extension to .txt. When you double-click on the file, it opens in your default text editor.

RunFilEx.ps in Windows

The syntax for directory paths in the PostScript code is different between Windows and the Macintosh, and on Windows varies somewhat from standard DOS syntax. When you open the RunFilEx.ps file in Windows WordPad or another text editor, the sample lines of code show directory paths and filenames for Macintosh users. The comments below the code provide a guideline for proper syntax when using Windows. In Figure 7-18, notice the comment line for Windows pathname syntax located toward the bottom of the figure. In Windows, identify your drive as a standard drive letter — for example, C:. After the drive letter, use a forward slash instead of a backslash to separate the drive name from the directory name. Nesting occurs in Windows the way it does later in the Macintosh example, but be certain to use forward slashes to separate the folder names. The filename should include the name and extension as it was written.

When describing drive, directory, and filenames, case sensitivity is not an issue. Any of these identifiers can be either upper- or lowercase. In Figure 7-18, I used my E: drive and a directory labeled RunPS. Only the file a.ps is noted for distillation, as it is the only file identified in the code. Notice the filename was changed from RunFilEx.ps to RunFilEx.txt, as you can see in the titlebar.

RunFilEx.ps on the Macintosh

The same file and location is used on the Macintosh as observed in the previous section with Windows. When you open the RunFilEx.ps in a text editor, the complete directory path, as described in the preceding section with Windows, needs to be supplied. In Figure 7-18, a description of a Macintosh directory path and filenames is shown.

It is critical to precisely code the directory path and filename(s) for Distiller to recognize the location and files to be distilled. The name of your volume (that is Macintosh HD, Hard Drive, and so on) would be the name you have provided for your hard drive. By default, many Macintosh hard drives are labeled Macintosh HD. If you have named your hard drive another name, enter it exactly as found on your Desktop. After the hard drive name, enter a colon (:) followed by a folder name. Folders are not necessary, but it is recommended you save the files to a folder below the root of your hard drive. Folders can be nested as long as you follow the proper syntax (in other words, *Hard Drive:FolderA:FolderB:FolderC*, and so on). The last entry for each line of code is the filename.

In TextEdit or any other text editor, save your file as text-only. Save the file with a descriptive name — you needn't use the RunFilEx.txt name of the original file. Be certain the file is a copy of the original, so you can return to the Examples folder and find this file again when needed.

In order to convert the named files in the RunFilEx.ps file, you need to open the newly edited file in Acrobat Distiller. You can drag the file on top of the Distiller window on either platform or launch Distiller and choose File ➪ Open. The instructions in the PostScript code direct Distiller to the files you listed for conversion to PDF.

Combining files in folders

The second file in the Examples folder used for concatenating PostScript files is RunDirEx.txt. Whereas RunFilEx.ps requires you to name all the PostScript files to be distilled, this file uses a wildcard character to distill all files with a common extension in a specified directory. The directory path for either the Mac or Windows uses the same syntax as illustrated previously; however, instead of filename(s), a wildcard character followed by the extension for the file-names is used. The wildcard is the standard asterisk (*), which is used to indicate all files with the same extension you specify in the line of code for the pathname.

In Figure 7-19, I specified my D: hard drive on my Windows computer and the ClientFolder directory. All the files with a .ps extension will be distilled by Acrobat Distiller. In this example for Windows, I used /PathName (D:/ClientFolder/*.ps). I then saved the file as MyFile.txt to the same ClientFolder directory.

After you edit the RunFilEx.ps or RunDirEx.txt file, it becomes the file that you open in Acrobat Distiller. This file tells Distiller where to go and what files to convert to PDF. The file can be located in any directory on your hard drive, because it instructs Distiller where to go to find the files for distillation. If the file is saved in the same folder where the files to be distilled are stored, it is important to provide a different extension for this filename from the extension of the files to be distilled when using RunDirEx.txt. If you name the file MyFile.ps and include it in a directory with a number of files also having a .ps extension, the PostScript code file for combining the other files is included in the final PDF file.

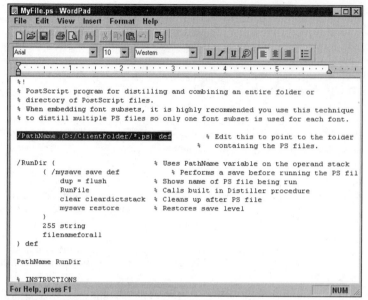

Figure 7-19: Following /*PathName* in the RunDirEx.txt file, enter the path and *.extension for all the files included in the distillation.

When you run MyFile.txt (or whatever name you have supplied for the file), the page order occurs in the same order as an alphanumeric character set. To help simplify understanding how the page order is applied, view your files in a folder as a list. Be certain the order is not date, type, or anything other than listed by name. The order you view is the same page order as the resulting PDF.

In Figure 7-20, the top of the list begins the page order. In my example, the 0.ps file is the first page in the PDF file, followed by 2.ps, and so on. All eight pages are distilled if the RunDirEx.txt file is used and includes all files ending in .ps in the ClientFolder directory.

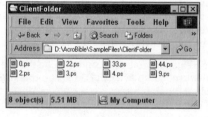

Figure 7-20: PostScript files in a Windows directory are viewed as a list, with the files arranged by name.

Note   As you examine the list in Figure 7-20, notice that 44.ps is followed by 9.ps. If you want these files to be consecutively ordered, the filenaming has to follow some different rules. Both Distiller and your operating system arrange the files according to the characters in left-to-right (dictionary) order. If two files have the same first character, the second character is examined and the file placed in the list accordingly. In this example, Windows doesn't care about 49 being larger than 9. It looks at the 4 in 49 and sees it as a lower order than 9.

To rearrange your files in the order you want to have them appear in an Acrobat viewer, rename them before distillation, taking into consideration the first character is the highest order of priority. For this example, I renamed my files as illustrated in Figure 7-21. When the PDF file is produced, the page order matches my new order as viewed in the folder.

Tip

To combine files in a page order where the file names are not listed in a folder in the order you want the pages to appear, you can use the Create PDF From Multiple Files command in Acrobat. You can add PostScript files to the Create PDF From Multiple Documents dialog box and order the .ps files as you want the page order to appear in the resulting PDF.

Cross-Reference

For more information on using Create PDF From Multiple Files, see Chapter 5.

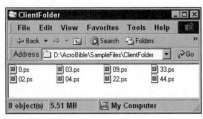

Figure 7-21: I renamed the files in the ClientFolder directory by including a zero (0) in front of the single-digit filenames so the two-digit filenames would follow in numerical order.

Tip

Because Distiller and your operating system order alphanumeric characters the same, view your folder contents as a list before distilling the files. The list order you see is the same order of the page numbers in the final PDF document.

Combining PostScript files on networks

If you want to develop a PDF workflow and use a server to collect all your PDF files on a local area network, you need to follow some simple guidelines in order to produce PDF documents. Whereas files can be printed to disk on remote systems and drives that are cross platform, Distiller can't follow cross-platform directory paths. Therefore, if you use RunDirEx.txt and want to distill files in C:\MyFolder*.ps, Distiller running on a Macintosh isn't able to execute instructions for following cross-platform directory paths. This also applies to Windows users who may want to use a file describing directory paths on a Macintosh. Distiller can be used cross platform to distill files on remote drives, and the RunDirEx.txt file works between two computers running the same operating system. Using Distiller and RunDirEx.txt on networks have the following capabilities and limitations:

✦ **Running Distiller across platforms:** Distiller can open PostScript files on local hard drives and across platforms. PDF files from distillation can be saved to local hard drives and across platforms. For example, using Distiller on a Macintosh, you can open a PostScript file on a PC and save it to either computer's hard drive.

✦ **RunDirEx.txt across platforms:** RunDirEx.txt cannot run across platforms where directory paths are specified for one platform while distilling on a different platform. For example, you can't open from a Macintosh the RunDirEx.txt file that resides on a PC with directory paths specified for the PC. The alternative solution is to either run Distiller on the platform consistent with the path identity or set up watched folders where the RunDirEx.txt file is introduced into a watched folder or create a virtual drive or hot folder and mount the drive/hot folder on both systems.

✦ **RunDirEx.txt in a common platform:** Distiller can open the RunDirEx.txt file that resides on one computer where the directory path includes files on another computer of the same platform. The RunDirEx.txt file can be located on either computer, the destination of the PDF can be saved to either computer, and the path to find the .ps files can be on either computer.

Summary

✦ PostScript is a streamed language that can contain many different dialects and is often redundant in describing page elements for imaging. PDF is a much more efficient file format, as it is structured like a database that offers logical order and eliminates redundancy.

✦ When creating PostScript files, the preferred PPD to use is the Acrobat Distiller PPDs, or print to the Adobe PDF Printer.

✦ Distiller Preferences enable you to establish settings for filenaming and overwriting.

✦ Acrobat Distiller has many Adobe PDF Settings enabling you to control font compression, image compression, color, high-end digital prepress output, and PDF/X compliance. All Adobe PDF Settings are available to Acrobat Standard users except PDF/X compliance.

✦ Additional font monitoring is established in the Distiller Settings menu for identifying different font locations on your computer.

✦ Watched folders enable you to create PDF workflows that automate the PDF creation process. Watched folders can be contained on local or remote storage systems in network environments. Use of watched folders with multiple-user access on a network requires strict compliance with Adobe's licensing agreements.

✦ Acrobat enables you to supply security passwords at the time of distillation. Security levels are applied consistent with PDF compatibility.

✦ Eastern language character sets and Asian text are supported font embedding features as long as font formats and font management are properly configured.

✦ Access to Acrobat Distiller is supported from within Acrobat 6.0, by using shortcuts or aliases, printer drivers, and through a variety of drag-and-drop procedures.

✦ You can join PostScript files in a single PDF document by using either the RunFilEx.ps or RunDirEx.txt PostScript file installed on your computer during the Acrobat installation. RunFilEx.ps concatenates files by filename, and RunDirEx.txt concatenates all files within a folder that have the same extension.

✦   ✦   ✦

Editing PDFs

◆ ◆ ◆ ◆

◆ ◆ ◆ ◆

Editing Text

Ideally, you should always return to an original document when you want to make changes on PDF pages that were converted from an authoring application. With all of Acrobat's impressive features, it is not designed to be used as a page layout program. The options you have in Acrobat for text editing are limited to tweaks and minor corrections. For major editing functions, returning to your authoring program, editing the pages, and converting them back to PDF is a preferred method.

For minor edits and for purposes of editing PDF files where original documents have been lost or are unavailable, Acrobat does provide you tools and means for text editing. As you look through this chapter, realize that the pages ahead are intended to describe methods for minor corrections and text editing when you don't have an option for returning to an original document.

Setting Up the Text Editing Environment

As you begin any editing session in Acrobat, you can benefit from customizing your working environment so you have immediate access to the tools you'll use during your session. As I explained in Chapter 1, both Acrobat Standard and Acrobat Professional offer you an extraordinary number of tools and commands. Rather than poke around for tools while editing a document, it is to your advantage to customize the Acrobat window ahead of time to show all the tools you anticipate using during your editing session.

Cross-Reference   For more information on organizing toolbars, see Chapter 1.

For text editing, there are several toolbars that you'll want to make visible and dock in the Toolbar Well or float in the Document Pane, depending on what is handier for you. Toolbars you need for text editing include

- ✦ **Zoom tools:** For zooming in and out of the Document Pane, use the Loupe, Pan and Zoom, and Dynamic Zoom tools. By default, the Zoom toolbar is docked in the Toolbar Well. You can expand the toolbar for easy access to any one of the Zoom tools by selecting the pull-down arrow adjacent to the Zoom In tool and choosing the Show Zoom Toolbar command. The toolbar expands in the Toolbar Well and makes all tools easily accessible.

✦ **Advanced Editing toolbar:** The Advanced Editing Toolbar contains the TouchUp Text tool used for editing short text passages and the TouchUp Object tool that permits you to move text blocks around a page, which are both handy when the toolbar is expanded. By default, the Advanced Editing Toolbar is hidden. To open the toolbar choose Tools ⇨ Advanced Editing ⇨ Show Advanced Editing Toolbar. To dock the toolbar in the Toolbar Well, click the vertical line adjacent to the left side of the toolbar and drag it to the Toolbar Well. Release the mouse button and the toolbar snaps within the Toolbar Well.

✦ **Selection tools:** A little more awkward to access, the Selection tools are nested in a submenu. By docking them in the Toolbar Well, they are much easier to work with. Choose Tools ⇨ Basic ⇨ Selections ⇨ Show Selection Toolbar. Dock the toolbar in the Toolbar Well and your Acrobat window should look something like Figure 8-1.

Note   If you need help at anytime, you can click on the How To button in the Toolbar Well to gain access to Acrobat Help. For an editing session, close the window to allow more room in the Document Pane to display your pages.

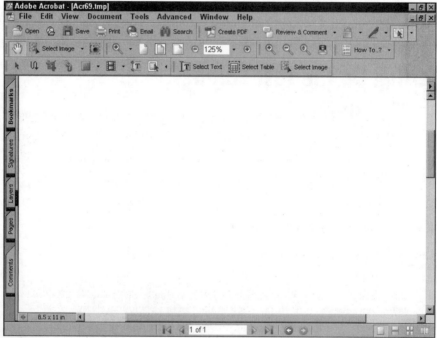

Figure 8-1: Before beginning any editing session it's more advantageous for working faster to show all the tools you anticipate using and docking them in the Toolbar Well.

Using the TouchUp Text Tool

 For minor text edits, the TouchUp Text tool on the Advanced Editing toolbar enables you to edit text along single lines of copy and edit bodies of text. Before you attempt to change text passages on a PDF page, you need to keep a few things in mind. Some of the considerations include

✦ **Font embedding:** If you attempt to edit an embedded font, Acrobat prompts you in a dialog box to unembed the font. Text editing is possible only after a font is unembedded. Depending on the permissions granted by the font manufacturer, some fonts can't be unembedded. If Acrobat informs you that font editing cannot occur, you need to make your changes in the original authoring document.

Cross-
Reference

For more information on font embedding, see Chapter 7.

✦ **Tagged and untagged PDF documents:** If you want to edit a body of text, such as text with two or more lines, using a tagged file is best because in an untagged file controlling text flow is much more difficult. When you edit tagged PDFs with document structure, the text blocks are divided into structured paragraphs. Editing one paragraph won't have an effect on the other paragraphs on a page. Untagged files appear in contiguous text blocks, which makes controlling text flow, indents and tabs, and paragraph structure difficult. Figure 8-2 shows text selected with the TouchUp Text tool in an untagged file. Figure 8-3 shows the same file created with tags. In a file created with tags, only single paragraphs can be selected with the TouchUp Text tool. In the untagged document, all text can be selected and remains a contiguous body of text.

Cross-
Reference

For more information on tagged and structured PDF documents, see Chapter 18. For information on creating tagged PDF files, see Chapter 6.

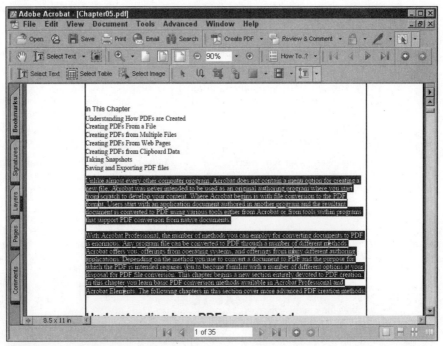

Figure 8-2: Untagged PDFs without any document structure are more difficult to edit because you lose some control over the text flow.

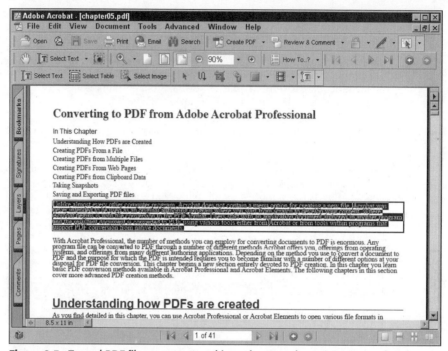

Figure 8-3: Tagged PDF files are structured into elements that are segmented and provide more control over editing single paragraphs without affecting the other paragraphs on a page.

✦ **Property changes:** You can apply property changes for fonts, such as color, size, and other attributes, to text without unembedding the font.

Fortunately, Acrobat alerts you ahead of time if you attempt to edit a PDF document with embedded fonts and those fonts aren't installed on your computer. To edit fonts on a page, select the TouchUp Text tool, and click and drag over a body of text to be changed. Acrobat pauses momentarily as it surveys your installed fonts and the font embedded in the PDF document. Enter your changes and the selected text is replaced with the new text you typed.

You'll be able to see onscreen whether your text editing results in an acceptable appearance and the edits are properly applied. If the text scrambles and you lose total control over the document page, you need to either find the original authoring document or export text from Acrobat into a word processor or layout program to make the changes.

Prepress

Editing text passages are fine for screen displays when the text flows in an acceptable manner. For high-end printing and prepress, you might be able to successfully make changes and minor edits without experiencing printing problems. However, for any kind of paragraph editing you are best off returning to the authoring application. You might get away with some edits in Acrobat, but eventually they will catch up with you. If you do make a spelling error change or other minor text edit be certain to re-embed the font (see Changing Text Attributes later in this chapter).

In addition to selecting the Properties menu command, a context menu opened from a TouchUp Text tool selection offers menu commands for insertion of special characters. Four choices are available to you when you open a context menu and select the Insert menu command. From the submenu you can choose

✦ **Line break:** This choice adds a line break from the cursor insertion. This command is handy when creating new text on a page or when pasting text. Text lines may extend beyond the page width when creating new text or pasting text. You can create line breaks to keep text within a specific area of the page.

✦ **Soft hyphen:** This choice adds a soft hyphen for text scrolling to a new line.

✦ **Non-breaking space:** To add spaces without line breaks, choose non-breaking space.

✦ **Em dash:** To add an em dash (—) at the cursor insertion, choose em dash.

When text is selected and you insert a special character, the selected text is deleted and the new character is added. If you use special characters in untagged PDF files, the results may be less than desirable. Line breaks can flow text into following paragraphs and the text can overlap, making the page unreadable. If you encounter such problems and the edits are necessary to make your files more readable, you must return the file to the authoring program, make the edits, and recreate the PDF document.

Caution   When using the TouchUp Text tool, you don't have access to the Undo command. All edits you make cannot be undone. If you inadvertently make a mistake, choose File ➪ Revert. The PDF reverts to the last save you made. When making many edits with the TouchUp Text tool, be certain to save regularly so the Revert command reverts to a recent save.

Changing Text Attributes

You can make many text-attribute changes without unembedding fonts. You can change colors, point sizes in lines of text, character and word spacing, and other similar text attributes, as well as changes related to the document structure. You make all of these changes in the TouchUp Properties dialog box.

To edit text properties, select the characters, words, or paragraph(s) you want to change. Be certain the text is highlighted and open a context menu as shown in Figure 8-4. From the menu options, select Properties.

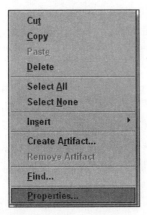

Figure 8-4: To change text properties, select the text to be changed with the TouchUp Text tool and select Properties from the menu options.

After you select Properties from the context menu, the TouchUp Properties dialog box opens as shown in Figure 8-5. The first two tabs relate to changing tags and document structure. Leave these alone for the moment and look at the third tab labeled Text. The properties contained here relate to changing font attributes for the selected text.

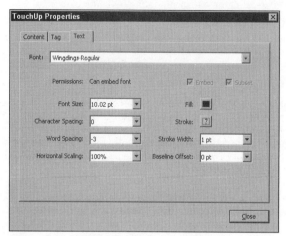

Figure 8-5: Select the Text tab in the TouchUp Properties dialog box to make changes to font attributes.

Cross-Reference   For information on using the Content and Tag tabs, see Chapter 18.

Items contained in the Text tab include

✦ **Font:** From the pull-down menu you have a list of fonts for all the fonts loaded in your system and fonts embedded in the document. One thing to keep in mind is that just because a font is listed in the pull-down menu doesn't mean you can select the font. If the font is an embedded/subsetted font and you don't have a compatible font loaded in your system, Acrobat won't let you use that font. Fonts loaded in your system can be selected to replace fonts that are both embedded and not embedded.

Note   The font list in the pull-down menu shows a line dividing the list at the top of the menu. All fonts appearing above the line are embedded fonts in the document. All fonts below the line are fonts loaded in your system.

✦ **Permissions:** A message is displayed for font permissions. If the font can be embedded, the message is *Can embed font.* If the font cannot be embedded, the message reads *Cannot embed font.* Some fonts may not be embedded due to licensing restrictions from a font manufacturer.

✦ **Font Size:** Font sizes are selected from the pull-down menu for preset sizes. To change the size where the desired size is not listed from among the menu choices, select the font size in the field box and type a new value.

✦ **Character Spacing:** You can move characters in a line of text closer together or farther apart. The values shown in the pull-down menu are measured in em spaces. Choose from the menu choices or type a value in the field box. Using negative (–) values moves the characters together.

✦ **Word Spacing:** This option controls the space between whole words. Choices for distance are made the same way as the preceding character spacing.

✦ **Horizontal Scaling:** Sizing of individual characters (narrower or wider) is set according to the percentage of the original size. Values above 100% scale characters larger than the original font. Values below 100% result in smaller characters.

✦ **Embed:** Check the box to embed the selected font.

✦ **Subset:** Check the box to subset the font.

Cross-Reference

For information on font embedding and subsetting, see Chapter 7.

Caution

In order to legally embed a font, you must own a copy of the font to be embedded and comply with the licensing restrictions of the font manufacturer. Be certain to review the licensing agreement that came with your fonts to be certain embedding the font(s) is permitted. Some manufacturers do not license fonts for embedding.

✦ **Fill:** The color swatch shows the default color of the selected font. Clicking on the color swatch opens a pop-up menu as shown in Figure 8-6. You select preset colors from the palette. When you click on Other Color, the system color palette opens. You can create custom colors from the system color palette and apply them to the text fill.

Prepress

If you intend to print your PDFs for color separations, don't make color changes in Acrobat. The color space for the preset colors and custom colors is RGB. You can experience color-matching problems if you attempt to convert RGB files to CMYK. If color changes to text are needed, you have to return to the authoring application and make the color changes, then recreate the PDF file.

✦ **Stroke:** Stroking text creates outlines for the font characters. You can make the same color choices for strokes as you can for the character fills.

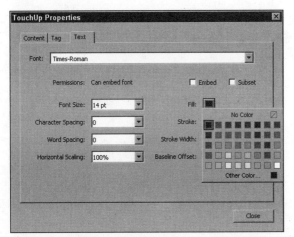

Figure 8-6: Click on the color swatch in the TouchUp Properties dialog box to open the pop-up menu used for making color selections.

✦ **Stroke Width:** You change the weight (in points) of the stroke outlines by making choices in the pull-down menu or by typing values in the field box.

Tip   If you want to create outline text, select No color from the Fill Color pop-up menu and add a stroke color and width. When stroke fills are set to No color, the fills appear transparent and show the background color.

✦ **Baseline Offset:** You can raise or lower text above the baseline or below it. To move text up, enter positive values in the field box. To move text below the baseline, use negative values.

After making choices in the TouchUp Properties dialog box, click on the Close button. The changes you make in the dialog box are reflected only on text you selected with the TouchUp Text tool.

Looking Up Definitions

Whether you're editing a PDF file or browsing documents, you can find the spelling and word definition for any text in an open document. This very nice little feature in Acrobat saves you time when looking up a definition. To employ the Look Up command, use the Select Text tool. With the cursor hovering over a word, or with the cursor inserted between characters in a word, or by selecting a word, open a context menu as shown in Figure 8-7. Select Look Up "your word" from the menu selections.

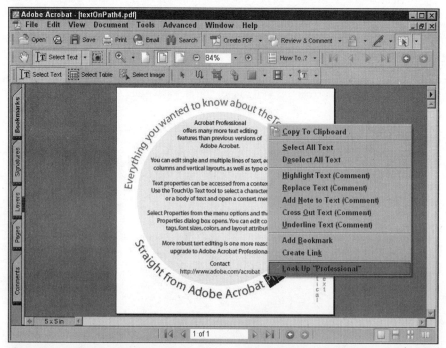

Figure 8-7: Select the Select Text tool and hover the cursor over a word, insert the cursor in a word, or select the word on a PDF page in the Document Pane. Open a context menu and select Look Up "..." at the bottom of the menu.

After you make your selection, Acrobat launches the default Web browser and the browser takes you to the Dictionary.com Web site. The Web page opens on the word selected in the PDF document. You can check for spelling errors, word definitions, pronunciation, and browse through a thesaurus. If you have an account for the Web site, you can click on the audio button shown in Figure 8-8 to hear an audio pronunciation output through your computer speaker(s).

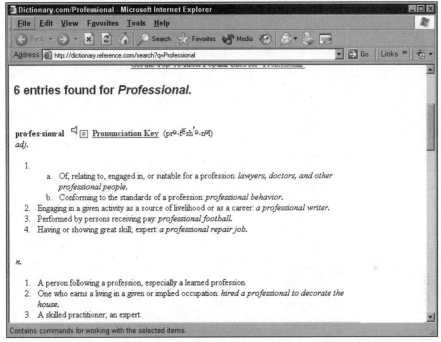

Figure 8-8: If you have an account at Dictionary.com, click on the audio button or the Pronunciation Key link to listen to the proper pronunciation of the word.

Currently, Acrobat supports only U.S. English as a language. Regardless of whether you have a foreign language kit installed, Acrobat launches the Dictionary.com Web site.

Editing Text on Layers

You can edit text on layered PDF documents. When layer data are visible, you can use the TouchUp Text tool to select text and edit the properties as described previously. If you have difficulty selecting text, you can hide layers and select just the text on visible layers. Figure 8-9 shows a PDF document with four layers. Only the Rotated Text layer is visible in the Layers palette. You can edit text selected on this layer without affecting any of the other layers.

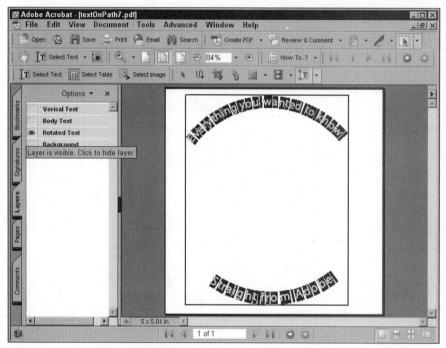

Figure 8-9: After hiding layers, select the text to be edited. When you select the TouchUp Text tool, only the text on visible layers is selected.

If you have text on separate layers, finessing the TouchUp Text tool can often help you select only text on a single layer. In Figure 8-10, the rotated text is selected while the body text remains unselected. Without hiding layers it was possible to select just the rotated text by moving the TouchUp Text tool around the page. However, if text on different layers overlaps, you'll need to hide layers before selecting the text.

After you select the text, open a context menu and select Properties. In Figure 8-11, the text on a path was changed to a different color and a stroke was applied to the text.

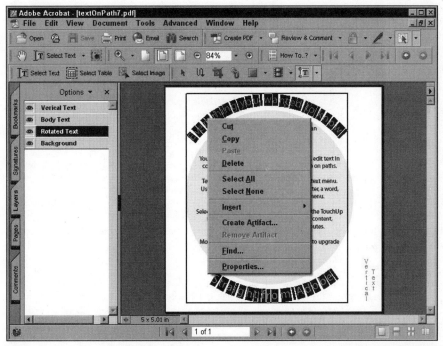

Figure 8-10: After selecting the text, open a context menu and select Properties. Make the text attribute changes in the TouchUp Properties dialog box shown earlier in this chapter.

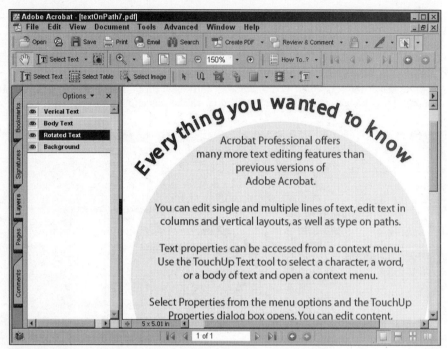

Figure 8-11: Text properties were changed for the font color and a stroke was applied to the text.

Tip
If you want to select text on a layer, hide all layers where text is not to be selected by clicking on the eye icon in the layers palette. Click the TouchUp Text tool in a text block and press Ctrl+A (⌘+A on a Mac) to select all. All the text on visible layers is selected, while text on hidden layers remains unselected.

You can select and edit text appearing on all visible layers. If text appears on all layers, the edits are applied to all layers. If text appears on a single layer, the text edits reflect changes only on the respective layer.

Engineering
Engineers working in AutoCAD and Microsoft Visio can export drawings as layered files. When opened in Acrobat, the layers created contain separate layer data in the PDF. If you anticipate changing text, try to keep all the text on a single layer for a given drawing if it's practical. You can then hide layers and select all the text on the text layer. Make your edits and the changes are reflected only on the layer(s) that was edited.

Cross-Reference
For more information on managing layers, see Chapter 17.

Adding New Text to a Document

You can also use the TouchUp Text tool to add a new line of text to a document. Select the TouchUp Text tool and press the Ctrl/Option key; then click the mouse button in the area you want to add new text. The New Text Font dialog box opens as shown in Figure 8-12.

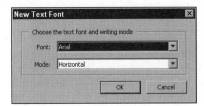

Figure 8-12: Press Ctrl/Option+click on a document page and the New Text Font dialog box opens. Select a font from the Font pull-down menu and select text alignment from the Mode pull-down menu (lad) choose between Horizontal or Vertical modes.

From the Font pull-down menu you can select any font loaded in your system. Fonts appearing below the horizontal line in the menu represent the current fonts loaded in your system. Fonts above the line are the embedded fonts in your PDF document. To use an embedded font, it needs to be unembedded and available in your system.

From the Mode pull-down menu you can select between Horizontal or Vertical alignment. Click OK in the dialog box and the cursor blinks at the location where you clicked the mouse button. The words "NEW TEXT" are pre-populated for you...(lad) Type the text you want to add and open the TouchUp Properties dialog box by choosing Properties from a context menu. Click in the check boxes for embedding and subsetting to embed the new text font in the document.

Selecting and Copying Text

You may want to copy and paste text from Acrobat PDFs to other programs. The best method of getting text into a word processor is using the copy/paste commands because they preserve more data integrity than using file export commands.

Depending on your needs, several ways exist for getting text out of Acrobat and into a program like Microsoft Word. The content you want to copy and how the content appears in Acrobat has an influence on the tool you choose to achieve the best results.

Copying text with the TouchUp Text tool

The TouchUp Text tool is probably the last tool you want to use for copying text and pasting the text into other programs. I mention it here so you know what limitations you have in Acrobat for copying text with this tool. Inasmuch as the TouchUp Text tool enables you to copy multiple lines of text, you are limited to single paragraphs or short blocks of text.

To copy text with the TouchUp Text tool, click and drag the tool through the text block(s) you want to copy. The text is selected as you drag the mouse cursor. After making a selection, open a context menu and select Copy from the menu commands as shown in Figure 8-13. You can also choose Edit ➪ Copy.

In Figure 8-13 the selected text block is the only block of text that can be selected when the cursor is positioned in the paragraph. If you want to copy and paste additional text blocks you need to individually select text blocks and copy/paste them. Obviously, if you have pages of text, this tool isn't the tool of choice. If you have a single line or a single paragraph of text, you achieve the same results for copying and pasting text as when using other tools.

To paste text is a word processor or other application where pasting text is permitted, open the application and select the Paste command. Typically, you find Paste under the Edit menu. When the text is pasted, the text formatting is preserved if you copy text from tagged PDF documents. Notice in Figure 8-14 that text pasted in Microsoft word the word wrap is preserved as can be seen when Show Formatting is toggled on.

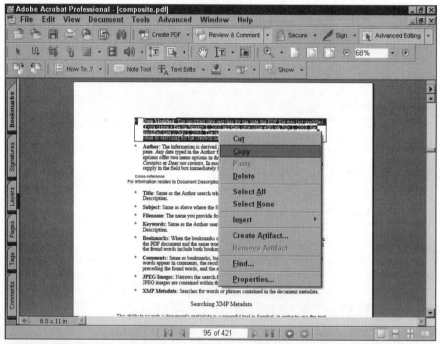

Figure 8-13: Select the TouchUp Text tool and drag through the text paragraphs you want to select. Acrobat 6.0 enables you to select multiple lines of text with the TouchUp Text tool.

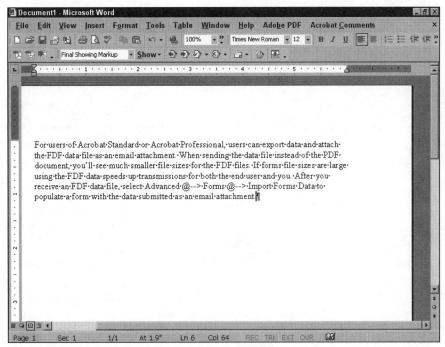

Figure 8-14: Text copied with the TouchUp Text tool from a tagged PDF document and pasted in Microsoft Word retains the paragraph structure.

Using the Select Text tool

The Select Text tool is a much better choice than the TouchUp Text tool for selecting text to be copied from a PDF document and pasted in an editor if you have multiple text blocks to copy. Users of earlier versions of Acrobat will notice that the Column Select tool is no longer available in Acrobat toolbar. Selecting text is more intelligent in Acrobat 6.0 and a single tool now lets you select body text in single or multiple columns.

To select text with the Select Text tool, click and drag the tool through the text on a page you want to copy. If a single column appears on the page, click just before the first character to be selected and drag down to the last character. If you want to copy a single column in a two-column layout, click the Select Text tool at the beginning of the column to be selected and drag down to the end of the column. Acrobat won't copy the text in the adjacent column as long as you stay within the boundaries of the column you are selecting. Figure 8-15 shows text selected with the Select Text tool where only one column in a three-column layout is selected.

Tip
The Column Select tool is still available in Acrobat 6.0 through the use of a shortcut key. Hold down the Alt/Option key to more precisely select text in columns, similar to using the Column Select tool in earlier versions of Acrobat. Although the tool doesn't exist in the toolbars, using the shortcut key turns the Select Text tool into a Column Select tool.

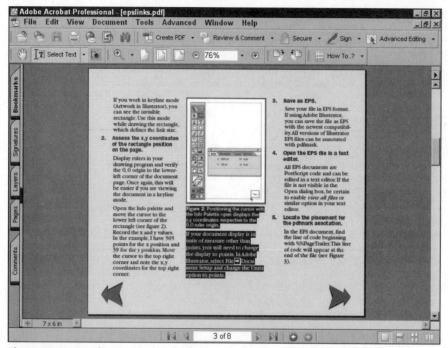

Figure 8-15: To select a column of text, use the Select Text tool and drag down the column length. Adjacent columns are not selected if you stay within the column boundaries. If the Select Text tool doesn't precisely select a column, hold the Alt/Option key down and drag through a column of text to select it.

In conjunction with the Select Text tool, shortcut keys and mouse clicks provide several ways to make various text selections including

- ✦ **Select a word:** Double-click on a word, space, or character.

- ✦ **Select a line of text:** Triple-click anywhere on a line of text.

- ✦ **Select all text on a page:** Click four times (rapid successive clicks) to select all text on a page.

- ✦ **Select a column of text:** Press Alt/Option and click and drag down a column of text. All text within the selection marquee is selected. (Use the shortcut key when text selection for a column selects unwanted text in adjacent columns.)

- ✦ **Select a contiguous block of text:** Click and drag through the block of text or click the cursor at the beginning of the text to be selected, press Shift, and click at the end of the text block.

- ✦ **Stop text selection and revert to the Hand tool:** Press the Esc key.

- ✦ **Deselect text:** Click outside of the text selection or press Ctrl/⌘+Shift+A.

Pasting text in a text editor preserves more paragraph formatting than pasting text copied from the TouchUp Tool selections. When copying and pasting text, using the Select Text tool works best for just about any edit jobs where text needs to be sent back to an authoring program. You can paste text in word processing programs and simple text editors that support character and paragraph formatting. In Figure 8-16, text was copied with the Select Text tool and pasted into Microsoft WordPad.

Figure 8-16: You can paste text copied with the Select Text tool into text editors with complete integrity when the text editor supports character and paragraph formatting.

Using the Select All menu command

If you have a need to select all the text on a page or throughout a PDF document, you can use the Select All menu command. Depending on the tool you use and the page view mode, text selections behave differently. You must first determine whether you want to select all the text on a page or all text in the document. When selecting text on a PDF page, be certain the page layout view is set to Single Page view. With the Text Select tool, click the cursor on any text and choose Edit ➪ Select All or press Ctrl/⌘+A. All the text on a single page is selected. To copy the text you just selected, open a context menu as described previously and select Copy to Clipboard. All the text is copied to the clipboard file and ready to paste into an editor.

If you want to select all text in a PDF document, change the page view to any one of the other three page views (Continuous, Continuous – Facing, or Facing). Click the cursor on any text and use the same Select All menu command. Any one of these views permits you to select all the text in the document. In Figure 8-17, the text was selected with the Facing Pages view mode on.

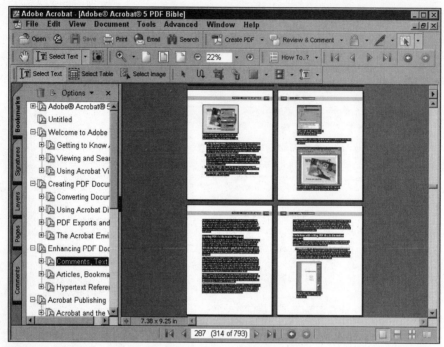

Figure 8-17: When you use the Select All menu command in any page layout view but the Single Page view, Acrobat selects the text on all pages.

The previous method works only when you use the Select Text tool. If you select all text using the TouchUp Text tool, the selected text is confined to a bounding box. On any given page there can be one or more bounding boxes and using Select All only selects all text within a single bounding box. Regardless of which page layout view you choose, the TouchUp Text tool doesn't permit text selections across multiple pages as shown in Figure 8-18.

To select text across several pages without selecting all the text in a document, set the page layout view to either Continuous or Continuous – Facing views, and click and drag the Select Text tool in a block of text until you reach the bottom of the page; the window scrolls. Continue to hold down the mouse button and drag until you reach the last page to be copied. The text on all scrolled pages is selected and ready for copying.

Tip

To copy several pages in a document, select the Continuous page layout and zoom out so you can see three or four pages in the Document Pane. Click the Select Text tool at the top of the page you want to start copying and drag down. The pages scroll as you hold your cursor at the bottom of the Document Pane and the page scrolling is much faster than when viewing single pages in the Document Pane.

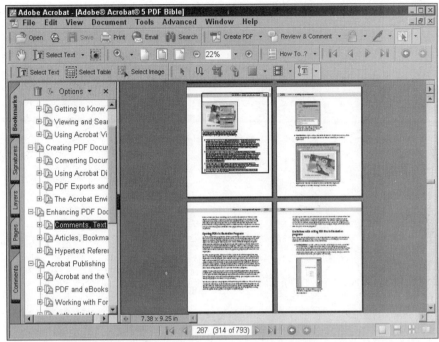

Figure 8-18: With the Facing Pages view mode on, click on the text with the TouchUp Text tool. After using the Select All menu command, only the text within the bounding box on the target page was selected.

Using the Hand tool for text selections

If you're editing text on a page, you can choose to make text selections with the Hand tool instead of the Select Text tool. A new feature in Acrobat 6 enables you to select text with the Hand tool when preference settings are adjusted to use the tool for text selections. Choose Edit Í Preferences or press Ctrl/Ô+K. In the Preferences dialog box, select General in the left pane. Check the box for Enable text selection for the Hand tool as shown in Figure 8-19.

Click OK in the Preferences dialog box and select the Hand tool. Move the cursor over a block of text and wait a moment. The Hand tool cursor changes to an I-beam cursor. Click and drag over a selection just as you would when using the Select Text tool.

With the Hand tool, you can move a page around in the Document Pane or scroll pages when they are viewed in page layout views other than Single Page view. If you move the cursor above any text, quickly drag the page around the Document Pane to move the page. If you wait a moment, the cursor changes and any dragging you do selects text. If you accidentally select text when you want to move the page, deselect the text by clicking outside a text block.

Tip

If you find it awkward toggling back and forth between the Hand tool and the Select Text tool when preferences are enabled for text selections with the Hand tool, disable the preference setting. Use the Select Text tool and press the Esc key when you want to return to the Hand tool.

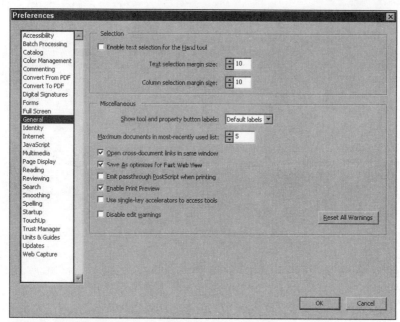

Figure 8-19: Open the Preferences dialog box and select General in the left column. Select the check box for Enable text selection for the Hand tool. You can now use the Hand tool to select text.

Copying a file to the clipboard

Clicking the Select Text tool and selecting all the text when the page view accommodates selecting text across all pages copies the entire file to the clipboard. You can also accomplish the same task by choosing Edit ⇨ Copy File to Clipboard. Open your word processor and you can paste the text into a new word processor document.

If you don't see the menu command, you don't have OLE (Object Linking and Embedding)-compliant applications installed on your computer. Microsoft's OLE is installed by default with Office applications on Windows. If the menu command does not appear, use the Select All menu command to achieve the same results.

Copying and pasting text in word processors is a better alternative for text editing than saving a file to RTF if the PDF was created as an untagged file. For tagged PDF documents, saving in RTF preserves much formatting, but may still be less desirable than copying and pasting text.

Cross-Reference

For a description of exporting to RTF, see the section on Exporting text later in this chapter.

Selecting tables

You can copy and paste formatted text in columns and rows with the Select Text tool in word processors; however, precise column tabs and formatting can fall apart when you attempt to paste the text in programs like spreadsheets. If you try to use the Select Text tool to copy a table in Acrobat and paste the data in Excel for example, the data are placed in a single cell. If you want to copy table data so the data spread to separate cells in a spreadsheet program from where the column and row breaks occur in Acrobat, you need to use another tool.

Making selections with a marquee

Select the Select Table tool and click and drag to open a marquee around the table to be copied. Dragging with this tool doesn't select any of the text; rather, a blue keyline border appears around the area you select. If the rectangle border is not sized properly after you release the mouse button, you can click on any of the small square handles and drag them in or out of the selected area to reshape the rectangle. When you see the cursor change to two parallel lines with opposing arrowheads, the handle below the cursor is ready to move.

The rectangle border you create does not have to exactly match the text within the border. You can extend the rectangle a few points outside the table and all the data within the border become selectable. You choose menu options from a context menu after selecting the table as shown in Figure 8-20.

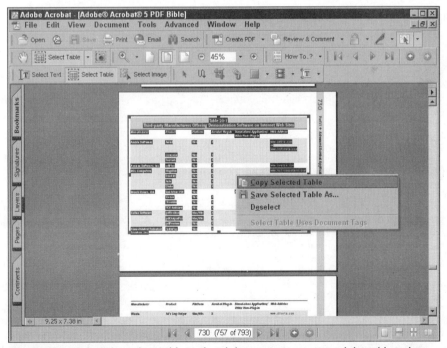

Figure 8-20: Select the Select Table tool and drag a marquee around the table to be copied. After you select the table, you can make choices for how to handle the selection from a context menu.

Making selections with a click

You can also select a table with a mouse click. Select the Select Table tool in the Basic toolbar and move the mouse cursor to the table to be selected. Click anywhere in the table and Acrobat assesses the table periphery and selects the entire table. If, for some reason, it doesn't grab all the data in a table, revert to the marquee method described in the "Making selections with a marquee" section.

Exporting data to a spreadsheet

After the table data are selected, you have a number of options for getting the data to another program. Among those options are exporting directly to a spreadsheet or saving the data as a file. If you want to introduce the data into a spreadsheet, you need to have Microsoft Excel installed on your computer. Open a context menu on a selected table and choose Open Table in Spreadsheet as shown in Figure 8-21. Acrobat launches Microsoft Excel and the table data are placed in separate cells.

Figure 8-21: Select a table and open a context menu. Select the Open Table in Spreadsheet option and the table data are copied to a new Microsoft Excel spreadsheet.

If you open a context menu and you don't see a menu command for opening a table in a spreadsheet, Acrobat can't find Microsoft Excel on your computer. Be certain to install all Microsoft Office programs first, and then install Adobe Acrobat. In Figure 8-20 you can see the same context menu without the menu command for opening a table in a spreadsheet. The computer used for the screenshot did not have Microsoft Excel installed.

Saving table data

If you want to export your data to a file and import the data in a program other than Microsoft Excel or perhaps keep the data around and open it in Excel at a later time, you can save table data in a variety of formats.

After selecting a table, open a context menu and select Save Selected Table As, which you can see in Figure 8-20. When you release the mouse button, the Acrobat Save As dialog box opens. From the Save as type (Windows) or Format (Macintosh) pull-down menu make a choice for a file format as shown in Figure 8-22. The file formats for table data include

- ✦ **Comma Separated Values (*.csv):** CSV-compliant applications can open files saved in this format. Microsoft Excel recognizes CSV data and you can open the files directly in Excel. If you use other applications recognizing the format, use CSV.

- ✦ **HTML 4.01 with CSS 1.0 (*.htm):** If you need to get table data to a Web page, you can save the data to HTML format.

- ✦ **Rich Text Format (*.rtf):** If you want to import data into programs like word processors, accounting programs and other applications that supports RTF, save the file as

RTF. If you want columns and rows of data without a table defined in the word processor, use the RTF format.

✦ **Text (Tab Delimited) (*.txt):** Where data need to be imported into a database management system (DBMS), export the data as tab delimited. Tab delimited tables import into programs like Microsoft Access and FileMaker Pro with data in separate fields and records.

✦ **Unicode Text (Tab Delimited) (*.txt):** If you use some foreign language kits, Unicode might be a better choice for your file exports. Select Unicode and import the data into applications supporting Unicode text data.

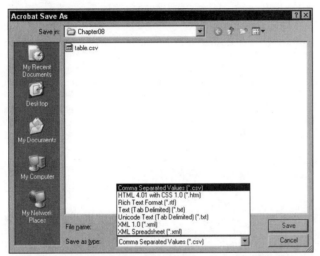

Figure 8-22: Select Save Selected Table As in a context menu and the Acrobat Save As dialog box opens. Select a file format from the Save as type (Windows) or Format (Macintosh) pull-down menu and click the Save button.

✦ **XML 1.0 (*.xml):** Acrobat supports exporting tables in Adobe XML format. XML data can be exchanged between many programs. If your workflow uses XML, save in this format.

✦ **XML Spreadsheet (*.xml):** This is an XML format defined by Microsoft. Use XML Spreadsheet when using XML data with spreadsheet applications like Microsoft Excel.

After exporting the data in a chosen format, you can open the file from an authoring application supporting the file type selected in the Acrobat Save As dialog box. If using Microsoft Excel, launch Excel and choose File ➪ Open. If the data import into single cells for each row, you didn't export the data with delimited values recognized by Excel. Return to Acrobat and choose a different format and try another import. For users working with Excel spreadsheets, CSV and Tab Delimited formats work well for data imports.

Exporting Text

Any major editing jobs with text in PDF documents are best accomplished with the copy and paste commands previously described. To completely rework a document and make edits on a number of pages, pasting text in a word processor and creating a new layout will, in the end, save you time.

You can export text in a file format such as RTF that can be opened in word processors, but much of the paragraph formatting is lost in the file conversion if you begin with an untagged file. Exporting text works very well when you begin with a tagged file in Acrobat. With tagged PDF documents use the Save As command and save in RTF. The structure of the document in terms of styles, paragraph breaks, and tables is preserved in text exports from tagged PDF documents.

If you work with legacy files that are untagged PDFs, for the purposes of text editing, you won't find much help in adding tags in Acrobat. There are two methods you can use to add tags. When you save a file to a format like RTF, Acrobat requires you to add tags during the conversion. To tag a file during conversion, click on the RTF format from the Save as type (Windows) or Format (Macintosh) pull-down menu and click on the Settings button. Another method for tagging an unstructured document is to access it by choosing the Advanced ⇨ Accessibility ⇨ Add Tags to Document menu command. Regardless of which way you add tags to your PDF, the result won't add the structure you need for an easy edit job back in your word processor.

| Cross-Reference | To learn more about tagged PDF files, see Chapter 18. |

Choose File ⇨ Save As and choose the RTF format for exporting the file in a text format you can edit in a program supporting RTF imports. When you save the file and open it in a word processor with the formatting revealed, the text appears similar to Figure 8-23. Notice in this figure all the paragraph hard returns at the end of each line of text.

Obviously, untagged files exported from Acrobat with the Save As command are the least desirable method for getting the data into a word processor. If you have untagged files that need to be re-edited, use the copy and paste methods described earlier in this chapter.

| Cross-Reference | For more information on exporting PDF data to different file formats, see Chapter 5. |

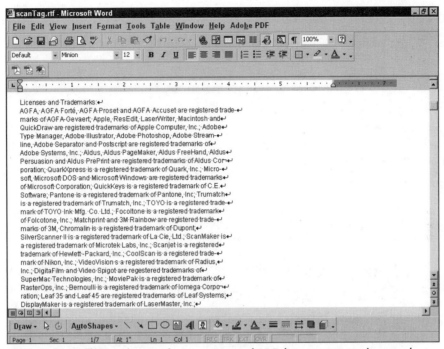

Figure 8-23: A file saved as RTF from an untagged PDF document opens in a word processor with line breaks. The file needs to be edited for paragraph formatting before it's converted back to PDF.

Reflowing Text

Reflowing text in Acrobat is a feature that's designed to reformat a page to a smaller or exploded view. Porting PDFs to hand-held devices requires pages to be reformatted so the text size can remain readable and the word wrap for paragraphs conforms to the screen size of the handheld device. Adaptive equipment that explodes text sizes to screen readers, such as Apollo readers for the visually impaired, needs files that can be reflowed to the screen size where lines of text word wrap like you see in word processing programs.

To reflow text you need to have a tagged PDF document. The PDF created with tags requires no editing in Acrobat and can be viewed with the View ➪ Reflow menu command selected. Untagged files require that you first add the tags. The process or reflowing text is easy and you can perform the steps to reflow a document and see the results on your computer monitor. Try following these steps to see how Reflow works:

STEPS: Reflowing text

1. **Check a document for tags.** Text cannot be reflowed unless a document is a tagged PDF file. You can easily check to see whether tags exist by opening the View menu and viewing the Reflow command. If the file is not tagged, the Reflow command is grayed out.

2. **Add tags to a document.** You can add tags to the PDF file for the purpose of reflowing the text. Choose Advanced ➪ Accessibility ➪ Add Tags to Document. Acrobat pauses a moment as tags are added to the file. Wait until all tags have been added before moving to the next step.

> **Note** Tags added via the menu command do not create the same structure as when exporting authoring documents to PDF with structure and tags. For more information on creating tagged PDFs, see Chapter 6.

3. **Reflow the text.** Choose View ➪ Reflow. If you start with a Fit in Window view and reflow text in the same view, you see the page without reflow as shown in Figure 8-24. When reflow is enabled, you see the page as shown in Figure 8-25.

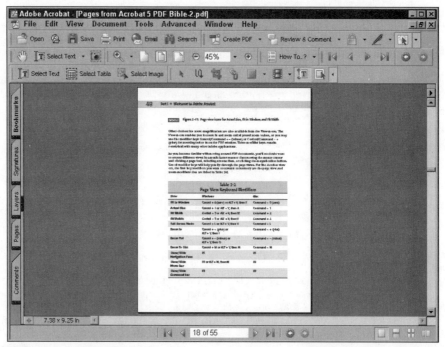

Figure 8-24: A PDF page is shown in a Fit in Window view without text reflow enabled.

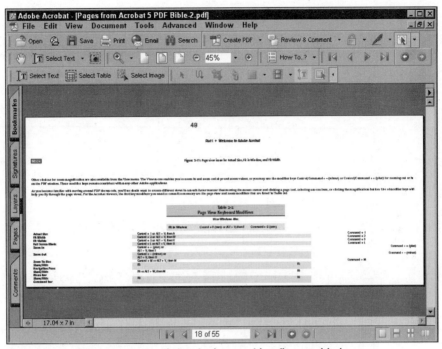

Figure 8-25: The same page and view is shown with reflow enabled.

4. **Zoom in on the page.** As you zoom in on the document page, the text reflow conforms to the size of your monitor screen. In Figure 8-26 the zoom level is 300%. In Figure 8-27 the zoom level is 200%. Notice the text flows to the zoom level without clipping and eliminates a need to scroll the window horizontally to see the complete passage.

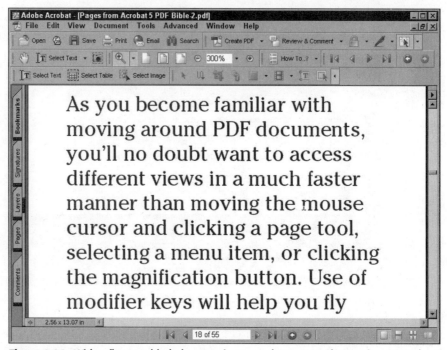

Figure 8-26: With reflow enabled, the page is zoomed to 200%. The text is wrapped horizontally to conform to the current zoom view.

PDF documents can be ported to handheld devices such as Palm Pilots, Pocket PC, and Symbian mobile devices. With the addition of the Acrobat for Palm software, a Palm Pilot can view PDFs. To read page content on such small devices requires you to add tags to a PDF document that enables text reflow so the text can be viewed on small screens without having to scroll screens horizontally. After you add tags to a PDF document that was created without tags, save the file. The tags added in Acrobat are saved with the file, and all subsequent Acrobat sessions enable you to use reflow without adding tags.

Cross-Reference   For more information on Acrobat Reader for Palm OS, see Chapter 2.

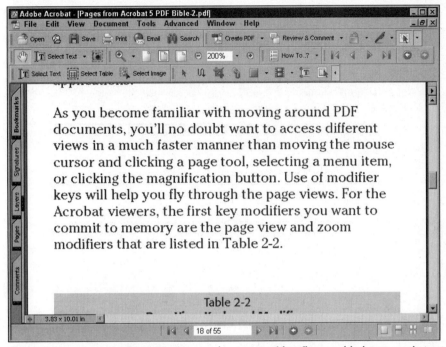

Figure 8-27: As you further zoom in on a document with reflow enabled, text continues to reform within the viewing space.

Summary

✦ When beginning an editing session, customizing your work environment and adding the toolbars you anticipate using to the Toolbar Well speeds up your editing sessions.

✦ You use the TouchUp Text tool to make minor edits on PDF pages. You can use the tool to change font attributes, add new lines of text, and access a Properties dialog box where fonts can be embedded and subsetted.

✦ Using the TouchUp Text tool is not well suited for copying and pasting text data into other programs. Text selections are limited and text formatting is lost when pasting text into other programs.

✦ The Select Text tool can select text on a page, across multiple pages, and all text in a document.

✦ When pasting text copied from a Select Text tool selection, the text data retains much integrity and can be edited with minimum character and paragraph reformatting.

✦ Text can be edited on visible layers. Text on hidden layers isn't selected with using the Select All command. Text appearing on all layers results in changes on all layers. Text on a single layer results in changes on a single layer.

✦ You use the Select Table tool to select table data. You can copy and paste tables in other applications and save the data to a number of different file formats.

✦ You can export text in a variety of file formats. Choose File ➪ Save As to gain access to the format options.

✦   ✦   ✦

Editing Images

Images and objects, such as raster images from programs like Photoshop, vector images like those created in Adobe Illustrator, and text, can be edited in external editors and dynamically updated in a PDF document. The process involves launching the external editor from within Acrobat, making changes in the external editor, and saving the file. The file is treated like a link to the PDF where the edits are updated. Acrobat itself doesn't have any image editing tools, but you can use the external editors provided through companion programs to help out when you need to make modifications to objects in a PDF file.

Like text edits discussed in Chapter 8, image editing with Acrobat is intended to be a minor task for last-minute small changes. For major editing tasks, you should return to the original authoring program. In circumstances where you do not have an original document, you may need to extend the editing a little further by updating documents or exporting them for new layouts. In this chapter you learn how to handle images and objects for editing and exporting purposes.

Setting Up the Editing Environment

Tools used for editing images and objects are found in the Basic Toolbar. It appears by default when you reset your toolbars. You also need the Advanced Editing Toolbar, which opens from the Tools menu. To open the Advanced Editing Toolbar, choose Tools ⇨ Advanced Editing ⇨ Show Advanced Editing Toolbar, or click on the Advanced Editing Task button in the Acrobat Toolbar Well. Drag the toolbar to the Toolbar Well to dock it and you're ready to handle most image and object editing jobs.

Note Toolbars are also accessed using a context menu. Open a context menu on the Acrobat Toolbar Well and select Advanced Editing.

Selecting Images

Two tools in Acrobat enable you to copy images and objects. An image element is considered to be a bitmap image, just like a photo you import in an authoring program from a scanned image or a document you edit in an image editor like Adobe Photoshop. Objects are illustrative elements, such as vector drawings you might create in an illustration or CAD program as well as lines that might appear in your document (such as table borders, or headers/footers). Acrobat also interprets text as objects when you select it with the TouchUp Object tool.

Using the Select Image tool

The Select Image tool is intelligent. You select the tool from the Selection Toolbar and click on an image. If Acrobat interprets the document area below the cursor as an image, the cursor icon changes to a plus symbol. As you move the cursor into the Document Pane, the default icon is a selection arrow. However, with a selection arrow you cannot make a selection by opening a marquee. You need to move the tool to an image; when the cursor changes shape, click the mouse button.

The image you select inverts all color and appears as a negative. Acrobat keeps you informed that the image is selected by inverting the appearance. Deselecting the image by clicking outside the image area or by selecting another tool and clicking in the Document Pane reverts the image color to its normal appearance.

From a context menu, you can either copy the image or save it to a file. Open a context menu on a selected image and choose Copy Image to Clipboard from the menu options as shown in Figure 9-1. You can paste the file into other programs; however, the data you copy with this tool cannot be used for pasting back into a PDF document.

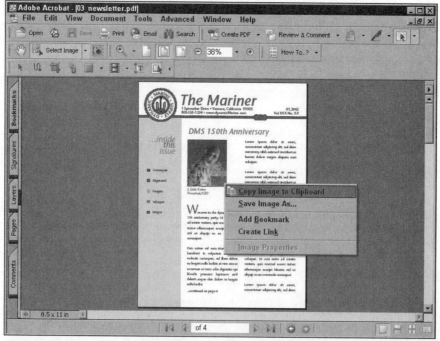

Figure 9-1: Select the Select Image tool and click on an image in a document. Open a context menu and select Copy Image to Clipboard. The image is ready to paste into another document.

Using the Snapshot tool

The Snapshot tool performs in some ways like the Graphics Select tool in earlier versions of Acrobat. You use this tool to create a marquee around any area on the document page. You can select text and graphics with the Snapshot tool. Select the tool from the Select Toolbar and click and drag a marquee around the area to be selected. When you release the mouse button, Acrobat takes a snapshot of the area within the marquee and copies it to the clipboard. A dialog box opens to inform you the data have been copied to the clipboard as shown in Figure 9-2.

After you click OK in the Alert dialog box, the marquee is still active on the document page. You can open a context menu where you have an option for copying the data or you can choose to print the selection. In addition, you can create a link to the snapshot by selecting Create Link in the context menu shown in Figure 9-3.

Cross-Reference
For more information on creating links from snapshots, see Chapter 15.

Caution
Taking a snapshot of a page containing images and text or text only creates a bitmap of the selected area. All text is converted to a raster image. If you intend to preserve text and edit it later, don't use the Snapshot tool. The text is not editable from Snapshot images.

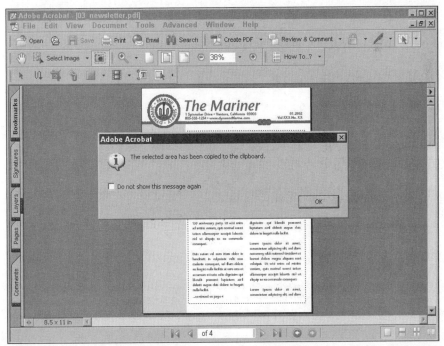

Figure 9-2: Select the Snapshot tool and draw a marquee over an area to be copied. When you release the mouse button, a dialog box informs you the marquee contents have been copied to the clipboard.

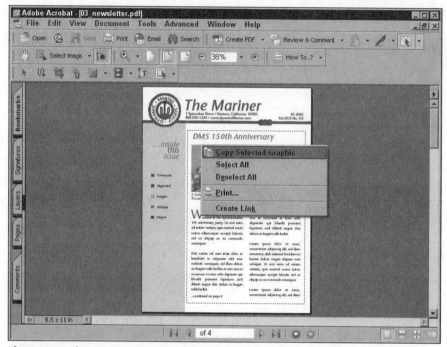

Figure 9-3: After you create a snapshot, the marquee remains active. Open a context menu to copy the data, print the selected area, or create a link.

Using the TouchUp Object tool

The TouchUp Object tool is used for selecting objects on a page. You select photo images, drawings and illustrations, and blocks of text with the tool. If the TouchUp Object tool is not visible when you open the Advanced Editing Toolbar, select the down arrow adjacent to the TouchUp Text tool. Select Expand This Button at the bottom of the pull-down menu. The toolbar expands and shows you both Touchup tools as shown in Figure 9-4.

Figure 9-4: After you expand the toolbar button for the TouchUp tools, you can view both tools together in the toolbar.

At the far left of the toolbar, notice the Select Object tool. The Select Object tool is used for selection of objects like form fields, links, movie clips, and other elements you add during an Acrobat session. The Touchup Object tool should be used for selecting objects that were part of the PDF before you began an editing session. Objects with regard to the Select Object tool should be used to select objects created in Acrobat.

The TouchUp Object tool copies image objects and pastes them back into a PDF or other PDF documents you open in Acrobat. The Select Image tool copies images to the clipboard for pasting into other programs. Copying selections with the TouchUp Object tool limits your pasting ability to documents in Acrobat. The minute you leave Acrobat, the data are lost from the clipboard.

You can also use the TouchUp Object tool to move or nudge objects. Click on a single object or marquee a group of objects on a page; then click and drag the selection to a new location. You are limited to moving objects on a single page. You can't select an object on one page and drag it to another PDF page. For moving objects to different pages you need to cut the selection, move to another page, and choose Edit ⇨ Paste. If you want to nudge objects, create a selection with the TouchUp Object tool and press the arrow keys on your keyboard to move the object right or left or up or down.

If you select a text block with the TouchUp Object tool, the bounding box for the text block is shown with a black keyline border. A text block can be one of many blocks on a page, a single block containing all text on a page, or a body of text spanning more than one page. When a text block is selected with the TouchUp Object tool, no text editing is possible. You need to use the TouchUp Text tool to edit the text. The TouchUp Object tool enables you to move text blocks or select them for editing in an external editor. (See "Object Editing" later in this chapter for more details.)

Cross-Reference   For more information on using the TouchUp Text tool, see Chapter 8.

Copying and Pasting Images

Acrobat provides you with different tools for different methods of copying and pasting data. The first decision to make in regard to copying images is determining what you want to do with the copied data. You can export data to other programs, modify data in the current PDF file, paste data to different pages, or create new PDF documents from the copied data. You perform all these tasks with the tools already discussed in this chapter.

Pasting images into authoring program documents

You export images by copying and pasting data, or saving data to new files. You need to use the right tool for pasting objects copied from a PDF document to other applications. For copying an image such as a photograph use the Select Image tool. After you copy the photo, you can paste it into another application document or save the photo as its own file. To copy a photo, use the Select Image tool, click on a photo or raster image, and open a context menu as shown in Figure 9-5. From the menu options, select Copy Image to Clipboard.

If you want to take a copied photo into an image editor, such as Adobe Photoshop, open your image editor and choose File ⇨ New. In a program like Photoshop, the new document you create defaults to the image size of the clipboard image. Choose Edit ⇨ Paste and the photo copied from the PDF is pasted in a new document window measuring the same size as the copied data. It also has the same resolution as the image copied from the PDF. This is to say that if you copy a 300 ppi image from the Acrobat PDF file, the new document in Photoshop where you paste the image defaults at 300 ppi.

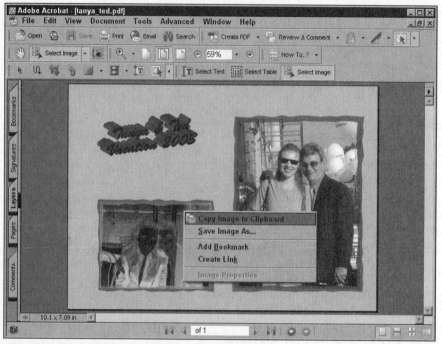

Figure 9-5: With the Select Image tool active, click on an image and open a context menu. From the menu options, select Copy Image to Clipboard.

Exporting images

Copying and pasting images is sometimes less desirable compared with image imports via menu commands. Layout programs, for example, are good candidates for using menu commands over copying and pasting data. When you copy data to the system clipboard, the data change to the format supported by your system. In a Windows system, pasted images become Windows Metafile format and in the Macintosh system, the formats change to PICT. These formats can present printing problems, especially on PostScript devices. Pasting images in a photo-imaging program offers you options for saving in different formats. Therefore, pasting in a program like Adobe Photoshop enables you to save in a file format suited to your output needs.

Prepress

For all high-end and commercial printing, avoid copying and pasting images. If you need to extract an image from a PDF document, copy or save the file from Acrobat. Open the file in Adobe Photoshop and set the color mode and file format best suited for prepress. Open your authoring program and place or import the image.

If you want to export directly from Acrobat in an image format, the Bitmap (BMP) and JPEG formats are supported (Windows) or PICT and JPEG formats (Macintosh) when you save a file from the context menu opened after you use the Select Image tool. If BMP is workable for your needs, select Save Image As from the context menu shown in Figure 9-5. The Save Image As dialog box opens where you supply a filename and locate a destination for the saved file.

Note Using the Save Image As command supports only BMP/PICT and JPEG as the export formats. If you need to change file format, open the saved BMP/PICT or JPEG file in Photoshop and save as a new format type. If your authoring program supports PDF documents, you can use the Create PDF From Clipboard Image command and create a new PDF document. Save as PDF and import the file into your authoring program. For more information on using Create PDF, see Chapter 5.

Pasting objects on PDF pages

To copy and paste objects, including photo images, illustrations and vector objects, and text blocks, you use the TouchUp Object tool. Whereas the Select Image tool is limited to single image selections and offers no support for pasting copied images onto other PDF pages, the TouchUp Object tool enables you to select multiple objects and paste the copied data into different pages in the open PDF document or other PDF documents.

To select a single object, click the object with the TouchUp Object tool. A keyline border shows the bounding box for the selected item. Open a context menu and you find menu options different from those available with the Select Image tool, as shown in Figure 9-6.

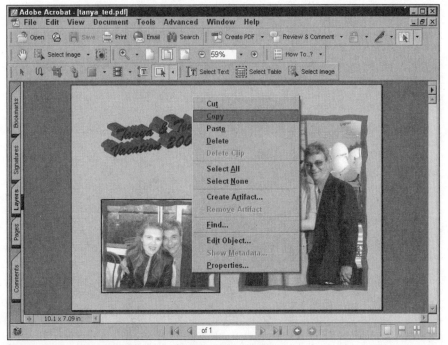

Figure 9-6: Select an image with the TouchUp Object tool and open a context menu. Select Copy from the menu choices to copy the selection.

To copy the selection, choose Copy from the context menu. Note that the menu command is Copy, while the menu command when using the Select Image tool is Copy File to Clipboard.

Acrobat makes a distinction between the two copy commands. When you copy a file to the clipboard with the Select Image tool, you can use Create PDF From Clipboard Image and convert the clipboard data to a PDF document. When you select the Copy command from the TouchUp Object tool context menu, the data cannot be converted to a PDF and you can't paste the data into another program.

To select multiple images with the Touchup Object tool, click and drag a marquee around the images you want to copy. If you include objects you want to eliminate from the selection, hold down the Shift key and click on selected objects to deselect them. To add objects to your selection, hold down Shift and click on any unselected image to add it to your selection.

Note

If two or more images or objects are spaced apart where each object is selectable, you can click and Shift+click to select multiple images/objects. If you have objects such as vector graphics where many paths are contained within the object or you have multiple overlapping objects, marquee the objects to be certain you select all you want to copy.

If dragging through a group of objects to select them moves the background object, start your marquee selection outside the document page and drag toward the objects you want to select. You can then hold down the Shift key and deselect any background items you don't want included in the selection. In Figure 9-7, the 3D type is comprised of many tiny objects. To select part of the type, I placed the cursor above the page and dragged the TouchUp Object tool down through the items shown with selection bounding boxes. I then held down the Shift key and clicked on the background color to deselect it.

Figure 9-7: To select multiple objects, drag a marquee around the items you want to select. Hold down the Shift key and click on any items you want to eliminate from the selection.

Acrobat lacks some editing tools you find in illustration programs where data can be hidden, locked, and sent to other layers. In Acrobat, you need to finesse the TouchUp Object tool when selecting objects surrounded by other objects. In some cases, creating a selection for only the objects you want to edit may not be possible. If you face this problem, you have two choices: Return to your editing program or edit objects in an external editor.

After copying an object or several objects, move to the page in the open PDF document where you want to paste the selection, or open another PDF file. Using the TouchUp Object tool, open a context menu and select Paste. The pasted object(s) remains selected. Make sure to click on a selected object if you need to move the selection around the document page. If you accidentally deselect the object(s), choose Edit ➪ Undo and paste again. Using the TouchUp tools enables you to choose a single Undo for any edits made with these tools.

Exporting images

If you need to completely overhaul a document and want to lay it out in an authoring program, you might want to copy and paste text into a word processor, format your text, save the file, and then import the text into a program best suited for layout design, such as Adobe InDesign. If your PDF document contains photo images, you need to export the images and add them to your layout. Having to individually export images with the Select Image tool would be tedious for a large layout project containing many images. Fortunately, Acrobat offers you a feature for exporting all images in a PDF with a single menu command.

Choose Advanced ➪ Export All Images. The Export All Images As dialog box opens where you can make selections for filename, destination, and the format you want to use for the exported images. In the Export All Images As dialog box, open the pull-down menu for Save as type (Windows) or Format (Macintosh). Four format options are available from the menu choices. You can choose from JPEG, PNG, TIFF, or JPEG2000. Select one of the format options and click on the Settings button to assign file attributes to the exported images.

For more information on image file format definitions, see Chapter 5.

When you select JPEG for the file type and click on the Settings button, the Export All Images As JPEG Settings dialog box opens as shown in Figure 9-8. The settings change according to the file type you select. Therefore, if you choose TIFF as a format, for example, you'll see changes for compression choices. The options for File Settings and Color Management are the same as those options discussed in Chapter 5. In addition to these settings, the Extraction item at the bottom of the dialog box enables you to eliminate certain files when the sizes are smaller than the size you choose from the pull-down menu.

You make preset choices from the pull-down menu for choosing an image's physical size. You might have icons or logos appearing on all pages constructed at .75-inch sizes. You can elect to exclude these images by selecting the 1.00 inches item in the pull-down menu. When you click OK in the Extract All Images As dialog box, all files above the size selected from the pull-down menu choice are saved as separate files in the specified format. If you want every image extracted, choose the No Limit item from the pull-down menu.

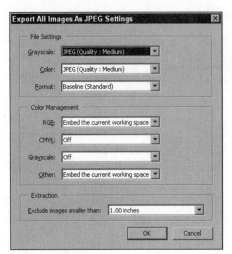

Figure 9-8: Make a choice for file format in the Export All Images As dialog box and click on the Settings button. Options are chosen in the Export All Images As (*file format*) Settings dialog box for File Settings, Color Management, and eliminating image extractions falling below user-defined values.

Object Editing

Acrobat offers you methods for copying and pasting images, moving them around the page, and exporting them to files. However, changing the physical attributes of images and shapes is not something you can do in Acrobat. To modify certain appearances or attributes of raster and vector objects you need to use an external editor. When you launch an editor from a menu command in Acrobat, you can make changes to images, text, and shapes and save your edits in the external editor. These saves are then dynamically updated in the PDF document. Acrobat treats external editing like many programs that support file links. When you edit linked files, the links are updated in the program where they are imported.

To access an external editor, you need to use the TouchUp Object tool. You cannot access external editors with any of the other selection tools.

TouchUp preferences

By default, Acrobat's external editors are Adobe Photoshop for image editing and Adobe Illustrator for object editing. When you install Acrobat, the installer locates these editors on your hard drive, if they are installed, and designates them as the default editors. If you install Photoshop and/or Illustrator after Acrobat, you need to instruct Acrobat where to look for the application files to use as your image/object editors.

Choose Edit ➪ Preferences to open the Preferences dialog box. Click on the TouchUp item on the left side of the Preferences dialog box. At the right side of the Preferences dialog box are two buttons as shown in Figure 9-9. Click Choose Image Editor to open the Choose Image Editor dialog box. The dialog box enables you to navigate your hard drive and locate Adobe Photoshop. Select the Photoshop application icon and click Open.

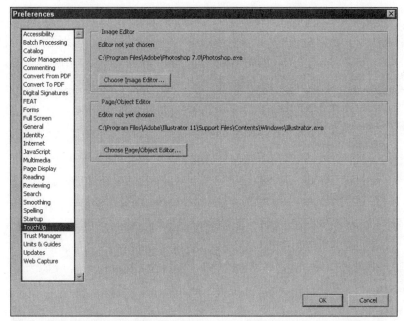

Figure 9-9: Click on TouchUp in the preferences list and the Choose buttons appear on the right side of the dialog box. Click on one of the buttons to navigate your hard drive and select the respective editor.

For page and object editing, Adobe Illustrator is the default tool. If you need to locate Illustrator, click on the Choose Page/Object Editor button. Find the Illustrator application on your hard drive and select it in the Choose Page/Object Editor dialog box. Click Open and Adobe Illustrator is enabled as your page/object editor.

After identifying your editors, click OK in the Preferences dialog box. The options choices made are immediately available. If Acrobat loses contact with either program, you are prompted in a dialog box that external editing cannot be done. If you see warning dialog boxes open as you attempt to use an external editor, return to the Preferences and reestablish the connection to your editors.

Editing images in Adobe Photoshop

You launch Adobe Photoshop from Acrobat by selecting an image with the TouchUp Object tool and opening a context menu. From the menu commands, select Edit Image. Depending on the speed of your computer and the amount of memory you have, Photoshop may take a few moments to launch. When the program opens, the image you selected is placed in a Photoshop document window.

You can change color modes and resolution, edit images for brightness and contrast, add effects, and just about anything you can do in Photoshop to a single layer file. If you add type, add layers, or create transparency, you need to flatten all layers before saving the file. Layers added to a Photoshop file require you to use the Save As command to update the file. When using Save As, the file is not updated in the PDF document. Flattening layers enables you to use the Save command that updates the PDF document when the file is saved. In Figure 9-10, a file in Photoshop was edited to add type and a drop shadow. As a final step, the layers were flattened before the file was saved.

Photoshop updates the PDF document dynamically according to the edits you make with the Save command. If you add a layer to the file, you are prompted by Photoshop to Save As a new filename. Selecting Save As and writing to a new file disrupts the link. If you save in this manner, your PDF document won't update. If the file is saved without writing a new file, the updates are dynamically recorded in the PDF when you return to Acrobat as shown in Figure 9-11.

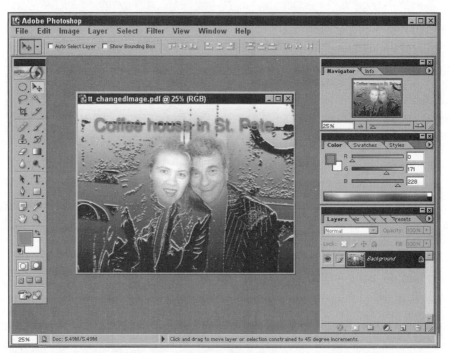

Figure 9-10: You can add type and effects in Photoshop, but be certain all layers are flattened before saving the file and returning to Acrobat.

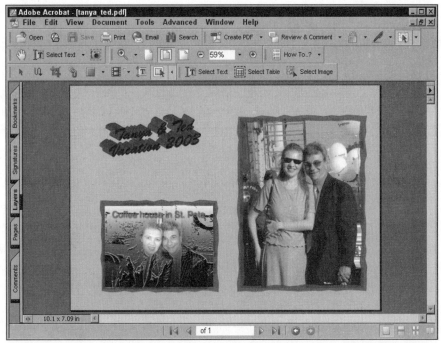

Figure 9-11: When you finish editing ad image, choose File ➪ Save in Photoshop and return to Acrobat. The image you edited is updated in the PDF file.

Note

For sending data to layers, you need to use programs supporting layers and the PDF 1.5 specification. If using a program such as Photoshop 7 and below, you need to be certain all layers are flattened to link the edits to the PDF file. For more on object editing with layers, see the section on Object Editing and Layers later in this chapter.

Editing objects in Adobe Illustrator

Objects, for the purposes of discussing external object editing, can be vector objects such as illustrations created in Adobe Illustrator, CorelDraw, or Macromedia Freehand. Objects can also be text. Both vector objects and text are edited in Adobe Illustrator when you select Edit Object(s) from a context menu with the TouchUp Object tool.

To edit a single object, select the object with the TouchUp Object tool and open a context menu. The Edit Image command changes to Edit Object in the context menu. Select Edit Object, and Adobe Illustrator launches. Changes you make to the object are dynamically updated when you save the file just as the file saves discussed with image editing are updated. If selecting a single object on the PDF page is difficult, you can marquee a group of objects and select Edit Objects.

If no object is selected and you open a context menu with the TouchUp Object tool, the menu command changes to Edit Page as shown in Figure 9-12. Edit Page appears as a menu command when no objects are selected.

To easily access the Edit Page command, you can also open a context menu outside the page boundary. When you click outside the page area, the Edit Page command appears in the context menu. Select Edit Page and all objects are opened in Adobe Illustrator as shown in Figure 9-13.

Be certain to not use the Save As command when editing objects. The procedures for saving files with object editing follow the same principles as described with image editing. Regardless of whether you edit a single object, multiple objects, or the entire page, only the edits you make in Illustrator are updated in the PDF document when you choose File ➪ Save.

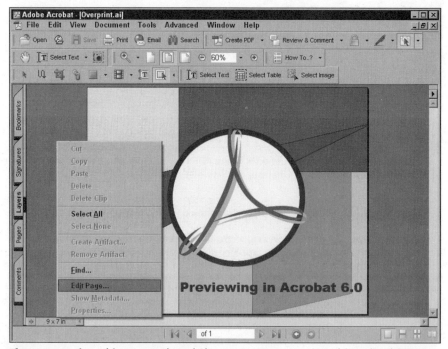

Figure 9-12: If no objects are selected, the context menu command for Edit Object(s) changes to Edit Page. Selecting the menu command places all objects in a new Adobe Illustrator document window.

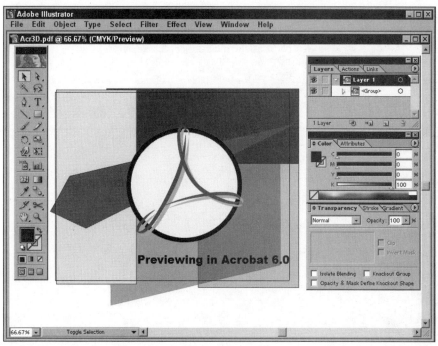

Figure 9-13: To edit a page, select Edit Page from the context menu options. All objects are opened in Adobe Illustrator.

Editing text in Adobe Illustrator

In some circumstances, you may find editing text in an external editor to prove more satisfactory than editing text with the TouchUp Text tool. Editing text in Adobe Illustrator requires you to have embedded fonts loaded on your computer. Keep in mind that returning to an authoring application to apply major edits to documents is more advantageous than using the TouchUp Text tool. But, for those jobs where you don't have a document available and using the TouchUp Text tool just doesn't do the job, here's a little workaround you can try. I offer a disclaimer and tell you upfront that these methods may not always work, but I've found more often than not that you can successfully edit text in Illustrator for some minor edit jobs. It's worth a try if you have no other alternatives.

As an example of a real-world experience, I had occasion to use the Edit Object feature in Acrobat on a file used recently at a PDF conference. In Figure 9-14, notice the type in the top-left corner gets lost against the lighter areas of the background. The yellow type and the background white areas don't create enough contrast to make the type legible. To polish up the layout, a drop shadow is needed. Rather than returning to the authoring program, I elected to use the Edit Object feature in Acrobat. Because the TouchUp Text tool won't add a new line of type behind the yellow text, the easiest solution is to take the file in Illustrator and add the drop shadow behind the original text.

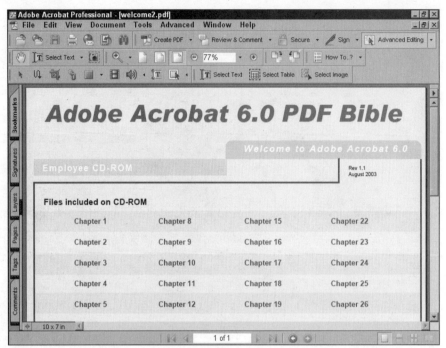

Figure 9-14: In this figure, the text needs to be edited to add contrast between the type and the background color. Rather than editing the text color with the TouchUp Text tool, I added a drop shadow in an external editor.

To understand how this file was edited using Adobe Illustrator as the object editor, follow these steps. If you don't have Illustrator, look over the steps to understand how object editing is handled when you launch the editor from within Acrobat.

STEPS: Editing text in Adobe Illustrator

1. **Open a PDF document to be edited.** Ideally, using a file that you created is best so you are certain all the fonts contained in the PDF document are loaded on your computer.

2. **Select the text block to be edited.** Select the TouchUp Object tool and click on the text block you want to edit. If you want to edit two or more text blocks, hold the Shift key down as you select additional text blocks.

3. **Select Edit Object(s).** Open a context menu and select Edit Object(s) as shown in Figure 9-15. In this example, I have two separate blocks of text selected for editing.

4. **Modify the type.** In this example, a drop shadow is added to show more contrast between the type and background. To add a drop shadow, copy the text block and paste behind the selected type. Add a black fill to the text and use the arrow keys to offset the text from the top text block. The results for adding a drop shadow should appear as shown in Figure 9-16.

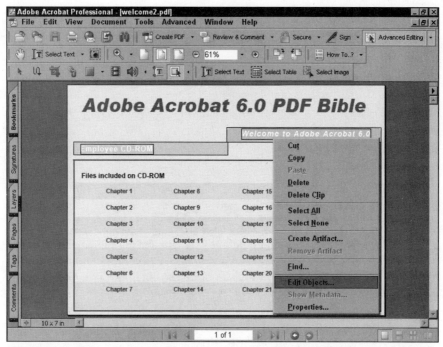

Figure 9-15: Click on the type with the TouchUp Object tool. Open a context menu and select Edit Object(s). Adobe Illustrator launches and the type is opened in a new document window.

Figure 9-16: The pasted text is filled black and offset from the top text block. The drop shadow helps add contrast between the type and the background.

5. **Save the file.** Choose File ⇨ Save. Be certain not to use Save As to write a new file. The file opened in Illustrator is linked to the PDF document. Saving the edits updates the PDF.

6. **Preview the results.** You can minimize the Illustrator window or quit the program. The edits applied in Illustrator are recorded when you select Save. Maximize the Acrobat window and review the changes. The result for the example described here is shown in Figure 9-17.

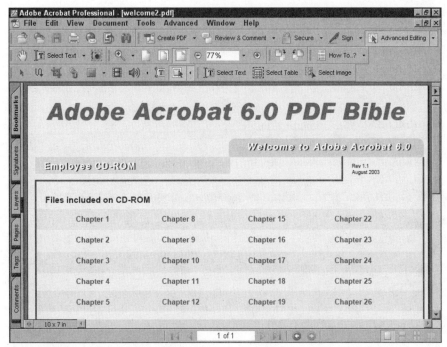

Figure 9-17: After saving the edits in Illustrator, quit the program and open the Acrobat window. The edits saved in Illustrator are updated in the PDF document.

Object Editing and Layers

You may have legacy PDF documents that could be better viewed with layers. Because earlier versions of Acrobat didn't support layers, you need to return to the authoring program and export to PDF in Acrobat 6.0-compatible format or use an external editor that supports saves to the PDF 1.5 format.

You need two essential items for creating layers: an authoring program that supports layers, and a program that supports exporting to PDF with Acrobat 6.0 compatibility. If your program of choice supports layers and PDF exports but you don't see an Acrobat 6.0-compatible file export option, you need to check for software updates. As of this writing, how many different authoring programs will support layers and Acrobat 6.0 compatibility is not yet known. Historically, software manufacturers have included compatible file exports with all new software releases. If the programs you use support exporting direct to PDF and they don't yet support exporting PDF 6.0-compatible files, keep checking your software manufacturer's Web site. When new releases are announced, in all likelihood, you should see PDF 1.5 and layers supported.

If you have a legacy file that needs to have layers throughout the document pages, obviously you need to return to the authoring program and modify the file, adding elements on pages to new layers. Export the file with Acrobat 6.0 compatibility and, if you have an option for preserving layers, be certain to enable the check box.

If you have a page or two and want to edit objects, here's a method that you can use to add layers in an object editor. Once again, your object editor needs to support layers and exporting to PDF 1.5 format.

Open the PDF to be edited in Acrobat. Select the TouchUp Object tool and either open a context menu while no objects are selected or while all objects are selected. If all objects are selected, the Edit Objects menu command appears in the context menu as shown in Figure 9-18. If no objects are selected, the Edit Page menu command appears.

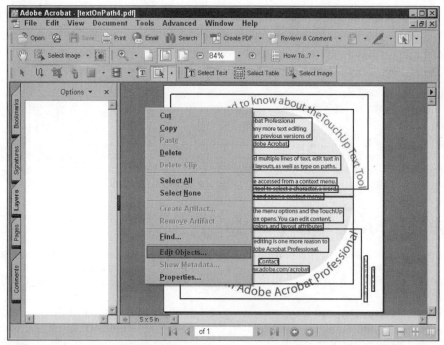

Figure 9-18: When all objects are selected, choose Edit Objects from the context menu opened with the TouchUp Object tool.

In your object editor, arrange the objects on separate layers. Edit the layer names to the names you want displayed in the PDF document. The default settings in your object editor should be set to save or export in PDF 1.5 format. After you add objects to new layers, choose File ⇨ Save.

Quit your object editor and maximize the Acrobat window. Click on the Layers tab when Acrobat comes to view. If you edited the layers properly and exported in PDF 1.5 format while preserving layers, the PDF document should look like the example shown in Figure 9-19.

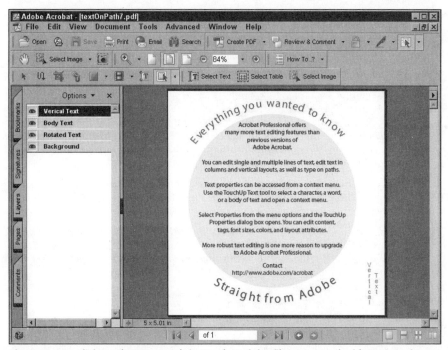

Figure 9-19: Click on the Layers tab in Acrobat. If the file was saved with PDF 1.5 format and layers were preserved, the individual layers appear in the Layers palette, with the names you provided for the layers in the object editor.

For quick edits, working with an object editor saves time when you want to rearrange data on different layers. With legacy files where you have no original authoring document, the method described previously might be your only solution.

Cross-Reference

For more information on creating and editing layers, see Chapter 17.

Summary

✦ You use the Select Image tool to select individual photo images on PDF pages. You can select only a single image with the tool. A single click on an image with the Select Image tool selects the image and copies it to the clipboard.

✦ You use the Snapshot tool to marquee an area on a page and select text, objects, and images within the selection marquee. Releasing the mouse button after you create a selection marquee copies the data within the marquee to the clipboard.

✦ To select objects use the TouchUp Object tool. Objects include photo images, illustrative artwork, and text. Dragging a marquee enables you to select multiple objects. Pressing the Shift key and clicking on an object toggles between adding and eliminating an object from a selection.

✦ Images copied with the Select Image tool can be converted to PDF with the Create PDF tool and you can paste them into authoring programs. The copied images cannot be pasted on PDF pages.

✦ Objects and images copied with the TouchUp Object tool can be pasted on PDF pages. They cannot be pasted into authoring application documents.

✦ External editing is handled by selecting an image or an object and opening a context menu. From the menu options, select Edit Image/Object. When you make the menu choice, the external editor launches. The default image editor is Adobe Photoshop and the default object editor is Adobe Illustrator. Select editors in the Preferences dialog box by clicking on the TouchUp item in the left list and clicking on the Change button on the right side of the dialog box.

✦ Unless a program supports exporting to the PDF 1.5 format, you must flatten all layers in external editors before saving edits. When a file is saved in an external editor, the PDF document is dynamically updated.

✦ If a program supports layers and exporting with Acrobat 6.0 compatibility, legacy PDF documents can be edited and have data applied to different layers with the Edit Object command. Edited files with new layers appear in Acrobat in the Layers palette with the new layer data and layer names.

✦   ✦   ✦

Editing Pages

Chapters 8 and 9 covered editing content on PDF pages. For text passages and image editing, you may have minor edits that can be completed with the tools discussed in the two previous chapters. If you want to modify larger portions of a PDF document, then you'll want to know something about the tools Acrobat offers you for page editing. If you return to an authoring application and edit text, graphics, and layouts, you may want to update your PDF document according to the page edits made in other applications. Rather than recreate the entire PDF file, Acrobat enables you to selectively append, replace, delete, and extract pages in a PDF document.

In addition to the number of different page editing tools found in earlier versions of Acrobat, the new version of Acrobat Professional offers some impressive features for creating headers and footers and adding backgrounds and watermarks. This chapter covers the page-editing tools in Acrobat and the new features that can help you modify documents.

Setting Up the Page Editing Environment

For page-editing tasks, you need to use some viewing tools, advanced tools, and perhaps some measurement tools. Move the cursor to the Toolbar Well and open a context menu. From the menu options select Reset Toolbars. If the How To Pane is open, select the Hide button or press F4.

Click on the pull-down menu adjacent to the Zoom In tool and select Show Zoom Toolbar from the menu options. When editing pages, zooming in and out with these tools is a frequent exercise.

Choose Tools ⇨ Advanced Editing ⇨ Show Advanced Editing Toolbar or click on the Advanced Editing Task Button. Follow up with Tools ⇨ Measuring ⇨ Show Measuring Toolbar and you wind up with three toolbars floating in the Document Pane. Dock the toolbars and the Toolbar Well should look something like Figure 10-1.

Note The Measuring toolbar is only available in Acrobat Professional.

Working with Thumbnails

Thumbnails are mini-views of PDF pages that can be displayed in various zoom sizes. Smaller and larger thumbnail sizes are supported in Acrobat 6.0 compared to earlier versions of Acrobat viewers, and the new size options are a great benefit for organizing pages in a PDF document and exchanging pages between documents. Thanks to the impressive size options available in the Pages palette, you don't have to squint your eyes to see page content when viewing the thumbnails of your document pages.

To see the thumbnail view of pages in an open document, click on the Pages palette tab to open the palette as shown in Figure 10-1. Thumbnail views are created on-the-fly when the palette is opened. Users of earlier versions of Acrobat will remember the palette was referred to as *Thumbnails.* In Acrobat 6.0 viewers the name has been changed for the palette, but the options you had in Acrobat 5 are the same as those available in Acrobat 6.0 with the addition of some features.

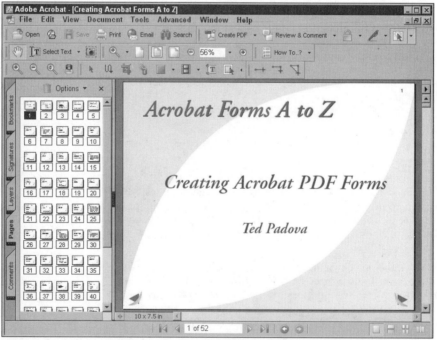

Figure 10-1: Click on the Pages tab to open the Pages palette where thumbnail views of the pages are created on-the fly.

Navigating pages

The Pages palette can be used to navigate pages. Clicking on a thumbnail takes you to the page associated with the thumbnail. The page opens in the Document Pane at the currently established zoom view. You can zoom in or out of pages in the Pages palette by dragging the lower-right handle on the rectangle appearing inside the page thumbnail. Changing zoom levels are reflected in the zoom view in the Document Pane. In Figure 10-2, a rectangle shows the current page view in the Document Pane. Click on the handle in the lower-right corner and drag it in to the center of the rectangle to zoom in on the page. Click and drag out and you zoom out of the page.

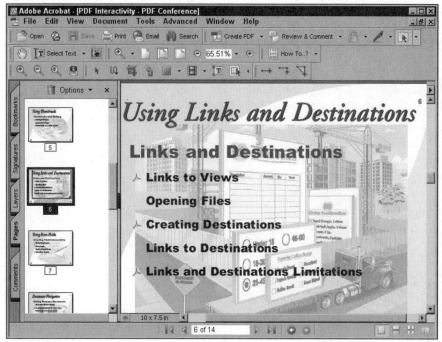

Figure 10-2: Thumbnails in the Pages palette are linked to the pages in the Document Pane. Click on a thumbnail and you navigate to the page link. Drag the rectangle to zoom in or out of the page displayed in the Document Pane.

The Pages palette and the Document Pane are two separate compartments in the open PDF document. If you click in the Pages palette, you activate the palette. Conversely, clicking in the Document Pane activates the area where pages are viewed. Unfortunately, Acrobat does not highlight any part of either pane to inform you when a pane is active. So you just have to remember to click first in the area you want to be active.

If you press the Page Down key or down-arrow key while the Document Pane is active, the pages in the Document Pane scroll. As each page is scrolled, the Pages palette likewise scrolls pages and the respective page thumbnails are highlighted. When you click in the Pages palette you experience a different behavior. Pressing the Page Down key scrolls several pages down only in the Pages palette. The respective pages in the Document Pane are not scrolled. As you scroll through page thumbnails in the Pages palette, the Document Pane remains fixed at its current view. The reason is that as you scroll in the Pages palette, thumbnails are not actually selected. The selected thumbnail is linked to the view in the Document Pane.

With reference to thumbnails, the term *selection* needs a little definition. When you click on a page thumbnail, the number appearing below the page icon is shown selected (highlighted) and the thumbnail is further highlighted with a keyline border around the icon. Likewise the respective page is placed in view in the Document Pane. In essence there are two selection messages Acrobat communicates to you. If you press the down-arrow key on your keyboard, the number below the thumbnail remains highlighted and the respective page remains open in the Document Pane. However, the keyline border moves to the next page down indicating the current thumbnail selection in the Pages palette. In Figure 10-3, page 8 in a PDF document is selected and page 8 is open in the Document Pane. When the down-arrow key is pressed, page 9 becomes selected in the Pages palette, while page 8 remains as the page viewed in the Document Pane.

Figure 10-3: Click the cursor in the Pages palette to activate the palette, and then press the down-arrow key. The keyline border shows the page selection in the Pages palette, while the highlighted page number on the previous page shows what page is in view in the Document Pane.

Tip   You can use the Pages palette and the Document Pane to compare pages in a PDF document. If you insert a new page that is similar to an existing page in the PDF file, click the thumbnail of one page to open it in the Document Pane. Use the arrow keys (up or down) to navigate to the inserted page. Enlarge the thumbnail view so you can clearly compare the thumbnail to the page in the Document Pane. For information on enlarging views and inserting pages, see the next section on changing thumbnail sizes.

Changing thumbnail sizes

In earlier versions of Acrobat you had a maximum of two zoom views for page thumbnails. Now in Acrobat 6.0 you can reduce the size of pages to a mini thumbnail view and enlarge the size up to a maximum view of about 300 percent. The support for increased thumbnail views in the Pages palette enables you to quickly find a page in a PDF document.

You access page thumbnail reduction and enlargements through menu commands. A context menu opened in the Pages palette or the palette pull-down menu includes the Enlarge Page Thumbnails and Reduce Page Thumbnails commands. Before using these commands, you should understand opening context menus.

If you click in the Pages palette on a page thumbnail and open a context menu, the Enlarge Page Thumbnails and Reduce Page Thumbnail commands are available as options in a menu with many different commands for page editing. If you click outside the page thumbnails, but still in the Pages palette, a different menu opens with fewer commands. However, the same menu commands for enlarging or reducing page thumbnails are still present. Likewise, the pull-down menu adjacent to Options at the top of the Pages palette offers the same commands. Regardless of which menu you use, you can enlarge or reduce page thumbnail views.

To enlarge the size of the page thumbnails click the mouse button outside the page thumbnails in the Pages palette and open a context menu. Select Enlarge Page Thumbnails from the menu options as shown in Figure 10-4. Return to the menu and select the same menu command to enlarge again. Repeat the steps to zoom in to the desired view.

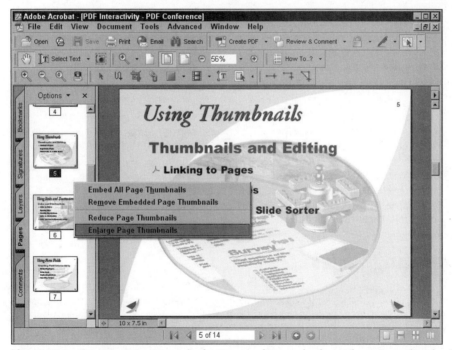

Figure 10-4: Open a context menu in the Pages palette and select Enlarge Page Thumbnails. Return to the context menu and repeat the steps several times to zoom in on a page thumbnail.

You'll notice that Acrobat makes no provision for selecting from among a number of preset zoom sizes. You need to return to the context menu or pull-down menu to successively increase or decrease page thumbnail views. If the zoom view in the Pages palette is larger than the palette width, click anywhere on the vertical bar on the right side of the palette and drag it to the right. The palette resizes horizontally to show more of the Pages palette while the Document Pane is reduced in size. In Figure 10-5, I enlarged the thumbnail view through repeated steps for enlarging the thumbnails and widened the palette so the entire thumbnail could be viewed.

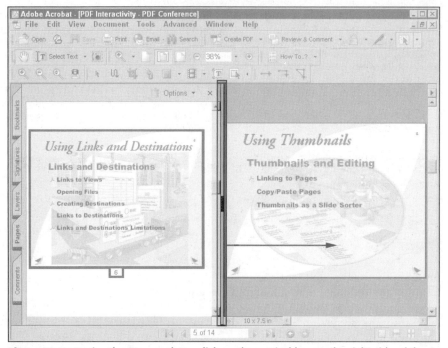

Figure 10-5: To size the Pages palette, click on the vertical bar on the right side of the palette and drag it to the right.

Organizing Pages

The Pages palette offers you a wealth of opportunity for sorting pages and reorganizing them. You can move pages around, copy and paste pages when you want to duplicate them, delete pages, print selected pages within a document, and a host of other options specific to page management.

Reordering pages

Acrobat provides you with a marvelous slide sorter where you can shuffle pages and reorder them in a page sequence suited to your needs. Now with an opportunity to view page thumbnails in much larger views, you can easily see the content of text only pages when no visible icons or graphics are present to distinguish differences in page content. Reorganizing pages in earlier versions of Acrobat was a little more difficult to view text pages in small thumbnail views; however, now you can manage page order more easily by zooming in on pages to clearly view the content.

To rearrange pages in a PDF document, open the Pages palette to the full width of your monitor by dragging the right side of the palette to the far right of the Document Pane. Open a context menu in the Pages palette and select Enlarge Page Thumbnails. Repeat the steps to enlarge the thumbnail views to a size that enables you to read text comfortably on the pages.

Click on a page and drag the page to a spot between the pages where you want to relocate the selected page. When you move a page around the Pages palette, a vertical bar appears where the page will be located. If the highlight bar is positioned in the area where you want to relocate a page, release the mouse button. Figure 10-6 shows page 8 selected. The page is moved to the area between pages 2 and 3. Notice the vertical highlight bar appearing between the pages.

Note   If you want to move pages between pages not in view in the Pages tab, move a page down or up and the Pages scroll to reveal hidden pages. Keep the mouse button depressed until you find the location where you want to move a page.

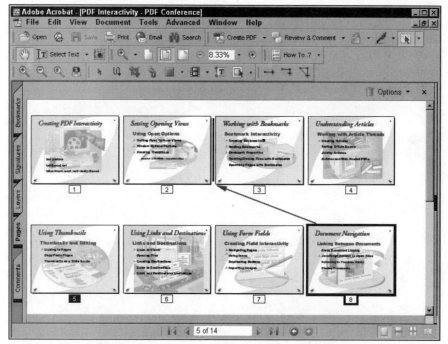

Figure 10-6: To move a page in a PDF document, click on a thumbnail and drag the thumbnail to the area you where you want to relocate the page. When you see a vertical highlight bar appear in the desired location, release the mouse button.

To select multiple pages, click on a page to select it. Hold down the Shift key and click on another page. If you want to select a block of contiguous pages, click on the first page to be selected, hold down the Shift key, and click on the last page within the group. All pages between the two selected pages are included in the selection. For noncontiguous selections, hold down the Control/Option key to individually add random pages to a selection. After you make your selection, click on one of the selected pages and drag to a new location to reorder the pages.

Tip   For a super slide sorter, open the Pages palette and view thumbnails in a large size. Place the mouse cursor over the vertical bar to the right of the Pages palette and drag to the right of your monitor screen. Press the F8 and F9 keys to hide the menu bar and toolbars. Resize the viewing window to fit the screen size. You'll get as much real estate on your monitor as possible. Shuffling pages is much easier in Acrobat than in almost any other program.

Copying pages

You can copy and paste pages within a PDF document or from one open PDF document to another. To copy a page with thumbnails, hold down the Control/Option key as you drag a page to a new location in the same PDF file. Release the mouse button when you see the vertical highlight bar appear at the desired location. To copy a page from one PDF to another, open both PDF files and view them tiled either vertically or horizontally. The Pages palette must be in view on both PDF documents. Click and drag the thumbnail from one file to the Thumbnail palette in the other document. The vertical highlight bar appears and the cursor changes, as shown in Figure 10-7. After the vertical bar is positioned at the desired location, release the mouse button, and the page drops into position.

Cross-Reference   For learning how to tile PDF documents, see Chapter 3.

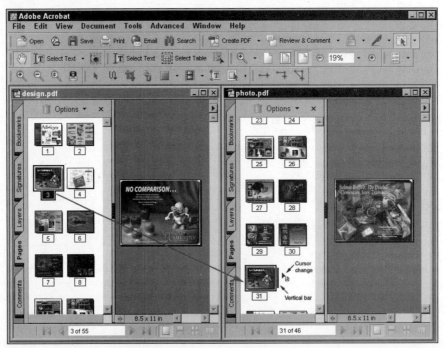

Figure 10-7: Dragging a thumbnail to a new location or copying between documents displays a horizontal highlight bar where the page will be placed.

Removing pages

The previous example behaves like a copy-and-paste sequence. You can also create a cut-and-paste action whereby the page is deleted from one PDF document and copied to another. To remove a page and place it in another PDF file, hold the down Control/Option key and then click and drag the page to another Pages palette in another file. The page is deleted from the original file and copied to the second file.

Caution　Be certain not to confuse the shortcut keys. If Control/Option is used with click and drag, the page is copied. If using the same keys between two documents, the page is deleted from the file of origin and copied to the destination file.

To delete a page with the Pages palette, use a context-sensitive menu or the palette Options menu. Select a single thumbnail or Shift+click to select multiple thumbnails in a contiguous order (Ctrl/⌘+click for a noncontiguous order), and select Delete Pages from the respective menu command. When the Delete Pages is selected, a dialog box opens, as shown in Figure 10-8.

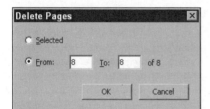

Figure 10-8: When you delete pages from the Pages context menu, the Delete Pages dialog box opens. Click OK to delete the selected pages.

In the Delete Pages dialog box, by default the selected page is marked for deletion. You can make a change in the dialog box by selecting the From button and entering a contiguous page number range in the field box. The Selected radio button deletes all pages selected in the Pages palette. You can click and select pages in a contiguous or noncontiguous group. Open the Delete Pages dialog box and click OK. The selected pages are deleted from the document.

Embedding thumbnails

Page thumbnails are created on the fly each time you open the Pages palette. In long documents, you may find your computer slowing down each time the Pages palette is opened and the thumbnails are recreated. If this proves to be a burden, you can choose to embed thumbnails when working with the Pages palette and avoid the delay for creating them.

Thumbnails add some overhead to your file. Each page thumbnail adds about 1K to the file size. Unless your files are to be viewed by users of earlier Acrobat viewers that don't support creating thumbnails on the fly, delete them as one of the final steps in your editing session.

To embed thumbnails, select the Embed All Page Thumbnails command from the Palette Options menu or a context-sensitive menu. Thumbnails can also be created by batch-processing PDF files using a Batch Sequence or at the time of distillation when using Acrobat Distiller.

You can delete thumbnails from PDF documents either individually in Acrobat or by using the Advanced ⇨ Edit Batch Sequences command in Acrobat Professional. If your work environment is such that you do a lot of editing in Acrobat and often use thumbnails, you may want to create them during distillation. When thumbnails are embedded, screen refreshes for multiple edits in long documents are faster. After you finish editing jobs and want to post PDF files on the Web or create CD-ROMs, you can batch-process the files for optimization and delete the thumbnails. When the Edit Batch Sequences command is run, multiple files are optimized and thumbnails are removed.

For information on creating and running Batch Sequences, see Chapter 13.

Modifying Pages

Users of earlier versions of Acrobat should pay special attention to the many options available from a context menu opened on a page thumbnail or in the palette Options menu. Certain commands formerly located in the Document menu in earlier versions of Acrobat have been moved to the Pages palette if they directly affect page editing.

In this context, *modifying pages* refers to the PDF page in its entirety and not individual page elements. Rather than look at changing single items on a page, this section examines some of the features for structuring pages as an extension of the commands found in the Pages palette. Page editing discussed here relates to the insertion, extraction, and replacement of PDF pages.

Before you go about creating a huge PDF document with links and buttons, understanding how Acrobat structures a page and related links is imperative. Bookmarks and other links are often created within a PDF document as user-defined navigation. Acrobat handles thumbnails and the link to the respective pages. You have no control over the links from a thumbnail to respective pages.

For information on creating bookmarks and links, see Chapter 15.

With regard to links and bookmarks, think of Acrobat as having separate layers where the navigation items are placed and the remaining layers handle the page content. This use of the term *layers* is different than the Adobe PDF layers that one might create from programs supporting layers and converting to PDF with Adobe PDF layers. In regard to a single layer PDF document a layer contains pages and contents, and a second layer hovering over the background content is where all the links appear. When viewing a PDF file, you don't see the navigation items independent of page content. This said, when you delete a page, all the links to the page are lost. Acrobat makes no provision to go to the page that follows a deleted page when links are deleted. Therefore, if you set up a bookmark to page four and later delete page four, the bookmark has no place to go. Such links are commonly referred to as *dead links*.

When editing pages in Acrobat, you can choose to insert a page, delete a page, extract a page, and replace a page. If you understand the page structure, you'll know which option is right for your situation. You access each of the following options described by choices available in the Pages Options menu, by selecting commands from the Document ⇨ Pages submenu, or by using a context sensitive menu (as shown in Figure 10-9) while clicking a thumbnail in the Pages palette.

Caution

Using the menu commands for page editing is available only when you work with PDF documents that are not password protected against page editing. If you attempt to edit pages in a secure PDF document, Acrobat prompts you for a password. This behavior applies to all the options listed here.

✦ **Insert Pages:** When you select this option, the Select File to Insert dialog box opens. Select a file to insert and click on the Select button in the dialog box. The Insert Pages dialog box opens next enabling you to choose the location for the insertion regardless of the current page viewed (see Figure 10-10). You can choose to insert a page either before or after the page in view, within a page range, or before or after the first or last page. Inserted pages do not affect any links in your document. All the pages shift left or right, depending on whether you select the Before or After option.

✦ **Delete Pages:** When you delete a page, you delete not only its contents but also its links. If a bookmark or other link is linked to a view in the deleted page, all links to the page become inoperable. When creating a presentation in Acrobat with multiple pages, you must exercise care when deleting pages to be certain no links are broken.

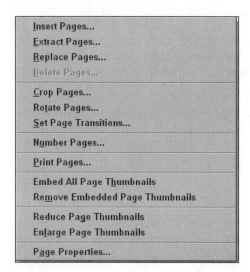

Figure 10-9: Move the cursor to a page thumbnail; click and open a context menu. All the commands used for page modification are contained in the menu. Be certain to open the menu on a thumbnail. If you open a context menu between thumbnails, menu choices for page editing are not accessible.

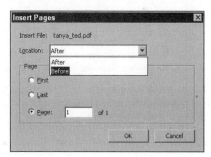

Figure 10-10: The Insert Pages dialog box enables you to locate the page that precedes or follows another page for the target location.

Select a single thumbnail or multiple thumbnails in the Pages palette. Pages can be selected in a contiguous or noncontiguous selection. Open a context menu or the Options pull-down menu and select the Delete Pages command. The Delete Pages dialog box opens where you can delete the selected pages by leaving the default Selected radio button active or by selecting a page range and clicking OK.

Acrobat opens a warning dialog box to confirm your choice. If you change your mind and want to keep the pages, click the Cancel button. To continue with the page deletion, click OK. (See Figure 10-8 earlier in the chapter).

Tip

If you begin an editing session and work on files where you insert and delete pages frequently, you may find the confirmation dialog box annoying. To eliminate the dialog box opening every time you delete a page, open the Preferences dialog box (Ctrl/⌘+K). Click on General in the left pane and check the box for Disable edit warnings. When you return to the Document Pane, all subsequent page deletions are performed without the warning dialog box opening. Be certain to exercise care when targeting pages for deletion if you are not using the edit warnings.

✦ **Extract Pages:** Extracting a page is like pulling out single or multiple pages and creating a new PDF file. Extracting pages has no effect on bookmarks or links for the destination pages in the original document unless you delete pages when extracting them. All links are operable for pages among the extracted pages. For example, if you extract 10 pages with bookmarks to each page, all the bookmarks within the extracted pages are functional in the new file. If you have a bookmark to a page not part of the extraction, the link is not operational.

When you select the Extract Pages command, the Extract Pages dialog box opens as shown in Figure 10-11. The page range is supplied in the From/To field boxes and a check box exists for Delete Pages After Extracting. When the check box is enabled, the extracted pages are deleted from the host document.

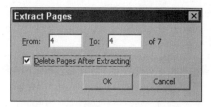

Figure 10-11: If you want to delete the pages extracted from the original file, check the box for Delete Pages After Extracting.

✦ **Replace Pages:** This option affects only the contents layer of a PDF page — the link layer is unaffected. If you have links going to or from the replaced page, all links are preserved. When editing PDF documents where page contents need to be changed, redistilled, and inserted in the final document, always use the Replace Pages command.

Replace Pages is particularly helpful when recreating Acrobat PDF forms. If you create a form in an authoring program and add all the form fields in Acrobat, then later decide you want to edit the appearance of the form, replacing the old design with a new design preserves the form fields.

You can click on a single page thumbnail or select multiple pages in a contiguous order and open a context menu. Select Replace Pages and the Select File With New Pages dialog box opens. Navigate to the file containing pages that are to replace pages in the open file, and click Select.

The Replace Pages dialog box opens. In the Original area of the dialog box shown in Figure 10-12, you select the page range in the open document for the target pages to be replaced. In the Replacement section of the Replace Pages dialog box, you select the first page number of the document selected in the Select Pages to Replace dialog box. The readout to the right of the field box automatically displays the range of pages that are targeted for replacement. At the bottom of each section, notice the filename listed for the open document and the selected document.

✦ If you disabled the edit warnings, the pages are replaced according to the selection made in the Replace Pages dialog box. If the edit warnings are not disabled (in this case, the check box not checked in the Preferences dialog box), a confirmation dialog box opens. Click OK and the pages are replaced.

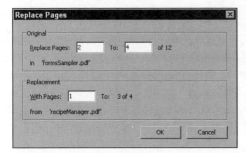

Figure 10-12: Specify the page range for the pages to be replaced in the first two field boxes. Enter the page number for the first page in the target file. The readout at the right of the With Pages field box shows the last page in the range used as a replacement page among the total number of pages in the document.

Tip

You can replace pages through drag-and-drop operations when viewing two documents in tiled views and when the Pages palette is opened for both documents. When you drag a page or a number of selected pages, move the cursor in the target document on top of the number below the thumbnail for the first page to be replaced. Rather than place the cursor between pages where the highlight bar is shown, be certain to drop the selection on top of the page number. The target page is highlighted in black when the cursor appears directly over the page number.

There are many ways you can approach page editing in Acrobat. Using the Pages palette helps you access menu commands quickly. You can also access the same commands just discussed with the Pages palette collapsed by choosing Document ⇨ Pages. In addition, you can open multiple documents, view them with horizontal or vertical tiling, and drag and drop pages to accomplish the same results. To help in understanding how page editing with tiled views is accomplished, try following these steps for a little practice.

STEPS: Editing pages with thumbnails

1. **Open two PDF documents where pages need to be arranged in a third document.** As an example for page editing, assume you have two files that need selected pages merged in a new, third file. Some of the pages need only to be copied to the new file and some pages need to be copied and deleted from the source document.

2. **Create a JavaScript.** Acrobat doesn't offer you a menu command for creating a new document, but you can use a JavaScript to create a file with a blank page. The routine is simple even if you haven't ever typed any JavaScript code. To open the JavaScript debugger, press Ctrl/⌘+J. The JavaScript Debugger opens. If any text appears in the window, select and delete the text. Enter the following code as shown in Figure 10-13:

```
app.newDoc();
```

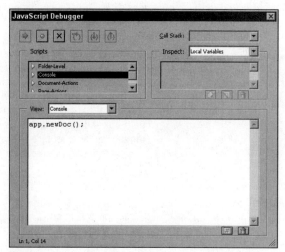

Figure 10-13: Open the JavaScript Debugger by pressing Ctrl/⌘+J. Delete any text in the window and type a new line of code.

3. **Create a new document.** With the cursor at the end of the line in the JavaScript Debugger, press the Enter key on the keyboard number pad. Be certain to press the number pad Enter key and not the Enter/Return key. A new blank document opens in the Document Pane.

Note　On notebook computers, use Control + Enter if a Num Pad Enter key is not available.

4. **Close the JavaScript Debugger.** Click on the close box in the JavaScript Debugger window.

5. **Tile the page views.** Choose Window ➪ Tile ➪ Vertically (or Ctrl+Shift+L). Click on the Pages palette in each file to open the palettes. The two files you opened and the new file you created should appear similar to Figure 10-14.

6. **Replace a page.** The new document you created with the JavaScript contains a blank page. One of the cover pages in the opened files will be used as the cover in the new document. Select a page from one of the open document Pages palette and drag the page to the top of *number 1* in the new document. When the page is targeted for replacement, the entire page is highlighted as shown in Figure 10-15.

7. **Insert pages.** Select a page in one of the open documents. Press the Ctrl/⌘ key and click on pages in a noncontiguous order. Drag one of the selected pages below the title page in the new document. Wait until you see a highlight bar appearing below the page before releasing the mouse button.

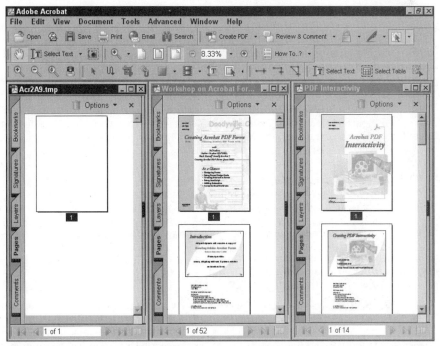

Figure 10-14: The two opened files and the new file created with the JavaScript appear with the Pages palettes open.

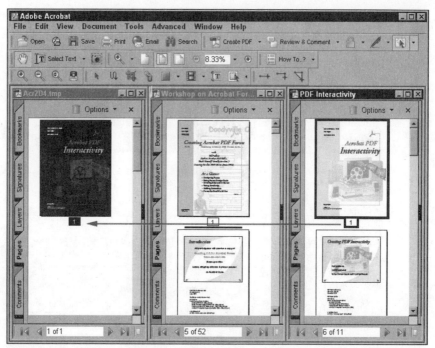

Figure 10-15: Drag a page thumbnail to the new document and place the cursor on top of the page number. The target page highlights. When you release the mouse button, the page is replaced.

8. **Extract pages with deletion.** Move to the second open file. In this document you copy pages to the new document while deleting them from the source document. Click on a contiguous or noncontiguous group of pages to select them. Press the Ctrl/Option key and drag the pages to the new document Pages palette. Pages are inserted in the new file and deleted from the source document.

9. **Close the original source documents.** Click on the close button or choose File ➪ Close to close the documents. If you want to save the file where you extracted and deleted pages, save the document and close the file.

10. **Sort the pages.** Open the Pages palette by dragging the right side of the palette to the right side of the Acrobat window. Open a context menu and select Enlarge Pages. Repeat the steps to enlarge pages until you have a comfortable view of the page content. Click and drag pages around the Pages palette to reorder the pages as shown in Figure 10-16.

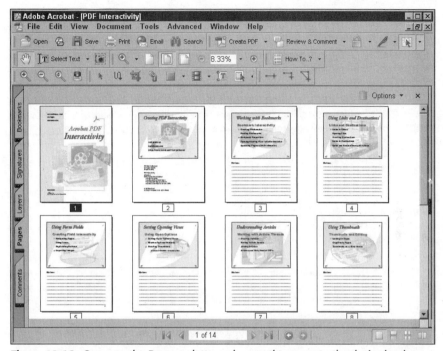

Figure 10-16: Open up the Pages palette and move the pages to the desired order.

11. **Save the file.** Choose File ➪ Save As. Supply a filename and select a destination in the Save As dialog box. Click on the Save button.

If you have a major editing job, periodically save your work. When you create a new file with a JavaScript, Acrobat supplies a temporary name, but the file is not actually saved to disk until you save the file. Save the file after a few edits; then repeat the Save command as you work on the file. When you finish the job, choose File ➪ Save As and rewrite the file. Page editing can add a lot of unnecessary data to a file during an editing job. When you rewrite the file, much of the redundancy is eliminated and the file size is reduced.

Cross-Reference

For information on rewriting files with the Save As command, see Chapter 3.

Appending Pages to PDF Documents

If you want to create a PDF document by combining multiple files that may have been created from multiple authors and multiple authoring programs, there are some alternatives you can choose in Acrobat that permit you to concatenate files to form a single PDF document.

When you use the Insert Pages command, the Select File to Insert dialog box enables you to select multiple files stored in a single folder. You can select multiple files by holding down the Shift key and clicking on the target files in a listed order from within a folder, or pressing the Ctrl/⌘ key to select files in a noncontiguous order.

However, when you use the Insert Pages command, the order the files are appended to the open PDF file does not follow the same order viewed as a list in the Select File to Insert dialog box. You have no control over rearranging the order or selecting additional files from within separate folders.

A much better alternative to use when appending pages is the Create PDF From Multiple Documents command. Select the Create PDF tool and open the pull-down menu. Select From Multiple Files to open the Create PDF from Multiple Documents dialog box. Note that you can start with no file open in the Document Pane.

Click on the Browse button to find the folder where files are located. In the Open dialog box, select a file or multiple files using the Shift or Ctrl/⌘ key to select a group of files. Click on the Add button to add the files to the Create PDF from Multiple Files dialog box as shown in the figure.

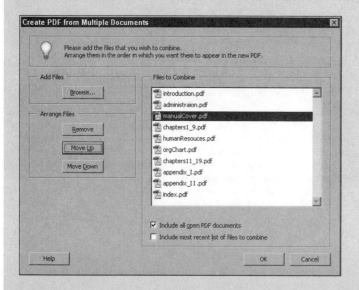

Add files to be concatenated in the Create PDF from Multiple Documents dialog box. If you want to add files from a different folder, click on the Browse button again.

If you need to add more files click on the Browse button again. Search your hard drive or network server for another folder and add more files. When all the files are listed in the dialog box shown in the figure, select individual files and click on the Move Up or Move Down buttons to rearrange the insertion order. Click OK and the files are concatenated to form a single PDF document. Choose File ⇨ Save As and save the file to your hard drive.

Cropping Pages

 In the Advanced Editing toolbar, you find the Crop tool. Cropping pages in Acrobat is performed with the Crop tool, or Document@–>Pages ⇨ Crop, or by selecting a menu command from the Pages palette. You can select the Crop tool and draw a marquee in the document window to define the crop region, double-click on the Crop tool in the Advanced Editing toolbar, or select the Crop Pages command from a context menu or palette menu in the Pages palette. Regardless of which manner you select to crop pages, the Crop Pages dialog box opens as shown in Figure 10-17.

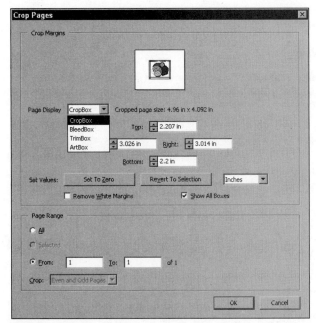

Figure 10-17: The Crop Pages dialog box displays a thumbnail image of the document page and offers options for crop margins and page ranges.

Tip　　To quickly access the Crop Pages dialog box, double-click on the Crop tool.

If you don't use the Crop tool from the Advanced Editing Toolbar, the Crop Pages dialog box opens with no crop zone specified. You can edit the margins numerically where a keyline border displays the crop area dynamically as you change the margins. When you use the Crop tool, open a rectangle marquee and move the mouse cursor inside the rectangle. The cursor changes to a selection arrow where you can double-click the mouse button to open the Crop Pages dialog box. The Crop Pages dialog box enables you to refine the page cropping. You can select from the following options:

✦ **Page Display:** Four options are available from a pull-down menu. When you choose one of the options, the keyline border displaying the crop region changes color according to the option selected. The four options are

- **CropBox:** This is the default selection. It is shown with a red keyline for the cropped page when displayed or printed.

- **BleedBox:** When you select the BleedBox option, the keyline showing the crop area is blue. Bleeds allow colors to extend off the finished page size so paper can be trimmed.

- **TrimBox:** The trim box is shown with a green rectangle. Trim areas are usually determined by the printer's marks indicating the finished paper size. The paper trim is made inside the bleed box.

- **ArtBox:** The art box is shown with a black rectangle. The art box size includes the entire bounding box for the page size.

✦ **Margins (Top/Left/Right/Bottom):** Choices for margins are available for each side of the page. In the field boxes for each side, you can use the up or down arrows and watch a preview in the thumbnail at the top of the dialog box. As you press the up or down arrow, the margin line is displayed in the thumbnail. If you want to supply numeric values, enter them in the field boxes.

Tip

To quickly adjust margins you can click in any field box and press the up and down arrow keys on your keyboard. The margins jump in increments according to the units you select from the pull-down menu adjacent to the Revert To Selection button.

✦ **Set to Zero:** This choice resets the crop margins to zero. If you change the dimensions with either of the preceding settings and want to regain the original dimensions of the crop boundary, click the Set to Zero button. From here you can redefine the margins. This button behaves much like a Reset button in other image editing programs.

✦ **Revert To Selection.** If you open a crop range and open the dialog box, then change the margins or click the Set to Zero button, the crop rectangle is restored to the size it was when the dialog box was opened. That is, it's restored to the original crop area. The view displays the crop area within the current page. In other words, the thumbnail preview displays the entire page with the crop area indicated by a red rectangle.

✦ **Inches (Units):** The pull-down menu enables you to change units of measure in the Crop Pages dialog box. In earlier versions of Acrobat you needed to change units before opening the dialog box. The default shown in Figure 10-17 is *Inches*. However, your default may be different as the units default to the settings you apply in the Preferences dialog box. Units preferences are made by selecting Units and Guides and making a selection from the Page & Ruler Units pull-down menu.

✦ **Remove White margins:** Acrobat makes an effort to eliminate white space on the page outside any visible data. Acrobat's interpretation is confined to true white space. If a slight bit of gray appears as a border, it is not cropped.

Tip   When creating PDFs for slide presentations or screen views, you may occasionally have an unwanted white border around the pages. This appearance may result from creating pages in layout or illustration programs when the image data doesn't precisely match the page size. To polish up the pages and eliminate any white lines, double-click the Crop tool or select the tool and double-click on the page. In the Crop Pages dialog box, select Remove White Margins and then select All for the page range. When the pages are cropped, the excess white lines are removed.

✦ **Page Range:** Pages identified for cropping can be handled in the Page Range options. If All is selected, all pages in the PDF file are cropped according to the sizes you specify in the dialog box. You can target specific pages for cropping by entering values in the Pages From and To field boxes. You select choices for Even and Odd Pages, Even Pages Only, and Odd Pages Only from the Crop pull-down menu.

Cropping pages does not eliminate data from the PDF document regardless of whether you use the Save or Save As command. If you return to the Crop Pages dialog box either after cropping or after cropping and saving, reopen the file and select Set To Zero. The PDF page is restored to the original size.

Tip   If you want to eliminate the excess data retained from the Crop tool, you can open the PDF in either Adobe Photoshop or Adobe Illustrator. Both programs honor the cropped regions of PDF files cropped in Acrobat. When a cropped page is opened in either program, resave as a PDF. Open the PDF in Acrobat. When you use the Crop tool and select the Set To Zero button, the page no longer has data remaining outside the page dimension. The new file size saved from Photoshop or Illustrator is smaller due to elimination of the excess data. If you crop raster images such as photos, you can save the PDF in an image file format such as TIFF. After saving the file, use the Create PDF From File command and open the TIFF image in Acrobat. The cropped region is eliminated and the file size is reduced proportional to the cropped image size.

When you crop a page in Acrobat, the original data beyond the crop range is still contained in the PDF file. If you view a cropped page in the Document Pane, you don't necessarily know that a page has been cropped unless you enable a preference setting to display the art, trim, and bleed boxes. Acrobat enables you to see the original page size through the display of a keyline color that matches the keyline border colors associated with the page display choices in the Crop Pages dialog box.

Choose Edit ⇨ Preferences to open the Preferences dialog box. In the left pane select Page Display and click on the check box for Display art, trim, bleed boxes. Click OK and view a page that has been cropped. A keyline border displays at the edge of the crop choice made in the Crop Pages dialog box.

In Figure 10-18, I cropped a page with the CropBox choice in the Page Display pull-down menu. The original image is shown on the left and the cropped page is shown on the right. When the Preference choice is enabled for Display art, trim, and bleed boxes, the red keyline on the right side of the screen shows the original page size.

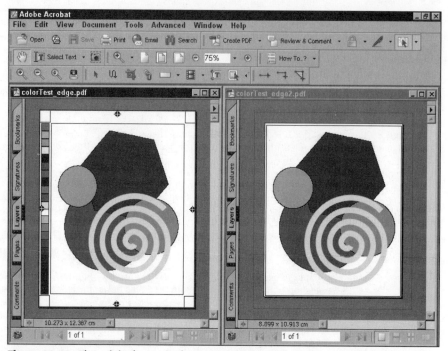

Figure 10-18: The original page is shown in the left window. The cropped image with the display for art, trim, and bleed boxes enabled in the Preferences dialog box shows the original page size with a red keyline border.

Rotating Pages

PDF documents can contain many pages with different page sizes. You can have a business card, a letter-sized page, a tabloid page, and a huge poster all contained in the same file. Depending on the authoring program of an original document and the way a PDF is created, you may experience problems with pages appearing rotated or inverted. Acrobat offers you tools to rotate pages for viewing and printing solutions to correct such appearance problems.

Rotating pages is handled with the Document ➪ Pages ➪ Rotate menu command or the Pages palette via context or Options menus. When you select Rotate Pages through any of these methods, the Rotate Pages dialog box opens. The direction of rotation is determined in a pull-down menu that enables you to rotate the page three different ways as shown in Figure 10-19. Options in the Rotate Pages dialog box include

Note   Rotate Pages is a menu command found in the menus discussed above. When you rotate pages with a menu command, the pages are rotated and the PDF can be saved with the new rotated appearances. You also have tools in the Acrobat Toolbar Well used for Rotate(ing) View(s). When using these tools to rotate a view, the page rotation is a temporary view and cannot be saved.

✦ **Direction:** Three choices appear from the Direction pull-down menu. Select from rotating pages clockwise 90 degrees, counterclockwise 90 degrees, or 180 degrees. Selecting clockwise or counterclockwise repeatedly rotates the page in 90 degree rotations.

✦ **Page Range:** Select All to rotate all pages in the PDF document.

✦ **Selection**: If you select pages in the Pages tab, the Rotate Pages dialog box offers you an option for rotating selected pages.

✦ **Pages:** Enter the page range you want to rotate in the From and To field boxes.

✦ **Rotate:** The pull-down menu for Rotate offers selections for Even and Odd Pages, Even Pages Only, or Odd Pages Only. The last pull-down menu offers choices for Portrait Pages, Landscape Pages, or Pages of Any Orientation.

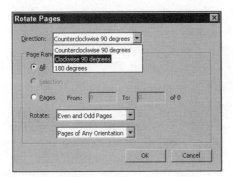

Figure 10-19: The Rotate Pages dialog box offers options for rotating pages in a range or by selecting even or odd pages. The Even/Odd choices can be helpful when printing to devices requiring page rotations for duplexing.

Rotating PDF elements

When you rotate a page, all page content is rotated. If you have any layers, visible or hidden, they are rotated. Acrobat provides no means for rotating individual layers.

If you create comments on a page and later rotate the page, the comment notes rotate at the point of origin, but the note displays are not rotated. For example, if you create a comment note in the top-left corner of a page and rotate the page 90 degrees counterclockwise, the note icon on the page is rotated, eventually ending up in the lower-left corner of the page. However, the open note is viewed at the default view with the note text in its original orientation.

Form fields behave differently than notes. If you create a form field containing text, the field and contents are rotated with the page. In Figure 10-20 a comment and field were added to a PDF document in the left window. When the page was rotated counterclockwise, the note origin and the field were rotated as shown in the right window.

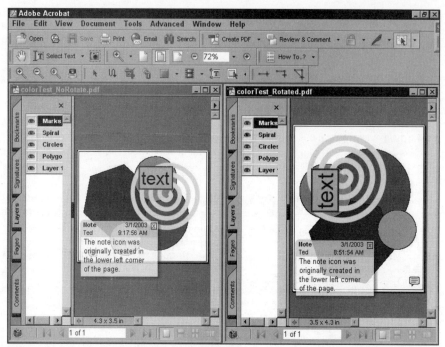

Figure 10-20: When you rotate pages, note icons and form fields are rotated with page content. All layers on the page rotate together.

Minimizing rotation problems

Among the major problems with PDF page rotation involves creating PDFs from layout programs. Layout programs such as Adobe InDesign or QuarkXPress enable you to transverse pages in the Print dialog box. This control is implemented for digital prepress and printing to high-end printing devices. In addition, many device PostScript Printer Description files (PPDs) used with high-end devices include transverse page options for page size selections.

As an example, a portrait page that prints transversed is rotated 90 degrees to conserve media on roll-fed devices. If you print files to disk as PostScript and distill the files in Acrobat Distiller, don't transverse the pages. When transversed pages are opened in Acrobat, even though the auto rotate feature is enabled during distillation, Acrobat interprets the page coordinates with a 90-degree rotation. The end result is a zero point (0,0) located in the lower-right corner of the page. This interpretation can lead to problems when you're trying to define x,y coordinates for JavaScripts, replacing pages, and copying and pasting data between documents.

If you set up a landscape page in a layout program, print the file as a portrait page with the horizontal width described in field boxes for custom page sizes. Print the file to disk and distill in Acrobat Distiller. The end product is a PDF that winds up with the proper page orientation and is interpreted by Acrobat with the zero point (0,0) located in the default lower-left corner.

Design and print professionals who seek to print files from PDFs can create the PDFs without transversing pages. When printing the PDFs for prepess, use the Acrobat Print dialog box to control printing and select device PPDs from within Acrobat. If you need to repurpose documents for Web or screen presentations, you can use the same file created for prepress without having to reprint and redistill the authoring document.

For more information on printing PostScript and using Acrobat Distiller, see Chapter 7.

Page Numbering

In Acrobat, page numbers appear in the Status Bar at the bottom of the Document Pane and in the Pages palette. When you open the Go To Page dialog box (View ➪ Go To Page or Ctrl/⌘+Alt/Option+N) and enter a value or type a value in the Status Bar and press Enter/Return, you may find the destination page not corresponding with the page number supplied in the dialog box. This is because certain documents may be designed for print where front matter, such as a table of contents, foreword, preface, and other such items precede the page numbering in a document. This is particularly true of books, pamphlets, essays, journals, and similar documents using numbering schemes other than integers for the front matter.

Acrobat provides you a choice for how to view and access page numbers in a document. Open the Preferences dialog box (Ctrl/⌘+K) and click on Page Display in the left pane. In the right panel, select Use logical page numbers. When you want to jump to a page using the Go To Page dialog box or the Status Bar, the number you type takes you to the logical page number. Logical page numbers begin at the first page in a document and consider the first page number one regardless of what numbering scheme is used to number pages. A nonlogical order considers the number of pages in Roman numbers in the document. If, for example, you have front matter with pages numbered with roman numerals I through X, and page 1 is actually the eleventh page, disabling Use logical page numbers in the Page Display preferences requires you to type 20 in the Go To Page dialog box to arrive at page 10. When the check box is enabled, typing 10 in the Go To Page dialog box takes you to page 10.

In Figure 10-21, I opened a document and typed 10 in the Status Bar, then pressed the Enter/Return key. The default setting in the Preferences dialog box was disabled for using logical page numbers. In the left window, page 10 is numbered page IX in the document, which is the actual tenth page in the file. I then enabled the preference setting for Use logical page numbers and again entered 10 in the Status Bar. After pressing the Enter/Return key, the page numbered page 10 in the document opened. At the bottom of the Document Pane the Status Bar reads: 10 (37 of 793). Page number 10 in this document is the thirty-seventh page in the file; therefore, 27 pages contain front matter using a numbering scheme different from the integers used for the body of the work.

You can make changes to the way page numbers are viewed in the Status Bar and the way you seek out pages in a document through use of the Go To Page dialog box and the Status Bar. Acrobat provides several options for renumbering pages and saving the renumbered order. The options are available in the Page Numbering dialog box accessed from the Pages palette.

Open the Pages palette in the Navigation Pane and open a context menu either from a page or from the palette pull-down menu. Select Number Pages from the menu options and the Page Numbering dialog box opens as shown in Figure 10-22.

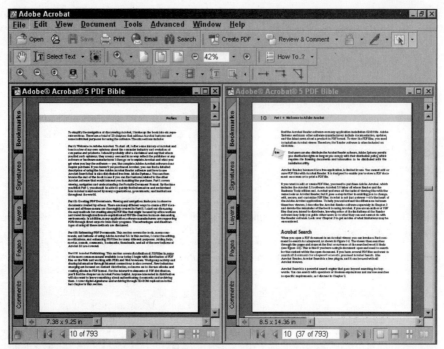

Figure 10-21: The left pane shows the tenth page in the document opened from an entry in the Status Bar when the Use logical page number preference setting is disabled. The right pane shows the page in the document numbered page 10 opened when the same action is invoked with the preference setting enabled.

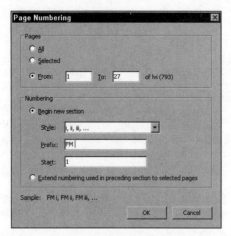

Figure 10-22: From a context menu opened on a page thumbnail in the Pages palette or the Options pull-down menu, select Number Pages to open the Page Numbering dialog box.

The Page Numbering dialog box offers options for selecting a range of pages and renumbering them in sections or throughout the entire document. The choices available to you include

✦ **Pages:** This area of the dialog box asks you to specify the page range. If you want to renumber all pages with the same numbering scheme, select the All radio button. This option might be used when numbering pages numerically with integers.

If you enable the radio button for Selected, only the pages selected in the Pages palette are affected. By default the Selected radio button is enabled if you click on a page or pages thumbnail in the Pages palette and open the dialog box. If no page thumbnail is selected the default radio button selection is From.

Enable the From radio button and supply a page range in the field boxes to select a page range numerically according to page position in the document. That is to say, pages 1 to 10 are interpreted as the first 10 pages in the file regardless of the page numbering scheme used before you open the dialog box. Perhaps you want to create a separate scheme for a document's front matter like the range specified in Figure 10-22. Specifying the scheme in the Numbering section of the dialog box renumbers the selection. Click OK to accept the changes. If you want to renumber another section, return to the dialog box and select a new section and new scheme. Repeat the process for all changes in page numbering according to different sections.

✦ **Numbering:** This portion of the dialog box offers you options for determining the page-numbering scheme you want to use. From the Style pull-down menu select a number style—the choices are shown in Figure 10-23.

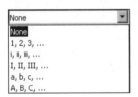

Figure 10-23: Select number styles from the Style pull-down menu.

- **Style:** If None is selected, no page number is assigned to the page. The readout in the Status Bar would appear similar to this: (10 of 100). The numbers within the parentheses represent the original page number order preceded by a blank space where no number (None) is specified. If you want to add a prefix, you could add alphanumeric data to the Prefix field box and supply a prefix with no number. Using the same example, the readout would appear something like this: A000 (10 of 100), where A000 is the prefix and no number follows.

  The remaining options in the Style pull-down menu are specific choices for styles of page numbers. If you have front matter where you want to use Roman numerals, you can choose between the two styles shown in Figure 10-23. Alpha characters offer you options for uppercase or lowercase letters, and integers are also available. You can combine these options with special characters by typing data in the Prefix field box.

- **Prefix:** Type any character, number, or combination of numbers and characters in the field box for a prefix value. The prefix precedes the numbering scheme defined in the Style pull-down menu.

- **Start:** The Start item is used to indicate the number a new section starts with. Typically you use 1 to start a new section, but you can begin sections with any number you want to type in the field box. Upon occasion you may have a document where page insertions might be added later. You can number pages in a section leaving room for new additions added in another editing session.

✦ **Extend numbering used in preceding section to selected pages:** For this option you need to select a range of page thumbnails in the Pages palette; then open the Page Numbering dialog box. Selecting the radio button and clicking OK removes the current assigned numbers and extends the previous section. For example, you may have Appendix A numbered A-1 through A-10. You later decide to combine Appendix B with Appendix A. Appendix B might be numbered B-1 through B-10. To extend the previous B numbered pages, you select the page thumbnails in the Pages palette, open the dialog box and click on the radio button. When you click OK, pages formerly numbered B-1 through B-10 are changed to A-11 through A-20.

Creating Headers and Footers

One of the most frequent questions I've had from readers over the past several years has been, "How can I number pages in a PDF file?" The page numbering previously discussed handles the structure of your PDF document and helps you navigate around pages, but once out of Acrobat and off to a desktop printer, all changes made to renumbering pages are not reflected in the printed output. All that has changed in Acrobat 6.0. Now you can add page numbers, time and date stamps, and brief text descriptions on pages that become part of the document content. These elements are assembled in the Add Headers and Footers dialog box. To add page numbers, a line of text, a date, or any combination of these, choose Document ➪ Add Headers & Footers. The Add Headers & Footers dialog box opens as shown in Figure 10-24. Two tabs appear in the top left of the dialog box. The default settings apply to document headers. Click on the Footer tab to add a footer to the bottom of your pages.

Page headers and footers are created in this dialog box. Options exist for adding a date stamp, a page number, and a line of custom text. Options for adding footers are identical to the settings provided for adding headers. Among your choices in the Add Headers & Footers dialog box are

✦ **Design Properties:** I refer to the top section of the dialog box as *Design Properties* to describe the miscellaneous settings area where you see three large windows and font settings below the windows. These three windows are a display of the settings you make for adding the insertion items in the lower portion of the dialog box. The windows themselves cannot be edited. Acrobat uses these windows to show you the results of the insertions you make from selecting the other options in the dialog box.

- **Font:** All the system fonts available to you from your operating system are displayed in a pull-down menu. Select the down-pointing arrow and make your font choice. You can assign a different font to each line of text in the listed items in the upper windows. After adding text from the Insert buttons in the lower portion of the dialog box, click on a line of text and make a font selection. If you use more than one font, select another line of text and choose another font.

- **Font Size:** Font sizes can be assigned individually to each line of text. If you want the Text to appear larger than the date or page number, select the item after clicking on an Insert button and choose a font size from the pull-down menu.

Fonts are selected from preset point sizes. You cannot edit the field box to add a point size other than the preset sizes.

- **Align:** The three large windows are associated with the Align radio buttons. If you click on the left align icon, any date entered appears in the left window. In Figure 10-24, the third align icon is active and the items in the dialog box appear in the last window. Once you add header or footer data, you can click on the Align icons and see the data move to the respective window for left, center, or right alignment. You can also individually add elements and use different alignments. For example, you can place the date with a left alignment, custom text center aligned, and page number right aligned.

- **Remove:** If you want to delete an item, select the line to be deleted and click on the Remove button. To remove several items, you need to select an item and click Remove, then select another item and click Remove. Acrobat does not permit you to select more than one item at a time.

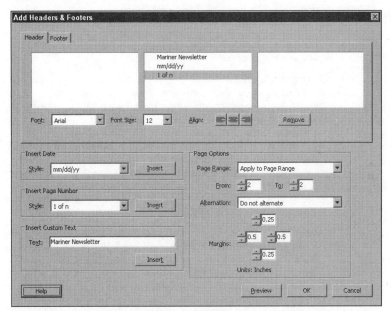

Figure 10-24: The default options are applied to document headers. Click on the Footers tab to select options for page footers.

Tip

If you want to reorder items after adding them to the Header or Footer lists, select an item and click on another alignment. For example, if date, page number, and custom text appear left aligned and you want to change the order to custom text, date, and page number, move the date to the center align position. Move the page number to the right aligned position. Custom text now appears at the top position in the left align window. Select the date and click on the Left Align icon and the date moves below the custom text. Click on the page number and click on the Left Align button and the page number moves below the date. Using this method, you can shuffle the items and reorder the lists.

✦ **Insert Date:** Down on the left side of the dialog box, the first item is the date style. From the pull-down menu you can select from thirteen different styles. Selecting a style does not add the date to an upper window. You make a choice for the style and then click on the Insert button adjacent to your style choice. As you add headers and footers you can make choices for all the styles, then click on each Insert button in the order you want to have them displayed.

✦ **Insert Page Number:** Five different styles are available from the pull-down menu. Open the menu and make the style choice. In Figure 10-24 the 1of n style is used. When the pages are shown, each page is represented by the respective page number out of the total number of pages in the document. Regardless of the numbering system you use from the settings made in the Page Numbering dialog box, the n value calculates the total number of pages and represents the number with an integer.

✦ **Insert Custom Text:** A title or message is added on the Text field. This is the only editable field among the insertion items. You type the desired text in the field box. You can only add characters in a single line of text. Scrolling text and using carriage returns is not permitted. The amount of text you can add is dependent on the horizontal size of the document page. Obviously a portrait page accepts less text than a landscape page.

✦ **Page Options:** The items in the lower-right quadrant offer options for text positions and where the text is applied in the document.

• **Page Range:** You choose between two options from the pull-down menu. If you select Apply to All Pages, the field boxes for From and To are not editable. The header, footer, or both are applied to all pages. If you select Apply to Page Range, the field boxes are editable and you specify in these boxes the page range where the header or footer text is applied. The field boxes accept values you type in each box, click on the up and down arrow keys to change page numbers, or select a field box and press the up or down arrow keys on your keyboard to change values. Acrobat knows how many pages are contained in your document before the Add Headers & Footers dialog box is opened. If you attempt to add a page number exceeding the total number of pages in the PDF file, the field boxes stop at the last page number in the document.

• **Alternation:** Three choices can be made from the pull-down menu for where the header, footer or both are applied to pages. If you select Do not alternate, the data are added to all pages in the document. If you select either of the other two options, for Even Pages Only or Odd Pages Only, Acrobat adds data only to the respective even/odd pages in the document.

• **Margins:** The four Margins field boxes are editable. You can physically position a header or footer at any location on a page. If you add a header, the options relate to the top, left, and right field boxes. Footers relate to all but the top field box. Entering values in the lower field box has no effect on the position where the text is added. If you use top = 5 inches, left = 3 inches, and click on the left alignment radio button, the text is added 5 inches from the top and 3 inches from the left side. Clicking on any other alignment radio changes the horizontal position.

• **Preview:** Before you close the dialog box, it's a good idea to preview the results of the options choices. If you click OK in the dialog box and the data encroaches on the space where page content appears, you may need to make alterations for the positioning of the header, footer, or both. When you click on Preview, a page preview opens (shown in Figure 10-25) while the Add Headers & Footers dialog box remains open in the background. Preview your settings and click OK in the preview to return to the Add Headers & Footers dialog box. You can use the Preview button to make adjustments and preview the settings again. When all the options appear correct, click on the OK button in the Add Headers & Footers dialog box.

Caution

Headers and footers changes can be made after closing the Add Headers and Footers dialog box in a single Acrobat Session. After you save a file and close the PDF, you cannot make changes to the headers and footers added in the saved file. When you open the dialog box it reverts to defaults. Before closing the PDF document, be certain your new headers and footers are properly defined. Be certain to work on a backup copy in case you need to start over.

When you open the Add Headers & Footers with a page displayed in the Document Pane and attempt to add a header, footer, or both to a different page, you specify the page number in the Add Headers & Footers dialog box. If the target page is different than the page in view in the Document Pane and you click on Preview, Acrobat intelligently shows you a preview of the target page.

Figure 10-25: Click on Preview to open the Preview window. The data applied in the Add Headers & Footers dialog box is shown on the Preview page. When you click OK, you return to the Add Headers & Footers dialog box, where you can change options before applying the data to pages.

Creating multiple headers and footers

You can add a header and footer to a page or range of pages in the Add Headers & Footers dialog box in a single session. Headers and footers can have different attributes assigned in a single session. When you add a header and select a font, font size, and custom text, the attributes are associated with headers applied to the defined page range. When you click on the Footer tab to create page footers, you can use different text, font styles and offset positions, and page ranges. Acrobat treats the header and footer as separate elements and, although you use the same dialog box with the same options, the settings are applied separately to the respective tab selections.

If you want to add a header, footer, or both to different pages with different fonts and styles, you need to reopen the Add Headers & Footers dialog box each time you change attributes. For example, if on page 1 you want the text aligned left for a header, you create the header for page 1. If you want page 2 aligned center, you create a new header with different attributes. If page 3 is treated differently, once again you return to the dialog box and select new options. Each time you open the Add Headers & Footers dialog box, all previous additions remain undisturbed as you add new page headers and footers.

Deleting headers and footers

After a header, footer, or both have been added to a document, you can delete the data by opening the Add Headers & Footers dialog box. The default choices for headers and footers are no specifications for any content. In other words, you won't find any text appearing in the design properties windows. When the three windows at the top of the page are empty, click OK and all data from pages and footers are deleted from the page range selected in the Add Headers & Footers dialog box.

If you want to delete all headers and footers, regardless of whether they were created separately with different options settings, open the Add Headers & Footers dialog box. Select Apply to All Pages from the Page range pull-down menu. Be certain no data are contained in the design properties windows and click OK. All page headers and footers are removed from the document.

If you save a document after creating headers and footers, you can remove them using the method just described. Acrobat interprets the data added with headers and footers in saved PDF documents the same as it does in an open file. You can change headers and footers or remove them in new Acrobat sessions by opening the saved file and applying the preceding methods for changing or removing the data.

Font handling

The downside of not creating headers and footers in your authoring program is that fonts are not embedded when you create the headers and footers in Acrobat. If you use a font loaded in your system and other users view your PDF documents, they need to have the same fonts to see the design as you created it. If other users don't have the same fonts, Acrobat uses font substitution. The result of substituting the fonts can often present problems with clear legibility. More often than not, embedding fonts assures you that end users see your PDF documents as you intend them to be viewed.

For an example of font substitution, look at Figure 10-26. In the top box, you see fonts I used on a Windows XP machine to create a page header and footer. The second box in the figure shows how the fonts displayed when I open the PDF file on my Macintosh computer.

For embedding fonts added to headers and footers, you have two choices. You can use the TouchUp Text tool and embed fonts in the TouchUp Text Properties dialog box, or you can repurpose the file and embed fonts with Acrobat Distiller.

Caution   You need to embed all fonts used for headers and footers. If you use a font that is already embedded in a PDF file and use that same font for in the Add Headers & Footers dialog box, the font used for headers and footers is not embedded after saving the file. Inasmuch as you have the same font embedded elsewhere in your file, the new fonts added to page headers and footers need to be embedded.

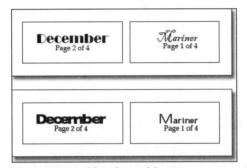

Figure 10-26: A header and footer were created in Windows XP. The top two boxes show the original font used in Windows. The two lower boxes show how Acrobat substituted the unembedded fonts when the file was opened in Acrobat on a Macintosh computer.

Embedding fonts with the TouchUp Text tool

After adding headers and footers, you embed fonts in the Document Pane. Navigate to a page containing a header or footer and select the TouchUp Text tool. Click on the header or footer text and open a context menu. From the menu options, select Properties to open the TouchUp Properties dialog box shown in Figure 10-27.

In the TouchUp Properties dialog box, click on the Text tab. Check the boxes for Embed and Subset as shown in Figure 10-27. When you embed a font on a given page, the font embeds for all pages in the PDF document. If you use a different font for other pages, for a footer, or for other text as part of a header or footer, you need to perform the same steps and embed all fonts. Acrobat doesn't permit selecting the header and footer text blocks together; therefore, be certain to embed fonts separately when the fonts are different between the headers and footers.

Cross-Reference   For more information on using the TouchUp Text tool and embedding fonts, see Chapter 8.

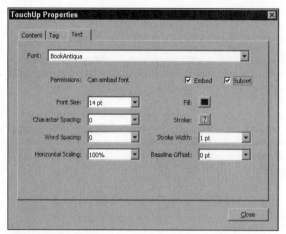

Figure 10-27: Click on a block of text for the header or footer with the TouchUp Text tool. Open a context menu and select Properties to open the TouchUp Properties dialog box.

Embedding fonts with Acrobat Distiller

The previous procedure for embedding fonts is adequate if you have only a few different fonts to embed. However, if for some reason you have an extraordinary number of different fonts across multiple pages, performing the same steps outlined previously will take you quite a bit of editing time. I can't imagine too many circumstances where you would add a considerable number of different fonts in a document; however, people do sometimes have extraordinary needs, and it's worth looking over the following helpful steps if the need arises.

Assume for a moment you have ten different sections of a document and need to add headers and footers to each section, all with different fonts. Rather than use the TouchUp Text tool and open the TouchUp Properties dialog box for each block of text, you can create a PostScript file and distill the PostScript in Acrobat Distiller.

Caution   Before you look over the steps that follow, I want to add a note of caution. Ideally, this method works best for documents you created and when you have all the fonts contained in the document loaded into your system. Upon occasion a font may not be embedded when you print the PostScript and re-distill the file. When you use the following method, be certain to examine the document carefully to be certain all font embedding is accomplished after distillation.

Choose File ➪ Save As and choose PostScript (*.ps) from the Save as type (Windows) or Format (Macintosh) pull-down menu. Be certain to click on the Settings button in the Save As dialog box after making the file type selection. When the Save As Settings dialog box opens, click on the down arrow to open the Font Inclusion pull-down menu. Select Embedded and Referenced Fonts from the menu options. The previously embedded fonts and any new fonts are embedded when you write the PostScript file.

Open Acrobat Distiller and select an Adobe PDF setting that has the Embed and Subset fonts enabled. Drag the PostScript file to the Distiller window to convert to PDF. Alternately, you could use the File ➪ Open command in Distiller or Create PDF From File within Acrobat.

The resulting PDF includes all the fonts added with headers and footers now embedded in the document. To double-check the font embedding, open the Fonts properties by choosing File ➪ Document Properties and click on Fonts in the left panel. Scroll through the font list to be certain all fonts are embedded.

For more information on using Acrobat Distiller, see Chapter 7. For more information on repurposing files, see Chapter 13. For saving files as PostScript with other options settings, see Chapter 5.

Headers and footers in layered PDF documents

If you have a layered PDF document, you can add headers and footers to the file. When a header, footer, or both are added to layered files, the data appears as though it resides on its own layer. A new layer is not created; however, if you hide all layers, the headers and footers are visible in the document. The header and footer are always displayed regardless of the choices you make in the layers palette for viewing layers.

If you want to edit a block of text in a header or footer, you can either return to the Add Headers & Footers dialog box or use the TouchUp Text tool. If you edit text with the TouchUp Text tool or in the Add Headers and Footers dialog box, the text changes are visible in all layer views.

If you want to add headers or footers independently to different layers, you need to return to your authoring program or use an object editor capable of saving in PDF 1.5 format and supporting layers.

For more information on editing layers, see Chapter 17. For more information on editing with the TouchUp Object tool and object editors, see Chapter 9.

Adding Watermarks and Backgrounds

Much like the issues related to numbering pages, watermarks and backgrounds used to require writing JavaScripts and spawning pages from templates in earlier versions of Acrobat. Now, in Acrobat Professional, you can easily modify content on pages by adding watermarks and background data through a menu command.

For information related to writing JavaScripts and spawning pages from templates, see Chapter 27.

Watermarks and backgrounds are added in the same dialog box, and the attributes for both items are identical. The distinction between a watermark and a background is that watermarks appear above all layers and backgrounds appear below all layers.

To add a watermark or background, choose Document ➪ Add Watermark & Background. The Add Watermark & Background dialog box opens as shown in Figure 10-28. In this dialog box you make a selection for adding a watermark, a background, or both. The attributes after making the decision(s) are the same for both watermarks and backgrounds:

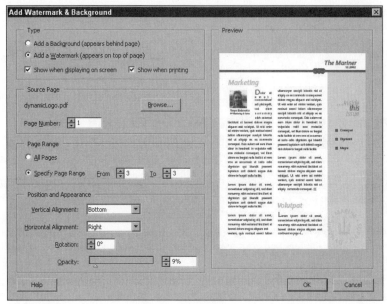

Figure 10-28: Choose Document ➪ Add Watermark & Background to open the Add Watermark and Background dialog box.

✦ **Type:** The first two radio buttons in the dialog box offer you choices for adding a watermark or a background. If you select the radio button for Add a Background (appears behind page), and apply settings in the dialog box to add the background, you can come back to the radio button choices and select Add a Watermark (appears on top of page). After making the selections below the radio button choices, both a background and watermark are added to the page range selected in the dialog box.

✦ **Show when displaying on screen:** When the check box is enabled, the watermark/background are displayed on your monitor. Disabling the check box hides the elements from the screen view.

✦ **Show when printing:** You may have occasion to use a watermark on pages for messages that you communicate among workgroup members and later decide to print the file for distribution without the watermark (or background). If this is the case, you can hide the elements when printing the file by disabling the check box.

✦ **Browse:** Click on the Browse button to locate a PDF file to import as a background or watermark. You can import PDF files only. Image file formats are not supported. If you select a multi-page document, you can select the source page that you want to import. When a page is imported from a multi-page document, the page number is supplied in the Page Number field box.

✦ **Page Number:** After selecting a file to import, you can toggle through the pages by changing the page number in the field box, clicking on the arrows in the field box, or clicking in the field box and pressing the up and down arrow keys.

✦ **Page Range:** Select All to apply a watermark or background on all pages. In the field boxes for From and To, you can restrict the watermark or background to selected pages within a page range by changing the values to only those pages on which you want to import the data.

✦ **Alignment:** There are four options available from the Vertical and Horizontal Alignment pull-down menus. If a page size of the imported page matches the page size of the destination page, alignment selections have no effect on the placement of the data. If the imported page is smaller or larger than the destination document, the alignment options offer choices for targeting a location where the imported data are displayed.

- **Top:** If an imported file is smaller or larger (width, height or both) than the destination file, the top of the imported image is aligned with the top of the page(s) receiving the data.

- **Center:** The page centers of the target file and the destination files are aligned to center.

- **Bottom:** The opposite of the top alignment, this option places the target file aligned to the bottom of the destination page(s).

- **Fit:** If the target file is smaller or larger than the destination file, the imported page is expanded or reduced to fit the page.

Note

You can set vertical and horizontal alignments independently. In Figure 10-29 various combinations of vertical and horizontal alignment settings were applied to a 3-inch by 3-inch document imported as a background on an 8.5-inch by 11-inch page.

- **Rotation:** You can rotate backgrounds and watermarks in 1-degree increments. Edit the field box for the rotation angle desired.

- **Opacity:** Opacity settings can be applied to raster and vector data contained in the PDF document used for a background or watermark. Move the slider to the left to add more transparency or type a number in the field box for the amount of transparency. In Figure 10-30, Fit was selected for both the vertical and horizontal alignments and the background was rotated. The figure on the right has an opacity adjustment.

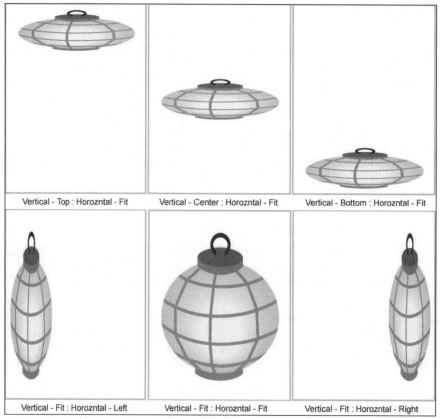

Figure 10-29: Different choices made in the horizontal and vertical alignment menus offer many different displays for small images added to larger pages.

Tip   Watermarks and backgrounds can be imported from multi-page PDF documents with differ-ent page sizes. If you routinely use logos, icons, symbols, and other such graphics in your workflow, you can create a library of images that all members in your workgroup can use. Create pages individually when you need to append pages to your library and use the Create PDF From File command. Add pages to the file and keep it handy when working on docu-ments to which you need to apply watermarks and change backgrounds.

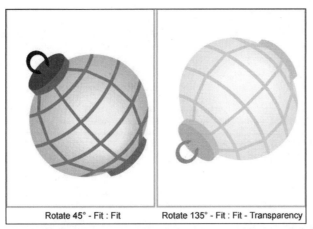

Rotate 45° - Fit : Fit   Rotate 135° - Fit : Fit - Transparency

Figure 10-30: The imported background was rotated 30 degrees on the left and 135 degrees on the right. The image on the right has an opacity adjustment.

Deleting watermarks and backgrounds

If you click the OK button in the Add Watermark & Background dialog box, the data are stamped on the document pages. You have one level of undo if you decide to change your mind. However, if you lose the Undo command or save the file, you cannot eliminate a watermark or background after it has been added to the target pages. To be on the safe side, choose File ➪ Save As and save your work to a new filename. In the event you want to begin again, open the original file and add new watermarks and backgrounds.

Watermarks and backgrounds in layered files

The treatment of watermarks and backgrounds is the same as when adding headers and footers. Watermarks and backgrounds are not applied to individual layers. If you have a layered file, the watermark and/or background is added to the document as if it is on its own layer. If you hide all layers, the watermark and/or background is visible on the document page(s). Individual watermarks and backgrounds need to be applied in an authoring program if you want to show and hide them in the Layers palette.

Cross-Reference   For more information on editing layers, see Chapter 17. For more information on editing with the TouchUp Object tool and object editors, see Chapter 9.

Watermarks and backgrounds can be used in many different ways, especially with legacy files where you want to change content without returning to an authoring application. To demonstrate some of the flexibility of working with backgrounds for changing design appearances, follow these steps:

STEPS: Adding a background to a legacy PDF document

1. **Create a background file.** You can use scanned photos, textures created in a program such as Adobe Photoshop, vector art drawings from a program such as Adobe Illustrator, or any other document you convert to PDF. For this exercise, I use a photo where I want to add a texture to an existing document and change the background design. Save the file as a PDF document from your authoring program.

2. **Open the destination file.** The file where you want to apply a new background needs to be opened in Adobe Acrobat. Open the file in the Document Pane.

3. **Open the Add Watermark & Background dialog box.** Choose Document ➪ Add Watermark and Background.

4. **Select the background PDF document.** Click on the radio button for Add Background (appears behind page). Click on the Browse button. In the Open dialog box select the PDF document you want to use for your new background and click Open.

5. **Select the page range.** If you want the background applied to all pages, select the All pages radio button. If you want to target a page range, enter the page range in the field boxes. In my example, I selected the All button.

6. **Position the background.** If the background page size matches the same page size as the destination pages, you can leave any settings for the alignment unchanged. If you have a smaller or larger page than the destination pages, select alignment options from the pull-down menus. You can check the display in the Preview as you make changes. In Figure 10-31 you can see the options I chose in the Add Watermark & Background dialog box.

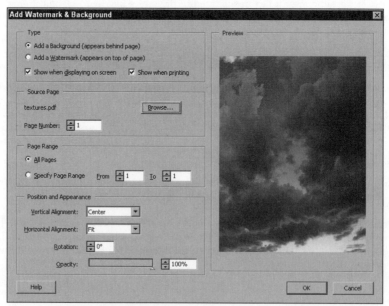

Figure 10-31: The All Pages radio button is enabled to apply the background to all the pages in the open PDF document. The Preview shows the data that will be used for the background at 100% opacity.

7. **Adjust transparency.** Move the slider for the Opacity item at the bottom of the Add Watermark & Background dialog box. Check the preview as you move the slider and rest it where you feel the right amount of transparency is applied so the background doesn't interfere with the foreground data.

8. **Apply the background.** Click OK in the dialog box and to return to the Document Pane. In Figure 10-32 the original file without a background is shown on the left side of the figure. On the right you can see the same layout with a new background.

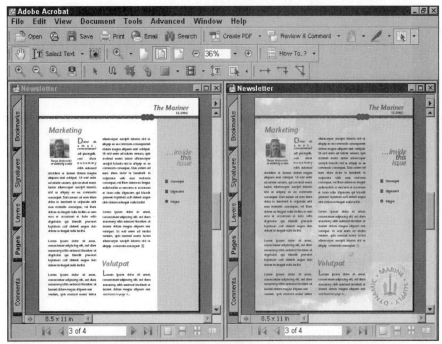

Figure 10-32: The newsletter page on the left is the original document created in Acrobat 5 with no background. On the right side of the figure the same newsletter page is shown with a new background.

Summary

✦ You can enlarge or reduce page thumbnails in size through successive menu commands in the Pages palette.

✦ You can open the Pages Pane to full screen size where you can sort and reorder pages.

✦ Page thumbnails can be used to navigate pages and zoom in on pages.

✦ Pages can be copied in a PDF document and between PDF documents with the use of page thumbnails.

✦ Page thumbnails are created on the fly when you open the Pages palette. If you want to speed up the screen refreshes when opening the Pages palette you can embed thumbnails from a menu option in the Pages palette and delete them after your editing sessions.

✦ Pages are inserted, deleted, extracted, and replaced through menu commands from the Pages palette context menu or the palette pull-down menu.

✦ You crop PDF pages with the Crop tool. When you crop a page, the page view is reduced to the crop region, but all the original data in terms of page size is still contained in the file. You can return to the Crop Page dialog box and undo crops even after a file has been saved.

✦ You can rotate PDF pages in 90- and 180-degree rotations via menu commands in the Pages submenu.

✦ Enabling a preference setting for viewing logical pages helps you navigate to pages numbered with integers.

✦ Opening the page Numbering dialog box from a context menu in the Pages palette enables you to renumber pages in a PDF file.

✦ To add page numbers to a PDF document use the Add Headers & Footers dialog box.

✦ You can add different headers and footers to different pages in a PDF document. Each time the content for headers and footers changes, you open the Add Headers & Footers dialog box, add the content and specify the page range.

✦ Fonts added in headers and footers are not automatically embedded in a PDF document. You can embed fonts with the TouchUp Text tool and the TouchUp Properties dialog box. You can alternately embed fonts by saving a PDF to PostScript and redistilling the file in Acrobat Distiller.

✦ To add watermarks and backgrounds to a document use the Add Watermarks & Backgrounds dialog box. A watermark appears on top of all page data and a background appears behind all page data.

✦ After you save a PDF with a watermark and/or background, the data are embedded in the PDF document. You cannot return to the Add Watermark & Background dialog box to remove them.

✦　　✦　　✦

Scanning and OCR Conversion

Acrobat's Optical Character Recognition (OCR) feature can be used to perform two jobs. First, you scan a document and convert it to a PDF file, and secondly employ the Paper Capture feature to convert the image file to rich text. Because scanning pages and converting to PDF is found under the Create PDF task button pull-down menu, you might think this chapter's information belongs back in Chapter 5 where the various methods of PDF creation were covered. The "Creating a PDF from a Scanner" section was added to this chapter because users typically scan from within Acrobat to convert scanned paper documents to searchable text. Accordingly, discussing these two Acrobat features together makes more sense.

When acquiring a scan in either Acrobat Standard or Acrobat Professional you are not limited to scanning documents for text conversions. Acrobat enables you to scan photos and images that might have some other uses. Therefore, this chapter covers all the aspects of scanning from within Acrobat and using Paper Capture to perform OCR.

Setting Up the Scanning Work Environment

For scanning and Paper Capture tasks you need access to the TouchUp Text tool. Choose Tools ➪ Advanced Editing ➪ Show Advanced Editing Toolbar. When the toolbar opens, dock it in the Toolbar Well.

During Paper Capture you may want to create several views where you can zoom in to see words requiring edits. Tools handy for displaying different views are found in the Zoom toolbar. Open the pull-down menu adjacent to the Zoom In tool and select Show Zoom Toolbar from the menu options.

Configuring Scanners

Before you can scan a page in Acrobat, you need to configure your scanner and be certain it functions properly. If you use a scanner regularly, after you complete your installation of Acrobat, it should recognize your scanner immediately. If all the scanner hardware is in place and operational and Acrobat still does not recognize it, the next step is to be certain the scanner's software is recognized by Acrobat. If Acrobat doesn't see your scanner, you may need to relocate software to another location on your hard drive or acquire a software update from your scanner manufacturer.

You get access to your scanner in Acrobat through one of two methods: TWAIN software or Acquire plug-ins. In earlier versions of Acrobat, support existed for ISIS software on Windows. Acrobat 6.0 no longer supports ISIS software; therefore, former ISIS users need to use one of the two supported methods in Acrobat 6.0 to access their scanner from within Acrobat.

TWAIN software

TWAIN (Technology With An Important Name) software is manufacturer supplied and should be available on the floppy disk or CD-ROM you receive with your scanner. In Windows, the TWAIN files are stored in the \WINNT\twain_32 folder. When you install scanner software, the TWAIN driver should find the proper folder through the installer routine. On the Macintosh you'll find TWAIN resources in the System\Library\Image Capture\TWAIN Data Sources folder.

Many scanner manufacturers produce the equipment but use third-party developers to write the software. Adobe has certainly not tested the Scan plug-in with all scanner manufacturers and all software developers. Theoretically, the TWAIN software should work in all cases. If you have problems accessing your scanner from within Acrobat, but can perform scans in other applications, then you most likely have a problem with the TWAIN software. If this is the case, contact your scanner manufacturer and see whether it has an upgrade or whether you can get some technical support. In many cases, you can download upgrades for registered software on the Internet.

Adobe Photoshop plug-in software

Acrobat 6.0 supports Acquire plug-ins you use with Adobe Photoshop. More prevalent than TWAIN drivers, Photoshop plug-ins are available from just about every scanner manufacturer. If you use Adobe Photoshop, you may need to copy your Photoshop Acquire plug-in to your Acrobat plug-ins folder. On Windows, copy the Photoshop Acquire plug-in and open the Acrobat\plug-ins\PaperCapture folder and paste your Acquire plug-in.

Mac OS X requires you to expand the Acrobat 6.0 Professional package in order to paste your Photoshop Acquire plug-in. To do so, follow these steps:

1. Open your Acrobat 6.0 Professional folder and select (not double-click) Acrobat 6.0 Professional.

2. Control+click to open a context menu, and select Show Package Contents.

   The Contents folder appears in the Acrobat 6.0 Professional folder.

3. Double-click on the Contents folder and double-click on the Plug-ins folder that comes into view.

4. Double-click again to open the Paper Capture folder and drag your Photoshop Acquire plug-in into this folder.

   When you close the folders, the package is restored.

Understanding Scanning Essentials

At this point you should have your scanner and Acrobat configured properly. Before I begin discussing how to use your scanner with Acrobat, take a moment to understand some of the essential issues to deal with in performing clean, accurate scans. A few items need to be discussed: the hardware and hardware-related issues; the types of scans to be produced; and understanding your scanner capabilities. A few moments here will save you much time in producing the best scans you can expect from your equipment.

Cross-Reference Preparing documents for scanning is discussed later in this chapter. See the section "Preparing a document."

The first hardware item is your scanner. The single most important issue with scanner hardware is keeping the platen clean. If you have dust and dirt on the glass, these particles show up in your scans. Keep the platen clean, and use a lint-free cloth to clean the glass. If you use a solvent, always apply the solvent to the cloth and not the scanner glass.

The second hardware item to consider is your computer. When performing scans, try to allocate as much memory as you can spare to Acrobat if your operating system allows memory allocations to programs. If you have multiple applications open simultaneously and subsequently experience crashes, then by all means, try using Acrobat alone when performing scans. Also related to your computer is virtual memory. Double-check the free space on your computer's hard drive before attempting to scan. Scans eat up memory fast, so be certain you have ample space before engaging in a scanning session. A scan of 300 pixels per inch (ppi) consumes about 24MB of hard drive space. You should plan on having three to five times that amount of free hard drive space for each page scanned at 300 ppi.

The third item to understand is your scanner and the technology used to manufacture the device. Flatbed consumer-grade scanners often use charge-coupled devices (CCDs), which are tiny little sensors placed along a horizontal plane in a number equal to the optical resolution of your scanner. Therefore, a 600-dpi scanner has 600 CCDs per inch. Each of these sensors picks up a pixel when the scanner pass is made. Where these sensors begin and end along the horizontal plane is important for you to know. If you experience some edge sharpness problems or degradation in your image at the edges, try placing the scanned source material a little farther from the edges of the scanner platen and toward the middle. When doing so, be certain to keep the material straight on the scanner bed.

Less expensive scanners that you can find today are CIS scanners. These scanners use contact image sensors instead of CCDs. They are well suited to scan text but you have to test the results to determine whether the scanner performs efficiently. In many cases, the low cost CIS scanners can produce text scans that work well with Paper Capture.

Preparing a document

Just as your scans can benefit from careful attention to your scanner, exercising a little care with the source material can help produce clean scans. Bits of dust, improperly aligned pages, poor contrast, and degraded originals affect your ability to create scans capable of being read without many errors by Paper Capture. A little preparation before scanning saves you much time in trying to clean up poorly scanned images.

Photocopying originals

Sometimes you can improve image and text contrast by photocopying original documents. Try some experiments to test your results. If you have large, bulky material, photocopies placed on the scanner bed ultimately result in better scans than the original material.

Ensuring straight alignment

If you have documents with frayed edges or pages torn from a magazine, then you should trim the edges and make them parallel to the text on the page. Precise placement of pages on the scanner bed facilitates clean scans. Even though Acrobat has a recognition capability within a 14-degree rotation, the straighter the page, the better the results.

Caution Be certain to observe copyright laws when scanning published material. If you scan text from books and magazines, you need to obtain permission from the publisher before using the material.

Tip A method I use with all flatbed scanning is to place the source material in a jig I created from poster board. If a standard US Letter (8.5 by 11 inches) page is your source material, get a large piece of poster board that extends past the edges of the scanner lid on the sides and bottom. Use a T-square and align a standard size page parallel to the top. Mark the edges for an 8.5 by 11 inch cutout in the center of the poster board. Cut out the marked area and use the waste as a lid on the poster board. You can tape the top so it opens much like your scanner lid. Use the cutout area as a template to place pages and ready them for scanning. Place the template under the scanner lid and preview a scan. If the preview is not straight, you can move the poster board because the edges extend beyond the scanner lid. When the preview appears straight, tape the poster board to the scanner. As you open the scanner lid, subsequently open the jig lid and place a page in the cutout area. Every scan you perform will have all the pages aligned precisely. The lid on the jig prevents the pages from rising in the cut out space and keeps them flat against the platen.

Try to remember the axiom "garbage in, garbage out" when you approach any kind of scanning. The better the source material, the better your scanned results. Exercise a little care in the beginning, and your Acrobat scanning sessions move along much faster.

Understanding Acrobat scan types

You can produce several different types of scans when converting to PDF from a scanner. Each of the scans you perform has different requirements and needs some special attention. Decisions related to image scans, color more, text conversion, and so on need to be made when you open a Scan dialog box and set attributes for the type of scan you want.

Text recognition

If you scan directly into Acrobat, more often than not your requirements are for text and OCR scanning. Given the fact that PDF pages are usually created with layout, illustration, and photo editing software, attempting to create PDF documents for final proofs by scanning them into Acrobat would be rare. If you create a page layout, scanning in Adobe Photoshop would be better than scanning in Acrobat, because Photoshop enables you to enhance and optimize image quality immediately after each scan. The area Acrobat excels in is searching text documents. For this situation, you would use the Create PDF From Scanner command and then the Paper Capture command or feature to recognize the text. When scanning text, you want to follow the few simple rules that follow.

Image mode

Image modes range from 1-bit line art or black-and-white scans to 24-bit color. The higher the bit depth, the larger the file size. For text scans, you need only 1-bit line art to recognize text. If your scanner software has a line art mode, use it to perform scans for text recognition.

Resolution

Resolution for text recognition needs to be high enough for good, clean scanning and tight pixels on the edges of characters, but not as high as you would need for output to high-end devices. As a general rule, you can scan normal body text at 300 dpi. Large text sizes can be sufficiently scanned at 200 dpi. For small text of 8 points or lower, you may want to raise the resolution higher than 300 dpi. In many cases, you need to run some tests for the target resolution for your particular type of scanner, software, and typical documents scanned. The maximum resolution supported by Acrobat is 600 dpi.

Grayscale scanning

Once again, scanning images is often the task of Photoshop. However, you may find grayscale scanning necessary or helpful when scanning for text recognition. The most important attribute of a scanned image for OCR software is a sharp contrast between the text and the background. If your line art scans aren't working out, try scanning in grayscale and applying contrast settings in your image editing software before completing the scan. Many software applications provide controls for brightness and contrast settings. Most software displays previews of the adjustments you make, which greatly speeds up the entire process.

If you want to scan photographic images in grayscale, be certain to lower the resolution. Try 200 dpi or lower. You should plan on testing resolutions to achieve the lowest possible resolution that maintains a good quality image. If you scan grayscale images in Acrobat, they should be for screen view only. To create PDF files that ultimately are to be printed, you should use Photoshop and a layout or illustration application. Then distill the images with Acrobat Distiller or use an application such as Adobe InDesign that supports direct exports to PDF.

Color scanning

If you have color documents and want to capture text from the pages, you might want to use a color mode if you can build up enough contrast during the scan. Large type of 12 points or higher in color images can be effectively recognized in 200 dpi scans.

Color images occupy the largest file sizes. For OCR conversion where retaining color is not required in the final output, converting color images to line art or grayscale saves considerable space on your hard drive. If you use an image editor like Adobe Photoshop and you have color images already scanned, you can run a Photoshop Action to automate the conversion of color to grayscale or line art. If existing scanned images are used for text recognition, you can use the Create PDF From Multiple Files command to convert to PDF and then use Paper Capture to convert the image files to text.

Creating a PDF from a Scanner

To scan a page from within Acrobat, select the pull-down menu from the Create PDF task button and select From Scanner. When you perform a scan within Acrobat, the scanned image opens as a PDF document. You can choose to leave the scan as an image and save it as a PDF file. However, to do nothing more than scan images in Acrobat is less efficient than scanning images in Adobe Photoshop and saving the Photoshop scans as Photoshop PDF files. Create PDF From Scanner is only half of the equation related to scanning in Acrobat. The real power of using Acrobat for scanning images lies in its capability to convert scanned text into readable and searchable text with Paper Capture. Raw image files with no text are referred to in Acrobat terms as *Formatted Text and Graphics* files. When you distill documents with Acrobat Distiller, create PDFs from files, or capture scanned pages with the Paper Capture command, the files contain text that can be indexed, searched, and selected. These files are known in Acrobat terms as *Formatted Text & Graphics documents*. When a scan is acquired in Acrobat, the file opens as a Formatted Text and Graphics PDF file.

Earlier versions of Acrobats Paper Capture feature were based on features found in Acrobat Capture 2. Acrobat Capture is a stand-alone product designed for industrial strength scanning and marketed as a separate product by Adobe Systems. With the introduction of Acrobat 6, the feature set in Paper Capture is now based on features found in Acrobat Capture 3. Among the changes is the change in what used to be referred to as a PDF Normal Image and terminology used to describe the types of image formats created with Paper Capture. PDF Normal is an old term *retired* with the introduction of Acrobat Capture 3.0 and is not present in any of the current documentation.

Cross-Reference   For information on PDF Normal Image and newer terms used to define the Paper Capture formats, see the section "Using Paper Capture" later in this chapter.

After you verify proper configuration for both your scanner and computer hardware and prepare your document, the rest of the scanning process is easy. To scan an image, open the pull-down menu from the Create PDF Task Button and select From Scanner. The Create PDF From Scanner dialog box opens as shown in Figure 11-1.

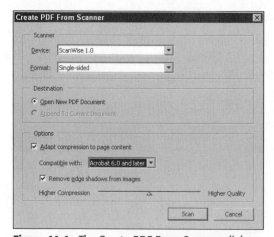

Figure 11-1: The Create PDF From Scanner dialog box opens after you select Create PDF From Scanner.

Look over the options in the Create PDF From Scanner dialog box. A few choices need to be made here before you convert a scan to searchable text.

✦ **Device.** If you have several Acquire plug-ins or TWAIN scanner drivers loaded on your system, they all appear in the pull-down menu after installation. Open the pull-down menu and make a choice for the scanner you want to use.

✦ **Format.** Options are available for single-sided or double-sided scanning. When you select double-sided scanning, a dialog box opens after the first scan and prompts you to select the next page as either the front side of the next page or the back side of the current page.

✦ **Open New PDF Document.** You can access the From Scanner menu command without a PDF opened in the Document Pane. If no file is open when the Create PDF From Scanner dialog box opens, the only selection for the destination is to open a new document. If a file is open in the Document Pane and you want the scan to open in a separate document, be certain to enable this radio button.

✦ **Append To Current Document.** If a file is open and you want the scan to be appended to the active document in the Document Pane, enable this radio button.

✦ **Adapt compression to page content.** If the check box is disabled, the items below the check box are not accessible. Check the box if you want to make choices for the remaining items.

✦ **Compatible with.** The PDF conversion creates a PDF document with PDF format compatibility. Select from Acrobat 4, 5, or 6 compatibility from the drop-down menu.

✦ **Remove edge shadows from images.** If you want to scan in grayscale or color mode, Acrobat can eliminate levels of gray where shadows appear around type. For cleaner text scans, enable this option. Note that you need to have crisp, clean originals to see much of a difference between scanning with the option enabled versus disabled.

✦ **Compression.** A slider at the bottom of the dialog box enables you to adjust compression. As the slider is moved left, the file is compressed more. The quality suffers with higher compression levels. As you move the slider right, the file sizes grow, but the quality improves. If you scan images, you can see immediate results for screen displays when the scans are opened in Acrobat. If compression is too high, you can see image degradation on screen. Rescan files with different compression levels to find a setting that appropriately suits your needs.

Many of the settings in the Create PDF From Scanner dialog box need to be tested in your own workflow, especially the Options items and when you scan for use with Paper Capture. There's no substitute for testing. Change settings and test the results when capturing pages. With a little practice, you can easily determine what settings work best in your workflow.

Creating Workflow Solutions

Scanning individual pages for limited use can easily be handled by the methods described previously. As you scan documents, you need to attend to feeding papers under the scanner lid and manually clicking buttons to continue scanning. If you need to convert large numbers of pages to digital content, you may want to explore other solutions. Depending on how much money you want to spend, you may want to invest in a commercial grade scanner with a document feeder.

Some scanners support automatic document feeders. If your workflow demands scanning volumes of papers, acquiring a good scanner with an automatic document feeder is a great advantage. When you scan in Acrobat, scanned pages are successively appended to a PDF. Therefore, you can leave a stack of papers in the scanner feeder and leave it unattended. Scanning can be performed automatically overnight. When you return to your computer, the PDF file is ready for saving and converting to text with Paper Capture. The only downside to this operation is that if your computer crashes, you lose everything because Acrobat won't save your PDF on the fly as new pages are appended.

A more expensive solution, but not out of the question for workflows needing automated means of capturing pages, is to purchase Adobe's stand-alone product, Adobe Acrobat Capture. Combined with a scanner and document feeder, the conversion of scanned images to text is handled in a single operation. You have other solutions from third-party vendors that support industrial-strength scanning and OCR conversion with the capability of converting the final file to PDF format.

Users in government and educational workflows seeking to scan volumes of text for document accessibility will find purchasing auto document feeding scanners and Adobe Acrobat Capture, or other software capable of batch scanning and OCR conversion, to be a much more effective means for converting publications and documents to accessible PDFs. Some hardware screen readers use proprietary software to read TIFF image files for document accessibility. Acrobat PDF is a much better solution over TIFF images and proprietary formats, as once converted to PDF, the document content is searchable and much smaller. If scanning textbooks and government papers is your task, PDF is a much better file format for document accessibility.

Using Paper Capture

After you either scan pages into Acrobat or open images as a PDF file by using the Create PDF From File command, you can convert the page to text through an OCR conversion. Acrobat's OCR utility is Paper Capture. To perform an OCR conversion on a file open in the Document Pane, choose Document ➪ Paper Capture ➪ Start Capture. The Paper Capture dialog box opens as shown in Figure 11-2. Before beginning a capture, you might want to review the settings in the Paper Capture dialog box. You can change the default settings for different options associated with the OCR conversion.

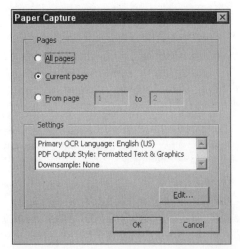

Figure 11-2: Choose Document ➪ Paper Capture ➪
Start Capture to open the Paper Capture dialog box.

Note Macintosh users were missed during the Acrobat 5.x life cycle and had no methods for OCR conversion from within Acrobat. In Acrobat 6.0, Paper Capture is available to users on both Windows and Macintosh platforms.

The first series of options in the Paper Capture dialog box offers you a page range for capturing pages. Select all pages, the current page only, or a specified page range. In the scrollable window you can see the default settings currently applied for your capture session. If you want to make further option choices, click on the Edit button in the Paper Capture dialog box. The Paper Capture Settings dialog box opens as shown in Figure 11-3.

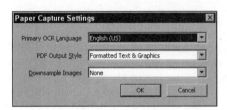

Figure 11-3: Click on the Edit button in the Paper Capture dialog box to open the Paper Capture Settings dialog box. In this dialog box you make options choices for the capture attributes.

Attribute choices available in the Paper Capture Settings dialog box include:

✦ **Primary OCR Language.** By default, Acrobat installs multiple languages in the Paper Capture folder. Seventeen different language dictionaries are included during installation. If you scan documents from any of the supported languages, select the appropriate language in the pull-down menu in the Paper Capture dialog box.

✦ **PDF Output Style.** You have three choices for PDF Output Style in the drop-down menu.

• *Searchable Image (Exact).* This option keeps the image scan in the foreground with text placed in the background. The appearance of the scanned image does not change. Text is added on a hidden layer that gives you the capability of creating indexes and performing searches. Use this option when you don't want to change a document's appearance, but you do want to be able to search the text of that document. Something on the order of a legal document or a certificate might be an example of such a document.

• *Searchable Image (Compact).* Text is also placed behind the original image, preserving the integrity of original documents. The image scan is compressed to reduce file size.

• *Formatted text and graphics.* The Graphic image (say TIFF) is discarded and replaced with formatted text and graphics. If there is an instance where the OCR engine does not have confidence, the original bitmap is left in place and the best guess is placed behind, mimicking the "Searchable Image" style.

Note See the "PDF Image versus PDF Formatted Text & Graphics" sidebar in this chapter for more detail on the differences among the PDF Output Styles.

✦ **Downsample Images.** This option enables you to downsample images or keep them at the original scanned resolution. If None is selected, no downsampling is applied to images. The remaining options offer downsampling values at 300 ppi, 150 ppi, and 72 ppi.

Cross-Reference For more information on image sampling, see Chapter 7.

PDF Image versus PDF Formatted Text & Graphics

When you capture pages with either Searchable Image (Exact) or Searchable Image (Compact), the captures are considered to be PDF Image with Hidden Text. The original file is an image file produced from your scan designed to be viewed as an original, unaltered document. This option enables you to electronically archive documents for legal purposes or when unaltered originals need to be preserved.

When you capture a document with Paper Capture, the OCR conversion places text behind the scan. The intent is for you to be able to archive files and search them either through using the Search Pane to search files on your hard disk or by searching an index where these documents have been catalogued.

The text behind PDF Image is not editable with Acrobat although you could buy Adobe Acrobat Capture 3.0 to edit text in a PDF Image file. If Paper Capture misinterprets a word, you cannot make corrections to the text. The text is selectable, and you can copy the text and paste it into a word processor or text editor. If you want to examine the Paper Capture suspects, paste the text into a word processor and review the document. Or buy a copy of Adobe Acrobat Capture 3.0 to do the edits from within the PDF file.

To copy text from a PDF Image format select the Select Text tool. Click the cursor anywhere in the text and choose Edit ⇨ Select All (Ctrl/⌘+A). Open a context menu and select Copy File to Clipboard. Open a word processor and choose Edit ⇨ Paste. You may find the number of suspects to be too many to be usable. If you want to improve the capture conversion, return to the Create PDF From Scanner dialog box and rescan the file with a higher resolution or different scanning mode.

PDF Formatted Text & Graphic files (previously referred to as PDF Normal) are scanned documents converted to text. When you select Formatted Text & Graphics in the Paper Capture dialog box, the file conversion is made to a PDF Formatted Text & Graphics document. Paper Capture reads the bitmap configuration of words and converts them to text. This text can be edited and altered on a page. When you make text corrections, you see the changes reflected on the document page.

When capturing pages be certain to view the options and know the difference between capturing pages as PDF Image With Hidden Text and PDF Formatted Text & Graphics.

After making your option choices in the Paper Capture Settings dialog box, click OK to return to the Paper Capture dialog box. Your new settings are displayed in the scrollable window. These settings become a new default and remain in effect until you revisit the Paper Capture Settings dialog box and make changes. Click OK in the dialog box and Paper Capture processes the page(s). Depending on the number of pages and the complexity of the document, you may need to wait before Paper Capture finishes the conversion.

The Paper Capture dialog box remains open during the capture and a display of the progress flashes by as various procedures are employed. When the conversion is finished, the dialog box closes. As a conversion from image file to text is made, Paper Capture analyzes the document and compares its interpretation of words to its dictionary. When Paper Capture finds a word where the interpretation doesn't quite match a word contained in the dictionary, it marks the word as a *suspect*. Your next task is to view the suspect words and make edits for all the words misunderstood by Paper Capture.

Editing Capture Suspects

A *suspect* word is one that Paper Capture interprets differently from the closest match found in the Paper Capture dictionary. The word is suspect because it may or may not be a correct interpretation. You might have proper names, industry terminology, abbreviations, and so on that Paper Capture marks as suspects. Simply because the word(s) is marked as a suspect doesn't necessarily require changing the word. Therefore, when you review suspects, you have two choices: Either change the word to a correct spelling or inform Acrobat to leave it as is and move to the next suspect.

After the Paper Capture dialog box disappears, the captured page(s) doesn't appear any different from before you began the capture. In order to see any words that may have been misinterpreted during the conversions, you need to access a menu command and tell Acrobat you want to view the suspect words. You have two choices in the Paper Capture submenu.

Note   In order to correct Paper Capture suspects in Acrobat, you need to capture pages with the Formatted Text & Graphics PDF Output Style.

If you choose Document ⇨ Paper Capture ⇨ Find First OCR Suspect, Acrobat shows the first word that it interprets as a suspect, which means the interpretation of Paper Capture did not exactly match a word in its dictionary. The suspect word is highlighted with a black border.

If you choose Document ⇨ Paper Capture ⇨ Find All OCR Suspects, all the suspect words are highlighted with a red border across all pages captured. At a glance you can see the number of suspects that need to be reviewed.

To begin editing suspect words, choose Document ⇨ Paper Capture ⇨ Find First OCR Suspect. Acrobat highlights the first suspect word and shows a bounding box for the paragraph where the suspect word resides as shown in Figure 11-4. When the Find Element dialog box opens, make a choice for accepting the word and moving to the next suspect. If the word needs to be edited, edit the suspect with the TouchUp Text tool. (The TouchUp Text tool is automatically selected when you open the Find Elements dialog box.) If you accept the word, the bitmap image is discarded.

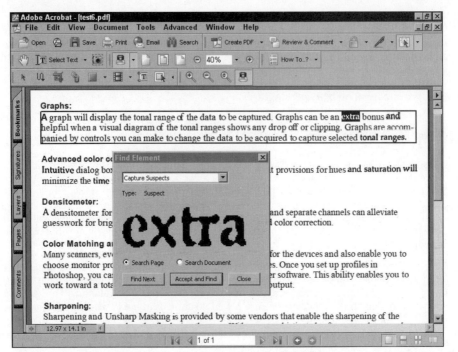

Figure 11-4: Choose Document ⇨ Paper Capture ⇨ Find First OCR Suspect to open the Find Element dialog box where the suspect word appears. You can choose to accept the word and move to the next suspect, or click on Next to move to the next suspect.

Tip   When examining suspect words you should plan on zooming in to the suspects. If you prefer to view a page in a zoomed out view, select the Loupe tool to zoom in on suspect words. You can keep the page view in a smaller view while zooming in on suspects with the Loupe tool as shown in Figure 11-5.

To leave a word unedited, you can choose either Find Next or Accept and Find. If you choose Find Next, the bitmap image of the text stays in place and the text behind the bitmap stays as is. When you click on the Accept and Find button, the bitmap is thrown away and the word behind the bitmap is promoted to the text location. As you work with the text corrections, realize that you have two layers. The bitmap is the scanned image and Paper Capture created the text above the scanned image. Therefore, as you edit the text corrections you can choose to throw away the bitmap image behind the text layer or choose to preserve it. To make a correction, edit a suspect word and click on Accept and Find. The new text you edited is promoted to the text layer while the bitmap behind the text is thrown away.

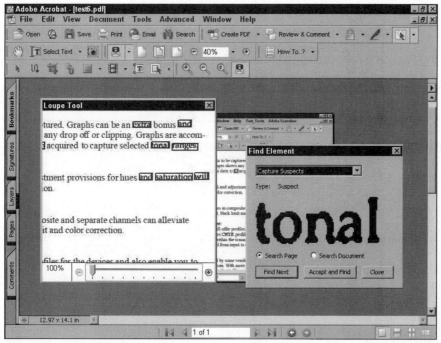

Figure 11-5: Select the Loupe tool and click on a suspect word to zoom in. You can keep the page view at a smaller view while examining suspects in larger views with the Loupe tool.

If you want to develop a workflow in an office environment, you may want to have several machines perform the function of scanning documents and have other computers perform OCR functions. You can scan images in software such as Adobe Photoshop and save your files in either an image format or as Photoshop PDFs. The scans can be routed to other workstations used for the OCR conversion.

When you begin a new Acrobat session and want to scan many pages with Paper Capture, scanning one or two pages representative of the pages you want to capture and examining the number of suspects in your sample scan is a good idea. If the suspects outnumber the number of correct interpretations, editing the suspect words could take you more time than typing the document in a word processor. At some point the ratio between the number of suspects to correct words can make capturing pages more of a burden than providing you a solution.

If the number of suspect words is extraordinary, you may want to scan another few pages using different settings. For example, increase the image resolution or scan in a different color mode. Change the attributes in the Create PDF From Scanner dialog box or adjust settings in your Acquire plug-in to produce scans more suitable for capturing pages. Run Paper Capture and examine the suspects. When a scan results in fewer suspects, you can then go about scanning the remaining pages. In Figure 11-6, I scanned a page at 200 ppi and captured the page with Paper Capture. After viewing the number of suspects, I decided to scan the page again with a higher resolution. The results of my capture suspects with a higher resolution were significantly reduced as you can see in Figure 11-7.

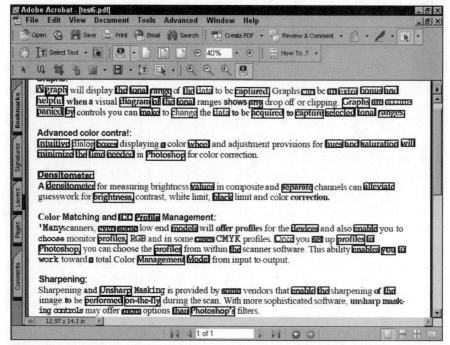

Figure 11-6: I scanned a page using Create PDF From Scanner and captured it with Paper Capture. After I chose Document ➪ Paper Capture ➪ Find All OCR Suspects, I determined that the number of suspects made this job too difficult to edit in Acrobat.

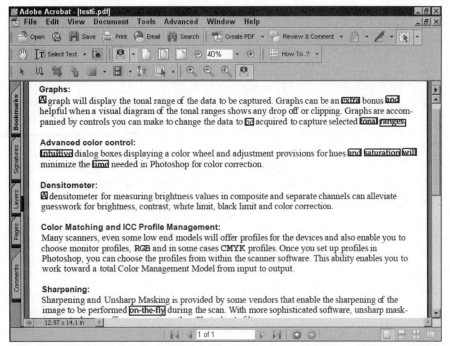

Figure 11-7: I scanned the same page from Figure 11-6 at a higher resolution and captured it again. Fewer suspects were found and the job of correcting the suspects was more manageable.

Summary

✦ Creating a PDF From Scanner uses TWAIN drivers or Adobe Photoshop Acquire plug-ins.

✦ Properly preparing the scanner and documents for scanning in Acrobat improves the quality of the scans. The scanner platen should be clean, the documents should be straight, and the contrast should be sharp.

✦ When scanning images in Acrobat, use the scanning software to establish resolution, image mode, and brightness controls before scanning. Test your results thoroughly to create a formula that works well for the type of documents you scan.

✦ Workflow automation can be greatly improved by purchasing Adobe's stand-alone product Adobe Acrobat Capture. When using Adobe Acrobat Capture with a scanner supporting a document feeder, the scanning and capturing can be performed with unattended operation.

✦ Acrobat Capture is a stand-alone application for optical character recognition used for converting scanned images into editable text.

✦ Text can be captured and saved as a PDF Image Only, where you can edit text and change the appearance of the original scan. Text can be captured and saved using the Searchable Image option, which preserves the original document appearance and adds a text layer behind the image.

✦ Paper Capture suspects are marked when Paper Capture does not find an exact word match in its dictionary. Text editing is performed with the TouchUp Text tool on PDF Formatted Text & Graphics documents.

✦   ✦   ✦

Exports and Imports

The ideal situation for making major edits to PDF content is to return to the original authoring application and make revisions, then re-create a PDF document or specific pages in a document. If you need to replace pages in a PDF file, the new edited pages can be converted to PDF and you can use either the Pages palette or the Document menu and select the Replace pages command.

However, if the original authoring application file is not available, you need to export PDF data to other applications for editing purposes. If you want to recompose PDF documents, you'll want to export the text and/or images and lay out a completely new document. Acrobat offers you many solutions for exporting PDF content.

Cross-Reference For more information on exporting PDF content, see Chapter 8.

You may also want to import PDFs in authoring applications so the PDF pages can be included as part of larger layouts. In this chapter you'll find information on how to export PDFs and include PDF documents in other applications.

Setting Up the Environment

Exports from Acrobat involve using menu commands. Occasionally you may want to select text and copy/paste the text to other applications, or you may want to select objects. Toolbars used for text and object selections are selected from the Advanced Editing and Selection toolbars. From a context menu opened from the Toolbar Well, select Advanced Editing or click on the Advanced Editing Task button. The Selection toolbar is loaded by default; however, only the Select Text tool is visible. From the pull-down menu adjacent to the Select Text toolbar, select Show Selection Toolbar. The Select Text tool remains visible in the Toolbar Well while the Selection toolbar opens as a floating toolbar.

Dock the toolbars individually in the Toolbar Well or open a context menu from the Toolbar Well and select Dock Toolbars. When you open the toolbars and dock them, your Acrobat window should look similar to Figure 12-1. This figure also has a document open in the Document Pane so you can see the tools active in the Toolbar Well.

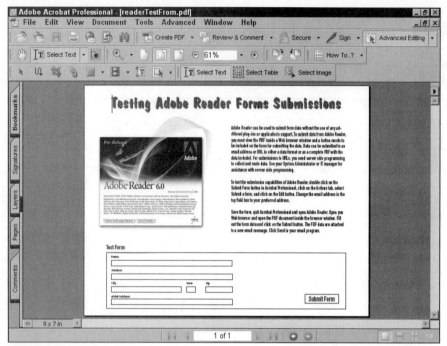

Figure 12-1: Open the Advanced Editing toolbar and the Selection toolbar. Dock the toolbars in the Toolbar Well.

Exporting PDFs

PDF as a file format can be read by many different authoring applications. Therefore, file conversion to other formats is not necessary when PDF imports are supported from authoring programs. You simply import the PDF document into the authoring program and add the content using tools in the authoring program to create new pages. When finished, you can convert the new pages back to the PDF format and view and/or print files from within Acrobat.

There are programs that don't support importing PDFs, and you may need to convert the PDF to a different file format in order to use the file with those applications. For exporting to recognizable formats by most other authoring programs, either the EPS format or an image format is your best solution.

Exporting to EPS

For authoring programs that support Encapsulated PostScript (EPS) formats, you can convert your PDF files to EPS and place the resulting EPS files in the authoring program. Some programs, by default, don't have PDF imports built into the program. In some cases, filters, extensions, and add-ons can offer you this support, but you may not have any readily available and might want to get your PDF documents into a layout without bothering to search for an available tool for PDF imports in your authoring application. Or, in other cases, such tools may simply not exist.

You can set up preferences for PDF exports to EPS in the Preferences dialog box by choosing Edit ➪ Preferences. In the left pane select Convert From PDF. In the right side of the dialog box select Encapsulated PostScript at the top of the list. To set up a new default, click on the Edit Settings button, and the Save As Settings dialog box opens as shown in Figure 12-2.

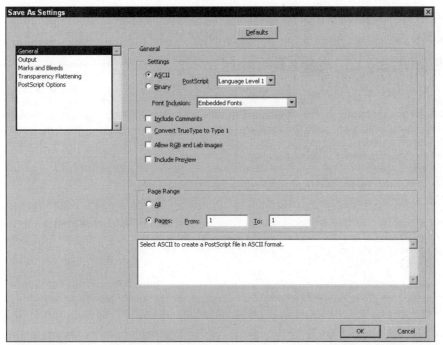

Figure 12-2: Open the Preferences dialog box and click on Convert From PDF in the left pane. Select the format to convert to in the right pane and click on the Edit Settings button.

Some important settings that need to be made in the Save As Settings dialog box include

✦ **Binary:** In most cases, you'll want to choose Binary encoding. Unless there's a special need for exporting to EPS with ASCII and Level 1 PostScript, such as with legacy files, use the Binary option.

✦ **PostScript:** Select Language Level 3 from the pull-down menu. Once again, you may need to use ASCII encoding and PostScript Level 1 for some legacy PDF documents. Be certain to try Binary/Language Level 3 settings first. If the exported file won't import in other applications, change the settings to ASCII and Level 1 PostScript.

✦ **Font inclusion:** Be certain to include all embedded fonts. You also have a pull-down menu option for Embedded and Referenced Fonts. If for some reason the referenced fonts give you problems when the EPS file is printed from another document, return to the Save As Settings dialog box and export the file with the Embedded Fonts menu selection enabled.

✦ **Include Preview:** Be certain to check the box so you can see a screen preview of the EPS file when importing in other applications. Failure to check the box results in imported documents displayed as a gray box with no preview image.

Adjusting the settings for the other options — Output, Marks and Bleeds, Transparency Flattening, and PostScript Options — are a matter of preference. If transparency creates a problem with printing, be certain to use the Transparency Flattener and move the slider toward the Rasters direction. Be aware that flattening transparency does not occur until you finally export the file.

For more information on Transparency Flattening, see Chapter 23.

Exporting to image formats

The most common format used for importing into other applications, as well as printing, is the TIFF format. You can choose from other image formats from the Save As dialog box and export to file formats such as JPEG and PNG. For each of the different file formats you make preference settings in much the same way as the settings you adjust for EPS files. Open the Preferences dialog box and select the image format that appears in the list that you want to export to; click on the Edit Settings button.

For more information on image formats, see Chapters 6 and 9.

After selecting the desired options, select Save As and choose the format from the Save As Type (Windows) or Format (Macintosh) pull-down menu. Once you have saved options in an image format, you can edit image sizes and crops in an image editor, such as Adobe Photoshop.

Whereas the EPS file preserves fonts and requires you to have all fonts installed on your computer in order to open the EPS document in a program like Adobe Illustrator, saving in image formats rasterizes the fonts and eliminates all text-editing capabilities in the resulting file.

For more information on rasterizing PDFs, see Chapter 6.

If you want to change image resolution in PDF documents, you need to use another method for converting files to image formats, rather than importing. The settings available to you in the Acrobat Preferences dialog box don't afford you the opportunity to specify resolutions for the saved file.

Rasterizing PDFs in Photoshop

For files that contain vector objects, you can upsize resolution without any image degradation. Because type is vector art, you can feel free to upsize the PDF during rasterization with excellent results. Suppose, for example, you have a PowerPoint slide presentation converted to PDF that contains text and some vector art illustrations and you want to take your 10 × 7-inch slides and expand them to 30 × 21 inches for trade show panels. Rasterize the PowerPoint PDFs at the necessary output resolution and you'll end up with images suitable for printing with crisp, clean type.

For more information on vector objects, see Chapters 6 and 23.

For raster objects contained in PDFs, upsizing images often produces less desirable results—especially if you want to take a small image and create a large-format display print. Both rasterizing PDFs and converting to image formats have their place and can be used effectively when you import into layout or other design applications where you want to create new designs. For a moment, imagine you want to convert some Web pages from your Web site and use the converted Web pages in a layout for a brochure. If you convert the pages to PDF, then save as an image format or rasterize the PDFs in Photoshop, you can downsize the files and increase resolution without image degradation. However, making the PDFs larger through rasterization when images are included in the document results in clean vector objects but poor-quality images. Therefore, before attempting any PDF conversion in Photoshop, be certain to know what the source document is composed of and what output needs you require. Upsizing images in Photoshop after rasterization results in the same poor-quality images; hence, you'll want to avoid upsizing in Photoshop as well.

For those conditions that produce good images when rasterized in Photoshop, follow the steps to convert a PDF to an image file by opening Photoshop and choosing File ⇨ Open. Select the PDF document to be converted and click on the Open button. The PDF Page Selector dialog box opens as shown in Figure 12-3.

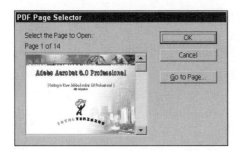

Figure 12-3: When you open a PDF in Photoshop, the PDF Page Selector dialog box opens, where you can select the page in a multi-page document that you want to convert.

The first dialog box appearing in Photoshop enables you to select the page to be converted from PDF to Photoshop's native format. If you have a single-page file, this dialog box is skipped. For multi-page files, you can select the page you want to convert by scrolling the elevator bar or clicking on the down and up arrows to navigate pages. A thumbnail appears for each page placed in view. If you know ahead of time what page you want to convert in longer documents, click on the Go To Page button, and another dialog box opens where you can type the page number and jump to the respective page.

When you select the page in the PDF Page Selector dialog box, click on the OK button. The next dialog box that opens (shown in Figure 12-4) is the Rasterize Generic PDF Format dialog box, where you set the size and resolution as well as color mode. Click OK and the file is rasterized and opens in a new Photoshop document window.

Note   If you open a PDF document that was saved originally as a Photoshop PDF, the document does not require rasterization. You won't see any of the dialog boxes discussed here, because the image data are already rasterized.

After you open the PDF document in Photoshop, you can save the file in any Photoshop-supported file format. Save in a format desired for importing in another application or a format you want to use for printing.

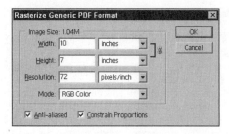

Figure 12-4: The Rasterize Generic PDF Format dialog box is used to define the size and resolution for rasterization. Enter the desired values and click OK to rasterize the file.

Tip   If you experience problems printing a PDF page on a desktop color printer, try rasterizing the file in Photoshop at the resolution recommended for your printer. The type on the page often appears much better than using the Print As Image setting in Acrobat's Advanced printing dialog box. For more information on printing PDFs, see Chapter 23.

Importing PDFs in Authoring Applications

If PDF document pages do not need editing but you want to use the pages in a different layout, you might find a need for importing the PDFs in other authoring applications. With some filters, extensions, or other add-ons, some programs offer you support for importing PDFs. In Adobe Software applications such as Illustrator, PageMaker, FrameMaker, and InDesign, the application support for importing PDFs is built into the programs without the need for additional plug-ins.

Note   Adobe PageMaker 7 supports importing PDFs in PageMaker without additional plug-ins. If you're using Adobe PageMaker 6.0 or 6.5, you need to download a plug-in from Adobe's Web site in order to import PDFs.

Adobe Illustrator supports both placing a PDF file and opening a PDF file. If you choose File ⇨ Place to import the PDF in Illustrator the PDF becomes a placed graphic with all fonts embedded. You cannot edit the graphic, but the advantage is you won't need to worry about font issues. If you choose File ⇨ Open in Illustrator and attempt to open a PDF without having the fonts installed, type characters are lost when the document is opened. Opening a file has an advantage as you can edit all the elements including changing fonts to fonts loaded in your system.

Situations where you might import PDF documents include using a PDF as an image file, adding a PDF for creating callouts, or perhaps creating slide notes if the PDF is used as a slide presentation. I often use PDF files for slide presentations when speaking at PDF conferences and I create speaker notes in Adobe InDesign with a PDF of each page placed on a separate page in the InDesign file along with some room for attendees to make notes. To create a handout document, follow these steps:

STEPS: Importing PDFs in Adobe InDesign

1. **Create master pages in InDesign.** For pages that need duplicate content on all pages, open a master page and add your elements on the master page as shown in Figure 12-5.

Note   You can create a new document with the number of pages needed for all the slides or insert pages after creating the master page template.

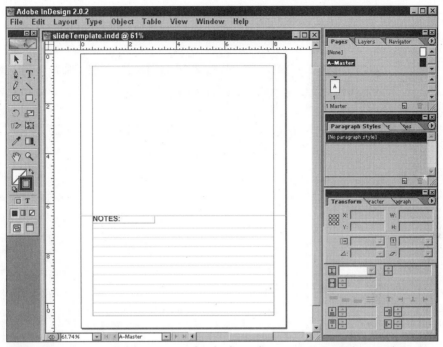

Figure 12-5: Create all the content to be duplicated on a master page in InDesign.

2. **Import the first page in the PDF document.** Navigate to the first page in the document and be certain the master page template is used for page 1. Choose File ➪ Place. In the Place dialog box, check the box for Show Import Options. Click Open, and the Place PDF dialog box shown in Figure 12-6 opens. The default page is page 1. Leave the default page alone, but be certain Bounding Box is shown in the Crop to pull-down menu. Click OK.

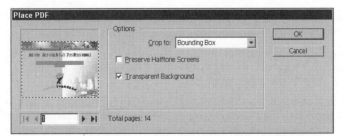

Figure 12-6: The Place PDF dialog box enables you to navigate pages in the PDF to select the page to place in the InDesign file. Leave the default page at 1 and click the OK button to import the first page.

3. **Size the imported PDF Page and position to fit.** In this example the page comes into the InDesign document in a larger size than desired. Use the Scale tool and size the image down. Drag the image to position as shown in Figure 12-7.

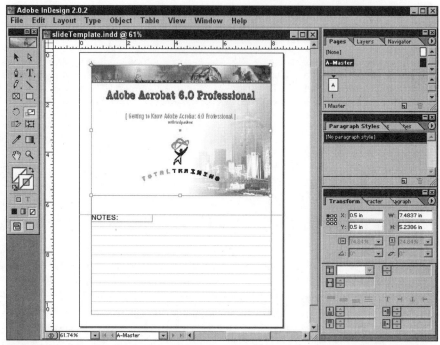

Figure 12-7: Size the PDF import and move to position.

4. **Copy and Paste the imported PDF page.** Choose Edit ➪ Copy. Move to the next page and choose Edit ➪ Paste in Place. The pasted copy is pasted at the same precise location as the image copied on page 1.

5. **Replace the selected item.** Be certain the copy on page 2 is selected and choose File ➪ Place. In the Place dialog box check the box for Replace Selected Item.

6. **Place the second page from the PDF File.** When the Place PDF dialog box opens, click on the right-pointing arrow to display the page 2 thumbnail in the dialog box. Click OK and page 2 replaces the copied page 1.

7. **Place the remaining pages.** Duplicate the process. Because you still have page 1 on the clipboard, there's no need to copy any pages. Move to the next page, and choose Edit ➪ Paste in Place; then choose File ➪ Place. Navigate to the next page in the Place PDF dialog box and place the page. Continue following the same steps until all pages have been placed.

8. **Convert to PDF.** When finished, choose File ➪ Export and select PDF as the format. The final file can be sent to other users, added to a Web site, or printed.

Although Acrobat is not designed specifically for presentations and there are no options for printing slide handouts from within the program, you can easily create handouts with this little workaround. Similar steps can be used with other applications supporting PDF imports such as Adobe Pagemaker, QuarkXPress, or Adobe FrameMaker.

Cross-Reference   For more information on using Acrobat for presentations, see Chapter 21.

Similar options exist for importing PDFs into other Adobe imaging applications such as Adobe PageMaker and Adobe FrameMaker. If you use QuarkXPress you can achieve the same results by downloading the free Import PDF Quark XTension. The programs vary a little with creating master pages and importing objects on pages, but you do have the opportunity to emulate the steps for creating similar master pages and replacing objects.

Summary

✦ You assign attributes for exporting PDFs to EPS format in the Preferences dialog box and select Convert From PDF in the left pane.

✦ When importing PDFs in Adobe Illustrator and fonts are not installed on your computer, use the Place command instead of opening the file.

✦ PDFs can be rasterized in Adobe Photoshop. When rasterizing PDFs with images, be certain to not upsample the resolution. Type and vector objects can be upsampled with good results.

✦ All Adobe layout applications support importing PDFs without the addition of special plug-ins. For other programs you can often find additional utilities that enable you to import PDF pages.

✦ Creating handouts for a PDF presentation can be easily developed in a program such as Adobe InDesign, where master pages are created and PDF pages are imported.

✦   ✦   ✦

Repurposing PDF Documents

PDF documents designed for one purpose, such as creating designs for prepress and printing, might need to be repurposed for other output intent such as Web hosting or copying files to CD-ROMs. Rather than going back to the original authoring program and recreating PDFs for each purpose, you can use tools in Acrobat that enable you to downsample file sizes and strip unnecessary content. The resulting documents can then be more efficiently viewed on Web sites or exchanged via e-mail.

In this chapter you learn how to repurpose PDF documents using some Acrobat tools and methods for downsizing file sizes and eliminating content unnecessary for other viewing purposes. In addition, you take a look at automating tasks by creating batch sequences.

Setting Up the Environment

For the purpose of downsizing files and optimizing them for other output circumstances, you don't need to access any special tools. The menu commands offer all the means for repurposing files. Therefore, set up your Acrobat work environment by opening a context menu and selecting Reset Toolbars from the menu options.

Reducing File Sizes

Reducing file sizes often occurs with downsampling images — that is to say, reducing the image resolution of all raster images or compressing images with higher compression options. In addition, you can reduce file sizes by eliminating redundant backgrounds; eliminating objects such as form fields, comments, bookmarks, and destinations; unembedding fonts; and/or compressing the document structure. You can handle file-size reductions at the time of PDF creation when you control file compression, image sampling, and font embedding for designing PDFs for a specific output purpose. However, if you create PDFs for one purpose such as commercial printing and later want to host the same file on a Web site, you need to either create a new PDF document specific for the new purpose or use Acrobat tools to create smaller file sizes more suited for other output purposes. Fortunately, several means are available to you for squeezing file sizes down and optimizing PDFs for multiple purposes.

Cross-Reference   For more information on understanding terms like *downsampling* and *resampling,* see Chapters 6 and 7.

Downsizing cropped images

If you scan a document in Acrobat using the Create PDF From Scanner command, the scanned image is sampled according to settings you apply when scanning pages. After a scan opens in Acrobat you may have a need to crop the scan using tools in Acrobat.

When you use the Crop tool in Acrobat, the cropped image data remain in the file; data are not eliminated. To reduce file sizes when cropping images, choose the File ➪ Save As menu command and save as a TIFF file. After saving the file, open it in Acrobat to convert back to PDF. The result is a document where the cropped area is completely eliminated from the file. Choose File ➪ Save As and overwrite the file to optimize it.

Using the Reduce File Size command

In Acrobat 6 a new menu command has been added to the program, enabling you to reduce file sizes with the simple selection of the command. Open a document and choose File ➪ Reduce File Size. The Reduce File Size dialog box opens as shown in Figure 13-1.

Figure 13-1: Choose File ➪ Reduce File Size to open the Reduce File Size dialog box, where you select options for Acrobat version compatibility.

In the Reduce File Size dialog box you have three options from the pull-down menu for selecting Acrobat compatibility. The default is Acrobat 5 compatibility. If your PDF documents are to be viewed by Acrobat users of version 5 or later, choose the Acrobat 5 compatibility. If all users are using Acrobat 6 viewers, use Acrobat 6 compatibility. Although Acrobat 4 compatibility is an option, there is little need to use the menu choice as Acrobat 4 users can view your Acrobat 5 files without problems if you don't introduce things like JavaScripts that only work in Acrobat 5 or greater viewers. For simply reducing file sizes, Acrobat 5 compatibility should work fine for all users of earlier versions of Acrobat.

After making the menu selection and clicking OK, the Save As dialog box opens. Provide a filename and save the file to disk. As a matter of practice it's a good idea to write a new file to disk in case the file reduction fails and you need to return to the original file to try another method of file reduction.

Using PDF Optimizer

In addition to the Reduce File Size command, you can use the PDF Optimizer to reduce file sizes through downsampling images and a variety of other settings that offer options for eliminating unnecessary data. The Reduce File Size command doesn't provide user-definable settings for what data are affected during file reductions. With PDF Optimizer you make the choices from a number of different settings in the PDF Optimizer dialog box for what data are affected during optimization. The PDF Optimizer also offers you an option for analyzing a file so you can see what part of the PDF document occupies higher percentages of memory.

Auditing space usage

The first step you want to perform when optimizing files with the PDF Optimizer is to analyze a file so you can see what content occupies the larger amounts of memory. Analyzing a document and using the PDF Optimizer is handled in the PDF Optimizer dialog box that opens when you choose Advanced ⇨ PDF Optimizer. The PDF Optimizer appears as shown in Figure 13-2.

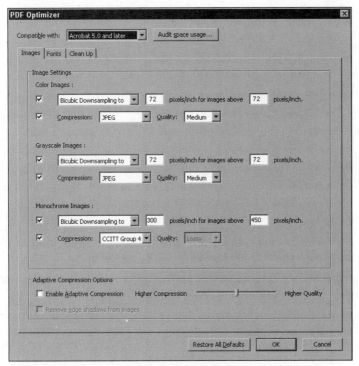

Figure 13-2: Choose Advanced ⇨ PDF Optimizer to open the PDF Optimizer dialog box. To analyze a file for the space usage, click on the Audit space usage button at the top of the dialog box.

Click on the button labeled Audit space usage. Depending on the size and complexity of the document, the analysis can take a little time. When the analysis completes, the dialog box shown in Figure 13-3 opens.

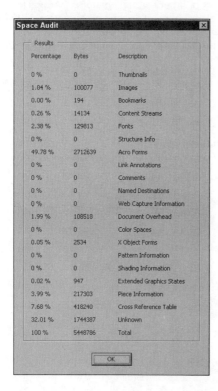

Figure 13-3: After the analysis is completed, the Space Audit dialog box opens, where space usage according to different objects/ elements are reported as a percentage of the total space.

Percentage	Bytes	Description
0 %	0	Thumbnails
1.84 %	100077	Images
0.00 %	194	Bookmarks
0.26 %	14134	Content Streams
2.38 %	129813	Fonts
0 %	0	Structure Info
49.78 %	2712639	Acro Forms
0 %	0	Link Annotations
0 %	0	Comments
0 %	0	Named Destinations
0 %	0	Web Capture Information
1.99 %	108518	Document Overhead
0 %	0	Color Spaces
0.05 %	2534	X Object Forms
0 %	0	Pattern Information
0 %	0	Shading Information
0.02 %	947	Extended Graphics States
3.99 %	217303	Piece Information
7.68 %	418240	Cross Reference Table
32.01 %	1744387	Unknown
100 %	5448786	Total

In the example shown in the preceding figure, notice almost half of the document space is used for form fields (Acro Forms in the dialog box description). The second largest space percentage is an item denoted as *Unknown*. This item is used for all elements not identified as any one of the other items described in the dialog box.

The analysis informs you that there would be little need to try to resample images because the image space is only 1.84% of the total space usage. Optimizing the file might best be achieved by resaving the file with the Save As command and doing something about all the form fields. If all the form fields are essential, then file reduction with either the Reduce File Size command or the PDF Optimizer might only be slight. Compare the first analysis (shown in Figure 13-3) with Figure 13-4. As you can see in the Space Audit report, images comprise more than 90% of the space usage. In this example you might see significant file reduction when using either the Reduce File Size command or the downsampling options of PDF Optimizer.

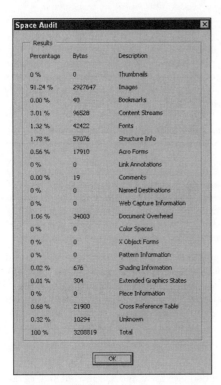

Figure 13-4: Another file analyzed for space usage shows that images occupy the highest percentage of space in the document.

Optimizing files

The file analyzed in Figure 13-4 was originally created for professional printing and the images are all sampled at 300 ppi (pixels per inch). To repurpose the document and reduce the file size for Web hosting, the images need to be resampled at 72 ppi. Using the PDF Optimizer, you can specify image-size reductions as well as perform cleanup of content that occupies space for unnecessary items like comments, bookmarks, destinations, or other items that add to overhead in the file.

Image settings

To reduce file size with the PDF Optimizer, use the first set of options that opens in the Images tab as shown in Figure 13-2. You can make choices for downsampling color, grayscale, and bitmap images by typing values in the field boxes for the sampling amounts desired. In my example, I edited the field boxes for color and grayscale images and chose 72 ppi as the amount of downsampling. To the right of the downsampling amount, another field box is used to identify images that are downsampled. In this box I added 72 ppi, which instructs Acrobat to look for any image above 72 ppi and downsample the file to the amount supplied in the first field box—in this example, to 72 ppi.

Cross-Reference

In the Images tab you have choices for the downsampling method. The default method is Bicubic Downsampling. Leave the choice for Bicubic Downsampling at the default selection. To learn more about the other methods and what they mean, see Chapter 7.

The Compression pull-down menu offers choices for JPEG2000 (Acrobat 6 setting only), JPEG, and Zip compression. For either form of JPEG compression you additionally have choices for the amount of compression from the Quality pull-down menu. If you choose a JPEG compression and use Minimum for the Quality choice, your images may appear severely degraded. As a general rule, Medium quality results in satisfactory image quality for Web hosting. If you try one setting and the images look too degraded you can return to the original file and apply a different Quality setting; then examine the results.

Cross-Reference For more information on the JPEG, JPEG2000, and Zip file formats, see Chapter 5.

Adaptive Compression Options at the bottom of the dialog box offer a means of adjusting the ratio between quality and compression. If you enable the check box for Enable Adaptive Compression, all other compression options are grayed out. This compression method uses advanced image processing such as edge shadow elimination and other effects not available with the downsampling models listed in the Image Settings area of the dialog box. If the check box for Remove edge shadows from images is enabled, shadows that may appear with scanned images are removed.

If you elect to choose Adaptive Compression Options, you may find that the file size reduction is not as compact as choosing from the Image Settings options. All depends on the files and whether the images contain data that are affected when using the Adaptive Compression Options. The best way to determine what settings result in the most compact suitable files is to test compression with Image Settings controls and then again with Adaptive Compression.

Fonts settings

Fonts won't always appear in a list in the Fonts tab when you click on the tab in the PDF Optimizer. Only fonts that are available for unembedding are listed. On the left side of the dialog box, fonts are listed that can be unembedded. If no fonts appear in the list, you can move on to the next tab. If fonts are listed in the left window, select the fonts to unembed and click the Move button adjacent to the right chevron.

On the right side of the dialog box are fonts listed for unembedding. If you want to keep the font embedded, select it in the right window and click on the Move button adjacent to left chevron. To select multiple fonts in either window, press Shift+click to select a list in a contiguous group, or press Ctrl/⌘+click to select fonts in a non-contiguous group.

Clean Up settings

Click on the Clean Up tab and you find a list of items checked by default that can be used safely without affecting the functionality of your document. All other items that appear unchecked can be enabled, but you should have an idea for what will happen to the PDF, in terms of functionality, if you optimize the file with any additional items checked. If you check one or more of the items and return to the PDF Optimizer, the new checked item(s) become a new set of default settings. To restore the dialog box to original defaults, click on the Restore All Defaults button at the bottom of the dialog box and the check boxes return to original defaults as shown in Figure 13-5.

Discarding items such as comments, form actions, JavaScript actions, cross references, and removing thumbnails affect document functionality as you might suspect. If the respective items are eliminated, any PDF interactivity created with these items is also eliminated. If you know that one or any group of these items won't have an effect on the way the repurposed document is viewed or printed, enable the check boxes for the items you want to remove.

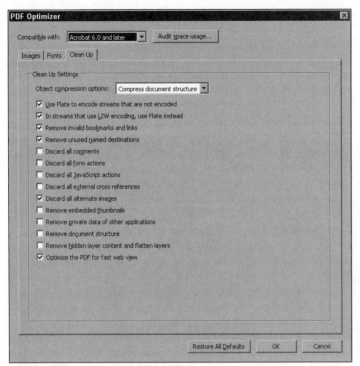

Figure 13-5: By default, a partial list of Clean Up settings is checked. The checked items won't disturb the PDF functionality.

Removing private data of other applications does not affect the PDF functionality. When the check box is enabled, the data removed affects only data useful to the original authoring application. For example, saving to PDF from Adobe Illustrator while preserving Illustrator editing capabilities contains data in the PDF file only useful to Adobe Illustrator. Removing document structure eliminates tags and structure and can affect accessibility and also can present problems with the document functionality. Removing hidden layers and flattening the layers results in a file where all hidden layers are discarded and the visible layers flattened.

After you make your preferred settings in the PDF Optimizer, click on the OK button and wait for the processing to finish. As a comparison between using Reduce File Size and the PDF Optimizer, using the same file with an original file size of 3.06 MB, I reduced the file size with the Reduce File Size command and produced a PDF that was resampled to 454 KB. The same file processed with PDF Optimizer was reduced to 285 KB. The increased file reduction from PDF Optimizer was due to eliminating some document overhead and structural information.

Redistilling Files

Creating a PostScript file from a PDF document and redistilling with Acrobat Distiller with different Adobe PDF options is something that may not always work. All depends on the fonts embedded in the file and whether you have fonts installed on your system that are not embedded in a PDF. In other words, it doesn't always work, but in many cases it's usually best to try if using the Reduce File Size or PDF Optimizer doesn't produce a sufficiently smaller file for your output consideration.

Using the file I analyzed earlier in this chapter in Figure 13-3, where almost one half the space is taken up by form fields, both the Reduce File Size command and the PDF Optimizer had little effect in reducing the file size. If the Clean Up item for Discard all form actions is selected in the PDF Optimizer dialog box, the file size is significantly smaller, but all the form field data are lost. Figure 13-6 shows one of 13 pages in the original 5.2 MB file.

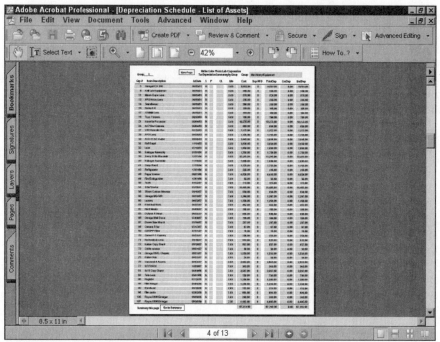

Figure 13-6: One of the 13 pages in a file at 5.2 MB is shown with all the form fields populated with data.

Before I discuss downsizing a file, there are a few assumptions to be made when using the redistilling downsampling method. The first assumption is that after the data are added to the document, the form fields are no longer needed. Second, the final document, complete with the data, is then used for e-mailing, hosting on a hard drive or network server, or hosting on a Web site for users to review. If changes are to be made, the original file is kept stored on a drive for editing purposes. With these assumptions in mind, the task at hand is to keep the data in the file while finding the most efficient means for downsizing the original 5.2 MB file.

Because neither the Reduce File Size command nor the PDF Optimizer does the job, the next option is to choose File ➪ Save As and save the file as a PostScript file. After it's in PostScript, open Acrobat Distiller and select an Adobe PDF Setting for the output desired.

Cross-Reference

For information on creating PostScript files from PDF documents, see Chapter 5. For information on using Acrobat Distiller and making choices for Adobe PDF Settings, see Chapter 7.

When you print a PostScript file to disk and redistill the file, the form fields are eliminated from the document; however, the form field data are stamped down on the background and all data originally supplied in form fields remain part of the newly created PDF with Acrobat Distiller. In the earlier example where the original file size was 5.2 MB, the file optimized with the PDF Optimizer reduced the file size to 3.45 MB. The file printed to disk and redistilled in Acrobat Distiller produced a file of 63 KB.

Tip

If you have interactive elements in a document such as bookmarks, form fields, destinations, and so on and want to preserve the interactive elements when redistilling PDFs, realize that all such items are lost in the new file created with Acrobat Distiller. To regain bookmarks, form fields, and so on, open the original file in Acrobat. Choose Document ➪ Pages ➪ Replace. Locate the new file created with Acrobat Distiller in the Select File With New Pages dialog box and replace all pages in the file. Choose File ➪ Save As to write a new optimized file to disk. The new file uses the optimized pages and the old file's interactive elements. You'll see a little increase in the file size due to the interactive elements, but the overall file size will be much smaller in your new file compared to the original file.

Once again, be aware that redistilling files is not always successful; however, in more circumstances than not, I've found the procedure described in this section to be successful when file reduction cannot be successfully accomplished via other means.

Note

You can also eliminate form fields while retaining the form data to reduce file sizes by using one of several different plug-ins you can purchase from third-party manufacturers. For a comprehensive list of third-party plug-ins, demonstration versions of the software, and a description for each third-party product, log on to /www.pdfstore.com and visit the Planet PDF store.

Batch Processing PDF Files

If you have multiple files that need to be refined for distribution on network servers, Web sites, or CD-ROM, then you'll want to create a batch sequence. *Batch sequences* are a defined series of commands in a specific order that can be run on multiple files. You create the batch sequence from a list of executable functions and determine the commands and order of the sequence.

Batch sequences help you automate tasks in Acrobat that might otherwise take considerable time to manually apply a common set of commands on many different files. After you develop one or more sequences, you can run the sequence(s) on selected PDF files, a folder of PDF files, or multiple folders of PDF files.

Tasks such as setting opening views of PDF documents, adding document descriptions, or adding page numbers can be applied to multiple files you might want to distribute on CD-ROM or on Web sites. Before distributing files you can run a batch sequence as a final step in your production workflow to be sure all files have common attributes.

Creating a batch sequence

To create a new sequence, choose Advanced ➪ Batch Processing. The Batch Sequences dialog box opens as shown in Figure 13-7. The dialog box lists several sequences predefined for you when you install Acrobat. From the list in the dialog box you can run a sequence, edit one of the listed sequences, rename a sequence, or delete any one or more sequences from the list. The first button in the dialog box is used to create a new sequence where you choose what commands you want to run from a list in other dialog boxes.

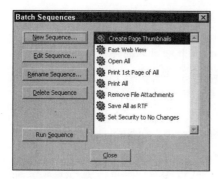

Figure 13-7: Choose Advanced ➪ Batch Processing to open the Batch Sequences dialog box.

Click on New Sequence and the Name Sequence dialog box shown in Figure 13-8 opens. The first step in creating a batch sequence is to provide a name for the sequence. The name supplied in the dialog box ultimately is added to the list in the Batch Sequence window. When you want to run the sequence you can open the Batch Sequences dialog box, select any one of the sequences you added to the list, and click on the Run Sequence button.

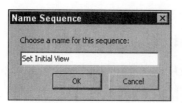

Figure 13-8: The first step in creating a new sequence is adding a name for the sequence. The names of new sequences are added to the list in the Batch Sequences dialog box.

Type a name in the field box and click OK. The next dialog box that opens is the Batch Edit Sequence - Set Initial View dialog box shown in Figure 13-9. Three items are listed in the dialog box. The next step (the Batch Sequence dialog box actually lists this step as the first step in creating a sequence) is to click on the Select Commands button. After you make choices for the commands added to the sequence, you are returned to this dialog box to make choices for items 2 and 3 where you identify the input location of files and the destination (output) location.

The Edit Sequence dialog box opens where you make choices for the commands added to your new sequence. From the scrollable list on the left side of the dialog box you select a command and click on the Add button to move the command to the right side of the dialog box. If you want more than one set of commands applied to your sequence, select a command and click the Add button; then select additional commands and click Add. In this example I added commands for setting the Initial View and adding a document Description as shown in Figure 13-10.

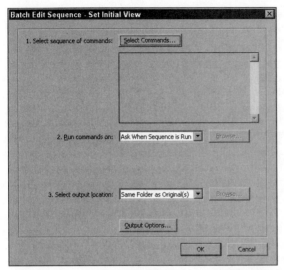

Figure 13-9: The Batch Edit Sequence-Set Initial View dialog box opens after you provide a name for a new sequence. Click on the Select Commands button to choose the commands executed in the sequence.

After the commands are added to the right window, you can make attribute choices for each command. From those commands in the right window, either select the command or double-click on the name to open dialog boxes where you make attribute choices. In Figure 13-11 I adjusted the Set Open Options dialog box to open PDF files in a Page Only view and Fit Page View with the Document Title displayed.

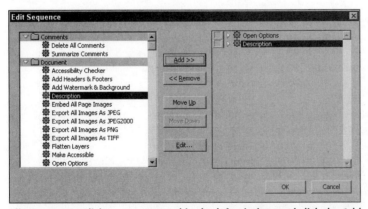

Figure 13-10: Click on a command in the left window and click the Add button. Continue adding commands that you want run as part of your new sequence.

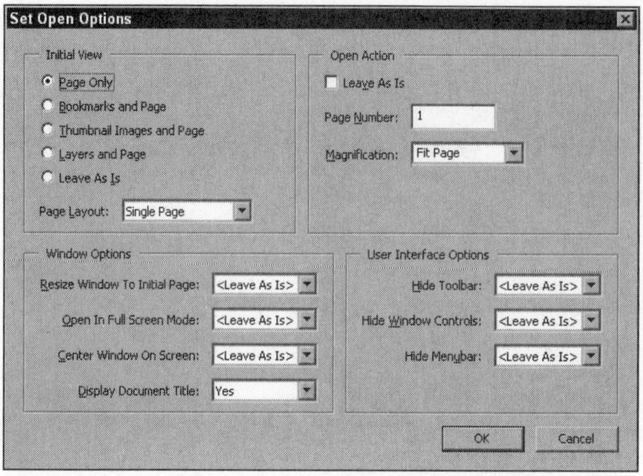

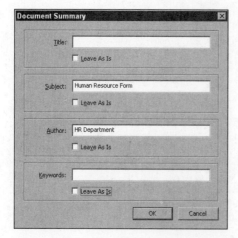

Figure 13-11: Initial View options are selected in the Set Open Options dialog box. To open the dialog box, double-click on the command in the right window in the Edit Sequence dialog box.

The settings applied for the Initial View are applied globally to files when you run the sequence. In some cases you'll want to supply data when each file is processed in a sequence to add unique settings for individual files. For example, the document Description fields for Subject and Author might be consistent among a group of PDF documents in a single folder; however, the Title and Keywords fields are unique for each file processed. In this example you can double-click on the Description item to open the Document Summary dialog box and add the common data to the fields that remain consistent across all PDFs processed when the sequence is run. In Figure 13-12 the common data are supplied in the Subject and Author fields while the Title and Keywords fields are left blank.

Figure 13-12: Add the data that are common in the PDFs processed when the sequence is run, and leave the fields requiring unique data blank.

In order to supply data individually to each file processed in the sequence, you need to set a flag in the Edit Sequence dialog box so each file pauses during processing and the Document Summary dialog box opens where the unique data are added. After adding the common data, exit the Document Summary dialog box to return to the Batch Edit Sequence dialog box. Click in the square adjacent to the command name to display a mini menu icon. This toggle sets the flag for Acrobat to pause on each file processed for user-supplied data. When you add the data and click OK, Acrobat continues running the sequence and pauses at the next file processed where you again add data and click OK, and so on. You can also see each attribute setting for any command by clicking on the right-pointing arrow to open the settings list associated with a command and review the settings. This feature is particularly helpful if you create a sequence and in some later Acrobat session want to review the settings before you run the sequence. In Figure 13-13 you can see the flag set for the Description command and the list of attributes assigned to the command in the expanded list.

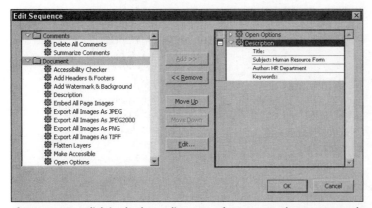

Figure 13-13: Click in the box adjacent to the command name to set the flag to pause processing where user-supplied data are added to a command. To review the attribute choices, open a list by clicking on the right-pointing arrow.

After adding all commands that you want to execute in a sequence, click on the OK button and you are returned to the Batch Edit Sequence dialog box. The remaining items to contend with are choices you make for selecting the location of the files to be processed and where the processed files are to be saved. The default for item 2 (Run commands on) is Ask When Sequence is Run. This option prompts you as you run each new sequence where you can select files or folders in a dialog box. If you have a predetermined location of files you can choose other options such as Selected Files, Selected Folders, or run the sequence on files open in Acrobat at the time you choose to run the sequence. If you intend to use the sequence many times in other Acrobat sessions, leave the default choice at Ask When Sequence is Run. This way you'll be prompted to identify files or folders as you run a sequence.

The output for files can be a Specific Folder, the Same Folder as Original Files processed in the sequence, or you can choose to be prompted when the sequence is run. In addition, a menu choice is available if you don't want to save the changes made. This choice is made for files processed from among the open files in Acrobat.

If you choose to write the processed files to the same directory where the original files reside, you can set up Output Options for adding a prefix or suffix to filenames so the original files won't be overwritten.

When you set all the attributes for a sequence, click OK and the new sequence is added to the list in the Batch Sequences dialog box.

Setting output options

When you select the Output Options button in the Batch Edit Sequence dialog box, you'll find choices for filenaming and output formats as well as file optimization. Click on the Output Options button when you create a new sequence in the Batch Edit Sequence dialog box and the Output Options dialog box opens as shown in Figure 13-14.

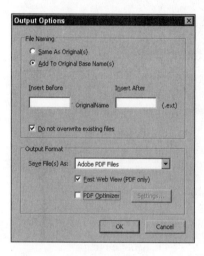

Figure 13-14: Output Options offer you choices for naming the processed files as well as saving in different formats and optimizing files with the PDF Optimizer.

You can add a suffix or prefix to filenames by clicking on the Add To Original Base Name(s) button and editing the field boxes for Insert Before and Insert After. If you enter data in the Insert After field box the data are added before the filename extension. Checking the box for Do not overwrite existing files ensures you that you won't inadvertently overwrite the original files.

From the Save File(s) As pull-down menu you have choices for the file formats to be exported. The default is Adobe PDF. If you want to save files in text formats (Word, RTF, text only, and so on), you can make the choice for the text format from the pull-down menu options. Additionally PostScript, EPS, image formats, HTML, and XML formats are available. You'll note that the Save As options in the Output Format Save File(s) pull-down menu offers the same options as when choosing the File ➪ Save As command.

You'll notice that to optimize files you find no options in the list of commands found in the Edit Sequence dialog box you can choose for simply optimizing files. For optimization, you make your choice here in the Output Options by selecting PDF Optimizer. Check the box and click on Settings to open the PDF Optimizer dialog box discussed earlier in this chapter. After making all the Output Options choices, click OK. Click OK in the Batch Edit Sequence dialog box, and your sequence is complete and ready to run.

Running sequences

Presuming you created a sequence and added the new sequence, you can open the Batch Sequence dialog box by choosing Advanced ➪ Batch Processing and selecting the sequence you want to run. Click on the Run Sequence button in the Batch Sequence dialog box and the Run Sequence Confirmation dialog box opens. A list of commands appears in the dialog box where you can review the settings for each command by clicking on the right-pointing arrow to display the settings as discussed earlier in this chapter. If all the settings are appropriate for the sequence you want to run, click OK and the Select Files to Process dialog box opens. You can select a file, a contiguous or non-contiguous group of files by using the Shift or Ctrl/⌘+Shift keys and clicking a folder, or a group of folders for processing. Click on the Select button, and the sequence runs. If you created a sequence to toggle open a dialog box for supplying unique data for each file, the dialog boxes open. Make changes in any dialog boxes, click the OK buttons, and the sequence continues. Files are saved according to the choices you made in the Output Options dialog box or the choice made from the Select output location pull-down menu in the Batch Edit Sequence dialog box.

After running a sequence, examine the files to ensure all files are created with the options you expect them to have. If there are any errors and you saved the new set of files without overwriting the original set, you can edit the sequence and run the edited version on the original files.

Editing sequences

If you create a sequence for one purpose and want to modify the sequence for another processing venture, you can edit the attributes of a command, add new commands, or delete commands from the original sequence. To edit a sequence, choose Advanced ➪ Batch Processing. In the Batch Sequences dialog box select the sequence you want to edit and click on the Edit Sequence button. The Batch Edit Sequences dialog box opens.

In order to edit the commands, add new commands, or delete commands, you first need to click on the Select Commands button. The Edit Sequence dialog box opens where you can add new commands, or edit existing commands, following the section explained earlier for creating sequences.

If you want to delete a sequence and all the commands associated with the sequence, click on the Delete Sequence button in the Batch Sequences dialog box. This action removes the sequence from the list. If you delete commands in the Edit Sequence dialog box and keep a modified version of a sequence listed in the Batch Sequences dialog box, you may want to rename a sequence to more closely relate to the modified version. Click on the Rename Sequence button in the Batch Sequence dialog box and edit the name in the Name Sequence dialog box.

Creating custom sequences

The batch sequences you create are chosen from the list of commands in the Edit Sequence dialog box. If you want to add a command that doesn't exist in the list in the Edit Sequence dialog box, you can create custom sequences from commands you add with JavaScripts.

JavaScripts offer you an infinite number of possibilities for automating commands and sequences applied to a group of PDF documents. As an example, suppose you want to add a Stamp comment to an assorted collection of PDFs designed to be documents in draft form.

After the files have been stamped with a Draft icon from the Stamp comment, you disperse the documents, collect feedback, and use another batch sequence to delete all comments from the documents. The sequence for deleting comments is a preset installed with Acrobat. Adding Stamp comments, however, is something you need to do with a JavaScript. To see how you handle adding a JavaScript to a batch sequence, and in particular, adding a Stamp comment to a collection of PDF files, follow these steps:

STEPS: Creating a JavaScript Batch Sequence

1. **Create a New Batch Sequence.** Choose Advanced ➪ Batch Processing. In the Batch Sequences dialog box, select New Sequence. When the Name Sequence dialog box opens, type a name for the sequence. In this example I use Add Stamp. Click OK.

2. **Select Execute JavaScript and Add it to the List of Sequences to be executed.** In the Batch Edit Sequence dialog box, click on Select Commands to open the Edit Sequence dialog box. In the Edit Sequence dialog box, select Execute JavaScript from the list on the left and click the Add button to move the command to the right window.

3. **Add the JavaScript code to execute the action.** Select the command in the right window and click on the Edit button. The JavaScript Editor dialog box opens. In the JavaScript Editor, type the following code (Note: The same code is shown as it should appear in the JavaScript Editor in Figure 13-15):

```
/* Add a Stamp to Page 1 in a File */
var annot = this.addAnnot
({
  page:0,
  type: "Stamp",
  name: "Draft",
  popupOpen: false,
  rect: [400, 725, 580, 760],
contents: "This is a draft document",
AP: "Draft"
})
```

4. **Save the JavaScript.** Click OK in the JavaScript Editor dialog box. Click OK in the Edit Sequence dialog box to return to the Batch Edit Sequence dialog box. The script is saved when you exit the JavaScript Editor dialog box.

5. **Set the Output Options.** Leave Run commands on at the default for Ask When Sequence is Run. In the Select output location pull-down menu, select the option you want to use for the saved files location. If you want to be prompted at the time the sequence is run, select Ask When Sequence is Run. Click OK in the Batch Edit Sequence dialog box and the sequence is added to the list of Batch Sequences.

6. **Run the Sequence.** Select the Add Stamp sequence in the Batch Sequences dialog box and click on Run Sequence. (Note if you closed the Batch Sequences dialog box after the last step, choose Advanced ➪ Batch Processing to reopen the dialog box).

7. **Examine the results.** Select a single file to process when the Select Files to Process dialog box opens. You should see a Stamp comment in the top-right corner of the document page. Double click on the Stamp icon to open the pop-up note window and observe the note contents as shown in Figure 13-16.

Cross-Reference

For more information on creating stamps and using pop-note windows, see Chapter 14.

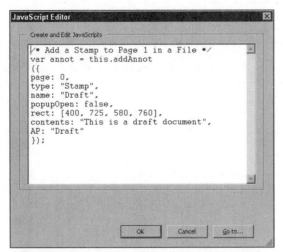

```
/* Add a Stamp to Page 1 in a File */
var annot = this.addAnnot
({
page: 0,
type: "Stamp",
name: "Draft",
popupOpen: false,
rect: [400, 725, 580, 760],
contents: "This is a draft document",
AP: "Draft"
});
```

Figure 13-15: Type the code in the JavaScript Editor dialog box.

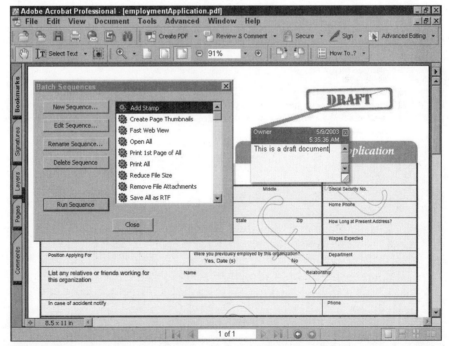

Figure 13-16: The Stamp comment is added to the first page of all documents processed with the Add Stamp routine created in the JavaScript Editor.

The preceding steps create a Stamp comment (Line 2) at the coordinates (Line 8)—note that the page size where the stamps are added is a standard US Letter 8.5 × 11 inches in portrait view. The note pop-up window is closed by default (Line 7), and the content of the note pop-up is *This is a draft document* (Line 9). You can change the position of the note by editing the coordinates in Line 8, change the contents in Line 9, or change the stamp type in Line 10. The code can be easily modified or you can copy and paste the code in the JavaScript Editor if you want to create other similar sequences.

Cross-Reference For more information on writing JavaScripts, see Chapter 26.

Summary

✦ File sizes can be reduced with the Reduce File Size menu command. If you're cropping image files in Acrobat, save the cropped image to an image format; then open the file in Acrobat to convert back to PDF.

✦ The PDF Optimizer is used to reduce file sizes and eliminate unnecessary data in PDF files. PDF Optimizer can often reduce file sizes more than when using the Reduce File Size command.

✦ Selecting options in the Clean Up tab in the PDF Optimizer other than the default options can interfere with the PDF functionality. Care must be exercised in selecting options to prevent potential problems.

✦ In some cases saving a PDF file to disk and redistilling with Acrobat Distiller can reduce file sizes. Redistillation can be used to stamp down data fields when form fields are no longer required.

✦ Batch sequences help you automate processing multiple PDF documents. From a standard set of sequence options you can create batch sequences for a limited number of actions. When custom options are needed, you can add JavaScripts for processing files with custom settings.

✦   ✦   ✦

PDF Interactivity

✦ ✦ ✦ ✦

✦ ✦ ✦ ✦

Review and Comment

Adobe Acrobat is the perfect tool for workgroup collaboration. With sophisticated tool sets and a number of menu options, Acrobat provides you the ability to comment, and markup PDF documents and share your annotations with users dynamically on Web sites or through file exchanges on servers or via e-mail. For example, you can mark up documents, send your comments to a group of colleagues, ask for return comments, and track the review history. Where PDF documents may be too large to efficiently exchange files in e-mails, you can export comments to smaller data files or summarize them and create new PDF documents from comment summaries that can be sent to members of your workgroup. You can compare documents for changes, for comment status, and for errors and omissions.

The review and comment tools and methods in Acrobat are extraordinary in number. Because Acrobat provides all these great tools doesn't necessarily mean you'll use all of them in your daily work activities. The best way to decide what tools work best for you and your colleagues is to review this chapter thoroughly and pick and choose the tools you favor and the features in review and markup that work best in your environment. In this chapter you learn how to use all the comment tools, exchange comments through email-based reviews, and compare documents for reviewing purposes.

All the tools and features discussed in this chapter are related to workflow environments. Regardless of what industry you work in, the many features related to review and comment and comparing documents can be applied to virtually all environments with two or more individuals collaborating on common projects.

This chapter deals exclusively with flattened PDF documents. Comments can be added to layered PDF documents. For a description of how Acrobat treats comments applied to layered PDFs, see Chapter 17.

Setting Up the Review and Comment Environment

You may be a user who adds comments infrequently with a few comment tools located in the Commenting toolbar, and you may not have much need for the Advanced Commenting tools. However to decide what tools work best in your workflow, you might want to add all the toolbars for review and markup to the Toolbar Well and look over all the tools in Acrobat Professional.

To set up the review and comment work environment, open the following tools:

✦ **Open Basic Commenting toolbar (A).** Two sets of commenting toolbars are in Acrobat, and require you to make separate selections to view both of them. To open the basic commenting tools, open a context menu on the Toolbar Well and choose Commenting.

✦ **Open Advanced toolbar (B).** Return to the context menu and choose Advanced Commenting.

✦ **Open Properties Bar (C).** You can easily access properties for all the commenting tools from the Properties toolbar. To show the Properties toolbar, open a context menu from the Toolbar Well and select Properties Bar.

✦ **Dock toolbars.** Open a context menu on the Toolbar Well and select Dock All Toolbars.

✦ **Expand Highlighting tools (D).** In the Commenting toolbar, select the pull-down menu beside the Highlighter tool and select Show Highlighting Toolbar. Move the toolbar to the Toolbar Well to dock it.

✦ **Expand Advanced Commenting tools.** On the Advanced Commenting toolbar, select the pull-down menu adjacent to the Rectangle tool and select Show Drawing Toolbar **(E).** Move to the Pencil tool and select Expand This Button **(F).** Adjacent to the Pencil tool is the Attach File Tool. Open the pull-down menu beside this tool and select Show Attach Toolbar **(G).** Move the toolbars to the Toolbar Well to dock them.

Note   The Cloud tool and the Arrow tool in the Drawing Toolbar are available only in Acrobat Professional. Acrobat Professional contains seven drawing tools while Acrobat Standard contains five drawing tools.

✦ **Open the Comments palette (H).** One more item used with commenting is the Comments palette in the Navigation Pane. Click on the palette tab to open the palette. Notice this palette opens in a horizontal view. Within the palette is the Commenting Palette Toolbar where you can select more tools for review and comment.

✦ **Hide Task Buttons.** If your monitor is small, you may want to toggle some of these tools on and off as you review one set of tools versus another in this chapter. You can acquire some more space in the Toolbar Well by hiding some Task Buttons. If you don't expect to use digital signatures, add security, or use any of the other Task Button, choose View ➪ Task Buttons and deselect any tools you care to hide. After hiding some Task Buttons and adding all the tools listed earlier, my Acrobat window appears as shown in Figure 14-1.

Notice that the tools are grouped together in logical collections. In a real-world scenario you might only use tools from a single group and not need to load all the tools in the Toolbar Well. If you work on a small monitor, you can see how expanding all the tools and the Comments palette can eat up a lot of screen real estate very quickly. If the view of your pages in the Document Pane is too small to comfortably annotate files, close the less frequently used tools to open up more space in the Document Pane.

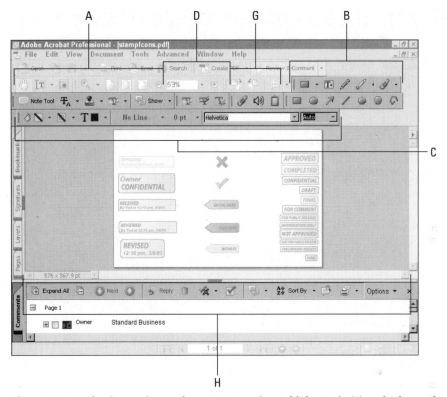

Figure 14-1: To begin a review and comment session, add the Basic (A) and Advanced commenting (B) toolbars to the Toolbar Well and dock them. Open the Properties Bar (C). Expand the Highlight tools (D), the Drawing tools (E), the Pencil Tool (F), and the Attach Tools (G) and dock them. Open the Comments palette (H) in the Navigation Pane. Hide any Task Buttons not commonly used and arrange toolbars according to your personal preference.

Setting Commenting Preferences

Acrobat provides an elaborate set of preference options that enable you to control comment views and behavior. As you draw comments on PDF pages you may see pop-up windows, connector lines across a page, changes in page views and a host of other strange behaviors that might confuse you. Before you begin a commenting session, you should familiarize yourself with the comment preferences and plan to return to the preference settings several times to completely understand how you control comment behavior in Acrobat.

Open the preference settings by pressing Ctrl/⌘+K or choosing Edit ➪ Preferences. In the left pane select Commenting. In the right pane you'll see a long list of preference settings as shown in Figure 14-2. Take a moment to review these settings before you begin a commenting session.

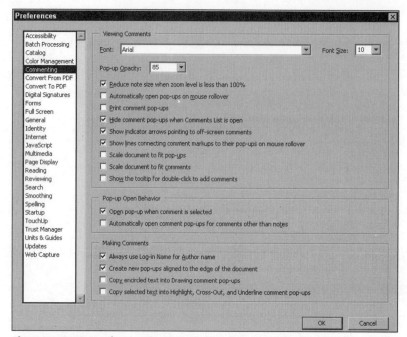

Figure 14-2: Open the Comment Preferences by pressing Ctrl/⌘+K or choosing Edit ➪ Preferences. When the Preferences dialog box opens, select Commenting in the left pane.

✦ **Font:** The comment tools are used to mark up text and create icons, symbols, and graphic objects on pages. Most of the comment tools have associated pop-up notes where you type remarks in a note window. By default the font used for the note text is Arial. To change the font, select another font from the pull-down menu. All fonts loaded in your system are available from the menu choices. The fonts you use are not embedded in the file. If you exchange PDFs containing comment notes with other users, the fonts default to another user's preference settings.

✦ **Font Size:** Font point sizes range from 4 points to 144 points. You can type a number between these values in the field box or select one from the preset point sizes from the pull-down menu.

✦ **Pop-up Opacity:** A pop-up note background color is white. At 100 percent opacity the note is opaque and hides underlying page data. You can change the opacity of pop-up notes for a transparent view so the background data can be seen when a pop-up note window is open. You adjust the level of transparency by typing a value in the field box or selecting one from the preset choices in the pull-down menu. The default is 85 percent.

✦ **Reduce note size when zoom level is less than 100%:** When a page view is reduced in the Navigation Pane, comment pop-up notes are sized proportionately to the zoom view. When zooming out to smaller views, pop-up note contents are difficult to read. If you want to fix the note size to a 100% view, disable the check box.

✦ **Automatically open pop-ups on mouse rollover:** Pop-up note windows can be opened or closed. Double-clicking on a collapsed pop-up note window opens the window. If you want to have a pop-up note window open automatically as the cursor is placed over a comment icon, enable this check box.

✦ **Print comment pop-ups:** Enabling this check box prints the pop-up note contents for all pop-up note windows regardless of whether they are opened or collapsed.

✦ **Hide comment pop-ups when Comments List is opened:** The Comments List is contained in the Comments palette. When you open the Comments palette, the list shows expanded comment notes with the content displayed in the palette window. To hide the pop-ups in the Document Pane when the Comments palette is opened, enable the check box. If you set this item as a default, you can expand comments in the Comments palette by clicking on icons to see content of the pop-ups.

✦ **Show indicator arrows pointing to off-screen comments:** Comment icons and pop-up notes are two separate elements. They can be individually located in different places in the Document Pane, either on a page or outside the page as shown in Figure 14-3. When you scroll through a document, arrows indicate that off-screen comments are present when the checkbox is enabled.

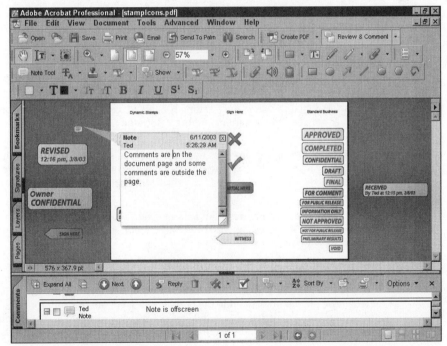

Figure 14-3: When the cursor moves over a comment icon, the cursor changes to a selection arrowhead indicating an off-screen comment.

✦ **Show lines connecting comment markups to their pop-ups on mouse rollover:** When you roll the mouse pointer over a comment markup (such as highlighting or a note icon), the shaded connector line between the comment and the open pop-up window appears (See Figure 14-4).

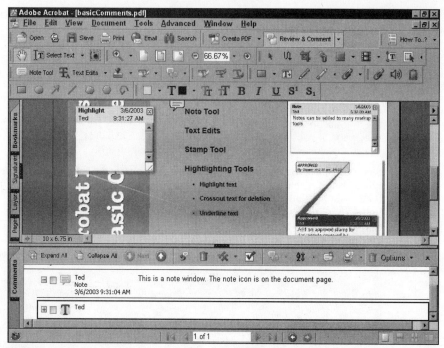

Figure 14-4: When the preference setting is enabled, connector lines are displayed on a mouseover between the comment and the associated note window.

✦ **Scale document to fit pop-ups:** The document page is scaled to the size of the open pop-up notes. If you have several open pop-up notes that appear off the page, the view in the Document Pane is scaled to fit the page and open pop-up note windows including pop-up notes outside the page boundaries.

✦ **Scale document to fit comments:** Adjusts the page zoom so that comments outside the page boundaries fit within the current view. This option applies to all comments except pop-up note windows.

✦ **Show the tooltip for double-click to add comments:** If a comment pop-up note contains a message, the Tool Tip displays the message when the cursor is placed over a comment icon while a pop-up note window is collapsed. If no note message is contained in the pop-up note, moving the cursor over a comment icon produces no message and no Tool Tip. If you enable this check box when the pop-up note window is blank, a Tool Tip is displayed with the message: *Double-click to add comments.*

✦ **Open pop-up when comment is selected:** You open pop-up note windows by double-clicking on a comment icon. For a single click operation to open the note window, check this box.

✦ Automatically open comment pop-ups for comments other than notes: As you create comments with drawing tools, the Text Box tool, or Pencil tool, the pop-up note windows are collapsed by default. If you want a pop-up note window opened and ready to accept type when creating comments with these tools, check the box.

✦ **Always use Log-in Name for Author name:** Another set of preferences appears when you click on Identity in the left pane. The Login Name specified in the Identity preferences is used for the author name on all comments when this check box is enabled. If you are a single user on a workstation, setting the Identity preferences and enabling this check box saves you time creating comments when you want to add your name as the author name.

✦ **Create new pop-ups aligned to the edge of the document.** By default the top-left corner of a pop-up note window is aligned to the top-left corner of the comment icon. If you enable this check box, no matter where you create the note icon, the pop-up notes are aligned to the right edge of the document.

✦ **Copy encircled text into Drawing comment pop-ups.** When proofreading a document and using the Text Edit tools you might strike through text, highlight text, or mark it for replacement or you may use drawing tools to encircle passages of text. When you select the text to be edited or encircle text with a drawing tool, the text selection is automatically added to the note pop-up window when this option is selected. You might use this option to show the author of the PDF document how the old text appears and follow up with your recommendations to change the text. In essence, the PDF author can see a before/after comparison.

✦ **Copy selected text into Highlight, Cross-Out, and Underline comment pop-ups:** This enables the text selected with tools in the Highlighting toolbar to automatically appear in the pop-up note window.

As you can see, there are many different preference settings. How you want to view comments and the methods used for review and comment is influenced by the options you set in the Commenting preferences. Take some time to play with these settings as you use the tools discussed in this chapter.

Using Commenting Tools

Users of either Acrobat Professional or Acrobat Standard can access the basic Commenting tools. Acrobat refers to these tools simply as Commenting tools; however, I make the reference to basic Commenting tools to distinguish these tools from the Advanced Commenting tools covered later in this chapter.

The basic Commenting tools are intended for use by anyone reviewing and marking up documents. Much like you might use a highlighter on paper documents, the commenting tools enable you to electronically mark up and comment PDF documents. A variety of tools with different icon symbols offer you an extensive library of tools that can help you facilitate a review process.

Most comment tools, whether they are among the basic or advanced group, have a symbol or icon that appears where the comment is created. Most comment tools also have a note pop-up window where you add text to clarify a meaning associated with the mark you add to a document. These pop-up note windows have identical attributes. How you manage note pop-ups and change the properties works the same regardless of the comment mark you create. I first explain how to use the Note tool in this section. All the features described next for the Note tool are the same as when handling note pop-up windows for all the comment tools that accommodate note pop-ups.

Note tool

The Note tool is the most common commenting tool used in Acrobat. To create a comment note, select the Note tool in the Commenting toolbar and drag open a note window. When you release the mouse button, the note pop-up aligns to the top-left corner of the note icon.

Alternately, you can click without dragging. When you release the mouse button, a pop-up note window is created adjacent to the note icon at a fixed size according to your monitor resolution. The higher you set your monitor resolution the smaller the pop-up note window appears. On an 800×600 display, the window size defaults to 360×266 pixels. In Figure 14-5, I drew a comment note with the Note tool on the left side of the page. On the right side of the page, I clicked the Note tool. Notice the left note is aligned with the note icon where the note on the right side of the page appears adjacent to the note icon.

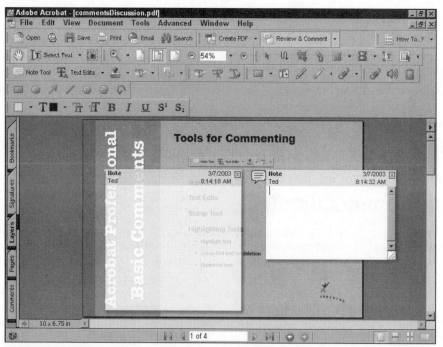

Figure 14-5: When clicking and dragging the Note tool, the pop-up note aligns to the top-left corner of the note icon. When clicking with the Note tool, a pop-up window is created at a fixed size and the pop-up note is aligned beside the note icon.

To add text to the pop-up note, begin typing. Acrobat places an I-beam cursor inside the pop-up note window immediately after creating the note. For font selection and font sizing, you need to address the Comment preference settings discussed earlier in this chapter.

Managing notes

The color of a note pop-up and the note icon is yellow by default. At the top of the note pop-up the title bar is colored yellow with the area where the contents are added in white. The title bar contains information supplied by Acrobat that includes the subject of the note, the author, and the date and time the note is created. You can move a note pop-up independently of the note icon by clicking and dragging the title bar.

The Subject of a note by default is titled *Note*. The default Author name is derived from either your computer log-on name or your Identity depending on how your preferences are established. For information on how to change the Subject and Author in the title bar, see "Note tool properties" later in this chapter.

You delete note pop-up windows and note icons either by selecting the note icon and pressing the Delete/Backspace or Del key on your keyboard or through a context menu selection. If you use a keystroke to delete a note, you must be certain to select the icon; then press the Delete/Backspace or Del key. Selecting the title bar in a note pop-up won't delete the note when using the same keys.

To resize a note pop-up window grab the lower-right corner of the window and drag in or out to resize smaller or larger, respectively. Note pop-ups containing more text that can be viewed in the current window size use elevator bars so you can scroll the window much like you would use when viewing pages in the Document Pane. Only vertical elevator bars are shown in the pop-up windows. As you type text in the window, text wraps to the horizontal width, thereby eliminating a need for horizontal scroll bars. As you size a note pop-up window horizontally, the text rewraps to conform to the horizontal width.

You open context menus from either the note icon or the note pop-up window. When opening a context menu from the note pop-up window, you have two choices: open the context menu from the title bar or open the context menu from inside the note window (below the title bar). Depending on where you open the context menu, the menu selections are different. Opening a context menu from the title bar or from the note icon shows identical menu options.

In Figure 14-6, I opened a context menu from the title bar on a pop-up note window. The menu options are the same as if I had opened the context menu from the note icon. In Figure 14-7, I opened the context menu from inside the note pop-up window. In both menus you can select Delete Comment to remove the note pop-up menu and the note icon.

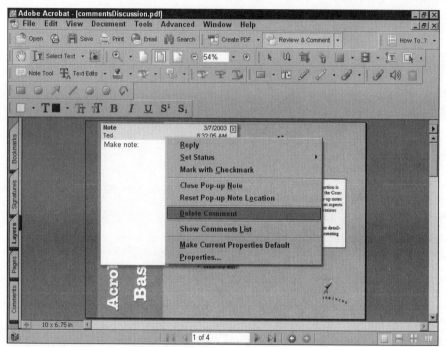

Figure 14-6: This context menu is opened from the note pop-up window title bar. From the menu options select Delete Comment to remove the note icon and the note pop-up menu.

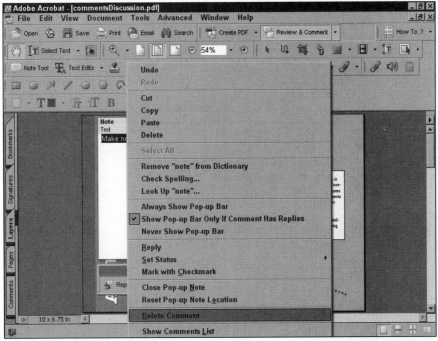

Figure 14-7: When you open a context menu from the note pop-up window below the title bar, menu options change. However, you can still delete a comment by selecting the same menu command as the context menu shown in the preceding figure.

The context menus are very similar and most commands existing in the smaller menu are the same as those found in the larger menu. The difference lies in the two menu selections at the bottom of the short menu. In Figure 14-6, notice the last two menu options. These commands exist for handling note properties. I discuss note properties a little later in this chapter.

In Figure 14-7 you see a long list of menu commands. Let's take a look at these commands; the same commands found in the context menu shown in Figure 14-6 operate the same way.

✦ **Undo:** When you type text in the pop-up menu and delete it, you can select the Undo command to regain your text. Deleting a comment note can also be undone. However, because deleting a comment note eliminates an opportunity to open a context menu from the note pop-up window, you need to select Edit ➪ Undo. If text was added to a pop-up note window and you delete the note, selecting Edit Undo returns the note and the text in the note pop-up window.

✦ **Redo:** If you type a block of text and select Undo, you can later select Redo and bring the text back.

✦ **Cut/Copy/Paste:** These items work as you might assume from using any text editor or word processor. The commands relate to typing text in the note pop-up window. You can also highlight text and use key modifiers (Ctrl/⌘+C for Copy; Ctrl/⌘+X for Cut; Ctrl/⌘+V for Paste).

✦ **Delete:** This item also relates to text typed in the note pop-up window. Don't confuse the Delete item here with Delete Comment. When you select Delete, the deletion only affects the contents of the note comment.

✦ **Select All:** Selects all the text typed in a note comment pop-up window. You can alternately use the key modifiers Ctrl/⌘+A.

✦ **Remove "..." from Dictionary:** This menu item is active only when you have a word selected in the note pop-up window. It's a nifty little feature in Acrobat 6.0. Because Acrobat automatically spell-checks text you type in the comment note pop-up window by matching your words to those found in its dictionary, words not found by Acrobat as a match in its dictionary are underlined in red with a wavy line like you might see in programs like Microsoft Word. If you want to have Acrobat flag you whenever you type a specific word, you can remove that word from the dictionary. Then Acrobat displays the word with a red underline each time it's used.

When would you use this feature? Assume for a moment that you want to use a generic reference to users as opposed to a masculine or feminine reference. Highlight the word *he* or *she* and open a context menu from the note pop-up window. Select Remove "*he*" from Dictionary. Each time you type the word *he*, Acrobat underlines the word because it can't find a match in the dictionary. When you review your notes, you might substitute *s/he* for the word *he*.

✦ **Check Spelling:** When you select Check Spelling in the note pop-up menu the Check Spelling dialog box opens, as shown in Figure 14-8. When the dialog box opens, click on the Start button and Acrobat checks the spelling for all the text typed in the note pop-up. When a word is found where Acrobat thinks the spelling is incorrect, the word is highlighted and a list of suggestions that closely match the spelling are shown in the lower window. Select a word where the spelling is correct and click the Change button.

✦ **Look Up Definition:** The default menu command is *Look Up Definition*. When a word is selected, the menu command changes to Look Up *selected word*. For example, if you select a word like *reply*, the menu command changes to Look Up "reply." Select the menu command and your Web browser launches and the Dictionary.com Web site opens in your Web browser where the word is searched and a definition is displayed on the Web page.

Cross-Reference For more information on looking up a definition and the Dictionary.com Web site, see Chapter 4.

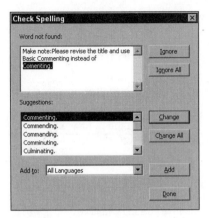

Figure 14-8: Select Check Spelling from a context menu and the Check Spelling dialog box opens. Click Start and Acrobat checks the spelling for the note pop-up contents. Suggestions are listed in the dialog box that you can choose from to replace the misspelled word(s).

✦ **Always Show Pop-up Bar:** A pop-up bar is only available when you share and review comments. The pop-up bar appears below a reply and helps you follow a thread in which others are participating in a review. If you want pop-up bars to always open when reviewing comments, select the menu command.

✦ **Show Pop-Up Bar Only If Comment Has Replies:** This is used under the same criteria as the preceding option. If you want the pop-up bar hidden unless the comment has a reply, select the menu command.

✦ **Never Show Pop-Up Bar:** Select the menu command to hide the pop-up bar whether the comment has a reply or not.

Cross-Reference The previous three menu commands and the next two commands relate to setting up a review and markup session where comments are exchanged between the PDF author and others in a collaborative work group. For reviewing and tracking comments, see the section in this chapter related to Creating an Email Review.

✦ **Reply:** When participating in a review, select the Reply command to reply to comments made from other users. A new window opens in which you type a reply message. From the pop-up bar you can review a thread and click the Reply button to send your comments to others via e-mail, to a network server, or to a Web-hosted server.

✦ **Set Status:** You as a PDF author may share a document for review with others. As comments are collected you may decide to determine a status for comments among your workgroup. You may want to mark a comment as *Accepted, Rejected, or Cancelled,* or mark a comment thread as *Completed.* These options are selected from the submenu that appears when you select the Set Status command. By default, a status is set to *None* when you begin a session.

✦ **Mark with Checkmark:** Whereas the Set Status items are communicated to others, a check mark you add to a comment is for your own purposes. You can mark a comment as checked to denote any comments that need attention, or that are completed and require no further annotation. Check marks are visible in the Comments palette and can be toggled on or off in the palette as well as the context menu. Check marks can be added to comments with or without your participation in a review session. Check marks can be sorted to list together all check marked comments and comments without checkmarks.

✦ **Delete Comment:** Deletes the comment pop-up note and the note icon.

✦ **Show Comments List:** Selecting this item opens the Comments palette. Any comments in the open document are expanded in a list view in the Comments palette. When the Comments palette is open, this open toggles to Hide Comments List.

Note tool properties

Each comment created from either the basic or advanced tools has properties that you can change in a properties dialog box. Properties changes are generally applied to note pop-up windows and icon shapes for a particular tool. In addition, a variety of properties are specific to different tools that offer you many options for viewing and displaying comments and tracking the history of the comments made on a document.

With respect to note pop-ups and those properties assigned to the Note tool, you have choices for changing the default color, opacity, author name, and a few other options. Keep in mind that not all property changes are contained in the properties dialog box. Attributes such as font selection and point sizes are globally applied to note pop-ups in the Comment Preferences dialog box discussed earlier in this chapter.

The properties dialog box is opened from a context menu. Be certain to place the cursor on a pop-up note title bar or the note icon before opening a context menu. Refer to the menu shown in Figure 14-6 to see the menu choices for handling pop-up note properties. Select Properties from the menu choices and the Note Properties dialog box shown in Figure 14-9 opens.

Note When you create a comment with any of the Comment tools, the Hand tool is automatically selected when you release the mouse button. You can select a comment mark/icon or pop-up note with the Hand tool or the Select Object tool. Either tool can be used to open a context menu where you can select Properties from the menu options. However, other menu items vary between the two context menus. For information regarding menu options from context menus opened with the Select Object tool, see the discussion on Drawing tools later in this chapter.

The Note Properties dialog box contains three tabs. Select a tab and make choices for the items contained in the dialog box. For pop-up note properties the items you can change include the following:

✦ **Appearance:** Options in the Appearance tab relate to the note icon appearances and the pop-up note window appearance.

- **Icon:** From the scrollable list select an item that changes the Note icon appearance. Selections you make in this list are dynamic and change the appearance of the icon in the Document Pane as you click on a name in the list. If you move the Note Properties dialog box out of the view of the note icon, you can see the appearance changes as you make selections in the list. Fifteen different icons are available to choose from as shown in Figure 14-10.

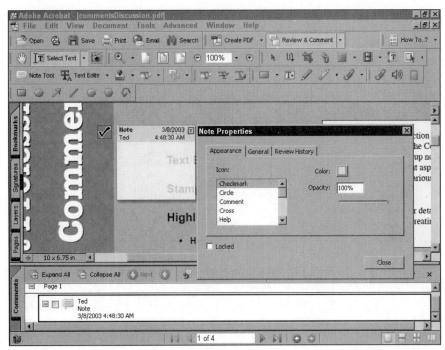

Figure 14-9: Open a context menu from a pop-up note title bar and select Properties.

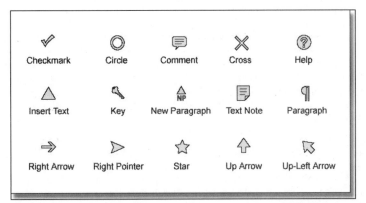

Figure 14-10: You select icon shapes from the Icon list in the Appearance tab in the Note Properties dialog box. You can choose from 15 different shapes.

- **Color:** Click on the color swatch to open the pop-up color palette shown in Figure 14-11. Preset colors are selected from the swatches in the palette. You add custom colors by selecting the Other Color item in the palette where the system color palette opens. In the system color palette, make color choices and the new custom color is applied to the note.

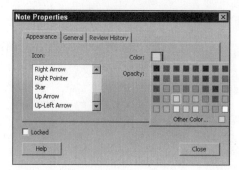

Figure 14-11: Click on the color swatch to select from preset colors or select Other Color to open the system color palette where custom colors are selected.

Changing color in the Appearance properties affects both the color of the note icon and the pop-up note title bar. If you mark up and review documents in workgroups, different colors assigned to different participants can help you ascertain at a glance which participant made a given comment.

- **Opacity:** Global opacity settings are applied in the Comment Preferences dialog box. You can override the default opacity setting in the Appearance properties for any given note pop-up window.

- **Locked:** Click on the Locked check box to lock a note. When notes are locked, the position of the note icon is fixed to the Document Pane and cannot be moved when you leave the Note Properties dialog box. All other options in the Note Properties dialog box are grayed out, preventing you from making any further attribute changes. If you Lock a note, you can move the pop-up window and resize it. The note contents however, are locked and no changes to the text in the pop-up note window can be made. If you want to make changes to the properties or the pop-up note contents, return to the Note Properties dialog box and uncheck the Locked check box.

✦ **General:** Click on the General tab to make changes for items appearing in the note pop-up title bar. Two editable fields are available as shown in Figure 14-12. As you edit the fields for Author and Subject, the changes you make in the General preferences are dynamic and reflected in the Document Pane when you edit a field and tab to the next field. You can see the changes you make here before leaving the Note Properties dialog box.

- **Author:** The Author name is supplied by default according to how you set your Comment preferences. If you use the Identity preferences, the Author name is supplied from the information added in the Identity preferences (see "Setting Commenting Preferences" earlier in this chapter). If you don't use Identity for the Author title, the name is derived from your computer log-on name. You might see names like Owner, Administrator, or a specific name you used in setting up your operating system.

If you want to change the Author name and override the preferences, select the General tab and edit the Author name. The name edited in the General preferences is applied to the selected note. All other notes are left undisturbed.

- **Subject:** By default, the Subject of a note is titled *Note* appearing in the top-left corner of the pop-up note title bar. You can change the subject in the General properties by typing text in the Subject line. You can add long text descriptions for the Subject; however, the text remains on a single line in the pop-up note properties dialog box. Text won't scroll to a second line. The amount of text shown for the Subject field relates to the horizontal width of the note window. As you expand the width, more text is visible in the title bar if you add a long Subject name. As you size down the width, text is clipped to accommodate the note size.

- **Modified:** This item is informational and supplied automatically by Acrobat from your system clock. The field is not editable. The readout displays the date and time the note was modified.

✦ **Review History:** The Review History lists all comment and status changes in a scrollable list. The list is informational and not editable.

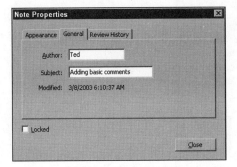

Figure 14-12: Make changes to the Author name and the pop-up note Subject in the General preferences.

Cross-Reference

For more information on review history, see the section later in this chapter called "Creating an Email Review."

After making changes in the Note Properties dialog box, click on the Close button to apply the changes. Clicking on the close box or pressing the Esc key also applies the changes you make in the Note properties dialog box.

Tip

The Properties dialog boxes for all Comment tools are dynamic and enable you to work in the Document Pane or the dialog box when the dialog is open. Make adjustments to properties and move the dialog box out of the way of your view of an object you edit. The updates are made when you tab out of fields in the dialog box. You have complete access to menu commands and other tools while the Properties dialog box remains open.

Using the Properties Bar

If you set up your work environment to view the Properties Bar while working in a review session, you can address several properties options from the Properties toolbar. Note color, icon type, and fixed opacity changes in 20% increments are accessible without opening the Properties dialog box.

As shown in Figure 14-13, from a pull-down menu on the Properties Bar, you can select the different note icons when the Note tool is selected. Clicking on the color swatch opens the same color selection pop-up window as it does in the Properties dialog box. The checkerboard to the right of the icon menu is the opacity selection. Click on the down arrow and preset opacity choices are listed in a menu.

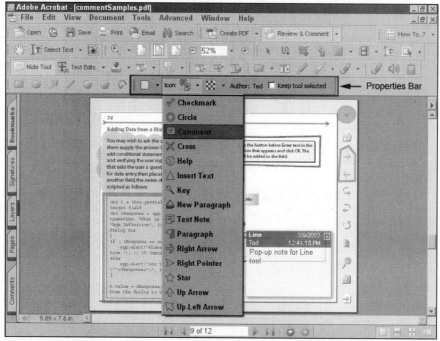

Figure 14-13: Some properties options can be changed in the Properties Bar. To open the toolbar, open a context menu on the Toolbar Well and select Properties Bar.

Notice the Author name appears in the Properties Bar; however, the name is not editable and you need to open the Properties dialog box to make an author name change. The last item in the Properties Bar is a check box. Click this box if you want to keep the Note tool selected. Disabling the check box causes the Hand tool to be selected each time a note is created. When you select a different comment tool from either the basic Commenting toolbar or the Advanced Commenting toolbar, the Properties Bar changes to reflect choices available for the selected tool.

Tip   Often you see a *More* button on the Properties Bar. Clicking on More opens the Properties dialog box.

Adding a note to a page

You can add notes to a page either inside a page in the Document Pane or outside the page boundary. Use the Note tool to add notes or add a note while browsing pages with the Hand tool selected. Open a context menu with the Hand tool and the menu options include Add Note as shown in Figure 14-14.

Add Note
Add Bookmark
▶ Next Page
◀ Previous Page
Select All
Deselect All
🖨 Print...
🔍 Search
Show How To Window   F4

Figure 14-14: Open a context menu with the Hand tool and select Add Note from the menu options. The note is added at the cursor position.

The new note is created at the position where the context menu is opened. You can use the Hand tool to browse pages by selecting the Next Page and Previous Page context menu commands and add a note when you want to comment on a page without changing tools.

You also can add notes to pages with a menu command. Choose Document ➪ Add a Comment. The note is added in the center of a document page regardless of the view in the Document Pane. All attributes for notes are changed, and these notes are also assigned in the Note Properties.

Tip

If you're proofreading a document and you think terms might be expressed better using different words and you want to find word definitions or access a thesaurus, open a context menu with the Hand tool and select Add Note. Type a word in the note pop-up window and highlight the word. Open a context menu from the highlighted word and select LookUp "...". The Dictionary.com Web site opens in your Web browser, with the word definition on the open Web page.

Text Edits

Adjacent to the Note tool in the basic Comments toolbar is an item labeled Text Edits. Text Edits in and of itself is not a tool. The tools are available from menu selections made from the pull-down menu shown in Figure 14-15. These tools are used for marking up documents when participating in a review. The different tools are similar to the way you might mark up a document with pen and paper as you review it for accuracy, opinions, and corrections. One of the advantages of using Acrobat for these kinds of markups is that you have pop-up note windows where you can amplify your reasons for marking a word, phrase, or body of text.

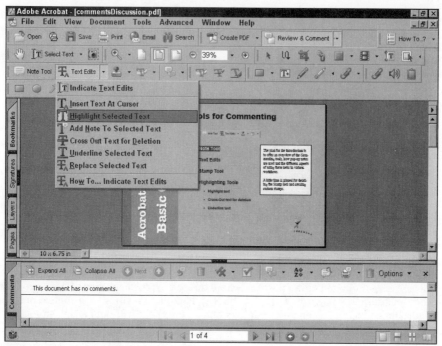

Figure 14-15: Select the Text Edit tools from a pull-down menu adjacent to the Text Edits label.

When you open the pull-down menu, be certain to select the down-pointing arrow to open the menu. Selecting the label *Text Edits* opens the How To Pane with a help section loaded in the pane for editing text. Be certain to keep in mind that Text Edits represents a menu category and not a tool. When you click on the down arrow to open the menu, select from one of the following to access a tool:

Indicate Text Edits: You'll notice the Indicate Text Edits tool looks like the Select Text tool. In actuality, Acrobat selects the Select Text tool when you make this menu choice. The procedure for adding any text edit is to first select this menu command or select the Select Text tool. You move the cursor to the document page and either click or click and drag through a block of text. Once the cursor appears inside a text block or text is selected, you then address one of the other menu commands to mark the text for commenting.

Note   All the tools below the Indicate Text Edit tools are grayed out unless you either select this menu command or select the Select Text tool and click or click and drag in a text block. Selecting either option without a cursor insertion on the document page or without high-lighting text does not enable any of the Text Edit tools.

Insert Text At Cursor: Select the menu command and move the cursor to the document page. The cursor appearance changes to an I-beam, informing you that text can be selected. Rather than selecting text, most often you'll find clicking the cursor at a specific location to be the method used with this tool. The intent is to suggest to a reviewer that text needs to be inserted at the cursor position. When you click on a document page, a caret is marked on the page at the insertion location and a note pop-up window opens. Type the text to be inserted in the note pop-up.

Highlight Selected Text: This tool works like the Highlight tool and similar to a yellow highlighter you might use on paper documents. Select the Highlight tool and drag across a block of text. The text is highlighted and a note pop-up window enables you to add comments.

Add Note to Selected Text: Select a word, a paragraph or a body of text. When you release the mouse button a note pop-up window opens in which you add a comment. Selecting the text does not include the selected text in the pop-up note.

Cross Out Text for Deletion: Select text and the text mark appears as a strikethrough. The symbol is used to mark text that needs to be deleted. A note pop-up window opens where you can add comments.

Underline Selected Text: Use this tool to underline the selected text. A note pop-up window opens where you can add comments.

Replace Selected Text: Use this tool to mark text for replacement. The line appears similar to the Cross Out Text for Deletion mark, but the caret at the end of the mark distinguishes this tool from the aforementioned one. A note pop-up window opens where you can add comments. The note contents do not include the text marked for replacement.

How To... Indicate Text Edits: The How To Pane opens with the Text Edits help page in view.

Figure 14-16 shows a sample of the different annotations made with the Text Edit tools. A single note pop-up window is open while the remaining note pop-ups are collapsed. On the right side of the Document Pane, the How To Pane shows the help page for Text Edits and at the bottom of the Document Pane the Comments palette is opened in the Navigation Pane.

Cross-Reference For more information on the Comments palette, see "Using the Comments Palette" later in this chapter.

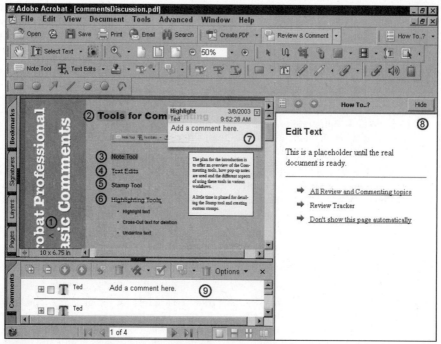

Figure 14-16: Text Edits are added to a document. The edits include the following — 1: Insert Text At Cursor; 2: Highlight Selected Text; 3: Add Note To Selected Text; 4: Cross Out Selected Text; 5: Underline Selected Text; 6: Replace Selected Text (notice the caret on the right side of the line); 7: Pop-up Note Window for Highlight Selected Text; 8: How To Pane with Text Edit help page; 9: Comments palette open.

Text Edits from a context menu

The Commenting toolbar doesn't offer you options for pulling individual tools out of the tool-bar, and the Text Edits tools don't offer you an expanded view of the tools for easy access in the toolbar. In order to select a tool, you need to open the pull-down menu and make menu selections. If you want to speed up a markup session, you might find using a context menu a better solution for accessing tools. Open the Text Edits pull-down menu and select Indicate Text Edits. As you move to text you want to mark, drag the cursor to highlight text to be annotated. When text is selected, open a context menu and options for text edits are available as menu choices as shown in Figure 14-17.

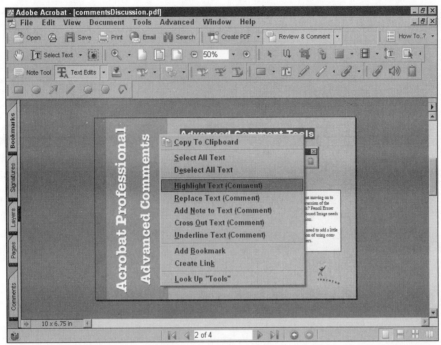

Figure 14-17: Select Indicate Text Edits in the Text Edits pull-down menu and drag the cursor through a block of text. Open a context menu and select a text edits command from the menu choices.

Notice that the item for Insert Text At Cursor is not among the menu selections. In order to open a context menu with choices for text edits, you need to select at least one character in a text block. Clicking the cursor without selecting text won't produce the same context menu choices.

Text Edits via the Highlighting tools

Another means of quickly accessing Text Edits tools is through the use of the Highlighting toolbar. The Highlight tool is the last tool in the basic Commenting toolbar and the tools are used like the same tools you can access in the Text Edits menu commands. If your work is limited to highlighting text, marking text for deletion, or underlining text, you can undock the toolbar and make it accessible as a floating toolbar. The means for creating the markups are similar to using the Text Edits menu commands; however, as tools they don't require you to select a text tool before adding the comment. Select any one of the three tools and drag across text. When you release the mouse button, the text is marked and a pop-up note window opens where you add comments.

Differences between Text Edit and Highlighting Tools

You may wonder why Acrobat offers you two toolbars with what appears to be identical tools performing the same functions. Although the appearances of the markups you make on PDF documents are the same for the Highlighting tools as the respective Text Edit tools, they are intended for different purposes.

When you make edits with the Text Edit tools, you can export comments directly to Microsoft Word (Windows XP and Word 2002 only). If you export the Text Edit comments to Word and accept changes, Word treats the comments as though you had created them in Word. For example, marking text for deletion and accepting changes deletes the marked text.

Although you can use the Text Edit tools to markup PDFs not intended for export to Word, the intent for using the tools is when working between Word and Acrobat. If you use either the Text Edit tools or the Highlighting tools on PDFs for comments designed for use in Acrobat, there is no difference between the markups.

Note that exporting comments to Word documents from comments made with the Text Edit tools is only available in Acrobat Professional.

Using the Stamp tool

The Stamp tool is part of the basic Commenting tools, but it differs greatly from the other tools found in the Commenting toolbar. Rather than mark data on a PDF page and add notes to the marks, Stamps enable you to apply icons of your own choosing to express statements about a document's status or add custom icons and symbols for communicating messages. Stamps offer you a wide range of flexibility for marking documents similar to analog stamps you might use for stamping approvals, drafts, confidentiality, and so on. You can use one of a number of different icons supplied by Acrobat when you install the program, or you can create your own custom icons tailored to your workflow or company needs.

Whether you use a preset stamp provided by Acrobat or create a custom stamp, each stamp has an associated note pop-up window where you add comments. You select stamps from menu options in the Stamp pull-down menu where stamps are organized by categories. Add a stamp to a page by clicking the Stamp tool after selecting a stamp from a category; or you can click and drag the Stamp tool to size the icon. After creating a Stamp, you access Stamp Properties the same as when using the Note comments.

Selecting stamps

Using a stamp begins with selecting from among many different stamp images found in submenus from the Stamp tool pull-down menu. Click the down arrow and the first three menu commands list categories for stamps installed with Acrobat. Selecting one of these three menu items opens a submenu where specific stamps are selected from the respective category as shown in Figure 14-18.

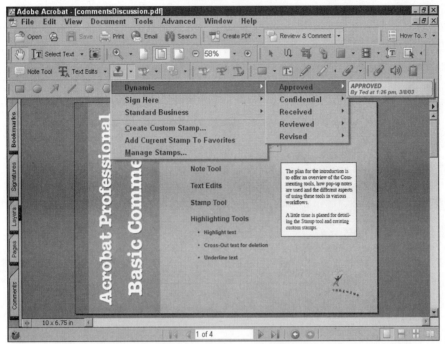

Figure 14-18: Select the pull-down menu from the Stamp tool and select a Stamp category. Select a subcategory and slide the mouse over to the Stamp name. Release the mouse button and the selection becomes the new default stamp.

Adding a stamp to a page

The stamp name you select in the menu becomes the new default stamp. When you click the Stamp tool or click and drag open a rectangle with the Stamp tool, the default stamp is added to the document page. Stamps are created by default with the pop-up note window collapsed unless you enable the Comment preferences for *Automatically open comment pop-ups for comments other than notes*. To open the pop-up note window, double-click the mouse button on the stamp image. The pop-up note opens and appears the same as other pop-up note windows for other Comment tools.

If you want to resize a stamp after creating it on a page, select the Hand tool and click on the stamp icon to select it. Move the cursor to a corner handle, shown in Figure 14-19, and drag in or out to resize the stamp.

Note   Stamps are always proportionately sized when dragging any one of the corner handles. You don't need to drag handles with a modifier key to proportionately size the image.

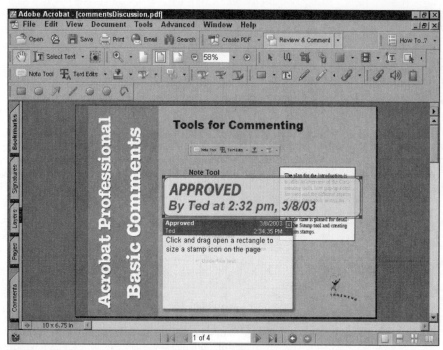

Figure 14-19: To resize a stamp, select the Hand tool and click on the stamp icon. Drag a corner handle on the selection marquee and drag in or out to size the icon.

Acrobat offers you an assortment of stamps you can select from the category submenus in the Stamp tool pull-down menu. These stamps are created for general office uses and you'll find many common stamp types among the sets. The three categories of stamps and their respective types and icons are shown in Figure 14-20.

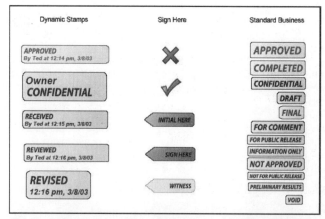

Figure 14-20: Choose stamps from three categories. The stamps installed with Acrobat are general office stamps used in many traditional workflows.

You should think of these stamps as a starter set and use them for some traditional office markups when the need arises. The real power of stamps, however, is when creating custom stamps where you can use virtually any illustration or photo image.

Stamp properties

You change stamp properties in the Stamp Properties dialog box. You have the same options in the Stamp Properties as those found in the Note Properties dialog box with one exception. In the Note Properties dialog box you make choices for the icon appearance from a list in the dialog box. Because stamps have appearances determined before you create the stamp, no options are available for changing properties.

If you want to change the appearance of a stamp, you need to delete the stamp and create a new stamp after selecting the category and stamp name from the category submenu. You delete stamps by opening a context menu and selecting Delete, or selecting the stamp icon and pressing the Backspace/Delete or Del key.

You make stamp icons opacity adjustments in the Stamp Properties dialog box and you can change opacity for stamps created from either vector art or raster art. Open the Stamp Properties dialog box and move the slider below the Opacity field box or edit the field box to change the level of opacity.

Creating custom stamps

Users of earlier versions of Acrobat will appreciate the ease in which custom stamps are created in Acrobat 6.0. Rather than creating PDF documents with page templates and setting up Document Properties for categories, you can now add stamps to categories you set up in Acrobat without bothering to open secondary documents and without a need to save your stamp files to a specific folder inside the Acrobat folder. The downside for creating custom stamps in Acrobat is you have to individually create each stamp. Acrobat 6.0 does not provide a means for converting a multi-page PDF to a stamp library if the document was not originally created as a file to be used as custom stamps.

You add custom stamps from the Stamp tool pull-down menu. Click the down arrow on the menu and select Create Custom Stamp or select Tools ➪ Commenting ➪ Stamp Tool ➪ Create Custom Stamp. The Custom Stamp dialog box opens as shown in Figure 14-21.

When you first create a custom stamp in Acrobat 6.0, the Create Stamp dialog box is empty. Although a pull-down menu is present, no options are available on your first visit to the dialog box. As you create new stamp libraries, the category names are added to the pull-down menu. Your first task in this menu is to add a name for a new category; then click on the Select button to open the Select dialog box as shown in Figure 14-22.

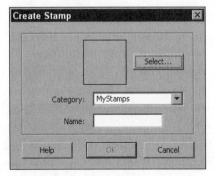

Figure 14-21: Select Create Custom Stamp from the Stamp tool pull-down menu. In the Create Stamp dialog box, type a name for a new category.

Figure 14-22: The next dialog box used for creating custom stamps is the Select dialog box. From here you click on the Browse button to locate a file to be used as your stamp.

Again, this dialog box is empty. Another step is required to identify the file to be used for your stamp. Click on the Browse button and the Open dialog box appears. The Open dialog box accessed from the Open command or the Create PDF From File command is a similar dialog box used for opening/converting PDF documents. Navigate your hard drive and find the file you want to use. Acrobat permits importing file types from the following file formats:

✦ **PDF:** All PDF documents can be used for Stamp icons; however, only single pages can be imported as a stamp. PDFs containing transparency are supported. Any PDF document imported as a custom stamp can have opacity applied in the Stamp Properties dialog box.

✦ **AI (Adobe Illustrator native files):** Acrobat supports native .ai files. Illustrator art can be layered and can have transparent elements. Importing Illustrator images with transparency displays transparent effects in Acrobat. All vector art including transparent objects can have transparency applied in Acrobat by making opacity adjustments in the Stamp Properties dialog box. Illustrator .ai files are not listed as a file type in the Open dialog box. In order to recognize Illustrator native files, type *.* in the File name field box in the Open dialog box.

✦ **BMP (Bitmap):** You can import 1-bit line art to 24-bit color images saved as BMP as a custom stamp. BMP files can be adjusted for opacity in the Stamp Properties dialog box.

✦ **EPS:** You can select an EPS file in the Select dialog box and subsequently the Open dialog box. When you open an EPS file, Acrobat Distiller is launched and the file is converted to PDF. The resultant PDF is then imported as a stamp and supports the same attributes as PDF listed earlier in this list.

✦ **GIF:** GIF files, including transparent GIFs, are supported. GIF files can be adjusted for opacity in the Stamp Properties dialog box.

✦ **JPEG/JPEG2000:** JPEG files are supported with the same options as GIFs and BMP files mentioned earlier.

✦ **PCX:** PCX files are supported. The file attributes are the same as those found with BMP and GIF mentioned earlier.

✦ **PICT (Macintosh only):** PICT (Picture Format) files from Mac OS can be imported. The attributes are the same as those applied to BMP and GIF images.

✦ **PNG:** PNG files and files saved as interlaced PNG are supported. Interlacing is not applied to the image once imported in Acrobat. The file attributes are the same as those found with BMP and GIF mentioned earlier.

Note Although several file formats are supported for importing layered files, the layers are flattened when imported as custom stamps. Transparency is preserved with these file types, but you can't have stamps applied to different layers in Acrobat.

Cross-Reference For information regarding comments and layered PDFs, see Chapter 17.

After selecting one of the file types listed here, click on the Select button in the Open dialog box. Acrobat returns you to the Select dialog box where you can see a preview of the image imported as your new stamp. In Figure 14-23, I used a JPEG image for a new stamp.

Figure 14-23: After selecting a file in the Open dialog box, Acrobat returns you to the Select dialog box where a thumbnail preview of the new stamp is shown. Click OK to return to the Create Stamp dialog box.

The last step in creating a new stamp is to supply a name for the stamp. When you click OK in the Select dialog box you are returned to the Create Stamp dialog box. The Create Stamp dialog box reflects all the additions you made by adding a Category name and importing a file for the stamp icon. In the Name field type a name for the new stamp as shown in Figure 14-24. The category is added to the Stamp tool pull-down menu and the Name for the stamp is added as a submenu option from the respective category. Click OK and you're finished.

To use the stamp, open the Stamp tool pull-down menu and select your category name. Acrobat automatically adds the category to the menu. Select the stamp name from the submenu and your new stamp is loaded in the Stamp tool. Click or click and drag with the Stamp tool and the new stamp is added to the document page. If you want to adjust properties such as opacity, open a context menu and choose your options. If you want to add a note, double-click the stamp icon and a pop-up note is opened.

Figure 14-24: When you return to the Create Stamp dialog box, type a name for the stamp. Click OK and you've successfully added a new category and a new stamp within the category.

Tip   If you aren't in a review and markup session and you don't have the Commenting tools open, you can apply a stamp from the top-level menus. Choose Tools ⇨ Commenting ⇨ Stamp Tool and select the desired stamp. All the stamp categories and stamps added to a favorite list are accessible from submenu choices.

Appending stamps to a new category

After creating a custom stamp and adding a new category, the next time you open the Create Stamp dialog box you have a choice for adding a new category or appending a new stamp to your existing category. When you open the Create Stamp dialog box, open the pull-down menu for Category and select your stamp category to add a stamp to the same category. If you want to create another category, type a new name in the Category field box. Follow the procedures in the preceding section for adding a stamp.

When you append stamps to a category, each stamp name opens from a submenu when you select the category name. In Figure 14-25, I added several stamps to a category I named *MyStamps*. When I open the Stamp tool pull-down menu and select my category, the submenu displays the stamp names. As I move the cursor to a stamp name, a preview of the stamp is displayed in another submenu as shown in Figure 14-25.

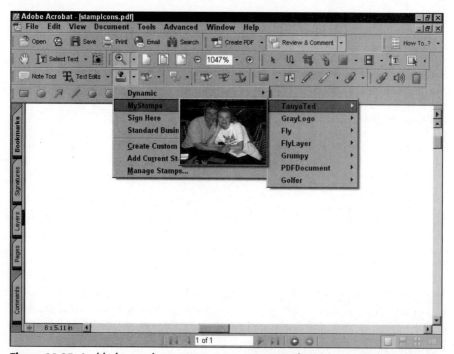

Figure 14-25: I added several stamps to a new category. When I want to use a custom stamp, I select the category and one of the stamps listed in the category. When the preview is shown, I select the stamp preview.

You can also append stamps by using page templates. In earlier versions of Acrobat, you created a custom stamp by creating a PDF document, making a page template of a page, and supplying the category name in the Document Properties dialog box. When you create a custom stamp in Acrobat 6, Acrobat creates a PDF file, adds a page template, and supplies the category name in the Description Pane in the Document Properties dialog box. This series of events is transparent to you when creating custom stamps in Acrobat 6.0.

If you want to add a number of stamp icons to an existing library you can open the PDF file and use the Create PDF From File or Insert Pages command to insert pages. Navigate to all newly inserted pages and choose Advanced ➪ Forms ➪ Page Templates. Add a page template for each appended image. When finished, save the file. When you return to the Stamp tool, you can import the newly appended stamps.

For more information on creating page templates, see Chapter 27.

Managing stamps

Acrobat offers you various options for handling stamps and making them easily accessible. The second half of the Stamp tool pull-down menu offers menu choices for managing stamps where you can append and delete stamps.

Using the Manage Stamps command

You may have some icon or symbol used frequently on PDF documents you edit. A logo, address, signature, watermark, or some visual representation of something you want displayed on many documents. If you use other Acrobat features such as adding watermarks and backgrounds, copying and pasting images, or importing PDF documents, you are required to know where these files reside on your hard drive. If you want to easily access an icon or symbol, you can create a custom stamp and the stamp icon is always accessible without your having to navigate your hard drive. For those frequently used images, you can add a list of favorites to the Stamp pull-down menu to further simplify easy access.

To add a favorite to the Stamp pull-down menu, select a stamp from a category and make it active in the Stamp tool. From the Stamp pull-down menu select Add Current Stamp to Favorites. The stamp name is added to the top of the menu. When you add a stamp listed in a submenu, the stamp still resides in the submenu as well as the location at the top of the menu.

If you want to add more stamps to your favorites, follow the same procedures and new stamp names are added to the menu. If you want to delete a stamp from the favorite list, you must first select the stamp and make it active in the Stamp tool. Return to the Stamp pull-down menu and select Remove Current Stamp From Favorites.

In Figure 14-26, I added a logo to my stamp favorites. To select the logo, I open the Stamp pull-down menu and select the stamp name and slide the cursor over to the thumbnail in the submenu. Notice the item listed as Remove Current Stamp From Favorites. Because the logo stamp is loaded, I can remove it from my favorite list by selecting the menu option.

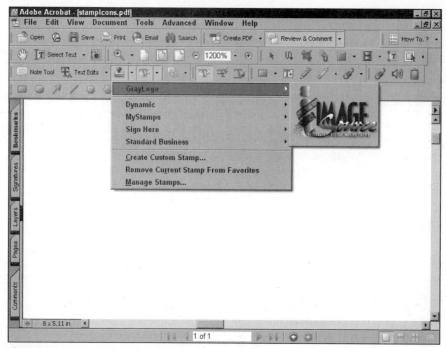

Figure 14-26: Stamps added as favorites appear at the top of the Stamp pull-down menu. When you select a favorite, the Remove Current Stamp From Favorites menu command becomes active.

Managing stamp libraries

You may want to edit category names, stamp names, or delete stamps after adding them to a category. To make these kinds of edits, select Manage Stamps from the Stamp tool pull-down menu. The Manage Stamps dialog box opens, as shown in Figure 14-27.

Figure 14-27: To edit category names, stamp names, or delete stamps, open the Manage Stamps dialog box.

Exchanging stamp libraries

If you work in an environment where you want to share custom stamp libraries, you can copy files created on any computer and port them across computers of the same or different platforms. The stamp files must be located in a folder where Acrobat can recognize the documents as stamps.

On Windows XP, stamp files are saved to the My Documents/Adobe/Acrobat/Stamps folder. On Mac OS X, stamps are located in the Library/Acrobat User Data/Stamps folder. Locate the file you want to send to other computer users and copy the file across your network or e-mail the file to a colleague. The user on the other end needs to copy the file to the same folder.

When you add a stamp file to the Stamps folder on either platform or you append the file using page templates, you may need to quit Acrobat and re-launch the program. If at first you don't see new stamps, be certain to re-launch Acrobat.

Advanced Commenting Tools

The Advanced Commenting tools offer you more options for marking up documents, attaching files, importing sound comments, and copying/pasting data to add as a comment. The Advanced Commenting tools are an extension of the basic Commenting tools but only available to Acrobat Professional users. Many of these tools also have associated note pop-up windows where descriptions for markups and icons can be added, and they all have various options choices in a properties dialog box.

Drawing tools

Drawing tools comprise a set of instruments that enable you to create geometric and freeform shapes. Each tool has a variety of options for appearance settings and they all support an associated pop-up note window. When you open the Advanced Commenting toolbar, select the pull-down menu beside the Rectangle tool and select Show Drawing Toolbar. A set of seven different tools opens in a separate toolbar. An example of the markings made from these tools is shown in Figure 14-28.

The drawing tools can be placed in two groups: lines and shapes. The options for applying property changes are the same among common tools in a group. That is to say, all the Line tools have common properties and all the Shape tools have common properties.

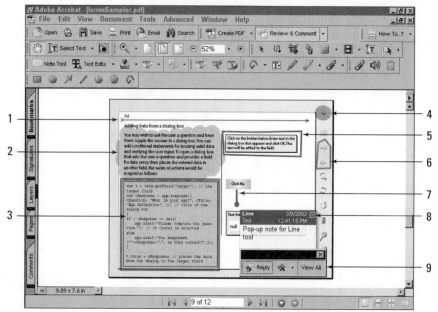

Figure 14-28: The drawing tools include the following—1: Arrow tool; 2: Cloud tool; 3: Rectangle tool; 4; Oval tool; 5: Polygon Line tool; 6: Polygon tool; 7: Line tool. In addition to the Drawing tools, 8: Pop-up note for Line tool and 9: Review Status Bar are shown.

Line tools

The Line tools are used for creating straight lines. You might use Line tools with or without arrowheads to illustrate points of interest, where background elements need to be moved, pointing to an object, or similar kinds of notations. These tools include

Arrow tool: The Arrow tool can be used with arrowheads, although applying arrowheads is a matter of user preference. You can draw straight lines on a 360-degree axis.

Line tool: The Line tool can have the same attributes assigned as the preceding Arrow tool, making them indistinguishable from each other. The intent is for the Arrow tool to provide you with a line for arrowheads while the line tool remains without arrowheads. When marking up a document and using both line tools you don't need to keep addressing the Line Properties dialog box each time you want to toggle on or off arrowheads. It's a matter of user preference, though, as you can choose to add or eliminate arrowheads from either tool.

Polygon Line tool: The Polygon Line tool also creates straight lines, but the lines are connected as you click the cursor to move in another direction. When you finish drawing a shape or lines with angles, double-click the mouse button to complete the line.

Line tools and context menus

When you use any of the Drawing tools to create a mark on a page, releasing the mouse button automatically selects the Hand tool. You can use either the Hand tool or the Select Object tool to open a context menu. The context menu options appear different depending on what tool you use to select the comment. In Figure 14-29, a context menu is opened on a line with the Hand tool.

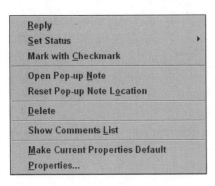

Figure 14-29: Menu options from a context menu opened with the Hand tool offer the same choices as found from context menus opened from basic Commenting tools and note pop-up windows.

When you create comments and add comment notes, note that the Hand tool context menu options are suited for initially annotating a document. You'll find that opening and closing notes, deleting notes, and accessing properties are frequent tasks you perform while reviewing a document.

After comments have been created you may want to manage comments for alignment, sizing, cutting, copying, and pasting. These options are available when you use the Select Object tool as shown in Figure 14-30. When you use the Hand tool you can select only a single comment. When using the Select Object tool you can select all the comments on a page or select a group of objects. Open a context menu and you can apply changes to all selected objects. This feature is particularly helpful when you want to align Drawing tool comments.

Figure 14-30: Open a context menu with the Select Object tool for menu options suited for managing multiple comments.

When comments share common properties options, you can use the Select Object tool to select the Properties dialog box for multiple comments. If you attempt to select objects where the properties options are different for the comments — for example the Line tool and the Cloud tool — the Properties dialog box offers only property changes that are common between the comments.

Line tools properties

With either the Hand tool or the Select Object tool, click on a line tool comment and open a context menu. Alternatively, you can open the Line Properties dialog box by selecting a comment with the Select Object tool and clicking on the More button in the Properties dialog box or double-clicking with the Select Object tool on a line. From the menu options select Properties. If you have more than one comment selected when using the Select Object tool, the Line Properties dialog box opens as shown in Figure 14-31.

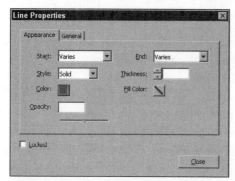

Figure 14-31: If you use the Select Object tool when opening a context menu and select Properties, the Line Properties dialog box displays two tabs.

The Line Properties dialog box opens with two tabs accessible for changing line attributes. If you use the Hand tool or select a single comment with the Select Object tool the third tab, Review History, is accessible. Review History is displayed only for individual comments. The Appearance tab includes the following options:

✦ **Start:** From the pull-down menu you select an arrowhead for the beginning of a line as shown in Figure 14-32. The default is None for no arrowhead.

✦ **End:** This is the same as the preceding option but applied to the end of the line. The pull-down menu choices are the same as for Start.

✦ **Thickness:** Line weights are selected from 0 to 12 points. Click on the arrows or type a value in the field box.

✦ **Color:** Represents the stroke color. Color choices are made from the pop-up swatches palette the same as used with Note tools.

✦ **Fill Color:** Represents the Fill color. For Drawing tools where a fill can be applied, the color choices are made from the color swatch pop-up menu.

✦ **Opacity:** Opacity is applied to both the stroke and fill colors. Move the slider the same as when adjusting opacity in the Note Properties dialog box.

✦ **Locked:** When Locked is checked, the line cannot be moved. Unlock a line to move it on the page.

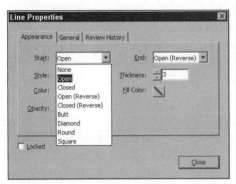

Figure 14-32: Open the pull-down menu for either the Start or End and select an arrowhead from the menu options.

The choices you make for arrowheads are obtainable from either the Properties dialog box or the Properties Bar. Not all choices are the same between the two tools. In Figure 14-33 you can see the results of choices from the Properties Bar and the Properties dialog box.

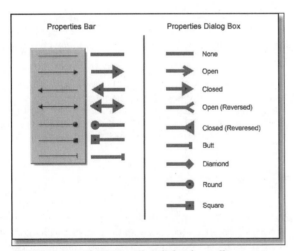

Figure 14-33: The Properties dialog box offers more selections for arrowheads. Click on the More button in the Properties Bar or select Properties from a context menu to open the Properties dialog box.

Figure 14-33 shows arrowheads applied to a single end. You can combine different shapes in the same line with a start and end selection.

The Style pull-down menu offers you choices for a line style. The default is Solid, as shown in Figure 14-33. The remaining line styles are dashed lines. Select from Dashed 1 through Dashed 6 for a different style as shown in Figure 14-34.

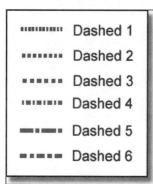

Figure 14-34: Six different dashed line styles are displayed in the Style pull-down menu. The default is Solid, while the remaining six styles are dashed lines.

The other two tabs in the Properties dialog box are the same as those found when using the Note tool. A Subject line is included in the General properties tab like the Note tool. The default name for the Subject is Line when using the Line tool. The default name changes according to the tool used to create the shape.

Managing line comments

To move drawing objects, align them, or reshape them, you need to select an object with the Hand tool. If you experience difficulty selecting a line it may be due to the preference option where you Enable text selection for the Hand tool. If selecting drawing tool objects is awkward, open the Preferences dialog box (Ctrl/⌘+K) and select General in the left pane. Disable the check box for Enable text selection for the Hand tool.

Cross-Reference   For more information on using the Hand tool for text selections, see Chapter 8.

Click on an object and you see handles appearing either at the ends of lines or at each end of line segments around polygon objects (see Figure 14-35). You can drag any handle in or out to resize or reshape objects. To move an object, click on a line or a fill color and drag the shape.

Drawing tools can be copied, cut, pasted, deleted, aligned, distributed, and sized. Use the Select Object tool and open a context menu while one or more objects are selected. Choose a menu command for the operation desired.

Tip   When selecting with the Select Object tool you can draw a marquee through objects to select them. You don't need to completely surround comments within a marquee to select them.

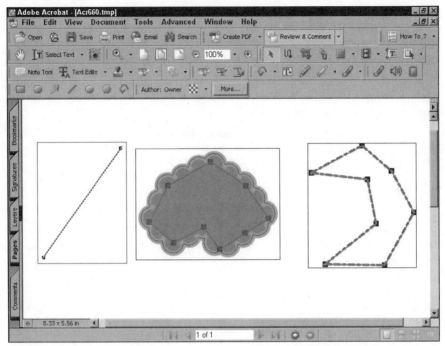

Figure 14-35: To reshape objects, select the Hand tool and click on a handle (square shape on a line) and drag to change the shape.

Shape tools

The remaining Drawing tools are used to draw shapes as opposed to lines. The objects can be filled as well as stroked. You can use different colors for the fills and strokes. Also found in the Drawing toolbar, these tools include the following:

Rectangle tool: Draw rectangle or square shapes. To keep the object constrained to a square, hold down the Shift key as you click and drag.

Oval tool: This involves the same process as the preceding for constraining objects to circles. Oval shapes are drawn without adding the Shift key.

Cloud tool: The Cloud tool is used like the Polygon Line tool where you click, release the mouse button, and move the cursor, click, and move the cursor again and continue until you draw a polygon shape. Return to the point of origin and release the mouse button and Acrobat closes the path. The paths appear as a cloud shape. The shape can be filled and stroked. (See Figure 14-35).

Polygon tool: Use the same sequence of clicking and moving as described in the preceding Cloud tool entry. When you release the mouse button back at the point of origin, the shape closes with flat edges instead of semi-circles like the Cloud tool.

Drawing shapes properties

The Properties dialog box and the Properties Bar offer options similar to the styles available with the Line tools. A solid line and six dashed lines are among the menu choices in either pull-down menu. Two additional options are added to these tools. The last two menu choices are Cloudy 1 and Cloudy 2. By default the Cloud tool uses a Cloudy line style. However the cloud effect can be applied to the other three tools in this group by selecting either Cloudy 1 or Cloudy 2 from the menu choices. Cloudy 1 renders smaller semi-circles along the edge of shapes. Cloudy 2 renders larger semi-circles.

Opacity settings made from either the Properties Bar or the tool's Properties dialog box applies equal levels of transparency to the strokes and the fills. Acrobat offers no option for rendering a stroke with a different level of transparency than the fill.

Text Box tool

The Text Box tool is used for creating text when more than a single line is created with the TouchUp Text tool or when adding messages in large blocks of text. You have more control over fonts, text attributes, and flexibility with the Text Box tool than when using a Note comment. Using the Text Box tool, as a comment tool you can track review history and see comments in the Comments list.

The Text Box tool offers you much more control over type than the type controls used with pop-up notes. As shown in Figure 14-36, you can bold, italicize, underline, strikethrough, superscript, subscript, and justify text left, right and center. You can change fonts and point sizes in the same text block and Acrobat checks spelling on-the-fly as you type.

In the Text Box Properties dialog box you can change opacity for text boxes, background colors, and line styles for borders. The remaining options are similar to properties for other comment tools.

Pencil tool

The Pencil tool is used to draw freeform lines. Whereas all the line tools draw straight lines, you use the Pencil tool for marking a page by drawing with a pencil, as you would with pencil and paper. The properties for pencil markings include choices for line weights, line colors, and line opacity settings.

Pencil comments are one contiguous line. If you stop drawing by releasing the mouse button, click, and drag again, a new comment is added to the document. After drawing a Pencil comment you can reshape the comment by selecting the line and dragging corner handles.

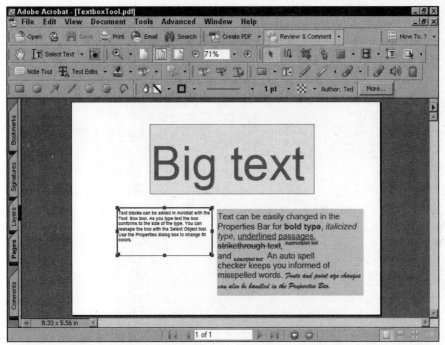

Figure 14-36: The Text Box tool enables you to add text on a page as a comment note or when you want to add passages of text to a file. You can change font attributes in the same text block, and an automatic spell-checker checks spelling as you type.

Pencil Eraser tool

The Pencil Eraser tool erases lines drawn with the Pencil tool. Lines drawn with other tools cannot be erased with this tool. When you draw a line with the Pencil tool and erase part of the line, the remaining portion of a Pencil comment is interpreted as a single comment. Broken lines where you may have several smaller lines remaining after erasing part of a Pencil comment are considered part of the same comment. A note pop-up is associated with the entire group of line segments. In Figure 14-37 I drew an oval shape with the Pencil tool and later used the Pencil Eraser tool to erase parts of the shape. The remaining line segments are grouped. When clicking on any segment, the comment is selected as a single group.

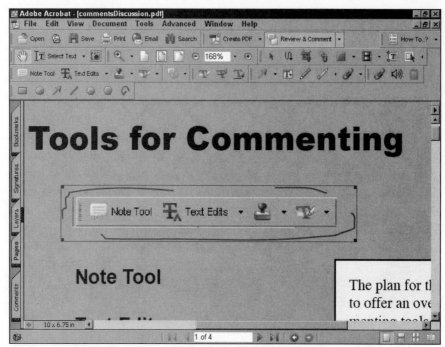

Figure 14-37: The Pencil Eraser tool is used to erase lines drawn with the Pencil tool. When you erase parts of a Pencil comment, the remaining line segments are grouped together and remain as a single comment.

Comment properties are associated with the Pencil comment. The Pencil Eraser tool itself has no properties.

Attach File tool

File attachments enable you to attach any document file on your hard drive to an open PDF file. Once attached, the file is embedded in the PDF document. Embedding a file provides other users the capability to view attachments on other computers and across platforms. At first it may appear as though the attachment is a link. However, if you transport the PDF document to another computer and open the attachment, the embedded file opens in the host application. Users on other computers need the original authoring application to view the embedded file.

To use the Attach File tool, select the tool and click in the document window. The Select file to attach dialog box opens, in which you navigate to a file and select it for the attachment. Any file on your computer can be used as a file attachment. Select a file and click Select. The File Attachment Properties dialog box opens with the Appearance tab in view as shown in Figure 14-38.

The Appearance properties for file attachments offer you choices for icon appearances to represent file attachments. Choose from one of the four icon choices shown in Figure 14-38. By default the Paperclip icon is used.

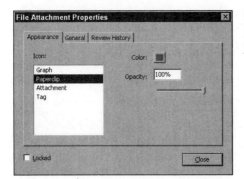

Figure 14-38: In the Appearance properties dialog box, the Description field contains the name of the file attachment.

By default the name of the file attachment is placed in the Description field box. You can edit the Description field, but leaving it at the default keeps you informed of what file is attached to the document. Figure 14-39 shows the General tab with the description noted as the name of the attached file.

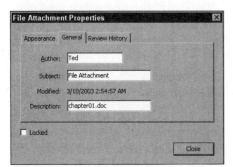

Figure 14-39: The General properties offer choices for author name, subject, and a description of the attached file.

If you place the cursor over a file attachment icon, a Tool Tip displays the attached filename. The name shown in the Tool Tip is related to the Description field in the General properties. As a matter of practice it's best to leave the descriptions at the default to be clear about what files are attached to documents.

The Attach File comment does not support an associated pop-up note. Double-clicking on an Attach File comment icon opens a dialog box where you are asked whether you want to open the file. Click Open in the dialog box. If the file is a file type other than PDF, the authoring application is launched and the file opened by the program that created it.

You can use PDF documents like a security wrapper for any file you want to exchange with colleagues and coworkers. Use the Attach File tool and attach one or more files to a PDF document. Secure the PDF with Password Security and use the Email tool to send the file to members of your workgroup. You can protect the document with password security and prevent unauthorized users from opening your PDF or extracting attached files. In this regard you can use Acrobat to secure any document you create from any authoring program.

Cross-Reference

For more information on using Password Security, see Chapter 19. For more information about using the Email tool, see Chapter 20.

File attachments are embedded in PDFs and double-clicking on the Attach File icon un-embeds the file. If you want to save an embedded file to disk without opening the file, open a context menu and select Save Embedded File to Disk. Acrobat opens a dialog box where you can navigate your hard drive and designate a location for the file save.

Attach Sound tool

Sound comments are recorded from within the PDF document or from prerecorded sounds saved in .WAV (Windows) or .AIFF or .WAV (Macintosh). For recording a sound, you must have a microphone connected to your computer. The resulting sound file is embedded in the PDF when you use the Attach Sound tool.

Attaching prerecorded sounds

Select the Attach Sound tool and click on a PDF page. The Sound Recorder (Windows shown in Figure 14-40) or Record Sound (Macintosh shown in Figure 14-41) dialog box opens. Click on Browse (Windows) or Choose (Macintosh).

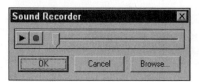

Figure 14-40: To select a sound file to attach to the PDF (Windows), click on the Browse button.

Figure 14-41: To select a sound file to attach to the PDF (Macintosh), click on the Choose button.

The Select Sound File dialog box opens after selecting Browse (Windows) or Choose (Macintosh). Navigate your hard drive and find a sound file to attach to the document. Select the sound file and click on the Select button. Acrobat returns you to the Sound Recorder (Windows) or Record Sound (Macintosh) dialog box. At this point you can play the sound or click OK to embed the sound in the PDF. Click on the right-pointing arrow (Windows) or Play (Macintosh) and you can verify the sound before importing it. After you click OK the Sound Attachment Properties dialog box opens.

After the sound file has been embedded in the PDF document you can play the sound by opening a context menu on the Attach Sound icon and selecting Play File.

Recording sounds

Click the mouse button with the Attach Sound tool to open the Sound Recorder (Windows) or Record Sound (Macintosh) dialog box. Click the record button and speak into the microphone connected to your computer. When you've finished recording the sound, click the OK button (Windows) or Stop button (Macintosh). The Sound Attachment Properties dialog box opens immediately after stopping the recording. The General properties are shown (Windows in Figure 14-42) or Appearance properties (Macintosh shown in Figure 14-43).

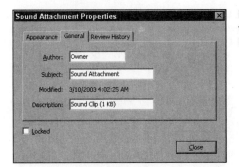

Figure 14-42: After stopping a recording, the Sound Attachment Properties dialog box opens (Windows).

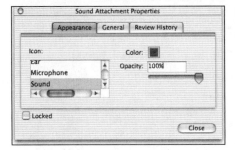

Figure 14-43: After stopping a recording, the Sound Attachment Properties dialog box opens (Macintosh).

When you close the Sound Attachment Properties dialog box, the sound can be played like imported sounds. Open a context menu and select Play Sound (or double-click on the Attach Sound icon). Because the sound becomes part of the PDF document, you can transport the PDF across platforms without having to include a sound file link. All sound files are audible on either platform once imported into PDFs.

Sound Attachment Properties

Properties for sound comments are made available in the same manner as with other comments. Open a context menu and select Properties to open the Sound Attachment Properties dialog box. The Sound Properties dialog box, shown in Figure 14-42, offers selections for adding a text description and editing the author name. By default, the Description field shows the file size of the sound clip. You can change the description by typing in the field box. All descriptions are also viewed in the Comments palette. (See "Using the Comments palette" later in this chapter).

The Appearance properties offer you options for three different icon appearances. The color swatch and opacity adjustment are used to change color for the icon.

Paste Clipboard Image tool

Paste Clipboard Image is great new addition to the comment tools in Acrobat 6.0. To use this tool you copy an image in another authoring application like Adobe Photoshop or Adobe Illustrator and paste the image in a PDF as a comment. As a comment, you have all the options for properties changes and review tracking. Keep in mind that pasting with this tool is much different from pasting data using menu and context menu commands.

In Figure 14-44 I copied a chart in Adobe Illustrator. I maximized Acrobat with a document open in the Document Pane and selected the Paste Clipboard Image tool. To paste the clipboard data as a new comment move the tool to the document page and click the mouse button. The image is pasted as a comment. You can then double-click on the image with the Hand tool to open a pop-up note and add a description for the message you want to communicate.

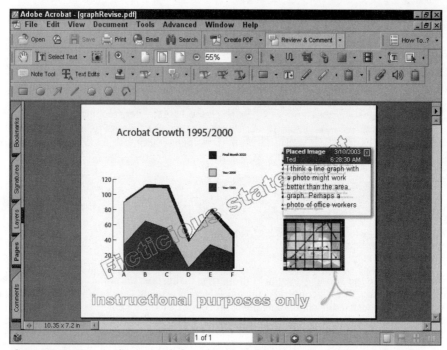

Figure 14-44: To use the Paste Clipboard Image tool, copy an image in an authoring program and click the tool on a page. The clipboard data becomes a comment where you can double-click on the image to open a comment note pop-up.

Pasting data with the Paste Clipboard Image tool requires you to copy image data. If you copy a passage of text, Acrobat doesn't recognize the text on the clipboard for use with the Clipboard tool. The tool is grayed out unless an image is copied to the clipboard.

Pasting PDF images and text

If you want to copy part of a PDF document page that includes an image, text, or both an image and text, you can use a couple of tools to create a comment from an image. This task can be particularly helpful if you want to comment about integrating data between PDF documents or suggest moving data between pages.

To copy an area on a PDF page, select the Snapshot tool. Marquee the area you want to include as your comment image. The selection you create can include text and images. Acrobat takes a snapshot and places the selection on the clipboard. In Figure 14-45 I copied the toolbars on page 2 in a PDF document.

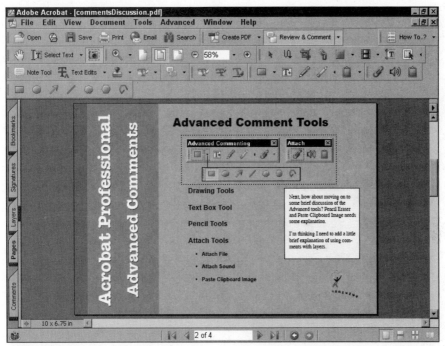

Figure 14-45: Use the Snapshot tool to copy an area on a PDF page. When you release the mouse button after creating a marquee, the data are copied to the clipboard.

Navigate to another PDF file or another page and select the Paste Clipboard Image tool. Click in the area you want to paste the image as a comment. If you want to add text in a pop-up note as shown in Figure 14-46, double-click the image with the Hand tool and type your message.

Tip You can stack comment notes and use transparency to create visuals that help communicate your message. As an example, in Figure 14-44 I wanted to communicate a message to use a photo behind a graph. When I opened my graph file I didn't have a photo handy. I copied the graph and opened my PDF document. Before I used the Paste Clipboard Image tool, I created a Stamp comment from a custom stamp where I had a photo readily available. I then pasted the chart image with the Paste Clipboard Image tool. I moved the objects and resized them, then went to the Stamp Properties dialog box and adjusted opacity to create transparency. On the page, it appears as though a single image is used; however, by stacking comments, you can create visuals when you don't have the right image to use at the moment you want to make a comment. When you create comments, keep in mind that they are created in a stacking order with the last comment created appearing as the front object.

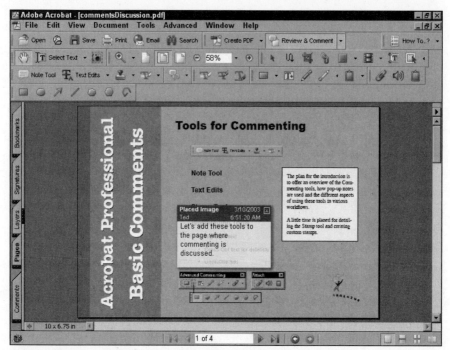

Figure 14-46: I moved to page 1 in my document and selected the Paste Clipboard Image tool. I clicked on the page where I wanted to place the image and double-clicked it to open the pop-up note window.

Stamp properties for Placed Image

Properties options when you create a stamp from the Paste Clipboard Image are the same properties options found with the Stamp tool. By default the Subject field in the General properties is titled *Placed Image*. The field is editable and you can type a new subject if desired. In the Appearance tab, you have choices for Color and Opacity. The color selections made from the color swatch pop-up menu relate to colors used for the pop-up notes. The pasted image itself does not change color. The opacity settings enable you to add transparency to the image.

Tip   If the Paste Clipboard Image tool is grayed out, you don't have an image copied to the clipboard. To verify content on the clipboard, open the Create PDF Task Button pull-down menu. If you see the From Clipboard menu item grayed out, you verified that no data exists on the clipboard.

Using the Comments Palette

The Comments palette conveniently contains many tools and options for managing comments. By default the Comments palette opens horizontally across the bottom of the Acrobat window and lists all the comments created in a PDF document. If you toggle views between several PDF files, the Comments palette dynamically updates the list of Comments to reflect comments on the file active in the Document Pane.

Depending on the size of your monitor, you'll find that viewing the palette occupies substantial space in the Acrobat window. If you're working on a small monitor, the amount of room left over for viewing pages, after loading toolbars in the Toolbar Well and expanding the Comment palette, can be very skimpy. Fortunately, you can view the palette docked in the Navigation Pane and control the size of the palette by dragging the horizontal bar at the top of the palette down to reduce size as shown in Figure 14-47.

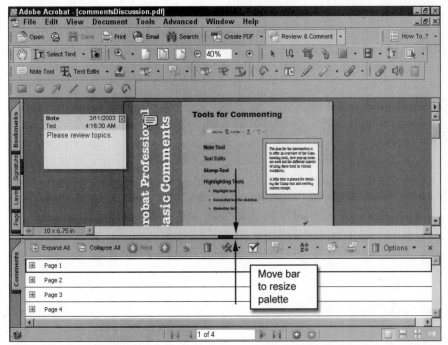

Figure 14-47: Click on the Comments tab to open the palette. Select the horizontal bar at the top of the palette and drag up or down to resize the palette.

You also have a choice for floating the palette by undocking it from the Navigation Pane and resizing the palette. To undock the Comments palette, click on the tab and drag the tab to the Document Pane as shown in Figure 14-48. The palette can be resized by dragging the lower-right corner in or out to reduce or expand the size.

Either way you choose to view the Comments palette, you'll find using it to be a great asset when reviewing documents and participating in review sessions. At first it may be a struggle to find the right size and location for the palette, but with a little practice you'll find the many tools contained in the palette much easier to access than using menu commands.

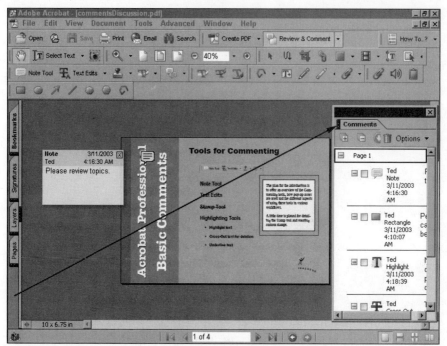

Figure 14-48: To undock the Comments palette from the Navigation Pane, click on the tab and drag it to the Document Pane. Drag the lower-right corner in or out to resize the palette.

Viewing comments

The Comments palette lists all the comments contained in the active document. By default the comments are listed by page. In a multi-page document, you'll see Page 1, Page 2, Page 3, and so on displayed in the list on the left side of the palette as shown in Figure 14-47.

You can view the list of comments expanded or collapsed. In Figure 14-47 the list is collapsed. In Figure 14-48 you see the list expanded. Expanded lists show comments in a hierarchy like bookmarks are shown in the Bookmarks palette. You can expand individual pages where comments are contained by clicking on the plus (+) symbol (Windows) or the right-pointing arrow (Macintosh). To expand all comments, click on the Expand All button in the Comments palette toolbar shown in Figure 14-47. Conversely, you can collapse all comments by clicking on the Collapse All button.

Comments are listed in a hierarchical order. If you have several comments on a page and you click on the icon to the left of the comment to expand the page comments, you see the Comment icon, author, and content of a note pop-up. You can further expand each comment in the expanded list by clicking on the plus (+) symbol (Windows) or right-pointing arrow (Macintosh). When further expanded, the comment subject and the creation date are displayed in the palette. Figure 14-49 shows Page 1 and Page 2 expanded. On Page 1 the first two comments are expanded and the second two comments are collapsed. Pages 3 and 4 are collapsed.

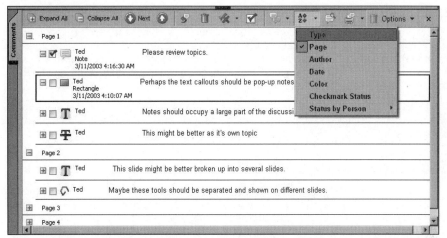

Figure 14-49: Comments are ordered in a hierarchical list. By default comments are viewed nested in a page order. The first two pages are expanded and the first two comments on Page 1 are expanded.

Sorting comments

Also shown in Figure 14-49 is the pull-down menu for Change how comments are sorted. You can change the default Page sorting to any of the following:

✦ **Type:** Comments are sorted together by the type of comment contained on pages. All Note comments appear together, highlight comments together, stamps together, and so on.

✦ **Page:** The default. Comments are listed together successively by page.

✦ **Author:** If a document has comments from several different authors, the comments are listed by author and sorted in an alpha order by author name.

✦ **Date:** The creation date is the sort order with the most recent date appearing first in the list.

✦ **Color:** Comments are sorted according to the color settings made in the comment Properties dialog boxes.

✦ **Checkmark Status:** You can check a comment for your own personal method of flagging a comment. Checking comments might be made for you to alert yourself to review comments, perhaps mark them for deletion, or to spend more time in a later editing session reviewing the comments made by others. The choice for what the check mark signals is a personal choice. When you view comments according to Checkmark Status, all unchecked Comments (Unmarked) are listed first followed by comments marked with a check mark.

✦ **Status by Person:** The menu option includes a submenu where you can select an author. Select an author name from the submenu and comments are sorted with the comments for the selected author appearing first. The unchecked comments are listed next by author name. You must have Status set on at least one comment to activate this command.

Navigating comments

 The up and down arrows in the Comments toolbar enable you to move back and forth between comments. Click the down-pointing arrow to move to the next comment in the list. Click the up-pointing arrow to navigate to a previous comment. The arrow tools are grayed out when comments are collapsed. In order to use the tools you need to have one or more groups of comments expanded and have a comment selected.

Double-clicking on a comment in the list takes you to the page where the comment appears. When you double-click on the comment in the Comments palette, an associated pop-up note also opens.

Searching comments

The contents of comment pop-up notes can be searched. To find a word in a pop-up note, click on the Search Comments tool. Enter the search criteria and click Search Comments. You can also open the Search Pane and select the Search in Comments check box. The Search Pane offers you the same search options used for searching open PDF documents. You can match case, search for whole words only, and other search criteria. The results of your search, however, return words found in the document as well as words found in comment pop-up notes.

When a word is found in a comment pop-up note, the page where the note appears opens and the pop-up note opens with the found word highlighted.

 For more information on using the Search Pane, see Chapter 4.

Printing comments

The Print Comments tool does more than print the comments in a document to your printer. When you select the Print Comments tool, a pull-down menu opens where you can choose from three menu options. These menu commands include the following:

✦ **Print Comments Summary:** Use this command to create a summary page as a new PDF file and print the summarized comments to your default printer. The comment summary is a temporary file that Acrobat creates while you print the summarized comments. After completing the print job the summary is deleted by Acrobat.

✦ **Create PDF of Comments Summary:** Use this command to create a new PDF document that summarizes the comments in your document, rather than print a file to your printer. You can save this file and keep it around to review a summary of the comments. This document is created with a Continuous-Facing page layout.

✦ **More Options:** This option opens a dialog box where you can choose from a number of different attributes for the way the comment summary is created. After making options choices in the Summarize Options dialog box, click OK. A PDF file is created according to the options you select in the dialog box.

From each of the menu commands, Acrobat handles comments with summarized pages. If you want to print pages with comments use the File ➪ Print with Comments menu command.

For details in regard to working with comment summaries, see the section "Creating Comment Summaries" later in this chapter.

Deleting comments

In addition to the context menus used when creating comments, you can delete them from within the Comments palette. Select a comment in the palette and click on the Trash icon to delete the selected comment. After deleting a comment you have one level of undo available to you. If you change your mind after deleting a comment, choose Edit ➪ Undo. Selecting multiple comments and clicking on the Trash icon can also be undone. Select Edit ➪ Undo Multiple Deletes if you change your mind after deleting multiple comments. In the event you loose the Undo command, you need to choose File ➪ Revert to bring back the comment. Be certain to update your PDF file after reviewing any comment deletions. The Revert command reverts back to the last saved version of the file.

Marking comments

The Mark the Current Comment with a Checkmark tool is used to mark comments for any comments you want to flag for a special purpose. You can select a comment in the Comments list in the palette and click on the tool to checkmark the current selection. Check marks are also applied to comments by clicking in the open check mark box when a comment is expanded (see Figure 14-49 to see a check mark applied to the first comment in Page 1). Between the expand/collapse icon and the comment icon is a check box. Click the box to checkmark a comment. Comments do not need to be selected to mark the check boxes when viewing an expanded list.

Setting comment status

Marking a comment with a check mark, described in the preceding section, is a method for you to keep track of comments for your own purposes. The Set the Comment Status tool is used to mark a comment's current status that is intended for use in comment reviews and when shared with other users. From the tool pull-down menu you have several options for marking the status of a comment. The five different choices are shown in Figure 14-50.

When you mark comments for status and view the comments sorted according to Status by Person, the comments are sorted according to the status groups. Beginning with Rejected, comments are listed for an author for all rejected comments appearing first in the list. Next the same author's Completed comments are listed, followed by Cancelled. Comments marked as None are listed last for each author. (Rejected, Completed, Cancelled, Accepted, None.)

Editing comment pop-up notes

A very handy feature available to you when viewing comments in an expanded list is the ability to edit note pop-up text. Rather than navigating to each page containing a comment and opening the associated note pop-up window to make your edits, you can delete, change, or modify text listed in the Comments palette.

When you select the note pop-up text in the Comments palette, the note pop-up window opens in the Document Pane as shown in Figure 14-51. As you make changes in the Comments palette, changes are reflected in the pop-up note window. If you edit text in the pop-up note window, the text edits are reflected in the Comments palette. To enable the dynamic viewing between the pop-up notes and the Comments palette, be certain to disable the check box in the Comment preferences for *Hide comment pop-ups when Comments List is open.*

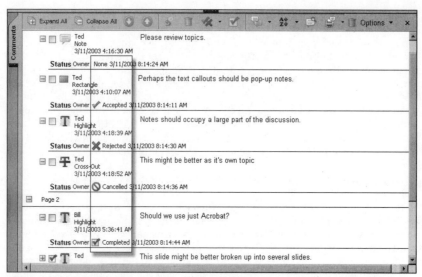

Figure 14-50: The Set the Comment Status pull-down menu contains five options for marking a comment's status. Beginning with the first item within the keyline in the figure, the options are None, Accepted, Rejected, Cancelled, and Completed.

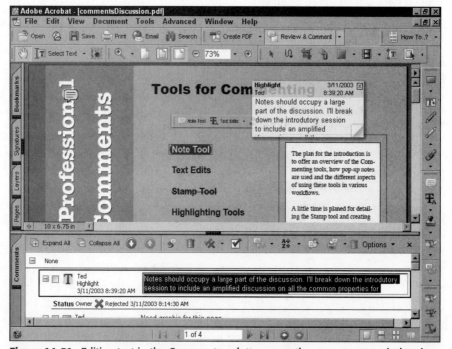

Figure 14-51: Editing text in the Comments palette opens the pop-up note window in the Document Pane. Changes to text are dynamically recorded regardless of which window you edit.

Creating an E-mail Review

The abundant number of comment tools, properties, and menu commands would be nothing more than overkill if all you want to do is add some comments on PDF pages for your own use. Acrobat is designed with much more sophistication when it comes to commenting, and the tools provided to you are intended to help you share comments in workgroups. You'll notice I skipped a few tools in the Comments palette and I haven't yet covered the Options menu. These remaining features are used for community reviews and summarizing comments. I first address setting up a review session here, and later in this chapter I cover comment summaries and filtering.

Comment and review among workgroups is handled in two ways. You can set up an e-mail review and exchange comments between your coworkers and colleagues where PDFs and data are exchanged through e-mail or you can set up a browser-based review where comments are uploaded and downloaded by participants to a Web server in the review process. In Acrobat 5 you were limited to collaboration with commenting on Web-hosted documents. If you didn't have the right Web server or server-side programming set up, there was no easy way to set up an online collaboration event.

Adobe engineers realized the problems for users configuring Web servers for online commenting and created this new feature for setting up e-mail reviews where virtually anyone with an e-mail account can start a review session and invite users to participate. What the e-mail review is intended for is when you want to distribute a document to reviewers for a single feedback session. You receive feedback from reviewers and make corrections on a document. At that point you either finalize the PDF or send a revised copy back to reviewers for another feedback session. E-mail review is not intended for use as a communication thread where users exchange comments back and forth. You can exchange comments back and forth between you and your reviewers, but the intent for e-mail-based reviews is for reviewers to comment once where you make document corrections based on the single one-time responses. This was the intent for engineers when they developed Acrobat 6, however, many users may use the email-based review for exchanging comments in multiple review sessions. There's nothing preventing you from doing so, but realize that there is another method available to you in the form of Browser-based reviews.

Browser-based reviews are designed for users to exchange comments back and forth where all participants comment and review each other's comments. The users start comment threads and exchange messages back and forth until the commenting event is completed. These two methods of collaboration have distinct roles and it's important to understand the differences.

 For information on setting up online reviews, see Chapter 20.

Initiating an e-mail review

An e-mail review is a method for you, the PDF author, to share a document with other users and ask them to make comments for feedback on a proposal or draft document that needs input from other users. As comments are submitted from other users, you can track comments from others and make decisions for how the comments are treated. Decisions like accepting or rejecting comments are part of this process. The comment exchanges between you and your workgroup members are handled through e-mail exchanges.

When you send a file for review, a modified FDF (Forms Data Format) and a copy of your original PDF is sent to users in an e-mail list. When a recipient receives the document it is received as an FDF (Forms Data Format) packaged with the PDF document. The recipients open the e-mail attachment in Acrobat and make comments. When a reviewer finishes commenting, the reviewer sends the data back to the PDF author. The data sent from the reviewers are also sent as FDF files, but the PDF document is not sent along with the comment data. If you start with a large PDF file, the comment exchanges require much less data transfers as the comment data are typically much smaller than original PDF files.

Note Before initiating a review, be certain to add your e-mail address in the Identity preferences. Open the Preferences dialog box and select Identity. Add your personal identity information including your e-mail address. The e-mail address supplied in the Identity preferences is used when e-mailing PDFs from within Acrobat. If the Identity preferences are not completed, Acrobat prompts you in a dialog box to type your e-mail address each time you start a review.

To begin a review session, open a PDF you want to use for the session and choose File ➪ Send by Email for Review. After selecting Send by Email for Review, the Send by Email for Review dialog box opens as shown in Figure 14-52. The dialog box offers you detailed instructions for starting a review session.

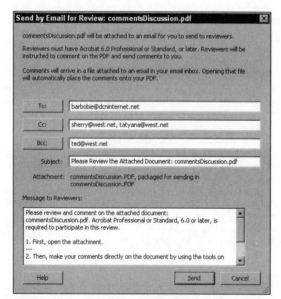

Figure 14-52: To start a review session, open the PDF to be used for the review and choose File ➪ Send by Email for Review. The Send by Email for Review dialog box opens containing instructions for starting a review.

Fill in the To and Cc field boxes with e-mail addresses of the reviewers you want to use. The message each recipient receives is displayed in the Message to Reviewers window of the Send by Email for Reviewers dialog box. If you want to add your own message, or modify the default message, insert the cursor in the window and type your message. Click Send and the file is attached to a message in your e-mail application. If your e-mail program is configured to send e-mail automatically, an outgoing mail message dialog box like Figure 14-53 may open.

Click Send and the file is sent to all recipients. If your e-mail program is not configured for auto-sending mail, you may need to first launch the e-mail application and later click on the Send button.

Figure 14-53: Click on the Send button in either a dialog box or from within your e-mail program. The file attachment and message are sent to the recipients.

Note   Initiating e-mail reviews can also be performed from within Microsoft Word and Microsoft Excel. The PDF maker macro includes a menu option for converting to PDF and e-mailing the converted document for a review. Use the Convert to Adobe PDF and Send for Review tool or menu command in Microsoft Word or Excel to initiate a review. For more information on using PDF Maker, see Chapter 6.

Participating in a review

Participants in a review include you, the PDF author and review initiator, and the people you select as reviewers. In your role, you field all comments from reviewers. If you use the e-mail–based review to send comments back to users, Acrobat does permit you to reply to users' comments. A review session is designed for a single set of responses; however, if you want, you can exchange comments back and forth between you and the reviews.

Before you begin a review, be certain to save any edits made on the PDF. If you insert pages, delete pages or perform a number of other edits without saving, the comments retrieved from others will appear out of place and make it difficult to understand where comments are made from the reviewers. Also, be certain to keep the original PDF in the same folder. If you decide to move the PDF to another folder, be certain to keep track of the location where the PDF resides. As you update comments, Acrobat needs to keep track of the directory path where the original PDF can be found. If Acrobat can't find the PDF, you will be prompted to search for it.

During a review period you and your recipients use tools in Acrobat designed for use with e-mail reviews. When starting an e-mail review, the first time you access the Send File for Email Review menu command, the FDF file with the PDF copy are sent to recipients. All subsequent comment exchanges between you and reviewers are handled with other tools. Be certain to not return to the command if you decide to respond to user comments. Doing so sends another FDF wrapper with the embedded PDF. If PDF files are large in file size the redundancy in sending the original PDF burdens users by having to download larger files when retrieving their e-mails.

Recipient participation

A recipient receiving your e-mail with the FDF attachment can open the attachment from the attachment folder or from directly within the e-mail message. Double-clicking on the file attachment launches Acrobat and loads the PDF in the Document Pane.

Avoiding Problems with E-mail Reviews

It is critical to understand what data are exchanged during an e-mail review. When you begin a review and select the Send by Email for Review command an FDF *wrapper* embeds a PDF document in the e-mail attachment. The PDF document is received by other participants who then add comments to the PDF document.

When the review participants send responses back to the PDF author, only FDF data are sent without an embedded PDF document. If a participant wants to add a reviewer and the participant sends the FDF data to a user who has not been invited to participate in a review, the new participant won't be able to open the FDF file.

If recipients want to invite additional users, the *unwrapped* PDF needs to be distributed to other users. If you want to send the FDF data, you need to send the FDF file *and* the PDF document to users who have not been invited for participation from the PDF author.

If you receive additional comments during a review, an FDF data file is sent to you. Double-clicking on the FDF data file opens the PDF document you originally sent (or started with) if you haven't deleted the file or changed the directory path. When working with e-mail reviews it's important to understand that two files exist. If you experience problems trying to open an FDF file in Acrobat you either don't have the PDF on your hard drive or Acrobat lost the connection to the file.

When the author wants to invite new users to participate in a review, it's important to make the invitation with the proper menu command. You add additional users to a review by opening the Review Tracker and selecting Invite More Reviewers from the Manage pull-down menu. When selecting this command, the PDF is contained in the FDF wrapper and sent to new users.

Note   When a recipient sees the file attachment in an e-mail message, the file appears as an FDF file. Although instructions are provided in the e-mail message on how to open the file, some users may become confused about the file received when they see the FDF extension on the filename. You may need to help users understand that although the file reads as an FDF file, the user can double-click on the file attachment to open the wrapped PDF document.

Reviewers make comments with any of the comment tools discussed earlier in this chapter. After a reviewer completes a review session, the reviewer clicks on the Send Comments button in the basic Commenting toolbar as shown in Figure 14-54. The tool appears in the Commenting toolbar when a recipient receives a file for review.

When the reviewer sends a response to the PDF author, the PDF author's e-mail address is automatically supplied in the To field in the e-mail program. The reviewer clicks Send and the FDF data are sent back to the PDF author.

Author participation

As comments are submitted from reviewers, you'll want to track reviews and decide to mark them for a status. If you want to reply to the recipients you can elect to send a reply to recipient comments; however, in most cases you'll want to make corrections and start a new review session. If you send a reply, each comment is treated like a separate thread in Acrobat. Rather than your having to select different tools to make responses scattered around a document page, Acrobat keeps each thread nestled together to make following a thread easier.

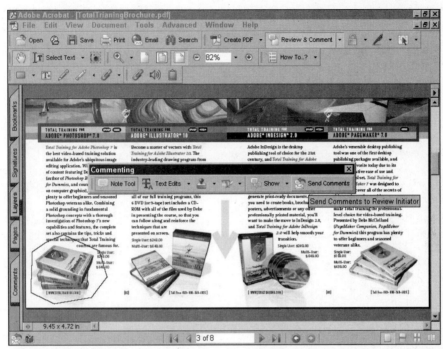

Figure 14-54: A reviewer clicks on Send Comments and the comment data are sent back to the PDF author.

To review comments added from recipients along a particular comment thread, select a comment with the Hand tool. The Review Status Bar opens where you can navigate through a comment thread as shown in Figure 14-55. You click on the left and right arrows to navigate through comments added by you or other recipients. If you want to set the status of a comment, open the pull-down menu from the Status tool and select from the menu options.

Updating comments

You send a file to recipients for review. The reviewers then send comments back to you. Your original document needs updating to reflect the new additions added by other reviewers. When you receive an e-mail attachment, the data are submitted to you in FDF format that contains all the comment information. Only a single PDF resides on your computer. If you want to merge the data sent by other reviewers with your existing PDF document, double-click the file attachment sent back to you. Acrobat updates your PDF document with the new comments.

Asking new reviewers to participate

You may begin a review and later decide you want to add new users to participate in the review. You can add new reviewers to a review at any time. To add a reviewer, open the Review Tracker by selecting the Review & Comment task button and choose Track Reviews from the menu options. The Review Tracker opens in the How To Pane. From the Manage pull-down menu, select Invite More Reviewers. The same dialog box opens as when you initiate a review. Add the recipient's e-mail address, and any additional message in the Message to Reviewers window and click OK.

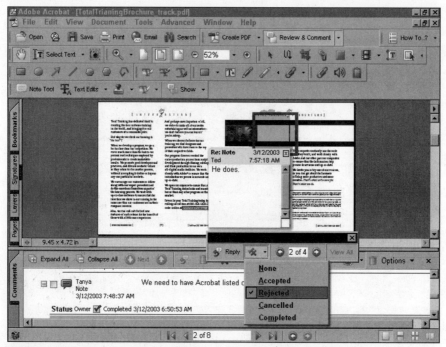

Figure 14-55: Select a comment with the Hand tool and the Track Reviews toolbar opens. Navigate through a comment thread by clicking on the arrow tools. If you want to mark a comment's status, select from the status states in the pull-down menu.

Cross-Reference

For a detailed description of the Review Tracker, see the next section in this chapter.

Replying to comments

You, the PDF author, and reviewers can reply to a comment that becomes part of a thread. The reply you create is the same comment type fixed to the same location on a page. For example, if a reviewer created a Note comment on a page, you can reply to the note with another note placed exactly on top of the original reviewer's note. Rather than selecting the Note tool, you click on the Reply tool in the Review Status Bar.

When you click on Reply, a new comment pop-up note is created on top of the pop-up note you reply to. Type your message in the pop-up note. The new note is associated with the same note icon. As more reviewers reply, new notes are added to the same thread. If you click and drag a note pop-up window, no underlying note pop-ups are visible. The only way to see other notes is to navigate through notes in the Review Status Bar or open the Comments palette and review the comments list.

Likewise, if you move the comment icon, only a single icon appears on the document page for the respective note pop-up. All note pop-ups in a thread are associated with a single icon. Both icons and notes can be moved to a different location on the page, but you can only select a single icon and a single note pop-up. Although Acrobat provides you a means for creating a comment thread in an e-mail-based review, these tasks are better handled in browser-based reviews.

Using the Review Tracker

The Review Tracker is a pane in the How To window where you find menu commands to help manage e-mail–based reviews and browser-based reviews. To open the Review Tracker, select Track Reviews from the Review & Comments task button pull-down menu or select Open Review Tracker from the Comments palette Options menu. The Review Tracker opens in the How To Pane as shown in Figure 14-56.

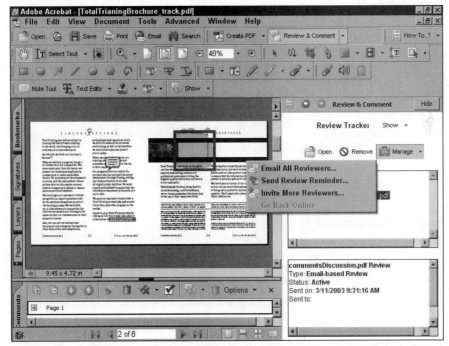

Figure 14-56: The Review Tracker is a pane that provides menu commands for helping you manage e-mail–and browser-based reviews.

Viewing documents in the Review Tracker

The pane contains two scrollable windows. You may have several reviews in progress at the same time and want to toggle between documents where a review is in progress. The top window lists current documents where reviews have been initiated. The list contains two groups that can be expanded and collapsed like comments listed in the Comments palette. One group contains all the e-mail reviews and the other group contains all browser-based reviews. To expand or collapse the list, click on the icon adjacent to the heading for Email-based or Browser-based.

To open a file currently being reviewed, select the filename in an expanded list and click on the Open button. As you select filenames and click Open, each document is opened in the Document Pane with the last file opened brought forward in the pane. To close a file, use the Close button in the Document Pane or choose File ➪ Close like you would with any other PDF document.

The lower scrollable window contains information specific to the document selected in the upper window. Filename, type of review (e-mail–based or browser-based), status, and creation date are listed as informational items. Below this information is a list of all recipients by e-mail address. If you need a reminder for who was included in your review invitation, scroll the list and observe the e-mail addresses.

Showing status

From the Show pull-down menu, you have several options for displaying the status of your reviews. These status options are different from the status options found with the Set Comment Status tool in the Comments palette. The Show commands include the following:

✦ **All:** Clicking All shows the status for all other menu options in the Show pull-down menu.

✦ **Active:** Until you mark a thread for completion, comments are active. When the check box is enabled and the other options are disabled, only the active comments are shown.

✦ **Completed:** If Active is disabled and Completed enabled, all comments you marked for completion are shown.

✦ **Sent:** Comments sent back to reviewers are shown. The responses from reviewers are hidden when the following option is disabled.

✦ **Received:** This is the opposite of the preceding menu command. All comments received from reviewers are shown while the comments you send are hidden when the preceding option is disabled.

Managing comments

The Manage pull-down menu offers you options for communicating with reviewers. In order to activate the menu commands, you need to select a document name in the first scrollable window where your list of active documents appears. Select a file and open the pull-down menu to choose from these options:

✦ **Email All Reviewers:** Selecting the menu command opens your e-mail program with all reviewers listed in the To, Cc, and Bcc fields. The position of the recipient's name corresponds to how you sent the original invitation to participate in the review. For example, if you supplied one name in the To field and three names in the Cc field, the names are placed in the respective fields in the original order you supplied them. The Subject line defaults to *Follow-up to <filename.pdf>*. Where *<filename>* is the name of the PDF document you sent to the reviewers. You can change the Subject field to any subject you want to use. Add a note and send the e-mail message to all your recipients.

✦ **Send Review Reminder:** The same action occurs as when selecting the preceding menu command. The difference between these commands is this command creates a message reminding reviewers to comment.

✦ **Invite More Reviewers:** This command opens the Send by Email for Review dialog box where the PDF document is automatically attached to an e-mail message.

✦ **Go Back Online:** For browser-based reviews, you can comment offline; then later reconnect to the server where the online commenting has been initiated. Select the command to reconnect to the server and upload your comments.

Cross-
Reference

For more information on online commenting, see Chapter 20.

Removing links to PDF documents

If you end a session or no longer want to continue collaboration, select the PDF in the list window and click on the Remove button in the Review Tracker Pane. The PDF document is removed only from the Review Tracker window and the link from Acrobat to the PDF document is broken. The file remains on your hard drive and you can open it by using the File ➪ Open command or Open tool.

Access to the menu commands is also available from context menu commands. To open a context menu, be certain to place the cursor in the first information window where the file-names are listed. Open a context menu and the same options for managing comments are listed in the menu.

Exporting and Importing Comments

If you ask a colleague to comment on a document, you can bypass the e-mail and browser-based reviews by having a reviewer export comments and e-mail the exported file to you. When you export comments from a PDF document the data are exported as an FDF file. The data file results in much smaller file sizes than PDF documents and can easily be imported back into the original PDF or copy of the original PDF document.

To export comments from a PDF document, choose Document ➪ Export Comments. The Export Comments dialog box opens. The dialog box behaves similarly to a Save As dialog box where you select a destination folder, provide a filename, and click on a Save button. Acrobat provides a default name by using the PDF filename with an .fdf extension. You can use the default name or change the name in the File Name field box. From the Save as Type (Windows) or Format (Macintosh) pull-down menu you can select between FDF formatted files and XFDF (XML-based FDF file). The default is FDF.

Click Save in the Export Comments dialog box. The resulting file can be exported to a user who has the same PDF document from which the FDF file was created. If you receive an FDF file and want to load the comments, choose Document ➪ Import Comments. The Import Comments dialog box opens. Navigate to the location where the data file is located and select it. Click on the Select button and the comments are imported into the open PDF document.

When you import comments in a PDF document, all the comments are imported in the exact location where they were originally created. If you delete a page in a PDF file and import comments, Acrobat ignores comments where it can't find matching pages. Note pop-ups and icons are matched with the way they appear in the file from which the comments were exported.

Exporting selected comments

You can select comments and choose to export only the selected comments to an FDF file. Open the Comments palette and select comments according to the sort order listed in the Comments palette. The default is by page. Select a page in the list and open the Options pull-down menu from the Comments palette toolbar. Select Export Selected Comments from the menu options as shown in Figure 14-57.

The Export Comments dialog box opens. Navigate your hard drive to find the folder where you want to save the FDF file, provide a name for the file, and click the Save button.

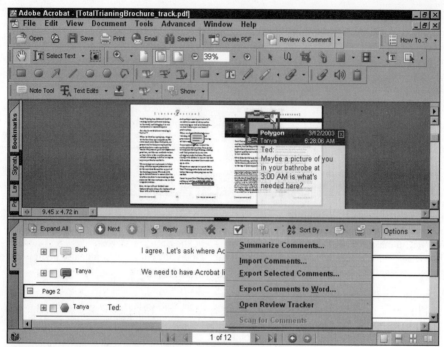

Figure 14-57: Select comments in the Comments palette and select Export Selected Comments from the Options pull-down menu. In the Export Comments dialog box, provide a filename and click the Save button.

Tip   When exporting all comments leave the filename for the FDF exported file at the default provided by Acrobat. When exporting Selected Comments, be certain to edit the filename. By default, Acrobat uses the same name. If you elect to export all comments and then want to export selected comments, you might mistakenly overwrite files with the same filename. By getting into a habit of being consistent when naming files, you'll prevent potential mistakes.

Exporting comments to Microsoft Word

If you create PDFs from Microsoft Word and use comments in Word and Acrobat, it may be easier to export comments directly back to your Word document. In order to take advantage of this feature you must be running Windows XP Service Pak 1 or above and you must be using Word 2002 or above. The feature is not supported on Macintosh OS X, nor in Windows 2000.

Be certain to use the Export Comments to Word feature on files that are not changed while importing or exporting comments. If you edit a Word document after creating the PDF file, or you edit the PDF document by inserting, deleting, or other page editing functions, the import/export operations may not work properly.

Comments that are exported from Acrobat to a Word document appear as comment bubbles in Word. Marking text for deletion and insertion are also supported in Word.

You can either start this process from within Acrobat with Export Comments to Word, or you can start this process from within MS Word with Import Comments from Acrobat. In both cases the Import Comments from Adobe Acrobat dialog box is launched. If you start from MS Word, the Word file is filled in and the PDF file is blank. If you start from Acrobat, the PDF file is filled in and the MS Word file is blank.

To export comments to a Word document from Acrobat, choose from one of several menu commands, such as File ➪ Export Comments to Word, Document ➪ Export Comments to Word, or use the Comments palette Options pull-down menu and select Export Comments to Word.

To import the exported comments in a Word document, in Word 2002 on Windows XP open the Word file that you converted to PDF. In Word choose Acrobat Comments ➪ Import Comments from Acrobat. The Import Comments from Adobe Acrobat dialog box opens. You can select the comments you want to import and choose from All Comments, All Comments with Checkmarks, and Text edits only: Insertions and Deletions. For a specific set of comments, select Custom Set and choose the filter options to filter the comments.

Cross-Reference

For information on comment filtering, see the next section in this chapter.

If you import text edit comments, Word prompts you for confirmation as each comment is imported. Be certain to track changes in Word or you won't see the dialog box appear. As you are prompted to accept changes, you can choose to apply changes or discard them as the comments are imported.

Filtering Comments

You can further enhance the features available to you for review and markup, exporting and importing comments, and viewing comments in the Comments palette, by filtering comments in groups. Filtering comments temporarily hides comments you don't want to use at the moment. You can choose to display all comments by an author, a date, a reviewer, selected types of comments, and a range of other criteria. When comments are filtered, exporting comments or creating comment summaries (explained in the next section) is applied only to those comments currently viewed. Any hidden comments are excluded from the task at hand.

Managing the comment filter is handled from pull-down menu selections made under the Filter the Comments Displayed tool in the Comments palette as shown in Figure 14-58. The assortment of options available to you includes the following:

✦ **Hide Comments List:** The first menu item hides the Comments palette. The command works the same as clicking on the Palette tab. To reopen the list select View ➪ Show Comments List.

✦ **Hide/Show All Comments:** This menu item enables you to hide comments while leaving the Comments palette open. By default you may have all options for filtering comments enabled. If you want to view comments contributed by a single author when you have a number of authors participating in a review, you might first select this menu item, then choose the author comments you want to see listed in the Comments List.

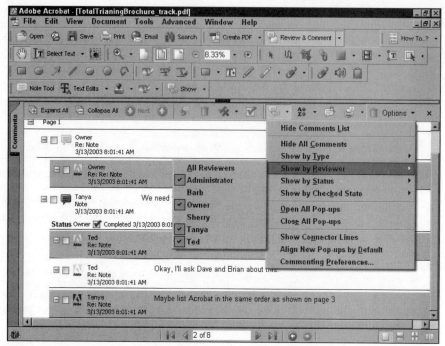

Figure 14-58: Open the pull-down menu beside the Filter the Comments Displayed tool and select menu options from the submenus to choose attributes for filtering comments.

✦ **Show by Type:** Presume you want to export all Text Edit comments. You make the selection for the comment type from the submenu. Among the comment types that you can select for filtering are All types, Notes, Drawing Markups, Text Editing Markups, Stamps, and Attachments. When you select All, all comment types are used. You can select one or more comment types from the other choices.

✦ **Show by Reviewer:** If you want to select something like comment Notes from three different reviewers and export the comments, you would select the comment type, then open the submenu for Reviewers and select those reviewers you want to include in the export. Each reviewer is listed as a separate name in the submenu. All Reviewers selects all reviewers that are subsequently shown in the Comments palette.

✦ **Show by Status:** The Status items you check during a review are applied to comments where you make the edits. To filter comments for status, you can choose from the submenu options All Status, None, Accepted, Rejected, Cancelled, and Completed.

✦ **Show by Checked State:** The check mark you use for your own purposes includes either checked or unchecked states. From the submenu items, choose from Checked and Unchecked, Checked, or Unchecked.

Tip

If you know ahead of time that you want to export edits back to Microsoft Word, you can mark only those comments received from reviewers that you intend to export to Word. When the review session is completed, select View ➪ Comments ➪ Hide All Comments. Open the menu again and choose Show by Type ➪ Text Editing Markups. Return to the menu and choose Show by Checked State ➪ Checked. Export the comments and only the Text Edit comments with the items you checked during the review are exported to Word.

The remaining menu options include non-filtering menu choices such as opening/closing note pop-ups, showing connector lines, aligning icons and pop-up notes, and accessing the Comment preferences. You can also make these menu selections from other tools and menus as described earlier in this chapter.

Creating Comment Summaries

If you create an extensive review from many participants over a period of time, the number of comments may become too many to comfortably manage in the Comments palette or on the document pages. Or you may have a need to create a comment summary you want to distribute to users after filtering out comments that you don't want included in a summary. Furthermore, you may want to print a hard copy of comments that show the PDF pages with connector lines to a summary description. All these tasks and more are provided when you create comment summaries.

To create a comment summary, you need to have a PDF document open in the Document Pane and comments in view in the Comments palette. The palette can be open or collapsed. Comments can be filtered according to the sorts and filtering you want to apply, but at least one comment with the criteria must exist for a summary report to contain comment information.

If the Comments palette is collapsed, you create a comment summary by choosing Document ➪ Summarize Comments. If the Comments Pane is open, you can choose the menu command from Options menu.

When you select Summarize Comments from either menu command, the Summarize Options dialog box opens as shown in Figure 14-59. Users of earlier versions of Acrobat can appreciate the many more options you have in Acrobat 6.0 for displaying comment summaries.

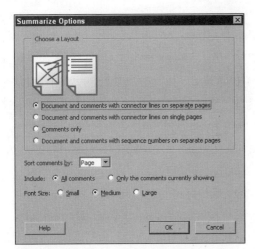

Figure 14-59: Select Summarize Comments from the Document menu or a context menu in the Comments palette to open the Summarize Options dialog box.

The first four radio buttons in the dialog box offer you choices for the way the summary pages are created and the page layout view that may contain single page views or page layout views in Continuous – Facing Pages. The resulting summaries are created as separate PDF documents.

Choices for creating a comment summary in the Summarize Options dialog box include

✦ **Document and comments with connector lines on separate pages:** The first choice is a comment summary created with each summary page aside the respective document page with connector lines from each comment on a page to the summarized item in a new summary. When the summary is created, Acrobat automatically switches to a Continuous – Facing Pages layout as shown in Figure 14-60.

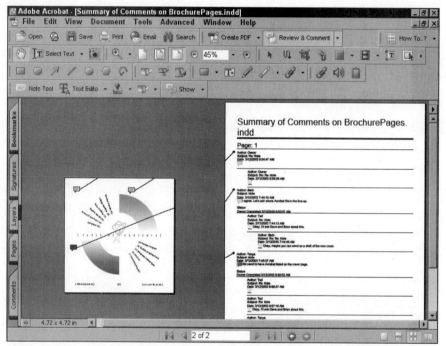

Figure 14-60: Summarized comments are shown with connector lines from original PDF pages and comments. Summary pages are created for each page in the PDF.

✦ **Document and comments with connector lines on single pages:** The summary is similar to the preceding option; however, the PDF document and the summary are created together on a single standard US letter landscape page as shown in Figure 14-61. One advantage for this summary view compared to the preceding summary is the comments, connector lines, and summary data require a little less room on your monitor to view the original file and the summary information. Furthermore, if you export summaries for other users, the summarized information and original file are assembled together in a single document.

✦ **Comments only:** This summary option is similar to summaries created in earlier versions of Acrobat. Only the summarized data are assembled together on single pages. The comment summaries are shown in a hierarchy according to the sort order you select in this dialog box. In Figure 14-62 the sort order is shown with comments sorted by Page. The page layout is a single page view.

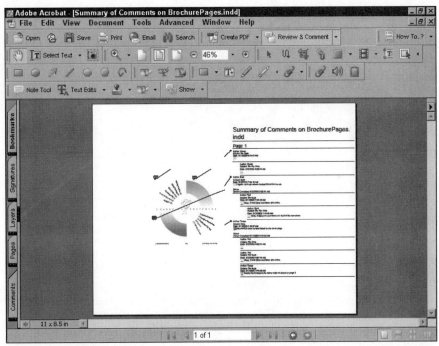

Figure 14-61: This is similar to the summary created in the preceding figure, but the PDF page and summary are created on new pages in a single document.

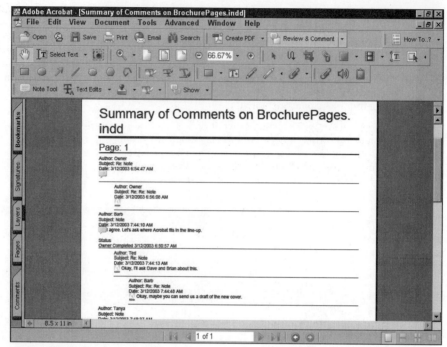

Figure 14-62: The Comment Summary is created as single pages in a hierarchical order according to the specified sort order.

✦ **Document and comments with sequence numbers on separate pages:** Summaries are created similarly to the method described in the preceding bullet, but with the addition of sequence numbers assigned to each comment according to the sort order and the order in which the comments were created. The page layout view is Continuous – Facing Pages, which shows the comments with sequence numbers and the resulting summary in the opposing page view as shown in Figure 14-63.

✦ **Sort comments by:** From the pull-down menu you can choose from four different options. The default is a sort according to Page. If you want another sort order, choose from Author, Type, or Date from the pull-down menu options. The sort order selected in the Summarize Options dialog box supercedes the sort order selected in the Comments palette.

✦ **Include:** All comments summarizes all comments on the PDF pages regardless of whether the comments are in view or hidden. The Only the comments showing option creates a comment summary from the comments visible in the Comments palette.

✦ **Font Size:** Applies to the font used in the comment summary description on the newly created pages. Depending on the size selected, the summary pages may be fewer (Small) or more pages (Large). The point size for small is 7.5 points, for medium 10 points, and for large 13.33 points.

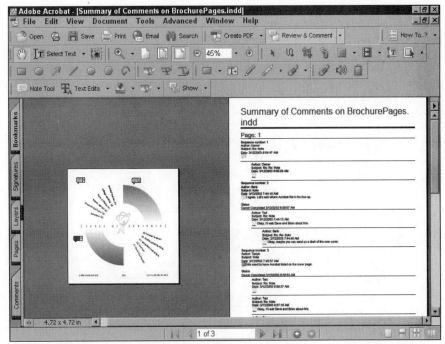

Figure 14-63: Sequence numbers are assigned to comments in the PDF file and the summary pages are shown in the same hierarchical structure as shown in Figure 14-62.

Comment summaries are particularly useful when sending PDF documents to Adobe Reader users. Although Reader users can see comments you create in a PDF document, they cannot create comment summaries. You can create a summary for a Reader user and append the new document to the existing PDF file, then send the file to other members in your workgroup. As an example for creating a summary, appending pages, and ultimately e-mailing a PDF document, take a look at how this workflow might be performed by following the steps in the next section.

STEPS: Creating and distributing comment summaries

1. **Create comments.** Open a PDF document and create some comments. Get creative and add a number of comments using the different tools discussed in this chapter.

2. **Create a comment summary.** Choose Document ➪ Summarize Comments. In the Summarize Comments dialog box, select Document and comments with connector lines on pages (second radio button).

3. **Save the comment summary.** The summary is created as a new PDF document. As yet the file is not saved. Choose File ➪ Save As and save the file to disk.

4. **View documents in a Tiled view.** When the summary is created it opens as a new PDF document. Your original PDF and the summary are open together in the Document Pane. To see both documents in the Document Pane, choose Window ➪ Tile ➪ Vertically.

5. **Append pages.** Click on the Pages tab in each document to open the palette and view page thumbnails. Select all the summary pages in the PDF file created as the comment summary and drag them to the pages palette in the original PDF document. As you drag to the original PDF document move the cursor below the last page as shown in Figure 14-64.

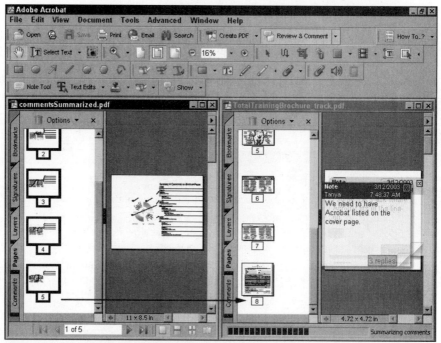

Figure 14-64: Drag the page thumbnails in the summarized document to the Pages palette in the original PDF document.

6. **Save the PDF document.** Update the original PDF document by choosing File ➪ Save As. Rewrite the file to optimize it and overwrite the original file. If you want to create a copy of the original file, use another filename in the Save As dialog box. Close the summarized file.

Cross-Reference For information on viewing tiled pages and copying/pasting pages in the Pages palette, see Chapter 10.

7. **E-mail the modified PDF document.** With your updated PDF in view in the Document Pane, click on the Email tool or choose File ➪ Email. Your default e-mail program is launched and the PDF document is attached to a new message as shown in Figure 14-65. Enter your own e-mail address so you can receive the PDF and review it in Acrobat.

8. **Open your mail and retrieve the file.** In your e-mail program, double-click on the file attachment. You should see the appended pages at the end of the document.

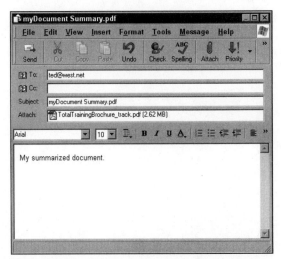

Figure 14-65: Click the Email tool and enter your own e-mail address in a new message window from your default e-mail program. Click on the Send button and send the e-mail with the attachment to yourself.

If you want to send just a comment summary instead of the appended PDF document, save the summary file and e-mail the file as described in the preceding steps. You can often use comment summaries with members of your workgroup who use the Adobe Reader software to keep them abreast of progress in a review process. Because Reader users can't import comments and take advantage of smaller FDF files, you can trim file sizes by sending comment summaries.

Comparing Documents

If you set up a review for users to provide feedback on a document, you may incorporate recommended changes in a file. As you work on modifying files, you may end up with several documents in different development stages. If you aren't quite certain which document contains your finished edits, you may have a need to compare files to check for the most recent updates. Acrobat's Compare feature provides you a method for analyzing two files and reporting all differences between them.

To compare two documents choose Document ➪ Compare Documents. The Compare Documents dialog box opens. You can open the dialog box without any file open in the Document Pane or open both files to compare and then select the menu command. In Figure 14-66 I have two files titled graph.pdf and grapha.pdf. Because these two files have similar names, I'm not certain which document contains revisions. Therefore, the documents are selected for comparison to check the differences.

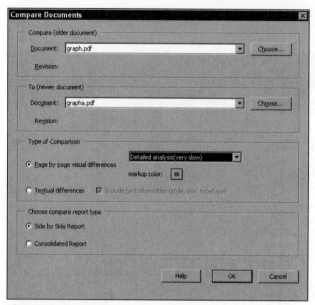

Figure 14-66: Choose Document ⇨ Compare Documents to open the Compare Documents dialog box.

The Compare Documents dialog box contains the following options:

✦ **Document:** The first two items are used to identify the documents for comparison. If no files are open in the Document Pane, click the Choose button and select a file in the Open dialog box that appears after clicking Choose. Click the second Choose button and open a second file. If you have the two documents to be compared open in the Document Pane before opening the Compare Documents dialog box, the pull-down menus show you both open files. Select one file in the top pull-down menu and the second file in the next pull-down menu.

✦ **Page by page visual difference:** Three options are available from pull-down menu choices. Depending on which item you choose, the reports are more or less detailed and the speed in which the documents are compared relate to how much detail you want to analyze. A detailed analysis takes more time than the other two options. Choose from Detailed analysis, Normal analysis, and Coarse analysis from the menu. Small visual differences between documents are reported when choosing the Detailed analysis (very slow) option. The resulting report shows differences in very small graphics. The Coarse analysis ignores small graphics that may appear on one document or another, and the Normal option falls somewhere in between the other two.

✦ **Textual differences:** Selecting this radio button deselects the preceding radio button selection. Use this option if your only interest is in comparing text in the document while ignoring graphics. If you want to compare fonts between documents, select the Include font information (style, size, typeface) check box.

✦ **markup color:** A report is created with markups. You can choose what color is used for the markups by clicking on the color swatch and selecting a preset color or a custom color.

✦ **Choose compare report type:** After comparing two files, Acrobat creates a report. The type of report can be either a Side by Side Report with the two documents displayed in a Continuous – Facing Page layout and comparison marks showing the differences, or a Consolidated Report where differences are marked with comment notes in a single PDF document. Choose the report type and click OK.

Acrobat compares the documents according to the attributes selected in the Compare Documents dialog box. When the comparison is finished, the report is created according to the report type selected in the Compare Documents dialog box. In Figure 14-67 a report is shown with markups where differences between the documents were reported in a Consolidated Report.

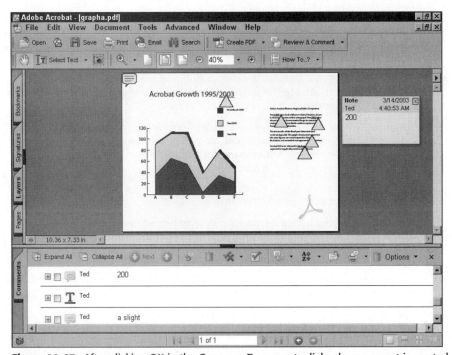

Figure 14-67: After clicking OK in the Compare Documents dialog box, a report is created, showing found differences between two documents. In this example, markups appear in a Consolidated Report.

Summary

✦ Acrobat provides an extensive set of Comment preferences. Before beginning any review session you should review the preference settings by choosing Edit ➪ Preferences and clicking on Commenting in the left pane.

✦ Two toolbars exist with commenting tools. The Commenting toolbar is available to Acrobat Standard and Acrobat Professional users. The Advanced Commenting toolbar is only available to Acrobat Professional users.

✦ Most comments created in Acrobat have associated note pop-up windows where you can type comments.

✦ You access comment properties by opening context menus from a note icon or pop-up note title bar.

✦ You can create custom stamps in Acrobat from a variety of different file formats.

✦ The new Paste Clipboard Image comment tool enables you to copy images to the clipboard and use the pasted image as a comment with an associated comment note.

✦ The Comments palette lists all comments in a PDF document. Additional tools are available in the Comments palette where you can mark status changes in comments, check comment status, and filter comments.

✦ The Review Tracker opens in the How To window. All active documents under review are listed in the Review Tracker Pane. You can select from a number of ways to communicate with reviewers from menu options in the Review Tracker.

✦ Anyone with an e-mail address can participate in an e-mail review. A PDF author sends a PDF document to selected members of a review team who comment on the document and send the comment data back to the PDF author.

✦ Comment threads are viewed by navigating comments in the Review Status Bar. A Comment thread contains a single note icon and pop-up window. Reviewer comments in a thread are viewed by clicking on arrows in the Review Status Bar.

✦ Comments can be filtered and sorted to isolate authors, types, dates, and other criteria. When exporting comments, only the sorted comments in view in the Comments palette are exported.

✦ Comments exported from a document can be imported in a matching PDF file. The comment data are saved as FDF and result in smaller file sizes.

✦ Comments can be exported directly to Microsoft Word files.

✦ Comment summaries are displayed in one of four different report styles. When a summary is created it can be sorted upon creation and saved as a separate PDF file.

✦ The Compare Documents command enables you to locate differences for text and images between two PDF documents. Reports are generated with comments describing found differences.

✦   ✦   ✦

Links and Actions

One of the truly great features Adobe Acrobat offers is the ability to create interactive documents where hot links invoke many different actions. Acrobat provides you with many tools and methods for making your PDFs come alive, and Acrobat helps you refine documents for user navigation and interactivity. Regardless of whether you post PDFs on Web servers, communicate via e-mail, replicate CD-ROMs, or work with documents on local network servers, Acrobat offers tools and features that help you create dynamic documents.

In this chapter you learn how to create links with a variety of Acrobat tools and learn some of the differences between several methods for linking views. With links originating from various elements such as bookmarks, page actions, links and destinations, you have a number of action tools that provide you with an almost limitless opportunity for handling views and relationships between documents. This chapter covers creating hot links and all the different actions you can associate with links.

Setting Up the Links and Actions Environment

Review and comment was the subject of the previous chapter. If you have read this book in a linear fashion, all the tools used in review and comment might be docked in your Toolbar Well. Because these tools take up so much room, you'll want to eliminate them and reset the toolbar. From a context menu, select Reset Toolbars to return to defaults.

Tools used for creating links come from the Advanced Editing tools and the Forms tools. To set up the environment for working with links and actions, open the Advanced Editing tools by clicking on the Advanced Editing Task Button and choose Tools ➪ Advanced Editing ➪ Forms ➪ Show Forms Toolbar. Open a context menu on the Toolbar Well and select Dock all Toolbars.

Note   Acrobat Form tools are available only in Acrobat Professional.

Tip   You can open the Forms toolbar when the Advanced Editing toolbar is in view. Select the pull-down menu adjacent to the Button tool and select Show Forms Toolbar.

When using these tools you continually address properties for each element you create. For easy access to properties, open a context menu on the Toolbar Well and select Properties Bar. Dock the toolbar after it opens. After docking toolbars in the Toolbar Well your editing environment for working with links and actions should look something like the Toolbar Well shown in Figure 15-1.

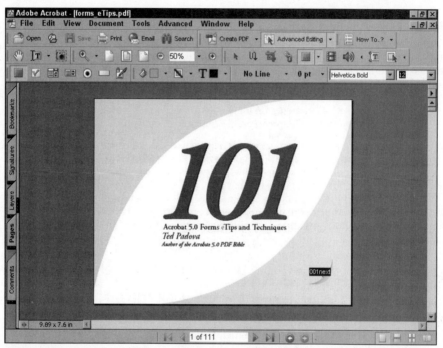

Figure 15-1: Open the Advanced Editing toolbar and the Forms toolbar, and dock them in the Toolbar Well. Select Properties Bar from a context menu opened on the Toolbar Well and dock it.

Working with Bookmarks

If you use programs that support exporting to PDF with structure, you can add Bookmarks automatically at the time PDF files are created. Programs such as Microsoft Word, Adobe PageMaker, Adobe InDesign, and Adobe FrameMaker support Bookmark creation from style sheets when you use export tools in the authoring programs. Ideally, in a workflow environment where these programs are used, creating Bookmarks from authoring applications when permitted by the program and when the Bookmark action relates to page views is advantageous. In other programs, or when editing PDFs with Bookmarks, you may need to reassign Bookmark actions, order Bookmarks in a hierarchy, or create additional Bookmarks.

Cross-Reference   For more information regarding Bookmark exports from authoring programs, see Chapter 6.

The most common Bookmark action in Acrobat is navigating page views. Whereas analog Bookmarks mark pages, the electronic Bookmarks in a PDF document enable you to navigate to different pages and different zoom views. You can capture various page views and zoom in on images, text, tables, and so on in Acrobat as Bookmark destinations. In a broader sense, you can use Bookmarks to invoke actions such as opening/closing files, opening secondary files, executing menu commands, submitting forms, playing sounds and movies, executing JavaScripts, and a host of other related actions.

Creating Bookmarks

As long as you understand the sequence of steps, creating Bookmarks is an easy task. Creating a Bookmark is like capturing a snapshot. The process involves navigating to the page and view you want to capture and then creating the Bookmark. Therefore, if you want to capture page 13 of a document in a Fit Page view, you navigate to page 13, click on the Fit Page tool, and then create the Bookmark.

You create Bookmarks from several options. When the page view is in place, open the Options menu in the Bookmarks palette and select New Bookmark. You can also open a context menu on a page and select Add Bookmark from the menu options. In Figure 15-2 the Bookmark Options menu is shown on the left and a context menu is shown on the right. Note that Figure 15-2 is used for illustration purposes — only one context menu can be opened at one time.

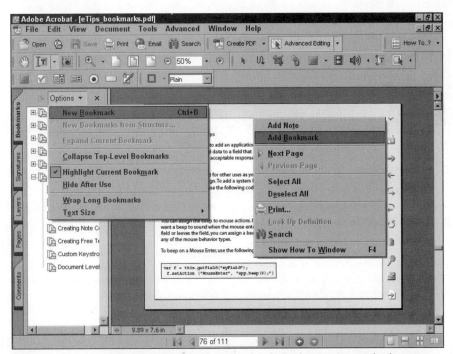

Figure 15-2: To create a Bookmark, navigate to the desired page view and select New Bookmark from the Options pull-down menu in the Bookmarks palette (left). or open a context menu when the Hand tool is selected and choose Add Bookmark from the menu (right).

Click on the Bookmarks tab and the Options menu for Bookmarks is accessible. Using a context menu, you can create a Bookmark when the Navigation Pane is collapsed. When a Bookmark is created from a context menu while the palette is collapsed, the Navigation Pane opens and the Bookmarks palette is placed in view.

If you open the Options menu without selecting a bookmark in the Bookmarks palette, the menu options appear as shown in Figure 15-2. However, if you first select a bookmark and then open the Options menu, the menu commands change to menu commands shown in Figure 15-3.

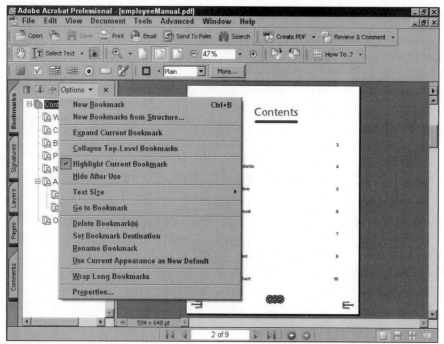

Figure 15-3: If you select a bookmark in the Bookmarks palette, then open the Options menu, the menu offers additional commands as compared to opening the menu without selecting a bookmark.

You can also use shortcut keys to create a Bookmark when the Bookmarks palette is either opened or closed. Press Ctrl+B or ⌘+B on your keyboard to create a Bookmark. In all of these methods, a Bookmark defaults to *Untitled*. Acrobat highlights the *Untitled* Bookmark name after the Bookmark is created. You type a name and press the Enter or Return key when finished typing.

If you have pages where titles on the pages correspond to names you want to use for Bookmarks, Acrobat helps simplify the naming process. Select the Text Select tool and highlight a title or words you want to use as your Bookmark name. From a context menu, select Add Bookmark. The Bookmark is created and the highlighted text is used as the Bookmark name. Figure 15-4 illustrates the stages of creating a Bookmark in this manner: 1) the page view is in place; 2) text is selected on the page and a context menu opened; 3) Add Bookmark is selected from the menu options; and 4) the Bookmark is created using the selected text for the Bookmark name. Using the Options menu or modifier keys for creating a Bookmark while text is selected creates the Bookmark in the same manner.

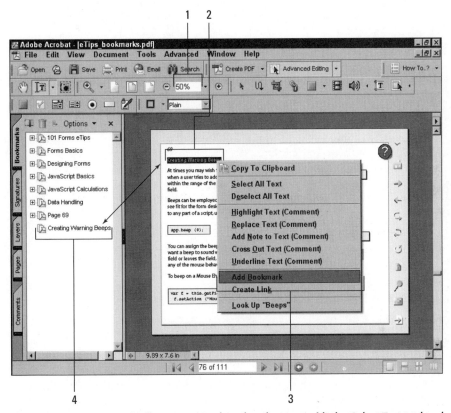

Figure 15-4: To automatically name a Bookmark, select text with the Select Text tool and create the Bookmark.

Managing Bookmarks

Bookmarks created in a document appear in the order they are created, regardless of the page order. For example, if you create a Bookmark on page 15, and then create another on page 12, the Bookmarks are listed with page 15 before page 12 in the Bookmarks palette. At times you may want to have the Bookmarks list displayed according to page order. Additionally, Bookmarks may appear more organized if they are nested in groups. If you have a category and a list of items to fit within that category, you may want to create a hierarchy that expands or collapses. Fortunately, Acrobat enables you to change the order of Bookmarks without recreating them. Additionally, you can categorize the Bookmarks into groups.

To reorder a Bookmark, select the page icon adjacent to the Bookmark name in the list and drag it up or down. A red triangle appears when you drag up or down, as shown in Figure 15-5. To nest a child Bookmark below a parent Bookmark, drag up or down and slightly to the left. Wait for a flag like the one shown in Figure 15-5 and release the mouse button.

Note   In Figure 15-5, three parent Bookmarks appear as the leftmost Bookmarks. Those Bookmarks indented to the right of each parent Bookmark are child Bookmarks. A Bookmark appears as a child Bookmark when you see the Bookmark appearing below and right of another Bookmark(s).

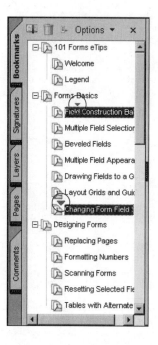

Figure 15-5: The triangle indicates a Bookmark is moved before or after another Bookmark. The flag indicates a Bookmark is moved to a child position below a parent Bookmark.

If you have a parent Bookmark with several child Bookmarks nested below it, you can move the parent to a new location. Drag the parent Bookmark, and all child Bookmarks below it move with the parent. If you want to remove a child Bookmark from a nest, click and drag the Bookmark to the left and either down or up to the location desired.

Multiple nesting is also available with Bookmark organization. A Bookmark can be subordinate to another Bookmark that is itself nested under a parent Bookmark. To subordinate a Bookmark under a child Bookmark, use the same method as described previously for creating the first order of children. As you drag right and up slightly, you can nest Bookmarks at several levels.

Multiple Bookmarks can also be relocated. To select several Bookmarks, Shift+click each Bookmark in a group. As you hold down the Shift key, you can add more Bookmarks to the selection. If you click one Bookmark at the top or bottom of a list and Shift+click, all Bookmarks between are selected. For a non-contiguous selection, Ctrl+click or ⌘+click. Once selected, drag the Bookmarks to a new location in the list. Once moved, their order remains the same.

By default, new Bookmarks appear at the end of a Bookmark list. If you want to place a Bookmark within a series of Bookmarks, select the Bookmark you want the new Bookmark to follow. When you select New Bookmark from the Bookmarks Options menu, from a context menu, or press Ctrl+B or ⌘+B, the new Bookmark is created after the one you selected.

Renaming Bookmarks

If you create a Bookmark and want to change the Bookmark name, select the Bookmark to be edited from the Bookmarks palette. From the Options menu, select Rename. Acrobat highlights the name in the Bookmarks palette. Type a new name and press the Return or Enter key on your keyboard to finish editing the Bookmark name. You can also click the cursor anywhere in the Document Pane to finish editing the name.

You can also rename Bookmarks by clicking on a Bookmark name and clicking again on the Bookmark. You can also use a context menu, but be certain you first select the bookmark; then open a context menu to select the menu option for *Rename Bookmark*. If you click on a bookmark, the first click takes you to the associated Bookmark view. Clicking a second time informs Acrobat you want to edit the name. To select the text, click and drag across the part of the name you want to edit or press Ctrl+A or ⌘+A to select all text. When you type a new name, the selected text is deleted and replaced with the new text you type.

Structured Bookmarks

Structured Bookmarks retain document structure in files generated from Microsoft Word, Web page captures, and programs supporting PDF creation with tags. Structured Bookmarks can be used to navigate PDF pages, reorganize the pages, and delete pages. If you create PDFs without tags, you can add structure to a document by choosing Advanced ➪ Accessibility ➪ Add Tags to Document. After you have a structured document and you create Bookmarks, more options are available to you. For example, moving a Bookmark in the Bookmarks palette only moves the Bookmark, and the page associated with the Bookmark is unaffected. When you move a structured Bookmark, the page associated with the Bookmark is moved. The same holds true for Bookmark deletions, extractions, and printing.

Depending on whether you have a Bookmark or a structured Bookmark, context menu commands appear different. When you open a context menu from a standard Bookmark, the menu commands appear as shown in Figure 15-6. When opening a context menu from a structured Bookmark, the menu commands are as they appear in Figure 15-7. Notice the items that relate to Print Pages, Delete Pages, and Extract pages that are available when you open a context menu from a structured Bookmark.

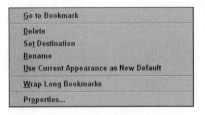

Figure 15-6: Menu commands shown when opening a Bookmark context menu

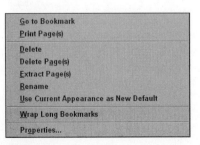

Figure 15-7: Menu commands shown when opening a structured Bookmark context menu

When you create a Bookmark, the destination for the Bookmark is a link to a page view. In the context menu for standard Bookmarks, you see the menu command for Set Destination. You can navigate to a new page and select this command to change the Bookmark link to a new view. With structured Bookmarks, you capture the page structure (a page view, a table, a head, and so on). No option to change the destination is available in the context menu. You need to delete a structured Bookmark and create a new one if you want to change the destination. In the context menu be certain to select Delete and not Delete Page(s). The Delete command deletes just the Bookmark. Delete Page(s) deletes the Bookmark and the page associated with the Bookmark.

Bookmark appearances

Both Bookmarks and structured Bookmarks contain menu options for Use Current Appearance as New Default. This menu choice is like a Bookmark style sheet where you first select the appearance of the Bookmark in terms of font style and color; then you select this menu option to set the attributes as a new default. For example, change the Bookmark to small text, italicized, in red; then open a context menu and select Use Current Appearance as New Default. All subsequent Bookmarks you create use the same style until you change the default.

The Wrap Long Bookmarks option from either menu creates a word wrap for the Bookmark name in the Bookmarks palette. By default a Bookmark appears on a single line. When you move the cursor to a Bookmark with a name longer than the palette width, a Tool Tip displays the complete Bookmark name across the page as shown in Figure 15-8. When you select Wrap Long Bookmarks, the Bookmark names appear as shown in Figure 15-9.

If you open the Options menu you have more choices for how the Bookmarks appear in the palette. In Figures 15-7 and 15-9, Bookmarks are collapsed. The plus (+) symbol (a right-pointing arrow on Macintosh) indicates a Bookmark has child Bookmarks nested below it. Click on the symbol and the Bookmark expands to show all child Bookmarks at the next level. If you want to show all top-level Bookmarks expanded, select Expand Top-Level Bookmarks from the Options pull-down menu. To collapse the Bookmark list, select Collapse Top-Level Bookmarks from the same menu. The latter menu command is dynamic and only appears accessible in the menu if you have first expanded Bookmarks.

Tip   To expand a Bookmark hierarchy, move the cursor to a parent Bookmark in the Bookmarks palette. Press the Ctrl or Option key and click. To collapse all Bookmarks, use the same shortcut keys when Bookmarks are expanded. This shortcut works well when you have multiple bookmarks nested as parent/child bookmarks.

Select Hide After Use from the Options menu if you want to hide the Bookmarks palette after selecting a Bookmark. To change text sizes, make selections from the Options pull-down menu. Select Text Size and choose from one of the three submenu items for Small, Medium, or Large point sizes.

Bookmark properties

The Options pull-down menu offers you choices for text sizes. For other text attribute changes you need to use the Bookmark Properties dialog box. Select Properties from a context menu and the Bookmark Properties dialog box shown in Figure 15-10 opens.

Figure 15-8: By default, Bookmark names are shown in a single line of text cut off at the end of the Bookmark palette. When the name is longer than the palette width, a Tool Tip shows the complete name extended beyond the palette width.

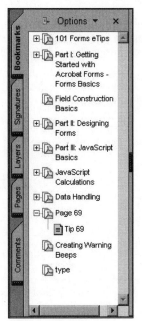

Figure 15-9: When Wrap Long Bookmarks is selected, Bookmark names are wrapped to the palette width and shown in multiple lines of text.

Figure 15-10: The Bookmarks Properties dialog box opens when you open a context menu from either a standard Bookmark or a structured Bookmark.

You select type styles from the Style pull-down menu. Select from Plain, Bold, Italic, or Bold & Italic. Clicking on the Color swatch opens the color pop-up window where you select preset colors or custom colors. You can capture changes from these style options when you select the Use Current Appearance as New Default menu command previously discussed.

The Actions tab enables you to change Bookmark actions. By default the Bookmark action is set to open a view within the active PDF document. You can assign many other actions to Bookmarks in the Actions properties.

For assigning Bookmark actions, see the section "Working with the Link Tool" later in this chapter.

Setting Bookmark opening views

If you create Bookmarks in a document and want the document to open with the Bookmarks palette open, you can save the PDF document in a manner where the Bookmarks palette opens in the Navigation Pane each time the PDF is opened.

Choose File ➪ Document Properties or press Ctrl+D or ⌘+D to open the Document Properties dialog box. Click on Initial View in the left pane. From the Show pull-down menu select Bookmarks Panel and Page. Save the file after making the properties change. The next time you open the document, the Bookmarks palette open.

The width of the Bookmarks palette is a user default specific to Acrobat on the end user's computer and not the file you save. If you open the Bookmarks palette to a wider view than the default, each time you open a PDF with the Bookmarks in view, the Bookmarks palette is opened at the width you last adjusted. If you save the file with the Initial View showing Bookmarks and pages, Acrobat does not take into consideration your Bookmarks palette width. Other users who open your files see the Bookmarks palette sized to their personal palette width default sizes. This default is made from the last time you adjusted the palette size.

Working with Articles

Acrobat offers a feature to link text blocks together for easy navigation through columns of text. User-specified ranges of text can be linked together, thereby forming an article. Articles help a user navigate through a PDF file, enabling the user to read logical sequences of paragraphs throughout a document. Working with articles is particularly helpful when you view PDF files on the World Wide Web. PDF files can be downloaded a page at a time in a Web browser. If you have a column or group of paragraphs of text that begins on page 1 and continues on page 54, an article thread can assist a reader in jumping from page 1 to page 54 without downloading the remaining pages in the document.

Viewing and navigating articles

If articles are included in a PDF, you need to know a few basics on navigating through an article. To determine whether articles exist, choose View ➪ Navigation Tabs ➪ Articles. A palette opens with tabs for Articles and Destinations, as shown in Figure 15-11.

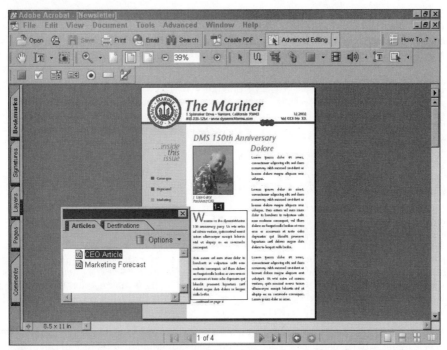

Figure 15-11: To determine whether Articles exist in a document, open the Articles Navigation tab.

Tip If you want to move the Articles palette to the Navigation Pane, click the tab and drag to the top of the Navigation Pane. The Articles palette can remain in the Navigation Pane for all subsequent Acrobat sessions as long as you leave it docked in the pane when quitting Acrobat.

When the Articles tab is in view, any articles existing in the PDF file are displayed in the palette list. If you select the Article tool from the Acrobat toolbar, the article definition boundaries are shown. In Figure 15-11, the Article tool is selected. The defined article is contained within a rectangular box with an identifier at the top of the box. In this example, 1-1 indicates this is article number 1 and the box is number 1. If the article is continued on another page, the subsequent boxes read 1-2, 1-3, 1-4, and so on, indicating they are continuations of the same article thread. If you create a second article, the article begins with number 2-1 indicating the second article in the document and the first box of the second article.

Article properties

The article properties are contained in a dialog box that opens immediately after you create an article or double-click an article with the Article tool. The Properties dialog box shown in Figure 15-12 is informational. When you view Article Properties, information supplied at the time the article was created is displayed for four data fields. The Title, Subject, Author, and Keywords fields are the same as those found in the Document Information dialog box.

Inasmuch as the data for these fields are identical to that found in document information, Acrobat Search does not take advantage of the article properties information. Properties are designed to help you find information about an article before you jump to the page where the article is contained. All the fields are editable when you open the Article Properties dialog box.

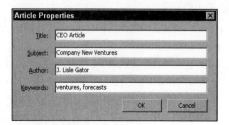

Figure 15-12: The Article Properties dialog box displays user-supplied information for Title, Subject, Author, and Keywords fields. These fields are not searchable with Acrobat Search.

Viewing articles

Articles are viewed at the maximum view established in the Preferences dialog box. When you view an article, you select the Hand tool and click on an article thread. The screen view jumps to the maximum view assigned in the Page Display Preferences. By default the zoom is set to an 800% view. In most situations this view is much larger than needed for comfortable viewing. Select Edit ⇨ Preferences and click on Page Display in the left pane. From the Max Fit Visible Zoom pull-down menu select a zoom view comfortable for reading on your monitor.

After you establish the zoom, open the Articles palette by choosing View ⇨ Navigation Tabs ⇨ Articles. The Articles palette can remain open as an individual palette, or you can drag it to the Navigation Pane and dock the palette. The palette pull-down menu in the Articles palette offers only one option. If you select Hide After Use from the palette pull-down menu, the palette disappears when you view an article. If you want to have the palette remain open, but want more viewing area in the document, dock the palette in the Navigation Pane.

Double-click an article to jump to the first view in the thread. Acrobat places the top-left corner where the article begins in view. You immediately see a right-pointing arrow blink on the left side of the first line of text. Once an article is in view, select the Hand tool and position the cursor over the article. The cursor changes to a Hand tool icon with an arrow pointing down. As you read articles, the cursor changes according to the direction Acrobat takes you when reading an article. For example, if viewing a column up instead of down, the cursor changes to inform you which direction is navigated. The different cursor views are shown in Figure 15-13.

Figure 15-13: Different cursors are used when viewing articles to inform you ahead of time the direction to be navigated.

To help navigation with the Article tool, several keyboard shortcuts can assist you when using the mouse. The cursor changes according to the following modifier keys:

✦ **Click:** The first click zooms to the Max Fit Visible preference setting. Click the cursor again to continue reading down a column. Click at the end of an article box, and the view takes you to the beginning of the next column.

✦ **Shift+click:** Moves backward or up a column.

✦ **Control+click or Option+click:** Moves to the beginning of the article.

✦ **Return or Enter:** Moves forward down the column or to the top of the next column.

✦ **Shift+Return or Shift+Enter:** Moves up or to the previous column.

Defining articles

Articles are defined by drawing rectangular boxes around the text you want to include as part of your article thread. While using the Article tool, the rectangular boxes are visible. When the tool is not active, the rectangular boxes are invisible.

Click and drag open a rectangle surrounding the column where you want to begin a new article. When you release the mouse button, the rectangular box displays on the page. At each corner and side of the article box are handles where you can grab a handle and move it to reshape the box. The lower-right corner of the article box contains a plus (+) symbol. When you finish your edits, deselect the Article tool to exit edit mode. You can return to edit mode and add more columns after reselecting the Article tool. Click the plus symbol, and Acrobat knows you want to extend the article thread.

Tip   Article threads can be created at the time the PDF file is either exported or distilled with Acrobat Distiller. Many layout applications support creating articles prior to exporting to PDF. In some cases you may want to have a single article thread used to help user navigation through your document. To practice, identify an article in one of the programs discussed in Chapter 6 then export to PDF either through the program's export feature or by printing to PostScript and later distilling in Acrobat Distiller.

Ending an article thread

When you reach the end of the article, Acrobat needs to know you want to finish creating the thread. To end an article thread, press Return, Enter, or Esc. Acrobat prompts you with a dialog box for supplying the Title, Subject, Author, and Keywords fields for the article properties. This dialog box appears immediately after defining an article. Supplying the information at the time the dialog box opens is a good idea because then you won't need to worry about returning to the Article Properties dialog box for last-minute cleanup.

Deleting articles

You might want to delete a portion of an article thread or an entire article. To delete either, select the Article tool and click an article box. Press the Backspace (Delete) key on your keyboard or open a context menu and select Delete from the menu options. A dialog box opens providing options for deleting the currently selected box or the entire article.

If you select the Box button, the deletion eliminates the box within the article thread you selected when you pressed the Backspace (Delete) key on the keyboard. Clicking the Article button deletes all boxes in the thread across all pages in the document.

Combining articles

At times you may want to join two articles to create a single article. To join two articles, you must first have them defined in the PDF document. Move to the last column of the first article and click the plus symbol in the last box. This click loads the Article tool. Next, move to the beginning of the article to be joined to the first article and Ctrl+click or Option+click inside the first box. While you press the shortcut keys, the cursor icon changes, as illustrated in Figure 15-14.

Figure 15-14: When you press the Ctrl or Option key while clicking the mouse button, the cursor changes to an icon, informing you that the selected articles are to be joined.

The numbering at the top of each box in the second article changes after joining articles. For example, if you have two articles, the first numbered 1-1, 1-2, 1-3, and the second article numbered 2-1, 2-2, the new numbering for the second article changes to 1-4 and 1-5. Article 2 takes on the attributes of Article 1 and assumes the next order of the article boxes. In addition, the properties identified in the second article are lost. Because the continuation of the thread is from Article 1, all attributes for Article 1 supersede those of Article 2. You can select multiple articles and they can all be joined together in a single article following the same steps.

 Tip   When combining two articles, always start with the article containing the attributes to be retained. For example, in the preceding case, to retain the attributes of article 2, select the plus symbol at the end of the last column in article 2 and click. Ctrl+click or Option+click in the first box for article 1. When the two articles are combined, the attributes of article 2 are retained.

Working with the Link tool

You use the Link tool to create links from a rectangle drawn with the tool to other pages, other documents, and a host of other link actions you can define in the Link Properties dialog box. The area within a link rectangle is the hot spot for invoking a link action. Links used with tools like Bookmarks and Form Field buttons have the same attribute choices for the actions associated with the objects created with the respective tools.

When creating links with the Link tool, you encounter two dialog boxes used to establish link actions. For link actions used in opening a view, opening a secondary document, or opening a Web page, the actions choices are contained in the Create Link dialog box that opens when you click and drag open a link rectangle and release the mouse button. If you want to assign different link actions, you create a custom link and make attribute choices in the Link Properties dialog box. The Create Link dialog box requires you to make all options choices in the dialog box before you can access any commands in the Document Pane. The dialog box is static, which means you need to cancel out of the dialog box or click OK to use menus, short-cut keys, or select objects on a page in the Document Pane. When you work with the Link Properties dialog box you can access tools, menu commands, and select items such as buttons and other links on pages while the dialog box remains open.

Linking to views

Select the Link tool and click and drag open a rectangle on a page where you want the link placed. When you release the mouse button, the Create Link dialog box opens as shown in Figure 15-15. In the Create link dialog box you make one of four radio button selections. The first three radio buttons enable you to specify link attributes in the Create Link dialog box. If you select the fourth radio button and click OK, the Link Properties dialog box opens where different actions are selected for the link behavior.

The first three radio button choices offer you options for selecting a page view or a file to open. Options shown in the Create Link dialog box include

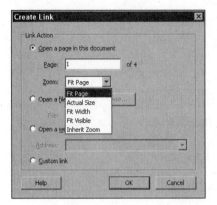

Figure 15-15: Select the Link tool and click and drag open a rectangle. The Create Link dialog box opens where you select link actions.

✦ **Open a page in this document:** The number of pages in the PDF document is reported below the radio button. You type a page number in the field and make a choice for the zoom level, and the link is fixed to the options choices. When using this dialog box you don't have access to navigation tools or page view zooms other than the menu options listed in the Zoom pull-down menu as shown in Figure 15-15. The link is created for pages in the open document only.

✦ **Open a file:** Select this option if you want to open a PDF document or any file from another authoring program. If you select a file other than files that can be opened in Acrobat, you (or your customer) must have the native authoring program installed in order to click on the link and open the file.

✦ **Open a web page:** When you select the radio button, the Address field is enabled. You type a URL in the Address field and the link is made to a PDF hosted on a Web site. When you add a URL, be certain to supply the complete Web address, including *http://www.* Once you add a URL, the address becomes a new default. Each time you create a new link, the last URL added to the Address field box is inherited and appears in the field box.

✦ **Custom Link:** Custom link in and of itself contains no properties. You select this radio button if you want to set a different action for a link. If you click on Custom Link and click the OK button, the Link Properties dialog box opens.

Tip

If you want to link from text on a PDF page, select the Select Text tool and highlight the text you want to use for a link button. Open a context menu and select Create Link. The Create Link from Selection dialog box opens with the same attribute choices found in the Create Link dialog box with the exception of the Custom Link option. If you want to edit text attributes such as text color after a link has been created, select the TouchUp Text tool and highlight the text. Open a context menu and select Attributes. Change the text color to a color that appears intuitive so a user knows a link is present. For example, blue text amidst black text communicates to a user that clicking on the blue texts invokes a link action. Links can also be created from the Select Image tool and the Snapshot tool by selecting images and/or after creating snapshots.

Cross-Reference

For more information on using the Select Image and Snapshot tools, see Chapter 9.

Editing a link action

If you create a link using any one of the first three radio buttons in the Create Link dialog box and later want to edit the link, you are not returned to the Create Link dialog box. The Create Link dialog box opens only after the first use of the Link tool when you initially create a link.

To change a link action, use either the Link tool or the Select Object tool. Double-click the mouse button with either tool to open the Link Properties. If you select the Hand tool and click on a link, the link action is employed.

Link appearance properties

The link appearance applies to the rectangle you draw when dragging the Link tool on a page in the Document Pane. Default appearances are established from the last appearance settings made for the link properties. To change properties you have two choices. You can use the Properties Bar (described when setting up the editing environment at the beginning of this chapter), or the Link Properties dialog box.

When using the Properties Bar, you make changes to link appearances for the items contained across the bar as shown in Figure 15-16. The choices in the Properties Bar include

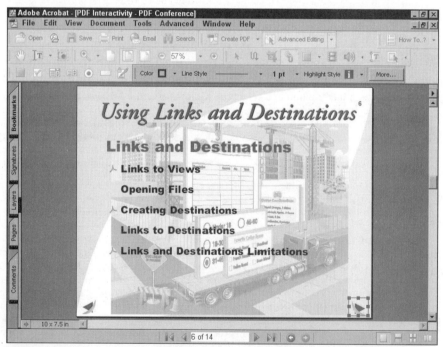

Figure 15-16: Select a link with the Link tool or the Select Object tool to enable the options choices in the Properties Bar.

✦ **Color:** The color pop-up window opens when you click on the stroked square at the far left side of the Properties Bar. Choices for color apply to strokes only and the options are the same as you find when changing colors in Note properties.

Cross-Reference

For more information on changing Note properties, see Chapter 14.

✦ **Line Style:** You have choices from the pull-down menu for No Line, Solid, Dashed, and Underline. No strokes might be used when you have a graphic image or text on a page and a link is apparent to a user. If text appears blue and underlined is one condition where you might use No Line for the line style.

✦ **Points:** The default shown in Figure 15-16 is 1 pt. You have choices for Thin, Medium, or Thick that translate to 1 pt, 2 pts, or 3 pts, respectively. The line weight you choose appears in the Properties Bar. If you select No Line, 0 pt appears listed in the Properties Bar.

✦ **Highlight Style:** Highlights are displayed when the mouse button is pressed. When you select the Hand tool and click on a link, the highlight is shown within the link rectangle while the mouse button is pressed. You can choose from No Highlight, Invert, Outline, and Inset.

✦ **More:** Clicking on the More button opens the Link Properties dialog box where the same appearance settings are available.

Link properties

To open the Link Properties dialog box, you can open a context menu and select Properties; double-click on a link with the Link tool or the Select Object tool; select a link and press the Enter or Return key; or, with a link selected, click on the More button in the Properties Bar. Opening context menus with the tools described previously performs two actions. A right-click in Windows or Control+click in Macintosh selects the link and opens the Link Properties dialog box. As you move the mouse cursor over a link with the Link tool or the Select Object tool, the link rectangle is highlighted in black with red handles. When you select the link, the highlight changes to red. Right clicking (Control+clicking on the Macintosh) selects the rectangle and opens a context menu.

When the Link Properties dialog box opens, you have options nested in two tabs: the Appearance tab and the Actions tab. By default the Appearance tab is placed in view as shown in Figure 15-17.

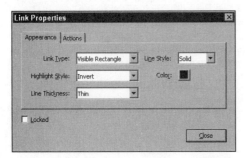

Figure 15-17: Two tabs exist in the Link Properties dialog box where you select appearance and actions options.

The same options offered in the Properties Bar for appearance settings are available in the Appearance tab with the addition of a check box for Locked. If you enable Locked, the link rectangle is locked to position on the document page and cannot be moved; however, when you select the Hand tool and click on a locked link, the action associated with the link still executes. Locking a link also disables all options choices in the Properties Bar and the Link Properties dialog box for that link. If you need to change properties for a locked link, open the Appearance tab and disable Locked.

Notice the dialog box uses a Close button instead of an OK button. Changes you make for either appearance settings or assigning action items are dynamic. You see the changes reflected in the Document Pane as you make changes. You can leave the Link Properties dialog box open while you create additional links and change properties and/or actions for each new link created. When finished editing links, use the Close button, check the box in the top-right corner, or press the Esc key. There is no Cancel button in the dialog box. If you make a change to a link's properties and want to revert back to the same properties assigned when the dialog box was opened, you must physically revert back to those changes before closing the Link Properties dialog box.

Link actions properties

Click on the Actions tab to assign an action to a link. The default link action is Go to a page in this document as shown in Figure 15-18 (the top item in the Actions list). After creating a link with another action type, the new action becomes the default.

Working in the Create Link and Link Properties dialog boxes for creating links to page views is handled differently. With the Create Link dialog box you need to specify a page number and click OK. The Create Link dialog box doesn't offer you a preview of the page link. When you open the Link Properties dialog box to reassign a page link, you can navigate pages while the dialog box is open. Find the page you want to link to, click the Edit button, type the viewed page number in the dialog box, and click the Close button in the Link Properties.

Tip

If you want to emulate the behavior more closely associated with earlier versions of Acrobat, create a link with the Link tool and select Custom link in the Create Link dialog box. Click OK and the Link Properties dialog box opens. Navigate to the page you want to assign the link action and click Add. When the action is listed in the Actions window, select it and click Edit. Type the page number in view and click Close. In this sequence, you see a preview of the page before you assign the link rather than trying to remember what page number to type in the Create Link dialog box.

The Select Action pull-down menu offers a number of link actions you can assign to a link. You can select an action and repeat a selection for a different action to nest action types that are executed in the order displayed in the Actions window. In Figure 15-18, three separate actions are associated with the same link. When you select the link with the Hand tool, a page opens, the article thread zooms to the Max Fit Visible Zoom established in the Preferences dialog box, and a sound plays. From the pull-down menu, you can choose action types such as the following.

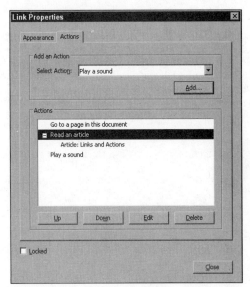

Figure 15-18: Click on the Actions tab to open the options settings for link actions.

Go to a page in this document

The default option is discussed in the last section. You can navigate to the destination page and click on the Add button. Click the Edit button, and the Go to a page in this document dialog box opens as shown in Figure 15-19. You need to type the page number and change the view if the current default does not match what you want. Click OK to close the Go to a page in this document dialog box. Click Close in the Link Properties dialog box after completing your edits.

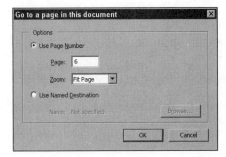

Figure 15-19: The Go to a page in this document dialog box allows you to select the page number and view for a link.

Go to a page in another document

This action type is a very nice addition to Acrobat 6.0. In earlier versions of Acrobat you needed to use JavaScript to open files on any page number other than the page assigned for the initial view. This new addition enables you to open another file and choose the page number to open in the linked file. Adobe engineers thought of everything in providing this new option in the links actions by offering choices for opening specific pages and how to handle the opening page behavior. When you select the action type in the Actions pull-down menu, the Go to a page in another document dialog box opens as shown in Figure 15-20.

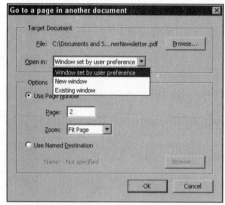

Figure 15-20: When you select the Go to page in another document action type, a dialog box opens where you set opening options.

✦ **Browse:** Click the Browse button to navigate your hard drive and find the PDF file you want to open.

Note Only PDF files are acceptable for the Browse action type.

✦ **Open in:** Three options are available from the pull-down menu.

- **Window set by user preference:** Opens the PDF document according to the preference choice made for handling cross-document links. Open the Preferences dialog box and click on General in the left pane. The check box for Open cross-document links in same window controls how files are managed from file open actions. If the check box is enabled, the current document in view with the Link button closes as the link destination opens. If the check box is disabled, the linked file opens on top of the open file and both remain open in the Document Pane. When you select Window set by user preference, the user preferences for handling cross-document viewing are enforced.

- **New window:** The linked file opens in a new window keeping the original file with the Link button open in Acrobat regardless of how the user preferences are established. The action is the same as when a user disables the preference setting.

- **Existing window:** The linked document opens while the original document closes regardless of how the user preferences are established. If you made any edits on the document with the link, Acrobat prompts you with a warning message asking whether you want to save your edits before the original document closes.

✦ **Options:** You select the page number and view from the Options settings. You can link to a named destination if you created destinations in the target document.

For information on working with destinations, see "Creating Destinations" later in this chapter.

Go to snapshot view

The first task you need to do before addressing the Link Properties when using the Go to snapshot view action is to create a snapshot. Navigate to the page you want to link to and select the Snapshot tool. Marquee the area for the zoom view and a snapshot is placed on the clipboard.

For more information on creating snapshots, see Chapter 9.

With a snapshot in place, select the Link tool and click and drag open a rectangle for the link hot spot. Click Custom Link in the Create Link dialog box and click OK. Select Go to snapshot view from the Select Action pull-down menu and click the Add button. The Create View from Snapshot dialog box opens confirming the snapshot view is converted to a link destination. Click OK in the dialog box shown in Figure 15-21 and click Close in the Link Properties dialog box.

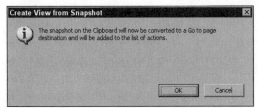

Figure 15-21: After creating a snapshot and adding a Go to snapshot view action type, the Create View from Snapshot dialog box opens, informing you that the link destination is added to the list of actions.

When you use the Go to snapshot view link action, be aware that no extra data such as destinations, pasted images, or other such matter are added to your document. Using this method simply captures the zoom view from the snapshot and adds a custom zoom size for the link destination. If you navigate to a page and click and drag to open a marquee with the Zoom tool and link to that zoom view, the results are the same as using a snapshot.

Open a file

You use Open a file to open any file on your computer. When you select the action type and click on the Add button, the Open dialog box opens. Browse your hard drive and select the file you want to open. If the file is other than a PDF file, you (or your customer) need to have the authoring application that created the file installed on your computer in order to execute the link action. Creating the link does not require you to have any external programs installed on your computer.

Read an article

When you select Read an article as the action type for a link, the Select Article dialog box opens when you click on the Add button. If no articles are present in the PDF document, you receive a dialog box alerting you that there are no articles present and you can't use this link action. When articles are present, select the article you want to associate with the link from the listed articles in the Select Article dialog box. When you select the link in the navigation mode, Acrobat opens the page where the first box in the article appears. Additionally, the cursor changes to the Article icon that enables you to continue reading the selected article.

Execute a menu item

You can use almost all the menu commands in Acrobat as link actions. If you want to open a file, convert to PDF, open or collapse palettes in the Navigation Pane, show or hide toolbars, or use any other menu command, you can use the Execute a menu item action.

On Windows a dialog box opens where the top-level menu commands are nestled together in the Menu Item Selection dialog box shown in Figure 15-22. In the dialog box, select a menu and scroll down the menu items to select an item. Figure 15-22 shows the Window ➪ Split menu command.

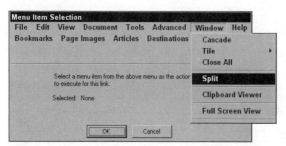

Figure 15-22: Select menu commands from the Menu Item Selection dialog box when using the Execute a menu item action type.

On the Macintosh, the Menu Item dialog box opens as shown in Figure 15-23. The dialog box is informational and instructs you to select menu commands from the top-level menus. While the dialog box remains open, select a menu and a menu command, as you normally would while editing in Acrobat. The menu selection you choose is set for the link destination.

Figure 15-23: When you choose Execute a menu item on the Macintosh, the Menu Item dialog box informs you to make menu selections from the menu bar at the top of the Acrobat window.

Set layer visibility

For PDF documents containing layers, you first create the layer view you want in the Layers palette. Open the Layers palette and show/hide the layers you want to display when a user clicks on the link. In Figure 15-24, two layers were hidden from the Layers palette. When a link is created using the Set layer visibility action type, the layers display the view when the link is created.

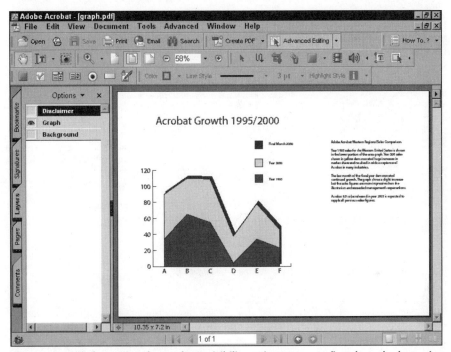

Figure 15-24: When using the Set layer visibility action type, you first show the layer view you want to display to assign it to the link action.

After setting your layer view for the display when the link button is selected, create a link and click on the Custom Link button. Select Set layer visibility from the Actions pull-down menu and a dialog box opens, informing you the current layer state has been captured, as shown in Figure 15-25.

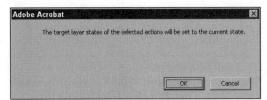

Figure 15-25: When you add the Set layer visibility action type, a dialog box opens, informing you the layer state has been captured.

When you return to the Document Pane, open the Layer palette Options menu and select Reset to Initial Visibility. This command resets the layer visibility to the default view. Presumably, your layer state is set to a different view when you create a link; therefore, the view should appear different when you reset the layers to initial visibility. In this example, all three layers are set back to initial visibility. The link rectangle appears in the top-right corner shown in Figure 15-26. When I click on the link button, two of the layers are hidden, as shown in Figure 15-24.

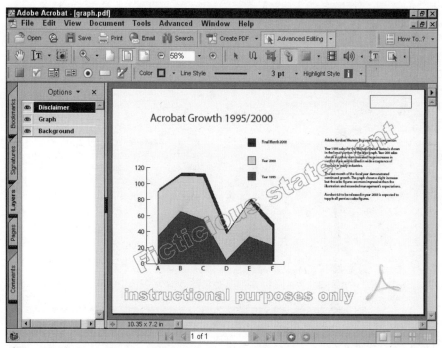

Figure 15-26: Open the Layers palette and select Reset to Initial Visibility from the Layer palette Options menu. When you click on the link button, the layer visibility changes to the state established when the link was created.

Cross-Reference

For more information on layer visibility, see Chapter 17.

Show/hide a field

The Show/hide a field action enables the user to hide selected form fields. Forms can be created to display and hide form fields for help menus, informational items, protecting data, and so on. You can make a hidden field visible by opening the Show/Hide Field dialog box and select the Hide radio button. Within this dialog box the options for both hiding and showing fields are enabled through radio buttons.

Cross-Reference

For more information on working with Acrobat PDF forms, see Part VI.

Submit a form

Form and comment data contained in PDF documents can be transported on the World Wide Web. When a user completes a form, the data can be submitted to a URL as a Form Data File (FDF), HTML, or XML data. The PDF author can then collect and process the data. Using form and comment data with Web servers has some requirements you need to work out with the ISP hosting your Web site. If you use forms on PDF Web pages, include a button that submits data after the user completes the form. Using the Submit a form action enables you to identify the URL where the data are submitted and determine which data type is exported from the PDF document. If comment data are to be submitted, a check box enabling comment delivery appears in the dialog box.

For more information on submitting PDF forms to Web servers, see Chapter 26.

Reset a form

The Reset a form link action relates to PDF documents with form fields. When a form is filled out, you can reset the form that removes all data contained in the form fields. Acrobat provides an opportunity to clear the data from all fields or from selected fields you identify individually. A Reset a form dialog box opens, enabling you to select the fields to clear.

For more information on resetting forms, see Chapter 25.

Import form data

When you select the Import form data option and click Add, the Select File Containing Form Data dialog box opens. Select the file containing the form data you want to import and click on the Select button. Imported form data are from files saved in FDF format that are exported from PDF documents and saved as FDF. When you click on the Select button, the data matching identical form fields are imported. Using Import form data limits you to importing data saved only in FDF format. If you use the Execute Menu Item action, data can be imported when saved as FDF, XFDF, and TXT.

Run a JavaScript

JavaScript adds great opportunity for making PDF documents interactive and dynamic. You can add JavaScripts to link button actions as well as form fields. When you select Run a JavaScript and click the Add button, the JavaScript Editor dialog box opens. You type the code in the dialog box, or copy and paste code from a text editor to the JavaScript Editor. Select OK to commit the JavaScript.

Play media (Acrobat 5 compatible)

To select the Play Media action type, a media file must be present in the PDF file. If there is no media file present, you are prompted with a dialog box. You import media clips with the Movie tool and at least one movie file needs to be present before you can create a link with the Play Media action type. After a movie is contained in a PDF file, create a link and select the action type. After you click Add, the Play Media (Acrobat 5 Compatible) dialog box opens. If you have several media clips in the PDF document, the Select Media pull-down menu lists all the clips by filename. Select a file and choose from one of four action types in the Select Operation pull-down menu shown in Figure 15-27. You may choose to play a movie, stop a movie, pause a movie during the play, or have it resume after it has been paused.

Figure 15-27: When the Play Media (Acrobat 5 Compatible) dialog box opens, select a media clip from the Select media pull-down menu and select the play option from the Select Operation pull-down menu.

Play a sound

You can create a button to play a sound in a PDF document. When you select the Play a sound action and click on the Add button, the Open dialog box opens where you locate a sound file on your hard drive and import the sound. Acrobat pauses a moment while the sound is converted to a format usable in Acrobat viewers. After it's imported in the PDF, the sound can be played across platforms. When the link button is selected, the sound plays. Sounds imported with the Play a Sound action and those added with the Sound Attach tool support only Acrobat 5 media. If you use the Sound tool you can choose to import either Acrobat 5 or Acrobat 6 compatible sounds.

Cross-Reference For importing sounds with the Sound Attach tool, see Chapter 14. For information on using Acrobat 5 and Acrobat 6 compatible sound and media see Chapter 16.

Notice the Advanced Editing toolbar contains a Sound tool. You can use the Sound tool to import sounds. In addition, the Attach Sound comment tool is used to import sound files. Playing sounds from any of these tools is identical. The Sound tool and the Attach Sound comment tool are limited to adding sounds on a page where a user needs to click or double-click a button to play the sound. The link action is more versatile as you can add sounds with nested link actions, page actions, and form fields. Sound files are supported from files saved as AIFF or WAV.

Cross-Reference For information on using the Sound tool, see Chapter 16, and for information on using the Attach Sound tool, see Chapter 9.

Play media (Acrobat 6 compatible)

Playing Acrobat 6-compatible media clips requires you to first import a movie (or import a Sound). When you import a movie with the Movie tool or import a sound with the Sound tool you have a choice for importing the media as an Acrobat 5- or Acrobat 6-compatible file. Acrobat 6 allows you to embed Acrobat 6-compatible media in the PDF document. All previous versions of Acrobat treated movie files as links. When you transport PDFs with Acrobat 5–compatible movie files you need to send the movie file along with the PDF whereas Acrobat 6–compatible files offer you a choice for importing the movie and embedding the file in the PDF document.

After you have imported a media clip with the Movie tool as an embedded file or a file link, select the Play media Acrobat 6 (Compatible) action and click on the Add button. The Play Media (Acrobat 6 Compatible) dialog box opens as shown in Figure 15-28. The operations available with Acrobat 6-compatible imports are the same as those used with Acrobat 5–compatible imports, with the exception of being able to add a Custom JavaScript and Play from beginning.

To add a JavaScript, select Custom JavaScript from the Operation to Perform pull-down menu and click on the Specify JavaScript button. Other dialog boxes open for specifying a rendition if you choose to do so and the JavaScript Editor dialog box opens where a custom JavaScript is written.

Figure 15-28: In addition to offering the same operations available with Acrobat 5–compatible imports, Acrobat 6 compatibility provides an option for adding a custom JavaScript.

You can use media clips saved in a variety of formats compatible with Acrobat 5 or the newer formats supported with Acrobat 6. When you use the Play Media (Acrobat 6 Compatible) action type, the file you select does not require Acrobat 6 compatibility for newer file types per se. However, Acrobat 6 compatibility enables you to embed files and use custom JavaScripts, and provides support for newer compression schemes.

When you use Acrobat 6 compatibility, be aware that users of earlier versions of Acrobat won't be able to use your PDF documents. If you need to work with users of older versions of Acrobat viewers, be certain to use Acrobat 5 compatibility.

Cross-Reference For more information on Acrobat 6 compatible files and new file formats, see Chapter 16.

Open a Web link

The World Wide Web Link option enables you to associate a link action to a Web address. Web links can be contained in PDF documents locally on your computer or within a PDF page where the PDF is hosted on a Web server. If a Web link is contained locally in a PDF document, selecting the link launches the browser configured with Acrobat and establishes a URL connection. Acrobat remains open in the background while the Web browser is viewed in the foreground. Like the Submit a form requirement mentioned a few paragraphs back, always use the complete URL to identify a Web address.

When you specify a URL in the Edit URL dialog box that opens after you click on the Add button in the Link Properties, you can add custom viewing in the URL address for the way you want to open a PDF document. For example, if you want to view a page other than the opening page you can add to the URL a request for opening any page number. To open a specific page, enter this text:

http://www.mycompany.com/myDoc.pdf#page=3

In this example the file myDoc.pdf opens on page 3 in the Web browser. In addition to opening a specific page you can add other viewing parameters such as zoom levels, page modes such as viewing layers or Bookmarks, opening named destinations, and other viewing options.

Cross-Reference For more information on setting viewing options with Web links, see Chapter 20.

Managing links

Acrobat 6.0 provides many menu options for link management that were not available in earlier versions of the program. You can now copy/paste, align, and distribute links and more through the use of a context menu. If you need to apply these editing tasks to multiple links, select the Select Object tool and click and drag through the links you want to manage. If you attempt to use the Link tool, you can select only a single link.

After selecting a link with the Link tool or selecting multiple links with the Select Object tool, open a context menu as shown in Figure 15-29. The context menu offers several menu categories with submenu items used for managing links. The menu items include

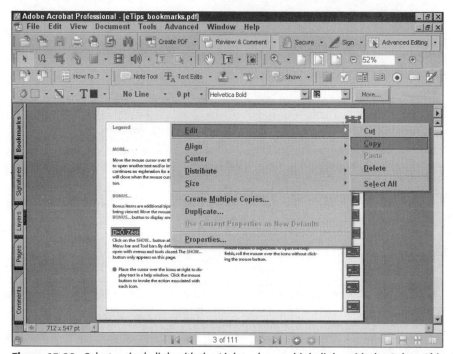

Figure 15-29: Select a single link with the Link tool or multiple links with the Select Object tool and open a context menu. Select a menu category and select from the submenu items the command you want to use.

✦ **Edit:** The Edit menu contains several items in a submenu for cut/copy/paste, as are accessible in the top-level Edit menu. You can delete a link or group of links by selecting Delete.

• **Select All:** Select All deserves some special comment. When you select a link with the Link tool choose Edit ➪ Select All, all links are selected on a page. If you click on a link with the Select Object tool and choose Select All from the Edit submenu, all objects selectable with the Select Object tool are selected on the page. For example, if you have links and form fields, Select All selects all links and form fields on the target page. If you want to edit the links for deletion, alignment, copying, and so on, be certain to click on the Link tool then use Edit ➪ Select All.

✦ **Align:** You can align multiple links Left, Right, Top, Bottom, and along the vertical and horizontal centers. Choose the respective submenu command for the alignment option of your choice.

✦ **Distribute:** If you have a row or column of links and you want to position them equidistant from each other, choose the Distribute command and select from either Vertically or Horizontally. Vertically distributes a column and Horizontally distributes a row of link objects.

✦ **Size:** As you create link rectangles, the rectangle size may differ from among a series of links you add to a page. To resize links on a given page to the same size, select one of the links with the Link tool. Using context menu select "Select All" Move the Link tool to the target size link rectangle and open a context menu. (The target link rectangle is displayed with a red keyline and red handles while the other rectangles in the selected group are highlighted blue). Select from the submenu Height, Width, or Both. The selected link rectangles are resized to the size of the target link.

✦ **Properties:** The Link Properties dialog box opens. If you select more than one link rectangle, the link actions shows Varies in the action list if the link actions are different from among the selected links. You can apply common appearance settings to all selected links or you can edit actions if the actions are all the same among the selected links.

STEPS: Creating links

To gain a little experience with creating and manipulating links, try practicing on any PDF document you have on your hard drive following these steps:

1. **Open a PDF document.** For this example, I use a PDF file containing a contents page. I want to create links from the contents headings on the contents page to the respective pages in the PDF document.

2. **Create a link from text.** Select the Text Select tool and click and drag through a word or line of text. Open a context menu and select Create Link as shown in Figure 15-30.

3. **Set the link action.** The link needs to open another page in the same document. In this example, I type 3 in the Create Link from Selection dialog box shown in Figure 15-31. Click OK when you are finished editing the options in the Create Link from Selection dialog box.

4. **Adjust appearance properties.** From the Properties Bar, select No Line from the Line Style pull-down menu. In this example the text itself is intuitive for the user to know a link exists; therefore, no keyline borders are needed.

5. **Create additional links.** Add additional links. If you use an example similar to this one for linking from a contents page, create links for the remaining text on the page. Repeat the previous steps for adding links and set the appearance properties to the same values.

Tip   If you forget to set link appearances when creating the links, you can change appearances on a group of links with common properties. Use the Link tool and select all the links from a context menu. In the Properties Bar select No Line from the Line Style pull-down menu.

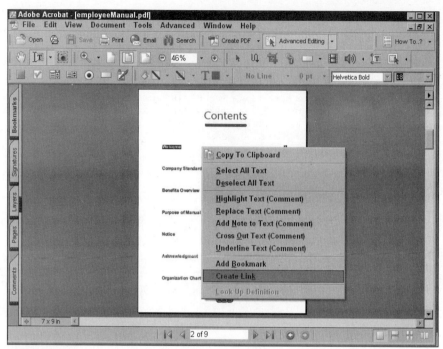

Figure 15-30: Select text with the Text Select tool. Open a context menu and select Create Link.

Figure 15-31: I left the default action at Open a page in this document and entered 3 for the page number.

6. **Link to a file.** The last item on my contents page requires the user to open a second file. For this example I need to create a link that opens another PDF document. Select text with the Select text tool on the text where you want to click to open a secondary file and select Create Link from a context menu. Select the Open a file radio button shown in Figure 15-31 and click on the Browse button. Locate the file to link to in the Select File to Open dialog box and click Select. The Specify Open Preference dialog box opens as shown in Figure 15-32. Select Existing window from the options and click OK.

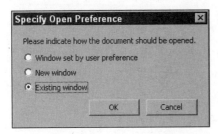

Figure 15-32: Select Existing Window in the Specify Open Preference dialog box to open the new file while closing the existing file.

7. **Save the document.** Before you execute any link actions, save the file. Choose File ➪ Save to update the file or File ➪ Save As to create a copy of the file.

8. **Click on the link to open a file.** Select the Hand tool and click on the link to open the second file. The current document closes as the new file opens.

9. **Create a link to a page in another document.** In this example I want to create a link that closes the file in view and takes me back to my contents page in my original file. My contents page is page 2 in the original file; therefore, I need to create a link to a specific page using the Go to page in another document link action.

   Select the Link tool and drag open a rectangle. Be certain to use the Link tool and do not select text with the Select Text tool. The Create Link from Selection dialog box doesn't offer you an option to link to a specific page in another document.

   When the Create Link dialog box opens, select Custom Link and click OK. In the Link Properties dialog box select Go to page in another document from the Select Action pull-down menu as shown in Figure 15-33.

10. **Specify the link destination page.** Click on the Add button in the Link Properties dialog box. The Go to a page in another document dialog box opens. Click on Browse and select the original file you opened.

    Enter a page number and select Existing window from the Open in pull-down menu as shown in Figure 15-34. Click OK and click Close to exit the Link Properties dialog box.

11. **Save the file.** Because the document closes when the link action is invoked, you'll want to save the file before continuing. If you make an edit, then click on a link that closes a fille while opening another, Acrobat prompts you for a save in a warning dialog box. If a dialog box opens asking you to save, be certain to click Yes.

12. **Click the link to return to the original file.** Test your link by selecting the Hand tool and clicking on the link. To be certain a file closes when the link destination opens, select the Window menu and view all open documents listed at the bottom of the window. If you created the link properly, you should see only the destination document listed in the Window menu.

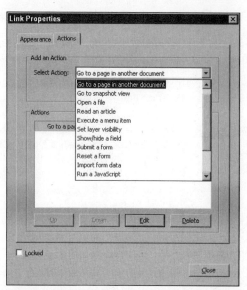

Figure 15-33: Click on Custom Link in the Create Link dialog box to open the Link Properties dialog box. Select Go to a page in another document from the Select Action pull-down menu. Click on the Add button to add the action to the Actions list.

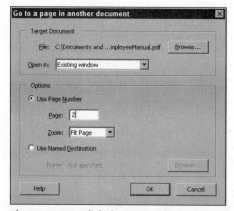

Figure 15-34: Click the Browse button to select a file to open. Select Existing window from the Open in pull-down menu and enter the page number for the link destination.

This example shows you how to create interactive documents by linking back and forth between files while controlling the document open options. As you practice creating links, try to understand some of the differences between using the Create Link dialog box and the Link Properties dialog box so you know when to use one set of options versus another.

Creating URL links from text

Acrobat provides a method for automatically creating links from text in a document where the text describes a URL. The text needs to contain the complete and precise URL including http://. If you have a Web address in a document on all pages, such as your company Web site address, you can create a link to the Web address the same way as when using the Edit URL dialog box when adding Link actions.

To add links to URLs across a range of pages, choose Advanced ⇨ Links ⇨ Create from URLs in Document. After making the menu selection the Create Web Links dialog box opens as shown in Figure 15-35.

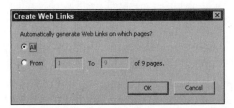

Figure 15-35: To automatically create links to Web pages across multiple pages, choose Advanced ⇨ Links ⇨ Create from URLs in Document. Select the page range in the Create Web Links dialog box and click OK.

You can choose to scan all pages or a selected group of pages in the Create Web Links dialog box. Click OK after making the page range selection and Acrobat analyzes the text in the document. When Acrobat encounters a bona fide URL, for example, http://www.mycompany.com, a link rectangle is created, with the destination specified as the URL in an Open Web Link action.

Note   Acceptable syntax for URLs includes using both *http://...* and *https://*.

If you have existing Web links in a document or you create Web links, you can automatically delete them using the same menu command with a different submenu selection. Choose Advanced ⇨ Links ⇨ Remove All Links from Document. The Remove Web Links dialog box opens where you make the same choices for scanning all pages or a selected range of pages. After making the page range selection, click OK and all links to URLs are removed from the document.

Working with Page Properties

If you were a fan of Page Actions in previous versions of Acrobat and you start looking around in Acrobat 6.0, you're going to spend a lot of time trying to figure out where they are. Page Actions are still available in Acrobat 6.0; they just went through a name change and are now found in the Page Properties.

For those new to Acrobat, a Page Action is like a link button that invokes an action when a page is opened or closed in the Document Pane. You don't have to click on anything, because the trigger for executing the action type is handled by Acrobat when the page opens or closes. All the action types you have available with links are the same actions that are associated with Page Actions.

To create a Page Action, open the Pages palette. Select a page with the Hand tool and open a context menu. From the menu options select Page Properties. The Page Properties dialog box opens with two sets of properties types available. The default page properties options are contained in the tab for Tab Order, but these settings don't have anything to do with setting a Page Action, so I'll skip them for the moment.

Cross-Reference   For information related to setting Tab Orders, see Chapter 26.

It is the second tab in the Page Properties dialog box that is used for setting Page Actions. Click on the Actions tab shown in Figure 15-36, and the options for defining actions to page behavior are displayed. Two areas are used for applying a Page Action to any page in a PDF document. You first select the Trigger for either Page Open or Page Close and then select the action from the Select Action pull-down menu. The options in this menu are the same as you have available with link actions.

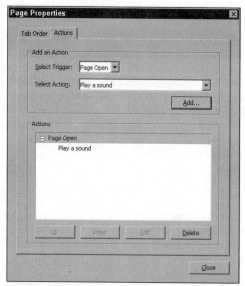

Figure 15-36: Open the Page Properties dialog box from a context menu on a page thumbnail. Click on the Actions tab to open the Page Actions options settings.

Page Actions help you make your PDF documents more automated. You might select a sound to play when a file opens as shown in Figure 15-36. You may want to set layer visibility, play a movie, or execute a menu item. Of all the options available for action types, with Page Actions you have the addition of an infinite number of choices when running JavaScripts. You might want to run a script that analyzes the Acrobat viewer version when a user opens a PDF document and alerts the user that Acrobat 6 is needed to properly view your document if the user opens the file in a viewer version earlier than Acrobat 6. This example and many more options are available to you when running JavaScripts from Page Actions.

To see examples of JavaScripts that analyze Acrobat viewer versions and viewer types, see Chapter 27.

Creating Destinations

A destination is a specific location in a document. Whereas a Bookmark and a link may link to page 5 in a file, a destination links to the location where page 5 resides. If you delete page 5, Bookmarks and links have no place to go and the links are often referred to as *dead links*. If you delete page 5 where a destination has been created, the destination remains at the same location — that is, following page 4 and preceding page 6. Furthermore, if you insert a page after page 4, the Bookmarks and links are linked to page 6. All pages shift to make room for a new page, but the links from Bookmarks and links remain fixed on a specific page. With destinations, if you insert a page after page 4, the destination takes you to the new page 5.

For users who have difficulty fully comprehending the difference between Bookmarks and destinations, let me say it another way. Assume for a moment that you have three ice cream cones seated in holder. The first cone is filled with strawberry, the second chocolate, and the third vanilla. If you Bookmark the chocolate cone, the Bookmark takes you to the second cone filled with chocolate. If someone eats the chocolate cone the vanilla cone slides left and occupies the second holder position, but the Bookmark is dead and has no place to go. If you create a destination, the destination is created to the holder where the chocolate cone resides. If someone eats the chocolate cone and the vanilla cone slides over to the second holder, the destination now goes to the vanilla cone.

Destinations are also used when you want to use JavaScripts for creating pop-up menus, creating smart forms, and adding other interactive features.

It all sounds pretty nifty but there's a downside to using named destinations. Adding many destinations in a PDF document adds a lot of overhead to the file size. Destinations can make a PDF bulky and slow if they are used extensively. Destinations should not be thought of as a substitute for Bookmarks and links, but rather, a complement to creating interactive documents when other methods don't support the same features.

Destination tools

You create, organize, and display destinations within the Destinations palette. To open the palette, choose View ➪ Navigation Tabs ➪ Destinations. If you want to use the Destinations palette frequently in an Acrobat session, you can drag the tab away from the palette and place it in the Navigation Pane. As a tab in the Navigation Pane it is visible and easily accessible until you remove it by dragging it out of the pane.

The palette contains a few icons and a pull-down menu as shown in Figure 15-37. In addition to the palette tools, context menus offer several menu options. You create, edit, and manage all destinations through this palette. The options include

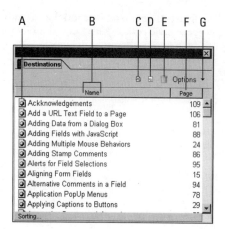

Figure 15-37: Open the Destinations palette by choosing View ➪ Navigation Tabs ➪ Destinations. Several icons and a list of destinations appear in the palette.

✦ **Destinations list (A):** When you create destinations, they are listed in the palette.

✦ **Name (B):** Name in the palette is a button. When you click the button, the destinations are sorted alphabetically according to name.

✦ **Scan Document (C):** Click the icon appearing first in the palette to scan the open document for any existing destinations. Destinations don't dynamically appear when you open a PDF. You must first scan the document to see them listed in the palette. From the Options pull-down menu the Scan Document menu command performs the same action. Another option for scanning a document is to open a context menu away from destination names.

✦ **New Destination (D):** You use the Adobe icon and a context menu option to create new destinations. You create a destination by first navigating to the page and view, then creating the destination, much like you create Bookmarks.

✦ **Delete (E):** You can use the Trashcan icon in the palette, as well as a menu command available when opening a context menu on a selected destination, to delete the destination.

✦ **Page (F):** Page is also a button. When you click it, the destinations are sorted according to page number and tab order on the page.

✦ **Pull-down menu (Options) (G):** Like other Acrobat palettes, a pull-down menu offers menu options for other commands. With destinations, the palette menu commands include Scan Document, New Destination, Sort by Name, and Sort by Page.

✦ **Go to Destination:** If you select a destination name and open a context menu, the first menu choice is Go to Destination, as shown in Figure 15-38. Keep in mind this context menu offers this option only when the menu is opened when a destination is selected. When you invoke the command, Acrobat opens the destination page.

✦ **Delete:** Select a destination and select either the Trashcan icon or the menu command to remove the destination from the document.

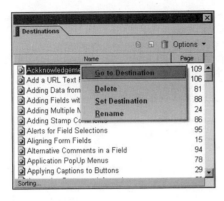

Figure 15-38: When named destinations have been created, selecting a destination and opening a context menu offers the same menu commands as found in the Options pull-down menu.

✦ **Set Destination:** If the current destination view is not what you want, navigate to the desired page and click on Set Destination. The destination is modified to open the current view when the destination is selected.

✦ **Rename:** You can change a destination name from any of those names listed in the palette. Select a destination name and select Rename. The text for the destination name is highlighted enabling you to edit the name.

Creating a pop-up menu

You can use destinations to create a pop-up menu on a page that displays menu options for navigating to other pages. To create a pop-up menu that links to other pages you create destinations then add some JavaScript to a link or button field. When a menu item is selected, the page destination opens in the Document Pane.

To create a pop-up menu with named destinations, open a PDF document containing several pages. Begin by creating a destination for each menu item you want to display in a pop-up menu. Navigate to a page and set the zoom view using the Zoom tool or Zoom toolbar.

Creating the destination links

Open the Destinations palette by choosing View ➪ Navigation Tabs ➪ Destinations. Scan the document for destinations by clicking on the Scan Document tool in the palette.

If the page and view are set, click the Create new destination button in the Destinations palette. Creating a Destination is like capturing a view. After creating a Destination, you need to name the destination in the Destinations palette. The default name is Untitled. Start typing after you create a destination and the Untitled text is replaced with the text you type. If you type and Acrobat does not accept the text, select the Untitled name and select Rename from a context menu. Continue navigating to new pages and zoom views and create new destinations.

When you finish adding new destinations, your Destinations palette should appear similar to Figure 15-39. In Figure 15-39 the destinations are sorted by name. You can also sort destinations by page number by clicking on the Page button in the palette.

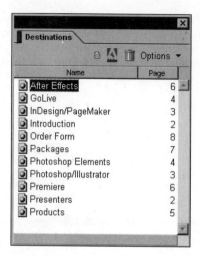

Figure 15-39: After you add destinations, the Destinations palette displays the names you used when creating each new destination. The destinations are sorted by name in the list. To sort the list by page number, click on the Page button in the Destinations palette.

Creating a JavaScript link action

After you have finished adding new destinations, the next step requires a little programming. If you haven't used the JavaScript Editor, don't panic. These steps are no more complicated than following a few simple directions.

Cross-Reference

For a better understanding on using JavaScript and the script created here, see Chapter 27.

Select the Link tool and click and drag open a link rectangle. Ideally, it's best if you have some text or an icon on the page indicating that a button or link is present. Without getting into button faces and icons, you can also simply use a keyline border to show where the link appears on the page. In the Create Link dialog box select Custom Link and click OK. The Link Properties dialog box opens with the Actions tab in view. From the Select Action pull-down menu, select Run a JavaScript.

Click Add and the JavaScript Editor opens. In the JavaScript Editor type the following code:

```
1. var c = app.popUpMenu
2. (["category_1", "item_1", "item_2", "item_3"],
3. ["category_1", "item_1", "item_2", "item_3"],
4. ["category_1", "item_1", "item_2", "item_3"]);
5. this.gotoNamedDest(c);
```

In the script, the first line of code sets a variable *c* for a pop-up menu. Regardless of what your destinations are named or the contents of your PDF, copy this line of code exactly as you see it into your JavaScript Editor.

Lines 2 to 4 contain the categories and submenu commands that link to the destinations you created. Here's where you need to modify your code. Where you see "category_x" replace the name with a category title of your choosing. You might want to use names like Personnel, Administration, and Finance, or you may use category names like Designs, Illustrations, and Photos, or any other combination of names that relate to the categories you want to use. Notice that line 2 begins with a open parenthesis — (—followed by a left bracket — [. These characters are important to include in your code.

Continuing with the data in lines 2 through 4 are three *item* numbers contained in quotes and separated by commas. These names need to replicate your destination names. Type the destination names exactly, including letter case, as you created them in your Destinations palette. The order in which you add the names is unimportant. Also notice that after the last destination name and quote mark no comma is inserted. Lines 2 and 3 end with a comma and line 4 ends with a semicolon. These characters are also important to type just as you see them in the sample code.

Line 5, the final line of code, is the instruction to take the user to the destination selected from the menu options. Type this line exactly as you see it in your JavaScript Editor. Click OK in the JavaScript Editor and click Close in the Link Properties dialog box. Select the Hand tool and click on the link. You should see a pop-up menu similar to Figure 15-40. In this example, I included six items in the first category by adding more destination names in quote marks. In Figure 15-41 you can see the code that produced the pop-up menu in Figure 15-40.

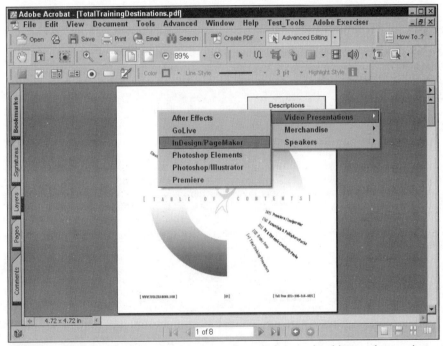

Figure 15-40: If the pop-up menu was created properly, you should see submenu items listed when selecting a category.

Note   To modify JavaScript code, select the Link tool and double-click on the link. In the Link Properties dialog box select the item denoted as Run a JavaScript in the Actions list and click on the Edit button. The JavaScript edit dialog box opens where you can make changes to the code.

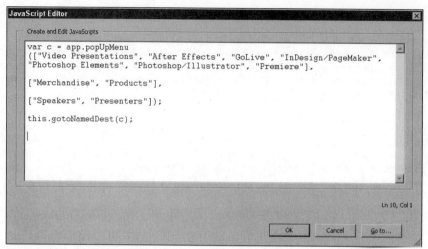

Figure 15-41: In the JavaScript Editor, I added the script that produced the pop-up menu shown in Figure 15-40. Select a name from the submenu and Acrobat should open the page associated with the destination. Check your work to be certain all menu items open the respective destinations. If you encounter an error, double-check the spelling and letter case for the destination name and the code you typed in the JavaScript Editor.

In this example, destinations are used to navigate pages in a PDF document via a pop-up menu. If the design of your PDF documents better suits pop-up menus, you have many options when using JavaScripts. You can also create pop-up menus with JavaScripts that open other PDF documents, specific pages in other PDF documents, and that execute many different menu commands.

Cross-Reference

For an example of a pop-up menu where secondary PDF documents are opened, see Chapter 27.

Working with Buttons

In the previous section you saw how to use the Link tool to navigate pages and open files. When links are created, you need some kind of icon or text that lets a user know that a link button exists. If you add links on a page in empty white space with no border keyline, users won't know where or when to click on a link button. If you want to use images or icons for button appearances, you can use another form of link tool with the Button tool that supports importing icons.

Using form fields instead of links has some advantages. You can add image icons to button fields, use rollover effects, copy and paste fields across multiple pages, and you have all the same action types accessible as those used with Bookmarks, links, and page actions.

Cross-Reference

The discussion of button fields in this chapter is limited to creating button fields with actions similar to those discussed in this chapter when creating link actions. For a more thorough discussion on using form fields in Acrobat, see Part VI.

Creating a button field

The Button tool is on the Forms toolbar. If you don't have the Forms toolbar open, choose Tools ➪ Advanced Editing ➪ Forms ➪ Show Forms Toolbar. Dock the toolbar in the Toolbar Well. The Button tool appears on the left side of the Forms toolbar. Select the tool and click and drag open a rectangle. Users of earlier versions of Acrobat will notice that the Field Properties dialog box does not open immediately.

To access the Button Properties dialog box click on the More button in the Properties Bar or double-click on the field. By default Acrobat automatically names the field for you beginning with Button 1, then Button 2 for the next button you create, and Button 3, and so on. When you open the Properties dialog box you can change the field name in the General tab. Highlight the default name and type a new name. In this example I want to create some navigation buttons. The name of the button I'll use is goNext as shown in Figure 15-42.

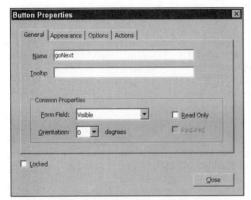

Figure 15-42: Double-click on the button field or click the More button on the Properties Bar to open the Button Properties dialog box. Click on General and type a name for the button field.

Button faces are handled in the Options settings. Click on Options and select Icon Only from the Layout pull-down menu. Click on the Choose Icon button and the Select Icon dialog box opens. From this dialog box you need to access yet another dialog box by clicking on the Browse button. The Open dialog box opens where you can navigate your hard drive and select a file to import as your button face. Any file format compatible with the Create PDF tool is acceptable. Click on a filename in the Open dialog box and click on Select. Acrobat returns you to the Select Icon dialog box where a preview of the imported file is displayed as shown in Figure 15-43.

If the preview looks like the file you want to use as a button face, click OK to return to the Button Properties dialog box. Click on the Actions tab where you assign the action type associated with your button. In this dialog box you make a choice for the trigger action. The default is Mouse Up, which means when the mouse button is released the action executes. Leave the Select Trigger menu option at the default and open the Select Action pull-down menu.

Select Execute a menu item from the pull-down menu. On Windows the Menu item selection dialog box opens. On the Macintosh make a menu item selection from the top-level menu bar. Choose View ➪ Go To ➪ Next Page. Click OK and click Close in the Button Properties dialog box.

Figure 15-43: The Select Icon dialog box displays a thumbnail preview of the imported file. Click OK to return to the Button Properties dialog box.

Repeat the same steps by creating a new button and adding an icon and choosing View ➪ Go To ➪ Previous Page from the Menu Item Selection dialog box (Windows) or top-level menu bar (Macintosh).

To move a button field, select either the Button tool or the Select Object tool. In the example here, two buttons are created to navigate back and forth between pages. If you want to move the two buttons together, you need to use the Select Object tool. Drag the buttons to an area where page navigation is easily performed when you click on the buttons to navigate pages.

Duplicating buttons

At this point there's an obvious advantage for using a button field over a link when you need some image contained within the link button. Another advantage for using button fields over links is the ability to duplicate button fields across pages. The hard part is finished after you create the fields and add the button faces. The next step is to duplicate buttons so you don't have to copy/paste them on each page.

With the button fields in place, select the Select Object tool and click and drag through both fields. Be certain to click and drag outside the first field so as not to select it while dragging. When both fields are selected, open a context menu and select Duplicate as shown in Figure 15-44.

When you release the mouse button, the Duplicate field dialog box opens as shown in Figure 15-45. In the dialog box select the page range for the duplicated fields. If you created fields on the first page, enter **2** in the first field box and enter the last page number in the second field box. Click OK and the fields with the same field properties are duplicated across the specified pages.

Click on the buttons to navigate pages. Notice that each button appears in the same relative position on each page.

The important thing to remember as you work with Bookmarks, links, page actions, destinations, and fields is that each is designed for different purposes. Although you can create the same results with one method or another, at times you'll favor one method over the others for a particular editing assignment. Acrobat offers many tools and features for creating dynamic interactive documents often limited only by your imagination. The more time you invest in learning all that Acrobat affords you, the more impressive results you'll produce.

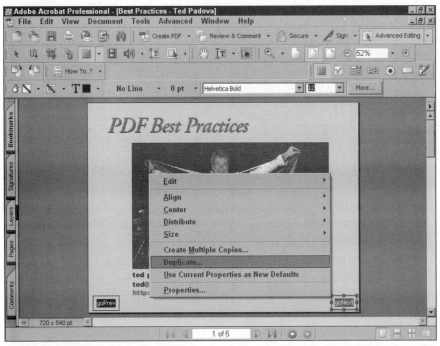

Figure 15-44: When the button fields are in place, select both fields with the Select Object tool and open a context menu. Select Duplicate from the menu options.

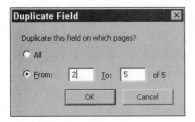

Figure 15-45: Enter the page range in the Duplicate Fields dialog box and click OK. The fields are duplicated on the pages you specified.

Summary

✦ You can name, organize, and create Bookmarks with different appearance properties. You can move, reassign, and delete standard Bookmarks without affecting page content. When you delete or move structured Bookmarks the respective pages are deleted or moved.

✦ Bookmarks support actions the same as found when creating link actions. Actions enable you to view pages, open documents, create Web links, and write JavaScripts and other types of commands that act as hypertext links.

✦ Article threads enable viewers to follow passages of text in a logical reading order.

✦ Links support many different actions from page navigation to running JavaScripts. Links can be copied and pasted and the link properties are retained in the pasted objects. Links cannot be duplicated across PDF pages and links do not support content files with colors or images.

✦ Acrobat 6.0 supports opening user-defined pages in external PDF documents via link actions.

✦ You select link properties in the Create Link dialog box, from a context menu command, or by double-clicking on a link. All link actions are changed in the Link Properties dialog box.

✦ You make links from text by selecting text with the Select Text tool and selecting Create Link from a context menu.

✦ All the actions assigned to links can also be assigned to page actions. Page actions are established in the Page Properties dialog box accessed by opening a context menu on a page thumbnail and selecting Properties.

✦ Page actions are invoked when a page opens or a page closes.

✦ Destinations are similar to Bookmarks. Destinations do not support actions. Destinations tend to make file sizes larger than when using Bookmarks and links.

✦ You can use destinations to create pop-up menus together with a JavaScript.

✦ You can assign form field buttons different button faces from external files.

✦ Form fields can be duplicated across multiple pages. Duplicated fields are placed on all pages in the same relative position as from where they were duplicated.

✦　　✦　　✦

Multimedia and PDFs

Acrobat offers you a wide range of possibilities with animation, motion, and sound. You can import sound files in PDFs, import movie files, convert Web pages with Flash animation, convert PowerPoint files with motion objects, and create animation by writing JavaScript routines. With the exception of writing JavaScripts, animation and sound are created in other applications and imported in PDF documents.

In this chapter you learn how to create animation and sound, import multimedia files into PDF documents, and create some motion effects by writing JavaScripts.

Setting Up the Multimedia Environment

You import sound and video files with the Movie and/or Sound tools available from the Advanced Editing toolbar. To open the toolbar, click on the Advanced Editing task button. When the toolbar opens, right-click to open a context menu from the Toolbar Well and select Dock All Toolbars.

The Movie tool is shown in the Advanced Editing toolbar by default. When working with sounds and movie clips, you'll want to use the Sound tool as well as the Movie tool. From the pull-down menu adjacent to the Movie tool, select Expand This Button. The Sound tool and the Movie tool both become visible.

If you write JavaScripts for creating animation effects, you'll most likely need to create form fields. Rather than open the Forms toolbar and the Properties Bar and dock them in the Toolbar Well, I'll open forms tools as needed from the pull-down menu in the Advanced Editing toolbar (see the section "Creating Animation Effects" later in this chapter). For now, limit the toolbars to the addition of the Advanced Editing toolbar to minimize the space occupied by the Toolbar Well.

Working with Sound Files

You import sounds in Acrobat in one of two ways. You can use the Attach Sound tool and record or import a message in the form of a comment. Once recorded, the sound is embedded in Acrobat and not accessible for importing via an Action. The other method of handling sound in PDF documents is to import sounds from files saved on your hard drive. By importing sounds you can invoke a sound with various action types; for example, using a Page Action to play a sound when the user opens or closes a page or clicks a button or link field.

Cross-Reference

For information on using the Sound Attach tool, see Chapter 14. For more information on Action types, see Chapter 3.

You import sound files with the Sound tool found on the Advanced Editing toolbar. Be certain to understand the difference between creating an audio comment and importing a sound with the Sound tool. Using the Attach Sound tool enables you to record a sound or import a sound file from your hard drive. Using the Sound tool enables you to import a sound from a file saved in a format compatible for importing sounds, but does not offer you an option for recording a sound. Before you can use the Sound tool, you need to either acquire or edit sounds and save them to a file format recognized by Acrobat.

Creating sound files

If you are so inclined you can purchase a commercial application for editing sound and saving recordings that Acrobat can recognize. If recording sounds is an infrequent task and does not warrant purchase of expensive commercial software, you can find sound recording applications as shareware and in the public domain that can satisfy almost any need you have for using sounds on forms.

Web sites change frequently, so you may need to do a search for public domain and shareware applications for your computer platform. As of this writing you can find sound editing programs at www.freewarefiles.com (Windows) or www.macupdate.com (Macintosh). You can find applications that enable you to record sounds and save them in formats acceptable to the platform you use that can then be recognized by Acrobat. The most common of the file types recognized by Acrobat is .wav for Windows and .aiff for Macintosh.

Note

You can import video and sound files that are compatible with Apple QuickTime, Flash Player, Windows Built-In Player, RealOne, and Windows Media Player.

Be certain you have a microphone properly connected to your computer according to your computer's user manual. Launch the sound-editing application you downloaded from a Web site or use a commercial application if you have one available. Most programs offer you a record button similar in appearance to a tape recorder or VCR. Click the Record button and speak into the microphone. When finished recording, click the Stop button. Depending on the application, you may be prompted in a dialog box to save the file or you may see a window where you can further edit the sound as shown in Figure 16-1.

If a dialog box does not prompt you to save the recording, select Save or Save As from a menu option. Typically the commands are under the File menu, but these may vary depending on the program you use. When you save the file, be certain to save in a format acceptable to Acrobat. A .wav (Windows) or .aiff (Macintosh) file format can be imported in Acrobat, but be careful of any file compression applied to the file when saved. You may need to test various compression options in order to find a format that Acrobat can recognize. After choosing the format, supply a name for the file with the proper extension as shown in Figure 16-2.

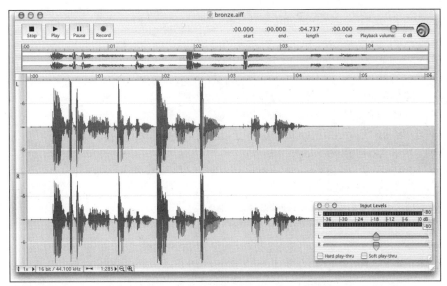

Figure 16-1: To record sounds and save the sound to a file available for importing in Acrobat, use a sound-editing program.

Figure 16-2: After editing a sound, save the file in either AIFF (Macintosh) or WAV (Windows).

Adding sounds to Page Actions

A sound might be added to a Page Open or a Page Close action to provide informational instructions to complete a form, play a music score, or other similar function. In order to add a sound to a Page Action, you must have the sound file saved to disk as described in the preceding section. To add a sound to a Page Action, follow these steps:

STEPS: Adding sounds to Page Actions

1. **Open the Page Properties.** Be certain your sound file is available in a directory on your hard drive and click on the Pages tab in the Navigation Pane. From a context menu opened on the page where you want the sound to play, select Properties. The Page Properties dialog box opens.

2. **Set the Action trigger.** Click on the Actions tab and select either Page Open or Page Close from the Select Trigger pull-down menu.

3. **Set the Action type.** Open the pull-down menu for Select Action and select Play a sound from the menu options as shown in Figure 16-3.

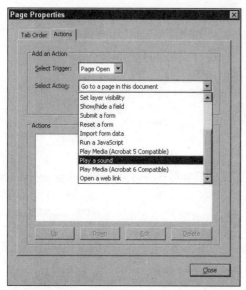

Figure 16-3: Select Play a sound from the Select Action pull-down menu.

Note

By default, the Select a sound menu item in the Select Action pull-down menu may not be in view. Scroll the menu down to show the command.

4. **Add the Action to the page trigger.** Click on the Add button in the Page Properties dialog box to add the sound to the lower window.

5. **Select the sound file.** The Select Sound File dialog box opens. Navigate your hard drive to find the sound to import, select it, and click on the Select button. After importing the sound, click Close in the Page Properties dialog box.

Note

Acrobat may pause momentarily. The sound file imported in Acrobat is converted during the import. When a sound is imported in a PDF file, the sound can then be played across platforms. Therefore, a .wav file can be played on a Macintosh computer and an .aiff file can be played on a Windows computer.

6. **Save the file.** Click OK in the Page Actions dialog box. Choose File ➪ Save As and rewrite the file to disk. Close the file and reopen it to test the Page Action.

After you save the PDF file and reopen it, the sound is played. You can also test the sound by scrolling a page in the PDF file and returning to the page where the sound was imported. The action is dynamic and the sound plays before you save the PDF file.

Adding sounds to form field actions

Of the mouse behavior types, you may find that Mouse Enter, On Focus, or On Blur behaviors work equally as well as using a Mouse Up or Mouse Down trigger. As an example, you might have a descriptive message display when the user places the cursor over a button field and before s/he clicks the mouse. Or you may want to invoke a sound when the user tabs out of a field as a reminder to verify data entry in a PDF form. In these situations and similar uses, the sound is played from a mouse behavior related to a data field. To understand how to use sound actions with data fields, follow these steps:

STEPS: Adding sounds to form fields

1. **Open a PDF document with form fields.** In Figure 16-4, I use a form with several check boxes. I want to create a sound when the user places the cursor over one of the check boxes or tabs to the field.

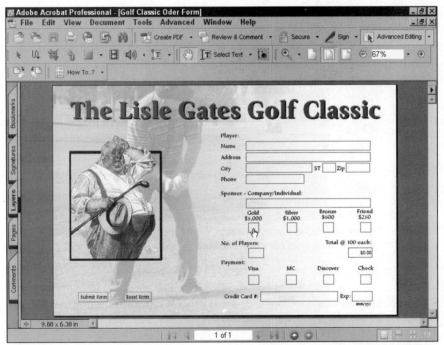

Figure 16-4: Four check boxes are to be configured to play a sound on a Mouse Enter trigger.

2. **Open the field properties.** Select the Select Object tool in the Advanced Editing toolbar and double-click on the field you want to edit. If no fields exist in your document, create a check box field.

Cross-Reference

For more information on creating form fields, see Chapters 25 and 26.

3. **Select the mouse trigger.** Select Mouse Enter in the field properties dialog box.

4. **Add a sound to the field.** Open the Select Action pull-down menu and select Play a sound.

5. **Select the Sound file.** Click on the Add button to open the Select Sound File dialog box. Select the file to import and click on the Select button.

6. **Close the Check Box Properties dialog box.** Check to be certain the mouse trigger is set to Mouse Enter as shown in Figure 16-5. Click Close in the Check Box Properties dialog box.

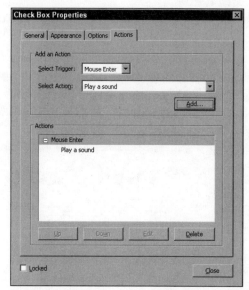

Figure 16-5: Check to be certain the mouse trigger and the action type are configured properly. Click the Close button when you're finished editing the properties.

7. **Test the sound.** Place the mouse cursor over the check box where the sound was added. (Note: To play the sound by tabbing to the field, use the On Focus mouse trigger.)

When the mouse enters one of the check boxes, the respective sound plays. The sound plays completely even if the cursor leaves the field. Sounds added to forms either for Page Actions or Field Actions can be played from any Acrobat viewer.

Tip

A sound continues to play to completion. If you want to stop the sound while editing a document, click on the Select Object tool or press the R key on your keyboard. (Note: You need to enable Use single-key accelerators to access tools in the General Preferences to use key modifiers to select tools.)

Using the Sound tool

 Importing sounds with a Page Actions, form fields, links, Bookmarks, and so on limits your import options to fewer file formats and limits the attributes you can assign to the imported file. In essence, you import the file and play the sound. Not much else is available when you use the Select Action command. Another method for importing sound files in PDF documents is using the Sound tool. When you use the Sound tool to import sounds, your options are much greater for the kinds of files you can import and attributes you can assign to the imported sounds.

To import a sound with the Sound tool, select the tool from the Advanced Editing toolbar and drag open a rectangle on a document page. The area contained within the rectangle becomes a trigger to play the sound. When you release the mouse button, the Add Sound dialog box opens as shown in Figure 16-6.

Tip You can manage sound and movie links similarly to links and form fields where context menu options enable you to size, align, copy, paste, and distribute fields. You can access these menu commands when you select sound and movie links in a group together with links and form fields.

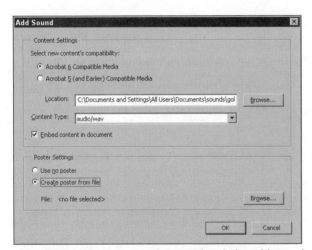

Figure 16-6: When you use the Sound tool, the Add Sound properties offer you many different file format import options and attribute choices for displaying and playing sounds.

You set the attributes for sound imports when you initially use the Sound tool. After specifying choices in the Add Sound dialog box, you can access the Multimedia Properties dialog box by opening a context menu. Your first stop is the Add Sound dialog box where the options include

✦ **Compatibility:** From the radio button choices you decide whether the sound import is Acrobat 6 or Acrobat 5 compatible. If you select Acrobat 5 compatible, the format options are limited to .WAV and .AIFF formats. If you use Acrobat 6 Compatible Media, the sound may not play with earlier Acrobat viewers depending on the file types you import and attributes assigned to the sound.

✦ **Browse:** Click on the Browse button to locate the sound you want to import.

✦ **Content Type:** By default the type of the file you import is listed automatically in the field box. By clicking on the down arrow you can open a pull-down menu where all compatible file formats are listed. A total of 27 different file formats are supported including newer MPEG4 and several midi formats. When you import files, let Acrobat interpret the file format and leave the format unchanged. If you click on a sound where Acrobat does not know the Content Type, Acrobat prompts you to click in a dialog box to select a content type.

✦ **Embed content in document:** Using Acrobat 5 compatibility automatically embeds sound files. If you use Acrobat 6 compatibility you can choose to link the sound file to the PDF or embed the sound in the PDF document. If you disable the check box for not embedding the file, you need to send the sound file to a user as well as the PDF in order for other users to play the sound.

✦ **Poster Settings:** The rectangle you create appears similar to a button field. If you leave the default at Use no poster, then the rectangle is invisible when the Hand tool is selected. A user can click anywhere within the rectangle boundary to play the sound. If you select Create poster from file, you can fit a graphic to the rectangle; for example, using button faces for form field buttons. You click on the Browse button to select the file you want to use for the poster. You can choose any file type that is compatible when using the Create PDF From File command. If the file type is other than PDF, Acrobat converts the file to PDF as it imports the image. If you're using a multipage PDF document for the poster, the first page in the PDF document is used for the poster.

Cross-Reference For information on creating button faces, see Chapter 25.

Click OK after selecting options in the Add Sound dialog box. When you return to the document page, the rectangle is visible. You assign additional properties when you open the sound properties from a context menu. Depending on what compatibility you chose when you added the sou nd file, the properties dialog boxes offer different options. When an Acrobat 5-compatible file is used, you open the Movie Properties by selecting Properties from a context menu. When you add an Acrobat 6-compatible sound to a document you open the Multimedia Properties dialog box by selecting Properties from a context menu. In either case, you open context menus by using the Sound tool, the Movie tool, or the Select Object tool.

Acrobat 5-compatible Movie (Sound) Properties

If you're using an Acrobat 5-compatible sound import, the Movie Properties dialog box opens when you select Properties from a context menu opened from the sound rectangle. As shown in Figure 16-7, the dialog box contains three tabs used for selecting further options than were available in the Add Sound dialog box.

Tip When you use either the Sound tool or the Movie tool and create a sound or movie field, the first dialog box that opens is the Add Sound or Add Movie dialog box. While selecting options in the dialog box, you have no opportunity to select objects on the document page or menu commands. However, after you create a sound or movie field and open the Properties dialog box, the Properties window functions similarly to the Link Properties and Form Field Properties windows where you can access objects on the page and menu commands. When editing properties for sound and movie files, you don't need to close the Properties window to select and edit additional fields.

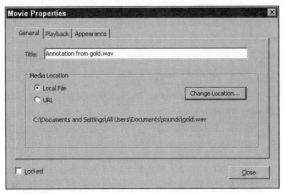

Figure 16-7: To open the Movie Properties dialog box, use the Sound tool, the Movie tool, or the Select object tool and select Properties from a context menu.

General Properties

The default properties are the General Movie Properties. In this dialog box you make selections for

✦ **Title:** By default the title of the sound clip is the filename. Edit the title name in the field box to change the title.

✦ **Media location:** Local files are stored locally on your hard drive. Although the sound file is embedded in the PDF, you can change the sound to another file by clicking the Change Location button. Click on the button and the Select Multimedia File dialog box opens. Select another file and click on the Select button and the sound is changed to another file. If you select URL, another dialog box opens asking you to specify a URL where a file is located. If importing sounds, you need to add the sound filename as part of the URL when using Acrobat 5 compatibility. When you deselect the option to embed the file with Acrobat 6 compatibility, the directory path is all you need to address in the line where the URL is specified.

Playback

The Playback tab offers options settings for playing sound clips and movies as shown in Figure 16-8:

Figure 16-8: Click on Playback to set options for playing sounds.

✦ **Show player controls:** A control palette opens when a sound is played if this check box is enabled. In the control palette you have a button to play/pause and a slider. Click and drag the slider to move forward or backward in the sound file.

✦ **Use floating window:** With sounds, the sound file is fixed to a location. With video clips you can select the Use floating window option to float a video clip in a window centered in the Acrobat window. If you select floating window for a sound file, the player control opens in a floating toolbar. In Figure 16-9 you can see the difference between using a floating window or disabling floating window when showing player controls. On the left is the player control with Use floating window disabled. On the right the same sound clip is played with the Use floating window check box enabled. In both examples, the Show player controls check box was enabled.

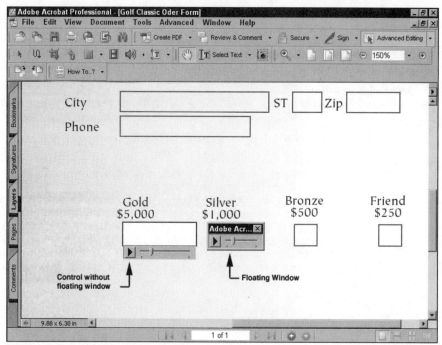

Figure 16-9: When Show player controls is checked, the control appears below the sound import (left). When Use floating window is checked, the player control opens in a floating toolbar (right).

✦ **Size:** For sound imports, the Size pull-down menu and field box are disabled. These options relate to sizing video clips, explained in the "Playback Options" section later in this chapter.

✦ **Play:** From the pull-down menu you can choose to play a sound Once; play a sound once and Keep the player open; Loop through the sound and continue playing it over and over again; and play Forward and backward, which provides an interesting way of hearing your voice played backward. This latter option is best used for video clips without sound.

Appearance

Many of the options for appearance settings are the same as those found for link and form field appearances. Click on the Appearance tab and make choices for the appearance of the rectangle border and the contents of the rectangle as shown in Figure 16-10.

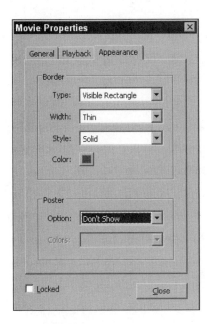

Figure 16-10: Click on the Appearance tab to change border colors and the poster image.

✦ **Type:** From the Type pull-down menu select from Visible Rectangle or Invisible Rectangle. If Invisible Rectangle is selected, the following options for Width, Style, and Color are grayed out.

✦ **Width:** The same three choices for link and form field rectangle widths of Thin, Medium, and Thick are listed in the pull-down menu.

✦ **Style:** Two choices appear for either setting the rectangle to a solid line or a dashed line.

✦ **Color:** You can choose from the same color options you have available for links and form fields by clicking on the color swatch and selecting either preset or custom colors.

✦ **Option:** The Option pull-down menu applies to movie files. If you select Put in Document from the pull-down menu when using a sound file, an error dialog box opens informing you that you can't use the poster option with the selected file type. Interestingly enough, if you select the third option, Retrieve From Movie, an icon appears in the sound rectangle as shown in Figure 16-11. Although the icon is intended to indicate a broken movie link, you can show the icon in lieu of a poster image.

✦ **Colors:** The Colors pull-down menu and field box are disabled for sound files.

Figure 16-11: When you select Retrieve From Movie, an icon is shown in the sound rectangle field indicating a broken link.

✦ **Locked:** The Locked check box is accessible from all tabs. When you check the Lock button the sound rectangle is locked to position on the document page and the attributes are locked. If you want to make any edits on the Movie Properties dialog box, you first need to uncheck the Locked item.

Acrobat 6–compatible Multimedia (Sound) Properties

If you elect to use Acrobat 6 compatibility, the options in the Add Sound dialog box are the same as discussed in the "Using the Sound Tool" section earlier in this chapter. After you create a sound import and select Properties from a context menu, a different set of property options appear in the Multimedia Properties dialog box. In Figure 16-12 the Multimedia Properties dialog box shows the default Settings tab options.

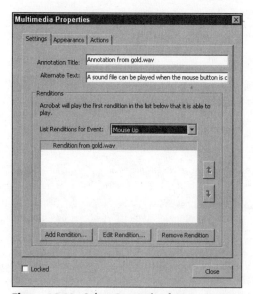

Figure 16-12: Select Properties from a context menu to open the Multimedia Properties dialog box for Acrobat 6–compatible sounds.

Settings

The Settings tab offers options for labels and renditions. By default the Settings tab is placed in view when you open the Multimedia Properties. As you can see in Figure 16-12, the Appearance tab is consistent with the Movie Properties dialog box, but the other two tabs offer options much different from those found with Acrobat 5-compatible sound files:

✦ **Annotation Title:** Add a title for the sound in this field. The title supplied here can be different from the filename.

✦ **Alternate Text:** When creating accessible files for vision- and motion-challenged users, you can add alternate text that can be read by screen-reading software.

Cross-Reference

For more information on creating Accessible PDFs, see Chapter 18.

✦ **Renditions:** A good number of options available when editing renditions apply to movie clips. For information on setting rendition options for sound files, see the section later in this chapter related to "Adding a rendition" for movie files.

Appearance

The Appearance tab (shown in Figure 16-13) in the Multimedia Properties dialog box offers similar options as those found in the Movie Properties for defining the attributes of a rectangle border for Type, Width, Style, and Color. In addition to these settings, other options include

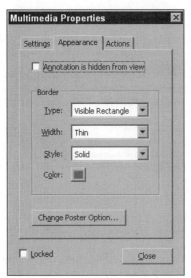

Figure 16-13: The Appearance tab offers options for setting the field rectangle appearance and a button to access the Change Poster Options dialog box.

✦ **Annotation is hidden from view:** The Annotation added to the field box in the Settings tab is visible by default. To hide the annotation, enable this check box.

✦ **Change Poster Option:** Options for the poster image are similar to those used with Acrobat 5-compatible files. The settings appear in a dialog box, shown in Figure 16-14, as opposed to a pull-down menu described earlier. When you click on the button for Change Poster Option, you'll find a few differences among the choices. The three options include

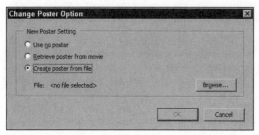

Figure 16-14: When you click on the Change Poster Options button, a dialog box opens, offering three choices for poster displays.

- **Use No Poster:** This choice is the same as selecting Don't Show in the Movie Properties dialog box. No poster is shown in the sound field.

- **Retrieve poster from movie:** Also a similar choice as you find in the Movie Properties dialog box. With sound files a dialog box opens informing you that no support for a poster is retrievable from sound files. For movie files the poster is retrieved from the first frame in the movie file.

- **Create poster from file:** The Movie Properties dialog box used with Acrobat 5–compatible files offers you an option for Retrieve From Movie as the third choice in the pull-down menu. This choice is the same as the preceding option and pulls the first frame in the movie clip as the poster image. With Acrobat 6 compatibility the Create poster from file option enables you to use a PDF or file compatible with the Create PDF From File command as the poster image. To add a poster from a file, click on the Browse button and select the file you want to import.

Actions

The Actions tab offers you options for setting an Action on Mouse Triggers much like you apply actions to links, Bookmarks, Page Actions, and form fields. Options from the Select Trigger pull-down menu differ slightly from those you select for links, Bookmarks, Page Actions, and form fields as you can see in Figure 16-15. Some of the triggers are available only to movie clips whereas others work with both sounds and movie files. The options in the Actions tab include

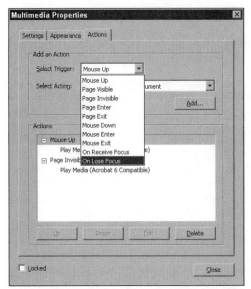

Figure 16-15: Click on the Actions tab to assign mouse triggers and action types to media files.

✦ **Select Trigger:** Open the pull-down menu and you see the trigger actions shown in Figure 16-15.

Cross-Reference

For more information on selecting trigger options, see Chapter 15.

- **Mouse Up:** This trigger belongs to both sound and video clips. The behavior is identical to the same trigger used for other items such as Page Actions, links, and buttons where actions are applied.

- **Page Visible:** A current page active in the Document Pane can be different than page visibility. When using Continuous page layout, Facing Pages, or Continuous – Facing Pages, you can have one page active while other pages are visible in the Document Pane. When this trigger is selected, the media clip plays dependent on page visibility and not necessarily the current page. This trigger is only available with video clips.

- **Page Invisible:** If a page is not visible in the Document Pane, the media clip can be played on an action such as a button, link, or Bookmark. This trigger is available only with video clips.

- **Page Enter:** Also available only with video clips, this trigger is like setting a Page Action. When the page becomes the current page, the video plays.

- **Page Exit:** The opposite of the preceding option. When you scroll to another page, only video clips play.

- **Mouse Down:** When the mouse button is pressed down, the trigger is invoked. This trigger is available to both sound and video clips.

- **Mouse Enter:** When the mouse cursor enters the focus rectangle either sound or video clips play.

- **Mouse Exit:** Opposite of the preceding option where the sound or video plays when the mouse cursor exits the focus rectangle.

- **On Receive Focus:** For video clips only, this trigger is like the On Focus mouse trigger used with form field buttons. Pressing the Tab key activates the focus rectangle and the video clip plays.

- **On Lose Focus:** The opposite of the preceding option and like the On Blur mouse trigger where a video clip plays when you tab out of the movie field.

✦ **Select Action:** From the Select Action pull-down menu you can select any action type that is also available to links, fields, Bookmarks, and Page Actions.

> **Cross-Reference**
>
> For more information on Select Action options, see Chapters 15 and 26.

✦ **Add:** When you select an action, click on the Add button to add the action to the Actions list window.

✦ **Actions:** The Actions list window shows all the trigger options and actions assigned to the sound or video clip. You can add multiple actions with different triggers and view all the additions in the Actions list.

✦ **Up/Down:** The buttons at the bottom of the Actions tab enable you to reorder multiple actions. Select an item in the Actions list and click on the Up or Down button to move the selected action before or after other items in the list. When the actions are invoked, the play is in the order shown in the Actions list.

✦ **Edit:** Select an item in the Actions list and click on the Edit button to edit action item attributes. If you select a sound or video file in the Actions list and click on the Edit button, the Play Media (Acrobat 6 Compatible) dialog box opens as shown in Figure 16-16. From the pull-down menu you make choices for changing the play options. Notice you also have an option for writing a custom JavaScript.

Figure 16-16: When you select Edit in the Actions tab for media files, the Play Media (Acrobat 6 Compatible) dialog box opens. Make choices in the dialog box for play options you want to change.

✦ **Delete:** If you want to delete an item in the Actions list, select the item to be removed and click on the Delete button.

✦ **Locked:** The Locked check box offers the same option as discussed earlier in the Movie Properties "Appearance" section.

Creating Movie Files

Like the sound files discussed earlier in this chapter, video files require that you create video clips in other authoring programs. No tools or features are contained in Acrobat for editing movies. However, after you create video clips in authoring applications you have the wealth of import options and play opportunities similar to those used with sound files.

Video editing at the high end is handled by sophisticated software like Final Cut Pro, Adobe Premiere, Adobe After Effects, and other similar professional programs designed to offer you limitless choices for editing video and audio channels. On the low end, you have some impressive features in programs that cost very little. For Windows, Adobe's new product, Adobe Photoshop Album, is a low-cost editing program designed to take your still images and video clips and create PDF presentations. On the professional side you can add still photos and sound clips to create presentations and demonstration projects. For personal use you can create entertaining presentations and videos for family and friends. The great advantage of using Photoshop Album for either purpose is that the program exports direct to PDF along with JavaScripts that allow the PDFs to be viewed in Full Screen mode with various player options.

For Macintosh users, Apple's own iMovie is a free application shipping with System X that produces QuickTime movies. You don't have the export options that Photoshop Album does, but iMovie offers many more features for video editing than Photoshop Album. iMovie supports PDF imports as well as still photos and video clips. If you happen to be a cross-platform user, the combination of using both programs offers you a sophisticated editing environment where you can produce PDF presentations and displays for just about any purpose.

Discussion in this chapter is related to multimedia authoring and working with video and sound in PDF documents. For additional information related to creating presentations and other application support for various kinds of animation, see Chapter 21.

You have many options for video and sound editing programs and different users will favor one application over another. I mention Adobe Photoshop Album in this chapter because Photoshop Album is optimized for direct export to PDF. I mention Apple Computer's iApplications because they ship free with the operating system. If you use other applications for creating video clips, look at the section "Importing Movies" where importing video in PDF files is covered to determine if Acrobat supports the programs you use.

Using Photoshop Album (Windows)

Although not a feature in Acrobat, the PDF support provided by Adobe Photoshop Album makes it worthwhile to talk about in a book on Acrobat. For less than $50 U.S. retail, Photoshop Album was designed for working with Acrobat. With easy-to-follow, step-by-step instructions for video creation and export to PDF, anyone not using professional video authoring applications will find Photoshop Album a favorite tool.

When you launch Photoshop Album, an easy-to-use help screen opens as a default. From the tabs shown in Figure 16-17 you select options for acquiring photos (Get Photos) and editing images with tools for cropping, image brightness, red-eye removal, and color saturation. After editing, select the images behind the Quick Guide window and click on the Create tab.

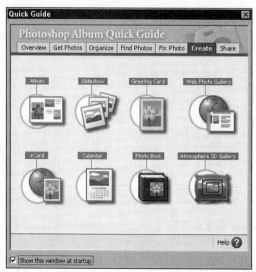

Figure 16-17: Photoshop Album opens with a Quick Guide window where you import photos and/or video clips, edit images, and create an album package.

Photoshop Album offers several ways to package your creations. Choose from one of the options in the Quick Guide made available after you click on the Create tab shown in Figure 16-18. Among some of your choices are exporting to a slide show, a greeting card, a calendar, or a photo album. If you use video imports, some of the layout options aren't available for exporting to PDF. If an option is not available, Photoshop Album warns you ahead of time.

After selecting your package option, the Workspace dialog box opens. You can examine the images/videos in the Workspace to ensure all photos are selected for export. Click on the Start Creations Wizard and a step-by-step Creations Wizard dialog box opens shown in Figure 16-19. You simply click on the Next buttons and make the edits you want for layout style, titles, transitions, music, and number of images per page.

Click the Next button until you arrive at Step 5 shown in Figure 16-19. The export options are shown on the right side of the Creations Wizard. Click on the Save as PDF button and the Save as PDF dialog box opens. You have options for Optimizing the file for onscreen viewing, printing, or preserving the full image resolution of the source files. Click OK in the dialog box and the Export PDF As dialog box opens. Find a location on your hard drive where you want the file saved and click on the Save button. The Photoshop Album document is exported to PDF.

Note   A special thank you to child film star of the early 1990s Jason Woliner for contributing a sample video. You'll find the video and the Photoshop Album PDF document contained on the CD accompanying this book.

Figure 16-18: When you click on the Create tab, several package options are made available. Select from the thumbnails in the Quick Guide and the Workspace dialog box opens.

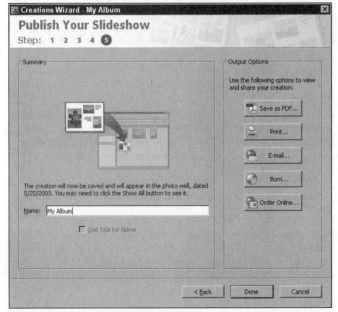

Figure 16-19: Photoshop Album walks you through five steps to produce your creation with easy-to-follow instructions.

When you open the file in Acrobat, the file opens in Full Screen view. Depending on the options you selected when you exported the file, you may have a control palette open in the Full Screen view window as shown in Figure 16-20. The Photoshop Album document plays through completion and returns you to edit mode after the last slide is viewed.

Cross-Reference   For more information on Full Screen views, see Chapter 21.

Figure 16-20: The PDF exported from Photoshop Album opens in Full Screen view in Acrobat.

The animation, controls, and buttons contained in the PDF exported from Photoshop Album are made possible with JavaScripts. Photoshop Album creates the JavaScripts and exports them in the PDF document. If you want to edit the JavaScript, you can edit the document-level scripts or the button Actions. In Figure 16-21 you can see some of the code added to the PDF from Photoshop Album.

Cross-Reference   For more information on writing and editing JavaScripts, see Chapter 27.

Exporting to PDF from Photoshop Album is a complete PDF package. The files you create in Photoshop Album don't provide you options for saving video clips you can import in Acrobat with the Movie tool. If you want to use a PDF exported from Photoshop Album as part of a larger presentation, you can use button links to open and close files while in Full Screen mode.

```
JavaScript Editor                                                    ×

┌─ Create and Edit JavaScripts ──────────────────────────────────┐
│                                                                 │
│  var haveSVG = typeof alternatePresentations != 'undefined' &&  │
│          alternatePresentations['Slideshow.svg'] != null;       │
│                                                                 │
│  var playButton;                                                │
│  var closeButton;                                               │
│  var upgradeButton;                                             │
│  var pluginButton;                                              │
│  var playMsg;                                                   │
│  var pluginMsg;                                                 │
│  var upgradeMsg;                                                │
│  var itv,timeout;                                               │
│  var doc = this;                                                │
│                                                                 │
│  if( typeof doAutostart == 'undefined' )                        │
│          doAutostart = false;                                   │
│                                                                 │
│  function hideAllButtons()                                      │
│  {                                                              │
└─────────────────────────────────────────────────────────────────┘

                          OK       Cancel     Go to...
```

Figure 16-21: Photoshop Album creates JavaScripts during the export to PDF. You can edit the JavaScripts in the JavaScript Editor in Acrobat.

> **Cross-Reference** For more information on creating link Actions while viewing PDFs in Full Screen mode, see the section "Creating play buttons" later in this chapter, and see Chapter 21.

Using iMovie (Macintosh)

When QuickTime movies are needed for importing into PDFs with the Movie tool, Macintosh users can create some impressive video clips with Apple Computer's iApplications. iMovie ships free with System X and together with the companion products of iTunes, iPhoto, and iDVD you have an elaborate editing environment for adding sounds and video to PDF documents and writing your creations to DVDs.

Windows users need to install QuickTime as the Acrobat 6 installer does not install the QuickTime player. QuickTime is part of the System X operating system files on the Macintosh so no additional installation is necessary. Once QuickTime is installed, users of either Windows or Macintosh operating systems can import QuickTime videos in PDF files. When using iMovie for video creation, you can export the source document to a QuickTime format. Be certain to regularly check Apple Computer's Web site at www.apple.com for upgrades. QuickTime is constantly being upgraded and you'll want to use the most recent version.

Like Photoshop Album, iMovie enables you to import video clips and still images. iMovie also offers you options for importing sounds, creating transitions and effects, and adding titles. You start by creating a new project and adding video and/or movie clips to the Clips Pane as shown in Figure 16-22. Choose File ➪ Import to select multiple files to add to the Clips Pane. From the Clips Pane, drag files to the timeline at the bottom of the window.

Figure 16-22: Start iMovie by importing still photos and/or video clips in the Clips Pane.

You add transitions, effects, titles, and sounds to the timeline by clicking on the Trans button and dragging effects to the timeline as in the example shown in Figure 16-23. You can control zooms, speed, and volume by moving sliders below the timeline. After assembling the movie clip, click on the Play movie button represented by a right-pointing arrow below the display window. When the preview looks like the final video you want to produce, choose File ➪ Export. In the iMovie:Export dialog box are options for file format and compression. Play with some different settings to determine the best compression and quality that works for your presentations.

The file you save from iMovie is a QuickTime .mov file. The resulting file can be imported in Acrobat. iMovie offers you a little more flexibility for sizing movie files and moving them around PDF documents. However, if a Photoshop Album package works for your presentation, you can import the QuickTime movie in Photoshop Album and create a PDF file as described in the previous section "Using Photoshop Album (Windows)".

Figure 16-23: Clips, transitions, effects, titles, and audio are added to the timeline by clicking on effects and dragging to the timeline. Click on the right-pointing arrow to preview the movie before exporting.

Importing Movies

 You use the Movie tool in the Advanced Editing toolbar to import movies. To import a movie, you create a movie link in the same way you create a link with the Sound tool. Select the Movie tool from the Toolbar Well and double-click the mouse button or click and drag open a rectangle. When you release the mouse button, the Add Movie dialog box opens as shown in Figure 16-24.

Select the compatibility you want to use and click on the Browse button to locate the movie to import. Import a movie file and click OK and the Add Movie dialog box. The Movie Properties dialog box opens as shown in Figure 16-25. In the Movie Properties dialog box, you can select from a number of attributes for how the movie is displayed and the types of play actions you want to assign to the movie file.

Tip
In Acrobat 6, when you double-click the mouse button or click and drag open a rectangle, the movie frame defaults to the size the video was compressed. If you want to size up or down the frame size, press the Shift key and drag one of the four handles with the Movie tool or the Select Object tool to reshape the rectangle. Be aware that if you size up the movie frame from the default size, the video may look distorted when played.

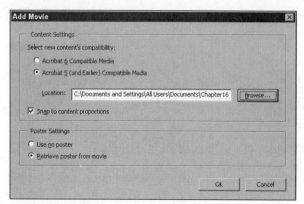

Figure 16-24: The Add Movie dialog box offers you options for selecting the content compatibility for either Acrobat 5–compatible media or Acrobat 6–compatible media.

Acrobat 5–compatible movies

Figure 16-24 shows the Add Movie dialog box options for Acrobat 5–compatible movies. You have options for selecting either Acrobat 5 or Acrobat 6 compatibility like you do with sound imports. When you select the Acrobat 5 (and Earlier) Compatible Media radio button, the dialog box reduces in size and displays only the options available when using Acrobat 5 or earlier compatibility.

Add Movie

You make choices in the Add Movie dialog box when you first create a movie field. After creating the field, you can make changes and select attributes in the Movie Properties dialog box that are similar to the Sound properties choices. In the Add Movie dialog box, you select from the following:

- ✦ **Compatibility:** Click on the compatibility for either Acrobat 5 or Acrobat 6 Compatible Media. If you select Acrobat 5 compatibility the movie clips cannot be embedded in the PDF file. Therefore, you need to send the PDF and the movie file to other users or host both on a Web site in order for users to view the movies. If using Acrobat 6–compatible media and embedding movie clips in a PDF, Acrobat users with viewers earlier than Acrobat 6 won't be able to see your movie files.

- ✦ **Location:** On local drives, the location of the movie file is added to the Location field box. When you first import a movie, identify the movie in the Add Movie dialog box and leave the Location at the default. After you create the movie rectangle, you can change the location to a URL for Web-hosted documents in the Movie Properties dialog box.

Note   If you move a movie file on your hard drive to another location, the path to the file is broken and the movie won't play. To reset the directory path, click on the Browse button, find the movie file, and click Select in the Select Movie File dialog box.

✦ **Snap to content proportions:** When enabled, the movie remains proportional as you drag open a rectangle, preventing distortion when the movie is played. The media file's original dimensions are preserved no matter how large you draw the rectangle.

✦ **Poster Settings:** Select the Use no poster option to show a blank video frame. Select the Retrieve poster from movie option to show the first movie frame in the movie rectangle when the movie is not playing.

Acrobat 5 Movie Properties

After you import a movie with Acrobat 5 compatibility, you can make further attribute choices in the Movie Properties dialog box. Select either the Movie tool or the Select Object tool and open a context menu. From the menu options, select Properties. The Movie Properties dialog box opens as shown in Figure 16-25.

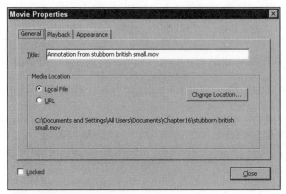

Figure 16-25: The General Movie Properties are identical to the Sound Properties.

General

Notice that options in the General tab are identical to the Sound Properties. For further definition of the options refer to the section in this chapter where Acrobat Movie (Sound) Properties were discussed.

If you want to link the movie to a URL location, click on the URL radio button. The Enter URL dialog box opens where you add the URL. Be certain to include the complete URL address, beginning with *http://*.

Playback

Playback options are also identical to the options found with Sound files. The pull-down menu for Size is accessible for movie files only. From the menu options you make choices for the size of the video frames during playback as shown in Figure 16-26. If you choose a size above the Default (1x) size, the video may be distorted when played.

If you choose Full Screen from the menu choices, the video plays at the largest possible size on your monitor in a separate window. However, the video playback does not change the view to Full Screen mode.

Figure 16-26: Playback options are identical to the Sound properties with the exception of the Size options. Choose the playback size from the menu choices.

Options for showing the player controls and using a floating window are handled a little different from when enabling the same options for sound files. The player controls are fixed at the bottom of the video clip for viewing movies either with or without a floating window. Also, rather than the player control being affected when you use the floating window option, the movie is shown in a floating window. In Figure 16-27 you can see the video frame playing with the player controls visible at the default size of the video. In Figure 16-28 the player controls are enabled as well as floating window.

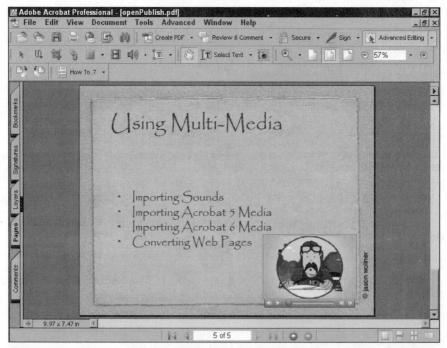

Figure 16-27: Player controls are enabled and the floating window option is disabled.

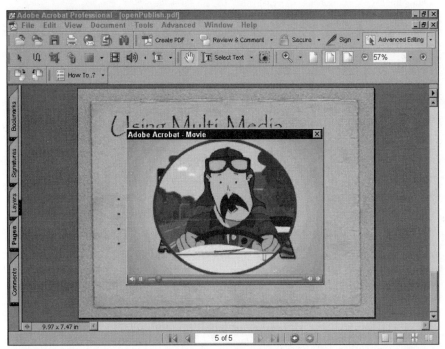

Figure 16-28: Player controls are enabled and the floating window option is enabled.

Appearance

Appearance options are also the same as those discussed for Sound properties. In the Appearance options, you have access to showing the movie poster in the file when the movie is still and not playing. If you choose to Put the Poster in the Document, you can also make choices for the color display of 8-bit (256 Colors) or 24-bit (Millions of Colors).

Acrobat 6–compatible movies

If you decide to use Acrobat 6 compatibility, you need to do it when you use the Movie tool to draw the field. If you create a movie field and specify Acrobat 5 compatibility, then change your mind and want to use Acrobat 6 compatibility, you need to delete the first movie field by clicking on it with the Movie tool or the Select Object tool. Press the Backspace/Delete key on your keyboard or open a context menu and choose Edit ➪ Delete. Double click the mouse button with the Movie tool and select Acrobat 6 compatibility and the dialog box changes to reflect the Acrobat 6-compatible options as shown in Figure 16-29.

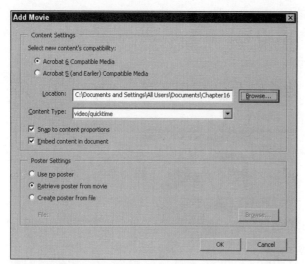

Figure 16-29: Select the Movie tool and draw a rectangle. In the Add Movie dialog box, select Acrobat 6 Compatible Media.

Add Movie

Select Acrobat 6 Compatible Media and you'll notice the dialog box expands to offer more options than when you use Acrobat 5–compatible files. The settings are the same as those discussed in the section "Acrobat 6 Compatible Multimedia (Sound) Properties." When adding movies you have options for the poster view in a still frame while the movie is not playing. Select from Use no poster, Retrieve poster from movie, or Create poster from file. These options are the same for sounds with the exception of the Retrieve poster from movie. Whereas sound files produce an error when you make this menu choice, movie files retrieve the first frame in the video for the poster image.

After making choices in the Add Movie dialog box, you have more options when accessing the Multimedia Properties dialog box. Click OK after selecting the Acrobat 6 compatible settings. Open a context menu with either the Movie tool or the Select Object tool and choose Properties from the menu options.

Acrobat 6 Multimedia Properties

The Multimedia Properties dialog box shown in Figure 16-30 contains the same options found when opening Acrobat 6–compatible sound files properties. The first stop is the Settings tab, where you see options for annotation text and alternate text. The items below the text fields contain options for Renditions. Because I didn't cover renditions earlier in the sounds discussion, I address the options you have for adding renditions here.

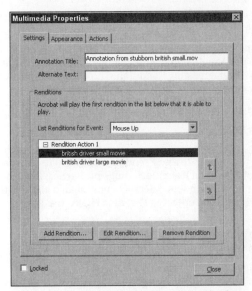

Figure 16-30: Open a context menu and select Properties to open the Multimedia Properties dialog box.

Understanding renditions

When you import a sound or video, the rendition of the clip is assigned to a Mouse Up trigger and plays according to the properties you enable for the play options. By default imported sounds and videos have a single default rendition. When using Acrobat 6-compatible media options, you have an opportunity to add different renditions to the same media clip or multiple media clips. For example, you may have a rendition that plays full screen from a large file and you may want to add an alternate clip of a duplicate movie with a smaller file size. If hosting the media on a Web site you can assign what media clip is downloaded to a user's computer based on the end user's connection speed. The movie field remains the same, but the attributes contain two different renditions for the same field.

You have options for editing existing renditions after importing a media clip or you can add new renditions to an imported file. When you add new renditions they are listed in the Settings tab in the Multimedia Properties dialog box.

Adding a rendition

By default a rendition is listed in the lower window in the Settings properties. To add a rendition, click on the Add Rendition button. A pull-down menu opens where you make choices for one of the following:

✦ **Using a File:** For local files select Using a File. The Select Multimedia File dialog box opens where you navigate your hard drive and select the file to use. This option might be used to select a duplicate file smaller or larger in size than the original rendition.

✦ **Using a URL:** If you want files downloaded from Web sites, select Using a URL. The Add a New Rendition Using a URL dialog box opens where you add the URL address for where the file is located. When you add the URL, a pull-down menu opens where you can select the content type for the media format.

✦ **By Copying an Existing Rendition:** If you want to use the same rendition as one listed in the Settings list window for the purpose of duplicating the rendition and providing alternate attributes, select By Copying an Existing Rendition. The Copy Rendition dialog box opens where you select the rendition to copy from a pull-down menu.

Select any one of the three options and click on the Edit button to open the Rendition Settings dialog box.

Editing a rendition

You can choose to edit an existing rendition or edit the new rendition added to the media file. If you want to edit a rendition, select Edit Rendition from the Settings properties. If you add a new rendition, the Rendition is added to the list window. Select a Rendition and click on the Edit button and the Renditions Settings dialog box opens as shown in Figure 16-31.

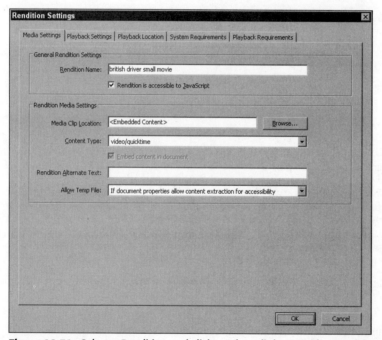

Figure 16-31: Select a Rendition and click on the Edit button. The Rendition Settings dialog box opens.

A considerable number of options are available in the various tabs of the Rendition Settings dialog box. By default the dialog box opens at the Media Settings tab. The various tabs and choices you have include

✦ **Media Settings:** Make choices from the Media Settings tab for the Rendition Name, the media location and content type, and the rendition for alternate text, and choose from the Allow Temp File pull-down menu for various options related to accessibility. If the media is to be made accessible to JavaScript, be certain to check the box for enabling JavaScript.

✦ **Playback Settings:** Click on the Playback Settings to make choices for the player window visibility, volume settings, showing player controls, continuous looping, or times played. In the list at the bottom of the Playback Settings, click on the Add button to add the type of media players you want users to use for playing the media. You have an option for enabling all players and a setting for the preferred player.

✦ **Playback Location:** Make choices for where the media is played such as in the document, floating window, or full screen. If floating window is selected, you have many different choices for document size and position.

✦ **System Requirements:** From a pull-down menu you have choices for connection speeds. If you want a particular rendition to be downloaded for all users with 384K connections or greater, you can make the choice in this dialog box. In addition you have choices for screen displays, captions, subtitles, and language choices.

✦ **Playback Requirements:** Based on options you selected in the other settings tabs, a list is displayed in the last settings tab. Each item has a check box for enabling a required condition. Check all the boxes for those items you want to make a required function.

Click OK in the Rendition Settings dialog box when you are finished setting the options in the various settings tabs. If you need to add another rendition with some alternate options to the last rendition you edited, copy the rendition and make the necessary edits. You can list as many different renditions as you like to provide much flexibility for your viewer audience and the systems they use.

Appearance

The Appearance tab in the Multimedia Properties dialog box offers the same options as those found when editing Sound Properties. You have choices available for poster display where you click on the Change Poster Option button shown in Figure 16-32 and the Change Poster Option dialog box opens. The poster options are the same as those available as discussed in the "Acrobat 6 Compatible Media (Sound) Properties" section described earlier in this chapter.

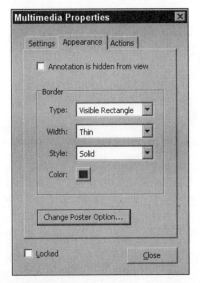

Figure 16-32: Click on Change Poster Option to change the poster image.

Actions

The Actions tab also offers the same choices as those available with sound files for adding an action to the media clip. You can choose an action from the Select Action pull-down menu shown in Figure 16-33.

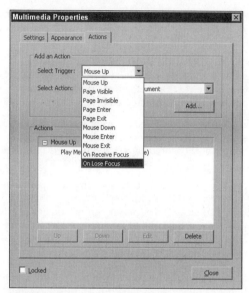

Figure 16-33: Click on the Actions tab and select the trigger from the Select Trigger pull-down menu.

Creating Play Buttons

As I explain in Chapter 21, you can create presentations from programs such as Microsoft PowerPoint where animated effects from PowerPoint are shown in PDF documents in Full Screen mode. If you want to add media clips to a presentation while showing slides in Full Screen mode you can set up some buttons to play, pause, and stop video clips.

Cross-Reference   For more information on converting PowerPoint files to PDF, see Chapter 21.

I started a new presentation from a file converted from PowerPoint. On one slide I wanted a media clip, so I used the Movie tool and imported a movie file using Acrobat 6 compatibility. After adding the media clip, I wanted the view of the video to appear without a poster, without player controls, and in Full Screen mode. To make these changes, I edited the rendition for Playback Settings as shown in Figure 16-34.

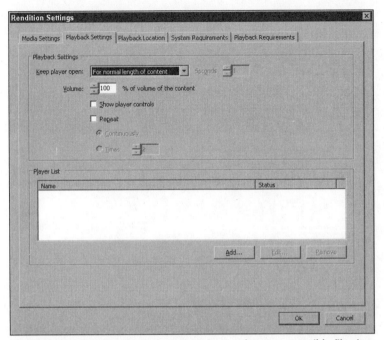

Figure 16-34: Set the playback settings for Acrobat 6–compatible files in the Rendition Settings dialog box. In the Playback Settings tab, I disabled the Show player controls.

The Show Player Controls check box was disabled and I clicked on the Playback Location tab to make a choice for the Playback Location. As shown in Figure 16-35, Floating Window is selected from the Playback Location pull-down menu. The position of the window is Center aligned relative to the document window as shown.

After making rendition changes, I selected the Appearance tab in the Multimedia Properties and selected Invisible for the Border type and changed the Poster Option to Use No Poster. After making the attribute changes in the Multimedia Properties, the rectangle was sized down to a small square on the document page. Because the video clip plays in a floating window, the size of the movie field is incidental.

Tip   When using a floating window the movie field size is of no importance to the video clip played in the floating window. Create a movie field and size it down to a half an inch or lower and move it to any location on the document page. When the movie plays in a floating window the window is positioned according to the attributes you assign to the playback location.

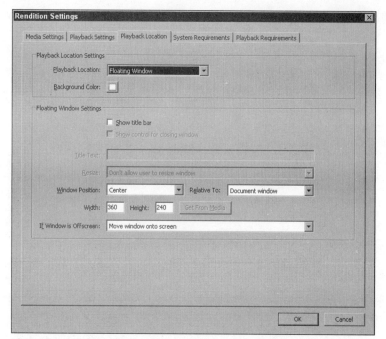

Figure 16-35: In the Playback Location tab the Playback Location was set to Floating Window mode and the position for Center was left at the default.

The next task is creating the buttons. Using the Button Field tool, I created a button field and set the appearance attributes to display text in the Options tab and selected No Border and no Fill Color in the Appearance tab. When you select Actions and choose the Play Media (Acrobat 6 Compatible) menu option from the Select Action pull-down menu, the Play Media (Acrobat 6 Compatible) dialog box opens. For the first button, I selected Play. With the Button Properties dialog box open, I duplicated the button field twice by using Ctrl/Option+Shift+drag and edited the field names and the action types for Pause and Stop in the dialog box shown in Figure 16-36.

After adding all the buttons, press Ctrl/⌘+L to open the Full Screen view. Click on the buttons to play, pause, and stop a video. If you select Pause and want to continue playing after a brief pause, click on the Play button again. In Figure 16-37 you can see the presentation in Full Screen view with the buttons added to the bottom-left side of the page. The text behind the page scrolls up line by line with mouse clicks. The text movement was created in PowerPoint and shows the animated effects in Full Screen mode.

Cross-Reference
For more information on creating button fields, see Chapters 25 and 26. For more information on Full Screen mode and button actions, see Chapter 21.

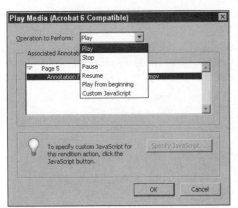

Figure 16-36: When you select the Play Media (Acrobat 6 Compatible) option from the Select Action pull-down menu, a dialog box opens where you make choices for the play action from a pull-down menu.

Figure 16-37: The presentation viewed in Full Screen mode shows the video clip displayed in a floating window. Because no controls are visible in the window, the play, pause, and stop buttons control the video play.

Creating Animation Effects

Although not multimedia in the sense of creating video, you can create animation in Acrobat with some programming in JavaScript. I offer this section as an example for what you can do with a little programming knowledge and not as a lesson in JavaScript.

In Figure 16-38 I added a tickertape type of effect to an opening page in a PDF document. The text scrolls in a field box like you might see on a tickertape or neon sign. The motion created in this document is handled with JavaScript.

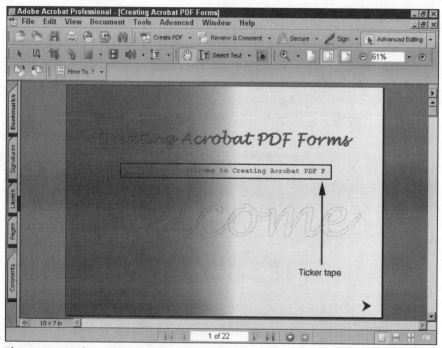

Figure 16-38: The moving text in a tickertape effect is created with JavaScript.

Cross-Reference   For more information on writing JavaScript, see Chapter 27.

To create a similar effect, you first begin by creating a text field and adding the text used for the display. If the Forms toolbar is not expanded, you can select the Text Field tool by opening the pull-down menu adjacent to the Button field in the Advanced Editing toolbar and selecting Text Field Tool. Create a text field and click on the Options tab when the Text Field Properties dialog box opens. Add the text you want for your message to the Default Value field box as shown in Figure 16-39. Be certain to also check the field name in the General properties and add a name of your choice rather than letting Acrobat auto-name the field.

Cross-Reference   For more information on creating form fields, see Chapters 25 and 26.

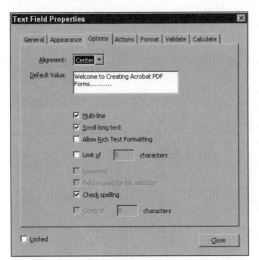

Figure 16-39: The text used for the message is added to the Default Value field in the Options properties for a text field.

After creating the field, it's time to add the scripts that make the motion possible. Three scripts are used in the file. One is a global script added to the document level; another starts the motion when the page is opened, and the last script is added to a Page Close action that stops the animation. To begin, add the first script as a JavaScript Function by choosing Advanced ➪ JavaScript ➪ Document JavaScripts. The JavaScript Functions dialog box opens. Add a name to the Script Name field and click on the Add button. In this example I used Motion for the script name as shown in Figure 16-40.

When you click on the Add button, the JavaScript Editor opens. The default view of the editor contains a few lines of code. You can delete the code or make insertions using the following script. The important thing to do is to type the script exactly as shown here:

```
1. function Motion(msg,n)
2. {
3. var f = new String(msg);
4. return f.substr(n)+f.substr(0,n);
5. }
```

The line numbers in the preceding code are used for clarification when I talk about specific lines of code. They are not included in the code written in the JavaScript Editor. Figure 16-41 shows the code as it should be written in the JavaScript Editor.

This function is addressed in the JavaScript that begins the motion. Click OK in the JavaScript Editor and the function is added to the list window shown in Figure 16-40. Click Close in the JavaScript Functions dialog box.

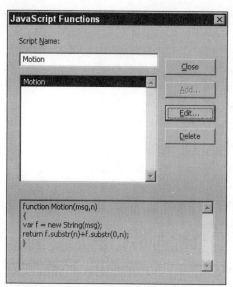

Figure 16-40: Open the JavaScript Functions dialog box and type a name for the script. Click on the Add button and write the script in the JavaScript Editor. When you return to the JavaScript Functions dialog box the script is listed in the window.

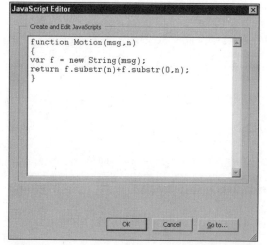

Figure 16-41: Enter the code in the JavaScript Editor and click OK.

You add the other two scripts to the Page Open action to start the motion and the Page Close action to stop the motion. To add the Page Actions, open a context menu on the page where the text field was created and click Actions in the Page Properties dialog box. The default Select Trigger item is Page Open. From the Select Action pull-down menu select Run a JavaScript. Click on the Add button and the JavaScript Editor dialog box opens. For the Page Open Action, type the following code in the JavaScript Editor:

```
1. var f = this.getField("openMessage");
2. var code = new String("this.getField('openMessage').value = \
3. Motion(this.getField('openMessage').value,3);\
4. ");
5. global.ttIsRunning = 1;
6. global.run = app.setInterval(code,150);
```

Cross-Reference   For more information on Page Actions, see Chapters 15 and 27.

Without getting into the detail of the JavaScript, there are a few things you should know. The first contains the name of the field you created on the page. Note the field is placed within quotes in the first, second, and third lines of code. If you use a different name, change the name for these three lines. In line third line the function is addressed. If you use a name other than `Motion` for the function, be certain to change it in line 3. In line 6 the value 150 determines the speed of the text moving in the field. You can change this value and play with it to see how the text is affected. The lower the value, the faster the text moves; conversely, the higher the value, the slower the text moves.

Click OK in the JavaScript Editor to return to the Page Properties dialog box. From the Select Trigger pull-down menu, select Page Close as shown in Figure 16-42. Select Run a JavaScript from the Select Action pull-down menu and click on the Add button. For the Page Close action, type the following code in the JavaScript Editor.

```
1. var f = this.getField("openMessage");
2. if (global.ttIsRunning == 1) {
3. app.clearInterval(global.run);
4. global.ttIsRunning = 0;
5. }
```

Once again the name of the field is noted in this script. If you use a different name, be certain to change the name in the first line of code. Click OK and close the Page Properties dialog box. Save your file and either scroll to a second page and back again to the page containing the Page Actions or close the file and reopen it. The motion starts when the page opens.

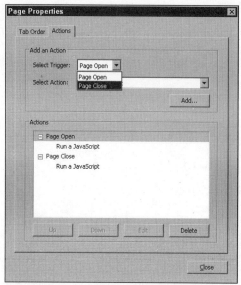

Figure 16-42: Select Page Close and add a JavaScript. When both scripts are added to the Page Properties dialog box, the list window shows the triggers and actions.

 Tip   If you have trouble accessing the Page Properties and the scripts when the motion is playing on the open page, navigate to a second page in your PDF. If you have only a single page, insert a page and navigate to the inserted page. Open the Pages palette and open a context menu on the page where the Page Actions were added. At times, the motion interferes with your access to the scripts. By viewing a different page in the Document Pane you can access Page Actions from any other page.

The scripts shown in this section can be modified to animate objects, rotate text, and so on. In many cases you need to implement JavaScript for certain animation effects you want to add to PDF documents. Although Acrobat 6 offers you the ability to capture Web pages with Flash animation the usability of the captured pages is confined to viewing the captured pages without options for integrating them in other PDF documents. For example, if you want to use an animation from a captured Web page, adding the captured Web page to a button face, watermark, or background doesn't preserve the animation. Animated GIFs are not supported in Acrobat as well. In the current version of Acrobat you'll need to rely on JavaScript to apply different animation effects to existing PDF pages.

 Cross-Reference   For more information on capturing Web pages with animation, see Chapters 5 and 20.

Summary

✦ Sound files can be imported with either Acrobat 5 or Acrobat 6 compatibility. Acrobat 5–compatible sound imports can be used with earlier Acrobat viewers. Acrobat 6–compatible sounds are only available to Acrobat 6 or later viewers. Acrobat 6 compatibility offers more options for attribute settings and file format compatibility.

✦ Sounds can be added to Page Actions, links, Bookmarks, and form fields or by using the Sound tool.

✦ Importing sounds on actions or with the Sound tool require you to have access to a sound file. Sound files are created and saved from sound-editing programs. A number of sound editing programs are available as freeware or shareware on the Internet.

✦ You edit movie files in multimedia authoring programs. Among low-cost alternatives for creating movie files are Adobe Photoshop Album (Windows) and Apple Computer's iMovie. Photoshop Album files are saved direct to PDF. iMovie files are saved in QuickTime format and are imported in PDFs with the Movie tool.

✦ Movie and sound files can have several renditions. Renditions offer you many options for assigning attributes to sound and media clips as well as providing end users with alternatives for downloading different versions of the same file.

✦ Create button fields to play, pause, and stop movies in Full Screen mode without showing the player controls.

✦ You can embed Acrobat 6-compatible media files in PDF documents. Acrobat 6–compatible media files offer much more support for importing different file formats.

✦ A poster is a still image that shows inside a sound or movie field. Posters for movie fields can be retrieved from a movie. Posters for sound and movie fields can be created from files including all file formats supported by the Create PDF From File menu command.

✦ You can add animation to PDF documents with JavaScripts.

✦ Although capturing different animation formats from Web pages is functional in Acrobat, PDFs with animation cannot be imported as button faces, watermarks, or backgrounds. No animated GIF support is provided by Acrobat 6.

✦　　✦　　✦

Working with Layers

Of the new features added to Acrobat 6.0, my favorite is the support for layered PDF documents. Layers are an integral part of many professional imaging applications and specialized technical programs, such as AutoCAD and Microsoft Visio. Now in Acrobat 6.0 you can view native layered documents and toggle on and off different layer views.

Design and creative, scientific, and engineering professionals can find many uses for communicating ideas and concepts with layered documents. To help simplify viewing layered documents, you can add interactive buttons for guiding users through various layer views. In this chapter you learn about what constitutes a PDF with layers, how to manage them, and how to create links to different layer views.

Setting Up the Work Environment

Viewing layers requires no special set of toolbars — the tools you need are dependent on what you intend to do with a PDF containing layers when you begin editing. If, for example, you intend to review and comment layered documents, you'll open the Commenting tools. In this chapter adding links to layer views and how to use the Measuring tools is explained. To prepare for this, you need to open the Advanced Editing toolbar, the Measuring toolbar, and it's also a good idea to open the Properties Bar.

As explained later in this chapter, the Measuring tools offer you options for creating annotations/comments. For some commenting issues, you may want to open the Commenting toolbar. Another option you may find helpful is a grid. To set up the grid, you might want to determine the distances for major and minor grid lines. These settings are available in the Preferences dialog box. Select Units and Guides in the left pane in the Preferences dialog box and define the grid height and width values as well as the offset and subdivisions.

After opening the toolbars, dock them in the Toolbar Well and your work environment should look like Figure 17-1. The following figure shows grid lines turned on so you can see how they are displayed in the Document Pane. For the remaining figures in the chapter the gridlines are off to make it easier to see objects drawn with the Measuring tools. You can easily toggle grid lines on and off by choosing View ➪ Grid or pressing Control/⌘+U.

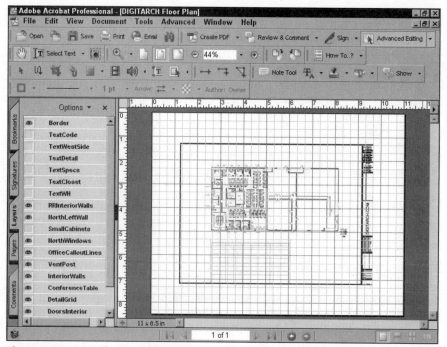

Figure 17-1: Open the Advanced Editing toolbar, the Measuring toolbar, and the Properties Bar, and dock the toolbars in the Toolbar Well.

Cross-Reference   For information on opening toolbars and docking them in the Toolbar Well, see Chapter 1.

Understanding Layers

Acrobat Professional supports the creation of layered documents from two authoring programs: Microsoft Visio and AutoDesk AutoCAD. When layers are created in these programs, the document can be converted to PDF with Adobe PDF layers and viewed in all Acrobat viewers with the layers intact. The creation of Adobe PDF layers requires Acrobat Professional; however, after the PDF creation, layers can be viewed in any Acrobat viewer. If you purchase Acrobat Professional and you use programs that support layers, you may wonder why your favorite application doesn't export a PDF with Adobe PDF layers. Note that conversion to PDF with from Microsoft Visio and AutoDesk AutoCAD is can be performed in Acrobat Standard, but the Adobe PDF layers are not created in the resultant PDF documents.

There are two important points to understand when creating layered PDF files. First, you must begin with an authoring program that supports layers — programs such as Adobe Photoshop, Adobe Illustrator, Adobe PageMaker, Adobe InDesign, CorelDraw, and Macromedia Freehand are some of the popular imaging programs that support layers. Secondly, the authoring application must export to the PDF 1.5 format (Acrobat 6 compatibility). Just because the authoring program supports layers is no guarantee that your resultant PDF will contain layers.

If you use a program that enables you to create and save layered documents and the program does not currently export to Acrobat 6 compatibility, log on to your software manufacturer's Web site and see whether a new version of the program is available and whether the latest release exports to PDF v1.5. As of this writing I cannot tell you what applications will or will not support conversion to PDF with layers. However, if, at the time you install Acrobat, you find no application software supporting exports to PDF with Adobe PDF layers, it is likely that you will eventually see all professional programs that support layers exporting to PDF with multiple layers. Historically, when new PDF specifications have been developed by Adobe Systems, most other programs evolve to support new specifications. If you use history as an indicator for what lies ahead, you'll see many software vendors rushing out new products to meet the new PDF format specifications.

If you don't have layer support now from your favorite authoring tools, be certain to continually visit manufacturer Web sites, Planet PDF, and Adobe's Web site to stay apprised of new developments in software updates, allowing you to take advantage of the new features in Acrobat Professional.

Layer Visibility

When you open a layered document in Acrobat and the Layer palette is open in the Navigation Pane, you see a list of all the layers contained in the document and an eye icon adjacent to each layer name when the respective layer is in view. A layer's visibility is either on or off as shown in the Layer palette.

Initial visibility is determined from the visibility shown in the original authoring program when the PDF is created. In Figure 17-2 you see a layered document with one layer visible as indicated by the eye icon in the Layers palette. The remaining layers in the document are hidden and the hidden state is expressed in the Layers palette by the absence of an eye icon adjacent to the layer names.

Figure 17-2: The initial visibility of layers in this file shows one layer in view, as indicated by the eye icon, and the remaining layers hidden.

Setting initial visibility

The initial layer visibility is the default view of visible layers when you open a PDF document. The layers in view when you open a layered PDF document are determined from the visibility of the layers in view in the original authoring application. If layers are hidden in the authoring application, the initial view in Acrobat viewers shows the same layers hidden as well. The initial view or *state* is the same view displayed in the authoring application at the time of PDF creation. As you browse a file in an Acrobat viewer and turn on and off different layer views, you may want to return to the initial state. Returning to the default view is handled with a menu command by opening the Options pull-down menu in the Layers palette as shown in Figure 17-3. Select this command and you return to the layer views when you first opened the PDF document.

Showing/hiding layers

You show and hide individual layers by clicking on the eye icon in the layers palette. When the eye icon is hidden, the respective layer is hidden. If you want to display a hidden layer, click in the box adjacent to a layer name; the eye icon appears, and the layer is made visible in the Document Pane.

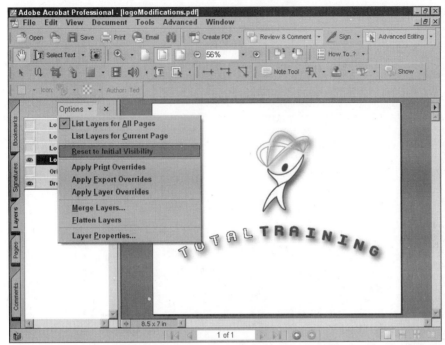

Figure 17-3: To return to the default layer visibility, open the Options pull-down menu in the Layers palette and select Reset to Initial Visibility.

At times you may have pages in a PDF with different layers associated with different pages. If you want to display all layers on the page in view in the Document Pane while hiding layers on other pages in your document, select List Layers for Current Page in the Options pull-down menu. All layers not contained on the page in view in the Document Pane are hidden. If the same layer spans more than one page and you select this menu command, the layer is made visible only when the layer is contained on the active page.

When you change layer visibility in the Layers palette and save the PDF document, the layer visibility is not recorded in the file save. When you open a file after saving with a different layer view, you are still returned to the initial visibility from your first editing session. To create a new default initial view, you need to change the Layer properties.

Initial views

You can open the Layer palette when the PDF is opened in the Document Pane by setting the initial view in the Document Properties. Choose File ➪ Document Properties and select Initial View in the left pane. From the Show pull-down menu, select Layers Panel and Page. Save the PDF document. When you reopen the file the Layer palette is expanded to show the layers.

Cross-Reference For more information on initial views, see Chapter 3.

You'll also notice a "slice of cake" icon in the lower-left corner of a PDF document containing Layers. Click on the icon and the Document Status dialog box opens. In the Document Status dialog box you can disable further appearances of the dialog box each time you open a file by clicking on the checkbox for *Don't show again*. If you want to open the Document Status dialog box at any time when a file is open, click on the slice of cake icon in the lower left corner of the Status Bar and the Document Status dialog box opens as shown in Figure 17-4. The dialog box informs you that the document contains layers and not all layers may be visible when the file is displayed in the Document Pane. This dialog box is more like a help item to inform users that they need to use the Layers palette to show and hide layers. As you first begin working in Acrobat, you may want to have the Document Status dialog box open. After a while though, it will be an annoyance. So be certain to check the preceding box for not showing the dialog box each time you open a layered PDF document. The fact that the slice of cake icon appears in the Status Bar is your clue that the document has special features.

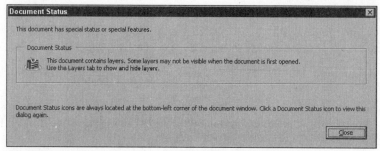

Figure 17-4: Click on the Document Status icon to open the Document Status dialog box. In the dialog box, users are informed that the open document contains layers and the Layers palette may be needed to view hidden layers.

Layer Properties

Layer properties are specific to each layer. To open the Layer Properties dialog box, you must have a layer selected in the Layers palette. Click on a layer name and open a context menu (or select Options ⇨ Layer Properties). The context menu contains two menu options — one for Show Layer and the other for Properties. Select Properties and the Layer Properties dialog box opens as shown in Figure 17-5.

Layer properties are adjusted for individual layers only. Acrobat does not permit you to select multiple layers. If you need to make changes in visibility for several layers, the Layer Properties dialog needs to be opened independently for each layer.

Changing the default state

The Default State pull-down menu contains menu options for either On or Off. The menu choice you make here determines the layer visibility when a file is opened. If you want to change the default state, select On or Off from the pull-down menu. When you click OK in the Layer Properties dialog box and save the PDF document, the default visibility changes according to the views you set in the Layer Properties.

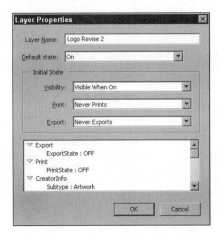

Figure 17-5: To open the Layer Properties dialog box, select a layer in the Layers palette and open a context menu. Select Properties from the menu options. The Layer Properties dialog box opens.

Changing the initial state

Initial states include Layer Visibility, Print, and Export. The default state described previously enables you to determine whether a layer is visible or hidden when a PDF document opens. The individual settings for layer states are applied when you enable a preference setting. Open the Preferences dialog box and select Startup in the left pane. Check the box for Allow Layer State to be set by user information. When this preference option is enabled, the layer state options chosen from the Initial State pull-down menus override the layer visibility set from the Default State pull-down menu. For example, if the default state is set to On and the preference item is deselected, the PDF opens with the layer visible. If you enable the preference settings and select Always Visible from the Visibility pull-down menu, the layer is always visible regardless of whether you have the default state On or Off.

The options for initial states include

✦ **Visibility:** Three choices are available from the pull-down menu. They include Visible When On, Never Visible, and Always Visible. The first option displays a layer according to whether you have the eye icon visible in the Layers palette. When toggled on, the layer is visible. When toggled off, the layer is hidden. Never Visible hides the layer data regardless of whether the default state is on or off. Always Visible always shows the layer.

✦ **Print:** You may have a watermark or message that you want to eliminate or display on a printed page. The three choices, Prints When Visible, Never Prints, and Always Prints, are similar to the options for visibility. Printing a layer does not require the layer to be in view in the Document Pane at the time you print the file if Always Prints is selected.

✦ **Export:** This setting applies to exporting PDF documents back into authoring programs using a Save As command and selecting a file format compatible with your intended authoring program. Export provides you the same three options when exporting layer data as are available for printing. You can eliminate layers exported by selecting Never Exports or hide or show a layer and choose Exports When Visible. Likewise, you can choose to always export a layer regardless of the visibility and print settings by selecting Always Exports.

Cross-Reference For information on exporting PDF data back to authoring programs, see Chapter 12.

The window at the bottom of the dialog box displays information according to the initial state(s) you select from the pull-down menu. When you open the Properties dialog box you can see, at a glance, the options for each initial state. At the bottom of the scrollable list is information related to the authoring document that was exported to PDF. If you want to export the PDF data back to an authoring program you can verify what program is needed for the export.

Overriding defaults

You can create PDF documents with layers that aren't visible in the Layers palette in your original authoring program. You can also hide layers in the Default State or the Initial State pull-down menus. If you change defaults to hide layers or a layer is not visible in the Layers palette, you can override all settings in the Options menu. If the Options menu shows a menu item for overriding a layer state grayed out, the menu choice is not available. To change the options you need to return to the Layer Properties dialog box.

Open the Options pull-down menu and three options are listed for overriding defaults. They include:

✦ **Apply Print Overrides:** When selected, any options you made for not printing layers are overridden. When the menu item is selected in the Options palette and you print the PDF all layers are printed.

✦ **Apply Export Overrides:** The preceding holds true for exporting layer data. When overridden, all layer data are exported.

✦ **Apply Layer Overrides:** Layer Overrides relates to the layer visibility. When enabled, all layers are visible in the Document Pane, but the individual layer visibility options are no longer available to you. You cannot click on an eye icon for hiding a layer when the override is enabled. To individually show or hide a layer you need to deselect the Apply Layer Overrides menu options and use the Layers palette for showing/hiding layers.

Managing layers

Layers can be edited for naming, merging, and flattening. To rename a layer, select the layer in the Layers palette and click a second time on the layer name. The layer name is highlighted. As you type, the highlighted text is replaced by the new text you type on the keyboard. You can click and drag across a layer name and edit a portion of the text much like you might change names in Bookmarks. Layer names are also edited in the Layer Properties dialog box. If you are changing properties and you additionally want to change a layer name, select the name in the Layer Name field in the Layer Properties dialog box and edit the name.

Merging layers

Layers can be merged whether they are visible or hidden. All layer merging takes place in the Merge Layers dialog box and is available only to users of Acrobat Professional. To open the dialog box select Merge Layers from the Options pull-down menu in the Layers palette. The Merge Layers dialog box opens as shown in Figure 17-6.

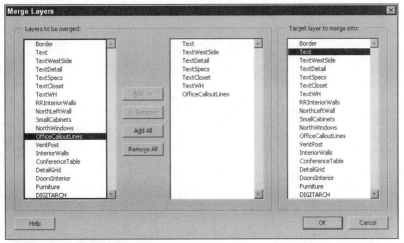

Figure 17-6: To merge layers, select Merge Layers from the Options pull-down menu. The Merge Layers dialog box opens where all layers (visible and hidden) are listed in the Layers to be merged column.

Regardless of whether a layer is visible or hidden, the list in the Layers to be merged column on the left side of the dialog box lists all layers in the document in a scrollable window. You can merge visible layers with hidden layers. To merge layers, select the layers to be merged into a single layer from the list on the left and click on the Add button. You can select multiple layers by holding down the Shift key for a contiguous selection or by using the Control key (Windows) or ⌘ key (Macintosh) to randomly select layer names in a noncontiguous group.

When the layers to be merged are visible in the center column, select the target layer in the Target layer to merge into: column. The name you select here is the name listed in the Layers palette and contains all the data from the other layers. The properties associated with the target layer become the properties in the merged layer. After merging layers, all previous layer names are removed from the Layers palette.

When adding layers to the list in the center of the dialog box (add list), you can move the target layer to the add list or elect to not move the target layer to the list. For example, if you have Text as a target layer where you want to merge Text02 and Text03 together with Text, you can add Text to the center window or not add Text to the list. When you select Text as the target layer and click OK, Text01 and Text 02 are added to Text regardless of whether Text was added to the center column.

Tip
If you want to merge a group of layers to a new layer name, you can edit the name of one of the layers to be merged in the Layers palette. Click, and click again on the layer name in the Layers palette to edit the layer name. Open the Merge Layers dialog box and merge the desired layers to the new target layer name.

Flattening layers

Layers can be flattened in a PDF document to combine a group of layers or all layers into a single layer for users of Acrobat Professional. Both merging layers discussed earlier and flattening layers are not available to Acrobat Standard users. You may want to flatten layers to simplify printing a document, exchange a PDF with users of an Acrobat viewer earlier than version 6, or reduce the file size. When flattening layers, the layer visibility is taken into account. If you have four layers and two layers are visible, the flattened PDF document results in combining the visible layers only. Be certain about what layer data you want to remain visible before selecting the Options menu and choosing Flatten Layers, as you won't be able to undo the operation and regain the data that was discarded from the hidden layers.

Using Measuring Tools

Although the use of the Measuring tools is not specific to PDF documents containing layers, it can be a great help to users creating engineering drawings and CAD documents for measuring distances and surface area. Therefore, I included the use of these tools along with layers. Keep in mind that the use of these tools can be applied to any PDF document you open in Acrobat regardless of whether there are layers present. Measuring tools however are not available in Acrobat Standard. This complete section on using the Measuring tools is related only to Acrobat Professional users.

The three tools available to you in the Measuring toolbar include

Distance tool: The Distance tool is used to measure linear distances between two x,y coordinates on a document page. To use the tool, click and release the mouse button. Move the cursor to a different location and click again. The measurement is calculated when you make the second click and is recorded in the Properties Bar.

Note

If you don't open the Properties Bar from a context menu or the View ➪ Toolbars submenu, clicking on a Measuring tool automatically opens the Properties Bar.

Perimeter tool: The Perimeter tool is used to measure the outside perimeter of any angle or polygon object. To use the tool, click and release the mouse button. Move the cursor and click again. Repeat the same steps to continue along a path (right angle, triangle, or polygon). When finished, make the last click and keep the mouse stationary. Click a second time when you see a small circle appear aside the cursor. The second click on the destination point informs Acrobat you're finished measuring. As each segment is drawn, the distance is reported in the Properties Bar and each new segment is added to the total distance. In essence, you continue to see the total distance from the point of origin as you keep adding new segments.

Area tool: The Area tool is used with any polygon object (three or more sides) and measures the surface area contained within the perimeter. When using the tool you need to draw line segments and return to the point of origin to close the path. Acrobat Professional informs you when you reach the point of origin by adding a small circle to the cursor. The circle appears only when you reach the point of origin when using the Area tool. After clicking at the point of origin, the surface area is calculated within the path you draw.

Measuring surface area

For measurements where you don't need a record of the results other than the distance reported in the Properties Bar, you can select one of the Measuring tools and move the cursor to the point where you want to begin a measurement. Click the mouse button and move to another location. If you use the Distance tool, click the mouse button at the destination. Before you move the mouse cursor, be certain to view the Properties Bar as shown in Figure 17-7. A readout is displayed in the toolbar that shows you the distance and angle of the measurement.

When you use the Perimeter tool, the distance is reported for each segment while the perimeter (angle is added between Distance & Angle to in Figure 17-7) readout reports the sum of each segment. For example, if you draw a 2-inch horizontal line, the distance and perimeter readings are the same. Click the mouse button and move down 1 inch; the distance reports 1 inch (the distance of the new segment), and the perimeter reports 3 inches (the sum of the two segments).

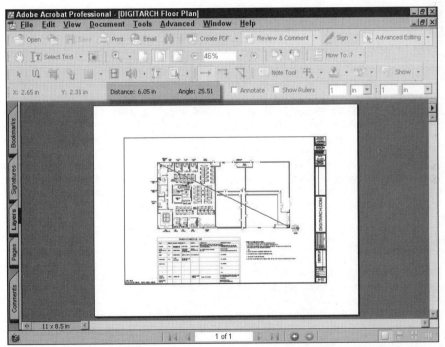

Figure 17-7: The Properties Bar displays the measurements for each of the Measuring tools for distance and angle, perimeter, or area according to which tool you use.

The Area tool reports distance and total area. As a line is drawn and you click the mouse button, the distance readout is shown in the Properties Bar. As each new segment is drawn, the readout reports the distance of the current segment, also in the Properties Bar. However, the area measurement is not displayed until you close the polygon by returning to the point of origin. As you move the cursor back to the point where you began the area measurement, a small circle is displayed beside the top right edge of the mouse cursor. Click and the path closes and the area readout displays in the Properties Bar.

Annotating measurements

When you use the Measuring tools, the minute you select another tool, the measurement disappears and you have no record of measuring distances or surface area. If you want to keep a record of measurements, Acrobat can create a comment note for each measurement when using any of the Measuring tools. To add a comment note and mark the path with a line or polygon comment, click on the Annotate check box in the Properties Bar.

When you draw a path with any of the measuring tools the line segments appear on the path you draw. The line is created with Line, Polygon Line, or Polygon comment tool and an associated pop-up note is available. Select the Hand tool after drawing a path and open a context menu on a line segment. From the menu options select Open Pop-Up Note or double click on the line. Pop-up notes record measurements each time you use one of the Measuring tools.

The note properties for author name and the color of the Pop-Up Note window are adjustable in the Properties dialog box. When you open a context menu on a line segment, the dialog box opens as Line Properties when the Distance tool is used, Polygon Line Properties when the Perimeter tool is used, and Polygon Properties when the Area tool is used. The properties options are the same as when using the respective comment tools. For example, a Polygon comment enables you to create a fill and set opacity for the fill and stroke. When using the Area tool, a Polygon comment is created that enables you to use these same properties options. In Figure 17-8, you can see examples of each measuring tool and different property options assigned to each comment. In addition to the Pop-Up Note windows, when either the Hand tool or a Measuring tool is selected, you can move the mouse cursor over any measurement line and a tooltip reports the measurement.

Cross-Reference For more information on comment pop-up notes; creating Line, Polygon Line, and Polygon comments; and setting properties, see Chapter 14.

The comments added when you select Annotate in the Properties Bar can be moved, deleted, and changed. Open a context menu and make the menu choices for the edits you want.

Engineering If you want to examine identical measurements for distances, perimeters, or areas, create a measurement with the Annotate check box enabled in the Properties Bar. Select the comment line with the Hand tool and drag it around the document page. You can move the path to different areas, assessing whether the background page contents fit the measurement reported in the pop-up note.

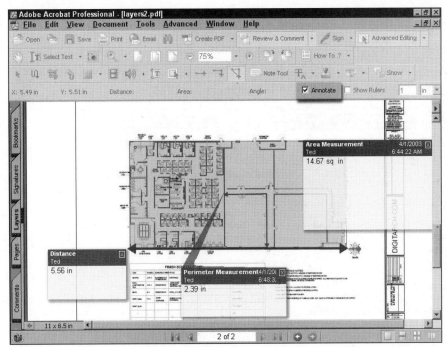

Figure 17-8: Click on the Annotate check box in the Properties Bar and draw a path with any of the Measuring tools. After completing a path, select the Hand tool and open a comment pop-up note. The measurement is recorded in the note window.

Adjusting units and scaling

The Properties Bar includes an option for showing rulers and a pull-down menu where units of measure are selected. Click on the check box for Rulers to show rulers and select the desired units of measure from a number of different menu options in one of two pull-down menus. The two field boxes are used for determining what scale you want to use in your document. For example if using a scale of 2:1, you type 2 in the first field box and 1 in the second field box.

When drawing measurements, the values are reported in the pop-up notes according to the scale and units selected in the Properties Bar. For example, if you want to use a scale of 2:1 and measure distances in centimeters, enter 2 in the first field box and 1 in the second field box. Select centimeters from the pull-down menu choices for both pull-down menus and measure a distance or surface area with one of the Measuring tools. In Figure 17-9 the Distance tool was used to measure a distance one centimeter long. Because the scale was set to 2:1, as shown in the Properties Bar, the pop-up note reported .5 centimeters.

Tip If you want to use two individual units of measure, say inches and centimeters, and want the results reported in the Pop-Up Note window to record one value or the other, be certain to select the unit of measure to be recorded in the second pull-down menu. The second value is recorded in the Pop-Up note window.

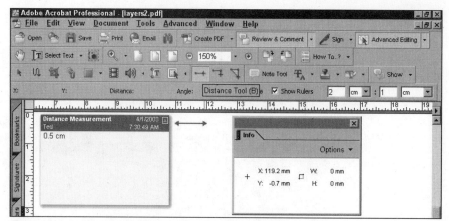

Figure 17-9: Select the units of measure from the pull-down menus and select the scaling by entering the values for the ratio in the two field boxes in the Properties Bar.

If you select your units of measure and the ratio for scaling, and want to change any values, you need to recreate the measurements in order to see the values reported correctly in the pop-up notes. Acrobat does not dynamically update values in the notes as you change units of measure or scaling ratios.

Units of measure can also be globally changed in the Info palette. If you want to change a default unit of measure, choose View ⇨ Navigation Tabs ⇨ Info to open the Info palette. From the Options pull-down menu you can make choices for the units of measure of Points, Inches, or Millimeters. The units changed in the Info palette globally change the units in an open PDF document. When you view the Properties Bar, the first pull-down menu reflects the units selected in the Info palette. However, if you change the units in the Properties Bar, the Info palette does not correspondingly change units. The palette holds true for headers and footers, backgrounds and watermarks, link buttons, and form fields. The content you add in Acrobat is not specific to a layer. Consider all the objects you add in Acrobat as residing on their own, separate layer. A new layer is not really created. The units remain fixed according to choices you make from the Options pull-down menu in the palette.

Comments, measurements, and layers

When you add measurement lines on layered documents and open pop-up notes, the lines and notes are visible on any layer in the document. If you hide all layers, the lines and pop-up notes are still visible.

If you have text that appears on all layers, the text can be edited regardless of what layer is visible. For example, adding a header to a document and selecting the TouchUp Text tool to change the text properties is one condition where the text is visible on all layers. Regardless of what layers are in view, the text can be edited and the changes are reflected in all layer views.

Cross-Reference For information on using the TouchUp Text tool, see Chapter 8.

If you want objects in terms of PDF content to appear on separate layers, you need to return to your authoring application and create the objects on specific layers. Objects and data created in Acrobat cannot become a part of individual layers or toggled on and off in the Layers palette.

Creating Visibility Buttons

You may have a document where you want to create navigation buttons to help a user easily navigate through different layer views. Inasmuch as the Document Status dialog box informs users how to view layers, some buttons that link to different layer views can help users understand the document structure and quickly navigate different views.

Creating buttons to layer visibility is much like creating Bookmarks. You first establish the view you want to be the destination view of a link action and then create the link button. In Figure 17-10, you can see a document displayed in the Navigation Pane at the layer initial visibility.

Cross-Reference   For more information on creating form fields, see Chapters 25 and 26.

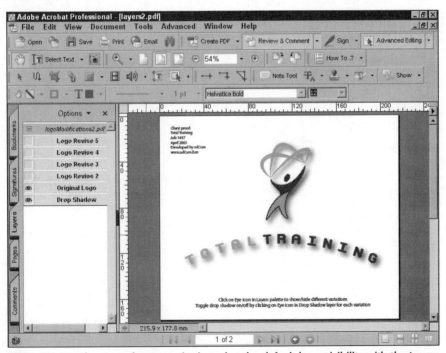

Figure 17-10: The open document is viewed at the default layer visibility with the Layers palette open.

The first step is to create the view that you want to display when a user clicks on a button. In the Layers palette you can toggle on or off different views to create the layer visibility you want as the final result of the link action. Then create a button using the button tool. Select the Actions tab in the Button Properties dialog box and select Set layer visibility from the Select Action pull-down menu options. In Figure 17-11 you can see the new visibility in the Layers palette where the Logo Revise 2 layer is visible as well as the Drop Shadow layer. This view is different than the initial view shown in Figure 17-10. After setting the view, create a button field and select Set layer visibility in the Select Action pull-down menu as shown in Figure 17-12.

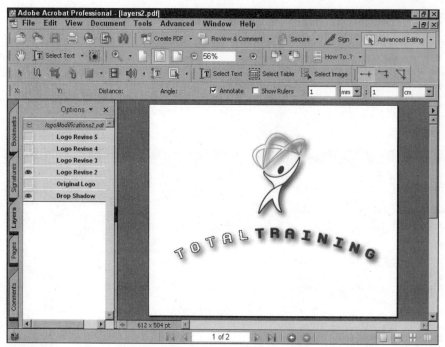

Figure 17-11: First set the visibility for the resultant view in the Layers palette.

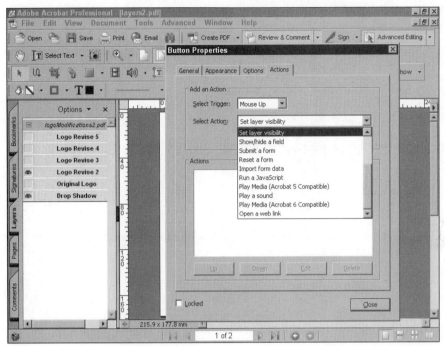

Figure 17-12: Select Set layer visibility from the menu option in the Select Action pull-down menu of the Button Properties dialog box. The link action captures the current view.

After clicking on the Close button, you can select the Options pull-down menu and choose Reset to Initial Visibility to return to the default view. You can select the Hand tool and click on the button to see the new view displayed in the Document Pane as shown in Figure 17-13.

The most difficult part of the process is to keep in mind that you first need to set the visibility you want as the result of clicking the button. After you create a few buttons, the process becomes second nature and creating links to layer visibility will become as easy as creating Bookmarks.

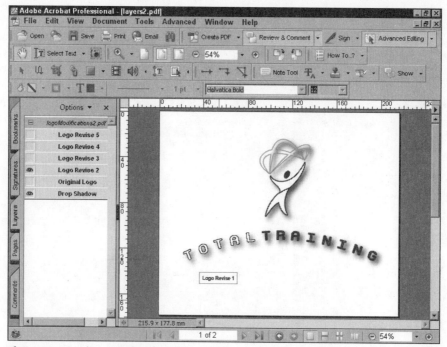

Figure 17-13: After resetting the initial visibility view, click the button you created and the new view is shown in the Document Pane.

Summary

✦ The PDF 1.5 format supports layers from authoring applications that are capable of creating layered files and exporting with Acrobat 6 compatibility.

✦ Individual layers can be viewed and hidden in Acrobat. The initial visibility for what layers are in view and what layers are hidden is determined at the time the PDF is created.

✦ Saving files after showing and hiding layers does not change initial visibility. Initial visibility is changed in the Layer Properties dialog box, where layers are toggled on and off.

✦ Layer states for visibility, printing, and exporting data are changed in the Layer properties. Layers can be printed or exported without visibility.

✦ Layers are merged and flattened using menu commands from the Options pull-down menu in the Layers palette.

✦ Measuring tools enable you to measure distances, perimeters, and surface area. Distances and area are displayed in the Properties Bar as you move the Measuring tools in the Document Pane.

✦ Associated comments and pop-up notes are assigned to measurement distances by selecting the Annotate check box in the Properties Bar. Comments properties are changed in a Properties dialog box accessed from a context menu opened on the comment or pop-up note.

✦ Measuring distances to scale is available by selecting options for scale values and units of measure in the Properties Bar.

✦ Link buttons can be created to display different layer visibility. To create a link action to a view, you first create the desired view in the Layers palette and then set the link action in the Button Properties dialog box.

✦　　✦　　✦

Accessibility and Tagged PDF Files

Adobe Acrobat 6 is compliant with United States federal code regulating document accessibility for vision- and motion-challenged persons. This means that screen readers can intelligently interpret the PDFs you create; in other words, PDF files can be read aloud in a reading order like a sighted person would read a document. Through an extensive set of keyboard modifiers available in Acrobat, almost anyone with vision or motion challenges can share your documents and read them.

In order for a document to be accessible, you must use authoring applications capable of delivering a document's structure to Acrobat. Hence, you need to know something about the internal structure of documents and what programs to use to create the structure required by Acrobat to make a document accessible. Not all the content in a document travels through the PDF creation process with information necessary to make a document completely accessible. Therefore you need to perform some work in Acrobat to either add accessibility or to polish up a document for delivery to a screen reader in a form that makes sense to the user. In this chapter I cover how to make documents accessible from authoring programs, as well as how to use Acrobat tools to make existing documents accessible.

Setting Up the Work Environment

The essential tool for working with document accessibility is the Tags tab. To view the Tags tab, choose Document ➪ Navigation Tabs ➪ Tags. The Tags tab opens in a palette nested between two other tabs. Click the Tags tab and drag it away from the other two tabs to undock it from the palette. Drag the tab to the Navigation Pane to dock it among the other tabs below the Layers tab. Click the close box in the top-right corner of the palette with the two remaining tabs to close it.

Although most of what you do with accessibility in Acrobat is handled with the Tags palette and the top-level menus, you may need to use the TouchUp Text tool and TouchUp Object tool. Click the Advanced Editing task button to open the Advanced Editing toolbar. From the pull-down menu adjacent to the TouchUp Text tool, select Expand this button. To dock the toolbar, select Dock All Toolbars from a context menu opened from the Toolbar Well.

Screen Readers

I use the term *screen reader* extensively in this chapter. When I use this term, I'm referring to tools created by third parties to read open documents aloud in Acrobat and other programs or from files in various formats saved to disk.

Screen readers range in price from $99 to over $1,000. The advantage of using third-party products with Acrobat PDF files is that they can read aloud single words as well as character by character. Through keyboard controls, users choose reading rates, audio output levels, voices, and navigation.

Screen readers are typically software programs installed on either Mac OS or Windows. More programs support Windows than Macintosh operating systems, but developers have been increasing support for both platforms. In past years, PDF documents were not supported by many developers. Today, much more support exists for reading PDF documents with the Adobe Reader software.

For a complete list of screen readers that have been tested with Acrobat, log on to Adobe's Web site at: http://access.adobe.com. From Adobe's Web page you'll find URL links to vendor sites as well as general information about accessibility.

Creating Accessible Documents

The terms *document accessibility, structure,* and *tagged PDFs* may be a mystery to you. If the term *accessibility* is new, then you need to begin with an understanding of what accessible documents are before working with them. After you know more about document accessibility, you can move forward to look at how to create an accessible document, and then look at how Acrobat can edit accessible documents. Therefore, the three areas to work with are understanding accessibility, creating accessible documents from authoring programs, and finally, working with accessible documents in Acrobat.

Understanding accessibility

Sighted people can view a document on the computer or read a printed page and easily discern the difference between titles, subtitles, columns, graphic images, graphic elements, and so on. With regard to Acrobat PDFs, you can easily see the difference between background designs, button links, bookmarks, animation, and form fields, and you typically see visual clues to know where buttons and fields exist.

With regard to screen-reading devices, which depend on software to generate audio output from an Acrobat PDF file, the software readers aren't intelligent enough to distinguish differences based on visual clues. For example, a screen reader may interpret a three-columned document as one continuous column and read the text from left to right across all three columns row by row. Obviously the output is useless to the end user working with a screen reader. Readers interpret headings, subheadings, and tables the same as body copy, and they offer no distinction in the structure unless the reader has some clue that these items are different from the body text.

Some authoring programs provide you an opportunity when creating the PDF file to retain the underlying structure of a document in the resulting PDF file. With a series of tags and retention of the document structure, screen readers use alternate text to make distinctions in the document much like the visual user would interpret a page. The document flow, alternate text for graphic elements, distinctions between headings, and so on, can all be managed in Acrobat when the internal document structural tree is included in the PDF export. When files are not exported with the document structure, you can use Acrobat commands to add structure to PDFs. In order to make it possible for people with screen readers to navigate your PDF documents correctly, the underlying structure must be present.

To gain more of a grasp on what I mean by terms like *structure* and *tagged PDF files*, a definition is warranted. PDF files fall into three categories when we are talking about a document's structure. The categories include

✦ **Unstructured PDF Files:** Unstructured PDF documents cannot be interpreted by screen readers with complete document integrity. For example, when exporting the PDF to other formats such as a Rich Text File (RTF), the basic paragraph structure is preserved, but tables, lists, and some text formatting are lost. Another kind of repurposing for PDF files is the ability to view them on handheld devices and various sized monitors with text reflows. Unstructured documents, however, cannot be reflowed on screens.

Cross-Reference

For more information on reflowing text, see Chapter 3.

✦ **Structured PDF Files:** Structured PDF files can be read by screen readers, but the reliability is much less than the next category of tagged PDF documents. When you export structured PDF files to other formats, more structural content is preserved, but tables and lists can be lost. Additionally, structured documents like the unstructured documents discussed previously do not support text reflows for different-sized devices.

✦ **Tagged PDF Files:** Tagged PDFs contain both the document structure and a hierarchical structure tree where all the internal structure about the document's content is interpreted. Tagged PDFs have the highest reliability when repurposing files for screen reader output and saving files in other formats such as RTF, HTML, XHTML, and XML. In addition, tagged PDF files support text reflow for viewing on different-sized screens and accommodating any zoom level on a monitor.

Cross-Reference

For more information on document reflow, see Chapter 3. For more information on exporting PDF content, see Chapter 5. For more on document structure, see "Understanding Structure" in this chapter.

The goal for you when creating PDF documents for accessibility is to be certain you use PDF documents that are not only structured, but also tagged PDFs. After you create tagged PDFs you can work with the structure tree and modify the contents for optimum use. In terms of making Acrobat PDFs accessible, you must consider several criteria to optimize files for effective handling by screen readers. These include

✦ **Assessing accessibility:** Fortunately, Acrobat provides tools for determining whether a PDF file is an accessible document. As a first order of business you should plan on assessing a file for accessibility. If you work with legacy files or files that are created from authoring programs that don't support the export of the document structure, be certain to make the document accessible before beginning an editing session.

Cross-Reference

For adding accessibility to PDF files from within Acrobat see the section "Making existing PDFs accessible" later in this chapter.

✦ **Logical reading order:** The text should follow a logical flow. You need to properly define column text in terms of the path that a screen reader follows (that is, down one column; then begin at the top of the second column, and so on). You should also mark headings and subheadings for distinction.

✦ **Alternative text descriptions for image and graphic elements:** Those familiar with HTML know that you can code an HTML document with alternate tags so users with text-only browsers can understand the structure of Web pages. The same principle for accessible documents applies. Alternate text needs to be inserted so the screen reader can interpret graphic elements.

✦ **Form field descriptions:** Form fields need to be described with text to inform a user with a screen reader that a form field is present.

✦ **Field tab order:** Setting the logical tab order for fields on a form is important for the visual user. With screen readers it is essential. The logical tab order for fields should be strictly followed.

✦ **Document security:** If documents are secured with Acrobat security, you must use 128-bit encryption compatible with Acrobat 5 and Acrobat 6. If you use compatibility less than Acrobat 5 or 40-bit encryption, the PDF is rendered inaccessible.

✦ **Links and interactivity:** Use form fields for link buttons with descriptions so the user knows that another destination or a link action is invoked if he or she selects the field.

✦ **Document language:** Screen readers typically deliver accessible documents in only one language. To protect your documents against inoperability with new releases, specify a document language when creating accessible PDFs. Document language specification is also important when using tools in Acrobat for checking accessibility.

For more information on field tab order, see Chapter 26. For more information on document security, see Chapter 19. For more information on links and interactivity see Chapter 15.

Adding accessibility in authoring applications

Not all authoring programs currently support accessibility. This phenomenon may change with new upgrades to software, so what is said today may change tomorrow. As of this writing the programs offering the best support for document accessibility include Microsoft Word version 2000 or higher, Adobe PageMaker 7.0 or higher, and Adobe InDesign 2.0 or higher. If you use other authoring applications you do have the option to make documents accessible with Acrobat Standard and Acrobat Professional.

When converting Microsoft Word files to PDF, be certain to use the PDFMaker in the Word toolbar or from the Acrobat menu. Set up the conversion settings for enabling accessibility and reflow with tagged PDF documents. This option is available in the Settings tab in the Acrobat PDFMaker dialog box.

For more on creating PDF files with accessibility and tags from Microsoft Office applications, see Chapter 6.

When creating documents with text, images, charts, diagrams, and so on, using a professional layout program often works better than a word processor. Adobe InDesign is an ideal tool for creating layouts that you need to make accessible. When you design a document for accessibility, be precise about how you add elements on each page. The order in which you lay out documents can have an effect on the order of the exported structure. For example, adding a block of text, then importing an image may result in the text appearing first in the structure tree and the image following the text even if you move the elements so the image appears first on the page. The only way to observe the results of how the document structure ultimately converts to PDF is to practice and examine the tags structure tree in Acrobat versus your layouts. You can develop a workflow that minimizes the work in Acrobat to properly create the structure needed for optimum performance when read by a screen reader.

Tip

> If you arrange objects in an authoring program like Adobe InDesign and the reading order is not following the viewing order, you can cut either text or images and paste them back into the document. If, for example, an image should be first in the structure tree followed by text, but the order is reversed when you examine the tags in Acrobat, cut the text block and paste it back into the document in InDesign. Recreate the PDF and you'll find the order changed according to the order that the elements were last placed on the page. This method is not always a precise solution for reordering elements, but can often be used to resolve problems.

When you export files to PDF from Adobe InDesign, be certain to use the File ⇨ Export command instead of printing a PostScript file and distilling in Acrobat Distiller. Distilling PostScript files does not retain document structure while exporting to PDF from programs like Adobe InDesign, Adobe PageMaker, Adobe FrameMaker, and the PDF Maker macro with Microsoft Office applications retains document structure and exports tagged PDF documents. When you open the Export dialog box, provide a name for the file and select Adobe PDF for the file format. Click the Save button and the Export PDF dialog box opens as shown in Figure 18-1. In the General settings click on the check box for Include eBook Tags.

The switch check box implies that the option is designed for creating eBooks, but this check box determines whether your exported file from Adobe InDesign is designed accessible with tags. Click on the Export button and the PDF file is created with tags.

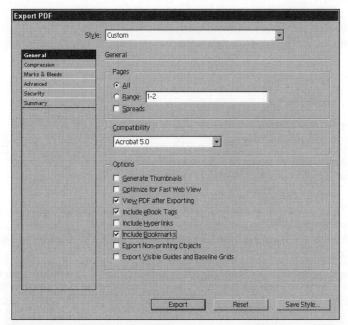

Figure 18-1: To add accessibility with Adobe InDesign files, enable the Include eBook Tags check box.

Making existing PDFs accessible

If you have PDF documents either from legacy files or from files converted from authoring applications that do not support exports to PDF with tags, you can use Acrobat commands to add structure to the document and make the files accessible. The first step is checking a document for accessibility. If the document contains no tags, then you can add tags in Acrobat Standard or Acrobat Professional.

Performing a Quick Check

To determine whether a document is accessible, in either Acrobat Standard, Acrobat Professional, or Adobe Reader, choose Advanced ➪ Accessibility ➪ Quick Check. This method of checking the PDF is a quick analysis to determine whether tags exist in the file. When the check is completed, a dialog box opens informing you of the accessibility status. If the document is not accessible, the dialog box message appears as shown in Figure 18-2.

Note   Document accessibility can be checked in Adobe Reader. Making a document accessible, however, requires Acrobat Standard or Acrobat Professional.

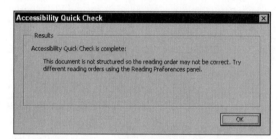

Figure 18-2: After running Quick Check on an unstructured document, the Accessibility Quick Check dialog box reports the findings.

Performing a Full Check

Acrobat Professional offers you a more sophisticated analysis where more file attributes are checked and a report is created either in a file, or by adding comments to the open PDF document, or both. To use the Full Check option:

STEPS: Checking Accessibility in Acrobat Professional

1. **Choose Advanced ➪ Accessibility ➪ Full Check.** The Accessibility Full Check dialog box shown in Figure 8-3 opens.

2. **Check the box for Create Accessibility Report and Create comments in document.** Checking these boxes creates a report and adds comment notes in the document pertaining to the results of the analysis. All errors found during the check are reported in comment notes.

3. **Select the Checking Options the items you want to check.** Enable checkboxes under Checking Options for items you want to check. In this example I checked all boxes.

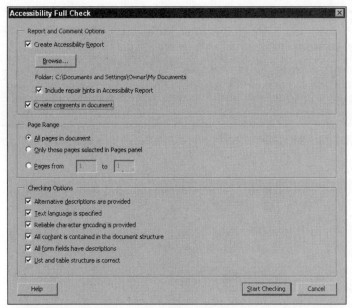

Figure 18-3: When you run a Full Check in Acrobat Professional, you can choose options for what content to check.

4. **Click the Browse button.** Identify the location for the report file if you want a report saved to a text file.

5. **When you set all the attributes, click Start Checking.** Acrobat opens a dialog box similar to Figure 18-4, reporting the findings.

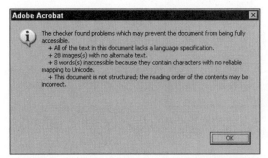

Figure 18-4: After running the Full Check, the findings are reported in a dialog box.

Adding accessibility

Keep in mind you are always best served by adding accessibility at the time a PDF document is created from authoring programs supporting exports to PDF with accessibility and tags. If you have files where either returning to the authoring program is impractical or the authoring program is incapable of exporting to PDF as tagged files, choose Advanced ➪ Accessibility ➪ Add Tags to Document. (If you are using Acrobat Standard, choose Advanced ➪ Accessibility ➪ Make Accessible.) Immediately after you select the menu command from either Acrobat Standard or Acrobat Professional, a slider bar opens displaying Acrobat's progress in adding tags to the document. After completion, no confirmation dialog box opens to report the status. If problems were encountered while adding the tags, a dialog box opens, reporting the problems found, as shown in Figure 18-5.

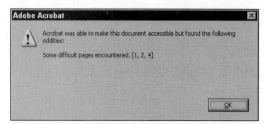

Figure 18-5: If problems are found while adding tags, a dialog box opens reporting the problems.

After adding the tags you can return to the Quick Check or Full Check menu command and check the document for accessibility. I performed a Full Check on a file that was made Accessible in Acrobat Professional and the dialog box shown in Figure 18-6 reported the findings.

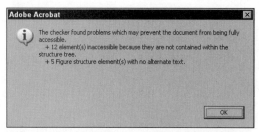

Figure 18-6: You can run a check on files made accessible in Acrobat to view the report findings.

If a file has tags and you choose Advanced ➪ Accessibility ➪ Add Tags to Document, Acrobat opens a dialog box informing you that the file already has tags. Adding tags is not permitted using the menu command.

Batch Processing for document accessibility

Using the Add Tags to Document menu command is sufficient for creating accessible documents for a few files. If you have many documents that you want to convert, you can use Acrobat's Batch Processing mode to convert a collection of PDFs from user-defined folders. Batch Processing is available only in Acrobat Professional.

STEPS: Adding Accessibility with a Batch Sequence

To create a batch sequence for making PDFs accessible:

1. **Choose Advanced ⇨ Batch Processing.** This opens the Batch Sequences dialog box.

2. **Click the New Sequence button in the dialog box.** This opens the Name Sequence dialog box.

3. **Provide a name for the sequence**. Add a descriptive name so you know what the sequence is used when returning to it in future Acrobat sessions.

4. **Click OK in the Name Sequence dialog box**. The Edit Sequence dialog box opens.

5. **Select the Make Accessible command from the list of commands in the left window**. See Figure 18-7.

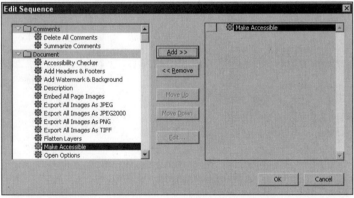

Figure 18-7: Select Make Accessible in the list of sequences and click on the Add button.

6. **Click the Add button.** This adds the command to the list of sequences on the right side of the dialog box.

7. **Click OK.** This returns you to the Batch Edit Sequence dialog box.

8. **Follow the same steps for selecting the output folder and run commands as you do with other batch sequences.** When you want to make PDF documents within a folder accessible, select the folder and run the sequence.

Cross-Reference

For information on creating and running batch sequences, see Chapter 13.

Understanding Structure

To understand more clearly the need for creating accessibility and adding tags to a document, look at Figure 18-8 as an example. This document contains several items that need attention to make the file accessible and comprehensible when read by a screen reader.

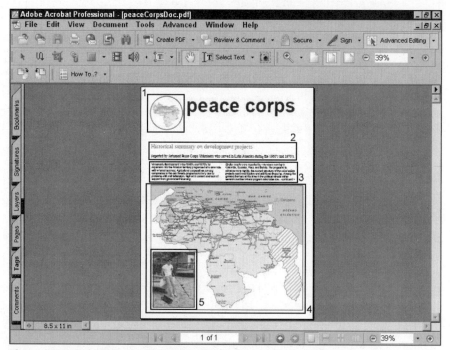

Figure 18-8: A document with images, illustrations, and text in multiple columns needs to have the structure modified for proper reading by a screen reader.

In Figure 18-8 the items of importance in regard to accessibility include the following:

1. **The first element on the page is a logo.** A screen reader won't interpret the logo unless you add some alternate text to the document describing the object. Adjacent to the logo on the right side is text that a screen reader can read after you make the document accessible. If the text does not read properly, the two lines of text need to be modified for the proper interpretation by the screen reader.

2. **The two lines of text are in a single column.** These lines should be read in logical order without any problems. They are shown here to illustrate the difference between the two lines and the two columns following.

3. **The text is blocked in two columns.** Unless the structure is established for the screen reader to read down one column before moving to the second column, the screen reader defaults at a left-to-right reading order, reading across both columns.

4. **Item four is a large map.** Alternate text for the illustration is needed for the screen reader to explain what graphic appears on the page.

5. **Item five is an inset photo.** The alternate text for the map can describe the photo or the photo can have an alternate text description. Either way, you need to create the alternate text for the screen reader to fully interpret the graphics.

When you export to PDF from authoring programs with tags, the structure of the document for the blocks of text in logical reading orders is preserved. In the example in Figure 18-8, the single and double-column text is typically not a problem when the file is read by a screen reader. Images, however, need some form of manual editing. Even the best source exporting with tags wouldn't be able to describe the visual elements in the layout. These are subjective items that need a description.

If using a program like Microsoft Word, you can add alternate text in Word before the file is exported to PDF. In other applications you need to create the alternate text in Acrobat.

Using the Tags palette

When you export a document from an authoring program with tags or use the Add Tags to Document menu command, a *structure tree* is created in the PDF file. The structure tree is a hierarchical order of the elements contained in the file. Elements may be in the form of heads, subheads, body text, figures, tables, annotations, and other items identified as separate individual structural elements. The hierarchy contains a nested order of the elements with parent/child relationships. A heading, for example, may have a subhead. The heading in this case is a parent element with the subheading a child element.

When a document contains tags, you view the tag elements and the structure tree in the Tags tab. Open the Tags tab and click on the top item. By default you see an icon labeled Tags with a plus (+) (Windows) or right-pointing arrow (Macintosh) symbol adjacent to it. Click the symbol and you open the tree at one level. Other child elements are nested below. Click several symbols and the structure tree appears similar to Figure 18-9.

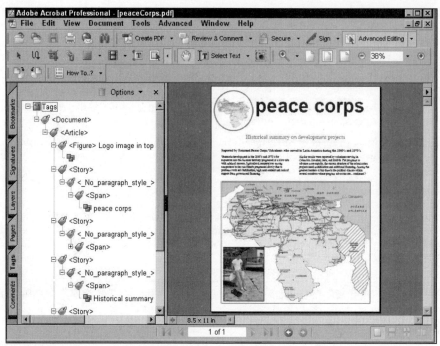

Figure 18-9: Open the Tags tab and click the plus symbols (Windows) or right-pointing arrows (Macintosh) adjacent to the tag element names. Expanding the tree gives you access to the individual elements.

The Tags palette may have an extensive list of elements depending on your document length and complexity. If you want to edit an element or find it in the document, you need some help from Acrobat to find out exactly what tag in the Tags palette is related to what element on a given page. The help comes in the form of a menu command in the Tags palette. Click the down-pointing arrow adjacent to Options in the Tags palette and select Highlight Content from the menu options as shown in Figure 18-10.

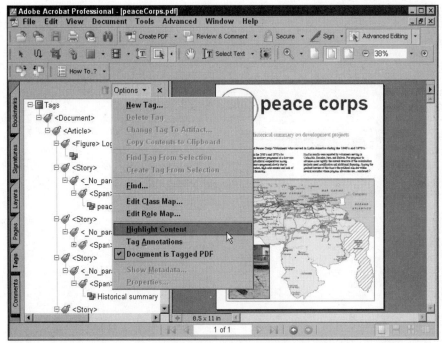

Figure 18-10: Open the Tags palette Options menu and select Highlight Content.

When you return to the structure tree, the items you select are highlighted on the respective elements on pages in the Document Pane. Click an element and Acrobat navigates to the page where the content is located. The object is highlighted with a keyline border as shown in Figure 18-11. In the Tags palette I clicked on Figure and the logo in the top-left corner is highlighted.

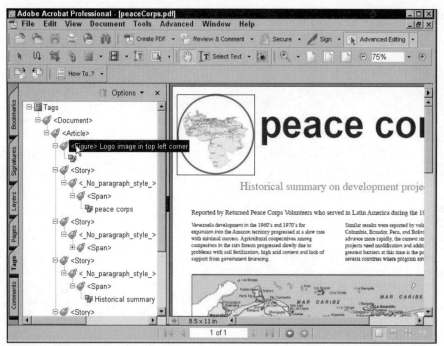

Figure 18-11: Click an element in the Tags palette and the related element is selected on the document page.

Adding alternate text

In the example in Figure 18-8, the logo appearing at the top of the page is an image file. When a screen reader reads the document, no specific instructions are contained in the document to interpret this image. As an option, you can create alternate text so a visually challenged person knows a graphic element exists on the page. To add alternate text in a tagged PDF document, follow these steps:

STEPS: Adding alternate text to tagged elements

1. **Open a tagged PDF file.** Or add tags to a document. Open the Tags tab in the Navigation Pane. Note: If you didn't set up the working environment as described in the beginning of the chapter, choose View ⇨ Navigation Tabs ⇨ Tags to open the Tags palette.

2. **Open the structure tree.** Click the Tags Root icon to the left of the text. On Windows a plus (+) symbol appears adjacent to the text. On the Macintosh, a right-pointing arrow appears next to the text. Clicking the icon opens the tags tree.

3. **Highlight Content.** If you haven't selected the menu command for highlighting content, open the Options palette in the Tags tab and select Highlight Content.

4. **Find the element where the alternate text is to be added.** In my example, the figure below the second paragraph (<P>) was selected. When you click the Figure tag, the logo at the top-left corner of the page highlights.

5. **Open the element's properties.** Select the TouchUp Object tool in the Advanced Editing toolbar. Click the element and open a context menu. Select Properties as shown in Figure 18-12. The TouchUp Properties dialog box opens.

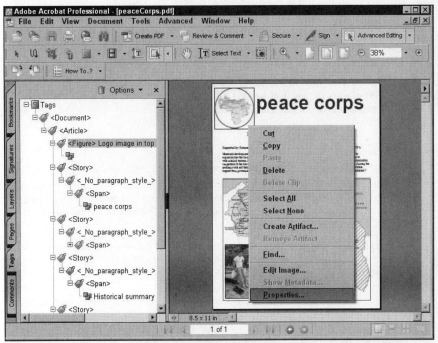

Figure 18-12: Select the element to edit with the TouchUp Object tool and open a context menu. Select Properties from the menu choices.

6. **Add alternate text.** Click the Tag tab. Add a title for the tag by typing a title in the Title field box. The title is not necessary for nor read by the screen reader. Add the text you want the screen reader to read out loud in the Alternate text field. Select the pull-down menu for Language and select a language. The edits made in this example are shown in Figure 18-13.

7. **Close the TouchUp Properties.** Click Close in the TouchUp Properties dialog box.

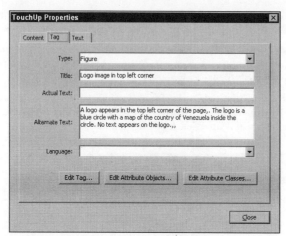

Figure 18-13: Fill in the fields for a title, alternate text, and select a language in the TouchUp Properties.

Checking accessible tags

You can check your work easily in Acrobat by having Acrobat read the document. Choose View ⇨ Read Out Loud ⇨ Read This Page Only. The default text-to-speech voice installed on your computer reads the text as a screen reader would interpret it. If you prepare files for screen readers, you can use Acrobat's built-in reading engine to read aloud the text in the document and the alternate tags you add to the file.

Although the Read Out Loud menu command is not intended to replace screen readers, the feature in all Acrobat viewers offers you a good means for checking files that meet accessible standards.

Cross-Reference

For more information on Read Out Loud and controlling voices and reading speeds, see Chapter 3.

In addition to using Acrobat's built-in function for reading documents aloud, you can acquire a low-cost plug-in from a third-party developer without purchasing a screen reader. PDFAloud, marketed by textHELP Systems (www.texthelp.com), is more robust than Acrobat's menu command. With PDFAloud you can read text a word, sentence, or paragraph at a time. The plug-in also offers you synchronized colored highlighting while the text is read.

Changing Text Color

Some accessibility requirements extend beyond text-to-speech reading. Individuals with assistive devices for visual impairments can view documents when text is zoomed and when text color significantly contrasts with background colors. In Acrobat's Accessibility Preference settings you can set color options for viewing documents:

Choose Edit ➪ Preferences and click the Accessibility item in the left pane. The right pane provides options for setting up the environment for some accessibility features as shown in Figure 18-14.

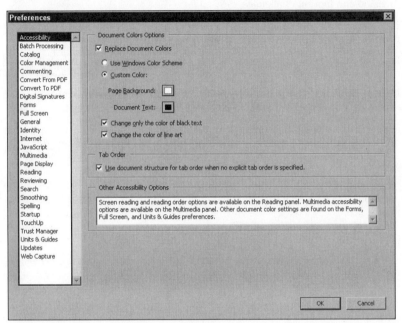

Figure 18-14: Open the Preferences dialog box and click Accessibility in the left pane. The right side of the dialog box offers options for changing color of the text and background.

In the Custom Color area, click the swatches to change color for Page Background and Document Text. You can use models for developing high contrast color for text similar to those used with Microsoft Windows on either the Macintosh or Windows system. An option is available for distinguishing a difference between black text and all text. If you want all text to be changed to the same color, deselect the Change only the color of black text check box.

When you create documents with tags, you can zoom in on pages and have the pages reflow on the screen to fit within the screen view. The text reforms to the view size and also on handheld devices. To enable reflow you must use a tagged PDF document. Choose View ➪ Reflow to enable the reflow feature.

Cross-Reference

For more information on text reflow, see Chapter 3

Summary

✦ Screen readers can interpret accessible PDF files and create audio output for people with vision and motion challenges.

✦ Microsoft Word, Adobe PageMaker 7 and higher, and Adobe InDesign 2.0 and higher are capable of creating tagged and accessible PDF forms.

✦ You can add tags to PDF documents from a menu command within Acrobat Standard and Acrobat Professional.

✦ You check files for accessibility with the Quick Check command in Acrobat Standard and Acrobat Professional or with a Full Check in Acrobat Professional.

✦ Tagged documents contain a structure tree. Elements in the tree locate respective elements in the document by enabling the Highlight Content menu command.

✦ Alternate text can be added to elements in Acrobat by addressing the element Properties.

✦ You can make text and background color changes in the Accessibility Preferences dialog box.

✦   ✦   ✦

PDF Publishing

Authentication and Security

Acrobat PDF documents can be secured with password protection using a host of different security methods and encryption tools to prevent unauthorized users from opening files and changing documents. Acrobat Security combined with digital signatures enables you to protect data and secure files for just about any purpose. There's a lot to Acrobat Security and using digital signatures, and it's important to know what levels of security are available to you and what kinds of security can be applied to many different circumstances. This chapter covers a broad description of security and digitally signing PDF documents and the methods you use to protect files against unauthorized viewing and editing.

Setting Up the Work Environment

You add security to a PDF document through menu commands and the Secure Task button that appears in the Tasks toolbar when you return to the default view. If all you want to do is add security to PDFs, you can open a context menu and select Reset Toolbars from the menu options.

If you want to add fields on a form where users can digitally sign documents, you need to use the Forms tools. Documents can be signed without signature fields, but when you want to add a field for signing the document, you'll want to have the Form tools immediately accessible. For the examples in this chapter, open the Tools menu and choose Advanced Editing ⇨ Forms ⇨ Show Forms Toolbar. In addition to the Forms tools, add the Properties Bar by opening a context menu on the Toolbar Well and selecting Properties Bar from the menu. After the toolbars open, dock them in the Toolbar Well.

Note   Use of the Forms tools is available only in Acrobat Professional. Acrobat Standard users can create digital signatures and electronically sign documents, but they cannot create signature fields.

If you follow along and use the same tools used in the examples, your Acrobat window should look something like Figure 19-1. In this figure the Button field is selected; therefore, the Properties Bar extends across the Toolbar Well.

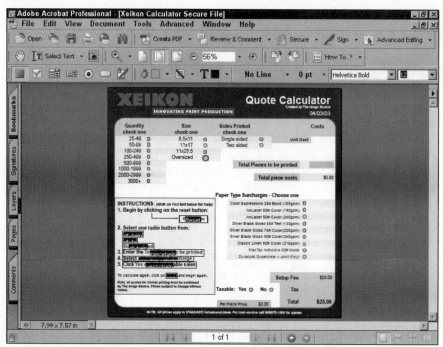

Figure 19-1: When creating digital signature fields, having the Forms toolbar and the Properties Bar docked in the Toolbar Well is handy.

Securing PDF Documents

Acrobat security comes in many different forms, allowing you to secure PDF files against user viewing and/or editing, in many ways based on the level of security you assign to a PDF document. However, depending on what level of security you apply to a file, the document may or may not be able to be opened by users of earlier versions of Acrobat. Therefore, when you add security, knowing your user audience and what versions of Acrobat they are using to view files is critical.

Methods of security available in Acrobat include two primary types of restrictions. You can secure a file against opening and editing by applying Acrobat Security at different levels of encryption or you can secure files using certificates that are acquired from users when they create digital IDs. The first method should be thought of as security you might apply globally to PDFs when you want the public to have a password to open your PDFs or you want to restrict certain Acrobat features such as content editing or printing. In this regard you secure documents for what is referred to as *unknown* users.

The second method of security should be thought of as restrictions you want to apply for a selected group of people or what are referred to as *known users*. You might want to restrict opening documents or PDF editing for a group of co-workers, colleagues, or individuals with whom you have direct communication. This method requires the use of digital IDs.

The discussion on Acrobat Security starts with the first method of applying security for a more global environment for unknown users. Later in this chapter, encryption using certificates for known users is covered along with digital signatures.

Restricting the Opening and Editing of Files

If you're familiar with earlier versions of Acrobat you'll notice the absence of Document Security in the File menu. The nomenclature has changed a little and the access to the Password Security dialog box has moved to the Secure Task Button pull-down menu. When you open the Password Security – Settings dialog box, you'll find some familiar options similar to those found in earlier versions of Acrobat.

Note You can apply security in the Document Properties dialog box in addition to using the Secure Task Button menu. Select File ➪ Document Properties. In the Left pane in the Document Properties dialog box, select Security. When you select Password Security from the Security Method pull-down menu and choose Password Security, the same dialog box shown in Figure 19-2 opens.

Click on the Secure Task Button to open the pull-down menu and select Restrict Opening and Editing. The Password Security – Settings dialog box opens as shown in Figure 19-2. Notice the Compatibility pull-down menu. Three options are listed in the menu as Acrobat compatibility selections. Depending on which compatibility option you select, the bottom of the dialog box lists additional options or removes options. In Figure 19-2 you can see that when choosing Acrobat 6 compatibility, all options are listed in the dialog box. If you select Acrobat 5 compatibility, the last line listed as Enable plaintext metadata is eliminated from the dialog box. When Acrobat 3 compatibility is selected, the options adjacent to the last two check boxes are also hidden from view in the dialog box.

Understanding Password Encryption

When you encrypt a file with password security, it's important to understand that methods exist that can be used to decrypt files. Just about anything that can be encrypted can be broken given enough time with the right tools. Software applications used for decryption run through cycles combining different characters to arrive at the right combination that accesses the encrypted file. What's needed is a tool that runs through all the possible permutations of character combinations and enough time to cycle through them.

If you use a three-character password, the amount of time to break your password by a sophisticated decryption tool might be a matter of a few hours or days. As you add characters to the password, the decryption tool requires more time to explore all combinations of characters. If you add 10 to 12 characters to a password, the most sophisticated tools on the fastest computers can take decades of constant running to come up with the right combination of characters to break a password.

As a matter of practice when assigning permissions for sensitive material, always use no fewer than eight characters to secure a file. Adobe Systems has provided a sophisticated tool that enables you to protect your content if you observe a few simple rules.

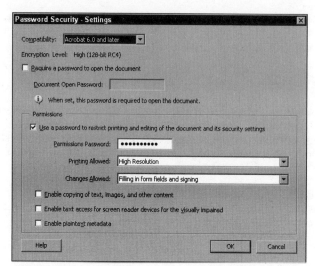

Figure 19-2: Depending on what level of compatibility you choose, the options change in the last three lines of options settings.

Adding Acrobat Security is handled in this dialog box any time you want to restrict a file from opening and/or making changes to the content. Users must know the password you add in this dialog box in order to open a file and/or make changes. The options available to you include:

✦ **Compatibility:** The options from the pull-down menu include Acrobat 3, Acrobat 5, and Acrobat 6 compatibility. If you select Acrobat 6 compatibility and save the PDF document, an Acrobat viewer of version 6 or greater viewer is needed to open the file. The same holds true when saving with Acrobat 5 compatibility for users who have Acrobat viewers lower than version 5.

✦ **Encryption level:** Below the pull-down menu Acrobat informs you what level of encryption is applied to the document based on the compatibility choice made in the pull-down menu. If you select Acrobat 3 and Later from the compatibility pull-down menu, the encryption level is 40-bit encryption. Acrobat 5 and Acrobat 6 compatibility are encrypted at 128-bit encryption. The higher encryption levels offer you more options for restricting printing and editing.

✦ **Require a password to open the document:** Click on the check box if you want a user to supply a password to open the PDF document. After clicking on the check box, the field box for Document Open Password becomes active and you can add a password. Before you exit the dialog box, Acrobat prompts you in another dialog box to confirm the password.

✦ **Use a password to restrict printing and editing of the document and its security settings:** You can choose to add a password for opening the PDF document and also restrict permissions from the items active in the Permissions area of the dialog box. You can also eliminate the option for using a password to open the PDF document and make permissions choices for printing and editing. Either way, you need to check this box to make choices in the Permissions options. If the check box is disabled no permissions options are available to you.

✦ **Permissions Password:** Fill in the field box with a password. If you apply permissions options for opening the PDF and restricting permissions, the passwords must be different. Acrobat opens a dialog box and informs you to make different password choices if you attempt to use the same password for opening the file and setting permissions.

✦ **Printing Allowed:** If you use Acrobat 3 compatibility, the options are available to either enable printing or disallow printing. The choices are None and High Resolution. Even though the choice reads High Resolution, the result simply enables users to print your file. With Acrobat 5 and 6 compatibility, you have a third choice for enabling printing at a lower resolution (150 dpi). If you select Low Resolution (150 dpi) from the menu options, users are restricted to printing the file at the lower resolution. This choice is typically something you might use for files intended for digital prepress and high-end printing or to protect your content from being printed and then re-scanned.

✦ **Changes Allowed:** From the pull-down menu you make choices for the kinds of changes you allow users to perform on the document. Acrobat 3 compatibility offers you four choices; Acrobat 5 and 6 compatibility offers you five choices. These options include

  • **None:** This option prevents a user from any kind of editing and content extraction.

  • **Inserting, deleting, and rotating pages (Acrobat 5 and Acrobat 6 compatibility only):** This option is not available when using Acrobat 3 compatibility. Users are permitted to insert, delete, and rotate pages. If you create PDFs for eBooks, allowing users to rotate pages can be helpful when they view PDFs on tablets and portable devices.

  • **Filling in form fields and signing:** If you create Acrobat Forms and want users to digitally sign documents, enable this check box. Forms are useless to users without the ability to fill in the form fields.

  • **Commenting, fill-in form fields, and signing:** You might use this option in a review process where you want to have users comment on a design but you don't want them to make changes in your file. You can secure the document against editing, but allow commenting and form field fill-in and signing. When you enable form fill-in with this option or the Filling in form fields and signing option, users are restricted against changing your forms design and cannot make edits other than filling in the fields.

  • **Any except extracting pages:** All the permissions are available to users except extracting pages from the document and creating separate PDFs from selected pages.

✦ **Enable copying of text, images, and other content and access for the visually impaired (Acrobat 3 only):** If you restrict permissions for any of the previous pull-down menu options, users aren't allowed to copy data. You can add permission for content copying by enabling this check box. This option is available to users of all Acrobat viewers version 3 and greater.

✦ **Enable text access for screen reader devices for the visually impaired (Acrobat 5 and 6 compatibility only):** As a matter of practice, checking this box is always a good idea. If you check this box, you can restrict all editing features while permitting users with screen reading devices the ability to read your files. If the check box is not enabled, screen readers are not able to read the PDF document and all the options for using the View ➭ Read Out Loud menu command are grayed out. Furthermore, users can index your files with Acrobat Professional by using Acrobat Catalog when this check box is enabled, regardless of the other items you prevent users from accessing.

Cross-Reference

For more information on screen readers and accessibility, see Chapter 18. For more information on creating index files, see Chapter 4.

✦ **Enable plaintext metadata (Acrobat 6 only):** If this check box is selected users can create search indexes from encrypted files. The document's metadata is made accessible to other applications.

Understanding Digital IDs

A digital ID is a file that you create in Acrobat or acquire from a third party signature provider. Your ID, also known as a *credential* or *profile*, is password protected and used to electronically sign or certify documents. Before you can digitally sign a document you need to create or acquire your own personal ID.

Digital IDs have two components important to understand (your personal digital ID and your public certificate). If you create your own personal *digital ID* in Acrobat, the file you create is used to sign or certify documents. After creating your personal ID, you can also create a *public certificate*. The public certificate is a file you share with other users so they can encrypt files that they send to you. In order to open such encrypted files you need to supply the password used when you created your personal profile.

Using Third Party Signature Handlers

Digital Signature handlers are available from third party providers and offer you many different options for securing PDF documents depending on the product and manufacturer. To find information on acquiring third party products for signature handling, take a look at a new area on Adobe's Web site at www.adobe.com/security. On the Adobe Web pages you find links to Digital Signature vendors worldwide.

In North America, the most popular third party products are offered by VeriSign® (www.verisign.com) and Entrust® (www.entrust.com). If you use Acrobat for languages other than US English, you can find other products suited for a given language. On the Adobe Web site you'll find a list of Adobe Partners according to language. You need to navigate through Web pages to find partners offering products in different languages. Using the search engine on the Adobe Web site can help you find an Adobe Partner offering products in a language suited to your needs.

When you create a Digital ID in Acrobat by selecting Advanced ➭ Manage Digital IDs ➭ My Digital ID, the Add Digital ID dialog box opens. Selecting the first button option in this dialog box opens your Web browser and takes you to Adobe's Web site where Adobe Document Security is explained and a list of Adobe partners appears. Click on a link on this Web page to take you to an Adobe partner offering signature handlers for US English and many other languages.

As a matter of understanding the security involved when using digital signatures, realize that every time you want to sign a document, you need to supply your password. Therefore, anyone having access to your computer cannot sign or certify a document on your behalf unless the user has your password. When a file is encrypted using your public certificate, the file is opened only when you supply your password. Again, anyone having access to your computer cannot open a document encrypted with your public certificate unless that user has access to your password. Digital signature IDs, both private and public, are used to secure PDF documents as well as sign and authenticate them.

Signature IDs can be created in Acrobat or acquired from other parties. The three kinds of IDs currently supported by Acrobat include

✦ **Default Certificate Security:** For many workflows, the built-in Default Certificate Security is sufficient for signing and validating documents. If you don't need advanced security features, Acrobat offers a sophisticated method for creating digital IDs and signing documents using the Default Certificate Security. When you create a digital ID in Acrobat, you need to send your public certificate to other users who use the public certificate to validate your signature. This method of signature handling is known as PPK — defined as private/public key. Your private key encrypts a *fingerprint* or data stored with the signature when you sign a document. The public key is used to decrypt the fingerprint when the document needs to be verified. Digitally signing documents would be meaningless unless you had a method for signature verification. Therefore the public key provides this method of verification.

✦ **Windows Certificate Security:** This method of signature handling is available for Windows 2000 and XP users only. Signature and verification are handled with client/server applications. Rather than keeping public certificates locally on your computer, you can authenticate documents using server-based profiles.

✦ **Third party signature handlers:** Private third parties also offer signature handling that can be used with Acrobat. The most popular among the third parties for signature handling are VeriSign® and Entrust®. These companies provide many advanced features for working with electronic signatures and develop some of the most sophisticated encryption schemes. Users can acquire signature handlers for enterprises, small businesses, and for individuals. For large business enterprises, government, education, and organizations, use of third-party vendors is like outsourcing all your security needs where the vendor handles digital ID assignments, certificate generation, validation, and renewals.

Using Default Certificate Security

Creating personal IDs and public certificates applies to using Default Certificate Security. If you don't have a Windows Certificate Security system in place or you aren't using a third-party vendor, you can use Acrobat's signature handling, also known as self-sign. To do so, your first step is to create a personal ID.

Acrobat offers you two different menu options for creating a digital ID and another menu option for customizing the appearance of digital IDs. The menu commands are selected from different Task Buttons and different menus. In essence, you can arrive at the same dialog box from different menus and Task Buttons. When you first create a new identity, you may be a little confused because different options are available in different menu commands and the appearances are added in a separate menu. Access to dialog boxes for Digital ID creation, appearance settings, and ID profile management are located in the following areas:

✦ **Security Preferences:** The Security Preferences are used to add appearances to digital IDs you create from different menu commands. If you want to add a logo, analog signature, symbol, or some text to an ID, you can handle the appearance settings by choosing Edit ➪ Preferences. Click on Digital Signatures in the left pane and the window on the right side of the dialog box lists all your currently configured signatures. You can select a signature profile and add a new appearance in this dialog box by clicking on the New button shown in Figure 19-3.

Secure Task Button: Open the pull-down menu from the Secure Task button and select Encrypt for Certain Identities Using Certificates. If no ID has been created, the Document Security – Digital ID Selection dialog box opens with no certificates listed as shown in Figure 19-4. Click on the Add Digital ID button to open the Add Digital ID dialog box shown in Figure 19-5. Here you can create a new ID or click on a button to open a Web page hosted by Adobe where you can obtain information on third-party signature handlers.

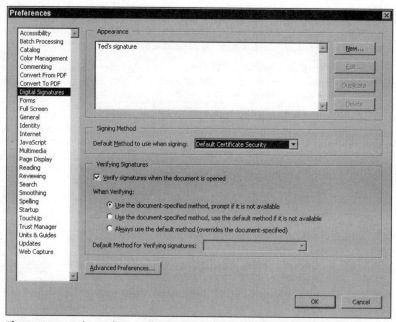

Figure 19-3: Select Edit ➪ Preferences and click on Digital Signatures in the Preferences dialog box. On the right side of the dialog box you can add an appearance to a digital ID. Adding appearances requires you to first create a digital ID.

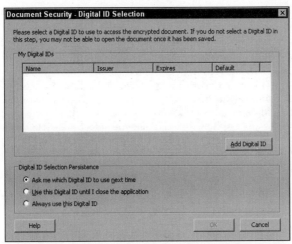

Figure 19-4: From the Secure Task button, select Encrypt for Certain Identities Using Certificates. If you have not yet created a Digital ID, the Document Security – Digital ID Selection dialog box shows an empty window. To continue, you need to click on the Add Digital ID button and open the dialog box shown in Figure 19-5.

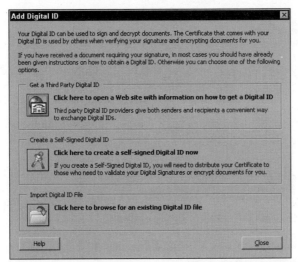

Figure 19-5: After clicking on Add Digital ID, the Add Digital ID dialog box opens. Click on the button shown below *Create a Self-Signed Digital ID* to create your personal digital ID.

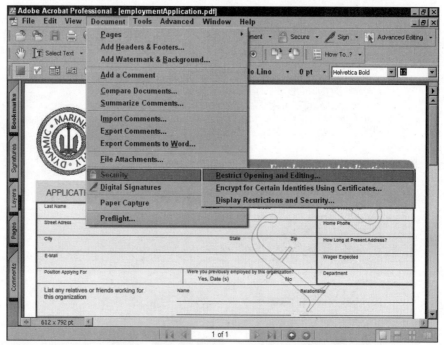 **Sign Task Button:** Menu commands appear in the pull-down menu accessed from the Sign Task button. You can sign a document and also validate signed documents from menu commands in the Sign Task button. If you have not created a digital ID navigation through several dialog boxes eventually takes you to the same dialog box shown in Figure 19-4 where you create your digital ID.

✦ **Document Menu:** The Document menu contains two menu items for handling security and signatures as shown in Figure 19-6. Select the Security menu item or the Digital Signatures menu item to open submenus with commands similar to the other options for securing documents and creating digital IDs. If you select Restrict Opening and Editing, the Password Security Settings dialog box shown in Figure 19-2 opens. If you select Encrypt For Certain Identities Using Certificates, the Document Security – Digital ID Selection dialog box shown in Figure 19-4 opens.

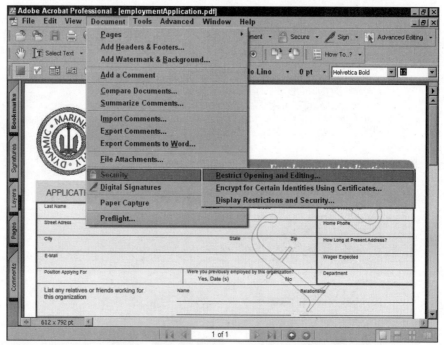

Figure 19-6: The Document menu contains two menu options for securing files and adding digital IDs.

✦ **Advanced Menu:** Under the Advanced menu, the Manage Digital IDs menu command opens a submenu where commands are used to manage your digital IDs as shown in Figure 19-7. Select My Digital ID from the submenu and the Manage My Digital IDs dialog box opens as shown in Figure 19-8. By default no IDs are listed in the dialog box. Click on the Add button and the Add Digital ID dialog box shown in Figure 19-5 opens.

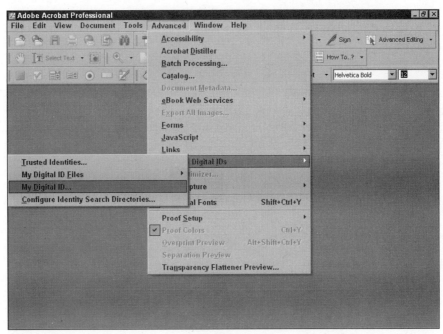

Figure 19-7: Select Advanced ⇨ Manage My Digital IDs to open the submenu where you select Manage Digital ID to open the Manage My Digital IDs dialog box.

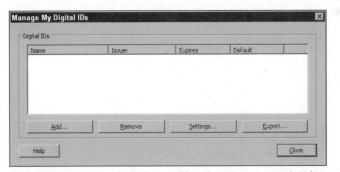

Figure 19-8: When you click on Add in the Manage My Digital IDs dialog box, the Add Digital ID dialog box shown in Figure 19-5 opens.

As you can see from all the dialog boxes shown in Figures 19-3 through 19-8, the creation and management of digital IDs can be accessed via many menu commands and through the use of Task Buttons. Where you arrive to create a digital ID is at the Add Digital ID dialog box. However, the path you use to arrive at the dialog box can be through many different menu commands.

Creating a digital ID

Choose Advanced ⇨ Manage Digital IDs ⇨ My Digital ID Files ⇨ Select My Digital ID File. The Select My Digital ID File dialog box opens as shown in Figure 19-9. By default, if you have not created any digital IDs the field boxes are empty.

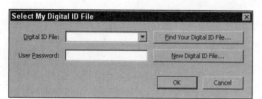

Figure 19-9: Open the Select My Digital ID File dialog box. By default, no IDs are listed in the Digital ID File pull-down menu.

To create your first ID, click on the New Digital ID File button. The Self-Signed Digital ID Disclaimer dialog box opens as shown in Figure 19-10. This dialog box displays disclaimer information informing you that if you want to have another individual validate your signature, the profile you create may not work if other users are using third-party products for signature validation. If other users work with Default Certificate Security, you should experience no problem as long as you send the authenticators your public certificate.

Figure 19-10: Before you move on to create your digital ID, a disclaimer dialog box opens where you are informed that your ID may not work properly with third-party products. Click Continue to move to the dialog box where you create your ID.

Click Continue in the disclaimer dialog box and the Create Self-Signed Digital ID dialog box opens as shown in Figure 19-11. In this dialog box you select options for creating your profile. The options include

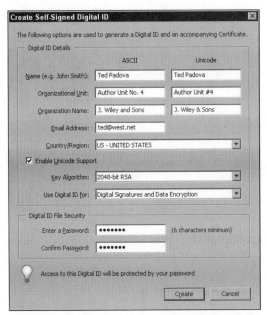

Figure 19-11: The Create Self-Signed Digital ID dialog box offers options for attributes assigned to your new profile.

✦ **ASCII:** Two columns are visible when you click on the check box for Enable Unicode Support. The left column is used for ASCII-only characters and doesn't support high ASCII values for special characters like #, /, *, and so on. If you want to use non-ASCII characters, enter them in the field boxes under the right column, Unicode. The first three field boxes are used to identify your name, organization unit, and organization name. If you want to eliminate the organization items, leave the field boxes blank.

✦ **Unicode:** Unicode is used for the field boxes listed in previous paragraphs where you want to use non-ASCII characters. You must have Enable Unicode Support selected in order to use the Unicode option.

✦ **Email Address:** Add your e-mail address to this field box.

✦ **Country/Region:** Countries are listed in a pull-down menu. There is an option for none if don't want to identify a country. The field box is not editable therefore you cannot add a new country name to specify a country not listed in the pull-down menu.

✦ **Enable Unicode Support:** If the check box is disabled, the Unicode field boxes above are hidden. Enable this checkbox only if you want to use Unicode characters.

✦ **Key Algorithm:** Two choices are available from the pull-down menu. If you use the higher bit encryption of 2048-bit the files are encrypted with a more reliable method; using 2048-bit encryption enables Acrobat 5 and 6 users to open the files. However, Acrobat 5 users won't be able to verify signatures when 2048-bit encryption is used.

✦ **Use Digital ID for:** Three choices are available in the pull-down menu. Choose to use your profile with Digital Signatures, for Data Encryption, or for both (Digital Signatures and Data Encryption). You can create multiple profiles and choose from among your list of profiles what kinds of uses you want to apply to them.

✦ **Password:** Two fields are listed for supplying a password. Enter a password in the Enter a Password field box and confirm your password by retyping it in the Confirm Password field box.

Set the attributes for your new digital ID and click on the Create button in the Create Self-Signed Digital ID dialog box. The New Self-Sign Digital ID File dialog box opens as shown in Figure 19-12. By default the name for your file is the name you used in the Create Self-Signed Digital ID dialog box with a .pfx extension. You can change the name for the file in the File name field, but be certain to leave the .pfx extension as the default. You can save your IDs to any directory on your hard drive. As a matter of practice, saving IDs to a common directory so you can easily back them up is a good idea.

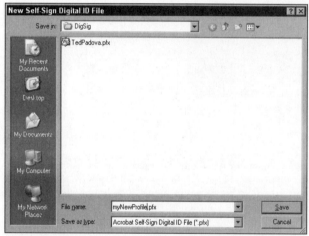

Figure 19-12: Provide a name and locate a directory for storing your digital ID. Click Save and the ID is ready for use.

After you click Save, you are logged in with the new digital ID. You can sign documents or secure them with data encryption according to the option selected for Use Digital ID for in the Create Self-Signed Digital ID dialog box. If you create multiple IDs, your list of IDs appears in the Select My Digital ID File dialog box in the Digital ID File pull-down menu as shown in Figure 19-13. In this example, two digital IDs were created and both are displayed in the pull-down menu. You can select and use Either ID and then use the ID within the use limitations in the Create Self-Signed Digital ID dialog box.

Users of earlier versions of Acrobat will notice that there is no menu option in Acrobat 6 for logging in as a user. When you want to log in as a new user, choose Advanced ⇨ Manage Digital IDs ⇨ Select My Digital ID File to open the Select My Digital ID File dialog box. Select the ID you want to use and you are logged in as a user. To log in, choose Advanced ⇨ Manage Digital IDs ⇨ My Digital IDs menu command and select Close My Digital ID File: *name of current open ID*. In Figure 19-14 the menu is opened displaying options for opening and closing IDs.

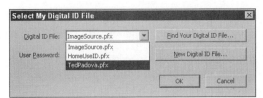

Figure 19-13: If you have multiple IDs, you can select from a list in the Digital ID File pull-down menu when you open the Select My Digital ID File dialog box.

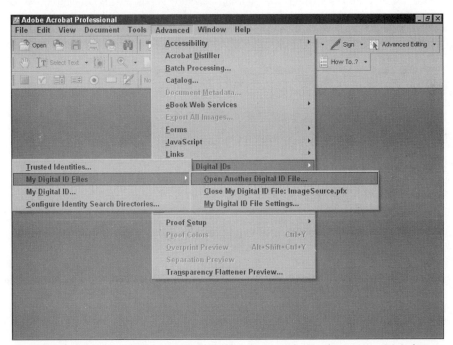

Figure 19-14: To open or close a digital ID file, choose Advanced ⇨ Manage Digital IDs ⇨ My Digital ID Files and choose from submenu options for opening and closing ID files.

Deleting IDs

If you add several digital IDs and the pull-down menu shown in Figure 19-7 displays a list of current IDs you created, you may want to edit an ID or delete one from your list. As you work through the dialog boxes for managing IDs, notice there is no option for deleting an ID from the Select My Digital ID File pull-down menu. If you want to delete an ID from this list, open the directory from the Desktop view where your digital IDs are stored. Select the file you want to delete and move it to the Trash. When you return to the Select My Digital ID File dialog box and open the pull-down menu, the menu lists only those IDs contained in the folder where the IDs are stored.

Managing multiple IDs

In Figure 19-14 the menu option for opening another ID is listed in the Manage Digital ID Files submenu. If you have several IDs and want to open a second ID file, the next file you open doesn't necessarily become a default for signing digital signature fields or encrypting documents. Priorities are assigned to IDs in the Set Digital ID Usage dialog box where priority options are defined for each ID.

Assume for a moment you have a digital signature field and you want to sign a document by clicking on the signature field. Further assume you have multiple digital IDs used for different signing purposes. You can use any one of your signatures or you can always use a default signature, depending on how your digital ID usage Selection Persistence is configured. The options for Selection Persistence are established in the Set Digital ID Usage dialog box. The first step in addressing the settings is to choose Advanced ➪ Manage Digital IDs ➪ My Digital ID. The first dialog box that opens is the Manage My Digital IDs dialog box shown in Figure 19-15.

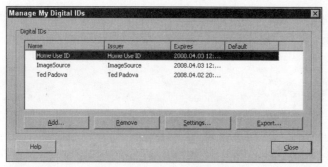

Figure 19-15: In the Manage My Digital IDs dialog box you Add IDs and define settings for each ID added to the list.

Figure 19-15 shows three IDs added to the list window. By default the window is empty and you need to manually add IDs you create in Acrobat or IDs you acquire from third-party providers. Click on the Add button and the Add Digital ID dialog box opens as shown in Figure 19-5. Click on the button listed below Import Digital ID File and the Locate Digital ID File dialog box opens. Navigate to the folder where your IDs are stored and select an ID. By default .pfx, *.p12, and *.apf files are listed in the dialog box. Click Open and Acrobat prompts you for a password. The password you enter is the same password used when you created your ID. Type the password and click OK. The ID is then added to the list window in the Manage My Digital IDs dialog box.

Note   Users of earlier versions of Acrobat who saved IDs with an .apf extension can import those IDs in Acrobat 6.

In the list window, select an ID and click on the Settings button. The Set Digital ID Usage dialog box opens. By default the Digital ID Selection Persistence is set to the first option, Ask me which Digital ID to use next time, as shown in Figure 19-16.

When you use the default setting, each time you digitally sign a document or encrypt a file with Default Certificate Security security, the Data Exchange File – Digital ID Selection dialog box opens as shown in Figure 19-17. Notice that the options appear similar to those in the Set Digital ID Usage dialog box shown in Figure 19-10.

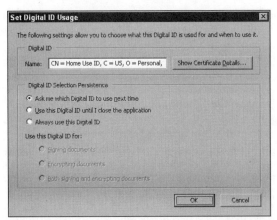

Figure 19-16: The Set Digital ID Usage dialog box offers you options for the Digital ID Selection Persistence. By default the first radio button is selected.

Note

When you sign or encrypt a document, an alert dialog box opens, asking you whether you want to certify the document with a certificate from an Adobe Partner or continue signing the document. If you click on the Continue Signing button, the dialog box shown in Figure 19-17 opens.

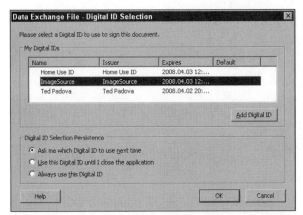

Figure 19-17: The Data Exchange File – Digital ID Selection dialog box offers you options for the Digital ID Selection Persistence. By default the first radio button is selected.

The three options in the Data Exchange File – Digital ID Selection dialog box are self-explanatory. Use the default when you want to be prompted to select an ID as you sign or encrypt documents with Default Certificate Security. The Use this Digital ID until I close the application option waives the subsequent opening of the Data Exchange File – Digital ID Selection dialog box and uses the ID for all signing and encryption until you quit Acrobat.

The Always use this Digital ID option sets a new default and the ID is used whenever you sign or encrypt a document with Default Certificate Security. When you quit Acrobat and re-launch the program it remains the default until you change the settings in the Set Digital ID Usage dialog box.

The Set Digital ID Usage dialog box shown in Figure 19-18 contains options for how your digital ID is used. These options are the same choices you made when you created your digital ID. If you want to edit the choices for using the ID for signing only, data encryption only, or both, you can make an option selection in this dialog box. Any options you chose when you originally created the ID are overridden by the choice made in this dialog box.

Also contained in the Set Digital ID Usage dialog box is a button that opens the Certificate Attributes dialog box shown in Figure 19-18. Click on the Show Certificate Details button in the Set Digital ID Usage dialog box and you can examine the attributes assigned to the ID and review items such as level of encryption (that is, 1024-bit or 2048-bit), the certificate serial number, the fingerprint and the usage key. If you need to edit the certificate attributes, for example changing the encryption level, you need to create a new profile with the desired attributes.

At first glance all these dialog boxes may be confusing to you. Realize that creating multiple IDs is not necessary in many workflows where Default Certificate Security is used. You may find that using Default Certificate Security is adequate for your needs and using a single ID is all you require. In this regard you won't need to manage multiple IDs. If you do need multiple digital IDs, a few practice runs through the dialog boxes will help you get up to speed and understand better how to manage your IDs.

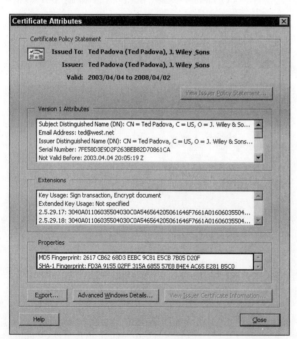

Figure 19-18: Click on Show Certificate Details in the Set Digital ID Usage dialog box and the Certificate Attributes dialog box opens.

Adding an appearance to a digital ID

Different appearances can be assigned to a signature. You might want to use an analog signature (your handwritten signature) that you scan in where your analog signature is added each time you digitally sign a document or you may want to use a logo or icon that's added as an appearance item to your signature certificate. As you review all the dialog boxes discussed thus far you'll notice that no options exist for importing images or defining text for a signature. Signature appearance configuration requires you to access another dialog box.

Note Appearances set in earlier versions of Acrobat required you to apply an appearance setting to each signature individually. If you used several signatures, you needed to define an appearance for each signature even if the appearance was identical for all your signatures. In Acrobat 6 you can use a single appearance and apply that appearance to all your signatures or a selected group of signatures. If you import signatures created in Acrobat versions lower than 6, all your appearances are lost. You need to reassign appearances in Acrobat 6 for all imported IDs created in earlier versions of Acrobat.

Open the Preferences dialog box by choosing Edit ➪ Preferences shown in Figure 19-3. In the left pane select Digital Signatures. On the right side of the dialog box you make some choices for the default method and the signature verification.

To add a new appearance, click on the New button in the top-right corner of the dialog box. The Configure Signature Appearance dialog box shown in Figure 19-19 opens. At the top of the dialog box, add a name for your appearance setting. In the dialog box you have choices for no graphic, importing a graphic, or adding a name to the appearance under the Configure Graphic title.

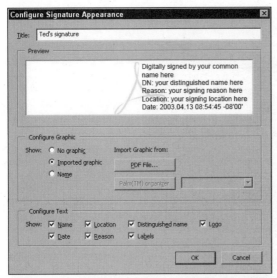

Figure 19-19: Add a name for your appearance setting in the Title field at the top of the Configure Signature Appearance dialog box.

Note   The name you supply in the Title field at the top of the Configure Signature Appearance dialog box applies only to the name you associate with the signature appearance. This name has nothing to do with the name you use for profiles. Many different profiles can use the same or different appearances.

If you want to add a graphic such as a logo or an analog signature, you can use any file type compatible with the Create PDF From File menu command. To select a file for the appearance, click on the Imported graphic radio button and click the PDF File button. Notice the button suggests that a PDF file must be used, but importing TIFF images, JPEG images, and a host of other formats are also options.

Cross-Reference   For more information on the Create PDF From File feature, see Chapter 5.

After you click on the PDF File button, the Select Picture dialog box opens. Click on the Browse button and you can search your hard drive to find the file to import. By default the Adobe PDF Files (*.pdf) format is selected in the Open dialog box that appears after you click on the Browse button. If you want to select another file type, open the Files of type (Windows) or Show (Macintosh) pull-down menu. Select the file format you used to save your appearance item and click the Select button.

The Select Picture dialog box displays a thumbnail view of the file selected for the appearance as shown in Figure 19-20. If you change your mind or you inadvertently selected the wrong item, click on Browse again and you can replace the current figure with a new image. When the right image is selected, click on the OK button to return to the Configure Signature Appearance dialog box.

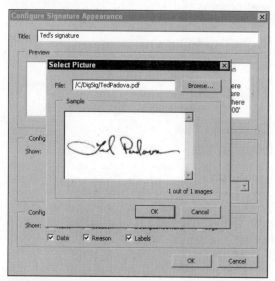

Figure 19-20: Select the appearance by clicking the Browse button. In the Open dialog box, select the file to be used and click Open. You are then returned to the Select Picture dialog box where a thumbnail preview of your image is displayed in the Sample window.

At the bottom of the Configure Signature Appearance dialog box are several check boxes for configuring the text displayed on the signatures you add to a document. By default, all check boxes are enabled. You can choose which text items you want to include or omit from signature appearances by enabling or disabling the check boxes. In Figure 19-19 all the checkboxes are enabled and the text items are displayed on the right side of the Preview window. As you disable various check boxes in the Configure Text area of the Digital Signatures Preferences dialog box, the respective items disappear.

Click OK in the Configure Signature Appearance dialog box and you're ready to apply the appearance settings to any signature(s) you use.

Signing a document

You have several methods available to you when signing documents. You can use an existing signature field and click on the field with the Hand tool, open the Task Button pull-down menu and choose Sign this Document, or use the Document Menu and choose Digital Signatures ➪ Sign this Document. All of the methods require you to have your digital ID created and available for use when signing a document. The methods vary in that you can use an existing field to sign a document, create a signature field while signing a document, or sign a document without the use of a signature field.

Using a signature field

To sign a document where a signature field exists, click on the field with the Hand tool. An alert dialog box opens providing information about the reliability of digital signatures. Click on the button *Continue Signing*. The Data Exchange File – Digital ID Selection dialog box shown in Figure 19-17 opens. Select your profile and click OK. After clicking OK, the Apply Signature dialog box opens as shown in Figure 19-21.

After you sign a field and arrive at the Apply Signature to Document dialog box, your last step is to save the file. In this dialog box you have options for Sign and Save the file to update it with your signature or Sign and Save As to save the file to a new name. Using this method protects your original document as you create a copy when using Save As and saving with a new file name.

Cross-Reference   For more information on creating signature fields, see Chapter 25.

Creating a signature field when signing a document

If no signature field appears on a document, you can sign a document by accessing Sign this Document from the Task Button pull-down menu or by choosing Document ➪ Digital Signatures ➪ Sigh this document. Using either command opens the same Sign Document dialog box. This method of signing prompts you to marquee an area on a page where you want to create a signature field. As you move through the same dialog boxes described previously for Using a signature field, you select options for making the same attribute. The difference lies in the fact that a signature field needs to be created when you use this method.

When using the Sign this Document menu command, the Sign Document dialog box shown in Figure 19-22 opens. In the dialog box you have options for how you want to sign the document.

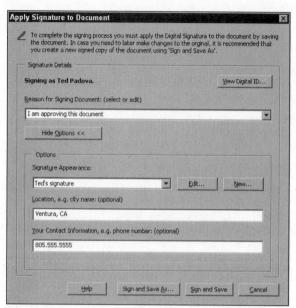

Figure 19-21: After selecting your profile and clicking OK in the Data Exchange File – Digital ID dialog box, the Apply Signature to Document dialog box opens. Here you make choices for the reason for signing the document, signature appearance, your location, and your phone number.

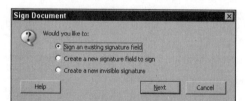

Figure 19-22: Select from either the Task Button pull-down menu or the Document ➪ Digital Signatures submenu the Sign this document menu command. The Sign Document dialog box opens.

The three radio-button options in the Sign Document dialog box offer the following choices:

✦ **Sign an existing signature field.** If you select this radio button and click on the Next button, a dialog box opens informing you that the page where a signature field is located is opened and the zoom level is changed to zoom in on an existing signature field. If more than one signature field exists, the dialog box informs you there are multiple signature fields and you need to manually navigate to a field and use the Hand tool for signing by clicking on a field. One reason you would use this item is if only a single signature field exists in a multi-page document and you want to easily navigate to the page containing the signature field. Otherwise, you'll find viewing signature fields in the Document Pane and clicking with the Hand tool as described previously in Using a signature field an easier method than accessing a menu command.

✦ **Create a new signature field.** This method is used when you want to sign a document that contains no signature field and you want your signature to be visible in the document. Select the radio button and click on the Next button. After clicking on Next a dialog box shown in Figure 19-23 opens. The dialog box is informational and is used to instruct you on following the next step. After clicking OK, the next step is to click and drag open a rectangle to create the signature field. When you release the mouse button the Data Exchange File – Digital ID dialog box opens where you follow the same steps noted previously when Using a signature field.

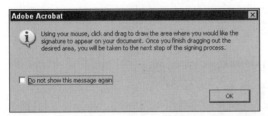

Figure 19-23: When you select Create a new signature field in the Sign Document dialog box and click Next, a dialog box opens informing you how to create a new signature field.

✦ **Create a new invisible signature.** The last radio button option enables you to create a *blind* signature. When you select this option and click on the Next button, you select your digital ID and sign the document without creating a signature field. If you select the Signature tool in the Form toolbar, you won't see a signature field on the page. These signatures do, however, appear in the Signatures palette where you can view the signature attributes and verify the signatures. (See the section Validating Signatures later in this chapter for more information.)

Access to the same options for signing a document or creating a blank signature field is also available in the Sign Task button. Open the pull-down menu from the Sign Task button and select Sign this Document to follow along through the dialog boxes that enable you to add a signature. Select Create a Blank Signature Field from the Task Button pull-down menu where Acrobat automatically selects the Digital Signature Field tool and you create a signature field for signing the document.

Certifying a document

To use a signature ID where you want to limit end users to certain editing tasks, use the File ➪ Save As Certified Document menu command. Certifying a document is typically a function of a PDF author who stamps the document for its authenticity. You might think of certification like a notary seal. The document is stamped with a certification that can be made visible on the document or invisible, and during the certification process the document is also marked with permissions restricting editing functions. Editing permissions are determined by you from several pull-down menu options when you select File ➪ Save as Certified Document.

When you save a file as a certified document you are not encrypting the file nor adding any type of security. Ultimately, certified documents lock out some editing features, but end users can alter the settings you choose to disallow. To do so requires a user to clear the document certificate and render the file uncertified. You can prevent users from editing PDF content as long as the document remains a certified document. If a user clears the document certification and edits the file, there is no way to get back the original certification and the PDF author always knows whether a document has had the certification altered.

When you select the Save As Certified Document menu command, the first dialog box that opens is the Save as Certified Document dialog box. Choices in the dialog box again offer you options for using a third-party ID or your ID created in Acrobat. Click OK to use Default Certificate Security and the Save as Certified Document – Choose Allowable Actions dialog box opens as shown in Figure 19-24. In this dialog box you make choices for what editing is allowable after saving the file. The choices available from the Allowed Actions pull-down menu are Disallow any changes to the document, Only allow form fill-in actions on this document, or Only allow commenting and form fill-in actions on this document.

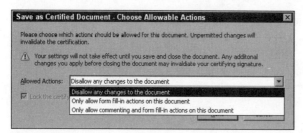

Figure 19-24: Make a choice for the edits you want to permit from choices available in the Allowed Actions pull-down menu and click Next to move to the next dialog box.

Select one of the three options and click Next. If you select Disallow any changes to the document, and click on the Next button, the Save as Certified Document – Select Visibility dialog box opens as shown in Figure 19-25. In this dialog box you make a choice for whether you want to Show Certification on document or Do not show Certification on document. Select a radio button and click the Next button.

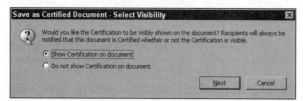

Figure 19-25: Make a choice for showing the certificate or not showing the certificate and click on the Next button.

If you choose to show the certification on the document, Acrobat opens a dialog box instructing you to click and drag open a signature field where the certification will appear on the document page. Click OK and you move to the Data Exchange File – Digital ID Selection dialog box to select you digital ID and sign the document using the same dialog box used when signing fields or signing documents described earlier in the section Signing a document.

If you choose Do not show Certification on document and click on the Next button, you arrive at the Data Exchange File – Digital ID Selection dialog box to select your digital ID and continue signing the document. This method works the same as choosing the Create a new invisible signature in Figure 19-23.

If you select either Only allow form fill-in actions on this document or Only allow commenting and form fill-in actions on this document in the Save as Certified Document – Choose Allowable Actions dialog box shown in Figure 19-24; then another dialog box opens as shown in Figure 19-26. The Save as Certified Document – Warnings dialog box informs you that the security could be compromised if you continue signing because of certain elements that may be included in your document such as layers, display settings and other items that appear listed in the dialog box. Acrobat informs you that to obtain greater security you should remove the items suggested in the list window.

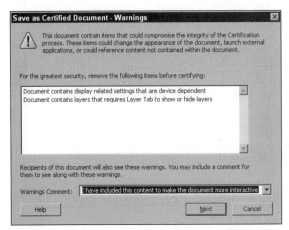

Figure 19-26: If you select Only allow form fill-in actions on this document or Only allow commenting and form fill-in actions on this document in the Save as Certified Document – Choose Allowable Actions dialog box, warnings are listed that may compromise your security.

If you want to continue signing, you can select <none> from the pull-down menu for Warnings Comment or the second option shown in Figure 19-26. If you want to include the content and add the warning comment choose the second pull-down menu option for *I have included this content to make the document more interactive.*

If you select Show Certification on document, you need to create a signature field where the signature is applied. Before you can create the rectangle you need to close the dialog box. Click OK and the mouse cursor changes enabling you to draw a signature field. Create a rectangle on a page and the location for the signature is defined; however, the signature is not yet added to the field box. When you release the mouse button the Data Exchange File – Digital ID Selection dialog opens. To apply the signature to the field, select your digital ID, click OK and the Save as Certified Document – Sign dialog box, just as if you were signing a document.

Certified document certificates are listed in the Signatures palette. Click on the Signatures tab to open the palette and you can see the signatures added to the document including those used in creating a certified document. In Figure 19-27 you can see the signature listed in the Signatures palette and the signed field on the document page.

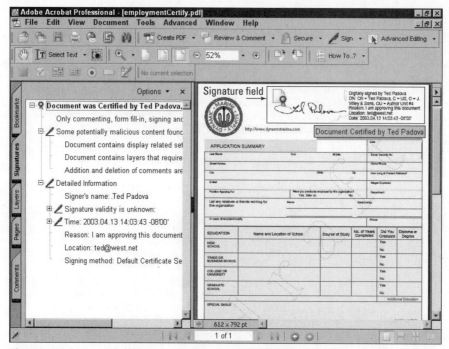

Figure 19-27: Open the Signatures palette to view all digital signatures used for signing fields and certifying documents.

Encryption Using Trusted Certificates

Encryption using *Trusted Certificates* is a means for you to add security for a selected group of users. The beauty of using trusted certificates is you can control the permissions settings individually for each user in the same PDF document. For example, you may want to allow a user to view your document, but restrict printing. For another user you may want to disallow editing, but enable printing. For a third user you may want to allow editing and printing. All these permissions can be set for each user in the same PDF document using trusted certificates.

To encrypt a file using trusted certificates, you need to collect the public identities for each user and load them in a recipient's list. After loading all the trusted certificates you specify permissions settings individually for each user. To handle this means of securing PDF files you need to understand creating public certificates, gathering them from users, managing the certificates, and loading them for use in a recipient's list.

Exporting public certificates

Public certificates are used for validating signatures and encrypting files with trusted certificates. For another user to validate your signature or encrypt a file unique to your profile you need to export your public certificate and share it with other users. Your public certificate does not compromise your password settings or ability to secure your own files. Public certificates are generated from your profile, but do not send along your password to other users.

To export a public certificate you need to start with a digital ID you have already configured. Choose Advanced ➪ Manage Digital IDs ➪ My Digital ID to open the Manage My Digital IDs dialog box. The same dialog box shown in Figure 19-8 opens. If you have more than one ID listed in the dialog box, select the ID you want to use and click the Export button. The Data Exchange File – Export Options dialog box opens as shown in Figure 19-28.

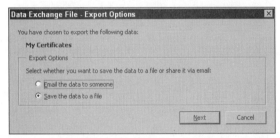

Figure 19-28: When exporting your certificate, you can choose to save the public certificate as a file or e-mail the certificate to another user.

In this dialog box you make a choice for saving your public certificate to disk or emailing the certificate to another user. If you elect to save the file to disk, you can later attach it to an email and send it to users as needed. If you select the radio button for Email the data to someone and click the Next button, the Compose Email dialog box opens where the recipient(s) email address is added. Enter an e-mail address and click the Email button and the data file is attached to a new e-mail message. Acrobat supplies a default message in the e-mail note for you providing instructions for the recipient, but you can edit if desired.

Whether you save the file to disk or send the file to another user, the file type is saved as an FDF (Form Data Format), Certificate Message Syntax – PKCS#7 (*.p7c), or Certificate File (*.cer) depending on which pull-down menu item you select in the Export Data As dialog box. This data file is used for signature validation and encrypting PDF documents using trusted certificates.

Trusted identity preferences

At some time before or after compiling a list of recipients from other users, you'll want to visit the Trust Manager Preferences. The permissions settings you assign to individual users don't cover handling file extractions or multimedia. For determining how these items are handled you need to choose options in the Trust Manager Preferences. Choose Edit ➪ Preferences (Windows) or Acrobat ➪ Preferences (Macintosh). Select Trust Manager in the left pane when the Preferences dialog box opens as shown in Figure 19-29.

In this dialog box you determine whether users can open file attachments and how multimedia operations are handled. In the list of multimedia operations, select the items individually and choose the permission setting from the pull-down menu. For example, if you wanted to restrict users to only using QuickTime, you would select all permissions lines except QuickTime and select Never from the pull-down menu. If you want users to have permission to use any of the listed applications to view multimedia, be certain either Always or Prompt is selected for each item. By default, all four applications are handled via a user prompt.

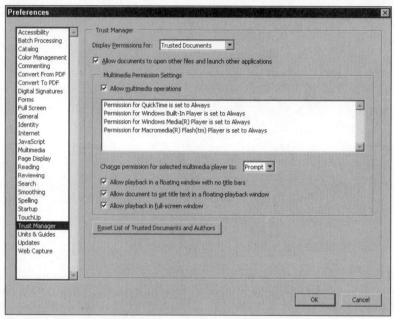

Figure 19-29: Select Trust Manager in the left pane to display the preference settings for handling trusted certificates.

Note   The list of multimedia players is derived from installed players on your system. If you do not see one of the options listed in Figure 19-29, you do not have the player installed or you may be using a version not compatible with Acrobat 6. If you want to restrict viewing to additional players, install them and verify that the player you want to use appears in the Preferences dialog box.

The three check box options at the bottom of the dialog box determine how media clips are viewed on screen. You can choose from a display in floating windows, displaying the title text in floating windows, and allowing the playback in a full-screen window. The settings in the Trusted Manager Preferences are intended more for the restrictions you want to employ to correspond with the way you intend media files to be viewed.

Click OK in the Preferences dialog box and you're ready to move on to loading recipients for either validating signatures or encrypting files for certain identities.

Encrypting files

After you collect public certificates, you need to load the certificates and assign permissions individually when encrypting files for certain identities. To load certificates, click the Secure Task button and open the pull-down menu (or choose Document ⇨ Security ⇨ Encrypt for Certain Identities Using Certificates). From the menu items select Encrypt for Certain Identities Using Certificates. If you haven't set a default for security handling you are prompted for which method is to be used in the Certificate Security – Choose Method dialog box. Select the method — either the Default Certificate Security or Windows Certificate Security (Windows only) or Third Party. Click OK and the Document Security – Digital ID Selection dialog box opens (if you've selected Default Certificate Security). Supply your password to log on and click OK. If you have more than one ID, select the ID to be used and click OK in the Document Security – Digital ID Selection dialog box. After logging in on and clicking OK, the Restrict Opening and Editing to Certain Identities dialog box opens as shown in Figure 19-30.

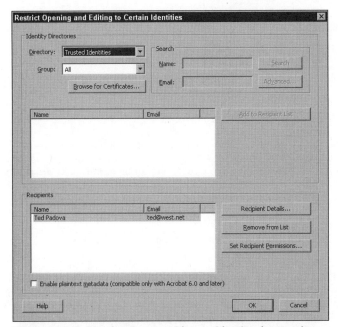

Figure 19-30: After logging on with your identity, the Restrict Opening and Editing to Certain Identities dialog box opens where you load certificates from other users in a recipient list. From the list of recipients you add individual permissions for the restrictions you want to apply to each user.

By default the directory for your identities is selected for you and appears as Trusted Identities. Groups are added when you manage trusted identities in another dialog box discussed later in this chapter. By default, All groups are selected in the dialog box. To add a recipient, click on the Browse for Certificates button. A dialog box opens where you can browse your hard drive or network server to locate certificates collected from other users. Select a certificate and click Open. The certificate loads into the first window. Select the name in the top window and click on the Add to Recipient List button. The certificate is then moved to the lower window list of recipients.

Add a certificate and return to the Browse for Certificates button and continue adding new certificates to your list of recipients. After all recipients have been added to the list, you apply individual permissions settings by selecting a recipient in the list and clicking on the Set Recipient Permissions button. The Recipient Permission Settings dialog box opens as shown in Figure 19-31.

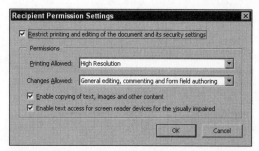

Figure 19-31: Permissions are assigned individually to each user in the Recipient Permission Settings dialog box.

Make the restriction choices according to what you want to allow for individual users. To change permissions from the default, check the box for Restrict printing and editing of the document and its security settings. Printing and document editing permissions are set from menu selections made from the pull-down menus. Your choices are the same as when securing files with 1028-bit or 2048-bit encryption. Click OK and you return to the Restrict Opening and Editing to Certain Identities dialog box.

Note   The encryption settings are compliant with either Acrobat 5 or later viewers.

After you establish permissions for a group of users, click OK in the Restrict Opening and Editing to Certain Identities dialog box. The file is not encrypted until you use the Save or Save As command to save the file; then close it. After you close the PDF, only designated recipients using their IDs and you (using your personal ID) can open the file. If a user attempts to open the file and does not supply a password consistent with one of the recipients a warning dialog box opens as shown in Figure 19-32.

By default, your personal identity is added to the recipient list. It is important to not remove your name from the list. If you delete your profile and encrypt the PDF for other users, all other users can open the file, but you can't.

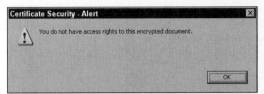

Figure 19-32: If a correct password is not added when you first attempt to open an encrypted document, a warning dialog box opens informing you that you don't have access to the file.

Managing identities

You manage trusted identities in the Manage Trusted Identities dialog box that opens when you choose Advanced ➪ Manage Digital IDs ➪ Trusted Identities. In the Manage Trusted Identities dialog box you can create different groups where you add individual recipients to one of the groups. Click on the New Group button and the dialog box shown in Figure 19-33 opens. After adding a new group, you can import collected certificates or request a certificate from users. Click on the Request Contact button and the Email a Request dialog box opens much like the e-mail you send when exporting certificates to other users.

When you request a contact and the user responds to you, your e-mail message from the other user contains an FDF file of the public certificate as an email attachment. Double-click on the file in your e-mail program and the recipient is automatically added to your list of recipients according to the group you selected when the request was submitted.

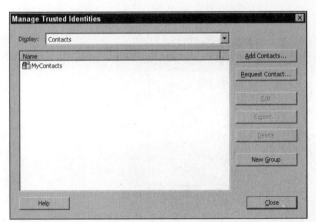

Figure 19-33: The Manage Trusted Identities dialog box enables you to create groups of recipients and import recipients into the newly created groups.

When you return to the Restrict Opening and Editing to Certain Identities dialog box shown in Figure 19-24, you select the group from the Group pull-down menu and all your recipients for that group are listed. Add them to the recipient list and you're ready to individually assign permissions.

Validating Signatures

Digital signatures would be of no value unless you could confirm that a document was signed by the individual claiming to have signed the document. For confirmation purposes you use tools to validate signatures. In order to validate a signature you need to collect the public certificate of all persons who sign a document if you are using Default Certificate Security. When the certificates are loaded in your trusted certificate list you can validate signatures.

Note   For third parties that have public Certificate Authorities (CAs), it is not necessary to validate a signature. The company you subscribe to for handling your digital IDs also handles signature validation.

To validate a signature you use the Sign Task button, the Signatures palette, or choose Document menu ➪ Digital Signatures ➪ Validate Signature or Validate All Signatures menu command. Choose any one of the menu commands from one of the three locations and Acrobat validates the signature(s) if the certificate is properly loaded in the list of trusted certificates.

When a signed document is opened and you view signatures in the Signatures palette, an icon with a question mark is displayed adjacent to the signature(s). In addition you'll notice the text below the signature icon states that the signature validity is unknown as shown in Figure 19-34.

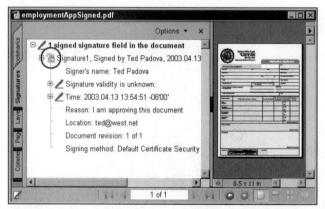

Figure 19-34: When you open the Signatures palette on a signed document, the signature validity is reported as unknown.

Note   When you open the Preferences dialog box and select Digital Signatures, a check box exists for *Verify signatures when the document is opened*. If the check box is enabled when you are viewing signed documents, the document is validated when opened. In this case, you do not need to manually access a menu command to validate a signature. You do, however, still need to have a trusted certificate from the individual who signed the document in order to validate upon opening the file.

When you validate a signature, Acrobat opens a dialog box reporting the validation status. If the public certificate is loaded and the validation is true, a dialog box as shown in Figure 19-35 opens, reporting the valid status.

Figure 19-35: When you validate a signature, Acrobat reports the status in a dialog box.

You can view the signature properties by clicking on the Signature Properties button to display all the properties of the certificate including the reason for signing, the e-mail address of the person signing the document, and the certificate fingerprint. Click Close in the Signature Validation Status dialog box and the Signatures palette reflects a valid signature as shown in Figure 19-36.

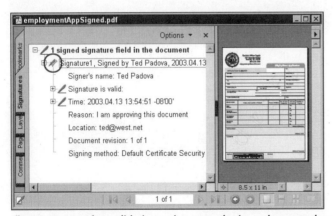

Figure 19-36: After validating a signature, the icon changes where a pen and checkmark appear adjacent to the signature name and the status is reported as valid.

Summary

✦ PDF documents can be secured with Acrobat Security and security handlers acquired from third party developers. Files can be secured from users opening documents, editing documents, or for both.

✦ Different levels of security can prevent users of Acrobat viewers earlier than version 6 from opening files. It is important to know your user audience and what version of Acrobat viewers they use before securing files.

✦ To digitally sign a document you need to create a Digital ID. Digital IDs are created and managed from several menu commands and menu options found in the Secure Task button pull-down menu.

✦ You can apply appearance settings to your signatures in the form of scanned documents, icons, and symbols from files saved as PDF or other file formats compatible with the Create PDF From File command. Adding Signature Appearances can be performed in the Digital Signature Preferences dialog box.

✦ You can digitally sign a document by using an existing signature field or by selecting a menu command where you are prompted to create a signature field.

✦ You can certify a document using your signature by selecting a menu command to certify the document. Certified documents are not password-protected files.

✦ Public Certificates are intended to be shared with other users. You can export your public certificate to a file or attach your public certificate to an email message from within Acrobat. When other users have your public certificate, they can validate your signature.

✦ You can encrypt files for a group of users by using other user identities you collect. A single PDF document can be secured for different users and with different permissions for each user.

✦ In order to validate a signature you need to collect the public certificates from all who signed the document. The public certificates need to be loaded in your trusted identities before validating any file.

✦　　✦　　✦

PDFs and the Web

Throughout this book the use of PDFs on the Web is addressed. As I discussed in Chapter 5, you can download selected Web pages or entire Web sites and have all the HTML pages converted to PDF. And now in Acrobat 6 you can convert media, animation, and sound to PDFs with the animated pages appearing the same in Acrobat viewers as when you see them on Web sites.

In Chapter 8 I discussed comments and hinted at collaboration through online reviews. Coming ahead in Chapter 22 I talk about eBooks and downloading books to the Acrobat Bookshelf, and in other chapters you find similar discussions on Acrobat PDFs hosted online. In short, the Web plays a major role with much of your Acrobat activity. In this chapter I cover more about how PDFs are used online for viewing in Web browsers, linking to PDF views on Web sites, creating PDFs with different Web tools, and commenting online.

Setting Up the Environment

To accomplish the tasks in this chapter, you use other authoring applications and set preferences for Acrobat viewers to accommodate viewing PDFs in Web browsers. When creating links and form fields in PDFs designed for Web viewing, you need to open several toolbars.

Click on the Advanced Editing Task button and the Advanced Editing Toolbar opens. Choose Tools ⇨ Advanced Editing ⇨ Forms ⇨ Show Forms Toolbar to open the Forms toolbar. When creating form fields and links, the Properties Bar can be helpful. To open the Properties Bar, open a context menu on the Toolbar Well and select Properties Bar.

When the toolbars are opened, open a context menu on the Toolbar Well and select Dock All Toolbars. If the space available in the Document Pane is too small for comfortable editing, you can collapse toolbars by hiding toolbar labels. Select Edit Preferences and click on General in the left pane. Select No Labels from the Show tool and property button labels. Click OK in the Preferences dialog box after making the menu selection.

When you dock the toolbars and select the menu option for hiding labels, your toolbars should look something like Figure 20-1. For illustration purposes, in this figure I opened a document in the Document Pane and selected the Button tool to show how the Properties Bar appears when using the form tools.

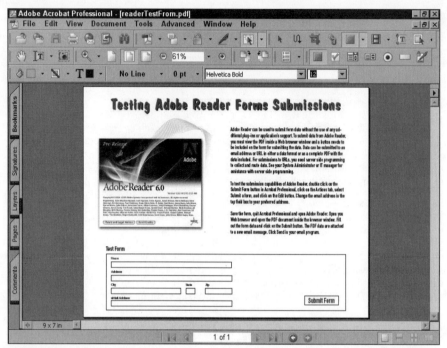

Figure 20-1: Open the Advanced Editing tools, the Forms tools, and the Properties Bar. When the tool labels are hidden by using a menu selection in the Preferences dialog box, the toolbars collapse and offer more room to consolidate the toolbars.

When viewing PDFs in Web browsers, you may need additional tools depending on what you do in Acrobat sessions related to viewing PDFs on the Web. As you need additional tools when viewing PDFs in a browser window, you can open toolbars as needed through the same context menu opened from the Toolbar Well in the browser window. Rather than set up the work environment ahead of time, leave the additional tools used for Web viewing PDFs hidden until they are needed during a Web-viewing session.

Viewing PDFs in Web Browsers

You have several ways to configure a Web browser for handling PDFs on Web servers. You can opt to view a PDF directly in an HTML file where the PDF appears as if it were actually created as HTML. You can save a PDF file to disk rather than view it from a Web connection, then later view it in an Acrobat viewer. A file can be viewed outside the Web browser in an Acrobat viewer window, and you can also view a PDF file through the use of an Acrobat viewer directly inside a Web browser, which is called inline viewing. You'll immediately notice an inline view in your Web browser when the Acrobat tools appear below the browser tools. This form of PDF viewing from Web-hosted documents is the most common use and the default view if you don't change preferences in your Web browser.

Viewing PDF documents in a Web browser

You open a PDF in a Web browser the same way you would open a file to view an HTML document. You specify a URL and filename to view the PDF directly in the browser or click on a Web link to open a URL where a PDF is hosted. For example, logging on to www.provider.com/file.pdf results in the display of the PDF page inside the browser window. As mentioned in the previous section, this is referred to as inline viewing, an example of which appears in Figure 20-2.

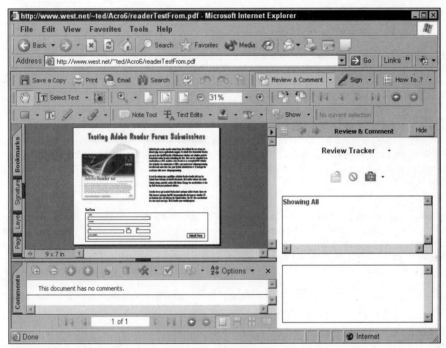

Figure 20-2: Inline viewing of PDFs offers you access to many Acrobat tools and the How To Pane.

In Figure 20-2 toolbars are open and docked in the Toolbar Well, the Review Tracker Pane is open, and the Comments palette is open. You have access to tools, commands, and preference settings while viewing PDFs online or locally from your hard drive directly in a browser window. You open toolbars in Web browsers the same way you open them in Acrobat: selecting them from a context menu opened from the Toolbar Well.

Inline viewing requires the proper configuration of components provided with the Acrobat installer CD and configuration of your Web browser. By default, viewer plug-ins are installed for Web browsers. Be certain to install your Web browser before you install Acrobat. If inline viewing is not the default when you view PDF files in your Web browser, you may need to configure the browser's helper applications. Be certain to review the applications in the browser preferences and select the viewer plug-in for handling PDFs.

PDF viewing on Windows

Adobe's first release of Acrobat 6 is much more compatible with Microsoft Internet Explorer running under Microsoft Windows when Web viewing. In Windows you have tools and features not accessible to Macintosh users, especially those who use Safari or other Web browsers. On Windows you can create PDF documents directly from within Explorer and open files in Internet Explorer easily with the Adobe PDF Explorer Bar.

To take advantage of the plug-ins that make inline viewing possible, you need to use Microsoft Internet Explorer version 5.0 or greater, Netscape Navigator version 7.0 or greater, or America Online 6.0 or greater. Users of earlier versions of Web browsers will find PDF viewing problematic, so be certain to upgrade your browser to one of the preceding versions and install Acrobat after your browser installation.

If your favorite browser is one other than Explorer, you may want to dedicate Explorer to PDF viewing and use your other browser for all other Web viewing. This is not a personal preference, but simply a reflection of the fact that Adobe has added much more functionality with Explorer than with other browsers.

PDF viewing on the Macintosh

As of this writing, support for Web viewing on the Macintosh is much more limited than when viewing PDFs in Web browsers on Windows. If you use Apple's Safari and PDFs appear to download but don't display properly in an Acrobat viewer, click the Save Task button and save the downloaded file to disk. You can often open the PDF directly in an Acrobat viewer after saving the file.

Microsoft Internet Explorer users can view PDFs only in Acrobat viewers. When you navigate to a URL and open a PDF document, the PDF is opened in the current open Acrobat viewer or launches your default viewer. If, for example, you have Adobe Reader and Acrobat Professional loaded on your computer and you open Adobe Reader, PDFs are viewed in Reader when you navigate to a PDF from within Internet Explorer. If no Acrobat viewer is open and your default viewer is Acrobat Professional, Acrobat Professional is launched when you navigate to a PDF on the Web. In essence, both your Web browser and your Acrobat viewer are opened simultaneously.

Regardless of whether you use Safari or Microsoft Internet Explorer, the first release of Acrobat 6.0 does not support inline viewing for either browser. This is a disadvantage for Macintosh users whom you intend to have forms completed from within Web browsers. However, forms can be designed with buttons to submit data via http for Macintosh users when PDFs are viewed in either Adobe Reader or Acrobat.

 Cross-Reference For information related to advantages of completing Acrobat PDF forms in Web browsers, see Chapters 26 and 27.

Users of earlier versions of Acrobat may attempt to adjust Internet Explorer preferences for viewing PDFs. If you open the Edit File Helper dialog box in Internet Explorer and try to change the viewing options for How to handle a PDF document as shown in Figure 20-3, PDFs open in your Acrobat viewer regardless of what setting you choose. Don't bother trying to adjust the preferences, as the only option you have is to view a PDF in an Acrobat viewer.

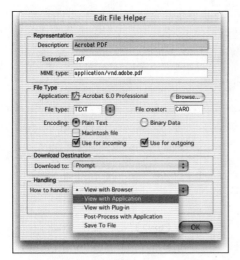

Figure 20-3: Regardless of the preference choice you make for handling helper applications, PDFs are opened only in Acrobat viewers on the Macintosh.

Macintosh users should plan on visiting the Adobe Web site regularly to see if a maintenance upgrade is available for download. The handling of Web viewing PDFs is a limitation in the first release of Acrobat 6 for Macintosh users and you can expect to see more support with future upgrades. If, at the time you purchase this book, you find that inline viewing is supported on the Macintosh, you should be able to take advantage of the features I discuss in this chapter related to viewing PDFs inside Web browsers.

Setting Web-viewing preferences (Windows)

On Windows, rather than setting preferences in your Web browser, you make preference choices for Web-viewing PDFs from within Acrobat viewers; to change preferences, choose Edit ➪ Preferences. In the Preferences dialog box, select Internet in the left pane. The viewing preferences appear in the right pane as shown in Figure 20-4.

Options for handling PDFs on Web sites with Acrobat viewers include the following:

✦ **Display PDF in browser:** When the check box is enabled, PDFs viewed on Web sites are displayed as inline views in browser applications. If you disable the check box, PDFs are displayed in Acrobat viewers. The default Acrobat viewer installed on your computer opens if no viewer is currently open and the target document is shown in the Acrobat viewer Document Pane.

✦ **Check browser settings when starting Acrobat:** Each time you launch an Acrobat viewer, your default browser settings are checked against the viewer application. If your default browser is not configured to use the Acrobat viewer, a dialog box opens asking whether you want to set the configuration to use Acrobat with the default Web browser.

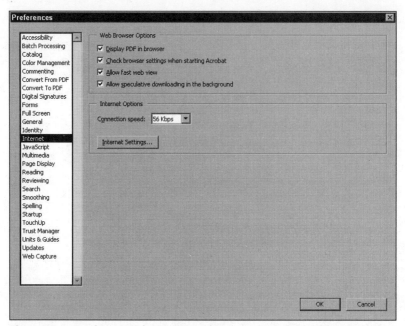

Figure 20-4: To change Web viewing preferences, open the Preferences dialog box and select Internet in the left pane.

✦ **Allow fast web view:** This option speeds up viewing PDFs on Web servers. When this option is enabled, a single page is downloaded to your computer and shown according to how you set your preferences — in the browser window or in an Acrobat viewer window. As you scroll pages in a PDF document, each new page downloads when the page is loaded in the Document Pane. If you deselect the check box, the entire PDF document is downloaded to your computer before the first page appears in the browser window or the Acrobat Document Pane.

✦ **Allow speculative downloading in the background:** If you select the preceding Allow fast web view option, and want to continue downloading multiple page PDF documents, check this box. As you view a page, the remaining pages continue to download until the complete PDF is downloaded from a Web site.

✦ **Connection Speed:** Select the speed of your Internet connection from the pull-down menu choices. This setting applies to viewing Web pages, but also influences the speed selection for viewing multimedia.

✦ **Internet Settings:** If you click on the Internet Settings button, the Internet Properties dialog box opens. In the Internet Properties dialog box you can make choices for configuring your Internet connection, choosing default applications for e-mail, making security settings choices, setting privacy attributes, and other such system-level configurations.

Working with Web Links

Web links to PDFs hosted on Web sites occur from within HTML documents and from within PDF files. If using an HTML editor like Adobe GoLive or Macromedia Dreamweaver, or writing HTML code, you create Web links the same as you link to Web pages. A PDF Web link in HTML might look like http://www.mycompany.com/brochure.pdf — where the link is made to the PDF instead of a document that ends with an .htm or .html extension.

Web addresses contained in the text of a PDF document can be hot links to URLs where PDFs are hosted. In order for links from text to be functional, the complete URL address must be supplied in the text, including http://. Text in PDF documents with complete URL addresses are converted to Web links via a menu command. To create Web links from text in PDF documents, choose Advanced ⇨ Links ⇨ Create from URLs in Document. Acrobat opens the Create Web Links dialog box shown in Figure 20-5. In the dialog box you make decisions for the pages where the links are created. Select All to create Web links from all pages in the PDF. The From button enables you to supply page ranges in the two field boxes.

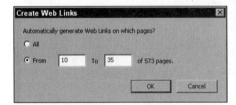

Figure 20-5: The Create Web Links dialog box enables you to determine what pages are targeted for creating Web links.

Acrobat can also globally remove Web links from all pages or a specified page range. To remove Web links, choose Advanced ⇨ Links ⇨ Remove All Links From Document. The same options are available in the Remove Web Links dialog box as those found in the Create Web Links dialog box.

Tip You can only create Web links from text that has been properly identified in the text of the PDF file. If you need to add a Web link, you can easily create the text in Acrobat without having to return to the authoring program. Select the TouchUp Text tool from the Advanced Editing toolbar. Hold down the Control key (Option key on Macintosh) and click. The text cursor blinks where you click and is ready for you to add new type on the page. Type the URL for the Web link and deselect the text by selecting the Hand tool; then click in the Document Pane. Choose Advanced ⇨ Links ⇨ Create from URLs in Document. Acrobat creates the Web link from the URL you added to the document.

Adding Web links to multiple pages

You may have documents that need Web links created across multiple pages. An example might be a document that has been repurposed from an original design that was created for output to prepress, then later downsampled and hosted on a Web site. In the original design you might have a Web link on the cover page, but for the Web-hosted document you may want to create a Web link to an order form or your home page on each page in the brochure document. Where the same URL is specified on each page and the location of the Web link is the same on every page, you can create the Web links in Acrobat after the PDF has been sampled for Web display. The following steps outline a procedure for creating Web links on multiple pages for similar designs or legacy files that don't have Web addresses added in the original authoring application document before a PDF has been created:

STEPS: Creating Web links on multiple PDF pages

1. **Add a header/footer to a multipage PDF document.** Open the file where the Web links are to be added and choose Document ➪ Add Headers & Footers. In the Add Headers & Footers dialog box, create a header or footer and set the type size, the alignment, and the offset distance desired. In this example I added a header (center aligned), used Arial 8-point text, and set the bottom offset to .1 inches as shown in Figure 20-6. Note: Be certain to add the complete URL in the Insert Custom Text field box.

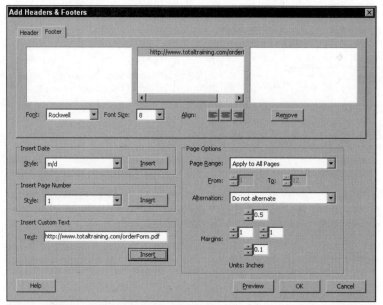

Figure 20-6: Click on the Header or Footer tab in the dialog box and add the URL text in the Insert Custom Text field box. Select a font, font size, alignment, and offset distance; then click the Insert button.

2. **Preview the header/footer.** Click the Preview button in the Add Headers & Footers dialog box. A preview of the text placement is shown in the Preview dialog box as illustrated in Figure 20-7.

3. **Embed the font.** Click OK in the Add Headers and Footers dialog box. Select the TouchUp Text tool in the Toolbar Well and select the text added as a header or footer on the first page in the PDF document. Open a context menu and select Properties. In the TouchUp Properties dialog box, check the boxes for Embed and Subset as shown in Figure 20-8. Click Close after checking the boxes.

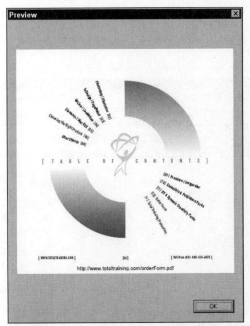

Figure 20-7: Click the Preview button before leaving the Add Headers & Footers dialog box to see how the text is placed on a page.

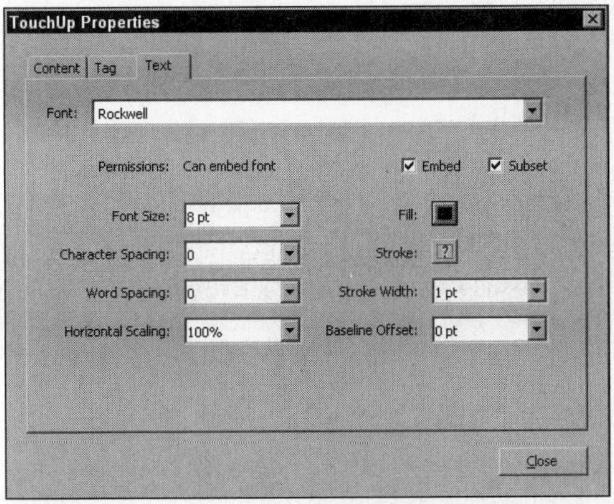

Figure 20-8: Open the TouchUp Properties dialog box and check the boxes for Embed and Subset.

4. **Create URL links.** Choose Advanced ⇨ Links ⇨ Create from URLs in Document. Select the All radio button in the Create Web Links dialog box and click OK. When you return to the Document Pane and place the Hand tool cursor over a Web link, a ToolTip shows the URL as shown in Figure 20-9.

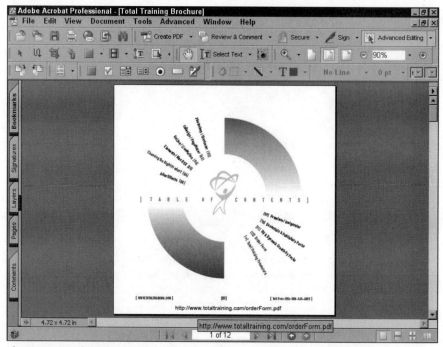

Figure 20-9: When the Hand tool is selected and the cursor is positioned over a Web link, the URL is displayed in a ToolTip.

Tip   If you want Web links to appear rotated along the left or right side of your PDF document, choose Document ⇨ Pages ⇨ Rotate Pages. Add a header or footer as described in the preceding steps and create the Web links described in step four. Choose Document ⇨ Pages ⇨ Rotate Pages and select the rotation option that turns the pages back to the original view. Save the document, and the Web links are positioned vertically on each page.

Adding Web links from form fields

The disadvantage you have when using the Add Headers and Footers dialog box is that you have limited control of setting font attributes when specifying type. For example, if you want your Web links to appear in a different color to make it a little more clear to a user that a Web link exists, you don't have the options for specifying font colors when creating headers and footers. To add more flexibility when assigning font attributes you can use form fields and set the font attributes in the form-field appearance properties.

To create Web links from form fields, select the Text Field tool in the Forms toolbar. Create a form field rectangle at the location on a page where you want the link to appear. By default the Text Field Properties dialog box opens. Click on the Appearance tab, select the font type, size, and color as shown in Figure 20-10. Click on the General tab and check the box for Read Only. Click Close to close the Text Field Properties dialog box.

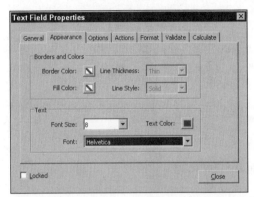

Figure 20-10: Set the Appearance properties and click Close in the Text Field Properties dialog box.

When you return to the Document Pane, select the Hand tool and add the URL text to the field. To duplicate the field on the remaining pages in your document, select the Select Object tool or the Text Field tool and click on the field to select it. Open a context menu and select Duplicate. In the Duplicate dialog box enter the page range by clicking on the From radio button and supplying the From and To page ranges. If you create the field on page 1 in the document and want to duplicate the field on the remaining pages, enter 2 in the From field box and the last page number in the To field box. In Figure 20-11, I duplicated a field from page 2 to page 12.

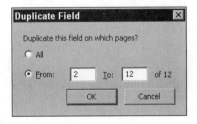

Figure 20-11: Enter the page range in the Duplicate Field dialog box to duplicate the field across the pages where you want the URL link to appear.

As a final step, choose Advanced ➪ Links ➪ Create from URLs in Document. Add the page range for all form fields including the first field you created. A link rectangle is placed over the form field rectangle with a link to the URL specified within the text field.

Cross-Reference

For more information on creating form fields, see Chapter 25.

Viewing Web links

Depending on how you have your Internet preferences set for Web-browser options, clicking on a URL link in Acrobat or in your Web browser either displays the PDF in the browser window or in an Acrobat viewer window. If the link is made to an HTML page, and the preferences are set to view the Web link in an Acrobat viewer, the Web page is converted to PDF with Web Capture. If you're using Adobe Reader, the PDF is displayed in the Web browser regardless of how you set your viewing preferences because Adobe Reader cannot convert Web pages to PDF.

 For more information on Web capture, see Chapter 5.

For an alternate view of where URL links are viewed, you can press the Ctrl/Option key when clicking on a link. If the preference settings are enabled for viewing links in a Web browser, using the modifier key displays the link in your Acrobat viewer and vice versa.

Controlling links to view behavior

By default, when you click on a URL link to a PDF document, whether from within your Web browser or from within Acrobat, the resulting view takes you to the same view established in your Initial View properties. Therefore, if your Initial View properties are set to Page Only, Single Page, Fit Page, and Page number 1, the PDF document opens in the Web browser according to these settings the same as you would view the file in Acrobat.

When you create links to open different documents and different pages in a PDF file, the links are often unusable when you're viewing PDFs in Web browsers. A link, for example, that opens a secondary PDF won't work in a Web browser unless you modify the link properties and link to the URL where the destination document resides. The Web browser needs URL links to open secondary files. Inasmuch as you may have all links working well for CD-ROM distribution, the links need to have some adjustments made before you can host the PDF documents with useable links on Web servers.

As an example, suppose you want to open page 2 in a PDF file on a Web server. You create a link in one document, and direct the link to the URL where the PDF is hosted and instruct the Web browser or Acrobat viewer to open page 2. To create the link, use either the Link tool or a form field button and enter the following code in an Open Web Link action:

```
http://www.west.net/~ted/pdf/manual.pdf#page=2
```

In this example, the #page=2 text following the PDF filename is the trigger to open page 2. In addition to accessing user-specified pages, you can control viewing behavior for page layouts, page views, zooms, linking to destinations, and a host of other attributes you assign to the Open Web Link action. Some examples of the code to use following the PDF document name in URL links include the following:

✦ **Zoom changes:** #zoom=50, #zoom=125, #zoom=200

✦ **Fit Page view:** #view=Fit

✦ **Destinations:** #nameddest=Section1

✦ **Open Bookmarks palette:** #pagemode:bookmarks

✦ **Open Pages palette:** #pagemode=thumbs

✦ **Collapsing palettes:** #pagemode=none

✦ **Combining viewing options:** #page=3&pagemode=bookmarks&zoom=125

The preceding are some examples for controlling view options when opening PDFs in Web browsers. For each item be aware that you need to use the complete URL address and add one of these options following the location where the PDF document is hosted. Using the pagemode example, the complete open action URL might look like: http://www.mycompany.com/file.pdf#pagemode=bookmarks.

Creating PDFs from Web Browsers (Windows)

As I mentioned earlier in the chapter, Acrobat on Windows with Microsoft Internet Explorer does offer more features than when using other browsers or operating systems. Of the advantages found with Explorer running under Windows is the ease of converting HTML pages to PDF. When you install Acrobat 6.0 Standard or Professional, the Convert Web Page tool is installed in the Explorer menu bar as shown in Figure 20-12. Clicking on the down-pointing arrow adjacent to the Convert Web Page tool opens a menu with options for converting and printing Web pages.

Figure 20-12: The Convert Web Page to PDF tool is installed in Microsoft Internet Explorer's menu bar when Acrobat is installed on Windows. Click on the down-pointing arrow adjacent to the tool to open a pull-down menu.

To convert the Web page in view in the Explorer window, click on the Convert Web Page to PDF tool and the Convert Web Page to Adobe PDF dialog box opens. Navigate to the desired location on your hard drive and click the Save button. The Web page is saved to disk much like when you use the Create PDF from Web Page tool in Acrobat.

Using Convert Web Page to PDF menu commands

If you want to open a Web page in Internet Explorer and convert the Web page to PDF as an appended page to an existing PDF, open the pull-down menu adjacent to the Convert Web Page to PDF tool. From the menu options, choose Add Web Page to Existing PDF. The Add Web Page to Existing Adobe PDF dialog box opens where you select the file to receive the page conversion as an appended page. All pages appended to documents are added after the document's last page. Click Save in the dialog box after selecting a PDF file stored on your hard drive. The current page in view in Internet Explorer is converted to PDF and added to the selected file.

When you append pages, the file that you select for adding a new page does not open in Acrobat. The new page is appended to the selected file and the file is updated without intervention from Acrobat.

Another menu command available from the Convert Web Page to PDF tool pull-down menu is the Print Web Page command. Rather than using the print engine supplied with Internet Explorer, you can print Web pages using Acrobat's Print command and dialog box. Options for page scaling, printing as image, and other choices available from the Acrobat Print dialog box are made available when you choose the Print Web Page command. When you select Print Web Page, the Web page is first converted to PDF and the Print dialog box opens after PDF conversion.

Using the Adobe PDF Explorer Bar

Another menu option available from the pull-down menu adjacent to the Convert Web Page to PDF tool is the Adobe PDF Explorer Bar. Select the menu item and the Adobe PDF Explorer window opens on the left side of the Internet Explorer window. The view appears similar to Windows Explorer where you can easily navigate your hard drive to find PDF and HTML documents as shown in Figure 20-13.

The tools visible at the top of the Explorer Bar offer the same options as when using the menu commands described earlier in this chapter for converting Web pages to PDF and appending pages. In the Explorer Bar you can easily navigate your hard drive to find the file you want to append to and make your selection in the Adobe Explorer Bar by clicking on the target file.

If you want to open a PDF document in Microsoft Internet Explorer, select the PDF in the Adobe PDF Explorer Bar and double-click on the file to open in MSIE. You might use this feature to participate in an online review where the PDF document needs to be viewed in a Web browser to share online comments while you work offline on adding comments before uploading them.

Cross-Reference   For more information on online commenting, see the "Sharing comments online" section later in this chapter.

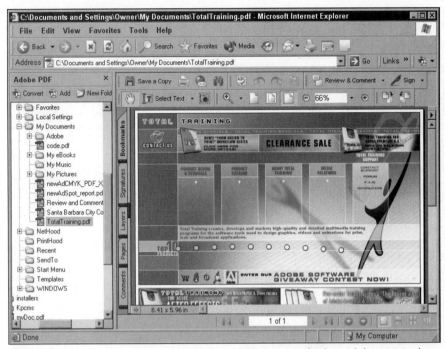

Figure 20-13: Open the Convert Web Page to PDF menu and select Adobe PDF Explorer Bar from the menu options. The Explorer Bar opens on the left side of the Internet Explorer window.

Alternatives for users of other browsers

The ability to create a PDF from a Web page within Microsoft Internet Explorer is a convenience feature added with Acrobat running in Microsoft Windows. However, you are not disadvantaged in any way if you don't use Explorer or other operating systems for Web page to PDF conversion. The same results are obtained by selecting the Create PDF From Web Page tool or Task Button menu command.

Cross-Reference

For more information on converting Web pages to PDF, see Chapter 5.

Creating PDFs in Outlook or Outlook Express (Windows)

Yet another means of simplifying workflows for PDF conversion is available to users of Outlook or Outlook Express running under Windows. Once again, the result of PDF creation can be handled with other methods, so users of other mail clients are not disadvantaged other than the loss of convenient one-click operations.

After installing Acrobat, the Attach Adobe PDF tool is installed in Microsoft Outlook or Outlook Express. Start a new e-mail letter and click on the tool. The Choose file to attach as Adobe PDF dialog box opens as shown in Figure 20-14.

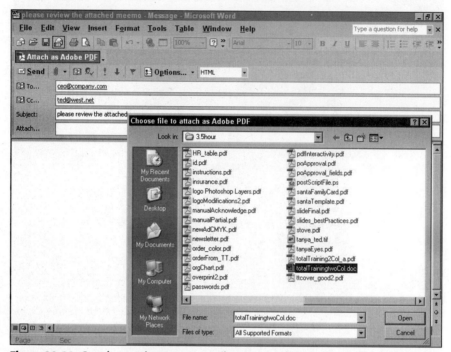

Figure 20-14: Start by creating a new e-mail message. Click on the Attach as Adobe PDF tool and a dialog box opens where you select a file to be converted to PDF and attached to your e-mail message in one step.

File formats you can attach are all the formats compatible with the Convert to PDF tools in Acrobat. If a file is formatted other than PDF, the document is converted to PDF and then attached to the e-mail message. You can convert/attach MS Office files, image files, scanned documents, HTML files, text files, and all other files that can be converted to PDF from within Acrobat.

When attaching files other than PDF, keep in mind that you need to have the native authoring application installed on your computer. Select the file for conversion, and the resulting PDF is added as an e-mail attachment. Click on the Send button in Outlook or Outlook Express and the message and file attachment are sent to the recipient(s).

Sharing comments online

In order to share comments online, you must use a Web browser and you must have Acrobat installed on your computer. The fundamental structure of comment sharing requires a PDF document to be present at a location on a network server or URL where work group members have access. As comments are added to the PDF file, the data are stored in individual fdf (Form Data File) files. The associated fdf data can be viewed and shared among users. An individual may delete or amend his/her own data, but won't be able to delete the data submitted by other users. The commenting tools for Send and Receive Comments are uniquely added to the Acrobat Toolbar Well when PDFs are viewed within a Web browser as shown in Figure 20-15. These tools enable you to upload and download the fdf data that are shared among workgroup members.

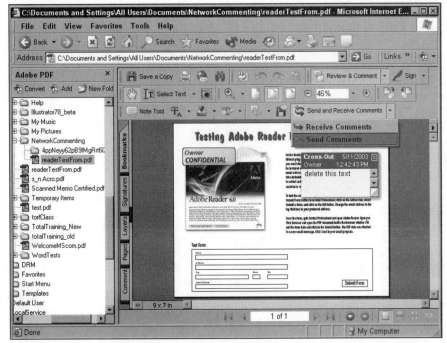

Figure 20-15: When you are sharing comments online, the PDF must be viewed in a Web browser. New tools are added to the Acrobat Toolbar Well when viewing PDFs in a Web browser and a location has been established for online commenting.

Comments on Web servers

Regardless of whether you elect to share comments on Web servers or on a local area network, you need to configure Acrobat properly for online commenting. To set up the configuration, choose Edit ➪ Preferences ➪ General and click on Reviewing in the left pane in the General Preferences dialog box. The first item to address is the Server Type by choosing an option from the pull-down menu.

For any comments shared on Web servers you'll need specific information from your Web administrator on how to set up the preferences and the URL to be used for those connection types that require a URL address. Database, Web Discussions, and WebDAV need special attention that requires assistance from your Web administrator. You'll also find information on the Acrobat installer CD and the Adobe Web site to help you configure your connection properly. If Web Discussions is selected from the menu options, you need to perform some configuration in Microsoft Internet Explorer.

After the connection type has been configured properly, you won't need to return to the Preferences dialog box. Until you change preferences, they remain active for all your online collaboration.

Comments on local area networks

Configuration for sharing comments on local servers requires no special assistance from network administrators. You can create a folder or directory on a server and identify the folder containing documents shared among users. For network collaboration, select the Network Folder menu command in the Reviewing Preferences. A browse button directly below the Server Type pull-down menu enables you to navigate your server and find the file or folder to be used for collaboration. If you change server settings, you'll need to return to the preferences. However, if you add PDFs to a folder where sharing comments is targeted, you can leave the preferences alone and select different files for sharing comments.

Sharing comments

After the configuration has been set up in Acrobat, open your Web browser and navigate to the location where the PDF file used for sharing is located. Be certain to use the most recent versions of either Netscape or Microsoft Internet Explorer.

You can use any of the comment tools among the tool groups in the Acrobat Toolbar Well that appears inside the browser window. For access to additional toolbars, open a context menu on the Toolbar Well and select the toolbars you want to use. After adding a comment, click on the pull-down menu beside the Send and Receive Comments tool and select Send Comments. If you want to view recent additions from other users in your group, click on the Receive Comments menu option. To synchronize uploading and downloading comments click on the Send and Receive Comments tool.

Caution   If you create a comment and quit your browser or you navigate to another page before uploading new comments, Acrobat automatically uploads the comments for you. This feature is handy, but it can also create problems if you have any second thoughts about sending a comment. Before you create a comment, be certain to think it out and add only those remarks you intend to submit to avoid inadvertently sending the wrong comments.

To delete a comment, you can use a context menu from either the Comments palette where the comments are displayed or select the comment in the Document Pane. When the context menu opens, select Delete. You can also address properties by opening a context menu. If you want to change author name or select a different icon for the comment appearance, options are available in the comment properties. If you want to use the Stamp tool, all the stamps accessible from Acrobat are also available from within the Web browser. In addition, the Text Edit tools, the drawing tools, and so on are all available inside your browser window.

Working offline

Acrobat also offers you an opportunity to work offline when sharing comments on any kind of server. You may be temporarily away from an Internet connection or network connection and want to organize comments and later submit them. To work offline, select File ⇨ Save and Work Offline. A copy of the PDF is saved to your hard drive. When you finish editing offline, choose either File ⇨ Go Back Online or Go Back Online from the Commenting toolbar. Your comments are then re-synced to the server.

Cross-Reference For additional information on commenting and using other tools such as the Review Tracker, see Chapter 14.

Summary

✦ PDFs can be viewed inside Web browser windows. When viewed as inline views in Web browsers, Acrobat toolbars and menu options are contained within the browser window.

✦ Although Adobe PDFs can be viewed in many different Web browsers, Windows users will find more functionality when using Microsoft Internet Explorer.

✦ Preferences settings for Web viewing PDFs in Windows are changed in the Acrobat viewer Preferences dialog box. Macintosh users can change viewing preferences in Web browsers.

✦ To make links from text in PDFs are made by choose Advanced ⇨ Links ⇨ Create from URLs in document. In order to create a link with the menu command, the complete URL address needs to be contained in the text, including http:// (or https://).

✦ To create multiple identical Web links across several pages, use the Add Headers and Footers dialog box. Specify a URL for a header or footer and use the Create from URLs in document menu command to add Web links.

✦ When you want to set type attributes for Web links, create a text or button field. Add the URL text in the field and set the type attributes. Duplicate the field across the pages where the link is to appear and use the menu command for creating URLs in the document.

✦ By modifying code in the Open Web Link Action properties you can control opening views and override Initial View defaults. Add the code following the URL link to adjust page views, zooms, page modes, and so on.

✦ With Microsoft Internet Explorer running under Windows, you can convert, print, and append Web pages from within the Web browser by using tools and menu commands.

✦ The Adobe PDF Explorer window enables you to navigate your hard drive and select files for appending the page in view in the Internet Explorer window to the selected file.

✦ PDF conversion can be handled directly in Microsoft Outlook Express running under Windows. File formats compatible with the Create PDF commands are converted to PDF and attached to an e-mail message in one step.

✦ Online commenting first requires you to identify the location where a PDF is stored for workgroup commenting. Open the Preferences dialog box and select Reviewing. Make choices for the type of connection from the pull-down menu for Server Type.

✦ Online comments can be made directly online inside a Web browser or offline in Acrobat Professional or Acrobat Standard. After making comments you need to log on to your server and select the Send and Receive Comments tool to upload and download comments. The comments are sent as fdf data.

✦   ✦   ✦

CHAPTER 21

PDF and Presentations

✦ ✦ ✦ ✦

In This Chapter

Setting up the environment

Using presentation authoring programs

Presentation documents and Adobe PDF Layers

Editing PDF presentation files

Using page transitions

Viewing presentations in Full Screen mode

✦ ✦ ✦ ✦

Among the many uses for Acrobat PDF files is for presentations. Acrobat does not provide the robust features for creating title slides, importing many different file formats in an open PDF document, or creating handouts such as those found in dedicated slide-authoring programs such as Microsoft PowerPoint. However, if you're willing to put in a little work in either designing a slide presentation in a layout program or converting a slide show from PowerPoint to PDF, you can explore many other opportunities in Acrobat for making slide presentations dynamic and suitable for any kind of audience through the use of file linking, JavaScripts, and other interactive elements. In this chapter you learn some helpful methods in producing PDF documents suited for presentations.

Setting Up the Work Environment

Interactivity is one element you'll want to add to documents designed for presentations. For adding interactive buttons and fields, open the Advanced Editing toolbar by clicking on the Advanced Editing Task Button. Open the Forms toolbar by choosing Tools ➪ Advanced Editing ➪ Forms ➪ Show Forms Toolbar. When using the Advanced Editing tools or the Forms tools, you'll find the Properties Bar a valuable asset. To open the toolbar, open a context menu from the Toolbar Well and select Properties Bar. After opening the toolbars, open a context menu on the Toolbar Well and select Dock Toolbars.

If you're familiar with the toolbar icons and don't need the tool labels, select Edit Preferences. Click on General in the left pane. Select the pull-down menu for Show tool and property button labels. Select No Labels from the menu options to hide the labels on the toolbars.

After setting up your work environment, the Acrobat window should appear similar to Figure 21-1. In the figure I selected the Button tool to view the Properties Bar expanded across the Document Pane.

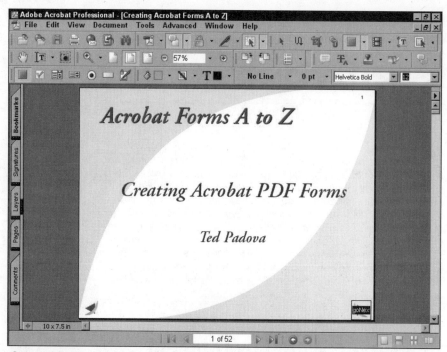

Figure 21-1: Open the Advanced Editing, Forms, and Properties Bar toolbars and dock them in the Toolbar Well.

Creating Presentation Documents

The first step in creating presentations for viewing in Acrobat is making a decision for what authoring program you want to use. If either Microsoft PowerPoint or Apple's Keynote is a tool you are familiar with, you can create a slide presentation and convert the authoring application file to PDF. In regard to using PowerPoint, you'll want to determine whether the PDF conversion is worthwhile. If the slide presentation you create is designed to discuss Adobe Acrobat, showing the slides in Acrobat makes sense. If the presentation is designed for another topic, you need to determine whether displaying the presentation is more beneficial in an Acrobat viewer or displayed directly in PowerPoint.

If PowerPoint or another slide application program is not a tool you use and you prefer other authoring applications, conversion to PDF for showing slides in an Acrobat viewer makes a lot of sense. Obviously, PDFs offer you more functionality when showing slide presentations than the original authoring applications. Ideally, the best authoring applications to create a slide presentation, if you don't use dedicated slide authoring programs, is a layout program such as Adobe PageMaker, Adobe InDesign, Adobe FrameMaker, or QuarkXPress. These programs offer you the ability to create documents with multiple pages and assign different backgrounds to pages via master pages. In addition, some programs offer you the ability to create text blocks on master pages so the text placement, font sizes, and paragraph properties are identical on each page.

Converting PowerPoint slides to PDF

Microsoft PowerPoint files are converted to PDF similar to the way you convert other Microsoft Office files. The Adobe PDFMaker macro is installed in PowerPoint just as you find with Word, Excel, and Visio. Keep in mind you must install your Office applications before installing Acrobat.

Cross-Reference For more information on conversion to PDF with the PDFMaker macro and Microsoft Office applications, see Chapter 6.

From the Adobe PDF menu, choose Change Conversion Settings as shown in Figure 21-2 to open the Adobe PDFMaker dialog box. Select the Adobe PDF Settings you want to use for your file conversion. For presentations, the Standard Adobe PDF Settings should work sufficiently for showing slides on screens and overheads as well as printing handouts for your audience. If you want to change the compatibility settings, click on the Advanced Settings button and you can custom-design Distiller JobOptions.

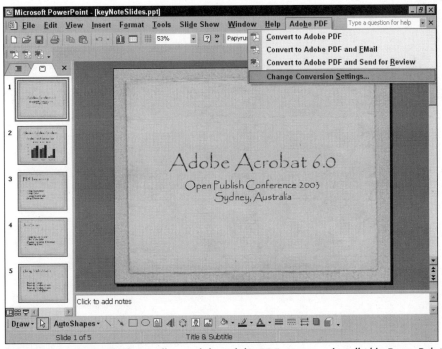

Figure 21-2: The PDFMaker toolbar and the Adobe PDF menu are installed in PowerPoint with the Acrobat installation. To be certain the tools appear in PowerPoint, install Acrobat after the PowerPoint installation.

Cross-Reference For more information on changing Adobe PDF settings and using Acrobat Distiller, see Chapter 7.

As with the other Office applications discussed in Chapter 6, you click on the Convert to Adobe PDF tool in the PowerPoint toolbar to convert the slides to a PDF file.

If you want to create notes for your audience, then you need to set up PowerPoint properly for printing Notes pages. Choose File ⇨ Print in PowerPoint. In the Print dialog box select the item you want to print. In this example, I chose Note Pages as shown in Figure 21-3. Make the choice for your printer from the name pull-down menu. Because you'll want the file set up for conversion to PDF, select the Adobe PDF printer. At the bottom of the dialog box, make choices for printing a keyline border (Frame slides), scaling if so desired, and including comments if you want to have any PowerPoint comments included in the resulting PDF.

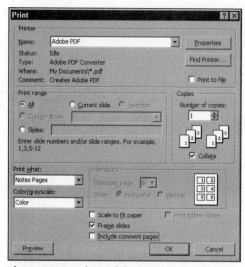

Figure 21-3: Select Adobe PDF as your target printer and choose Notes Pages from the pull-down menu choices for Print what.

Click Print when finished setting the attributes, and the PDF is created. If you elect to view the file immediately in Acrobat, the converted slides appear in the Acrobat viewer Document Pane as shown in Figure 21-4. In this example the white space at the bottom of the note pages is empty. If you want to add lines and any graphic elements after the PDF conversion, you can handle these edits in Acrobat.

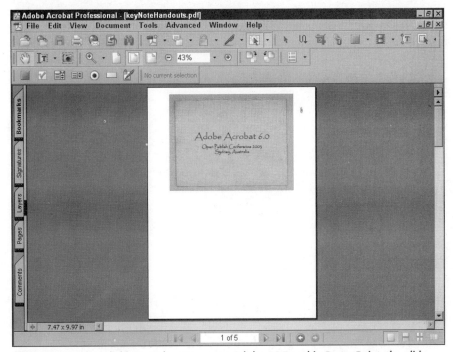

Figure 21-4: After clicking on the Convert to Adobe PDF tool in PowerPoint, the slide presentation is converted to PDF and opens in Acrobat.

To add a graphic and lines for the note takers, create a single-page PDF document in any authoring application that supports graphic imports and conversion to PDF. In this example I used Adobe Illustrator and added the conference logo and some lines at the bottom half of a standard US Letter size page as shown in Figure 21-5.

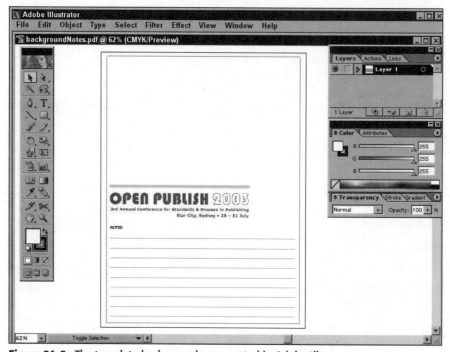

Figure 21-5: The template background was created in Adobe Illustrator.

After it's converted to PDF, open the slide show in Acrobat and choose Document ➪ Add Watermark & Background.

The PowerPoint conversion created pages with an opaque background; therefore, the tool to use is a Watermark that appears on top of the background data. In the Add Watermark & Background dialog box, I selected Add a Watermark so the new page is positioned on top of the slides as shown in Figure 21-6. Because I used Adobe Illustrator, all white space outside the graphic object and lines remains transparent and doesn't interfere with the view of the slides.

Cross-Reference   For more information on adding watermarks and backgrounds to PDFs, see Chapter 10.

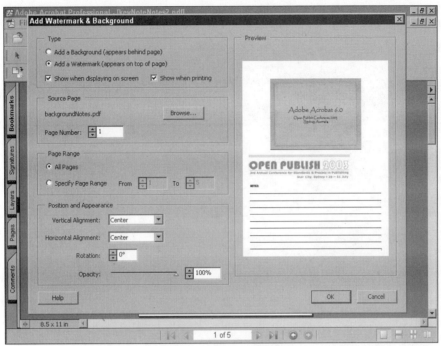

Figure 21-6: I added a Watermark by selecting the radio button for Add a Watermark and clicking on the Browse button. I selected my Adobe Illustrator file saved as a PDF and opened it in the Add Watermark & Background dialog box.

Be certain All Pages is selected for the Page Range and click OK in the Add Watermark & Background dialog box. The file in Acrobat is updated to include the new data introduced with the Add Watermark & Background options as shown in Figure 21-7. After adding the data, you can send the file, along with your slide presentation, to a conference promoter for duplication and be confident all file links and fonts are contained in the document.

Note   Keep in mind that you end up with two files. One file is created as a PDF from PowerPoint for the presentation, whereas the other file is created for handout notes.

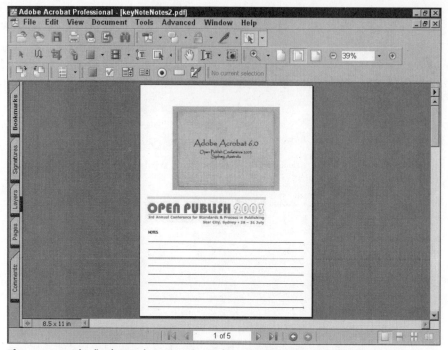

Figure 21-7: The final PDF document is ready to duplicate for attendee handouts.

Converting Apple Keynote slides to PDF (Macintosh)

A nice new addition to Apple Computer's lineup of software is Keynote. Keynote is a dedicated slide presentation authoring application that offers a robust authoring environment with simplicity and ease in creating slide shows. The charting features in Keynote are easy to use with intuitive palettes for editing chart types and data as shown in Figure 21-8.

Keynote supports file imports for many image formats, video and sound, and PDF imports that can be sized and scaled. The templates installed with the program are attractive and well designed. After creating a slide show in Keynote, choose File ➪ Export. A dialog box drops down from the application menu bar where you are offered format options for exporting to QuickTime, PowerPoint, or PDF formats as shown in Figure 21-9. To export directly to PDF format, select the PDF radio button and click Next. Locate the folder where you want the PDF file saved and click on the Export button.

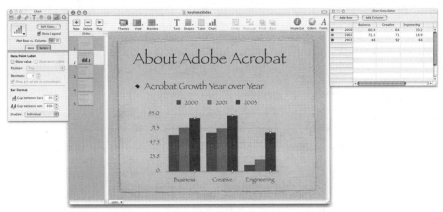

Figure 21-8: Keynote provides many attractive templates and supports charting with easy-to-use palettes for selecting chart types and editing data.

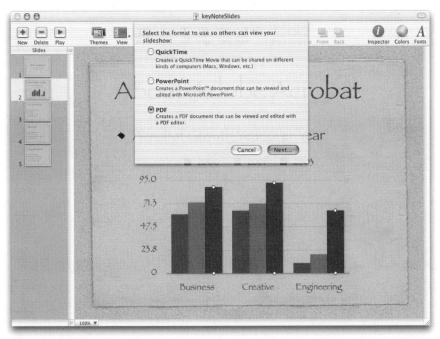

Figure 21-9: To save Keynote slide presentations to PDF, choose File ➪ Export. Select the PDF radio button and click Next. Locate a folder where the file is to be saved and click on the Export button.

If you want to create a PDF for handout notes, choose File ⇨ Print Slides. From the pull-down menu below the Presets pull-down menus, select Keynote. Select Adobe PDF to create the PDF file using the Adobe PDF settings options. As described in converting PowerPoint presentations to PDF, the Standard preset works well for slide presentations. Select Slides with Notes and make choices as desired from the set of Options shown in Figure 21-10.

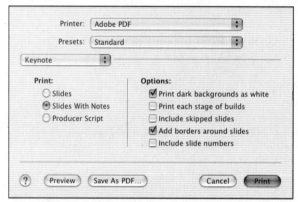

Figure 21-10: Select Keynote from the pull-down menu in the Print dialog box to open the options settings for printing the Keynote slides with notes.

As is the case with any application on Mac OS X, you also have an option to create a PDF document by clicking on the Save As PDF button. For PDF creation, you'll find writing PDFs to the Adobe PDF printer to be a better choice. When using the Adobe PDF printer you have choices for selecting the Adobe PDF settings. Using the Save As PDF option in the Mac OS X print dialog box uses a fixed set of options to create PDF files.

In addition to the PDF creation from Keynote documents, you can export to PowerPoint. If you are sending Keynote files to Windows users who want to edit slides, you can send an exported PowerPoint document to workgroup members who finalize your slide presentation in PowerPoint. For comments and review, your best choice is converting to PDF and starting an Email-based Review or a Browser-based commenting session.

Converting authoring application documents to PDF

Many creative professionals use layout programs for a variety of purposes including slide presentations. If you use QuarkXPress, Adobe InDesign, Adobe PageMaker, or Adobe FrameMaker for creating a slide presentation, you can export your documents to PDF via the same methods used for PDF exports when preparing files for print. For creating notes and handouts, you can create master pages in any one of the applications with the graphics, lines, and style you want to use for the note appearances and import the PDF document into the layout application. Each of the aforementioned programs supports PDF imports.

Cross-Reference   For more information on converting layout program documents to PDF, see Chapter 6.

Depending on the program you use, you can set up either master pages with graphic place-holders or place and size PDF pages individually. In a program such as Adobe InDesign, creating Note pages is a snap. You begin by creating a master page with the design you want to use for the note handouts. In Figure 21-11, I started by adding the graphic elements such as the lines, text, and logo. I then created a rectangle with the Rectangle Frame tool. In this example the slide pages need to be sized down to 75%; therefore, I created the rectangle and used the Transformation palette to size the rectangle to 75% to accommodate the PDF slide pages.

After creating the template, I added pages to the document and assigned the template to each page. When it came time to import the slide file, I chose File ➪ Place. In the Place dialog box, be certain to select Show Import Options. When the check box is enabled, InDesign opens the Place PDF dialog box where you determine what page is placed. After clicking OK in the Place dialog box with the Show Import Options check box enabled, the Place PDF dialog box opens as shown in Figure 21-12.

In the Show Import Options dialog box, click on the left- or right-pointing arrows to scroll pages. Select a page and click OK. Click the cursor in the area where the rectangle frame was drawn on the master page and the PDF page is placed and sized to the exact fit, including scaling. When the page is placed as shown in Figure 21-13, move to the next InDesign page and place the next PDF page.

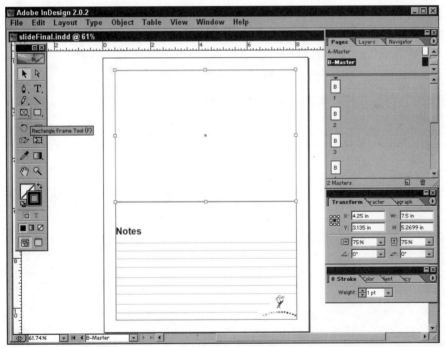

Figure 21-11: The master page was created with all the graphic elements and a box for the placeholder for the imported PDF pages. The rectangle frame box was sized to 75% to fit the slides to the page width.

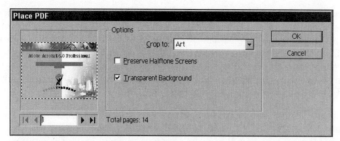

Figure 21-12: To make choices for what page to place in the InDesign file, be certain to enable Show Import Options in the Place dialog box. After clicking OK in the Place dialog box, the Place PDF dialog box opens where you can scroll pages to place the page of choice.

A nice feature in InDesign is that each time you visit the Place PDF dialog box for placing the next page, the last placed page is the new default in the dialog box. Therefore, all you need to remember is to click on the Next Page arrow to place the next successive page. This feature helps you avoid confusion about what page needs to follow the previous placed page.

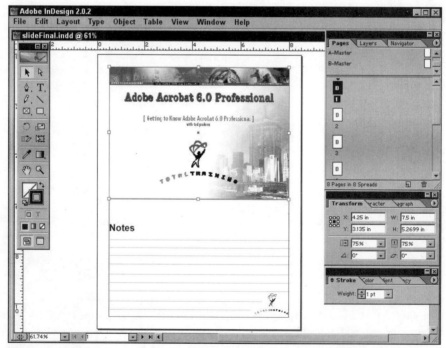

Figure 21-13: Click the cursor in the rectangle frame area after loading the page to be placed, and the PDF page drops into the frame at the size, scaling, and location prescribed on the master page.

Although InDesign happens to be my personal preference for creating a slide presentation when using a layout program, you can create similar workflows with other programs. Take advantage of the master page options in your layout program and find the simplest method for getting the PDF pages sized and placed on individual pages.

After completing PDF page imports, convert the file to PDF and you can be certain that all font embedding, image links, and a reduced file size is preserved in the resulting PDF file. You can send off the document to a conference promoter or a workgroup for commenting; the recipients won't need your original file, fonts, or links to view and print the handouts.

Using Layers with Presentations

Layers offer a new dimension when creating slide presentations. The power of presentation programs, with text popping up as you cover topics in a presentation, can be simulated by using layers and toggling on and off layer views. To create presentations using layers you need support for two essential ingredients. First, the authoring program you use needs to support layers. Second, the authoring program needs to support writing to the PDF 1.5 format while preserving the layers. If, at the time you read this book, your favorite authoring program does not support either of the preceding criteria, you'll need to wait for a product upgrade. Although it's not known as of this writing what programs will eventually support writing to PDF 1.5 format with layers preserved, software development history tells us that all programs supporting PDF exports are most likely going to support these new Acrobat 6 features.

If you find an upgrade to a program where layers are supported in the PDF file, you can approach viewing layers in several ways. A simple approach is to use the Link tool and create a link to set a new layer visibility. After discussing one topic, click the Link tool to show the next line of text while either hiding the previous line or showing the previous line of text with another color or tint of the color used for the text so the topic you discuss at the moment appears with visual emphasis.

When you navigate to a second page, you can use a page action to return to the default layer visibility state. Set either a Page Open or a Page Close action for Set layer visibility and collapse the layers. Thus, each time you show the slide presentation, the layers return to the default you want to use when addressing a new audience.

In Figure 21-14, I created a slide presentation with layers. The bullets at the bottom of the slide trigger layer visibility. The last line of text is the current topic being discussed. The four lines of text above the last line are subjects already discussed. Each bullet contains a link that shows a new layer state. When the page opens, a page action hides all the text below the slide title.

Cross-Reference For information on showing and hiding layers and changing layer states, see Chapter 17.

One thing to remember when creating files with layers in authoring programs is to set the layer visibility in the original authoring program to the visibility you want to appear in the Acrobat PDF document before conversion to PDF. In the earlier example, all layers where hidden before the file was converted to PDF except the Background, Logo, and HeadType layers. The link buttons were added to show the text from the hidden layers created in the original authoring application.

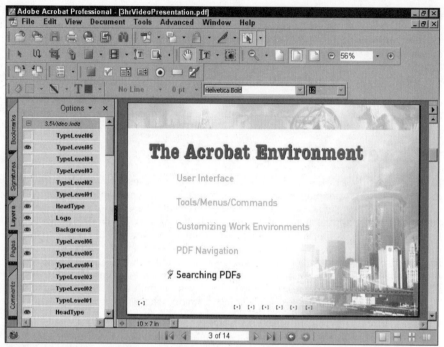

Figure 21-14: Link buttons are used to show different layer states. When the page opens, a page action sets the layer state to the initial view.

Editing Slides in Acrobat

Invariably, you will need to edit slides after PDF creation and after adding all the interactive elements in the final PDF presentation. You may be speaking at a conference or seminar and find out at the last minute that one topic or another won't fit your assigned session or that someone asks you to cover another topic. Or you may have everything well prepared and need to do a little tweak on rewording a topic, moving a graphic, or introducing a new graphic. Rather than returning to the authoring program, you can make these minor edits in Acrobat.

For text editing, be certain that all fonts are loaded before opening Acrobat. If you open Acrobat first and load a font using a utility such as Adobe Type Manager or Extensis Suitcase, the font isn't recognized by Acrobat until you quit the program and re-launch it after loading the font. When transferring files to laptop computers for presentations, be certain you have all the needed fonts installed on the computer and the tool you use to handle font management.

Tip For a super font-management tool, log on to www.extensis.com and download Suitcase for either the Macintosh or Windows. You can try out the software for 30 days without buying the product. After assessing the product for your use, you can purchase Suitcase online and obtain the serial number to continue use. Suitcase does a superb job on both Macintosh OS X and Windows 2000 and XP.

Editing text

As an example for editing text in PDF documents, take a look at Figure 21-15. The title of the slide has two blocks of text. One text block is a drop shadow and the other text appears in a color above the drop shadow. In order to edit the text, the two different lines need to be separated so the TouchUp Text tool can edit each line of text. In this example, I used the TouchUp Object tool to move the top line of the title text down toward the bottom of the page.

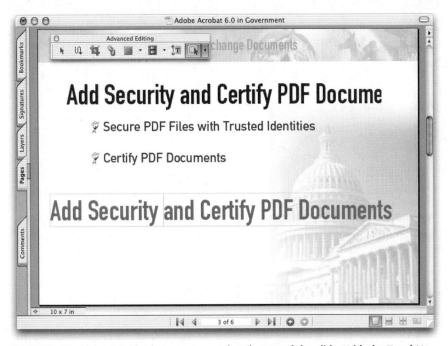

Figure 21-15: The original title text appeared at the top of the slide. With the TouchUp Object tool, the top line of text was moved to the bottom of the slide.

After the text is moved and is easily accessed, select the TouchUp Text tool and click in a line of text. Press the Ctrl/⌘+A keys to select all the text in the line and type the new line of text. In this example I changed the entire line of text and repeated the steps for each line used as the slide title. When you complete the text edit, select the TouchUp Object tool to move the text to position. To nudge a line of text press the arrow keys on your keyboard. The finished edit in this example appears in Figure 21-16.

As you make text edits in a file you'll find that text blocks may have some structural problems, and editing a line of text and moving it around the slide won't always be easy. You may need to cut a line of text and use Ctrl/Option+click with the TouchUp Text tool and paste the line of text into a new text block. You can then select the TouchUp Object tool and move the text around the page as a single line of text apart from the paragraph from which it was copied.

Figure 21-16: Edit text with the TouchUp Text tool and move the text back to position with the TouchUp Object tool.

Copying/pasting text and images

Continuing with the example slide discussed in the preceding section, I need to add a third line of text for another topic. In this case I need to duplicate a line of text and the graphic beside the subheads. To duplicate the objects, select the TouchUp Object tool and drag through the objects to select them. Choose Edit ➪ Copy. While the objects are selected, you can't paste them back into the document. First, click outside the selection to deselect everything; then choose Edit ➪ Paste.

The pasted objects are placed in the center of the page. To move the objects to a precise location, press Ctrl/⌘+R to show rulers. Drag the ruler guides to mark the alignment for the pasted objects; then drag the objects to position with the TouchUp Object tool as shown in Figure 21-17.

As a final step, edit the text line with the TouchUp Text tool. Choose File ➪ Save As and overwrite the file to optimize it.

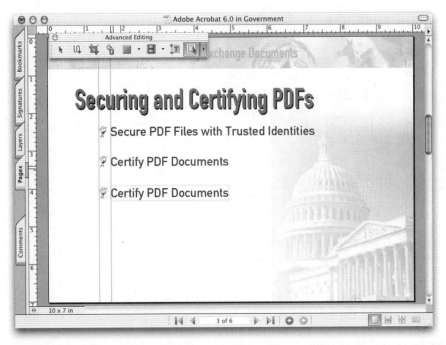

Figure 21-17: After pasting the objects, show the rulers and drag guidelines for positioning the pasted objects. Drag to position with the TouchUp Object tool.

Adding Page Transitions

Page transitions are available in both Edit mode and Full Screen mode in Acrobat 6. You can set page transitions for all pages in a file or from selected pages in the Pages palette. You can batch-process files and apply transitions on a group of documents with a batch command.

Cross-Reference

For more information on creating batch sequences, see Chapter 13.

To set transitions on all pages or a specified range of pages in a document while remaining in Edit mode (as opposed to Full Screen mode), choose Document ⇨ Pages ⇨ Set Page Transitions. If you want to set transitions for pages in a noncontiguous order, open the Pages palette and Ctrl/⌘+click on the individual pages where you want page transitions. After making the page selections, choose Document ⇨ Pages ⇨ Set Page Transitions. The Set Transitions dialog box opens as shown in Figure 21-18.

Note

You can also set Page Transitions by right clicking (Windows) or Control + click (Macintosh) on a page thumbnail and selecting Set Page Transitions to open the Set Page Transitions dialog box. Also, select the Options pull-down menu in the Pages palette and select Set Page Transitions to open the same dialog box.

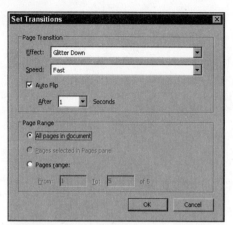

Figure 21-18: The Set Transitions dialog box offers you a wide range of choices for transition effects you can apply to pages while viewing documents in Edit mode.

From the Effect pull-down menu you select the transition effect to be applied for the pages selected either in the dialog box or from the range of pages selected in the Pages palette. Acrobat offers you a total of 50 different choices. One choice is to set no transition, with the remaining 49 choices being different effects.

If you enable Auto Flip, pages are scrolled at an automatic interval according to the number of seconds you select from the pull-down menu below the Auto Flip check box. Choices for the interval are between 1 and 32767 seconds. You can select fixed interval options or type a value within the acceptable range. If you want to manually scroll pages, leave the check box disabled.

If you don't select pages in the Pages palette, you make choices for applying transitions to All pages in document, or you can specify a page range in a contiguous order by clicking on the Pages range and typing in the page From and To field boxes. When you select pages in the Pages palette, the Pages selected in the Pages panel check box becomes active by default and the transitions are applied to the selected pages.

After setting the effects and page range, click OK and transitions are applied to the pages when you scroll pages in Edit mode.

Although it isn't necessary with all the new features in Acrobat 6, you can apply page transitions in authoring applications prior to PDF conversion. If you happen to have an old Acrobat 3 installer CD you'll find a folder on the CD titled Transitions. The Transitions folder contains EPS files with PostScript code to create transitions when pages are scrolled in Edit mode. If you use a layout application to create your slide presentations, place one of the EPS transition effects on a master page in your layout program and convert to PDF. The transitions are applied to all the pages as you scroll through the document. If you elect to use this method, you don't have the flexibility for quickly changing transition effects. The one advantage is that any user of older versions of Acrobat can create PDF documents with transitions by using this method.

Using Full Screen Views

Full Screen mode offers you many different viewing options when you want to show a slide presentation where viewing in Edit mode is not necessary. If your presentation requires a discussion of Acrobat and you want to access tools and menu commands, working in Edit mode is the most obvious choice. When you use Full Screen mode, the menu bar and tools are hidden from view, but the viewing options and alternatives for showing slides in Acrobat are much greater.

Setting Full Screen preferences

The first task in working with Full Screen mode is to set up the environment for showing slides by setting the Full Screen preferences. Choose Edit ⇨ Preferences (Acrobat ⇨ Preferences on the Macintosh). In the left pane, select Full Screen and the preference choices appear as shown in Figure 21-19.

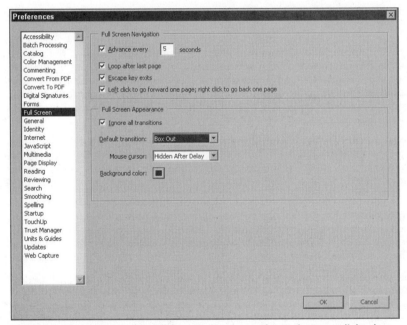

Figure 21-19: To set up the Full Screen view, open the Preferences dialog box and click on Full Screen in the left panel.

The preference choices include

✦ **Advance every:** If you enable the check box, the slide presentation automatically scrolls pages at the interval specified in the field box adjacent to the check box. The values permitted for the interval are between 1 and 60 seconds.

✦ **Loop after last page:** Using this option and the preceding setting for auto advancing, you can set up a kiosk and have the slide presentation continue with auto repetition. After the last page is viewed, the presentation begins again, showing the first page and continuing in an infinite loop.

✦ **Escape key exists:** Entering the Full Screen mode is handled by setting the Initial View options or pressing Ctrl/⌘+L. If you want to exit Full Screen view you can press the Esc key when this check box is enabled. Be certain to leave the check box at the default switch. If you disable the check box, you need to remember to use Ctrl/⌘+L to exit Full Screen view.

✦ **Left click to go forward one page; right click to go back one page:** When the check box is enabled, you can navigate pages with mouse clicks. For both Windows and Macintosh users who use a two-button mouse, clicking on the left or right button navigates pages in the respective direction.

✦ **Ignore all transitions:** If you set transitions while in Edit mode and want to eliminate the transition effects while in Full Screen view, enable the check box.

✦ **Default transition:** From the pull-down menu you have choices for one of the same 49 different transition effects. If you apply a transition in the Full Screen preferences, all pages use the same transition. Selecting Random from the menu choices offers you effects that change randomly as you move through slide pages. If you want to use specific transitions that change for selected pages, set the transitions from the Document ➪ Pages ➪ Page Transitions menu command before opening the Preferences dialog box. Disable Ignore all transitions and the effects you choose for page transitions applied to selected pages in the Pages palette are used when you enter Full Screen mode.

✦ **Mouse cursor:** You have three choices from the pull-down menu for the mouse cursor display while viewing slides in Full Screen mode. You can choose from Always Visible, Always Hidden, or Hidden After Delay. The Hidden After Delay menu choice shows the cursor position when you scroll pages, and then hides it after a short delay (usually a two to three second delay).

✦ **Background color:** Click on the color swatch and the preset color palette opens where you can make choices for the background color. The background color appears outside the slide pages on all pages that do not fit precisely within the monitor frame. If you want to use a custom color, click on Other Color at the bottom of the palette and select a custom color from your system palette.

After setting the Preferences, you can enter Full Screen mode by pressing Ctrl/⌘+L. If you want your PDF document to always open in Full Screen view, open the Document Properties dialog box (File ➪ Document Properties) and click on Initial View. Enable the check box in the Window Options for Open in Full Screen mode. Save the file and each time it opens, the document starts in Full Screen mode.

For more information on setting the Initial View options, see Chapter 3.

Scrolling pages

To advance through slides when in Full Screen mode you can use the preference setting to scroll pages with mouse clicks. If the preference choice for Left click to go forward one page;

right click to go back one page is disabled, you scroll pages with keystrokes. Press the Page Down or Page Up keys to move forward and backward through slides. In addition, you can use the up or left arrow keys to move backward and the down or right arrow keys to move forward. Use the Home key to move to the first page and the End key to move to the last page. If you want to move to a specific page without leaving Full Screen mode, press Shift+Ctrl/⌘+N and the Go to Page dialog box opens. Enter the page number to open in the field box and click OK.

Using PowerPoint effects

PDF documents have never been more dynamic than what's been made available in Acrobat 6. With all the new animation and multimedia support, you can view motion in PDF documents in new ways. It stands to reason, therefore, that support for moving text, flying bullets, and motion objects created in Microsoft PowerPoint are now viewed in Acrobat as you might see them in PowerPoint.

If you start in PowerPoint and add animation to slides such as Entrance, Emphasis, Exit, or Motion Paths, and create a PDF document with PDFMaker, the effects are shown in Acrobat when the PDF is viewed in Full Screen mode. In Figure 21-20, I created a slide presentation in PowerPoint and applied motion paths to text on slides.

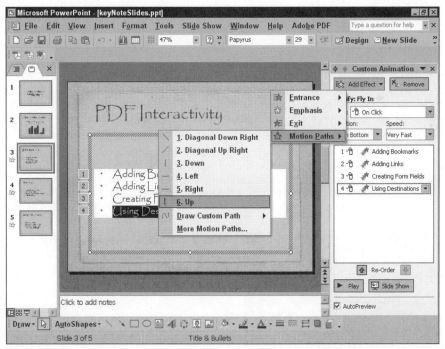

Figure 21-20: In PowerPoint, add all the type and object effects you want to display in the PDF document and convert to PDF with PDFMaker. View the PDF document in Full Screen mode and the animation is shown in Acrobat according to the effects applied in PowerPoint.

After converting the PowerPoint document to PDF, open the Preferences dialog box in Acrobat and disable the Ignore all transitions check box. If you enable the check box, the slides are shown as a flat file with all the text on a slide in view as you scroll pages. When the check box is disabled, the slide begins with the slide title in view. As you scroll pages, the animation shows the text on the slide with the motion applied in PowerPoint.

Tip

If you want to apply page transitions after converting a PowerPoint slide to PDF with the motion objects defined, leave the Ignore all transitions check box disabled in the Preferences dialog box. In Edit mode choose Document ⇨ Pages ⇨ Set Page Transitions. Select the transition effect you want to show in Full Screen mode and click OK. If you want different transitions applied to different pages, select the pages in the Pages palette and apply transition effects to specific pages, then open the Set Transitions dialog box, select Pages selected in Pages panel, and click OK. When you view the PDF in Full Screen mode, the slides are viewed with transitions along the PowerPoint motion effects.

Creating interactivity in Full Screen mode

You may have a slide presentation that does not require access to Acrobat menus and tools, but you want to show cross-document links. Perhaps you have a presentation about a company's financial status, economic growth, or projected growth and you want to show a financial spreadsheet, another PDF document, or a scanned image of a memo or report. The slideshow created in PowerPoint with the motion objects and viewing in Full Screen view is what you want, but you also want the flexibility for opening other files without leaving Full Screen mode.

Creating links and buttons for cross-document linking

If you want to open a secondary document while in Full Screen mode, you can create links or form field buttons to secondary files. When you click on the link, the link action is invoked. If opening a secondary file, the file link opens in Full Screen mode. After viewing the file, press Ctrl/⌘+W to close the file and you are returned to the last slide view also in Full Screen mode.

To set up a file link, create a link or form field button and select Open a file in the Select Action pull-down menu. Click the Add button and select the file to open. When the Specify Open Preference dialog box opens, select New window as shown in Figure 21-21. Click OK and click on the Close button. When you view the file in Full Screen mode and click on the button, the secondary file opens in Full Screen mode, leaving the slide presentation open in Acrobat.

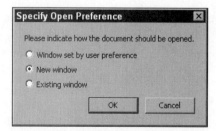

Figure 21-21: Select New window in the Specify Open Preference dialog box. When you click on the link, the secondary file opens in Full Screen mode.

The same behavior exists with other link actions. You can create a URL link to display a Web site while in Full Screen mode by using the Open a web link action. Click on the link and your Web browser opens at the specified URL. When you quit the Web browser, you are returned to the slide presentation in Full Screen mode. If you use PowerPoint effects, the effects are not disturbed.

Cross-Reference   To learn more about setting link actions, see Chapter 15.

Using interactive devices

Another interactivity tool that can be used with Full Screen view is a remote control device. For about $50 to $75 US, you can purchase a handheld remote control. The control comes in two parts. The control device has two buttons used for moving forward and backward in the slide presentation. The companion unit is plugged into a USB port on your laptop or desktop computer. You open the slide presentation in Full Screen view and click the left or right button to navigate slides while you walk across a stage. Some devices also have a button for cursor control. You can remotely move the cursor on a slide and click on a button that opens a secondary file, Web link, or other action associated with the button or link.

When using remote devices, be certain to set your Full Screen preferences to left click to go forward one page; right click to go back one page. The USB devices have two buttons enabling you to move backward and forward through your slide presentation. When the check boxes are enabled, the back and forward buttons on the handheld device are supported.

Summary

✦ PowerPoint slides are converted to PDF with the PDFMaker macro.

✦ To create note handouts from PowerPoint, use the Print dialog box and print the file to the Adobe PDF printer after making the attribute choices in the Print dialog box for the type of handouts you want to create.

✦ Apple Keynote slides can be exported to PDF and PowerPoint formats. Keynote offers Macintosh users a robust slide creation program with easy, intuitive palettes and tools.

✦ Layout programs can be used to create slide presentations. For creating handout notes, set up a master page with objects and elements to be added to each page. Import the PDF slide presentation and convert to PDF to distribute handouts.

✦ Layered PDFs add additional viewing options in slide presentations. To create layered PDFs you need to use programs supporting layers and exporting to the PDF 1.5 format.

✦ Minor edits can be effectively made in Acrobat without returning to an authoring program. For last-minute changes use the TouchUp Text tool to edit text and the TouchUp Object tool to move text, and copy and paste text and objects.

✦ Page transitions are applied to pages individually using the Document ➪ Pages ➪ Set Page Transitions command. To apply different transitions to different pages, select pages in the Pages palette and adjust the transitions in the Set Transitions dialog box.

✦ When using Full Screen mode, open the Preferences dialog box and select Full Screen. Make choices for options used in Full Screen viewing and click OK.

✦ Full Screen views support file linking with link and button actions, Microsoft PowerPoint animation, and transitions applied to pages with either the Full Screen preferences or the Set Page Transitions command.

✦   ✦   ✦

PDF and eBooks

The promise of eBooks has been a roller coaster ride for users, providers, and would-be authors in recent years. The fall of some important content providers, coupled with some not-so-impressive display mechanisms, has slowed down an industry that many thought had a lot of promise. Notwithstanding hardware-display mechanisms and user acceptability, the software used to secure eBooks and make them accessible to every potential consumer was not as robust as viewing documents in Acrobat viewers.

With the introduction of Acrobat 6, Adobe Systems waved good-bye to the Adobe eBook Reader software and now offers users, content providers, and content authors a much more attractive means of creation, protection, and delivery of eBooks. Built into the Acrobat viewers including Adobe Reader, Acrobat Standard, and Acrobat Professional is the new eBook support for borrowing, purchasing, managing, and reading eBooks. In this chapter you take a look at how to set up an account to acquire eBooks and how to manage them in Acrobat.

Setting Up the eBook Work Environment

To access eBook features in Acrobat choose File ⇨ My Bookshelf or use the eBook Task Button pull-down menu. By default the task button is hidden from the toolbars. To open the eBook Task Button, select View ⇨ Task Buttons ⇨ eBooks. The task button and pull-down menu for making menu choices for eBook management is loaded in the Tasks toolbar.

If you want to edit a book stored on the eBook Bookshelf, you need to access tools according to the edits you want to make. For acquiring eBook publications and reading eBooks, no other tools are necessary.

Setting Up an Account

When you install Acrobat you are provided an option for setting up an Activator Account for handling eBook borrowing and purchasing. If you elect to postpone activation you can set up an account at any time by choosing Advanced ⇨ eBook Web Services ⇨ Adobe DRM Activator. In Adobe Reader choose Tools ⇨ eBook Web Services ⇨ Adobe DRM Activator.

Your default Web browser launches, and the activation page on Adobe's Web site appears in your browser window. If you have an existing account you can click on a button for Activate and your account is updated to include the eBook activation. If you haven't set up an account you are provided options for activating an account with Adobe Systems or with Microsoft.Net. Supply a user name and password and you are taken to the activation page where you click Activate to create your account with your new user name and password. Activating an account either with Adobe Systems or Microsoft.Net is done without any fees for services.

Activating multiple devices

If you have an account on one computer and want to open eBooks on another computer, you need to activate all devices. Follow the same steps noted previously for "Setting Up an Account" and log on to Adobe's Web site. Follow the onscreen information for activating your second device and you're ready to view and manage eBooks on your other computer(s). If you have a handheld device such as a Palm Pilot, you need to activate your account on it. To activate a Palm device, place the unit in its synchronization cradle and choose Advanced ➪ eBook Web Services ➪ Adobe DRM Activator. On the Adobe Web site, click on the Activate Palm OS Device button.

The activation must be made before you can download eBooks designed to be used with Acrobat viewers. If you attempt to download an eBook without activation, Adobe's Web site and activation page opens in your Web browser where you follow the same steps mentioned earlier for "Setting Up an Account" to create an account. You can receive eBooks from other users who send you content via e-mails or downloads. If the file is encrypted with Adobe DRM (Digital Rights Management), again you are required to create an account and comply with the purchase requirements before gaining access to the content.

Adobe Content Server 3

The default Digital Rights Management (DRM) for eBooks viewed with Acrobat viewers is handled with Adobe's server-side software. The Adobe Content Server 3 enterprise solution is designed for content providers to encrypt and manage electronic content with the highest levels of security. End users need not be concerned with the product. Your task is the acquisition of content encrypted with the Adobe Content Server 3 product.

 Note   Adobe partners such as FileOpen Systems, Authentica, SealMedia, and Docurights offer third-party solutions that legally use the Adobe Reader technology.

For enterprises, however, your mission is to protect against unauthorized distribution of your products. With the Adobe Content Server 3 product or other third-party solutions you can protect documents and distribute them to users meeting your requirements for distribution. If a user exchanges your content with another user who has not obtained permission to access the content, the user is directed to the Web site where purchases are made. Enterprises interested in finding out more about the Adobe Content Server 3 product can log on to www.adobe.com/products/contentserver.

Acquiring eBooks

After setting up your activation account, you're ready to download eBooks and store them on your Bookshelf—a feature built into all Acrobat viewers. You can test the activation and eBook download procedures by downloading sample eBooks free of charge from Adobe's Web site.

To download an eBook, select the pull-down menu for the eBook Task Button and select Get eBooks Online. Your Web browser is launched and takes you to the Adobe eBook Mall. On the Web page you find helpful information about purchasing eBooks and some sample books you can download without purchasing the content. From a pull-down menu you can select the country where you live and download eBooks in other languages. The default location is for USA and Canadian users.

Click on a book to download, and a progress bar displays the download progress. When the download completes, you are prompted in a dialog box whether you want to read the downloaded book. Click OK and the book opens in your Acrobat viewer as shown in Figure 22-1. If you select No when asked whether you want to read an eBook, the downloaded material is stored on your Bookshelf. Depending on the borrowing time frame, you can read the book at any time by opening your Bookshelf and double-clicking on the book you want to read. The Bookshelf is used to store all downloaded eBooks and any other PDF documents you want to organize and store in an easily accessible and organized manner. To open your Bookshelf, open the eBook Task Button pull-down menu and select My Bookshelf or select File ➪ My Bookshelf. The Bookshelf opens as a floating window on top of the Document Pane as shown in Figure 22-2.

Acquiring eBooks in PDF format is not limited to downloads from the Adobe Systems Web site. When you log on to the Adobe eBook Mall, Adobe partner Web sites and third-party links take you to other Web sites hosting eBooks. In addition, you can browse the Internet and download eBooks from content providers using the Adobe Content Server 3 software or other third-party solutions for eBook management and distribution.

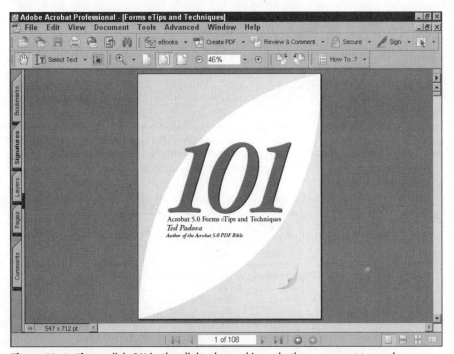

Figure 22-1: If you click OK in the dialog box asking whether you want to read a downloaded eBook, the eBook opens in the Document Pane.

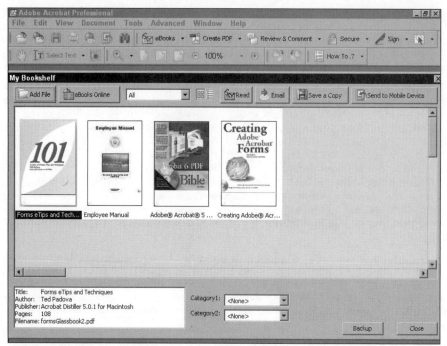

Figure 22-2: To view, organize, and read eBooks, open My Bookshelf and view all content stored in your personal library.

Managing eBooks

eBooks are managed in the My Bookshelf window shown in Figure 22-2. Downloading an eBook automatically adds the eBook to My Bookshelf with the most recent download appearing first in the default thumbnail list. In the Bookshelf window you have several tools and commands to help you organize books, acquire new content, and create category listings for storing books according to preset or custom topics. The options contained in the My Bookshelf window include

- ✦ **Add File:** The first button at the top-left corner of the My Bookshelf window enables you to add any PDF document to the Bookshelf. Click on the Add button and a dialog box opens where you navigate your hard drive and select a document to add to the list. Click the Add File button and the new acquisition is placed at the first position on the left side of the current thumbnail.

- ✦ **eBooks Online:** Click on the eBooks Online button and you are returned to the Adobe Web site eBook Mall in your Web browser.

- ✦ **Category views:** The default is All. From the pull-down menu you select which category you want to view on the Bookshelf. Each eBook can be categorized with one of the preset categories created when you installed Acrobat or a custom category you create in the My Bookshelf window.

✦ **Views:** The two icons adjacent to the pull-down menu offer viewing options in the Bookshelf. By default, thumbnail views are shown in the list. Thumbnails are created from the first page in a document. If you select the second icon the books are listed alphabetically by eBook titles.

✦ **Read:** To read a book you can double-click on one of the books in the list or select an eBook and click on the Read button. When books are read, they open in the Acrobat Document Pane and the Bookshelf window is hidden. To reopen the Bookshelf, select the pull-down menu command from the eBook Task Button or select File ➪ My Bookshelf.

✦ **Save a Copy:** Click Save a Copy and save a duplicate of a selected eBook. Be certain to click on the book you want to copy before clicking on the Save button.

✦ **Send to Mobile Device:** This button is only installed when you install Adobe software for handheld devices. By default the button is not installed with Acrobat. Click on the button if you install software to read PDFs on handheld devices and want to copy a document to your handheld device. You must first activate your device for eBooks as described earlier in this chapter before copying an eBook to the device.

✦ **Summary window:** The window in the lower-left corner of the Bookshelf lists information relative to a selected document. Some information is derived from the Document Summary of the PDF file, and other information may include total pages in the book, filename, ISBN number, publisher, and so on.

✦ **Category:** There are two category lists. You apply a category by selecting a document and opening the pull-down menu for one of the categories. The document is assigned to one or two different categories. If you make selections from both pull-down menus the book is categorized for two categories and appears when books are sorted for either category. When you return to the category views at the top of the window and select a category, only those documents specified for the respective category are shown in either the thumbnail list or the alpha list.

✦ **Time-out:** Notice in Figure 22-2 the tiny clock icon in the top-right corner of the first three eBooks and the last eBook on the Bookshelf. These books are borrowed for a limited-time use. After reading a borrowed book, click on the clock icon and the Document Expiration dialog box opens as shown in Figure 22-3. You can view the information about the lending period or choose to return the book. If you select Return To Lender, the book is eliminated from your Bookshelf. If you click OK, the book remains on your Bookshelf until you return it, delete it, or refresh the Bookshelf.

Figure 22-3: Click on a clock icon on a book in the Bookshelf and the Document Expiration dialog box opens. Click OK to keep the book on the Bookshelf or click Return To Lender to eliminate the book from the Bookshelf.

Categorizing documents

The term *documents* is used here to globally refer to both PDF documents you add to the Bookshelf and eBooks you acquire. Acrobat enables you to add both eBooks you download from content providers and PDF documents you add from files on your hard drive to the Bookshelf. If you want to view all eBooks, open the pull-down menu for the category views and select All eBooks. Likewise, if you want to open all documents (as opposed to only your eBooks), select All Documents from the pull-down menu. In addition, you'll notice the separate listings for categories such as Fiction, History, Mystery, and so on.

When you download an eBook it may have a category associated with the book and fall into one of the category listings. If you want to reorganize an eBook or document from one category to another, select the thumbnail for the item to be reorganized, and open the Category1 pull-down menu. Make the category selection from the list of menu items while the item is selected in the thumbnail list or when viewing the books in a list view.

If you want to create a new category, open the pull-down menu for the category views at the top of the window and select Edit Categories. The Bookshelf Categories dialog box opens as shown in Figure 22-4. Type a new category name and click on the Add button. The new category listing is added to the pull-down menu and also added to the Category1 and Category2 pull-down menus. To place a book in the new category, select it in the Bookshelf and open either the Category1 or Category2 pull-down menu. Select the new category name, and the book is categorized according to the new listing.

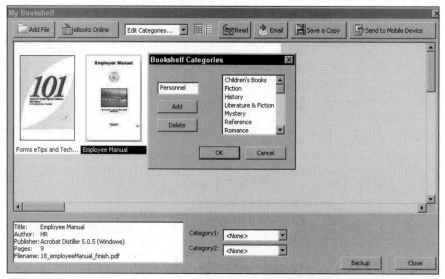

Figure 22-4: To create a new category, select Edit Categories from the category views pull-down menu. Add a name to the field box and click on the Add button in the Bookshelf Categories dialog box.

Using a context menu

You can manage eBooks through the choice of menu commands by opening a context menu on the Bookshelf. As shown in Figure 22-5, you have several menu choices for working with eBooks.

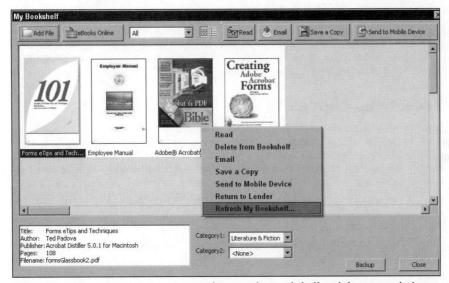

Figure 22-5: Open a context menu anywhere on the Bookshelf and the menu choices offer you options for working with eBooks and documents.

The menu choices include

✦ **Read:** Selecting the Read command results in the same action as double-clicking on a book. The document opens in the Document Pane.

✦ **Delete from Bookshelf:** Selecting the menu option deletes the currently selected item from the Bookshelf. Only single books can be deleted at one time.

✦ **Email:** When you select the menu choice and the publisher has given permission to enable e-mailing of the document, the Document Email Options dialog box opens. You have two choices available in the dialog box. Select the Mail a copy of the document as an attachment radio button or the Mail a link to a Web site where the recipient can obtain a copy of the document radio button. If you choose the first option, the entire eBook is attached to a new e-mail message in your default e-mail application. If you choose the second option, your e-mail application opens with a URL link to where the recipient can download the eBook. For either choice you can add to the message window in your e-mail application and specify recipient address(es) and copies of the message. If you e-mail a copy of a document secured with the Adobe Content Server 3 software, the recipient is instructed on how to purchase and activate the content.

✦ **Save a Copy:** The menu option is the same as clicking on the Save a Copy button in the Bookshelf toolbar.

✦ **Send to Mobile Device:** This menu option also performs the same operation as clicking on the Send to Mobile Device button.

✦ **Return to Lender:** This operates the same as when clicking on the clock icon and selecting the Return to Lender button.

✦ **Refresh My Bookshelf:** For any books that have expired and are no longer accessible, you can choose to refresh the Bookshelf to eliminate all expired books from the Bookshelf. If you have many expirations and many books on the Bookshelf, the refresh action can take some time to complete.

Backing up eBooks

In the lower-right corner of the Bookshelf is a button you can use to back up your books. Click on Backup and the Backup and Restore Bookshelf dialog box opens. If you have content you purchased and other content that's hard to replace, you'll want to copy your books to another source. You can copy to a server, another computer on your network, another hard drive attached to your computer, or an external media storage device.

In the Backup and Restore Bookshelf dialog box, select Backup and choose the categories you want to back up from the pull-down menu. For backing up all eBooks, leave the default menu choice at All. If you added comments to books, you can choose to back up your comments by clicking on the check box for Include user comments and markup, as shown in Figure 22-6.

Figure 22-6: Make choices for what categories to back up and whether to include comments and markups in your backup. Click OK and the Browse for Folder dialog box opens.

Click OK in the dialog box and the Browse for Folder dialog box opens where you can navigate to the destination where all the eBooks are saved. In the Browse for Folder dialog box, a button offers you an option for creating a new folder. Create a folder and click OK, and all your books are backed up to the device selected in the Browse for Folder dialog box.

Copying eBooks to Handheld Devices

To copy files to a handheld device such as a Palm Pilot, you need to download the Adobe Reader for Palm OS software. Visit Adobe's Web site at www.adobe.com/products/

`acrobat/readermain.html`. Click on the Get Acrobat Reader for Palm OS button on the Adobe Reader page and follow the directions to download the Adobe Reader software on your Palm OS device.

Note   Be certain to upgrade to an Acrobat viewer 6.0 or greater and Palm OS 3.0 or greater.

After Adobe Reader is installed on your handheld, you need to activate your device for downloading eBooks. Open Acrobat and choose Advanced ➪ eBook Web Services ➪ Adobe DRM Activator. If you've already set up an account, you'll see the Adobe DRM Activator Web page with a button for activating a Palm OS device. Click on the button to activate your Palm device.

After activation, open Acrobat and select My Bookshelf from the eBooks Task Button pull-down menu. The button for Send to Mobile device is added to the Bookshelf toolbar when you install the Adobe Reader for Palm OS software. If you haven't downloaded an eBook to your Bookshelf for copying to your Palm device, you need to first download the eBook and store it on your Bookshelf. When the book appears in the Bookshelf, select it and click on the Send to Mobile Device button. A dialog box opens with instructions on how to prepare the file for copying to the mobile device as shown in Figure 22-7.

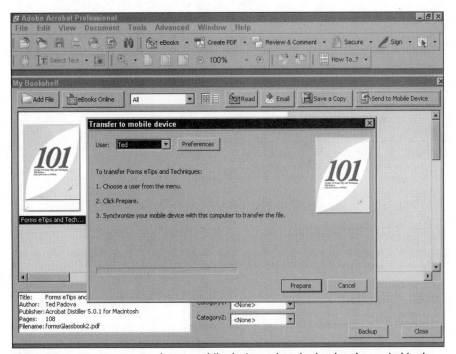

Figure 22-7: To copy an eBook to a mobile device, select the book to be copied in the Bookshelf and click on the Send to Mobile Device button.

In the Transfer to mobile device dialog box, click on Prepare. Acrobat prepares the file for delivery to the mobile device by restructuring the document. A progress bar shows the status of preparation and eventually you'll see the Adobe Reader for Palm OS dialog box open with your file added to the Files to Transfer list. If you want to add files stored on your computer to be copied to your handheld device, click on the Add button shown in Figure 22-8. When all files have been added to the transfer list, synchronize your device by clicking on the Hot Sync cradle button. Be certain your handheld is properly seated in the cradle before attempting to synchronize the unit.

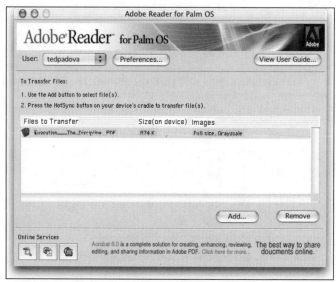

Figure 22-8: To transfer PDF files and eBooks, be certain the files to copy are listed in the Adobe Reader for Palm OS dialog box. Press the Hot Sync button on the Palm device cradle and the listed files are copied to your device.

To read eBooks on your Palm device, select the main menu and tap on the Adobe Reader icon. Adobe Reader for Palm OS loads into memory and lists the PDF documents stored on the device. Tap the book you want to read and the book opens in the Reader software. Scroll pages as you would in any document on your mobile device.

Reading eBooks

Reading an eBook on your computer or laptop is handled much the same as when viewing any PDF document. For LCD displays you have some options for viewing type that adjust to your display in various ways by making choices in the Preferences dialog box. To change the preferences, choose Edit ➪ Preferences. In the left pane, select Smoothing; the right pane changes as shown in Figure 22-9.

In the Smoothing preferences you can make choices for the font appearance by checking the box for Use CoolType. When the check box is enabled, the CoolType options are accessible.

Click on the Next button for more options and select from the opening preferences options or the Next options the type view that looks best on your display.

By default Smooth line art and Smooth images are enabled. You can deselect the check boxes and compare views on your device. Make changes in the dialog box and test the view. If the appearance is not improved, return to the preferences and make other choices. By testing the views you can make selections for the best view on your device.

eBooks can also take advantage of the Read Out Loud command. By choosing View ⇨ Read Out Loud you can listen as the book is read to you using your operating system's Text to Speech engine. For accessibility and leisure reading or group activity, the Read Out Loud feature in Acrobat 6 is a great new addition to the program.

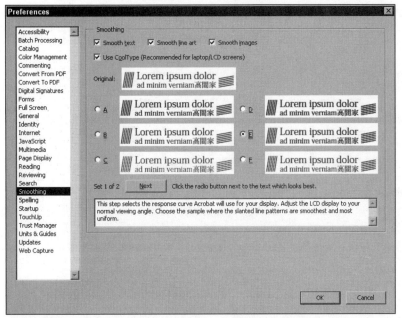

Figure 22-9: Select Smoothing in the left pane where options are shown for changing font displays for better reading on LCD screens and laptop computers.

Cross-Reference

For more information on Read Out Loud options settings, see Chapter 3.

When reading eBooks or any PDF document with many pages, you may want to return to the place where you stopped reading in a previous Acrobat session. Acrobat offers you a method to return to the last viewed page by making a choice in the Preferences dialog box. Select Edit ⇨ Preferences (Windows) or Acrobat ⇨ Preferences (Macintosh) and click on Startup in the left column. On the right side of the Preferences dialog box, open the pull-down menu for Reopen Documents to Last Viewed Page and select either the eBooks Only choice or the Marked Files and eBooks Only choice from the menu as shown in Figure 22-10. When you close an eBook and reopen it in another Acrobat session, the book opens on the last viewed page.

If you select Marked Files and eBooks Only from the pull-down menu in the Startup Preferences, all PDF documents you open, whether they are opened from the Bookshelf or by choosing File ➪ Open, can be returned to the last viewed page. If you select Marked Files and eBooks Only in the Startup Preferences, open a file and navigate pages, and then close the document, a dialog box opens as shown in Figure 22-11 where you confirm opening the document again on the last viewed page. Select Yes to open the current document on the last viewed page or select Yes to All to set the preferences to view all documents you open in Acrobat to the last viewed page. If you select Yes to All and check the box for *Do not show this message again*, the defaults are set to open all PDF documents on the last viewed page without being prompted to confirm the action.

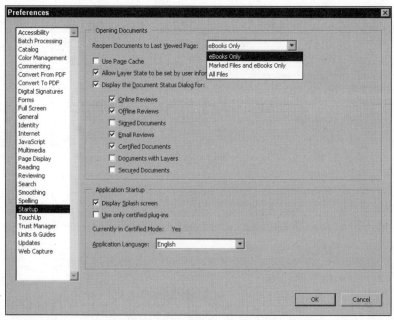

Figure 22-10: Open the Preferences dialog box and select Startup. Select either eBooks Only or Marked Files and eBooks Only to open an eBook on the last viewed page.

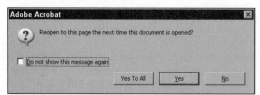

Figure 22-11: When you select Marked Files and eBooks Only in the Startup Preferences, and close a PDF document, Acrobat prompts you to confirm opening the PDF document in another session on the last viewed page.

Commenting on eBooks

Depending on the permissions granted when an eBook was secured, you may have options for editing content and marking up a document with highlights, notes, and references you want to keep stored in the book. To see what options you have when you acquire an eBook, open the Security settings by choosing File ⇨ Document Properties. Select Security in the left pane and the right side of the dialog box shows you the security settings and permissions as shown in Figure 22-12.

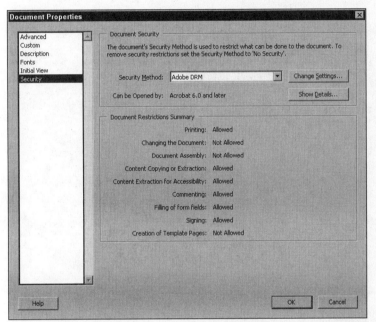

Figure 22-12: To find out what permissions are granted with an eBook you download from a Web site, open the Security Document Properties settings.

In this example, permissions for content copying and extraction, commenting, and some other permissions are allowed. However, commenting is limited to using the Highlight, Underline, StrikeOut, Note, and Attach tools. The toolbar is visible and these tools are accessible when the eBook has been encrypted with Adobe DRM.

To view the book publisher's permissions, click on the Show Details button in the Security preferences dialog box. The Permissions Set by the Publisher dialog box opens where additional permissions are listed. Notice in Figure 22-13 that the permissions include limited copying and a notice for when the document expires.

To add comments to an eBook, use the commenting tools as you would with any Acrobat PDF file. In Figure 22-14, I added a note and rectangle comment to the cover page in an eBook.

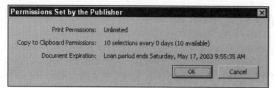

Figure 22-13: To view additional permissions, click Show Details for permissions established from the publisher for printing and the lending period.

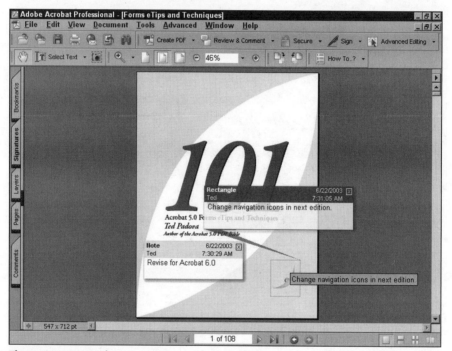

Figure 22-14: Use the commenting tools to mark up a book as you would with any other PDF document.

How you use comments for eBooks is identical to how you use them in other PDF documents. You can open the Comments palette and organize comments, mark them for a status, and print the comments. You can summarize comments and export/import comments as long as the permissions grant you commenting on the document.

When you finish commenting, you don't need to save the file. Close the document, and the PDF is stored back on the Bookshelf. Reopening the book shows you the comments added in your previous Acrobat sessions.

Summary

✦ Before you can access eBooks online, you need to activate an account either with Adobe Systems or Microsoft.Net. Activation can be performed at the time you install Acrobat or by choosing Advanced ➪ eBook Web Services ➪ Adobe DRM Activator.

✦ Each computer device you use needs to have an activated account in order for you to read downloaded eBooks on that device. Again use the Advanced ➪ eBook Web Services ➪ Adobe DRM Activator menu command to activate additional computers.

✦ eBooks are stored and managed in the My Bookshelf window. You access your Bookshelf through the File menu or eBook Task Button pull-down menu.

✦ You use tools in the My Bookshelf window to manage, read, and return books borrowed from content providers.

✦ You can organize eBooks into categories and subcategories by making menu choices from the Category1 and Category2 pull-down menus. You create custom categories with the Edit Categories command.

✦ Opening a context menu on the Bookshelf offers additional commands to manage eBooks.

✦ When you activate an account for a handheld device, eBooks can be prepared and copied to handheld devices.

✦ For reading eBooks on LCD screens and laptop computers, open the Smoothing preferences and select the text views that appear best on your device.

✦ You view security and publisher permissions in the Document Properties Security dialog box.

✦ When the appropriate eBook permissions are granted you can copy content, add comments, and print files.

✦   ✦   ✦

Printing and Prepress

Regardless of why you create PDF files, at one time or another you'll want to print hard copy. You might be interested in printing documents to office laser printers, personal color printers, or you may be a creative professional or service center technician who wants to print to commercial printing equipment.

All Acrobat viewers including Adobe Reader offer the ability to print documents to personal desktop printers. For high-end digital prepress and commercial printing, Acrobat Professional now includes all the print controls long desired by the commercial printing community. Combined with new features for previewing color, preflighting jobs, and printing color separations, Acrobat Professional ranks as a strong competitor against any layout or other professional applications designed to serve creative professionals. In this chapter I cover printing from Acrobat viewers, soft proofing, preflighting, and commercial printing.

Setting Up the Work Environment

You print files from Acrobat either with default tools or menu commands. You also handle all the other options for color proofing and preflighting with menu commands.

Start by opening a context menu from the Toolbar Well and selecting Reset Toolbars. For printing large documents, one set of tools that comes in handy is the Zoom toolbar. To view all the Zoom tools, open the pull-down menu adjacent to the Zoom In tool and select Show Zoom Toolbar. Dock the Zoom toolbar in the Toolbar Well.

Soft Proofing Color

Soft proofing color is viewing color on your monitor with a screen preview for the way color is printed to hard copy. Rather than print a test proof and consume paper and ink, soft proofing is a digital process whereby you use your computer monitor screen to preview things like proper color assignments, overprints, separations, transparency, and similar issues that might cause problems on printing devices.

With the exception of previewing overprints, all soft proofing options are contained only in Acrobat Professional. Most of the options you find for soft proofing apply to high-end commercial printing; however, some features can be useful when you're printing to desktop color printers.

Printing and soft proofing in Acrobat Professional is a quantum leap in Acrobat development, and the new features added to the program rival the best applications used today for commercial printing.

Proof Setup

The soft proofing commands in Acrobat Professional are contained in the Advanced menu. Select Advanced and choose from options for Custom, Proof Colors, or Overprint Preview.

Custom

Custom enables you to select from a list of ICC (International Color Consortium) profiles. A number of preset profiles are available from which to choose and you can also create your own custom profiles and add them to the list. You create custom profiles with either software applications like Adobe Gamma or hardware/software devices that are designed specifically for calibrating monitors and creating ICC profiles. As a profile is created, it is saved as a file to your hard drive.

In order for Acrobat to recognize the ICC profiles you create, you must be certain that the profiles are stored in the proper directory. By default, utilities and commercial devices used for calibrating color save profiles to a directory that makes them accessible to Acrobat. If you want to remove ICC profiles so fewer profiles show up in the Proof Colors dialog box or you have problems getting a profile to the right directory, open the folder where the profiles are stored. On Windows the path is System32\Spool\Drivers:Color. On Macintosh OS X look in Macintosh HD:Library:ColorSync:Profiles:Displays. When new profiles are added to the folder according to your operating system, you can access the profiles in Acrobat after you quit the program and relaunch it if the profile was added while Acrobat was open.

To select a profile for color proofing, choose Advanced ➪ Proof Colors ➪ Custom and the Proof Setup dialog box shown in Figure 23-1 opens.

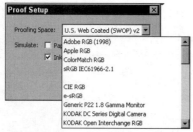

Figure 23-1: Choose Advanced ➪ Proof Setup ➪ Custom to open the Proof Setup dialog box.

Creating Color Profiles

Covering all the aspects of creating and using color profiles is beyond the scope of this book. For a brief introduction let me say that you have two choices for creating profiles: Use a program that is shipped with an application you use for editing color images, like the Adobe Gamma utility (Windows) or the Display Calculator Assistant (Macintosh), or purchase a calibration system. A calibration device is usually a hardware device that attaches to your computer monitor and a software program that analyzes the color from the hardware device. The result of analyzing color and making monitor hardware adjustments for correcting color is the creation of a color profile suited to an individual monitor. The systems are expensive, starting at around $3,000 U.S. Fortunately, you can calibrate monitors throughout your company with a single system.

If you use a program such as Adobe Gamma to adjust monitor brightness, the idea is to bring the monitor in sync with the printed output. You need to measure a print on the device you commonly print to against your monitor brightness and color balance. Hold a print with a wide range of color beside your monitor as you follow the steps in the calibration utility. As a general rule with quality monitors you can come close to balancing color between your screen and printed work; however, no off-the-shelf program will do the job as well as a professional calibration system.

If you use flat screen displays, adjustments with Adobe Gamma are cruder. Check your monitor's user manual for information on color calibration or look for a disk that ships with your monitor containing ICC profiles. If you don't have software support for your monitor, check your manufacturer's Web site for information or software downloads to help you calibrate your system.

From the pull-down menu you'll see a number of different profiles appear in a long list. If you have an ICC profile developed for your system as the result of calibrating your monitor, select the profile in the list. If you haven't created a profile, you can choose from one of the preinstalled profiles. As a general rule, select a CMYK proofing profile such as U.S. Web Coated (SWOP) 2 for files you intend to print as process (CMYK) color. For Web and screen uses, select sRGB IEC61966-2.1. You can make a number of other selections, but be certain to test results of selecting one profile over another. If you select profiles like Apple RGB or Wide Gamut RGB, you may find the color works well for your screen viewing but other Acrobat users will see much different color if they are using a different profile.

If you want to preview the PDF document as it theoretically is printed on paper, choose from either an ICC profile you created or from the preset profiles such as Euroscale, SWOP, and so on. For printing on offset press on coated stock use U.S. Web Coated (SWOP) v2. When you select one of the presets for soft proofing prints, the two check boxes for simulating ink and paper become accessible.

Tip   To ensure your color proofing uses the same profile each time you view a file onscreen, open a document in Acrobat. Choose Advanced ⇨ Proof Setup ⇨ Custom and choose the profile that works best in your workflow. Quit Acrobat and re-launch the program. The last choice you made becomes the new default. You don't need to quit the program to make the profile choice a new default, but if the program crashes during a session, you lose preferences applied in that session. Quitting after making a preference choice ensures you that the preference is held in all subsequent Acrobat sessions.

Simulate Paper White

If the check box for Paper White is enabled in the Proof Setup dialog box, the preview shows you a particular shade of gray as simulated for the paper color by the profile you choose. You may find that the preview looks too gray or has too much black. This result may not be the profile used, but rather the brightness adjustment on your monitor. If your monitor is calibrated properly and the profile accurately displays the paper color, the preview should show you an accurate representation of the document as it is printed on paper.

Simulate Ink Black

When the Ink Black check box is enabled, the preview shows you the dynamic range of the document's profile. Dynamic range is measured in values usually between 0 and 4, although some scanner manufacturers claim dynamic ranges of 4.1, 4.2, or higher. A dynamic range of something like 3.8 yields a wide range of grays between the white point and the black point in a scanned image. If the dynamic range is high, you see details in shadows and highlights. If the dynamic range is low, highlights can get blown out and shadows lose detail. When you enable the Ink Black check box look for the distinct tonal differences in the preview and detail in shadows and highlights.

Proof Colors

Choose Advanced ➪ Proof Colors to preview the document using a profile you selected in the Proof Setup submenu. If you select the Proof Colors dialog box and choose a profile, the Proof Colors menu command is selected for you. You can turn off proofing without affecting your profile choice by returning to the Advanced menu and selecting Proof Colors again to turn the proofing off.

Overprint Preview

Overprints are often used to *trap* colors when files are intended for printing separations. Trapping a color creates an overlap between colors so any movement of the paper when printed on a printing press prevents printing colors without gaps between the colors. In other cases, overprints may be assigned to colors in illustrations intentionally where a designer wants to eliminate potential trapping problems. For example, you might assign an overprint to text to avoid any trapping problems where black text is printed on top of a background color. In other cases, a designer might unintentionally assign an overprint to a color during the creative process. As a measure of checking overprints for those colors that you properly assign and to review a document for potential problems, you can use Acrobat's Overprint Preview to display on your monitor all the overprints created in a file. To view overprints in a PDF document, select Advanced ➪ Overprint Preview.

Note   Overprint Preview is available in both Acrobat Standard and Acrobat Professional.

To understand what happens with overprints and knockouts, look at Figure 23-2. The composite image is created for printing two colors. These colors are printed on separate plates for two different inks. When the file is separated, the type is *knocked out* of the background, leaving holes in the background as in Figure 23-3. Because the two colors butt up against each other, any slight movement of the paper creates a gap between where one ink color ends and the other begins. To prevent the problem, a slight bit of overprinting is added to the type. In an exaggerated view in Figure 23-4 you can see the stroke around one of the type characters. The stroke is assigned an overprint so its color, which is the foreground color, prints on top of the background color without a knockout.

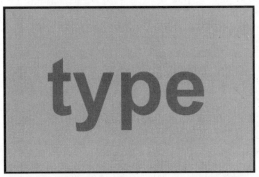

Figure 23-2: Type is set over a background. Two colors are used and the file is color separated so each color appears on a separate printing plate.

Figure 23-3: When color is separated and the background color is printed, the background appears with the type *knocked out*.

Designers can apply overprints in programs like Adobe Illustrator. If a designer inadvertently makes a mistake and selects the fill color to overprint, the color of the foreground image results in a different color created by the mix of the two colors. In Figure 23-5 a file is opened in Acrobat and viewed without an Overprint Preview. The figure shows the document as it should be printed. When Advanced ⇨ Overprint Preview is selected the overprints shown in Figure 23-6 appear. As you can see by comparing the figures, the overprints assigned in the file were a mistake. By using Acrobat's Overprint Preview command you can check for any overprint errors contained in your illustrations.

Figure 23-4: If an overprint is assigned to the type, the overprint area of the type color prints on top of the background color. If the paper moves slightly, the overprint prevents any paper color showing through gaps created by the misregistration.

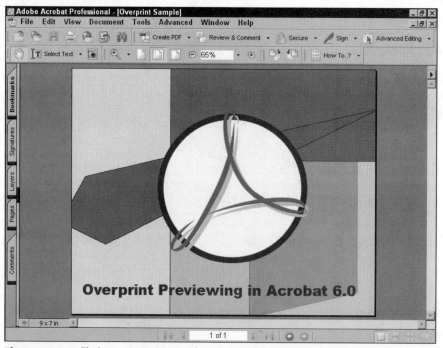

Figure 23-5: A file is previewed in Acrobat without an Overprint Preview. The file appears as it is intended to be printed.

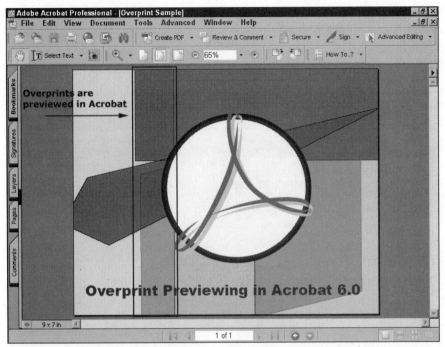

Figure 23-6: When you select Advanced ➪ Overprint Preview, all colors assigned an overprint are previewed on your monitor. In this example, the overprint assignments were a mistake.

Tip
To carefully examine overprints assigned to type characters, select the Loupe tool in the Zoom toolbar. Move the cursor around the document to preview overprints on small type.

Separation Preview

One of the great new features for softproofing color in Acrobat Professional is the addition of the Separation Preview. To preview a color separation, choose Advanced ➪ Separation Preview. The Separation Preview dialog box opens as shown in Figure 23-7.

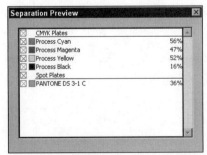

Figure 23-7: Separation Preview shows all colors contained in a file.

Assessing Ink Values

As you move the cursor around a document, the values for each colorant are reported according to the profile you select in the Color Management Preferences. To open the Color Management Preferences, select Edit ➪ Preferences. Click on Color Management and make choices for your working spaces from the profiles you select from pull-down menus as shown in the figure. The profiles available to you are the same as those you choose in the Proof Setup dialog box discussed in the "Proof Setup" section earlier in this chapter.

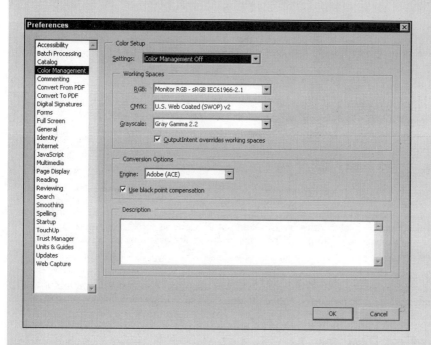

While assessing colors in the Separation Preview dialog box is fine in most cases, there are situations where you might assess a color and the printed result is different from the value reported in the Separation Preview dialog box. Achieving accurate proofing all depends on the proper creation of the PDF file, selecting the proper profile in the Color Management Setup preferences, and the output space that is selected when you print the file.

If you intend to print a file in four-color process, the Separation Preview dialog box helps you identify any potential problems if spot colors are contained in the file. Likewise, if a spot color job contains colors not intended to be printed, they also show up.

You can selectively view individual colors by disabling the check boxes adjacent to each color name, view selected colors only, and view spot colors converted to CMYK. When you click on the X in a check box for a spot color, the first preview is a process equivalent. Click again and the color is hidden in the document. Click a third time and the color returns as a spot color.

You evaluate color values by moving the cursor around the document with the Separation Preview dialog box open. Notice the percentage values on the far right side of Figure 23-7. These values represent the percent of ink at the cursor position.

Tip   Color management is a complex issue and requires much research and study to fully comprehend managing color on computer systems and how color is reproduced on printing devices. To learn more about color management, click on the Search tool in the Acrobat toolbar and add *color management* as your search criteria. Click on Search PDFs on the Internet in the Search Pane and the Google.com search engine reports all PDF documents on the Internet where color management is found. You can download many PDF documents that offer you definitions of terms and thoroughly explain color management.

Tip   For color proofing multiple files, open them in Acrobat Professional and choose Window ⇨ Tile ⇨ Vertically (or Horizontally). Open the Separation Preview dialog box. Move the cursor from one document to another. As the cursor enters a page in the tiled view, the separation preview displays the colors relative to the cursor position. As you move the cursor to a different document with different colors, the colors are dynamically reflected in the Separation Preview dialog box.

Transparency Flattener Preview

Transparency creates problems when printing to various PostScript devices. For resolving printing problems with transparency, you need to flatten the transparency, resulting in files that print successfully on almost any kind of PostScript device. When transparency is flattened in a file the vector objects are converted to raster images. Through the conversion to raster images the colors meld together to form a simulated view of transparent objects. The amount of blending transparent colors depends on the amount of transparency you apply to a file. As the transparency slider is moved to the left to flatten transparency all vector objects are rasterized. When the slider is moved to the right, the transparency flattener maintains as many vector objects as needed in order to successfully print the file.

You can flatten transparency in degrees, and objects in a document are affected according to the degree of transparency flattening you apply. Determining how the other objects are affected is the purpose of the transparency flattener in Acrobat. The one thing to keep in mind when soft proofing files with transparent objects is the transparency preview does not flatten objects in the file. Flattening only occurs in Acrobat at the time you print the file.

Choose Advanced ⇨ Preview Transparency and the Flattener Preview dialog box initially opens with an empty view in the preview area. Click on the Refresh button and the preview appears as shown in Figure 23-8. For the purpose of illustration, the darker objects in the preview are transparent objects and the background is ghosted to show the contrast between transparent objects and nontransparent objects.

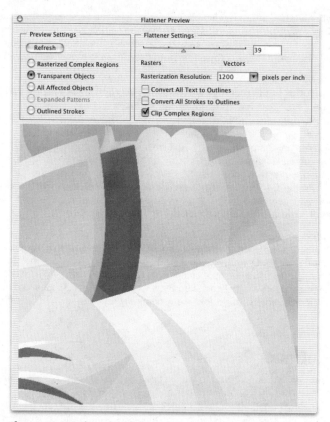

Figure 23-8: When the Flattener Preview dialog box opens, click Refresh to see a preview of the document page.

Previews are displayed only for PostScript printing devices. Be certain you have a PostScript printer selected in your Page Setup dialog box before previewing transparency. On the left side of the dialog box, check boxes offer options for

✦ **Rasterized Complex Regions:** On the top right side of the dialog box the slider is moved to the left to show previews with rasterization. The farther the slider is moved to the left, the more rasterization is applied to objects. Click on the Refresh button after moving the slider. Each adjustment requires you to click the Refresh button again to display the preview.

✦ **Transparent Objects:** All objects containing a degree of transparency, objects with blending modes, and masks with opacity are previewed. If you have overprints in the file, the overprints may also be treated as transparent objects. When you click on the Transparent Objects radio button and click Refresh, all objects containing transparency are displayed with a red mask in the preview area.

✦ **All Affected Objects:** Flattening transparency affects both the transparent objects and other objects overlapping the objects assigned transparency. When type is converted to outlines and the type objects contain transparency, the entire page may be affected. When you select the radio button, all objects that are affected when the transparency is flattened are shown with the same red mask described in the preceding bullet.

✦ **Expanded Patterns:** If you have patterns contained in the artwork, the patterns are expanded when transparency is flattened. Gradient blends, for example, are viewed as expanded objects.

✦ **Outlined Strokes:** If type is converted to outlines, or you select the Convert All Strokes to Outlines option on the right side of the dialog box, the strokes involved with transparency are previewed.

✦ **Flattener Settings:** In addition to the slider, edit the field box to change the amount of flattening. With either adjustment, click the Refresh button to preview again with new settings.

✦ **Rasterization Resolution:** From the pull-down menu or by editing the field box, select the resolution for rasterizing complex objects. Rasterized objects require the same considerations for output resolutions assigned to raster images.

✦ **Convert All Strokes to Outlines:** If you intend to convert text to outlines, you can see a preview for how text objects are affected in complex regions. When printing a file, you'll want to avoid globally converting text to outlines as the files are more difficult to print and small text on output devices that print at lower resolutions may appear unsatisfactory.

✦ **Clip Complex Regions:** The boundaries between vector objects and raster objects change as you move the slider. Some objects remain in vector form according to the degree of rasterization you apply. This option ensures the boundaries between the vector and raster objects fall within clipping paths preventing artifacts appearing outside the path boundaries. As with any illustration artwork, the more clipping paths used in a file, the more difficult the printing.

The first time you open the Flattener Preview dialog box, you may find no changes appearing in the preview window no matter how much you move the slider or change the options. Double-check the radio button for Rasterized Complex Regions. If the choice is grayed out, no complex regions exist in the file and the only previews you'll see are those related to the display of transparent objects and the affected objects. Moving the slider won't change the preview.

When complex regions are present, the preview changes with every movement of the slider or other options selected in the Flattener Preview. In Figure 23-9, I selected the Rasterized Complex Regions radio button. Compare the view to the preview of transparent objects in Figure 23-8. In Figure 23-10, I select All Affected Objects for the same level of rasterization. Notice the objects affected when the Flattener Settings are adjusted as shown in the figure.

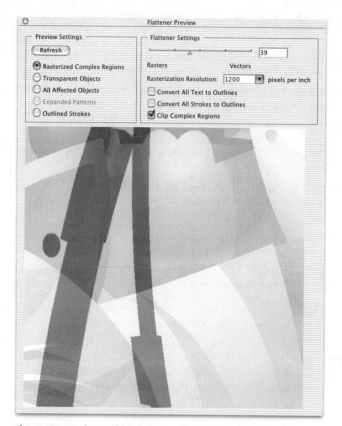

Figure 23-9: If complex regions are present, the preview changes when different options are selected, here shown with Rasterized Complex Regions selected.

If you have complex drawings, the time to refresh the preview can take some time. Think out the previews you want to see before clicking on the Refresh button. If you want to zoom into an area, click the mouse cursor in the preview window. To move around the window, hold the spacebar down and drag the image around the window.

Keep in mind that what you see is not applied to the open PDF document. The Flattener Preview shows what happens if you apply flattening settings. After previewing when you find the right amount of transparency you want to apply, enter the value in the field box beside the slider. You add this same value later in the Advanced Print Setup dialog box for flattening the transparency when you print the file.

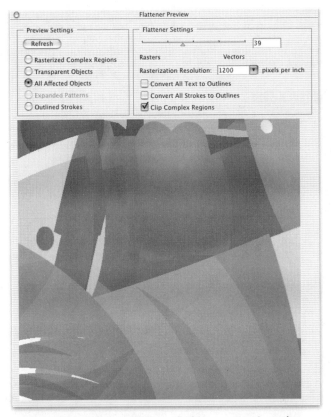

Figure 23-10: Click on All Affected Objects to preview what objects are affected by flattening the transparency according to the current Flattener Settings.

Preflighting PDF Files

Preflighting is a term used by creative professionals and service technicians to analyze a file for suitability in printing. A preflight assessment might examine a file for the proper color mode of images, whether images are compressed, whether fonts are accessible either embedded or accessible to the operating system, or any number of other conditions that might interfere with successfully printing a job.

The tools used to preflight files might be stand-alone applications or features built into programs used for printing to commercial printing equipment. Prior to Acrobat 6 you needed to preflight a file before converting to PDF with a standalone product that analyzed the original authoring application file prior to conversion to PDF or a third-party plug-in for Acrobat that performed preflighting on PDF files. Now in Acrobat 6 Professional, preflighting is built into the program.

To preflight a PDF document, choose Document ➪ Preflight. Notice the preflight option is contained in the Document menu and not in the Advanced menu. Preflighting is only available in Acrobat Professional. When you select the menu command, Acrobat pauses momentarily to load profiles already created as presets from your initial Acrobat installation. After the profiles are loaded the Preflight: Profiles dialog box shown in Figure 23-11 opens.

Figure 23-11: After you select the Preflight menu command in Acrobat Professional, preflight profiles load and the Preflight: Profiles dialog box opens.

Preflight profiles

A preflight profile contains one or more *conditions* that are contained within *rules*. A condition might be something like *is not a spot color*. A rule may contain a single condition or multiple conditions. For example, a rule like *ProcessColor* might contain conditions like *is not spot color, is not grayscale, is not RGB color*. The profile is created from a single or several rules. For example a profile might contain *ProcessColor, Not Compressed, Fonts not Embedded*. A profile containing rules and conditions is listed in the opening dialog box when you select the Preflight menu command.

When you install Acrobat Professional, a list of preset profiles appears in the Preflight: Profile dialog box. You can use one of these profiles to preflight a job, you can create your own custom profile and add it to the list, or you can acquire a profile developed by a service center or print shop and add it to the list. After a profile appears in the list, you use all the rules and conditions contained in the profile to analyze the current open document in Acrobat Professional. If problems are found, Acrobat reports all conditions not met as measured against the conditions in the profile.

Creating a new profile

Before moving on to actually preflighting a document, start by looking at how profiles are created. Click the Edit button in the Preflight: Profiles dialog box. After you click Edit, the Preflight: Edit Profiles dialog box shown in Figure 23-12 opens.

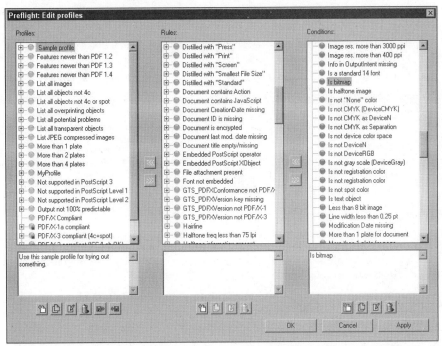

Figure 23-12: Click on Edit in the Preflight: Profiles dialog box and the Preflight: Edit Profiles dialog box opens where you create new profiles or edit existing profiles.

At the top of the dialog box you see three column headings for Profiles, Rules, and Conditions. In this dialog box, you work from right to left. In the column at the right you create a new Condition, or select an existing Condition from the list. In the Rules column you create a new rule or select a rule from the list. In the Profiles column you create a new profile or select a profile from the list. When an item in a list is selected it is moved to the selected item in the column to the left. For example, if I select a rule, then select a condition, I click on the left-pointing chevron and my condition is added to the selected rule. I then select a profile, and select a rule to add to the profile. You can add multiple conditions to a single rule and add multiple rules to a single profile. However, you add conditions and rules one at a time. Repeat the steps to add one to the other with successive selections and clicks on the left chevrons.

You can modify any one of the existing profiles or rules. You can choose from presets in the columns and move items from one column to selected items in the other columns. If none of the existing presets work for you, you can create new rules, conditions, and profiles. The icons at the bottom of the dialog box enable you to manage the conditions, rules, and profiles. They include

 New (condition, rule, profile): Click on the icon in the respective column to create a new condition, rule, or profile.

 Duplicate (condition, rule, profile): Select an item in the respective list and the condition, rule, or profile is duplicated.

Edit: Select an item in the respective list and the condition, rule, or profile edit dialog box opens.

 Delete (condition, rule, profile): Select an item in the respective list and the condition, rule, or profile is deleted.

For profiles only, two other buttons appear at the bottom of the column. The tools are

 Import: Select a profile and click on the Import button. A profile created by a print shop or service center can be e-mailed to you and you can load profiles from vendors who send you their recommended conditions for preflighting jobs.

 Export: If you are responsible for creating profiles at a service center or in a company where you want to implement a set of standards, click on the Export button. The profile selected when you click on the button is exported to a file that you can send to other users who in turn import the profile.

Creating conditions

Click on the New Condition button at the bottom of the Conditions column in the Preflight: Edit profiles dialog box. The Preflight: Edit this condition dialog box opens as shown in Figure 23-13. You make decisions in this dialog box for adding descriptive information in field boxes and selecting a group and property as they apply to conditions.

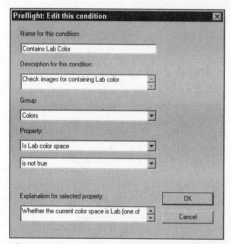

Figure 23-13: Click on the Edit button in the Conditions column and the Preflight: Edit this condition dialog box opens.

The options include

✦ **Name this condition:** Type a name for the new condition. Use any name you want. Try to add a name that describes the condition so it is clear to you what condition you're selecting when you return to the Conditions list.

✦ **Description for this condition:** The text you type in this field box is only visible when you return to the edit dialog box. Add a description for what the condition does or why you're using it.

✦ **Group:** Conditions are made up of selections from Groups and Properties. The Group pull-down menu contains categorical items that are further defined in the Properties pull-down menu choices. Select a group by opening the pull-down menu and make a menu selection. In Figure 23-14, I chose Colors from the pull-down menu.

✦ **Property:** After selecting the Group item, open the Property pull-down menu and select an item. In the example, I selected Is Lab Color Space. The second pull-down menu is the conditional item. For my Lab color analysis, I want the preflight to pass if there are no Lab color images in the file. Therefore I select *is not true* from the pull-down menu. When the condition is checked, a problem is reported if the condition *is true*. If all images are not Lab color, the preflight reports no problems.

✦ **Explanation for selected property:** The message at the bottom of the dialog box is informational. A help message is reported for any condition you select. Before creating a new condition, you can check the definition to be certain what you select preflights the condition you want.

After choosing the options, click OK to add the new condition to the Conditions list.

Creating rules

You create rules by either duplicating an existing rule or creating a new rule. The composition of a rule is the addition of one or more conditions. When you click on the New rule button at the bottom of the Rules column in the Preflight: Edit profiles dialog box, the Preflight: Edit rule dialog box shown in Figure 23-14 opens.

Figure 23-14: Click on New rule and the Preflight: Edit rule dialog box opens.

Notice that no preflight conditions are added in the edit dialog box. You add a name for the rule in the dialog box and supply a description. After you click on OK, the rule is empty. To add conditions to the rule, you select it in the Rules column and select one or more conditions to move to the rule by clicking on the left chevron. The rule must be selected to receive the conditions you move from the Conditions column.

Also in the Preflight: Edit rule dialog box is a check box titled For information only (no error). If you want the report to show if a condition was not met but still pass the preflight without reporting problems, check the box.

Creating profiles

After adding all the conditions to one or more rules, the last step is to create a profile to use for preflighting a job. Click on the New profile button at the bottom of the Profiles column in the Preflight: Edit profiles dialog box, and a dialog box similar to the dialog box used when creating rules opens. Add the name for the profile and a description as shown in Figure 23-15.

Figure 23-15: Click on the New profile button to open the Preflight: Edit profile dialog box.

After naming the profile and adding a description, click OK and the profile is added to the Profiles column in the Preflight: Edit profiles dialog box. Select the profile and select a rule to add to the profile. Click on the left chevron between the columns and the rule is added to the profile. Note that only a single profile is moved at one time. To add additional rules to the same profile, click on the next rule to add and click the left chevron.

Note   Preflighting PDF documents is intended primarily for assessing a document's reliability in printing properly. The number of rules and conditions, however, go beyond print conditions and may be used for checking files suitable for other output modes such as distributing files on Web servers or CD-ROMs. Be certain to check the conditions available to you for preflight options other than printing.

Importing/exporting profiles

After creating a profile, you may want to send the profile to another user. Select the profile you want to export from the list of profiles in the Preflight: Edit profiles dialog box and click on the Export button. The Export profile as package dialog box opens. Find a location on your hard drive where you want to save the file and click on the Save button. The file is saved with a default extension of .kfp.

Importing profiles are handled similarly. Click on the Import button and locate a file to import. Only .kfp files are listed in the Import profile from package dialog box. Select the file to import and click Open. The imported profile is added to the list of profiles in the Preflight: Profiles dialog box shown in Figure 23-11.

Tip   If you want to e-mail a profile to another user, create a PDF document with a description of the profile and how to load it. Any help information you want to add in the document might make it easier for other users. In the PDF file, select the Attach tool from the Advanced Commenting toolbar and attach the .kfp file to the PDF document. Click on the Email tool in the Toolbar Well to attach the PDF with the file attachment to a new e-mail message.

Cross-Reference   For information on attaching files to PDFs see Chapter 14. For information on e-mailing PDF files, see Chapter 20.

Analyzing a file

To see the profiles you've created for preflighting jobs you want to send off to a commercial printer, choose Document ➪ Preflight. To check a document against the conditions and rules specified in the profile, select the profile from the list in the Preflight: Profiles dialog box and click on the Analyze button. After a few moments Acrobat opens the Preflight: Results dialog box shown in Figure 23-16.

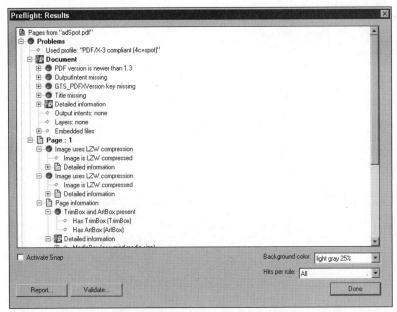

Figure 23-16: After you click Analyze in the Preflight: Profiles dialog box, a report in the Preflight: Results dialog box shows any problems found during preflight.

A report shows you a list of items described as problems if the conditions in the profile were not met during preflight. Click on any + (plus) shown in the list to expand an item and review the detail associated with the item. If more than one page exists in the document, problems are reported according to each page.

If problems are reported that prevent successful printing, you need to return to the authoring program, resolve the problems, and create a new PDF document. For example, if images are RGB color and you analyze a file for four-color process printing, you need to go back to the original images and convert them to CMYK color, update the links, and create a new PDF document.

Validating a file

When you preflight a file and the report shows No Problems Found, you can create a validation stamp that can be viewed by a service center printing your file. The validation stamp is embedded in the PDF document and won't interfere with printing the file. While still in the Preflight: Results dialog box, click on the Validate button. A dialog box opens asking whether you want to append a Validation stamp to the file. In Figure 23-17, the Do you want to continue? dialog box is shown.

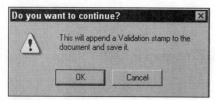

Figure 23-17: After you click on the Validate button a dialog box opens to confirm adding a Validation stamp to the file.

Click OK in the dialog box to add the Validation stamp to the document. You can view the Validation stamp by clicking Validation in the Preflight: Profiles dialog box. You need to return to the original dialog box when you began the preflight. When you click Validation, the Preflight: Validations dialog box opens as shown in Figure 23-18.

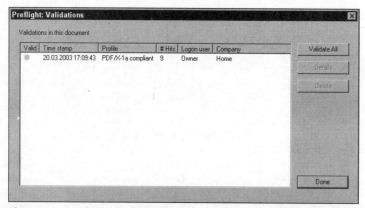

Figure 23-18: The embedded validation is visible when you click on Validation in the Preflight: Profiles dialog box.

The validation is time-and-date stamped and shows the user viewing the validation what profile was used to validate the document. If you want to create a validation report, you have another option. In the Preflight: Results dialog box click on the Report button. The Preflight: Report dialog box opens as shown in Figure 23-19.

Note   To see the Report button you need to preflight the job again. You don't have an option for returning to the Preflight: Results dialog box. Return to the Preflight: Profiles dialog box, click on Analyze, and click on Report in the Preflight: Results dialog box to see the dialog box shown in Figure 23-19.

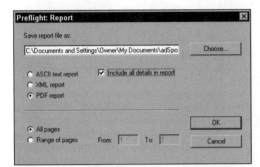

Figure 23-19: The Preflight: Reports dialog box offers you options for exporting the report to several different file types.

In the Preflight: Reports dialog box, select the file format you want to use for the report from among ASCII text report, XML report, or PDF report. Check the box for Include all details in report if you want a detailed report. Select the page range and click OK to produce the report. In Figure 23-20, I created a PDF report.

The report lists all problems and descriptions as Bookmarks. Expand the Bookmarks to show details for items listed in the Bookmarks tab. If you have images where problems are found, the images are converted to separate document pages.

Producing a PDF/X-compliant file

When you successfully pass a preflight for suitable printing, you can produce a PDF/X-compliant file. After running the preflight, return again to the Preflight: Profiles dialog box. Click on the PDF/X button and the Preflight: PDF/X dialog box opens as shown in Figure 23-21.

Cross-Reference   For professional printing, you'll want to use PDF/X files. For a detailed description of PDF/X, see Chapter 7.

From the top of the dialog box, select either Use PDF/X-3 specification or Use PDF/X-1a specification. For each button on the right side of the dialog box you'll see a description for the results of clicking on the button. If you select the PDF/X (1a or 3) Sets, another dialog box opens where you can add a new set based on an ICC profile calibrated for your system as shown in Figure 23-22.

Cross-Reference   For more information on ICC profiles, see Chapter 7.

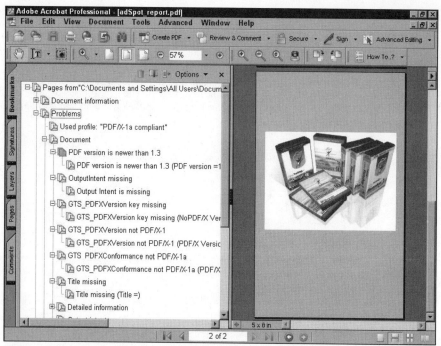

Figure 23-20: When creating a PDF report, the problems are listed in the Bookmarks tab. Any images where problems are found are shown on document pages.

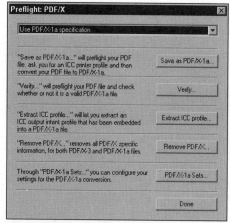

Figure 23-21: Click on PDF/X in the Preflight: Profiles dialog box and the Preflight: PDF/X dialog box opens.

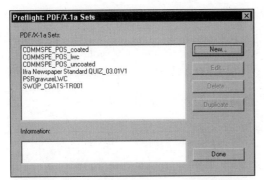

Figure 23-22: Click on PDF/X (1a or 3) Sets, and a dialog box opens where you add a custom set based on the ICC profile you use.

Click on the New button, and another dialog box opens where you provide a name for the set and select the ICC profile for your output intent. Clicking on the Browse button in Figure 23-23 enables you to navigate your hard drive and find the ICC profile to add to the set. Add a check for the number of plates, the minimum and maximum resolution for halftone and bitmap images in the dialog box, and a description to complete the set.

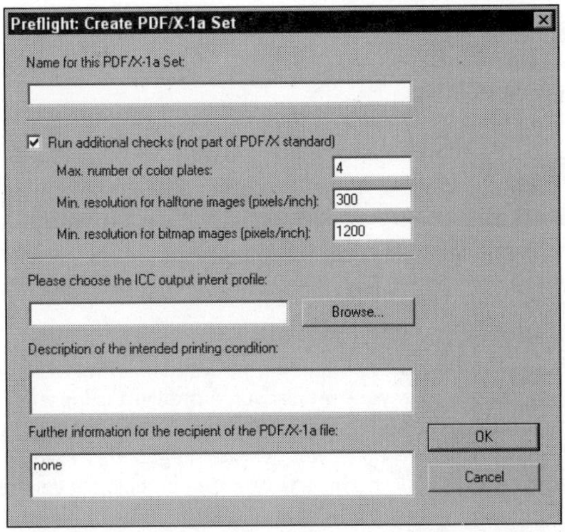

Figure 23-23: Add a name for the set and add any custom checks for number of color plates, halftone and bitmap resolutions, and an ICC profile selection.

Click OK and click OK again in the first dialog box that opened to return to the Preflight PDF/X dialog box. To create the PDF/X-compliant file, click on Save As PDF/X (1a or 3). The Save As PDF/X dialog box opens as shown in Figure 23-24. (Depending on whether you select PDF/X-1a or PDF/X-3, the dialog box appears as Save as PDF/X-1a or Save as PDF/X-3). Be certain to select one of the sets in the scrollable window at the top of the dialog box and click on the check box to run additional checks if desired. Click Save and a dialog box opens where you are prompted to supply a file and location. By default Acrobat adds an extension after the filename before the file extension so you won't inadvertently overwrite your existing file. Change the name or click Save to save the file.

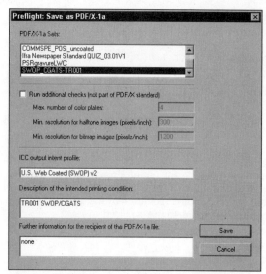

Figure 23-24: Select a profile for your output intent and click on the Save button to save the file as a PDF/X complaint document.

If the file is not PDF/X compliant, you won't be able to save the file. You need to return to the Preflight: Profiles dialog box and begin again by either viewing the Validation report or analyzing the file. Locate the problems in the file and make changes back in the authoring program. When you fix the problems, return and create a PDF/X file.

Note
You may preflight a file with a profile you created or obtained from a service center that fails PDF/X compliance. After preflighting the job with your profile, run a preflight using a PDF/X profile and review problems in the report. You need to resolve the problems before you can save the file with PDF/X compliance. Ideally, the profiles you use should include the rules for the PDF/X version you use so a single preflight is all you have to do when preflighitng your files.

The files you create from saving PDF/X-compliant files are optimum for digital prepress and printing. If you follow the steps and produce files that pass the preflights with no problems and you create PDF/X-compliant files, you'll rarely experience any problems when placing orders at commercial print shops.

Preflighting batches of files

Using the Preflight command in Acrobat Professional is handy for a single file or a few files you want to preflight or save as PDF/X compliant. If you have many files that need to be preflighted, you can set up a batch sequence and preflight a folder of PDF documents.

To create a batch sequence for preflighting files, choose Advanced ➪ Batch Processing. Click on the New Sequence button in the Batch Sequence dialog box and type a name in the Name Sequence dialog box. Click OK and select Preflight, Save As PDF/X-1a, or Save As PDF/X-3 from the Edit Sequence dialog box. Click on the Add button in the Edit Sequence dialog box and the sequence moves to the list of sequences in the right pane as shown in Figure 23-25.

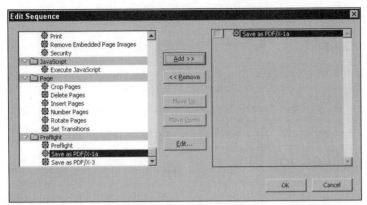

Figure 23-25: Click on PDF/X in the Preflight: Profiles dialog box and the Preflight: PDF/X dialog box opens.

You can edit the preflight sequence by double-clicking on the name in the right pane and selecting the Preflight Profile, then creating reports and adding sets to PDF/X files as described earlier. Follow the same path to create batch sequences as you do with other sequences for selecting the output options and run commands.

Cross-Reference For a detailed description on creating and running batch sequences, see Chapter 13.

Printing PDFs to Office Printers

You may browse the preceding information and find that you don't need to either preflight or create PDF/X files because you're only interested in printing to office and personal printers — either laser printers or desktop color printers. If that's the case, you don't need to be concerned about creating any special PDF-compliant file or running any preflight checks. However, you can check files you distribute to others for desktop printing for issues such as embedded fonts, image resolutions, and problems with features related to printing to personal printers.

Print Setup

Choose File ➪ Print Setup to open the Print Setup dialog box shown in Figure 23-26. From the Name pull-down menu select a printer on your network or a local printer. Select the Orientation and Size. You can click on Properties and make additional choices specific to your printer such as manual feeds, paper trays, and so on. If you want to print the file to a specific paper size and orientation listed in the Print Setup, just click OK after checking these settings. Whenever you begin a new print job, double-checking the settings, particularly for orientation and page size, is a good idea.

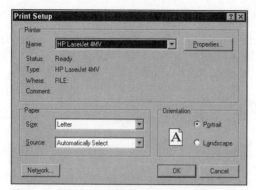

Figure 23-26: Open the Print Setup dialog box and select the paper size and orientation.

Using the Print dialog box

Choose File ➪ Print or click on the Print tool in any Acrobat viewer to open the Print dialog box shown in Figure 23-27. After visiting the Page Setup dialog box and selecting the Page Orientation, you'll notice that you can select the printer in this dialog box as well as the Page Setup dialog box. If you change your mind and want to print to a different printer, make a selection from the Name pull-down menu.

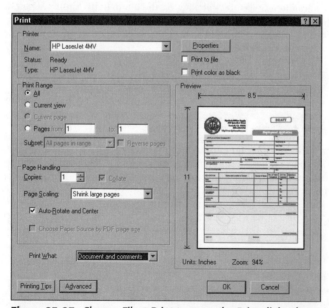

Figure 23-27: Choose File ➪ Print to open the Print dialog box.

The Print dialog box offers many controls for printing to any printer. These include

✦ **Print to file:** If you check the box, the file is printed to disk as a PostScript file. You might use this option to send a PostScript file to a PostScript printer. As you set all the other print options in the dialog box, the PostScript file captures the print settings. This file can then be sent to a PostScript printer with a downloading utility. You might use this option for preparing multiple files to print at a later time in a batch download.

For more information about creating PostScript files, see Chapter 7.

✦ **Print color as black:** Check the box to print the file with black ink only on color desktop printers.

✦ **Print Range:** Select All to print all pages in the document. Select Current View to print a portion of a page in a zoomed view in the Document Pane. Select Current page to print the page in view in the Document Pane. Select the range of pages (Pages) to print within a specified range. If Pages is selected you also have options from the Subset pull-down menu for All pages in a range, Odd pages only, or Even pages only. Click on the Reversed check box to print pages in back-to-front order.

✦ **Page Handling:** Enter the number of copies you want to print. If you're printing more than one copy with more than one page per copy, click on the Collate check box to collate the copies as they are printed.

✦ **Page Scaling:** Page Scaling offers options for None, Fit to paper, Shrink large pages, Tile large pages, and Tile all pages. Select the option you want from the pull-down menu choices. Note that all the options listed here are available in Acrobat Professional and Acrobat Standard. Adobe Reader offers fewer options.

✦ **Auto-Rotate and Center:** When the check box is enabled, pages are auto-rotated and centered.

✦ **Print What:** From the pull-down menu you have choices for printing the document as you might print any document. The Document and comments option prints the document and comments. When the item is selected, the comments on the first page, if they exist, are displayed in the Preview area. The Form fields only option prints only the form fields in an Acrobat form.

✦ **Preview:** A document preview shows the first page in the file (or current page) in a page preview as it prints. Notice in Figure 23-24 that the stamp comment (draft) in the top-right corner of the page is in view in the Preview when the Document and comments item is selected for printing comments, too.

Click OK after choosing the options, and the file prints to your local or network printer as defined in the Print dialog box.

Printing layers

Printing individual layers in a file is dependent on the Layer state options you set in the Layers tab and the visibility of layers. As you visit the Print dialog box in all Acrobat viewers, there are no options for selecting layers to print. Be certain you open the Layers tab and select the layer that you want to print. If a Layer state is defined for printing layers when layers are visible, you can print the selected layer by accessing the Print dialog box and printing the layer as you would any PDF document. If the Layer state is set to Never Print, the layer doesn't print even though it may be visible. To enable printing for a layer that isn't printing, open the Layer Properties dialog box and change the Print layer state.

 Cross-Reference   For more information on layers and Layer states, see Chapter 17.

Print with Comments

When you select Print with Comments from the File menu, Acrobat Standard or Acrobat Professional performs a task similar to creating a comment summary although a PDF file is not created. Choose File ➪ Print with Comments and the Summarize Options dialog box opens as shown in Figure 23-28.

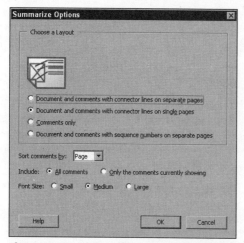

Figure 23-28: Choose File ➪ Print with Comments, and the Summarize Options dialog box opens.

Make a selection for the type of comment summary you want to print. You have all the options for summary comments as you do when summarizing comments from menu options in the Comments tab. Click OK and the Print dialog box opens. The preview shown in the Print dialog box displays the preview of the document with the comment summary. If you select an option for printing the summary as a second document, the PDF file prints, and the summary prints on separate pages.

 Cross-Reference   For information on creating comment summaries, see Chapter 14.

PrintMe Internet printing

PrintMe is a network for printing from computers, handheld devices, and fax machines to any device on the PrintMe network. You can print from within any Acrobat viewer including Adobe Reader to any device on the network and store files on a network-connected computer for on-demand printing. To use the service, you first need to set up an account.

Choose File ➪ PrintMe Internet Printing. In the PrintMe Networks dialog box, click on the New Users radio button and click on Signup Now if you don't already have an account. The PrintMe New user Signup dialog box opens as shown in Figure 23-29.

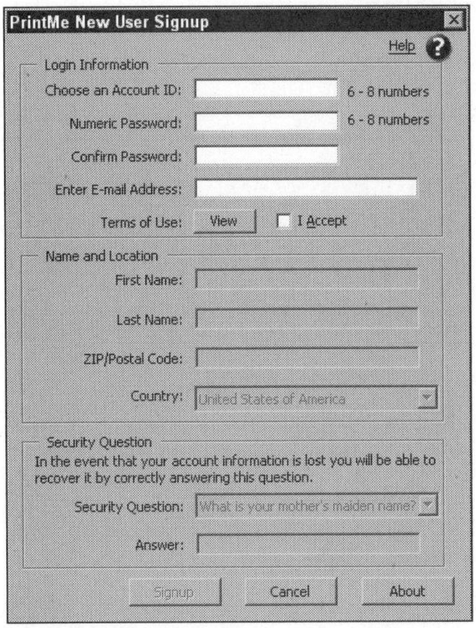

Figure 23-29: Create a new account to start using the service.

After creating an account, your password is e-mailed to you and you can log on and begin using the service. Return to the PrintMe Internet Printing command and the PrintMe Networks dialog box opens as shown in Figure 23-30. Enter your login information and click on the Login button.

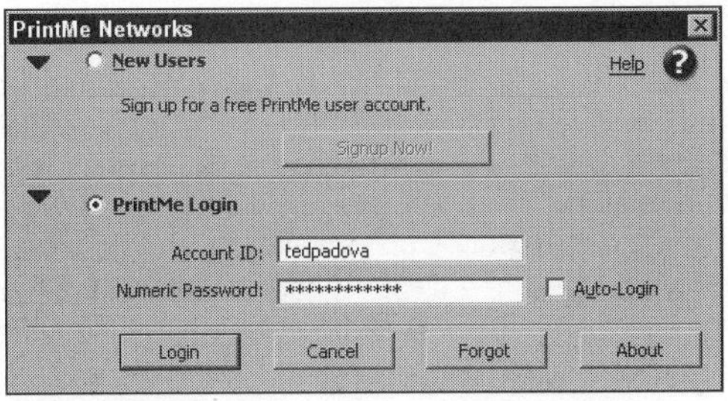

Figure 23-30: Log on to the PrintMe network with your account number and password.

The PrintMe Networks dialog box changes after you create an account and log in as shown in Figure 23-31. In the dialog box, you can designate a printer or fax number. The devices require PrintMe ID numbers and must be a participant in the network service. Click on PrintMe and your file is sent to the account ID you supply in the dialog box.

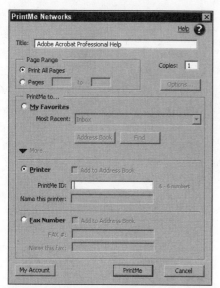

Figure 23-31: After logging on to the PrintMe Network, identify the target printer or fax machine using a PrintMe account and click PrintMe.

Windows users can download a universal driver that enables you to use the PrintMe service with any program installed on your computer. After setting up an account, from the Start Menu in Windows choose PrintMe Internet Printing ➪ Download Driver. A software download commences and the PrintMeDriverforWindows.exe file downloads to your computer. Launch the executable file and the driver is installed on your computer.

Printing PDFs for Commercial Printing

Most of the settings in the Print dialog box are the same for all Acrobat viewers including Adobe Reader. With the exception of Print color in Black, fewer choices for Print What, and no support for printing fields, Adobe Reader uses the same print options as Acrobat Standard and Acrobat Professional. The distinction between Acrobat Professional and the other Acrobat viewers is found in the Advanced Print Setup dialog box. Advanced print options are available in Adobe Reader and Acrobat Standard, but only a few other options for printing as image, language-level choice, and downloading Asian character sets are found in the other Acrobat viewers.

For printing files to commercial devices, Acrobat Professional contains all the print controls you need for commercial printing. To access the options, choose File ➪ Print or click on the Print tool in the Toolbar Well. In the Print dialog box, click on the Advanced button.

Advanced Print Options

When you select Advanced in the Print dialog box in Acrobat Professional, the Advanced Print Setup dialog box shown in Figure 23-32 opens. There are four categories in the left pane. When you select a category, the right pane changes, just as the Preferences dialog box changes when you select a category.

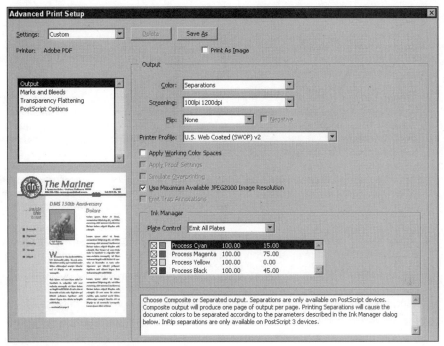

Figure 23-32: Click on the Advanced button in the Print dialog box and the Advanced Print Setup dialog box opens.

Output

Output options are where you set the color and frequency controls for the output. At the top of the dialog box a check box is available for printing the document as an image. For desktop printing when you have trouble printing the file, you can use the Print As Image option as a last resort. Print as Image rasterizes the PDF document and type usually looks poor on the final output. Don't enable the check box for professional printing. This option is also available in the Advanced print options for Adobe Reader and Acrobat Standard. The remaining items are used for commercial printing and they include

✦ **Color:** Select from composite or separations. Users with PostScript 3 RIPs can choose either Separations or In-Rip Separations depending on how you set up your RIP defaults. For creative professionals printing separation proofs to desktop printers, select Separations. For composite color, select Composite from the pull-down menu. For printing RC Paper or composite images to film, select Composite Gray.

Note   If Separations is not available, you don't have a PostScript printer capable of printing separations selected for your printer. If you don't see separations active, cancel out of the dialog box and select the Adobe PDF printer in the Print dialog box; then click on Advanced to return to the Advanced Print Settings.

✦ **Screening:** If you're using the Adobe PDF printer as the printer driver, the screening options won't match the device where you print your job. If you're using a device printer, the screening options for the device are derived from the PPD (PostScript Printer Description). If the frequency is not available from the pull-down menu, you select custom screens and angles from the Ink Manager (discussed later in this list).

✦ **Flip:** For emulsion control, select the Flip item for horizontal to print emulsion down. You have options for flip vertical and flip vertical & horizontal.

Note   Adobe's new print controls in Acrobat Professional are *almost* perfect. However, one limitation does exist. There is no emulsion control for composite printing. Emulsion control is only available when printing separations. Therefore service centers needing to print emulsion-down composites on LexJet, mylar, transwhite, and other substrates on large format inkjet printers need to flip files prior to PDF creation.

✦ **Apply Working Color Spaces:** This setting in effect applies the profile you select in the Color Management Preferences dialog box as the source space to the PDF document in the PDF is defined in Device Colors. If the PDF is calibrated, it uses the Calibrated color spaces in the PDF document as the source.

✦ **Apply Proof Settings:** This setting is available for composite printing only. If you want to apply settings made in the Proof Setup for a simulated print, enable the check box.

✦ **Simulate Overprinting:** This option, also available for composite, prints only the print results in a proof showing the results of overprints assigned in the document. This feature emulates the overprinting previews of high-end color proofers, such as what was introduced with the Imation Rainbow printer.

✦ **Use Maximum Available JPEG2000 Image Resolution:** When the check box is enabled, the maximum usable resolution contained in JPEG2000 images is used.

✦ **Emit Trap Annotations:** Only applies to documents where trap annotations are included in the file. The trap annotations are sent to RIPs when In-Rip separations are used on PostScript 3 devices.

✦ **Ink Manager:** If spot colors or RGB colors are contained in the file you can convert spot or RGB to CMYK color by clicking on the check box. The spot color converts to CMYK color when the X in the check box turns to a fill with CMYK color. To edit the frequency and angle for each plate, double-click on a color and the Edit Frequency and Angle dialog box opens. Supply the desired frequency and angle for each color by successively opening the dialog box individually for each color.

Marks and Bleeds

Select Marks and Bleeds in the left pane of the Advanced Print Setup dialog box, and the right pane changes to show the options as shown in Figure 23-33.

Select All to show all printer's marks. If you want individual marks, deselect All Marks and click individually on the check boxes below the Marks Style pull-down menu. From the pull-down menu options, you can choose Western Style or Eastern Style. Use Eastern Style for printing files in far-eastern countries.

Marks and Bleeds are also available for composite proofs as well as separations.

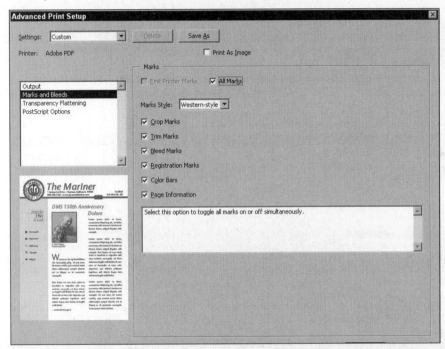

Figure 23-33: Select Marks and Bleeds in the left pane of the Advanced Print Setup dialog box to change options for adding printer's marks.

Using Save as PostScript for High-End Printing

Commercial printers should note that although you can successfully print files from the Print dialog box using the Advanced print settings, there are many circumstances where saving a file to PostScript and downloading the PostScript file offers you more options and may be necessary to successfully print a job. For example, to send a PostScript file to other post-processing programs that require DCS (Desktop Color Separation) compliant PostScript requires you to download a PostScript file and not use the print path. In addition, PPD (PostScript Printer Description) selection is also provided in the Save As PostScript advanced settings dialog box.

Selecting File ➪ Save As ➪ PostScript (.ps) and assigning attribute choices in the Save as Settings dialog box is the path high end commercial printers should use instead of printing files direct from the Print dialog box.

For more information on assigning attribute choices in the Save as PostScript dialog box and saving files as PostScript, see Chapters 5 and 7.

Transparency Flattening

Click on Transparency Flattening in the Advanced Print Setup dialog box to apply settings you determined for flattening transparency in the Flattener Preview dialog box. As you move the slider toward Rasters, you'll notice the preview does not change. The transparency flattening preview is only available in the Flattener Preview dialog box. Set the options here from those determined earlier when you soft proofed the file. The flattening of the transparency occurs only when the file is printed or when you save a file as PostScript.

PostScript Options

Click on PostScript Options in the Advanced Print Setup dialog box, and the right pane changes as shown in Figure 23-34. From the options available, select the PostScript settings for the output you want.

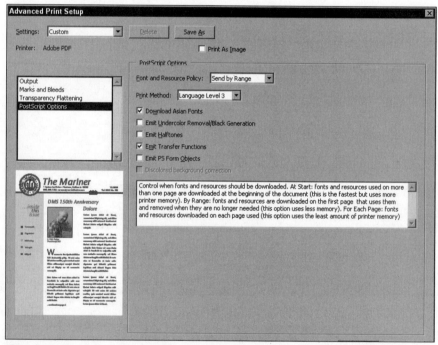

Figure 23-34: Click on the PostScript Options to open the PostScript Options settings.

The PostScript Options include

✦ **Font and Resource Policy:** Three options are available from the pull-down menu. Select Send at Start to send all fonts to the printer as the print job starts. Select Send by Range to send fonts as they are encountered on the pages as new pages print and where the fonts stay in memory until the job finishes printing, or select Send for Each page to conserve memory where the fonts are flushed after each page prints. The last selection takes more time to print but can overcome problems when experiencing difficulty in printing a job.

✦ **Print Method:** Choose from PostScript Level 2 or PostScript 3 depending on the level of PostScript used by the RIP.

✦ **Download Asian Fonts:** Check the box if Asian characters are in the document and not available at the RIP.

✦ **Emit Undercolor Removal/Black Generation:** GCR/UCR removal is necessary only if the original file contained embedded settings. Deselect the box to remove any embedded settings that might have been inadvertently added and saved in Photoshop. If you want to apply any embedded settings, checking the box to Emit the settings applies them as they were embedded in the authoring program.

✦ **Emit Halftones:** In the event that the PostScript file contained embedded halftones, you can preserve them here, and the frequency assigned in the Output options is used to print the file. Check the box to apply the frequency embedded in a file. When you want to preserve halftones is when you want an embedded halftone frequency in an image to print at a different frequency than the rest of the job.

✦ **Emit Transfer Functions:** Deselect the box to eliminate any transfer functions that might have been embedded in Photoshop images. If you know you want images to print with embedded transfer functions you may have applied according to instructions provided from a publication house, check the box to preserve the transfer functions.

✦ **Emit PS Form Objects:** PostScript XObject stores common information in a document. Things like backgrounds, headers, footers, etc. When PostScript XObjects are used, the printing is faster, but it requires more memory. To speed up the printing, check the box to emit PostScript XObjects.

To understand more about XObjects, see Chapter 7.

✦ **Discolored background correction:** Enable this option only when printing composite proofs where backgrounds print darker or with a discolored appearance like a yellow tint.

Save As

You can capture and save the settings you select in the Advanced Print Setup dialog box as a printing profile. Click the Save As button and the Save Print Settings dialog box opens. Provide a name and click OK. You select the profiles from the pull-down menu for Settings in the top-left corner of the Advanced Print Setup dialog box.

If you create a setting and want to later delete it from the Settings pull-down menu, select the setting to delete and click on the Delete button.

Printing Tips

The Printing Tips button appearing in all Acrobat viewers is a link button to Adobe's Web site. Click on Printing Tips, and the troubleshooting Web page for printing PDF files opens in your Web browser. Before calling for technical support, look over the information posted on Adobe's Web site. Chances are that some of the problems you experience printing PDF documents are listed on the Web pages with solutions on how to overcome them.

Summary

✦ Soft proofing color in Acrobat Professional provides several menu commands for proofing color, overprints, separation previews, and transparency flattening. Acrobat Standard offers only overprint previews.

✦ Preflighting files is a manner of checking a document for potential errors in printing. Acrobat Professional offers you an extended set of rules and conditions to check files before sending them to prepress centers and print shops.

✦ A set of preset profiles is installed with Acrobat Professional for preflighting jobs. You can create custom profiles by adding preset conditions or creating custom conditions and adding them to rules and adding the rules to a new profile.

✦ You can import and export profiles. You can acquire profiles from service centers and add them to your profile list for preflighting files.

✦ You save PDF/X-compliant files from the Preflight: PDF/X dialog box. Sending PDF/X files to service centers and print shops optimizes your chances for successful output when printing to commercial printing devices.

✦ All Acrobat viewers are capable of printing composite prints to office and personal printers. Only Acrobat Professional offers high-end printing and color separations.

✦ The Advanced Print Setup dialog box in Acrobat Professional offers you options for color separations, printer's marks, frequency control, emulsion control, and other print attributes associated with commercial printing.

✦ Clicking the Printing Tips button in the Print dialog box in all Acrobat viewers launches your default Web browser and opens a Web page on Adobe's Web site that contains printing tips and problem solutions.

✦   ✦   ✦

Distributing PDF Documents

For distribution of collections of PDF documents, you have basically two choices: store files on Web servers or copy documents to various media devices. For Internet uses you may be exchanging files with colleagues or uploading documents to your company's Web site. For external media storage the most common form of storage device is CD-ROM. In this chapter I talk about uploading PDF documents to Web servers and replicating CD-ROMs.

Setting Up the Work Environment

For most of what you do with document exchanges and copying files to media devices, the tools provided on default toolbars are sufficient. If you add button fields for submitting form data or PDF documents, you can open the Advanced Editing toolbar and use the Button Field tool appearing as the default form tool in the toolbar.

Hosting Forms on Web Servers

To send PDF files to Web servers from a remote location you need a software application program that enables you to submit files to Web servers. Most of the programs used today for submitting PDFs to Web servers are available as shareware programs. In years past, many freeware programs were around for FTPing files to Web servers, but now almost any worthwhile application requires a nominal purchase. You can find Web sites hosting software applications as shareware or public domain programs and download them to your computer. Windows users can visit www.tucows.com for an extensive list of programs for almost any purpose. Among the programs available are FTP client software applications designed to FTP files to Web servers. The list is extensive, so read the comments and try out a few to find one that you can easily understand and use.

You can usually find sites that rate software according to popularity and usability. Furthermore, most applications are offered with a free 30-day trial program with full functionality that enables you to thoroughly evaluate the products.

The typical FTP program offers you drag-and-drop operations where you log on to your Web site by clicking on an activation button or from a dialog box and then see your logon site and host computer in a split pane or two separate windows. When the logon is successful, navigate your hard drive and locate the files or folders to upload. Drag the files from your host computer to a directory on your Web server. In Figure 24-1, the PrimaSoft AutoFTP client shows a logon Web site and a host drive. From the top window you drag files to the lower window for uploading.

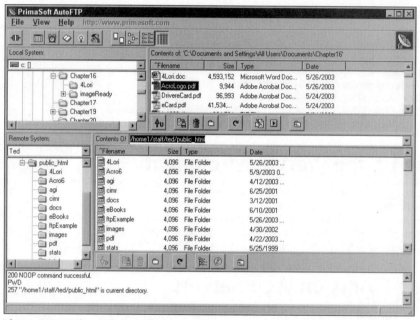

Figure 24-1: PrimaSoft AutoFTP is an application that enables drag-and-drop file uploading. After logging on, drag files from your hard drive to your Web server.

On the Macintosh, the most popular FTP client is Fetch. Fetch is available on many different Web sites as a free download. Download the program and install it. When you launch the program you are prompted for identifying a Host (http://mycompany.com — this is the URL where your company Web site is located), User ID (typically this is your name used in your e-mail address or your authorization to gain access to your Web pages), Password (your password to access your Web site), and Directory (in most cases the root directory is *public_html* plus a subfolder where you want to send your files). If you experience difficulty contact your system administrator for the directory where your files should be delivered.

Fetch also offers you drag-and-drop methods for file uploading. After you log on, the Fetch window opens at the specified URL as shown in Figure 24-2. Drag files from your desktop to the window for uploading.

Figure 24-2: The most popular FTP application on the Macintosh is Fetch. Fetch offers drag-and-drop uploading/downloading and the newer version runs native in System X.

If you used software with older operating systems, be certain to invest a few dollars in upgrading your client FTP applications to newer operating systems. These programs cost between $30 to $40 U.S. and are worth the investment if you make routine visits to your Web site to upload and download files. Mac OS X users especially will find Fetch 4.x a much greater tool to work with than using older freeware versions in the Classic environment.

After sending files to the Web server, you enter the URL in HTML on a Web page for a button action that opens the PDF file. For example, you may have text or a button with a hypertext link (in a simplified version) specified as

```
< a href = "http://www.mycompany.com/directory/file.pdf"> text or
button goes here </a>
```

This code instructs the browser to go to the company Web site (mycompany.com), to a directory you specify (/directory) and open the PDF file specified (/file.pdf).

Cross-Reference

For more information on creating links to Web-hosted PDFs, see Chapter 20.

Getting PDF files on your Web server and creating hypertext links to the files are the easy parts. Where you encounter problems is with many users who experience difficulties in viewing your PDFs. These problems are generally on the users' end and not with your hosting of the PDF files. Web-hosted PDFs may be designed for inline viewing, which means a PDF file viewed inside the browser window. If users aren't seeing the PDFs as inline views, they most likely have a configuration problem on their end. In other cases, you may want to have a user download a file from your Web site and use it offline. In such cases, you'll want the user to be able to save a file to disk.

The best way to overcome problems users may experience in working with your PDF documents is to design several help pages in HTML, describing how your files are viewed as inline PDFs, saved as copies from the Adobe Reader software, and special considerations for completing forms online and offline. Try to address viewing PDFs from several browsers and different versions in your help files. With a little guidance for the end user, you can minimize the number of inquiries users have regarding accessing your documents.

Another link you'll want to create on your Web site is for users to acquire the Adobe Reader software. If you create PDFs in Acrobat Standard or Acrobat Professional, you'll want the individuals viewing your PDFs to be updated with the most recent Acrobat viewer. Wherever you host a collection of PDF documents, create a Web link to www.adobe.com/products/acrobat/readermain.html. As a precaution against violating restrictions, be certain to review Adobe's requirements for posting links to the Adobe Reader download page and any special restrictions for using the *Get Adobe Reader* image you may acquire from Adobe Systems.

Writing PDFs to CD-ROMs

The advantage in hosting PDFs on the Web is the ability to keep them updated and current as they are changed. With CD-ROMs you lose this advantage. However, CD-ROMs have their own advantages that you can't duplicate with Web-hosted documents. For example, you can eliminate any problems for users accessing your PDFs and you can create search indexes for faster searches. You can eliminate long download times for large files and you can minimize confusion when several PDFs are interactive and need to be housed in the same directory to work properly. With some of these advantages you may find replicating CD-ROMs a viable solution for distributing your PDFs.

If you replicate CD-ROMs for distributing your Acrobat PDF documents, you'll want to exercise some care in creating a master CD that works properly and provides users with all the features you want them to enjoy.

 Cross-Reference   This chapter assumes you have optimized PDF documents, set up initial views, and provided Document Summary data for your files. To learn more about optimizing PDF documents, setting the Initial View, and adding Document Summaries, see Chapter 13.

Organizing a CD-ROM collection of PDFs

When organizing your documents for CD-ROM replication, you must consider two important measures. First, you must preserve the directory path for all actions that open and close files. If you use a button, a Page Action, a Bookmark, a Link, a JavaScript, or any interactive element that opens another file, the path that Acrobat searches is absolute. If you relocate files after creating links and copy them to a CD-ROM, Acrobat won't be able to find the linked files. The best way to prevent a potential problem is to create a single folder on your hard drive, then nest subfolders below the main folder. Create the links and test them thoroughly before creating a master used to replicate the CD-ROMs. You can copy all the files and subfolders from the main folder on your hard drive to the root location on the CD-ROM, but don't move any files from the subfolders. The folders and folder names need to be preserved.

The second precaution is to ensure all filenames are preserved when copying PDFs to a CD-ROM. This issue is related to the software used to write the CD. You must use naming conventions that preserve long names. Writing CDs for a cross-platform audience is always best. Therefore, if you use a Macintosh, be certain the filenames are not disturbed when files are viewed on a Windows machine and vice versa. As a matter of practice, using standard DOS naming conventions (eight-character maximum name with three-character maximum extension) is always successful. As a final step you should test a CD-ROM before replication on both platforms.

Adding search indexes

Search indexes enable users to find information in large collections fast. If your files are distributed to Acrobat Standard or Adobe Reader users, adding a search index is certain to be appreciated by users. Fortunately, in Acrobat 6 a search index is not absolutely necessary, but it can save time for users who want to find keywords among the CD files. In Acrobat 6 you have to be concerned only with copying a single folder, as opposed to nine separate folders you had to copy in earlier versions of Acrobat, and the index file. After copying the index file, be certain it is functional and test it before replicating CD-ROMs.

For more information on using Acrobat Search, see Chapter 4.

With Acrobat 6 you also have an option for all users of the Acrobat Professional software to create their own index files. Make sure you enable Document Accessibility when securing files so end users can index your password-protected files.

For more information on securing PDF documents, see Chapter 19.

A good example of how to enable users to create their own index files is by using the book you're reading. Rather than risk a chance for creating an index that might not work properly, as may happen if left in the hands of others, users of Acrobat Professional can index the PDF version of this book, which can be found on the CD-ROM.

Acrobat Catalog is great for creating search indexes for PDFs. However, if your needs extend beyond PDF documents, you need another application that indexes multiple file formats. DocuQuest from A1A Software (www.docuquest.com) offers such a solution. In environments where volumes of multiple file formats exist, an index-creation tool such as DocuQuest can save mountains of time. The product is available in personal and network site license versions. If you keep your PDF documents within the confines of your company or organization, then DocuQuest just might serve your needs. If you need to distribute CDs to clients and individuals outside your company, you need to find other solutions.

Search indexes are created with Acrobat Catalog in Acrobat Professional only. The index files created by Acrobat Catalog however work in all Acrobat viewers.

For more information on using Acrobat Catalog with Acrobat Professional, see Chapter 4.

Replicating CD-ROMs

If you have a limited number of CD-ROMs to copy, a personal CD-R device can satisfy your needs. These devices come with different interfaces where the write speed varies greatly according to the interface type. USB devices are extremely slow, whereas FireWire drives are the top of the line. Even if your CD-ROM write needs are occasional, you'll appreciate the much faster completion time of a FireWire drive.

If your CD-ROM replication involves writing many CDs, you will want to use a replication center. The cost of replicating CD-ROMs can be reduced to less than $1.00 U.S. apiece, depending on the number of CDs you order. For a replication source, search the Internet and compare the costs of the services. When you find a service, send them a CD-ROM of the PDF files you want replicated. In order to ensure the filenames and directory paths are properly specified on the destination media, thoroughly test your own CD to be certain everything works properly before submitting the files to the replication center.

Adding a Web page for updates

After you distribute a CD-ROM to clients or employees you have no idea how long people may use the files. You might go through several updates of the same files before someone updates your CD to the latest version. To guard against obsolescence, create a folder with an HTML file to be included on the CD. For all the button and text links, make the hypertext references to the pages on your Web site where updates are routinely reported. You can add a *readme* file or a PDF to instruct users they should frequent your Web site for updated forms. Be certain to keep the directory paths fixed on your Web site so even a user with an antiquated CD can easily access the pages without having to search your site.

> **Note**   Readme files are text-only documents. On Windows use Windows WordPad or Notepad and type your help information. Save the file as text only. On the Macintosh type your help information in TextEdit and save the file as text only.

Creating a welcome file

A file that describes the CD, its contents, and a general statement about visiting your Web site can be made as a text-only file or a PDF document. If you create a PDF file, the user needs to have an Acrobat viewer installed on his/her computer. Any computer user can read a text file, so you may want to add both.

Unfortunately, everyone won't view the readme files. Some users will avoid them and jump right into your documents. If you want to ensure that every user sees your welcome file at least one time, then you can add an autoplay file that automatically launches your welcome file when the CD-ROM is inserted in the CD drive. I explain how to create and set up an autoplay file in the next section.

Adding Adobe Reader

Before I talk about the inclusion of the Adobe Reader software, you should always check with Adobe's Web site for the current rules and licensing restrictions before distributing software like Adobe Reader. The distribution policy can change at any time, so what is said today may not be true tomorrow.

As of this writing Adobe permits you to copy the Adobe Reader software installer to a media source for distribution. You must comply with the licensing policy and include all licensing information with the installer application. For specifics related to the distribution of the Acrobat Reader software, visit Adobe's Web site at http://www.adobe.com/products/acrobat/distribute.html to get the most recent copy of Adobe Reader and the current distribution policy.

If you include the Adobe Reader installer on a CD-ROM, also create a Web page that is linked to the download page of the current Reader software. If your CD is out for a long time, Reader may go through several versions before a user updates to your latest CD-ROM version.

Setting up an autoplay

An autoplay directs the operating system to launch an application or a document within an application at the time the CD-ROM is read by the system software. You have probably seen autoplays on CDs you have purchased for application software. A window opens and directs you to the installer buttons to install software or browse a CD for the contents. You can create a similar effect by adding your own autoplay to the CD-ROMs you distribute.

For a more professional look, you may want to add a few bells and whistles to your CD-ROM by developing an autoplay, creating a custom icon, and perhaps even searching a hard drive to see whether an Acrobat viewer is installed. Take a look at some of the options available to you for creating an autoplay with some of these features.

Creating an autoplay (Windows)

Autoplays are created differently according to your platform. On the Macintosh you create an autoplay at the time the CD-ROM is written. Autoplay features are available in newer versions of CD-writing software. Not all software is capable of creating an autoplay so be certain to check the features of software before you make a purchase. If you already have software to write CDs and an autoplay feature is not available, you'll need to acquire a new application.

Windows users have more flexibility in adding an autoplay to CDs as you can write a very simple routine to run an autoplay. The method is to create a text file in any text editor and add the following code:

```
[AutoRun]
open=C:\Program Files\Adobe\Acrobat 5.0\Acrobat\Acrobat.exe welcome.pdf
icon=myicon.ico
```

In the code, AutoRun tells the operating system to launch the following lines of code. The line beginning with open= specifies the location of the application and the executable application to be launched. The document name welcome.pdf is the file that opens in an Acrobat viewer (a space separates the executable application name and the document filename).

The last line of code is optional. This line specifies the icon that appears on the CD drive when the CD is inserted in the drive. When you finish writing the code, save the file as text only as *autorun.inf* (be certain to use an .inf extension). Write the text file along with your other files to a CD. When you insert the CD in the CD drive, Acrobat launches the welcome.pdf file.

The aforementioned routine is fine if you're working with your own system and you know you have Acrobat installed and you know the absolute directory path for the application. However, when distributing CDs you won't know the directory path for every user and you won't know whether they have an Acrobat viewer loaded. Thus, your welcome file won't be launched.

You could write all the code necessary to search a user's hard drive for an Acrobat viewer, prompt the user to install an Acrobat viewer if one does not exist, and find a viewer through a search if one does exist. Writing the routine is more complex, but you can write the code in a text editor. Fortunately, there's an easier way.

A number of applications are designed specifically for creating an .inf file based on criteria you supply in dialog boxes. When you finish responding to all the options, the file is written for you. Among the many applications available is GS Technologies AcroPDF Launch 2. This program specifically addresses PDF documents. The product sells for $59.00 in the U.S. A fully functional demonstration version is available for download from the Internet at www.autorun-autoplay-tools.com.

The easy-to-use directions are supplied in dialog boxes you navigate to define the attributes for your autorun file. As you move through the dialog boxes you are prompted to identify files to be included on the CD. You can copy files to the folder from the desktop or add them in the dialog boxes offered by AcroPDF Launch 2. When you move on to the next screen after loading files, you are prompted to identify the file to be used as the launch file when the CD is inserted in the CD drive as shown in Figure 24-3.

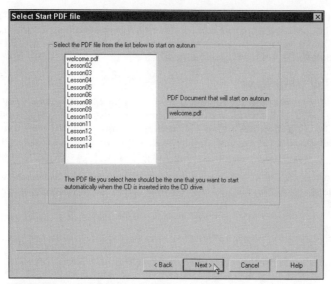

Figure 24-3: A dialog box prompts you to identify the PDF file to be launched by the autorun file. In this example, the file welcome.pdf is selected.

The next dialog box enables you to identify the Adobe Reader installer. If you intend to add the Reader installer, you specify the name of the installer in the dialog box. Figure 24-4 shows the dialog box to acquire the Reader installer and a message that opens to inform a user that the Reader software will be installed. If you want to change the message, edit the text in the field box at the bottom of the dialog box.

When you finish with all the attribute settings, the autorun files are written to the folder where the PDFs are contained that you ultimately copy to the CD-ROM.

An option to include a Flash graphic is also available in the options settings when you create the autorun file. If you elect to use a graphic, it is displayed onscreen and subsequently the PDF identified for launch opens in an Acrobat viewer.

When using a welcome file you can create pop-up menus and file links from the welcome page to all other PDF documents copied to the CD-ROM. Each time a user inserts the CD, the welcome page opens in an Acrobat viewer so there's no room for error, making the PDF navigation easy for any novice user.

Cross-Reference For information on creating pop-up menus and navigating to other PDF files from a central content page, see Chapter 27.

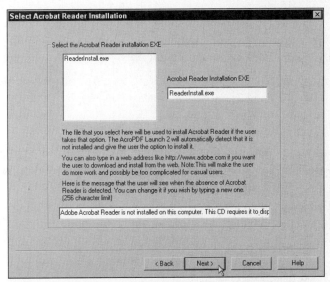

Figure 24-4: You can add the Adobe Reader installer to the autorun file. If autorun does not detect an Acrobat viewer, a dialog box opens, prompting the user to install Adobe Reader from the CD-ROM.

Creating image icons

Many applications are available for creating custom icons you can use for the display of your CD-ROM when it is inserted in the CD drive. Search for *icon maker* or *icon editor* and you can find literally hundreds of utilities for creating custom icons for both Macintosh and Widows systems. On the Macintosh, add a custom icon in the CD-writing application. On Windows you can include the icon in the .inf file as described earlier in the "Creating an autoplay (Windows)" section.

To create an icon for use in Windows without the use of an editor, select a file with the icon you want to use. If you save files from Adobe Photoshop with an Icon Image Preview, the icon is displayed on the file when viewed as icons on the Desktop or within folders. Create a short-cut for the file with the icon and right-click the mouse button on the shortcut to open a con-text menu. Select Properties from the menu options. In the Shortcut to *<filename>* Properties dialog box, click on the button for Change Icon. The Change Icon dialog box opens where you can select a system icon or click on the Browse button to browse your hard drive and find the file to use as the icon. Select the file and click Open in the Change Icon dialog box. The new icon is displayed and ready for use as shown in Figure 24-5. Add the line of code mentioned earlier for creating an autoplay to use the new icon. When you insert the CD-ROM, the CD drive icon changes to your custom icon.

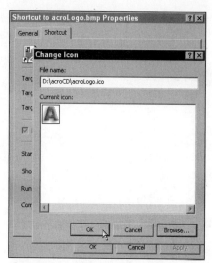

Figure 24-5: Click OK in the Change Icon dialog box and the new icon is ready to be included in the autorun routine.

Adding security to CD-ROMs

Securing PDF documents, whether it be Acrobat Certificate Authority or third-party signature handlers, works great for protecting content in PDF documents and for protecting files from being opened when a user doesn't have access to a password. But what if you want to encrypt files against content copying, changing, and so on and don't want the encrypted documents circulated? Providing a user with a password to open the PDF does not guarantee that your documents won't be distributed along with the password to open them. Something like eBooks might be a good example of where you want to license a single copy of your content to a single user.

We've been around the mill—so to speak—with securing PDF files. Without going into detail, there was a little misunderstanding a few years ago between a Russian company that managed to decrypt some secure files and a few American software development companies. All has been resolved, DRM (Digital Rights Management) has been improved, and hopefully all the wounds have healed.

Who better than a group of Russian engineers and cryptologists to develop sophisticated algorithms to protect PDF documents distributed on CD-ROMs? The company is StarForce (no relation to the company mentioned previously) and the product is PDF Pro 1.1.

Note   Contact the manufacturer at: www.star-force.com in San Francisco, CA, USA; and www.star-force.ru in Moscow, Russia.

PDF Pro 1.1 is a marvelous tool for anyone who wants to license a single copy of PDF documents contained on CD-ROMs. The product was designed especially for publishers and government, corporate, and small business users who want to distribute eBooks, eZines, reports, statistical data, scientific data, and any type of sensitive material that needs to be protected against copying, extraction, modification, and distribution.

The protection of each PDF document incorporates a unique algorithm with encryption. The end user installs the Protection Plug-in that initiates the StarForce PDF protection module each time the user's Adobe Reader application is launched. The plug-in module cannot be used by another user and anyone who attempts to view any of the protected CD-ROM contents is denied access. The behind-the-scenes encryption actually uses the physical parameters of the CD-ROM drive and a unique 24-byte key on each batch of licensed CD-ROMs. StarForce claims that CD-ROMs duplicated from individual users or through plant manufacturing are completely unusable.

If a user tries to access PDF files with other Acrobat viewers or applications supporting imports of PDF documents, the user is likewise denied access. The manufacturer claims the product is effective against any kind of workaround where a user may attempt to extract the content from an encrypted CD-ROM and circulate the data. If your needs include mass-copy protection, this product is worth examining.

Summary

✦ PDF documents are uploaded to Web servers with FTP client applications. Many FTP applications can be purchased as shareware programs for nominal costs.

✦ Any Acrobat view user can use search indexes. Creating a search index is limited to users of the Acrobat Professional software.

✦ Autoplay files help you direct a user to a central navigation page. Autoplay routines are developed with CD-ROM authoring programs, writing scripts, or by using applications designed for the specific purpose of creating autoplays.

✦ Through the use of a third-party application, CD-ROMs can be secured against copying and distributing PDF documents.

✦   ✦   ✦

Acrobat PDF Forms

Understanding the Form Tools

Certainly one of the most popular uses of the Portable Document Format has to be Acrobat PDF forms. As a matter of fact, the creation of PDF forms is so complex that I wrote a book of more than 600 pages dedicated just to creating forms in Acrobat.

Because the PDF format is so widely accepted, people often design forms documents in authoring programs, convert to PDF, and call the end result a PDF form. In a way, these documents might be termed *forms*, but to take full advantage of the power in Acrobat, you need to add live form fields and interactive elements and make your forms more dynamic with tools specifically provided for forms authoring. In this chapter you learn how to create forms with the Forms tools and how to fill-in forms in Acrobat viewers.

Note Creating, modifying, and working with form fields requires the use of Acrobat Professional. Acrobat Standard does not support PDF forms creation or editing.

Setting Up the Environment

Working with PDF forms requires the use of the Forms tools. To open the Forms toolbar, choose Tools ➪ Advanced Editing ➪ Forms ➪ Show Forms Toolbar. The Select Object tool in the Advanced Editing toolbar is an essential tool to use when creating forms in Acrobat 6. To gain access to the tool, open the Advanced Editing toolbar by clicking on the Advanced Editing Task Button or by choosing Tools ➪ Advanced Editing ➪ Show Advanced Editing Toolbar. As a last item, open a context menu on the Toolbar Well and select Properties Bar. When all toolbars are visible in the Document Pane, select Dock All Toolbars from a context menu opened from the Toolbar Well.

In addition to tools, you have available a Fields palette that offers more options for editing forms. By default the Fields palette is hidden. To open the palette, choose View ➪ Navigation Tabs ➪ Fields. The Fields palette opens with two other palettes nested in the same window. Click on the Fields tab and drag it to the Navigation Pane.

After setting up your environment, the toolbars and view should appear something like Figure 25-1. In this figure, I opened a populated form with the Fields palette opened in the Navigation Pane. The Text Field tool is selected to show the Properties Bar options and the text fields on the form.

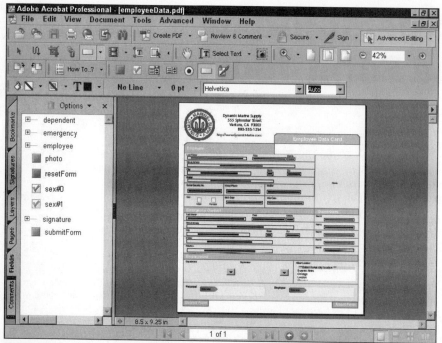

Figure 25-1: Setting up your work environment for creating PDF forms includes showing the Forms toolbar, the Advanced Editing toolbar, and the Properties Bar.

If you plan to engage in a review session for soliciting comments on draft forms, you might want to open the comment toolbars after creating the forms and resetting the toolbar. Creating forms requires a lot of real estate at the top of the Acrobat window and adding the comment tools leaves much less room for editing forms or creating comments. If you need to edit form fields later when you participate in a review, you can use the Select Object tool to modify fields, thereby needing only the Advanced Editing toolbar along with the comment tools.

What Are Acrobat Forms?

Forms in Acrobat are PDF files with data fields that appear as placeholders for user-supplied data. In Acrobat, you can use text string fields, numeric fields, date fields, calculation fields, signature fields, and a variety of custom fields created with JavaScripts. The advantage of using forms in Acrobat is that doing so enables you to maintain design integrity for the appearance of a form while providing you powerful control over data management. Rather than using a database manager, which may limit your ability to control fonts and graphics, Acrobat PDFs preserve all the design attributes of a document while behaving like a data manager.

Forms are created and in Acrobat Professional. Form field data can be saved with Acrobat Standard or with Adobe Reader when used with Adobe Reader Extensions. The Adobe Reader software without Reader Extensions enables you to edit field data, but no provisions exist for saving the edited form, nor do you have an opportunity to export form data without the assistance of plug-ins or server-side programming. In developing PDF workflows for a company or organization, all users expected to design forms in Acrobat need to use the Acrobat Professional software.

The one thing to keep in mind regarding Acrobat and forms is that a form in the context of PDF is not a paper form scanned as an image and saved as PDF. Tons of these so-called forms are around offices and on the Internet. The documents originated as forms, but hopefully by the time you understand all the features available to you with Acrobat, you'll understand these scanned documents could hardly be called forms. Simply put, they're scanned images saved to PDF. The power of Acrobat gives you the tools to create *smart forms*. These forms can be dynamic, intuitive, and interactive, and save both you and the end user much time in providing and gathering information.

Understanding Form Fields

Forms contain different types of data fields that hold data, act as buttons that invoke actions, and call scripts to execute a series of actions. Form fields can assume different appearances as well as possess the capability to include graphic icons and images to represent hot links that invoke actions. Acrobat forms are more than a static data filing system — they can be as vivid and dynamic as your imagination. When designing a form in Acrobat, you are well advised to plan your work ahead of time. As you will see, with the many different choices available for field contents and appearances, creating form fields in Acrobat Professional offers an enormous number of options.

To learn how forms function in Acrobat, you need to understand how forms are developed and, ultimately, how you go about creating form fields. As Acrobat cannot be effectively used as a layout application, nor can it be used to draw rules and design elements, creation of a form begins in another application. You can use illustration or layout software for designing a form that ultimately is converted to PDF. In Acrobat, the form data fields are created with the Form tool, and options are selected from the Field Properties window. Form fields can be of several different types:

 Button: A button is usually used to invoke an action or hyperlink. A button face created as a graphic element in other programs can be applied as an appearance to the button or you can use difference appearance settings in the button properties for adding stroke and fill colors as well as adding text. Buttons are also used to import images.

 Check boxes: Check boxes typically appear in groups to offer the user a selection of choices. Yes and no items or a group of check boxes might be created for multiple-choice selections.

 Combo box: When you view an Acrobat form, you may see a down-pointing arrow similar to the arrows appearing in palette menus. Such an arrow in a PDF form indicates the presence of a combo box. When you click the arrow, a pull-down menu opens with a list of choices. Users are limited to selecting a single choice from combo boxes.

 List box: A list box displays a box with scroll bars, much like windows you see in application software documents. As you scroll through a list box, you make a choice of one or more of the alternatives available by selecting items in the list.

 Radio buttons: Radio buttons perform the same function in PDF forms as radio buttons do in dialog boxes. Usually you have two or more choices for a category. Forms are usually designed so that when one radio button in a group is turned on, the other buttons in the group are turned off.

 Signature fields: Digital signatures can be applied to fields, PDF pages, and PDF documents. A digital signature can be used to lock out fields on a form.

 Text: Text fields are boxes in which text is typed by the end user when filling out the form. Text fields can contain alpha characters, numbers, or a combination of both.

All these form field types are available to you when you create a form in Acrobat. From the end user's point of view, one needs to examine a form and understand how to make choices for the field types in order to accurately complete a form. Fortunately, Acrobat field types relate similarly to the metaphors used by most applications designed with a graphic user interface. An example of an Acrobat form with several form field types is shown in Figure 25-2.

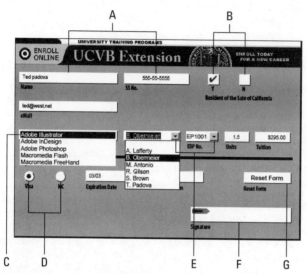

Figure 25-2: Different field types include A) text fields; B) check boxes; C) list box; D) radio buttons; E) combo boxes; F) Digital Signature field; G) button.

Filling in Forms

As you view the form shown in Figure 25-2, notice it contains several text fields, a combo box, a list box, and a least one each of the other field types. To fill out a text field, you need to select the Hand tool, place the cursor over the field, and click the mouse button. When you click, a blinking I-beam cursor appears, indicating text can be added by typing on your keyboard.

Tip   To begin filling in a form, press the Tab key on your keyboard. When the Hand tool is selected and the cursor is not active in any field, pressing the Tab key places the cursor in the first field on the form.

To navigate to the next field for more text entry, you can make one of two choices: Click in the next field or press the Tab key on your keyboard. When you press the Tab key, the cursor jumps to the next field, according to an order you specify in Acrobat when you design the form. Be certain the Hand tool is selected and a cursor appears in a field box when you press the Tab key. If you have any other tool selected, you can tab through the fields and type data in the field boxes; however, if you click with the mouse when another tool is selected, you make edits according to the active tool.

Cross-Reference For understanding more about tab orders, see the section "Setting field tab orders" later in this chapter.

When selecting from choices in radio button or check box fields, click in the radio button or check box. The display changes to show a small solid circle or check mark within a box. When using a combo box, click the down-pointing arrow in the field and select from one of several pull-down menu choices.

Form field navigation keystrokes

As mentioned in the preceding section, to move to the next field, you need to either click in the field or press the Tab key. Following is a list of other keystrokes that can help you move through forms to complete them:

✦ **Shift+Tab:** Moves to the previous field.

✦ **Esc:** Ends text entry.

✦ **Return:** Ends text entry.

✦ **Shift+click:** Ends text entry.

✦ **Double-click a word in a field:** Selects the word.

✦ **Ctrl/⌘+A:** Selects all the text in a field.

✦ **Left/right arrow keys:** Moves the cursor one character at a time left or right.

✦ **Up arrow:** Moves to the beginning of the text field.

✦ **Down arrow:** Moves to the end of the text field.

✦ **Up/down arrow with combo and list boxes selected:** Moves up and down the list. When the list is collapsed, pressing the down-arrow key opens the list.

✦ **Ctrl/⌘+Tab:** Accepts new entry and exits all fields. The next tab places the cursor in the first field.

Setting viewing preferences

If you design forms where fields are not distinguished from background colors by contrasting borders and/or fills, users of all Acrobat viewers can set preferences to show all fields in a high-light color. By default the preference setting for highlights is enabled. If highlights on fields are disturbing or not necessary, you can turn the highlight off in the Preferences dialog box. In Figure 25-3, a form is shown in the Document Pane without the field highlights.

Choose Edit ➪ Preferences (Acrobat Preferences on Macintosh). Click on Forms in the left pane and the forms preference options are shown on the right side of the dialog box. Enable the check box on the right side of the Form preferences where you see Show background, and hover color for form fields. If you want to use a color other than the default highlight color, click on the color swatch below the check box and select a color from the preset options or click on Other Color to add a custom color from the system palette. Click OK in the Preferences dialog box and the form fields appear with a highlight color as shown in Figure 25-4.

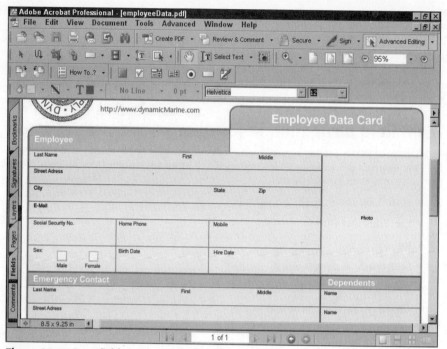

Figure 25-3: Form fields are not visible on this form without showing the field highlights.

Using Auto-Complete features

While filling in a form, you can let Acrobat record common responses you supply in form fields. After recording responses, each time you return to similar fields, the fields are automatically filled in or a list is offered to you for selecting an option for auto-completing fields.

To turn the recording mechanism on, you need to address the Forms preference settings. Open the Preferences dialog box by choosing Edit ➪ Preferences (Acrobat Preferences on Macintosh) and select Forms. In the right pane, open the pull-down menu under the Auto-Complete section of the Forms preferences. You can make menu choices from Off, Basic, and Advanced as shown in Figure 25-5. Selecting Off turns the Auto-Complete feature off. Selecting Basic stores information entered in fields and uses the entries to make relevant suggestions. Select Advanced from the pull-down menu and suggestions are provided from the stored list as you Tab into a field.

By default, numeric data are eliminated from the data stored for the suggestions. If you want to include numeric data for telephone numbers, addresses, and the like, check the Remember numerical data box.

The list grows as you complete forms when either the Basic or Advanced choice is enabled in the pull-down menu. You can examine the list of stored entries by clicking the Edit Entry List button; the Auto-Complete Entry List dialog box opens as shown in Figure 25-6. To remove an item from the list, select it and click on the Remove button. To remove all entries click on the Remove All button.

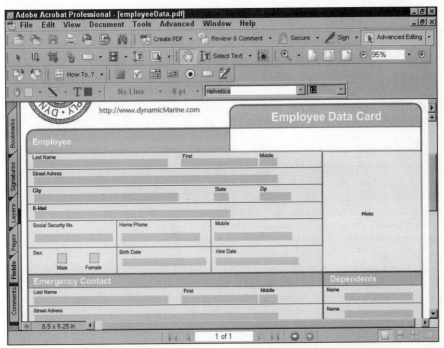

Figure 25-4: Select the check box for showing field highlight colors in the Forms preferences dialog box and all form fields appear with a highlight.

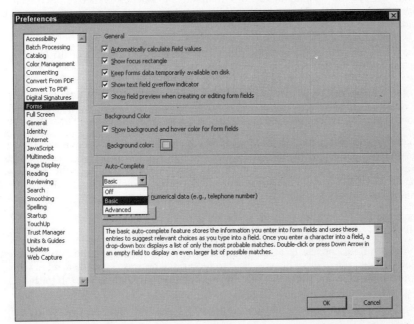

Figure 25-5: Click on Forms in the Preferences dialog box and select Basic or Advanced from the Auto-Complete pull-down menu to use the auto completion feature.

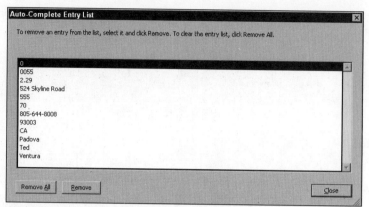

Figure 25-6: To remove entries from your suggestion list, click on the Edit Entry List button in the Forms preferences. Select items in the Auto-Complete Entry List and click on the Remove button.

In order to record entries, you need to first make the selection for using either the Basic or Advanced Auto-Complete feature. To have suggestions for entries submitted as you type in fields, one of the two menu options needs to be enabled. When you select Off in the pull-down menu, both recording entered data and offering suggestions is turned off. To see how the Auto-Complete operation works, follow these steps:

STEPS: Using Auto-Complete

1. **Set preferences.** Open the Preferences dialog box and click on Forms in the left pane. Open the pull-down menu under Auto-Complete and select Advanced from the menu options. Click on the check box to enable adding numeric data to the field entries. Click Close to exit the Preferences dialog box.

Note   If you have any data in your entry list, click on the Edit Entry List and click on the Remove All button to clear the data while performing these steps.

2. **Fill-in a form with your personal identifying information.** You need to create or acquire a form with fields used for name, address, phone, and so on. With the preferences set to Auto-Complete, fill in the data fields as shown in Figure 25-7.

3. **Examine your entry list.** After filling in the data fields, open the Preferences dialog box. If you haven't changed the last preference settings, the Forms preferences should be in view. Click on the Edit Entry List button and examine the entries in the list as shown in Figure 25-8. Click Close in the Auto-Complete Entry List and click Close in the Preferences dialog box.

4. **Save the file.** To keep the entries recorded in the Entry List, choose File ⇨ Save As and save the file under a new name. Close the file.

5. **Type new field entries.** To see the results of your entries and use the Auto-Complete feature, open the original file you used to record the entries. Type in each field the appropriate data and press the Tab key on your keyboard. When you tab to the next

field, the list of probable responses is displayed in a menu as shown in Figure 25-9. Select the correct response for a given field from the list and tab to the next field. Continue selecting responses and tabbing until you complete the form.

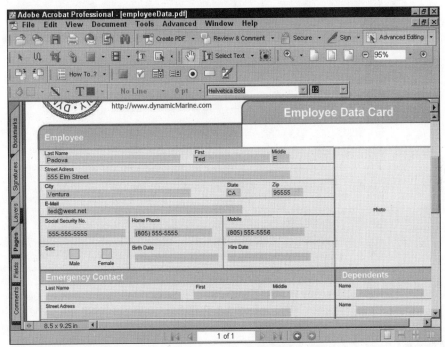

Figure 25-7: Fill in a form to record data for the entry list.

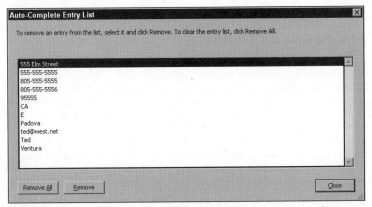

Figure 25-8: Click on the Edit Entry List button in the Forms preferences and examine your list of new entries.

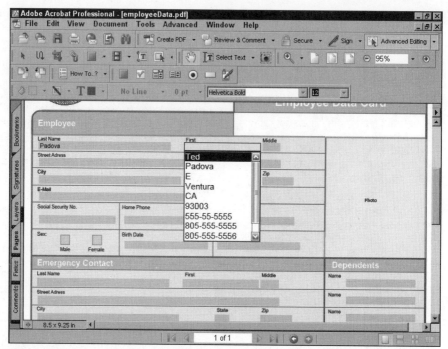

Figure 25-9: Tab to a field, and a list of probable responses is shown. Click on the correct response, and the field is populated from the selection you make in the menu.

Creating Form Fields

Now that you know something about filling out a form, it's time to learn about the attributes associated with each field type in Acrobat Professional. Creating forms in Acrobat begins with a template or PDF document and requires use of the seven Form tools. Users of earlier versions of Acrobat will notice that a single tool for creating the different fields has been replaced with separate tools to create the seven different field types.

To help with precise placement of data fields, you can use Grids and Guides and define attributes in the Preferences dialog box. You set major and minor gridlines in the Units preferences by choosing Edit ➪ Preferences and selecting Units & Guides. Showing a forms grid and snapping to a grid are enabled by selecting the View menu and choosing Grid and Snap to Grid, respectively. When creating forms, showing the forms grid and using the Snap to Grid feature can be helpful. If you are not using the Grid and Snap to Grid views, you can show rulers by choosing View ➪ Rulers and dragging guidelines from the ruler wells.

Cross-Reference
For more information on showing rulers, creating guidelines, and editing guides and grids, see Chapter 3.

All the form field types are created with the different forms tools. Select the tool of choice in the Forms toolbar and draw a rectangle. When the Snap to Forms Grid option is enabled, the rectangle snaps to the gridlines. The moment you release the mouse button after drawing a rectangle, the Field Properties window opens.

Tip   While editing a given field type, you can leave the Properties dialog box open; you don't have to close it to create more fields or edit field properties.

Field properties

The field properties vary according to the field type you create using the field tools. You change field types by creating new fields with your tool of choice. After a field has been created, you don't have an option in Acrobat 6 for changing the field type or assigning attributes that uniquely belong to a different field type. If you want to change a field type, delete the field to be changed and use the tool for the field type you want to create. Users of previous versions of Acrobat will notice that no menu option exists in Acrobat 6 for changing different field types.

When you want to edit fields in Acrobat 6, you select a specific field type with either the form tool used when creating the field or by using the Select Object tool. If you have several field types on a single page and want to modify fields, remember to use the Select Object tool to select fields where a given field's properties need to be edited. If you use the form tools, only form fields respective to the selected tool can be selected on the page. For example, when you're using the Text Field tool, only text fields are selected. If you want to change the attributes of a button field, you need to select the Button Field tool. By using the Select Object tool, you can select all field types and make edits for the selected field properties.

Naming fields

Use the Name item in the General tab (shown in Figure 25-10) for each field type's properties to enter a name for the field. The name that appears here provides a name for the field irrespective of the field contents. By default, Acrobat 6 adds a name for every field created on a page. The default name starts at Text1, Button1, Combo Box1, and so on for the respective field type and adds to the number following the field name as more fields are created. For example, when creating text fields, the names are created as Text1, Text2, Text3, and so on.

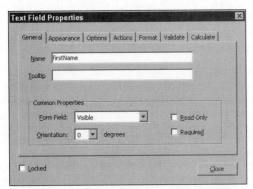

Figure 25-10: The General tab is where field names are added. By default Acrobat supplies a name in the Name field box. You can change the name at the time the field is created or later when editing field properties.

As fields are created (or after the fact), you can edit the default field name supplied by Acrobat. You can provide any name you want to use for the fields. In practice, using an identifier that closely resembles the contents of the field — something such as *First* or *FirstName* for a field where a user's first name is to be typed — is best. You could use any other identifier such as *1*, *F1*, *First Field*, and so on. The name you enter is used to identify the field when data are exported or imported, using JavaScripts, and creating calculations. If you use forms for importing data into other PDF forms, the names of fields play an important role when swapping data. It's critical that you understand the importance of field names and keep naming conventions and case sensitivity consistent among files and applications.

Tip   When naming fields, the most important thing to remember is to be consistent. Case sensitivity is important in regard to importing and exporting data. Always use the same letter case for all fields.

Using proper naming conventions will mean the difference between creating some complex forms in a short time and having them gobble up every one of your waking moments. You can choose to allow Acrobat to name fields automatically or you can name fields by editing the field names in the General tab in the Field Properties. Regardless of which method you use, you need to be aware of the advantages and disadvantages regarding field-naming conventions.

When you supply names to fields with parent/child names, you have much more opportunity to make changes to the field names when duplicating fields and when calculating fields with JavaScripts. A parent/child name contains a root name and a numeric character following the root or subroot name. Fields like total.0, total.1, total.2 or employee.name.last, employee. name.first, and employee.name.middle are examples of field names with parent/child relationships. In the first example you can create calculations on the root name of *total* and use this name in performing calculations and when writing JavaScripts. In the second example you can use the root name *employee* to globally change the name by changing just the parent name.

If you leave the default names provided by Acrobat as Text1, Text2, Text3, and so on the names do not contain parent/child relationships. Creating calculations or writing JavaScripts requires you to identify all field names in the calculation or script as opposed to using only a parent name. If you add 10, 20, or more fields that need to be calculated, the calculation or script requires more time because each field needs to be identified individually in the calculation or script.

ToolTip

As previously stated, the Name item in the Field Properties window identifies a particular field and plays an important part in importing and exporting form data. You must use a field name when creating fields. Tooltip, located beneath the Name field, is optional. When you add text to this field, the text you supply appears as a ToolTip when the mouse cursor hovers over the field. The Tooltip field is helpful to users when completing forms. For example, you could name a field *name.1* that you want to be the field in which users type a first name. In the Tooltip field, enter the text *First Name*. When a user moves the cursor over the field box, First Name appears as a ToolTip. As the mouse cursor moves over fields, ToolTips change to the short description added in the Tooltip field box.

Note When creating accessible forms for documents read by screen readers, be certain to provide descriptive names for tool tips. Screen readers read the text in the tool tip and can be helpful to people with vision challenges understand your forms. For more information on creating accessible documents and understanding screen readers, see Chapter 18.

Common Properties

The seven field types have the same attribute choices for Common Field Properties. Four item choices are available in the Common Properties section of the General tab of the Text Field Properties dialog box shown in Figure 25-10. The options include

✦ **Form Field:** From the pull-down menu you have choices for visibility onscreen and when printing fields. By default the choice is Visible. The Hidden menu item hides a field from view onscreen and when printing the form. Visible but Doesn't Print shows the field onscreen but the field and its contents are not printed. The last item, Hidden but printable, hides the field onscreen but the field and its contents are printed.

✦ **Orientation:** A field and a field's contents can be rotated in 90-degree rotations. By default fields are at a 0 (zero)-degree rotation. Select from 90, 180, and 270 to rotate fields in fixed rotations.

✦ **Read Only:** When a field is marked as Read Only, the field is not editable. The user is locked out of the field. Use of a Read Only field might be something you use to show fixed price costs where you don't want users changing a fixed purchase price on an order form. Another example is a value that is pre-populated from a database.

✦ **Required:** If a field needs to be filled in before the data is submitted, check the Required box.

In the General tab of the properties dialog box for each field type are two additional items. The check box for Locked appears on all tabs for all field types. Check this box to lock a field position on a page. When a field is locked, the field sizing, movement, and attributes cannot be changed. Disable the Locked check box to edit, move, or resize a field.

The Close button in all field properties dialog boxes close the dialog box. Notice that the button is not an OK button. Clicking the Close button simply eliminates the dialog box from view. Clicking on Close is not required to change values for any field properties. The changes are dynamic and are made as you work through the options among the various tabs.

Appearance

The Appearance tab relates to form field appearances. The rectangle links you draw can be assigned border colors and content fills. The text added to a field box or default text you use for a field can be assigned different fonts, font sizes, and font colors. These options exist in the Appearance properties for all field types. Figure 25-11 shows the Appearance properties for a selected text field.

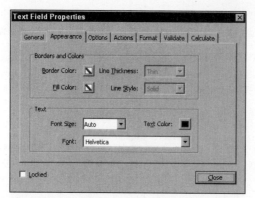

Figure 25-11: Click on the Appearance tab for any field properties and make choices for the appearance of fields and text.

The Appearance options include the following:

✦ **Border Color:** The keyline created for a field is made visible with a rectangular border assigned by clicking on the Border Color swatch and choosing a color.

✦ **Background Color:** The field box can be assigned a background color. If you want the field box displayed in a color, enable this option, click the color swatch next to it, and choose a color the same way you do for the borders. When the check box is disabled, the background appears transparent.

✦ **Line Thickness:** Options are the same as those available for link rectangles. Select the pull-down menu and choose from Thin, Medium, or Thick. The pull-down menu is grayed out unless you first select a Border Color.

✦ **Line Style:** You can choose from five style types from the pull-down menu. The Solid option shows the border as a keyline at the width specified in the Width setting. Dashed shows a dashed line; Beveled appears as a box with a beveled edge; Inset makes the field look recessed, and Underline eliminates the keyline and shows an underline for the text across the width of the field box. See Figure 25-12 for an example of these style types.

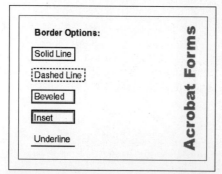

Figure 25-12: Five choices for a border style are available in the Appearance tab when selecting from the Line Style pull-down menu.

✦ **Font Size:** Depending on the size of the form fields you create, you may have a need to choose a different point size for the text. The default is Auto, which automatically adjusts point sizes according to the height of the field box. Choices are available for manually setting the point size for text ranges between 2 and 300 points.

✦ **Text Color:** If you identify a color for text by selecting the swatch adjacent to Text Color, the field contents supplied by the end user change to the selected color.

✦ **Font:** From the pull-down menu, select a font for the field data. All the fonts installed in your system are accessible from the pull-0down menu. When designing forms for screen displays, try to use sans serif fonts for better screen views.

Note   When designing forms for cross-platform use, use one of the Base Fonts. Custom fonts loaded in your system may not be available to other users. Base Fonts appear at the top of the font list and are separated from the fonts installed on your system with a space between the Base Fonts and your system fonts. For more information about Base Fonts, see Chapter 7.

The Appearance settings are identical for all field types except Digital Signature fields, Radio Button fields, and Check Box fields. The latter two field types use fixed fonts for displaying characters in the field box. Choices for what characters are used are made in the Options tab. When creating Radio Button and Check Box fields you don't have a choice for Font in the Appearance properties. By default, the AdobePi font is used.

Options

The Options tab provides selections for specific attributes respective to the type of fields you add to a page. Options are available for all fields except the Digital Signatures field. Options tab attributes for the other six field types include options for text, radio buttons, combo and list boxes, and buttons.

Text options

When you use the Text Field tool to create a field and you click on the Options tab, the Properties window appears as shown in Figure 25-13.

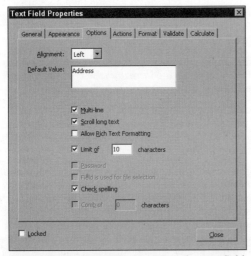

Figure 25-13: The Options settings for Text field properties.

Each of the following attribute settings is optional when creating text fields:

✦ **Alignment:** The Alignment pull-down menu has two functions. First, any text entered in the Default field is aligned according to the option you specify from the pull-down menu choices. Alignment choices include Left, Center, and Right. Second, regardless of whether text is used in the Default field, when the end user fills out the form the cursor is positioned at the alignment selected from the pull-down menu choices. Therefore, if you select Center from the Alignment options, the text entered when filling out the form is centered within the field box.

✦ **Default Value:** The Default Value field can be left blank or you can enter text that appears in the field when viewing the form. The Default item has nothing to do with the name of the field. This option is used to provide helpful information when the user fills out the form data. If no text is entered in the Default field, when you return to the form, the field appears empty. If you enter text in the Default field, the text you enter appears inside the field box and can be deleted, edited, or replaced.

✦ **Multi-line:** If your text field contains more than one line of text, select the Multi-line option. When you press the Return key after entering a line of text, the cursor jumps to the second line where additional text is added to the same field. Multi-line text fields might be used, for example, as an address field to accommodate a second address line.

✦ **Scrolling long text:** If Multi-line is selected and text entries exceed the height of the field, you may want to add scroll bars to the field. Enable the check box to permit users to scroll lines of text. If the check box is disabled, users won't be able to scroll, but as text is added, automatic scrolling accommodates the amount of text typed in the field.

✦ **Allow Rich Text Formatting:** When you check this box, users can style text with bold, italic, and bold italic font styles. You may want to enable the checkbox if you want users to emphasize a field's contents.

✦ **Limit of [ ] characters:** The box for this option provides for user character limits for a given field. If you want the user to add a state value of two characters, for example, check the box and type 2 in the field box. If the user attempts to go beyond the limit, a system warning beep alerts the user that no more text can be added to the field.

✦ **Password:** When this option is enabled, all the text entered in the field appears as a series of asterisks when the user fills in the form. The field is not secure in the sense that you must have a given password to complete the form; it merely protects the data entry from being seen by an onlooker.

✦ **Field is used for file selection:** This option permits you to specify a file path as part of the field's value. The file is submitted along with the form data. Be certain to enable the Scrolling long text option described earlier in this list to enable this option.

✦ **Check spelling:** Spell checking is available for comments and form fields. When the check box is enabled, the field is included in a spell check. This can be helpful so the spell checker doesn't get caught up with stopping at proper names, unique identifiers, and abbreviations that may be included in those fields.

✦ **Comb of [ ] characters:** This is a great new addition in Acrobat 6 for users designing forms with comb fields. When you create a text field box and enable this check box, Acrobat automatically creates a text field box with subdivision lines according to the value you supply in the Characters field box. Be certain to disable all other check boxes. You can set the alignment of the characters by making a choice from the alignment pull-down menu, but all other check boxes need to be disabled to access the Comb of check box. In Figure 25-14, I created a comb field center aligned with eight characters. Notice the subdivision lines added to the text field box.

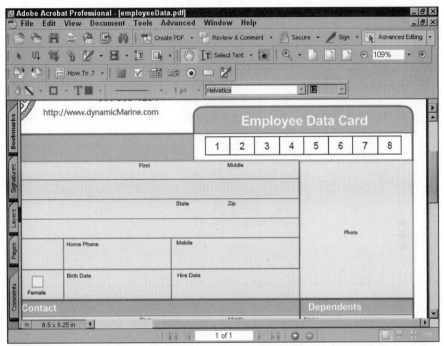

Figure 25-14: By enabling the Comb of [ ] characters check box and adding the number of characters, a single field box is created with subdivision lines.

Note   Comb fields are limited to single characters. If you need to create comb fields where two characters are contained in each subdivision, you need to create separate field boxes for each pair of characters.

Check box and radio button options

Check boxes and radio buttons have similar Options attribute choices. When you select either field and click on the Options tab, the settings common to both field types include

✦ **Button/Check Box Style:** If a radio button is selected, the title is Button Style. If the field is a check box, the title is listed as Check Box Style as shown in Figure 25-15. From the pull-down menu, you select the style you want to use for the check mark inside the radio button or check box field.

✦ **Export Value:** When creating either a check box or radio button, use the same field name for all fields in a common group where you want one check box enabled while all the other check boxes or radio buttons are disabled in the same group. To distinguish the fields from each other, add an export value that differs in each field box. You can use export values like Yes and No or other text, or number values like 1, 2, 3, 4, and so on.

The creation of radio buttons and check boxes on Acrobat forms has been confusing to many users and users often inappropriately create workarounds for check boxes and radio buttons to toggle them on and off. To help eliminate confusion, notice the Options properties in Figure 25-16 includes a help message informing you to name fields the same name but use different export values.

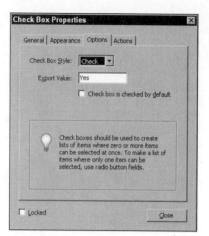

Figure 25-15: You can choose various options for radio buttons and check boxes, including those for the style of the check marks or radio buttons.

✦ **Button/Check box is checked by default:** If you want a default value to be applied for either field type, like Yes for example, enter the export value and check the box to make the value the default.

As you can see in Figure 25-16, an additional option is made available in the Radio Button Options properties.

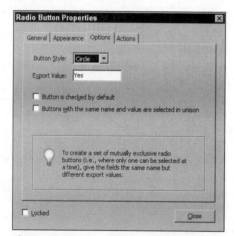

Figure 25-16: An additional option for radio buttons differs from the check box options.

✦ **Buttons with the same name and value are selected in unison:** As an extra item to help users avoid confusion when creating radio buttons, by default Acrobat 6 radio buttons toggle on and off companion buttons with the same name regardless of what export value you provide. Therefore, you don't need separate export values when you click on one field to disable another field with an exact name. If, for some reason, you want all radio buttons with the same name to be enabled when you click on one of the fields, check this option.

In the Options tab for the check boxes or radio buttons, use the Check box/Button is checked by default item to place a mark in all data fields by default. When the user fills out a form, she or he needs to click a check box or radio button field to toggle the check mark on and off. Among the different marks applied to the field boxes are six different characters shown in Figure 25-17.

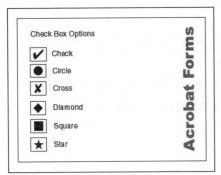

Figure 25-17: Six icon options are available for check boxes and radio buttons.

Combo box and list box options

Combo boxes enable you to create form fields with a list of selections appearing in a pull-down window. The user completing a form makes a selection from the menu items. If all items are not visible, the menu contains scroll bars made visible after selecting the down-pointing arrow to open the menu. A list box is designed as a scrollable window with an elevator bar and arrows like you see in authoring application documents as shown in Figure 25-18.

The two field types differ in several ways. First, combo boxes require less space for the form field. The combo box menu drops down from a narrow field height where the menu options are shown. List boxes require more height to make them functional to the point where at least two or three options are in view before the user attempts to scroll the window. Second, you can select only one menu option from a combo box. List boxes enable users to select multiple items. Finally, combo boxes can be designed for users to add text for a custom choice by editing any of the menu items. List boxes provide no option for users to type text in the field box and the menu items are not editable.

The data exported with the file include the selected item from the combo boxes and all selected items for list boxes. The item choices and menu designs for the field types are created in the Options tab for the respective field type. Attributes for list boxes, shown in Figure 25-19, are also available for combo boxes. The options include

✦ **Item:** The name of an entry you want to appear in the scrollable list is entered in the Item field.

✦ **Export Value:** When the data are exported, the name entered in this field box is the exported value. If the field is left blank, the exported value is the name used in the item description typed in the Item field. If you want different export values than the name descriptions, type a value in this field box. As an example, suppose you created a consumer satisfaction survey form. In that form, the user can choose from list items such as Very Satisfied, Satisfied, and Unsatisfied, and you've specified the export values for these items to be 1, 2, and 3, respectively. When the data are analyzed, the frequency of the three items would be tabulated and defined in a legend as 1=Very Satisfied, 2=Satisfied, and 3=Unsatisfied.

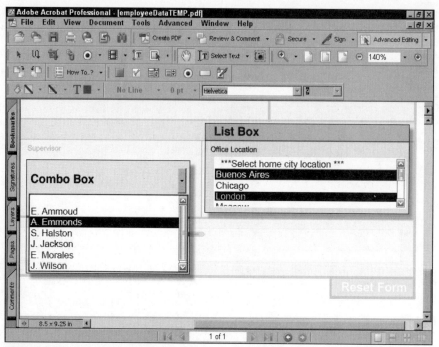

Figure 25-18: The combo box items are viewed by selecting the down arrow. After opening the menu the scrollbars are made visible. List boxes enable users to select multiple items in the scrollable window.

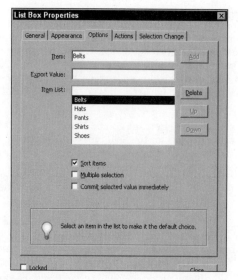

Figure 25-19: The Options settings for list boxes have common properties also found in combo boxes.

✦ **Add:** After the Item and Export Values are entered, click the Add button to place the item in the Item List. After adding an item, you can return to the Item field and type a new item in the field box and, in turn, a new export value.

✦ **Delete:** If an item has been added to the list and you want to delete it, first select the item in the list. Click the Delete button to remove it from the list.

✦ **Up/Down:** Items are placed in the list according to the order in which they are entered. The order displayed in the list is shown in the combo box or list box when you return to the document page. If you want to reorganize items, select the item in the list and click the Up or Down button to move one level up or down, respectively. To enable the Up and Down buttons, the Sort Items option must be disabled.

✦ **Sort items:** When checked, the list is alphabetically sorted in ascending order. As new items are added to the list, the new fields are dynamically sorted while the option is enabled.

✦ **Multiple selection (List box only):** Any number of options can be selected by using modifier keys and clicking on the list items. Use Shift+click for contiguous selections and Ctrl/⌘+click for non-contiguous selections. This option applies only to list boxes.

✦ **Commit selected value immediately:** The choice made in the field box is saved immediately. If the check box is disabled, the choice is saved after the user exits the field by tabbing out or clicking the mouse cursor on another field.

With the exception of the multiple selection item, the preceding options are also available for combo boxes. In addition to these options, combo boxes offer two more items as shown in Figure 25-20.

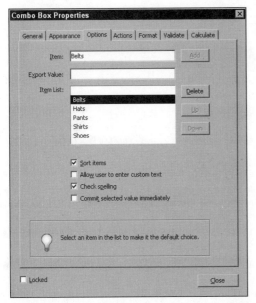

Figure 25-20: The Options settings for combo boxes also include custom field editing and spell checking.

✦ **Allow user to enter custom text:** The items listed in the Options tab are fixed in the combo·box on the Acrobat form by default. If this check box is enabled, the user can edit all items in the list. Acrobat makes no provision for some items to be edited and others locked out from editing.

✦ **Check spelling:** Spell checking is performed when the list items have been added to the field and when a user edits an item and types in new text.

Button options

Buttons differ from all other fields when it comes to appearance. You can create and use custom icons for button displays from PDF documents or file types compatible with Convert to PDF from File. Rather than entering data or toggling a data field, buttons typically execute an action. You might use a button to clear a form, export data, import data from a data file, or use buttons as navigation links. When a button is added to a page, the Options tab attributes change to those shown in Figure 25-21.

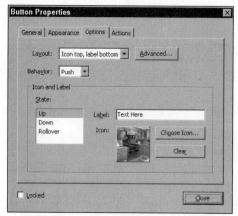

Figure 25-21: The Options tab for the Button field properties includes options for button face displays and several different mouse behaviors.

When you create a button, you make choices from the Options tab for the highlight view of the button, the behavior of the mouse cursor, and the text and icon views. The Options attributes for buttons are as follows:

✦ **Layout:** Several views are available for displaying a button with or without a label, which you add in the Label field described later in this list. The choices from the pull-down menu for Layout offer options for displaying a button icon with text appearing at the top, bottom, left, right side of the icon, or over the icon. Figure 25-22 shows the different Layout options.

✦ **Behavior:** The Behavior options affect the appearance of the button when the button is clicked. The None option specifies no highlight when the button is clicked. Invert momentarily inverts the colors of the button when clicked. Outline displays a keyline border around the button, and Push makes the button appear to move in on Mouse Down and out on Mouse Up.

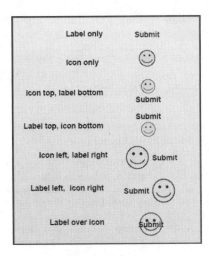

Figure 25-22: The Layout options include Label only; Icon only; Icon top, label bottom; Label top, icon bottom; Icon left, label right; Label left, icon right; and Label over icon.

✦ **Icon and Label State:** Three choices in the list are available when you select Push in the Behavior pull-down menu. Up displays the highlight action when the mouse button is released. Down displays the highlight action when the mouse button is pressed. Rollover offers an option to use a second icon. When the mouse cursor moves over the button without clicking, the image changes to the second icon you choose — much like a rollover effect you see on Web pages.

✦ **Label:** Type text in the field box for the label you want to use. Labels are shown when one of the options for the layout includes a label view with or without the icon.

✦ **Choose Icon:** When an icon is used for a button display, click Choose Icon to open the Select Icon dialog box. In the Select Icon dialog box, use a Browse button to open a navigation dialog box where you locate a file to select for the button face. The file can be a PDF document or a file compatible with converting to PDF from within Acrobat. The size of the file can be as small as the actual icon size or a letter-size page or larger. Acrobat automatically scales the image to fit within the form field rectangle drawn with the Button tool. When you select an icon, it is displayed as a thumbnail in the Select Icon dialog box like the thumbnail shown in Figure 25-23.

Figure 25-23: After clicking the Browse button and opening a file, the image is shown as a thumbnail in the Select Icon dialog box.

Tip

An icon library can be easily created from drawings using a font such as Zapf Dingbats or Wingdings or patterns and drawings from an illustration program. Create or place images on several pages in a layout application. Distill the file to create a multiple-page PDF document. When you select an icon to use for a button face, the Select Icon dialog box enables you to scroll pages in the document. You view each icon in the Sample window as a thumbnail of the currently selected page. When the desired icon is in view, click the OK button. The respective page is used as the icon.

✦ **Clear:** You can eliminate a selected icon by clicking the Clear button. Clear eliminates the icon without affecting any text you added in the Layout field box.

✦ **Advanced:** Notice the Advanced button at the top of the Options tab. Clicking the Advanced button opens the Icon Placement dialog box, shown in Figure 25-24, where you select attributes related to scaling an icon. You can choose from icon scaling for Always, Never, When the icon is too big to fit in the form field, or When the icon is too small to fit in the form field. The Scale option offers choices between Proportional and Non-proportional scaling. Click Fit to bounds to ensure the icon placement fits to the bounds of the field rectangle. Sliders provide a visual scaling reference for positioning the icon within a field rectangle.

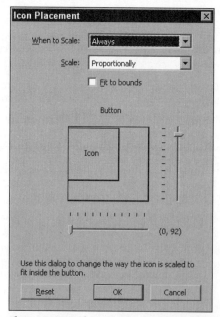

Figure 25-24: The Icon Placement dialog box offers options for positioning and scaling icons.

Actions

The Actions tab, shown in Figure 25-25, enables you to set an action for any one of the seven field types; the attribute choices are identical for all fields.

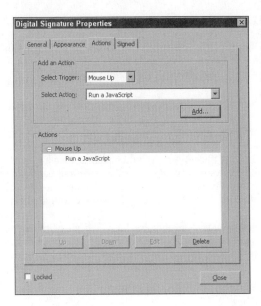

Figure 25-25: The Actions tab provides options for invoking an action from a trigger mouse behavior you choose from pull-down menu options in the dialog box.

From the Select Trigger pull-down menu, you make choices for different mouse behaviors that are assigned to invoke the action. From the menu options you have choices for

✦ **Mouse Up:** When the user releases the mouse button, the action is invoked.

✦ **Mouse Down:** When the user presses the mouse button, the action is invoked.

✦ **Mouse Enter:** When the user moves the mouse cursor over the field, the action is invoked.

✦ **Mouse Exit:** When the user moves the mouse cursor away from the field, the action is invoked.

✦ **On Focus:** Specifies moving into the field boundaries through mouse movement or by tabbing to the field. As the cursor enters the field, the action is invoked.

✦ **On Blur:** Specifies moving away from the field boundaries through mouse movement or by tabbing to the field. As the cursor exits the field, the action is invoked.

Actions assigned to the cursor movements are similar to those in the context of creating links. You first select the trigger, and then select an action type from the Select Action pull-down menu. Click the Add button to add the action to the Actions list.

Cross-Reference For more information on mouse behaviors and actions, see Chapter 15.

The action is assigned to the mouse cursor option when you click Add. The default is Mouse Up. When Mouse Up is selected, the action is invoked when the mouse button is released.

Caution Trigger choices other than Mouse Up may sometimes complicate filling in form fields for end users. Just about any program dealing with link buttons has adopted the Mouse Up response to invoke an action. Many users often click down, think about what they are doing, and then move the mouse away without releasing the button. This behavior enables the user to change his/her mind at the last minute. If you deviate from the adopted standard, it might be annoying for a user.

When you click the Add button, a dialog box specific to the action type you are adding opens. The actions listed in this dialog box are the same as those in the Link Properties dialog box discussed in Chapter 15. Turn back to Chapter 15 for examples of how the following action types work. A few of the more important action types used with form fields include importing form data, resetting a form, submitting a form, and showing and hiding a field.

Importing form data

You can export the raw data from a PDF file as a Form Data File (FDF) that can later be imported into other PDF forms. To import data, you use a menu command, a JavaScript, or use the Execute Menu Item action and select the Import Forms Data command. Rather than retyping the data in each form, you can import the same field data into new forms where the field names match exactly. Therefore, if a form contains field names such as First, Last, Address, City, State, and so on, all common field names from the exported data can be imported into the current form. Those field names without exact matches are ignored by Acrobat.

The Import Form Data command enables you to develop forms for an office environment or Web server where the same data can easily be included in several documents. When designing forms, using the same field names for all common data is essential. If you import data and some fields remain blank, recheck your field names. Any part of a form design or action can be edited to correct errors.

Resetting a form

This action is handy for forms that need to be cleared of data and resubmitted. When the Reset a form action is invoked, data fields specified for clearing data when the field was added are cleared. When you select Reset a form and click the Add button, the Reset Form dialog box opens. You make choices in this dialog box for what fields you want to clear. Click on the Select All button and all data fields are cleared when a user clicks on the button you assign with a Reset a form action. When you use this action, associating it with Mouse Up to prevent accidental cursor movements that might clear the data and require the user to begin over again is best. Reset a form can also be used with a Page Action command. If you want a form to be reset every time the file is opened, the latter may be a better choice than creating a button.

For more information on using Page Actions, see Chapter 27.

Submitting a form

Form data can be e-mailed or submitted to Web servers. You can design forms so users of the Adobe Reader software can submit data via e-mail or to Web servers when the PDF is viewed as an inline view in a Web browser. When using the Submit a form action, you have access to option choices for the type of data format you want to submit.

For more information on submitting form data, see Chapter 26. For more information on viewing PDFs as inline views in Web browsers, see Chapter 20.

Showing/hiding a field

You'll find many uses for the Show/hide a field action type. You may want to set up conditional responses in which a user answers a question, and based on the answer, another field is made visible. Or you may want to add some help information where a user can click on a

Acrobat's Data Search

When a data file is identified for an import action, Acrobat looks to the location you specified when creating the action. Acrobat also searches other directories for the data. On the Macintosh, Acrobat looks to the Reader and Acrobat User Data directories for the data file. On Windows, Acrobat looks to the Acrobat directory, Reader directory, current directory, and the Windows directory. If Acrobat cannot find the data file, a dialog box opens containing a Browse button to prompt the user to locate the data file.

button to show a field containing a description to help the user complete the form. These actions occur with showing fields that are hidden when you select Hidden in the field General tab and create a button to show the hidden field(s). From a dialog box, you select what fields are to be made visible.

Format

The tabs General, Appearance, and Actions are available for all field types. Option attributes are available for all field types except digital signatures. The options vary significantly depending on which field type is used. For a quick glance at the tab differences according to field type, take a look at Table 25-1.

As shown in Table 25-1, the Format, Validate, and Calculate tab options are only available for Combo Box and Text field types. To access the Format tab, select either of these field types. The Format options are the same for both field types.

When you click the Format tab, you'll find a pull-down menu for selecting a format category. To define a format, open the Select format category and choose from the menu choices the format you want to assign to the Text or Combo Box field. As each item is selected, various options pertaining to the selected category appear directly below the pull-down menu. When you select Number from the menu choices, the Number Options appear as shown in Figure 25-26.

The Select format category menu options include

+ **None:** No options are available when None is selected. Select this item if no formatting is needed for the field. An example of where None applies would be a text field where you want text data like name, address, and so on.

+ **Number:** When you select Number, the Number Options choices appear below the Select format category pull-down menu. The options for displaying numeric fields include defining the number of decimal places, indicating how the digits are separated (for example, by commas or by decimal points), and specifying any currency symbols. The Negative Number Style check boxes enable you to display negative numbers with parentheses and/or red text.

+ **Percentage:** The number of decimal places you want to display for percentages is available when you select Percentage from the pull-down menu. The options are listed for number of decimal places and the separator style.

+ **Date:** The date choices offer different selections for month, day, year, and time formats.

+ **Time:** If you want to eliminate the date and identify only time, the Time category enables you to do so, offering choices to express time in standard and 24-hour units and a custom setting where custom formats are user-prescribed in a field box.

✦ **Special:** The Special category offers formatting selections for Social Security number, Zip code, extended Zip codes, phone numbers, and an arbitrary mask. When you select Arbitrary Mask, a field box is added where you define the mask. The acceptable values for setting up an arbitrary mask include

- **A:** Add *A* to the arbitrary mask field box and only the alpha characters A–Z and a–z are acceptable for user input.

- **X:** When you add *X* to the arbitrary mask field box, most printable characters from an alphameric character set are acceptable. ANSI values between 32–166 and 128–255 are permitted. (To learn more about what ANSI character values 32–166 and 128–255 are translated to, search the Internet for ANSI character tables. You can capture Web pages and use the tables as reference guides.)

- **O:** The letter *O* accepts all alpha and numeric characters (A–Z, a–z, and 0–9).

- **9:** If you want the user to be limited to filling in numbers only, enter *9* in the Arbitrary Mask field box.

✦ **Custom:** Custom formatting is available by using a JavaScript. To edit the JavaScript code, click the Edit button and create a custom format script. The JavaScript Editor dialog box opens where you type the code. As an example of using a custom JavaScript, assume that you want to add leading zeros to field numbers. You might create a JavaScript with the following code:

```
event.value = "000" + event.value;
```

The preceding code adds three leading zeros to all values supplied by the end user who completes the form field. If you want to add different characters as a suffix or prefix, enter the values you want within the quotation marks. To add a suffix, use

```
event.value = event.value + "000";
```

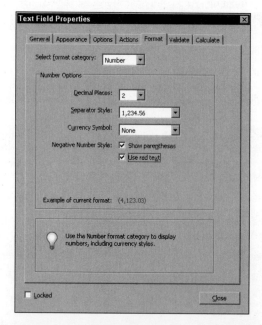

Figure 25-26: When you choose either Combo Box or Text as the field type, you can select data format options from the Format tab.

Validate

Validate helps ensure proper information is added on the form. If a value must be within a certain minimum and maximum range, check the radio button for validating the data within the accepted values (see Figure 25-27). The field boxes are used to enter the minimum and maximum values. If the user attempts to enter a value outside the specified range, a warning dialog box opens, informing the user that the values entered on the form are unacceptable.

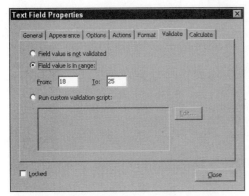

Figure 25-27: Validate is used with Combo Box and Text field types to ensure acceptable responses from user-supplied values.

Selecting the Run custom validation script radio button and clicking on the Edit button enables you to add a JavaScript. Scripts that you may want to include in this window would be those for validating comparative data fields. A password, for example, may need to be validated. If the response does not meet the condition, the user is denied access to supply information in the field.

Calculate

The Calculate tab in the Field Properties window enables you to calculate two or more data fields. You can choose from preset calculation formulas or add a custom JavaScript for calculating fields as shown in Figure 25-28.

The preset calculation formulas are limited to addition, multiplication, averaging, assessing the minimum in a range of fields, and assessing the maximum in a range of fields. For all other calculations you need to select the Custom calculation script radio button and click on the Edit button. In the JavaScript Editor you write JavaScripts to perform other calculations not available from the preset formulas.

Cross-Reference   For more information on calculating data, see Chapter 26.

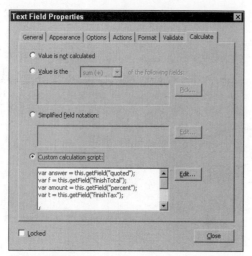

Figure 25-28: The Calculate tab offers options for calculating fields for summing data, multiplying data, and finding the average, minimum, and maximum values for selected fields. In addition, you can add custom calculations by writing JavaScripts.

Selection Change

The Selection Change tab shown in Figure 25-29 is only available for List Box fields. If a list box item is selected, and then a new item from the list is selected, JavaScript code can be programmed to execute an action when the change is made. Like the other dialog boxes, clicking the Edit button opens the JavaScript Editor dialog box where you create the JavaScript code.

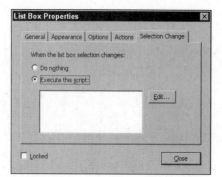

Figure 25-29: The Selection Change tab is available only for List Box fields. When using a Selection Change option, you'll need to program JavaScript code to reflect the action when a change in selection occurs.

A variety of uses exist for the Selection Change option. You might want to create a form for consumer responses for a given product — something such as an automobile. Depending on information preceding the list box selection, some options may not be available. For example, a user specifies "four-door automobile" as one of the form choices, and then from a list, that user selects "convertible." If the manufacturer does not offer a convertible for four-door automobiles, then through use of a JavaScript in the Selection Change tab, the user is informed that this selection cannot be made based on previous information supplied in the form. The displayed warning could include information on alternative selections that can be made.

Signature fields

The Digital Signature Field tool enables you to create a field used for electronically signing a document with a digital signature. The Signed tab offers options for behavior with digital signatures as follows:

+ **Nothing happens when signed:** As the item description suggests, the field is signed but no action will take place upon signing.

+ **Mark as read-only:** When signed, the selected fields are changed to read-only fields, locking them against further edits. You can mark all fields by selecting the radio button and choosing All fields from the pull-down menu. Choose All fields except these to isolate a few fields not marked for read-only, or select Just these fields to mark a few fields for read-only.

+ **This script executes when field is signed:** Select the radio button and click on the Edit button to open the JavaScript Editor. You write a script in the JavaScript Editor that executes when the field is signed.

Digital signatures may appear as secured data fields. They can also be used to indicate approval from users or PDF authors or you may want to display a message after a user signs a form. In Figure 25-30, a JavaScript was added to the Digital Signature Signed Properties.

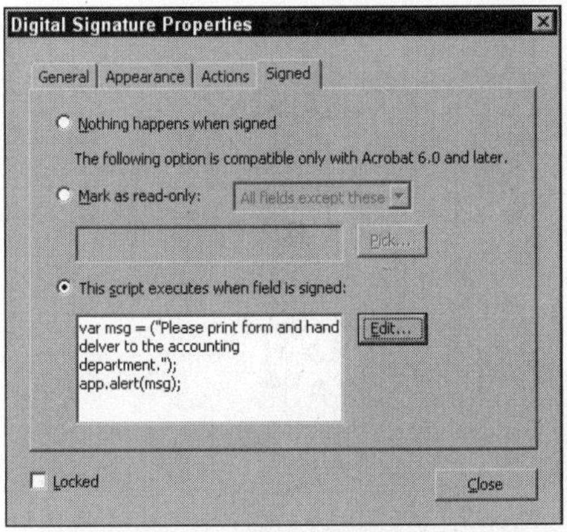

Figure 25-30: For custom actions when a user signs a form, use a JavaScript.

The script in this example instructs a user to print the form and hand-deliver it to the accounting department. The dialog box (shown in Figure 25-31) opens after the user signs the form.

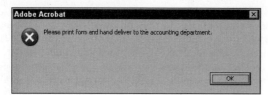

Figure 25-31: The custom JavaScript is written to open a dialog box containing a message after the form is signed.

Cross-Reference For setting up digital signatures and understanding more related to signing documents, see Chapter 19.

Table 25-1: Tab Options for Field Types in the Field Properties Window

Field Type	Appearance	Options	Actions	Format	Validate Change	Calculate	Selection Change	Signed
Button	X	X	X					
Check box	X	X	X					
Combo box	X	X	X	X	X	X		
List box	X	X	X				X	
Radio button	X	X	X					
Signature	X	X	X					X
Text	X	X	X	X	X	X		

Using the Properties Bar

Many of the appearance attributes you apply in the Field Properties Appearance settings you can also apply with the Properties Bar. The Properties Bar can be used if the Field Properties window is either opened or closed. As a matter of standard practice, you'll often use the Properties Bar while the Field Properties window is closed. Notwithstanding the options excluded for font selection with check boxes and radio buttons, the options in the Properties Bar are identical for all form tools.

The options available to you include changing field appearances and text. You can make selections for field fills and strokes, line widths, font selection, and font point sizes. To make an appearance change on a field, select the field with the Select Object tool. Make appearance and font changes by clicking on buttons in the Properties Bar or making selections from pull-down menus.

Editing fields

For purposes of explanation, I'll use the term *editing fields* to mean dealing with field duplication, deleting fields, and modifying field attributes. After a field is created on a PDF page, you may want to alter its size, position, or attributes. Editing form fields in Acrobat Professional is made possible by using one of several menu commands or returning to the respective Field Properties window.

To edit a form field's properties, use the Select Object tool or the form tool for the respective field type and double-click the field rectangle. The Properties window opens after double-clicking with either tool. You can also use a context-sensitive menu opened from using either tool and clicking on the form field to be edited. At the bottom of the context-sensitive menu, select the Properties command as shown in Figure 25-32.

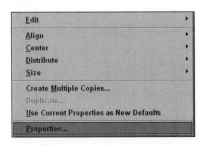

Figure 25-32: Double-click on a field with either the Select Object tool or the tool used to create the field, or open a context menu from the selected field with either tool and choose Properties from the menu options to open the Field Properties.

To select multiple fields you must use the Select Object tool if you want to select fields of different types. If the same field types are selected, you can use the tool that was used to originally create the fields. Ctrl/Shift+click each field to be selected. You can drag through fields to select them, but dragging through a group of fields is only enabled with the Select Object tool.

When multiple fields are selected and Properties is chosen from the context-sensitive menu, options in the General tab, the Appearance tab, and the Actions tab are available for editing. Specific options for each different field type require that you select only common field types. For example, you can edit the appearance settings for a group of fields where the field types are different. However, to edit something like radio button field options for check mark style, you need to select only radio button fields in order to gain access to the Options tab.

Tip   If the fields you want to select are located next to each other or many fields are to be selected, use the Ctrl key (Windows) or ⌘ key (Macintosh) and drag with the Select Object tool to place a marquee through the fields to be selected. When you release the mouse button, the fields inside the marquee and any fields intersected by the marquee are selected. The marquee does not need to completely surround fields for selection — just include a part of the field box within the marquee.

Duplicating fields

You can duplicate a field by selecting it and holding down the Ctrl/Option key while clicking and dragging the field box. Fields can also be copied and pasted on a PDF page, between PDF pages, and between PDF documents. Select a field or multiple fields, and then choose Edit ➪ Copy. Move to another page or open another PDF document and choose Edit ➪ Paste. The field names and attributes are pasted together on a new page.

Tip   To ensure exact field names match between forms, create one form with all the fields used on other forms. Copy the fields from the original form and paste the fields in other forms requiring the same fields. By pasting the fields, you ensure all field names are identical between forms and can easily swap data between them.

Moving fields

You can relocate fields on the PDF page by selecting the Select Object tool in the Advanced Editing Toolbar, and then clicking and dragging the field to a new location. To constrain the angle of movement, select a field with the Select Object tool, press the Shift key, and drag the field to a new location. For precise movement, use the arrow keys to move a field box left, right, up, or down. When using the arrow keys to move a field, be certain to not use the Shift key while pressing the arrow keys because it resizes field boxes as opposed to moving them.

Deleting fields

Fields are deleted from PDF documents in three ways. Select the field and press the Backspace key (Windows) or Delete key (Macintosh). You can also select the field and then choose Edit ➪ Delete, or open a context menu and choose Edit ➪ Delete. In all cases, Acrobat removes the field without warning. If you inadvertently delete a field, you can Undo the operation by choosing Edit ➪ Undo.

Aligning fields

Even when you view the grids on the PDF page, aligning fields can sometimes be challenging. Acrobat simplifies field alignment by offering menu commands for aligning the field rectangles at the left, right, top, and bottom sides as well as for specifying horizontal and vertical alignment on the PDF page. To align fields, select two or more fields and then open a context menu and select Align. The options for left, right, top, bottom, horizontal, and vertical alignment appear in a submenu. Acrobat aligns fields according to the first field selected (the anchor field appearing with a red highlight). In other words, the first field's vertical position is used to align all subsequently selected fields to the same vertical position. The same holds true for left, right, and top alignment positions. When using the horizontal and vertical alignments, the first field selected determines the center alignment position for all subsequently selected fields. All fields are center aligned either vertically or horizontally to the anchor field.

Tip   Fields are aligned to an anchor field when multiple fields are selected and you use the align, center, distribute, and size commands. The anchor field appears with a red border whereas the remaining selected field highlights are blue. If you want to change the anchor (the field to be used for alignment, sizing, and so on), click on any other field in the selected group. Unlike other multiple object selections, you don't need to use the Shift key when selecting different fields from among a group of selected fields. All fields remain selected until you click outside the field boundaries of any selected field.

You can distribute fields on a PDF page by selecting multiple fields and choosing Distribute from a context-sensitive menu. Select either Horizontal or Vertical for the distribution type. The first and last fields in the group determine the beginning and ending of the field distribution. All fields within the two extremes are distributed equidistant between the first and last fields.

For an example of how to use the Distribute command, see "Creating multiple copies of fields" later in this chapter.

Center alignment is another menu command available from a context menu. When you choose Center ⇨ Vertically or Horizontally from a context menu, the selected field aligns to the horizontal or vertical center of the page. Choose Center ⇨ Both to align a field to the center of a page. If multiple fields are selected, the alignment options take into account the relative positions of the field boxes and center the selected fields as a group while preserving their relative positions.

Sizing fields

Field rectangles can be sized to a common physical size. Once again, the anchor field determines the size attributes for the remaining fields selected. To size fields, select multiple field boxes, and then open a context menu and choose Size ⇨ Height, Width, or Both. Size changes are made horizontally, vertically, or both horizontally and vertically, depending on which menu option you choose. To size field boxes individually in small increments, hold down the Shift key and move the arrow keys. The left and right arrow keys size field boxes horizontally, while the up and down arrow keys size field boxes vertically.

Creating multiple copies of fields

In Acrobat 5 you had a means of creating table arrays by selecting a group of fields and dragging a rectangle to cover the table distance. After you released the mouse button Acrobat created new fields to fill the array. The method was a nice new introduction in Acrobat 5, but performance was a little crude. Now in Acrobat 6 you have a new command for creating table arrays with much more precision and an intuitive sense of operation.

To create a table array, select fields either in a single row or single column and open a context menu. From the menu options select Create Multiple Copies. The Create Multiple Copies of Fields dialog box opens as shown in Figure 25-33.

You can also create a table array by first creating a single field and selecting options for both Copy Selected Fields down and Copy Selected Fields across.

In the Create Multiple Copies of Fields dialog box, enter a value in the field box for Copy selected fields down (for creating rows of fields) or Copy selected fields across (to create columns of fields). If you want to add both rows and columns, you can supply values in both field boxes for the desired number of columns and rows. The Change Width and Change Height field boxes enable you to adjust the field distance respective to each other — editing the values does not change the physical sizes of the fields. Click on the Up/Down buttons for moving all fields vertically or the Left/Right buttons to move fields horizontally. When the preview box is enabled, you'll see a preview of the duplicated rows/columns before you accept the attribute choices by clicking the OK button.

If, after you click OK you need to polish the position of the new fields, you can move the top and bottom fields (for aligning single columns), then open a context menu and choose Distribute ⇨ Vertically or Horizontally — depending on whether you're adjusting a row or column. In Figure 25-34 you can see the Vertical adjustment of the second column being applied.

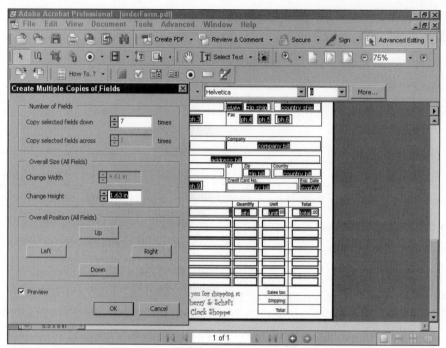

Figure 25-33: To create a table array, select a row or column of fields and open a context menu. Select Create Multiple Copies and make selections in the Create Multiple Copies of Fields dialog box for the number of rows or columns to be duplicated.

When using the Distribute command, you can only distribute single rows or columns. If you attempt to select all fields in a table and distribute several rows or columns at once, the results render an offset distribution that most likely creates an unusable alignment.

Duplicating fields

Using the Create Multiple Copies menu command from a context menu enables you to create table arrays or individual columns or rows only on a single page. If you want to duplicate fields either on a page or through a number of pages, another menu command exists for field duplication.

After creating a field, open a context menu and select Duplicate. The Duplicate Field dialog box opens as shown in Figure 25-35. Most often you'll use the Duplicate command when duplicating copies of fields throughout all pages or selected pages in a document.

Duplicating fields is particularly helpful when you create navigation buttons and want to duplicate buttons for navigating to the next and previous pages. By combining button faces and rollover effects, you can add some creative design buttons for users to easily navigate pages.

Cross-Reference   For information on creating navigation buttons and duplicating buttons in a PDF document, see Chapter 15.

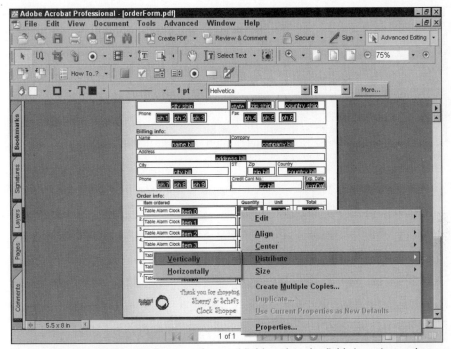

Figure 25-34: To evenly distribute a column of fields, select the fields in a given column and open a context menu. Choose Distribute ⇨ Vertically to position the fields equidistant between the first and last fields.

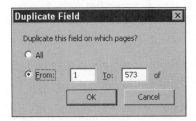

Figure 25-35: To duplicate fields across a range of pages, select From and enter the page numbers where you want to duplicate the fields.

Setting attribute defaults

If you spend time formatting attributes for field appearances, options, and actions, you may want to assign a default attribute set for all subsequent fields created with the same form tool. After creating a field with the attributes you want, open a context menu and select Use Current Properties as New Defaults. The properties options used for the field selected when you choose the menu command becomes a new default for that field type. As you change form tools and create different fields, you can assign different defaults to different field types.

Setting field tab orders

Setting tab orders in Acrobat 6 is a step back in development. The Tab Order options in earlier versions of Acrobat provided a more customizable ordering method, and I suspect you'll see some maintenance upgrade eventually to add more sophistication for setting the tab order among fields. Until then, you're stuck with much more limited methods for setting field tab orders when designing forms in Acrobat Professional.

To set tab order, open the Pages palette and open a context menu on the page where you want to set tab order. Select Properties from the menu options and the page Properties dialog box opens as shown in Figure 25-36. Click on the Tab Order tab and the options for setting tab order appear as radio button selections.

Figure 25-36: To set tab order, open the Pages palette and open a context menu on the page where you want to edit the tab order. Select Properties from the menu choices and click on Tab Order in the Pages Properties dialog box.

The options for setting tab order include

✦ **Use Row Order:** Tabs through rows from left to right. If you want to change the direction for tabbing through fields, choose File ➪ Document Properties. Click on Advanced in the left pane and select Right Edge from the Binding pull-down menu. When you select Use Row Order and the document binding is set to Right Edge, the tab order moves from right to left.

✦ **Use Column Order:** Tabs through columns from left to right, or right to left if you change the binding as described in the preceding bullet.

✦ **Use Document Structure:** When selecting this option, you first need to use a PDF document with structure and tags. The tab order is determined by the structure tree created by the original authoring application when the file was exported to PDF.

✦ **Unspecified:** The default for all documents you created in earlier versions of Acrobat that you open in Acrobat 6 have the Unspecified option selected. Unless you physically change the tab order to one of the preceding options, the tab order remains true to the order set in Acrobat 5 or earlier.

As fields are added to a page, the field tab order is recorded according to the field creation order. If you happen to create a row of fields, then change your mind and want to add a new field in the middle of the row, Acrobat tabs to the last field in the row from the last field created. Changing the tab orders in the Page Properties won't help you fix the problem when the fields need to be reordered.

As a workaround, follow these steps to fix tab order problems:

STEPS: Fixing tab order problems

1. **Create a row or column of fields.** Select the Text Field tool and create four or five fields in a row or column.

2. **Set the tab order.** Open the Pages palette and open a context menu on the page thumbnail. Select Properties from the menu options. In the Page Properties dialog box click on the Tab Order tab. Click on Use Row order (if creating a row of fields) or Column Order (if creating a column of fields). Click on Close after setting the order.

3. **Save the file.** Choose File ➪ Save to update the edits.

4. **Add a new field.** Move a few fields over to the right or down a column so you have room to insert a new field in the row or column. Use the Text Field tool and create a new field positioned between the existing fields.

5. **Tab through the fields.** Press the Tab key on your keyboard and the cursor jumps to the first field in the row or column. Press the Tab key and tab through the remaining fields. Notice that the last field created is where the cursor stops.

6. **Cut the fields to reorder.** Select the Select Object tool and drag through the fields following the last field created. If, for example, you created four fields, then moved fields three and four aside to insert a field before field three, select the fields following the new field — in this case, fields three and four. Choose Edit ➪ Cut to cut the fields from the page.

7. **Paste the fields back on the page.** Choose Edit ➪ Paste.

8. **Check the tab order.** Press the Tab key and keep pressing Tab through all fields. Notice the tab order now moves the cursor through all fields in logical order on the page.

Using the Fields Palette

To access the Fields palette, choose View ➪ Navigation Tabs ➪ Fields. The Fields palette contains a list of all fields in a PDF document. The fields are listed in hierarchical order much like bookmarks. For fields where parent/child names are used, you can expand or collapse the list of child names by clicking on the icon adjacent to the parent name. In Figure 25-37 the Fields palette is opened with a list of field names and expanded views.

If no fields are contained in a document, the palette appears empty. As you add new fields, each field is dynamically listed in the palette. From the Options menu you have choices for Importing/Exporting form data, creating multiple copies of fields or duplicating them, creating page templates, and setting the calculation order of fields.

If you open a context menu on a field name in the palette you have more menu options for navigating to a selected field, renaming a field, deleting fields, or opening the fields properties. If you elect to rename a field, you can choose to rename a parent name and all child names in the field group are renamed. For example, if you have field names like total.1, total.2, and total.3, you can rename the fields to subtotal.1, subtotal.2, subtotal.3, and so on by simply selecting the parent name *total* and renaming it to *subtotal*. All child names are renamed according to the new name you modified for the parent name.

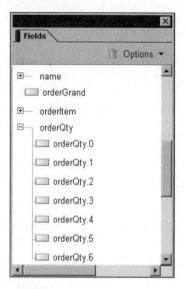

Figure 25-37: The Fields palette shows all fields in the document. You can expand child names by clicking on the plus (+) symbol (Windows) or the right-pointing arrow (Macintosh).

Summary

✦ Acrobat forms are not scanned documents converted to PDF. They are dynamic and can include interactive elements, data fields, buttons, and JavaScripts.

✦ Automatic form fill-in is enabled in the Preferences dialog box. Form fields can be displayed on PDF pages with a highlight color to help identify field locations.

✦ Data fields are created from many different field types including text, buttons, combo boxes, list boxes, signatures, check boxes, and radio buttons.

✦ You set all data field attributes in the Field Properties window. Properties can be described for fields by selecting the tabs labeled Appearance, Options, Actions, Calculations, or other tabs associated with specific field types.

✦ You can edit fields with a context-sensitive menu. Acrobat has several editing commands used for aligning fields, distributing fields, and centering fields on a PDF page.

✦ Field duplication is handled in a context menu. You can duplicate fields on a page to create tables with the Create Multiple Copies command, or duplicate fields across multiple pages with the Duplicate command.

✦ The Forms palette dynamically lists all fields created in a PDF file. The palette menus and options can be of much assistance in editing field names and locating fields.

✦ Field names need to be unique for each field added to a form. By using root names and extensions, you can reduce the amount of time needed for designing forms and creating calculations.

✦ More functionality with many field types can be created with JavaScripts. The Field Properties window enables the user to add JavaScript code for all field types.

✦   ✦   ✦

Working with Form Data

After you get a handle on creating form fields as covered in Chapter 25, you'll want to know some things about managing data to help economize your efforts when working with forms and performing routine calculations on data fields. When forms are completed, you have the option of printing a form or sending the data off to a host that processes the field data. In this chapter I cover data management from calculating field data to importing, exporting, and submitting data.

Setting Up the Environment

As described in the previous chapter, creating form fields requires use of the Forms tools. The same toolbars used in Chapter 25 are used to handle form field editing and field creation. For setting up the Toolbar Well, refer to Chapter 25.

In addition to using form fields, having access to menu commands helps you manage data while working with forms. Nothing specific needs to be opened for menu access. As you move through this chapter, I'll cover the various menu options used for data management.

Calculating Field Data

More often than not, you'll want to create forms that use some kind of calculation for data fields. Calculations might be used for summing data, calculating averages, adding complex formulas, assessing field responses, or many other conditions where results need to be placed in separate fields.

Acrobat offers you a few limited built-in functions for performing math operations. When your needs extend beyond these simple functions, you need to write JavaScripts. Some math operations, as simple as subtracting data or producing a dividend, require use of a JavaScript.

Even though JavaScript is addressed in detail in the next chapter, you need to begin learning about JavaScript when calculating data. Therefore, I'll start this chapter with some details on using the built-in functions for calculations in Acrobat and move on, later in this section, to cover some JavaScript basics.

Formatting for calculations

Math operations can be performed on data fields without any formatting applied to either the fields to be calculated or the result field. In earlier versions of Acrobat, access to formulas required you to at least format the result field with a number in order to specify a formula. In Acrobat 6 you can leave the format for a text field at the default of None and still create a calculation in the result field.

Although doing so is not required, as a matter of practice it's a good idea to apply formats to all fields where calculations are made and to those fields participating in the calculation result. As you create a PDF form, you may need to use a particular format that eventually is required either in the formula or for the text appearance in the result field. Rather than go back to the fields and change the format, you'll save time by supplying proper formats as you create fields.

When creating text fields, open the Format tab in the Text Field Properties window and select the format you want for the field. If Number is the desired format, select Number from the pull-down menu and make choices for the number of decimal places, the display for negative numbers if it applies, and the use of a currency symbol if it applies.

Cross-Reference   For more information on using the Text from tool, see Chapter 25.

When you set the attributes for one field, select the field with the Text Field tool or the Select Object tool and open a context menu. Select Use Current Properties as New Defaults. As you create additional fields, the new defaults are applied to all subsequent text fields. If you create a field that needs a different format, you can change the format for the new field without affecting the defaults.

Using the preset calculation formulas

Preset math calculations include sum, product, average, minimum, and maximum. After formatting fields, select the field where you want the result to appear and click on the Calculate tab in the Text Field Properties dialog box as shown in Figure 26-1. For adding a column or row of data, click on the radio button where you see *Value is the*. The default is sum (+). Click the down-pointing arrow to open the pull-down menu to make formula choices from the list of other preset formulas.

For summing data, leave the default as it appears and click on the Pick button. The Field Selection dialog box opens as shown in Figure 26-2. You can see the fields added to your form and grouped together. To sum a group of fields, click on the check box to the left side of each field you want to add to the formula.

Click OK to leave the Field Selection dialog box and you are returned to the Calculate properties. Click Close and the calculation is ready. In this example the sum of the data for the selected fields updates as you enter data in the fields assigned to the calculation.

For performing other preset calculations, you follow the same steps. Select the formula you want to use from the pull-down menu options and click on the check boxes for all fields you want to add to the calculation.

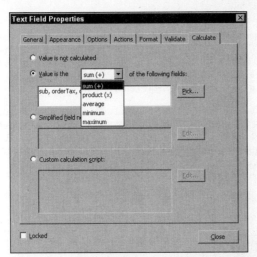

Figure 26-1: To add a preset calculation to a field, click on the Calculate tab in the Text Field Properties dialog box. Select the calculation formula from the value pull-down menu.

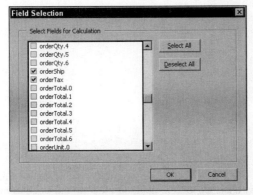

Figure 26-2: Identify the fields used for the calculation in the Field Selection dialog box by clicking on the check box for each field name.

Note

When using the Average formula, Acrobat averages all fields regardless of whether the fields used in the formula contain data. If you have three fields, but only two have values — for example 3 and 3 — Acrobat returns a result of 2 ((3+3+0) ÷ 3=2). The preset formula doesn't take into consideration whether or not a field has data in it. To perform an average calculation where you want to average only fields containing a response, you need to write a JavaScript.

Summing data on parent names

If you've read Chapter 25 you may remember that I mentioned advantages when using parent/child names for form fields. As you can see in Figure 26-2, all the fields in your form are listed in the Field Selection dialog box. If you want to sum data in large tables, clicking on all the boxes in the Field Selection dialog box to select fields for columns or rows in a table can take some time. However, when you use parent/child names, the task is much easier.

Assume you have fields with names like total.1, total.2, total.3, and so on. You want to calculate the sum of all the fields with the parent name *total*. In a *subTotal* field, open the Calculate properties and type the parent name of the fields you want to sum — in this case, *total*. Be certain to use the sum(+) menu option and type the parent name in the field box below the pull-down menu as shown in Figure 26-3.

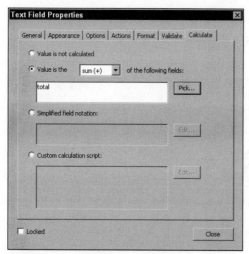

Figure 26-3: Open the Calculate tab, select sum (+) from the Value in the pull-down menu, and type the parent name in the field box.

Imagine a table that contains 25 rows of data with a total field at the bottom of each column; you have 10 columns across the page. By using the parent name in the formula, you can easily create total fields at the bottom of the page by duplicating fields and editing the parent names in the Calculate properties.

Note   You cannot type values in the field box in the Calculate properties. This feature was deleted in the first release of Acrobat 6. Be certain to check Adobe's Web site for a maintenance upgrade as you can expect this feature to be added to Acrobat Professional.

Using hidden fields

Complex formulas can be written in the JavaScript Editor. However, if you aren't up to speed in JavaScript programming or you want to simplify the code you write, you may want to break down a series of calculations and place results in separate fields. For example, suppose you want to calculate the result of A - B * C. If you don't know the code to create the calculation to first subtract two values and multiply the result times another value, you can use separate fields to hold results. In this example you need a field to hold the result of A - B. In another calculation you take the result field containing A - B and multiply it by C.

On the PDF form, the result of A - B is not needed for user input — it's simply a container to use as part of the larger formula. To help avoid confusion, you can hide the field. When data are contained in hidden fields, the data can still be used for calculations.

To create such a field, add a text field anywhere on a page and add the calculation in the Calculate properties. In the General properties, select Hidden from the Form Field pull-down menu. If you need to edit a hidden field, you can do so with either the Text Field tool or the Select Object tool.

When using hidden fields, you can create calculations and access the fields in the Field Selection dialog box or use parent names in the Calculate properties as described in the preceding section.

Using Simplified field notation

A new item added to the Calculate properties is Simplified field notation. When you click the radio button and click Edit, the JavaScript Editor dialog box opens. In the dialog box you don't write JavaScript code. The code added for this calculation type is based on principles used with spreadsheet formulas.

Simplified field notation can be used in lieu of writing JavaScripts for many different math operations. As an example, suppose you want to calculate a sales tax for a subtotal field. To calculate an 8% sales tax with a JavaScript on the result of a subtotal field you would open the JavaScript Editor and type the following code:

```
1. var f = this.getField("subtotal");
2. event.value = Math.round(f.value * 8) / 100;
```

As an alternative to using JavaScript, click on the Simplified field notation radio button and select the Edit button. In the JavaScript Editor you type the following code to produce the same sales tax calculation:

```
1. subTotal * .08
```

Notice in the JavaScript code you need to identify each field used in a calculation and assign a variable to the field name. Line 1 of the preceding JavaScript code assigns the variable "f" to the field *subtotal*. Notice that in the Simplified field notation the field name does not get assigned to a variable. You simply use all field names as they appear on the form and introduce them in your formulas.

Using JavaScripts

You need to write JavaScripts for all calculations that cannot be made with either the preset formulas or the Simplified field notation method. If you are a novice, you'll find writing simple JavaScripts to be a relatively easy task if you understand a few basic concepts in regard to performing simple calculations.

✦ **Variables:** Variables consist of using characters (alpha and numeric) to identify a field, a result, or other variable used in the formula. You can use something as simple as a character name or a long descriptive name. Variables might be *f, amt, item0, discount.1, grandTotal, Price Amount,* and so on.

✦ **Identifying fields:** You need to tell Acrobat in the JavaScript code that you want to assign a variable name to a field that exists on your form. The syntax for assigning a field to a variable name might look like

```
var f = this.getField("item");
```

In the preceding code the field name appears in quote marks and the quote marks are contained within parentheses. The variable f is assigned to the field name item on this (the current open) document.

✦ **Algebraic formulas:** After identifying the variables, you use standard algebraic notation. Therefore, to divide one value by another (something not available to you with the preset formulas), you might enter the code shown in Figure 26-4 in the JavaScript Editor as

```
1. var f = this.getField("amount");
2. var g = this.getField("itemNumber");
3. event.value = f.value / g.value;
```

The first line assigns the variable f to the field amount. The second line of code assigns the variable g to the field itemNumber. The third line of code is the formula where f is divided by g. The result is placed in the field where you add this script in the JavaScript Editor. The trigger to put the result in the field where the calculation is coded is the event.value item.

Figure 26-4: Select Custom calculation script in the Calculation properties and type the code to perform the calculation in the JavaScript Editor.

Without going into loops and more complex formulas, the beginning Acrobat forms designer can do quite a bit by just following the preceding simple example. The code is all case sensitive and your field names need to be identical to the name of the field on the form as you code in the JavaScript Editor.

Managing Form Data

The field boxes in an Acrobat form are placeholders for data. After data are added to a form, they can be exported. When the data are exported from Acrobat, they are written to a new file as a Form Data File (FDF), XFDF, or XML. These files can be imported in a PDF document or managed in an application that can recognize the data formats. When submitting data to a Web server, the server must have a Common Gateway Interface (CGI) application that can collect and route the data to a database. Using form data on the Web requires advanced programming skills and use of the Adobe FDF Toolkit. You can acquire more information about handling data on Web servers at `http://partners.adobe.com/asn/acrobat/forms.jsp`. On the Adobe Web site, you'll find samples of CGIs and information for contacting Adobe's Developer Support program.

Enterprise solutions for managing form data

Large enterprises will want to use industrial-strength solutions for managing forms and data. Inasmuch as Acrobat supports Acrobat Database Connectivity (ADBC) where you can connect PDF documents and form data to databases using JavaScript and Structured Query Language (SQL), the programming is complex and requires much assistance from programming engineers. The forms designer and non-programming personnel will want to use much easier solutions that you can manage and configure to suit your company's needs.

Many third-party solutions exist to help you design, manage, and handle forms data. Among some of the most powerful solutions with simplified approaches to data management are Adobe's own server products. For a complete description of a host of server products offered by Adobe Systems, visit `www.adobe.com/products/server`. On the Web page you'll find a pull-down menu listing the different server products available from Adobe for document handling, forms management, and many different workflow solutions.

Among the server products available from Adobe Systems is the Adobe Form Designer. Form Designer is a WYSIWYG (What You See Is What You Get) design tool that lets you develop and maintain data in a simple user-friendly environment. Adobe Form Designer enables you to create links to databases and the JavaScript associated with the data links are automatically generated for you. Coupled with Adobe Reader extensions, Adobe Server products can save you time, money, and aggravation for managing the largest organizations with powerful but more simplified methods. For information on Adobe Form Designer, access the Web page from the pull-down menu at the URL mentioned earlier or go directly to `www.adobe.com/products/server/formdesigner`.

Importing and exporting data

One of the great benefits of importing and exporting data is the ability to eliminate redundancy in recreating common data used in different forms. Among the most common redundant data entries is your personal identifying information. Adding your name, address, phone number, and so on to forms is often a common practice. In an environment where you need to supply your personal identity information, you could keep an FDF file on your hard drive and load it into different PDF forms, thereby eliminating the need to re-key the data.

In order to swap data between forms, you need to observe one precaution. All data fields used to import FDF data must have identically matched names to the fields from which the data were exported, including case sensitivity. Therefore, the data from a field called *Name* in a PDF that exports to FDF cannot be introduced in a PDF with a field called *name*. Setting up the fields is your first task, and then you can move on to data exports and imports. To clarify this concept further, I first show you how to design forms with common fields, then export and import data.

Creating common fields

To be certain your field names match exactly between two forms, the easiest and most efficient way to duplicate the fields is to copy fields from one form and paste them into another form. In Figure 26-5, I have a form used for customer identity. In Figure 26-6, I have a form that uses the same data for customer identity. As yet, the fields on this form have not been created. The customer identity form has all the identifying information, but nothing specific for placing an order. This form is designed to be the source for a customer's individual identity. From this form, I want to take the data and place it on order forms when the customer places an order. To do so requires all forms to have the exact same field names for the identity information.

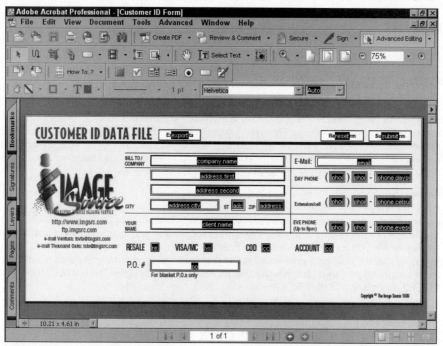

Figure 26-5: The customerID.pdf file contains all the fields used for a customer's identity. Field names on the form you're importing need to match field names on the form where the data were exported.

To ensure the field names have an exact match in other files, copy and paste the fields from the original document to the secondary documents. Open the document where the fields are to be pasted and keep it in the background. On the form containing the fields, select the Select Object tool and marquee the fields to be copied. After you select the fields, open a context menu and choose Edit ⇨ Copy from the menu choices or choose Edit ⇨ Copy from the main menu.

Tip

If you need to copy all fields on the form, click on the Select Object tool and press Ctrl+A (Windows) or ⌘+A (Macintosh) to select all fields. Press Ctrl+C (Windows) or ⌘+C (Macintosh) and all the selected fields are copied to the Clipboard.

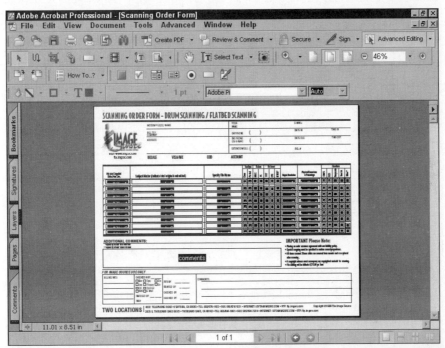

Figure 26-6: The order form uses the same identifying information as the customerID.pdf file. As yet, the form contains no fields for customer identity.

Choose Window ⇨ *filename* where filename is the name of the file where the fields are to be pasted. When the destination PDF appears in the Document Pane, choose Edit ⇨ Paste. If the forms are not pasted to exact position, you need to move the fields to the proper location on the form. Click and drag the group into position or nudge the fields with the arrow keys on your keyboard. Be certain to keep the fields selected if they overlap existing fields on the page. In Figure 25-7, I pasted fields from my customerID.pdf form to an order form and moved the fields into proper position.

The appearance of the fields may change with different form designs. In my example, a beveled style was used on the customerID.pdf form. The order form has much less space for fields and a beveled style crowds the form too much. Therefore, I use a solid style on the order form to occupy less space. As a result, the appearance of the fields needs to be changed. With all the fields selected, open a context menu using the Select Object tool on any selected field. The Field Properties window opens. Click on the Appearance tab and select the Border and Fill colors as shown in Figure 26-8.

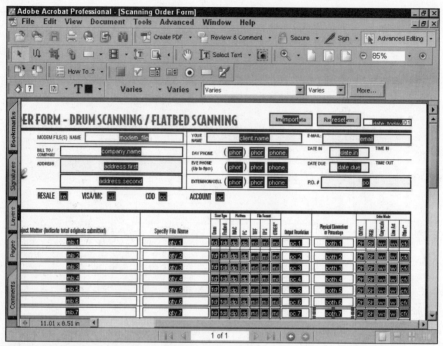

Figure 26-7: After pasting the fields, move them into position on the form. The pasted fields have the same names as the fields in the document where they originated.

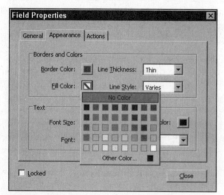

Figure 26-8: With multiple fields selected, select Properties from a context menu. Change the attributes for the desired appearance.

Exporting FDF data

After the forms have been created with matching fields, complete a form and fill-in all the data fields. If you have some fields on one form that have been excluded on a second form, Acrobat ignores any field data where it can't find a matching field name. Therefore you need not worry about having the same number of fields on both documents.

Exporting data from a PDF file is handled with a menu command. If you want to export the data from a form choose Advanced ➪ Forms ➪ Export Forms Data. A dialog box opens where you name the file and designate a destination for the FDF data. If you want a user to export data from a button action, create a Button field on the form. Click on the Actions tab and select Execute Menu Item from the Select Action pull-down menu. In the Menu Item Selection dialog box (Windows) or the top-level menu bar (Macintosh), choose Advanced ➪ Forms ➪ Export Forms Data, as shown in Figure 26-9.

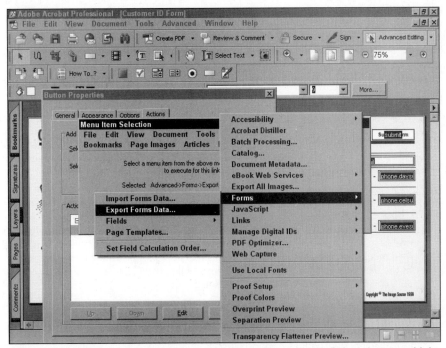

Figure 26-9: Select Execute Menu Item from the Select Action pull-down menu. Add the menu command to export the form data.

Click OK and you are returned to the Button Properties. When you click on the button or select the menu command, the Export Form Data As dialog box opens. By default the name of your PDF file and an .fdf extension are supplied in the File name field box. This name is used as the FDF filename. If you want to change the name, edit the File name, but be certain to leave an .fdf extension after the filename. Click Save and the file is saved as a Forms Data Format file.

The file you save as FDF contains only the data from the form fields. Therefore, the file size is considerably smaller than the PDF that produced the data. The file can be stored on a local disk, network server, or sent as an e-mail attachment to another user. If another user has a PDF with the same field names, the data can be imported with either Acrobat Standard or Acrobat Professional.

Importing FDF data

As with form data exports, importing FDF data in PDF forms is handled with menu commands. Choose Advanced ➪ Forms ➪ Import Forms Data or create a button like the export button mentioned in the preceding section. In either case the Select File Containing Form Data dialog box opens where you can navigate your hard drive and find the FDF file to import.

To create a button, follow the same steps used for exporting form data (see the preceding section). In the Menu Item Selection dialog box (Windows) or the top-level menu bar (Macintosh) choose Advanced ⇨ Forms ⇨ Import Forms Data.

Click OK and click Close in the Field Properties dialog box to complete creating a Button field. When you click on the button the Select File Containing Form Data dialog box opens. The default file type from the Files of type pull-down menu is Acrobat FDF Files (*.fdf). When the dialog box opens, only files saved as FDF appear in the window list.

Select the FDF file to be imported and click on the Select button in the dialog box. When you import data from common field names the fields are populated for all matching fields. Acrobat ignores all data where no matching fields are found.

Importing text data

The discussion thus far has been limited to FDF data in Acrobat forms. In addition to using FDF data, you have other options available with different data types. You may receive data files created in database managers or spreadsheets that you want to use in your Acrobat forms. As long as the data exports are properly formatted with text-delimited fields, you can import data saved as text from spreadsheet and database programs.

To understand how Acrobat supports text data, follow these steps:

STEPS: Importing text data

1. **Create a database.** You can use any program capable of exporting data as a text file. In this example, I use Microsoft Excel to create a data file with three records and a row for field names. For the first row in a spreadsheet application, add the exact same names as the field names used in the Acrobat form. All subsequent records (rows) contain the data like the example shown in Figure 26-10.

2. **Add export values for radio buttons and check boxes.** For fields such as check boxes, the data used to denote a checked box is equal to the export value associated with the field in Acrobat. If you use export values like Yes and No, add Yes or No in a data field for the data imported in Check Box fields.

3. **Save the spreadsheet**. Save as text only from your database manager. In this example I chose File ⇨ Save As and selected Text (tab delimited)(*.txt) in the Microsoft Excel Save As dialog box.

4. **Open the PDF document.** Quit your database manager and open the form to import the data in Adobe Acrobat.

5. **Open the text file.** Choose Advanced ⇨ Forms ⇨ Import Forms Data. The Select File Containing Form Data dialog box opens. From the Objects of type pull-down menu, select Text Files (*txt). Find the file exported from the database manager and select it. Click on the Select button to open the file.

Note   Each time you use the Advanced ⇨ Forms ⇨ Import Forms Data menu command, Acrobat defaults to the *.fdf Files of type, expecting you to select an FDF file. Be certain to select Text Files (*.txt) from the Files of type pull-down menu when importing text data. You need to manually access the pull-down menu choice each time you want to import data other than FDF.

6. **Import the data.** The Import Data From Delimited Text File dialog box opens. In the dialog box you see the names of the fields appearing at the top of the dialog box. Below the title fields are the records in the database. Only one record can be imported in the form. Therefore, you need to tell Acrobat which record you want to import. Click on the first field in a record row to select the desired record as shown in Figure 26-11. In this example, the first record data is selected for import. Click OK and the data are imported in the form for all matching field names.

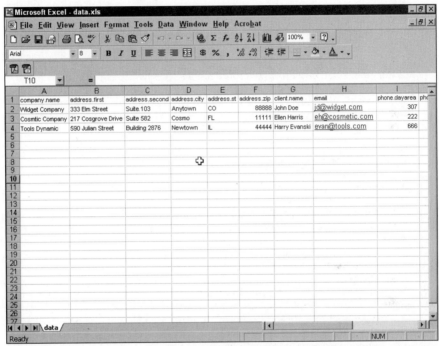

Figure 26-10: A data file is created in Microsoft Excel with three data records. Each row is a separate record and the cells across each row horizontally represent the field data for the respective record.

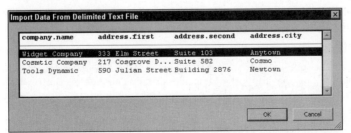

Figure 26-11: Select a record to import by clicking on the first field in the record row you want to import.

Creating and Using Submission Buttons

All the previous discussions for importing and exporting data work well on local hard drives and network servers. When you use the Internet for data transfers and extend data submission to users of the Adobe Reader software, then you need to use other measures. Users of any Acrobat viewer can submit adobe form data. This feature offers you a powerful tool when collecting data from anyone. Because the Adobe Reader is a free download from Adobe Systems, you can be assured all potential customers can place orders for your products or any employee can remotely complete any form you create and submit the data to you.

The primary thing to understand with regard to submitting data to Web servers is that after the data leave Acrobat, Acrobat is no longer in control of the data. Whatever programming you add to a PDF file, remember that after Acrobat executes its action to send the data to a destination, some other form of programming is needed to collect the data and route it to the proper location. If you find errors in submitting PDFs or FDF data on servers and the data disappear, you most likely have a problem in the programming outside of Acrobat. Look to your system administrator or individual responsible for server-side programming to help you with a solution.

Submitting data to URLs

Data from a PDF form can be sent to a Web server in several different formats and with different attributes. You can also use either an Acrobat built-in action type or a JavaScript action. The submission of data, regardless of the format exported, is a relatively simple process. Things get more complex with scripting actions; however, the real complexity is involved at the server end. In terms of a simple explanation—you need a script at the server to know what to do with your data. For the server-side issues, you can find a wealth of information on the Web related to CGIs (Common Gateway Interface) and scripting languages like Perl, which is one of the most popular scripting languages for writing CGI scripts. Start your browsing by logging on to www.perl.com and downloading the free Perl software for your platform. Next, log on to www.planetpdf.com and search for Perl on the Web site. You can find examples of how to process PDF data and using Perl scripts for collecting PDF data. If Planet PDF doesn't answer your questions, start searching the Web for PDF and Perl or PDF and CGIs. Many sites offer sample code and documentation to help you get started.

If you are a forms designer and not a programmer, you'll be best served by passing on the preceding information to your system administrator. The task at hand is not to be concerned with what happens at the server end, but how to get the data from the PDF file on your computer to the server. In this regard, the next section discusses using a Submit Form action and some JavaScript actions.

Using the Submit Form action type

The Submit Form action type is created from a choice in the Select Action pull-down menu for all interactive functions that support adding actions. You can create a Button field, a link, use a Page Action, or use a Document Action to invoke the Submit Form action. Most often you'll want to use a Button field so the user knows when the data are submitted to the server. Submit buttons work equally from all Acrobat viewers and you can submit any of the data types from the free Adobe Reader software.

Note   Adobe Reader prior to version 6 required you to submit data from within a Web browser. In Acrobat 6 Professional, you can create submit buttons that enable users of Adobe Reader 6 and enhance the ability to submit data without using a Web browser.

Cross-Reference For more information on inline views in Web browsers, see Chapter 20.

To create a submit button on a PDF form start with creating a Button field and select the Actions tab. Select Submit a form from the Select Action pull-down menu and click on the Add button. The Submit Form Selections dialog box opens as shown in Figure 26-12.

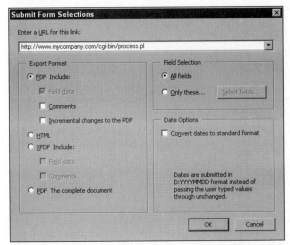

Figure 26-12: Select Submit a form in the Select Action pull-down menu and click on the Add button. The Submit Form Selections dialog box opens, offering you many different options for the type of data to be submitted.

At the top of the dialog box, enter the URL where the data are to be sent. Include the script name for the script that post processes the form data. Under the Export Format section on the left side of the dialog box you have four data type options from which to choose.

The four data options include

✦ **FDF Include:** The FDF data are sent to the server. The three options below the FDF Include item offer you choices for sending the Field data; Comments, which includes any comments created on a form; and Incremental changes to the PDF, which should be used when digital signatures have been used to save updates. Any one or all of the selections can be made for this data type.

✦ **HTML:** The data are sent in HTML format. Much as you might create a form on a Web page using HTML and JavaScript, the HTML option processes the same data type.

✦ **XFDF Include:** The data are sent in XML format. Two options are available for sending the Field data or the Comments data or both.

✦ **PDF The complete document:** This option enables you to submit the PDF populated with the field data.

On the right side of the dialog box are options for including all or selected field data in your submission. If there are fields to be eliminated, click on the Only these button and then click on the Select fields button. The Field Selection dialog box opens where you select which fields are used for the data export. Dates are converted from the format specified on the form to standard date formats when the Date Options check box is enabled.

When the user clicks on the button, the form data from the choices you made in the dialog box are sent to the specified URL. Keep in mind that if you do not have the necessary server-side programming, nothing happens to the data and it won't be found on your server. You need intervention from the host to collect and route the data.

Tip   If you have a form containing button fields and you want to export the buttons as well as the text field data, select the Only these radio buttons in the Submit Form Selections dialog box. The Field Selection dialog box opens after you click on the Select Fields button. In the Field Selection dialog box, check the box for all fields you want to submit.

Using a JavaScript action

One of the best reasons to use a JavaScript over a Submit Form action is that part of the JavaScript routine can check your form and validate it prior to submitting the data. If you want to verify all fields have been completed, you can instruct Acrobat via JavaScript to check the form. If the form is complete, a JavaScript instruction submits the data in any format you specify in the JavaScript code. If the form is not completed properly, you can instruct Acrobat via JavaScript to halt the submission action and advise a user what problem needs to be overcome before the data are submitted.

You need a routine to check the data fields before you add the submit action in the JavaScript code. For a sample of a script to check for empty fields, see the Acrobat Tips eBook on the CD-ROM accompanying this book. For the code to submit forms to Web servers, look over the following examples:

✦ **Submit FDF Data:** Use the following:

```
this.submitForm("http://www.mycompany.com/cgi-bin/process.pl#FDF");
```

The #FDF item instructs Acrobat to submit FDF data. If you add

```
1. this.submitForm({
2. cURL: "http://myserver/cgi-bin/myscript.cgi#FDF",
3. aFields: aSubmitFields,
4. cSubmitAs: "FDF"
5. )};
```

The three button options for FDF data are enabled.

✦ **Submit HTML Data:** Use the following:

```
1. this.submitForm({
2. cURL: "http://myserver/cgi-bin/myscript.cgi#bHTML",
3. aFields: aSubmitFields,
4. cSubmitAs: "bHTML"
5. )};
```

✦ **Submit XML Data:** Use the following:

```
1. this.submitForm({
2. cURL: "http://myserver/cgi-bin/myscript.cgi#bXML",
```

```
3. aFields: aSubmitFields,
4. cSubmitAs: "bXML"
5. )};
```

Where true, `true` enables the radio button options for XML data files.

✦ **Submit a PDF file:** Use the following:

```
1. this.submitForm({
2. cURL: "http://myserver/cgi-bin/myscript.cgi#PDF",
3. aFields: aSubmitFields,
4. cSubmitAs: "bPDF"
5. )};
```

Any one of these routines is placed after a loop that checks for empty fields. If the fields are populated, Acrobat continues to one of the preceding instructions according to the data type that you want to submit. If empty fields are found, Acrobat breaks out of the loop and stops the execution.

E-mailing forms

For a simple exchange of data between you and a limited number of users you might want to have data submitted via e-mail attachments. Any user of the Adobe Reader software as well as other users can e-mail forms to you by adding a simple statement in the Enter a URL for this link field box in the Submit Forms Selections dialog box. Rather than send the form to a Web address, change the line of code in the field box to

```
mailto:you@company.com
```

Enter your own e-mail address after the `mailto:` item in the preceding line of code and the PDF from is e-mailed to you. Users of the Adobe Reader software viewing your PDF document either in or outside a browser window can e-mail the form back to you by clicking on the submit button you added to the form with one of the statements in the preceding section.

Users of Acrobat Standard or Acrobat Professional can export data and attach the FDF data file as an e-mail attachment. When sending the data file instead of the PDF document, you'll see much smaller file sizes for the FDF files. If forms file sizes are large, using the FDF data speeds up transmissions for both the end user and you. After you receive an FDF data file, choose Advanced ⇨ Forms ⇨ Import Forms Data to populate a form with the data submitted as an e-mail attachment.

Summary

✦ Acrobat offers a few preset calculation formulas used for calculating data. For more sophisticated calculations, you need to use JavaScripts.

✦ When using parent/child names you can easily sum data by adding a parent name in the Calculate properties and selecting the sum (+) menu command.

✦ Acrobat Professional offers you a new option for calculating data by offering support for calculation formulas common among spreadsheet applications.

✦ Form data can be exported from populated PDF forms to an FDF file. The data can be introduced into any form having matching field names as from where the data were exported.

✦ To ensure creating fields with exact names between different forms, copy fields from one document and paste the fields in all other documents for the matching fields.

✦ Button fields can be created to submit form data from any Acrobat viewer. Once the data leaves an Acrobat PDF file, a server side application needs to collect and route the data.

✦ Submitting data from JavaScripts offers the ability to check forms for required data before submitting the data to a server.

✦ By adding a simple line of code in the Submit Forms Selections dialog box, users of the Adobe Reader software can e-mail PDF form data when viewing the forms in a Web browser.

✦   ✦   ✦

Understanding JavaScript

With JavaScript you can create dynamic documents for not only forms, but also many other uses such as adding interactivity to files, viewing options, animation, and similar features not available with Acrobat tools. JavaScript helps you add flare and pizzazz to your PDF files. JavaScripts can be edited in Acrobat Standard and JavaScripts can be created using bookmarks, links, and Page Actions in Acrobat Standard. However, to get the full range of JavaScript editing and apply JavaScripts to form fields, you need to use Acrobat Professional.

This chapter offers you a brief introduction to using JavaScript by example. The contents of this chapter are intended only to provide the novice some examples that can be easily duplicated without much description for understanding coding syntax and programming methods. For more sophisticated uses and some sound reasoning for coding forms, look at the Acrobat JavaScript Scripting Reference and the Acrobat JavaScript Scripting Guide. Both documents are available from Adobe Systems by logging on to: `http://partners.adobe.com/asn/acrobat/docs.jsp#javascript`.

Setting Up the Environment

As described in Chapter 25, creating form fields requires use of the Forms tools. You also use the same toolbars used in Chapter 25 to handle form fields where you add JavaScripts. For setting up the Toolbar Well, refer to Chapter 25.

In addition to using form fields, you'll find several menu commands related to writing JavaScripts. As you move through the chapter, the menu options related to accessing and writing JavaScripts are covered.

Getting Started with Acrobat JavaScript

Before I begin to explain some coding, let me start by making a few suggestions to the novice user who may find the programming aspects of Acrobat confusing and beyond your reach. For those who haven't coded a single line, you can easily search and find samples of code used in Acrobat forms that can be copied and pasted into your designs. Search the Internet and find PDF forms that are not secure, which enables you to examine the code. If, for example, you need a calculation for sales tax, you can find many examples of forms where a sales tax calculation is coded in a form field. You can copy and paste fields into your designs and often only need to change a variable name to make it work. Poke around and experiment, and you'll find some worthwhile routines in existing PDF forms.

Tip

Create a blank page in a program and convert it to PDF. To create a blank new page, press Ctrl/⌘+J to open the JavaScript Editor and type the following code:

```
app.newDoc();
```

Press the Num Pad Enter key (or Control+Enter if you are on a laptop) on your keyboard with the cursor at the beginning or end of the line of code and a new page is created in the Document Pane. On the PDF blank page you can paste JavaScript form fields and add comments as to what the JavaScripts do. A collection of common scripts will make your task easier when it comes time to code a new form. Open the file and search through the comments to find the routine you want for a given task. Copy the form field, complete with the JavaScript, and paste it into your new form design. Test it out and make changes that might be needed to get the routines to work in your form.

Finding JavaScripts

As you peruse documents searching for JavaScripts either to paste into your own designs or to learn more about using JavaScript in Acrobat, you need to know where scripts are contained. You might copy and paste a script and find that the script doesn't execute properly. One reason is that the script relies on a function contained in another area in the document. Therefore, to gain a complete understanding of how a form works, you need to examine all the potential containers for scripts. As a matter of practice, you'll want to examine several areas in a form where JavaScripts are found.

Examining field scripts

The most frequent use of JavaScript in Acrobat forms is when scripts are written for field Actions. To examine JavaScripts associated with fields, select the Select Object tool and open the Field Properties. Depending on the field Type, there may be several places where a script can be located. The first logical place to look is the Actions tab. Actions can contain JavaScripts for all field types. Click on the Actions tab to see what Actions are assigned to the field as shown in Figure 27-1.

If you see JavaScript assigned to a mouse behavior, click on Run a JavaScript in the Actions list and click the Edit button. Acrobat opens the JavaScript Editor and displays the code written for the script as shown in Figure 27-2. The code in the JavaScript Editor can be copied from one field and pasted into the editor when you assign a script to another field. In addition, the field can be copied and pasted into another form. When pasting fields with JavaScript in them, the code is preserved in the pasted field.

Button Properties
General
Appearance
Options
Actions
Add an Action
Select Trigger:
Mouse Up
Select Action:
Go to a page in this document
Add...
Actions
Mouse Up
Run a JavaScript
Up
Down
Edit
Delete
Locked
Close

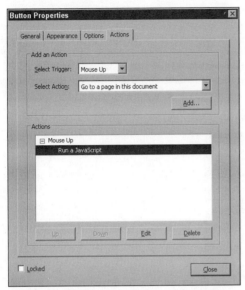

Figure 27-1: Click on the Actions tab to see whether a JavaScript action has been added to the field.

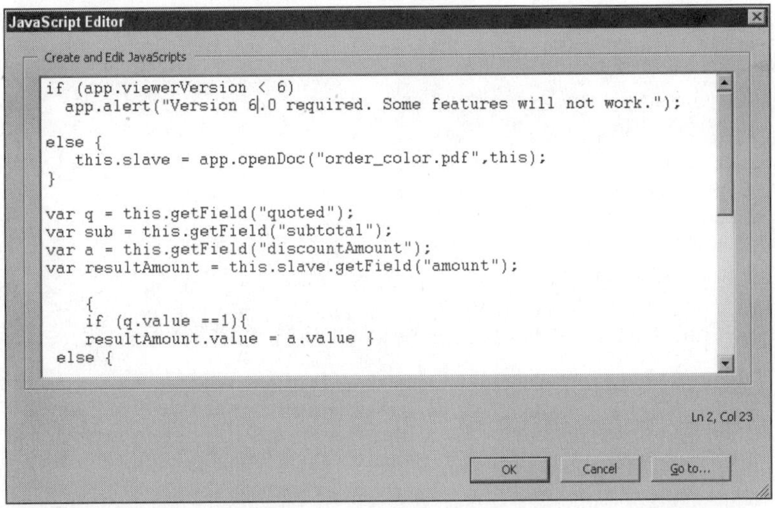

JavaScript Editor
Create and Edit JavaScripts
if (app.viewerVersion < 6)
app.alert("Version 6.0 required. Some features will not work.");
else {
this.slave = app.openDoc("order_color.pdf",this);
}
var q = this.getField("quoted");
var sub = this.getField("subtotal");
var a = this.getField("discountAmount");
var resultAmount = this.slave.getField("amount");
{
if (q.value ==1){
resultAmount.value = a.value }
else {
Ln 2, Col 23
OK
Cancel
Go to...

Figure 27-2: Select JavaScript in the Actions tab and click on the Edit button. The JavaScript Edit dialog box opens, displaying the code.

With Text and Combo Box fields you can find JavaScripts in the Actions properties as well as the Format, Validate, and Calculate properties. If you are examining a form to understand how the field actions are executed, be certain to select each of these tabs to see whether any custom formatting or validation is used. Click on the Format tab and look for Custom selected in the Select format category pull-down menu as shown in Figure 27-3. If a JavaScript appears in either the Custom Format Script window or the Custom Keystroke Script window, click on the Edit button adjacent to where the script is written. The JavaScript Editor opens where you can edit the script or copy the text.

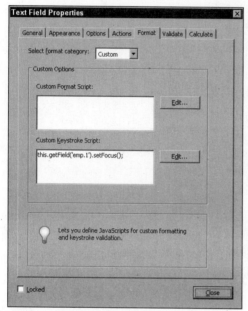

Figure 27-3: Select the Format tab and click Edit where a script appears in the dialog box.

The Validate properties offer the same options. Follow the same procedures as described earlier in this section by clicking on the Validate tab and clicking on Edit where you see a JavaScript in the Run custom validation script window to open the JavaScript Editor dialog box.

Field calculations are often handled in the Calculate properties. When JavaScript produces data calculations, be certain to examine the Calculate properties as shown in Figure 27-4. Not all field calculations are assigned to the Calculate properties, so be certain to check the Actions properties as well as Calculate in the event a calculation is performed on an action.

List Boxes offer different properties. If a List Box is used, click on the Selection Change tab. A JavaScript can be executed when a selection in the List Box changes. If a script appears in the dialog box, click on the Edit button to open the JavaScript Edit dialog box.

Digital signatures can also be assigned custom JavaScripts. Click on the Signed tab for a Digital Signature field and examine the dialog box for a custom script.

Buttons, Radio Buttons, and Check Boxes can only have JavaScripts added to the Actions properties. When opening these field types, click on the Actions tab described earlier.

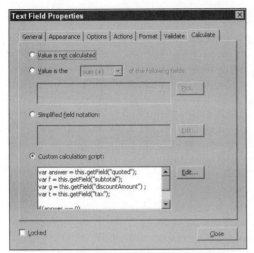

Figure 27-4: Click Calculate to see whether a custom calculation script has been added to the field. If a script appears in the dialog box, click Edit to open the JavaScript Editor dialog box.

Bookmarks and links

Both Bookmarks and links use the same action types as form fields. You might use a Bookmark for navigating documents rather than creating form field buttons or links on every page to open and close files. When the Bookmarks tab is open, users can click on a Bookmark to open secondary files or perform other actions such as spawning pages.

To check for JavaScripts contained in Bookmark actions, open the Bookmark Properties dialog box and click on the Actions tab. JavaScripts are listed the same as when examining actions for form fields (described in the preceding section). Likewise, when you open Link Properties you can check to see whether a JavaScript has been added as a Link Action.

Examining document-level JavaScripts

You may copy a field and paste it into another document and find an error reported when executing the JavaScript action. Notwithstanding variable names that are explained later, you can experience problems like this because the routine in the JavaScript might be calling a JavaScript function or global action that was contained in the original document as a document-level JavaScript. Among your tasks in dissecting a form should be an examination of any document-level JavaScripts. To find JavaScript functions contained in a form, choose Advanced ⇨ JavaScript ⇨ Document JavaScripts. The JavaScript Functions dialog box opens as shown in Figure 27-5.

In the JavaScript Functions dialog box, search for any names in the box below the Script Name box. All document-level functions are listed in this dialog box. To examine a script, select the script name and click on the Edit button. The JavaScript Edit window opens where you can examine the script.

Writing functions and accessing them in JavaScript code written for field actions is much more complex. If you are new to JavaScript you may want to start with simple scripts in form fields until you learn more about how JavaScript is coded and implemented in Acrobat. As you learn more you can develop more sophisticated routines that include functions.

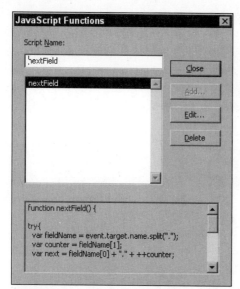

Figure 27-5: Open JavaScript functions by choosing Advanced ⇨ JavaScript ⇨ Document JavaScripts.

Examining Page Actions

Page Actions execute when a user opens or closes a PDF page. You can assign any Action type available from the Select Action types for field actions including Run a JavaScript. When examining forms, open the Page Properties dialog box by opening a context menu in the Pages tab and selecting Properties. Click on Actions when the Page Properties dialog box opens. If a JavaScript or any other Page Action is assigned to either the Page Open or the Page Close action, the action types are listed in the Actions window. Notice in Figure 27-6 that both a Page Open and Page Close action appear in the Actions window showing Run a JavaScript for both Page Actions.

Like the other dialog boxes described earlier in this chapter, click on Run a JavaScript and select the Edit button. The JavaScript Editor window opens where you can view, edit, and/or copy the JavaScript.

Examining Document Actions

Document Actions execute JavaScripts for any one of five different Acrobat functions. On a document close, during a save, after a save, during a print, or after a print a JavaScript action can be executed. To view any Document Actions assigned to the PDF document, choose Advanced ⇨ JavaScript ⇨ Set Document Actions.

The Document Actions dialog box opens. If a JavaScript is assigned to a Document Action an icon appears adjacent to the action type. You can view a script in the dialog box as shown in Figure 27-7 or you can open the JavaScript Editor window by selecting the action name and clicking Edit.

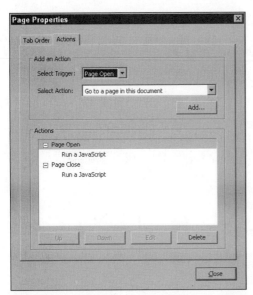

Figure 27-6: When you open the Page Properties dialog box and click on the Actions tab, both Page Open and Page Close Actions are shown in the Actions window.

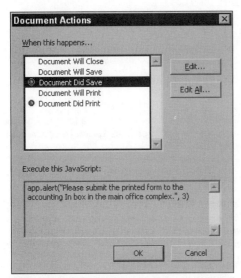

Figure 27-7: Any Document Actions assigned to the PDF are displayed with a green circle adjacent to an action type in the Document Actions dialog box.

Searching for page templates

Although not a JavaScript action, page templates can be called upon by JavaScript routines or additional fields can be created from template pages. Because templates can be hidden, the only way to examine JavaScripts on template pages is to first display a hidden template. As a matter of routine, you should search for page templates when examining forms.

To display a hidden template, choose Advanced ➪ Forms ➪ Page Templates. The Page Templates dialog box opens. If a Page Template is used in the PDF file a template name appears in a list box in the Page Templates dialog box. If the Page Template is hidden the square adjacent to the template name appears empty. To show the template page, click on the icon adjacent to the template name. The icon changes to an eye icon inside the square as shown in Figure 27-8.

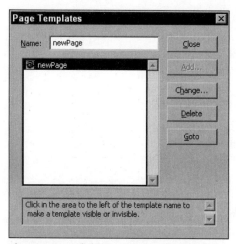

Figure 27-8: Clicking on the icon to the left of a template name for hidden templates makes the template visible in the PDF.

The template likely appears at the end of the document. After you make a template visible, click the GoTo button to navigate to that page. If form fields or links are on the page, you can open them and examine them for JavaScripts.

Using the JavaScript Debugger

All of the aforementioned JavaScript locations can also be found in the JavaScript Debugger. The JavaScript Debugger dialog box enables you to examine JavaScripts from a list in the Scripts window shown in Figure 27-9. Select an item in the list and click on the arrows to open scripts nested in a hierarchical order. When you select the script, the code is shown in the View window.

At the top of the hierarchy in the Scripts window, you'll see all the scripts associated with different actions. Click on the right-pointing arrow to expand a listed item. You can expand individual items until you arrive at the Action. Select the Action, and the code for the item is listed in the lower View window when you select either Script or Script and Console from the pull-down menu options.

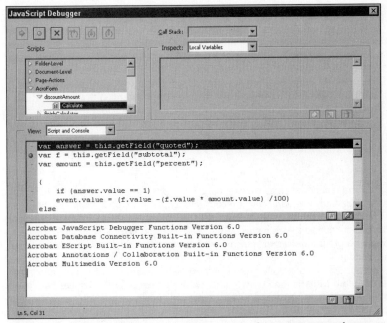

Figure 27-9: Open the JavaScript Debugger and select AcroForm at the top of the hierarchy. Click on the right-pointing arrows for a given item and select the Action associated with the mouse behavior. You can see the script in the View window when you select either Script or Script and Console from the View pull-down menu.

The JavaScript Debugger also helps you debug scripts you write. You can set break points that halt routines to help narrow down bugs in your code. To set a break point, click on the left side of each line of code where you want a break to occur. A red circle appears after you set a break point. Notice in Figure 27-9 that a break point was set at the second line of code for the discountAmount field selected in the Scripts window.

Using the JavaScript Console

The JavaScript Console is a part of the same dialog box where you find the JavaScript Debugger. In the console window you can type a line of code to test it for errors or you can copy code from a field and paste it into the console window. To execute a segment in a routine, select the segment to be tested and press the Num Pad Enter key (or press Control+Enter).

You can also execute a statement by placing the cursor at the beginning of the line to be executed. Press the Enter key on the Num Pad and the routine runs.

Be certain to check the Preferences dialog box when using the JavaScript Debugger and Console. Open the Preferences dialog box and click on JavaScript in the left pane. On the right side of the dialog box you have options for enabling the Debugger and the Console. Be certain these items are enabled before you begin editing scripts.

Creating Viewer Options Warning Alerts

There are some circumstances where it will be helpful for users to know the limitations of completing your forms before they attempt filling in data fields. If users open your forms in Adobe Reader, they cannot save the data after filling in the form. In other cases, some scripts you add to a form cannot be performed in Adobe Reader. Some examples of such scripts might be adding a Comment note from a button action or spawning a page from a template. These actions require Acrobat. In other cases, new features in Acrobat 6 make some actions unusable for users with viewers earlier than Acrobat 6. Therefore, you may want to assess the viewer type and viewer version when a user opens your forms. If a version or viewer type cannot be used with the form you created, you can alert the user immediately when the file opens.

Tip   Although some features such as viewing page templates or creating fields are not available in Acrobat Standard, you can often execute JavaScripts in Acrobat Standard that produce actions not available through menu commands. For example, you cannot add templates or write JavaScript code to spawn pages from templates using Acrobat Standard. However, you can write a script for a button to spawn a page from a template in Acrobat Professional. An Acrobat Standard user can open the file, click on the button, and a page is spawned via the button action. Before you create viewer version alerts, you need to run all your scripts in Acrobat Standard to determine what scripts cannot be executed in Acrobat Standard. Use viewer version alerts for Acrobat Standard users only when scripts don't execute properly. You can also find a key in the JavaScript Reference Guide that describes which objects and methods work in Acrobat Standard.

Creating viewer type alerts

A viewer type is the Acrobat viewer used to view the PDF form. Adobe Reader, Acrobat Standard, and Acrobat Professional are the viewer types that are used in filling out PDF forms. If you have forms submitted via an Internet connection, any viewer type is capable of submitting data if you have the proper server-side programming and create a button to submit the data to a URL.

Cross-Reference   For more information on submitting data, look over Chapter 26.

In a local environment where PDF forms may be completed on local hard drives or network servers, users of the Adobe Reader software may not be aware that they cannot save the form data after completion. If a user realizes this only after filling in a long form, users are likely to become annoyed and frustrated. To help the user out, follow these steps to create an alert dialog box informing a user that the current viewer type has limitations:

STEPS: Adding viewer type alerts

1. **Open the Page Properties dialog box.** Open a PDF and navigate to the default page view when the file is opened. Open the Pages tab and from a context menu opened on the first page, select Properties. The warning message you create appears immediately after a user opens the PDF form. To ensure the message is displayed upon opening the file, be certain to navigate to the first page and open the context menu. Unless the default has been overridden in the Initial View Options dialog box, the opening page is always the first page in the PDF file.

2. **Add a Page Action.** Click on the Actions tab. Select Page Open from the Select Trigger pull-down menu and select Run a JavaScript from the Select Action pull-down menu. Click on the Add button to open the JavaScript Editor.

3. **Add a JavaScript.** Enter the following code in the JavaScript Editor dialog box:

```
1. //is Reader (as opposed to Acrobat)
2. if (typeof(app.viewerType)!="undefined")
3.  if(app.viewerType == "Reader")
4.  {
5.   var msg = "To save form data you need to purchase Adobe Acrobat
Standard or Adobe Acrobat Professional. This form can be completed
and printed from Reader; however to save the data, you need one of
the viewers noted above.";
6.   app.alert(msg);
7.  }
```

Note   The preceding line numbers are for clarification only. The line numbers are not included in the code you write in the JavaScript Editor.

This routine begins with a comment denoted by // where a programmer's comment is added to the script. In line 2, the `if` statement assesses the viewer. If the viewer type in line 3 is equal (==) to Adobe Reader ("`Reader`"), then an alert dialog box opens — line 6: `app.alert(msg)`. The variable `msg` is defined in the line 5 `var msg` statement. Therefore, the variable `msg` value appears when the alert dialog box opens. If the viewer type is not `Reader`, the warning dialog box does not open.

4. **Save the file.** Select Save or Save As and save the file.

5. **Open the file in Adobe Reader.** Click OK in the JavaScript Editor dialog box and click Close in the Page Properties dialog box. Save the file and close it. Open the file in Adobe Reader and you see an alert dialog box open when the file is launched as shown in Figure 27-10.

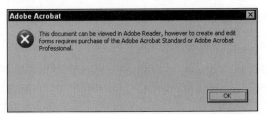

Figure 27-10: When the PDF is opened in Acrobat Reader, the alert dialog box displays the message created in the JavaScript routine.

Creating viewer version alerts

You may create JavaScripts to perform actions that are not available in earlier versions of Acrobat. The newer Acrobat 6.0 implementation of JavaScript adds more statements and reserved words than earlier versions. If it is essential for a user to complete your form in Acrobat 6, you can add a Page Action and inform the user in an alert dialog box that Acrobat 6 is needed to complete the form. Follow these steps to assess the viewer version:

STEPS: Create a viewer version alert

1. **Create a Page Action.** Create a Page Action following the steps listed earlier for opening the Page Properties dialog box. Select Run a JavaScript from the Select Action pull-down menu and click on the Edit button.

2. **Add a JavaScript.** Type the following code in the JavaScript Editor:

```
1. if (typeof(app.viewerVersion)!="undefined")
2.  if(app.viewerVersion < 6.0)
3.  {
4.   var msg = "Not all features in this document work in Acrobat
viewers lower than version 6.0. Upgrade to Adobe Acrobat Standard 6.0
or Adobe Acrobat Professional 6.0 before proceeding.";
5.   app.alert(msg);
```

In line 1, `app.viewerType` is used instead of the viewer version noted in the earlier example. This routine assesses the current Acrobat viewer version and displays the message in line 4 if the viewer version is less than Acrobat 6.0.

JavaScript Calculations

Going back to the form created in the previous chapter where I discussed calculating sales tax with a Simplified Field Notation, assume you want to create a sum of a total column and add sales tax with a JavaScript. For the sales tax, you need to first create the sum of values in a column or row. If you aren't up to speed in writing complex formulas, you can create a temporary field for summing the data and use the temporary field data to compute the sales tax. The field can be placed anywhere on the form and be hidden from the user.

To create a temporary field, drag open a field with the Text Field tool and the Text Field Properties dialog box opens. I'll call this field `subtotal`. Click on the Calculate tab and either use the Select Field dialog box to select fields for summing a group of fields, or type the parent name in the field box as described in Chapter 26. To hide the field, select the General tab and choose Hidden from the Form Field pull-down menu at the bottom of the dialog box.

The field name is `subtotal` and the field is now hidden. I'll use this field data to calculate my sales tax. For the sales tax field, I create a new form field and name it `tax`. In the Calculate dialog box I enter the following code:

```
1. var f=this.getField("subtotal");
2. event.value=Math.round(f.value*7.25)/100
```

The variable name `f` gets the contents of the `subtotal` field. The second line of code performs the calculation for variable `f` to compute sales tax for a tax rate of 7.25%. If you want to duplicate the code for one of your forms, change the tax rate accordingly.

Calculating dates

You can add a date to a form with a simple JavaScript. To add a date to a form, create a text field. Set the attributes for the text appearance and font in the Appearance tab and click on the Calculate tab. Add a JavaScript Action and enter the following code:

```
1. event.value = util.printd ("mm/dd/yy", new Date());
```

In the preceding example the date is reported in the format 07/31/03. You can change date formats by editing the text within quotes. For example, change the text to read "mmm dd, yyyy" and the date is reported in the format Jul 04, 2003.

Using loops

For summing columns of data you can use the sum + preset formulas where you need results at the end of a column or row. However, at times, summing column or row data with a JavaScript is necessary. You might have a need to multiply an item by a quantity for a subtotal, and then add all the subtotals together to create a grand total. For summing data in columns, you need to create a loop that loops through all the fields used in the calculation.

For a simple loop to calculate a row of data, use the following example:

```
1. var amount = "price";
2. var sum = 0;
3. for (var i=0; i < 12; i++)
4. {
5.   var total = amount + "." + i;
6.   sum += this.getField(total).value;
7. }
8. event.value = sum;
```

Line 1 assigns the variable amount to a parent name price. The fields in a column are named price.1, price.2, price.3, and so on. Line 2 assigns the variable sum to zero. Line 3 begins the loop and the loop continues through 12 iterations (< 12). Line 5 inside the loop assigns variable total to price.1 — the first pass through the loop. Line 6 takes the variable sum and collects the value of total with each pass through the loop. Line 8 places the total value sum in the field where the script is written.

In Figure 27-11 a form contains two columns where data are added for a quantity and price. Assume you want to calculate a grand total and place the result in the grand total field. A loop like the following example is used to take the product of each row and calculate the sum of the products:

```
1. var quantity = "qty";
2. var amount = "unit";
3. var sum = 0;
4. for (var i=0; i < 12; i++)
5. {
6.   var total = quantity + "." + i;
7.   var unit + "." + i;
8.   sum += this.getField(total).value * this.getField(amount).value;
9. }
10. event.value = sum;
```

In the preceding code, I added a second variable item and used it along with the amount variable from the earlier example. The sum variable takes the product of item and amount with each pass through the loop and sums the values until the loop halts.

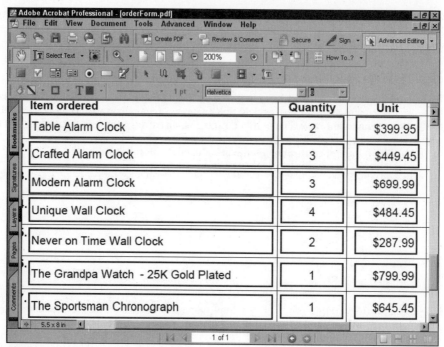

Figure 27-11: Each row needs a product of the quantity and unit fields calculated and the sum of the values placed in a total field.

Using Document Actions

Document Actions are actions from JavaScript routines that are implemented when a file is printed, saved, or closed. Rather than using a button to execute an action, Acrobat executes the action during one of five conditions. A Document Action is executed when a file closes, when a file is saved, after a file is saved, when a file is printed, and after a file is printed. There are many uses for executing actions on one of the Document Action items. You might want to delete unused fields on a form, delete all page templates, or perhaps offer a message to the user after a form has been saved or printed. In environments where Adobe Reader is used, users can't delete fields or page templates, but alert dialog boxes can be displayed from Reader on all the Document Action types.

As an example, suppose forms need to be routed in printed form. You can provide instructions on what to do with the form after it finishes printing. You may have Adobe Reader users who cannot save data. For the Adobe Reader users it is necessary to circulate printed documents. In this case, you can set up a Document Action after a file has finished printing. You are assured the user sees the message because the form needs to be printed as the last step in completing the form.

Follow these steps for creating an alert dialog box with a message to instruct a user what to do with a form after it has printed:

STEPS: Create a Document Action showing an alert dialog box

1. **Open the Document Actions dialog box.** Open a PDF file by choosing Advanced ➪ JavaScript ➪ Set Document Actions. The Document Actions dialog box opens.

2. **Select the Document Did Print action type.** Select one of the five items in the list box for the type of action to be used. In this example, I'll use Document Did Print as the action type as shown in Figure 27-12. After the form prints, the action executes.

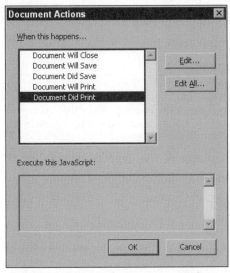

Figure 27-12: Open the Document Actions dialog box and select Document Did Print. Click on the Edit button to open the JavaScript Editor.

3. **Open the JavaScript Editor.** Click Edit in the Document Actions dialog box. The JavaScript Editor dialog box opens.

4. **Code the script.** Enter the following code:

```
app.alert("Please submit the printed form to the accounting In box in
the main office complex.",1)
```

5. **Exit the JavaScript Editor.** Click OK in the JavaScript Editor.

Note

The Document Actions dialog box displays an icon adjacent to the action type and the code appears in the window below Execute this JavaScript. If you later want to delete the script, click the Edit button and highlight the text in the JavaScript Editor. Press Delete (Backspace) on the keyboard to eliminate the text.

6. Print the form. Print the document to your desktop printer. After the PDF finishes printing, the dialog box shown in Figure 27-13 opens.

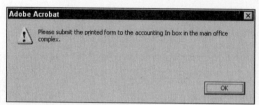

Figure 27-13: An alert dialog box opens after the file prints.

Working with Page Templates

One very useful tool available to you with page templates and JavaScript is the ability to create new pages from a template page. You can make templates either visible or hidden in your forms. You create new pages from template pages by spawning a page from a template. The spawned pages are duplicates of the template pages, but any fields on spawned pages are created with new field names. The scripts and actions for fields added to template pages are duplicated when you spawn pages from templates. The only changes that occur are field names, so each field in your new document contains unique field names.

Creating a page template

To create a page template, open a PDF form where you want to convert one of the pages to a template. You may have a form where you want to add pages for users to make comments. As more comments are needed, the user can create new pages by spawning new pages from the template page. In the following example, I have a form where one page on the form is a page designed for comments. In Figure 27-14 I designed an employee application form. At the bottom of the section for education history is a button used to create a new page if the applicant needs to add comments.

Figure 27-15 shows a page used to amplify comments regarding educational background. The page is optional and all potential candidates won't need to fill out this page. To eliminate the page from view, you can create a page template and then hide the template. When a user needs to fill in the template page, the button action creates a new page from the template.

To create a template, be certain to navigate to the page in the document that needs to be converted to a template. Choose Advanced ➪ Forms ➪ Page Templates. In the Page Templates dialog box, provide a name in the Name field and click on the Add button. To hide the template, click on the icon adjacent to the template name in the list window. By default templates added to the list window appear with an eye icon (Windows and Macintosh). Click on the eye icon and the icon disappears as shown in Figure 27-16. The page template is hidden in the PDF document and you can see the page disappear when you click the icon.

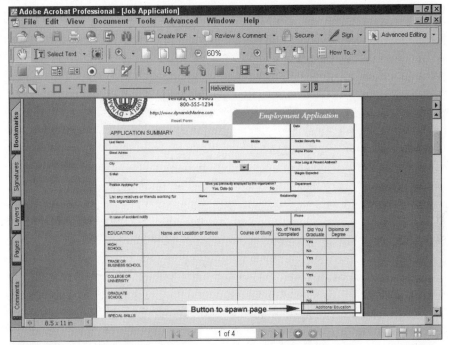

Figure 27-14: The employee application form contains a button to spawn a page from a template for adding additional comments related to education history.

Spawning a page from a template

To create new pages from your template, create a button on the page from which you want the user to spawn a new page. Either a link button or form field can be used. In the link or button properties dialog box select Run a JavaScript as the action type. In the JavaScript Editor dialog box enter the following code:

```
this.spawnPageFromTemplate(additionalEducation);
```

The code within the parentheses is the name of the template. In this example, I created a template called *additionalEducation*. When the user clicks on the button a new page is added to the PDF. The template remains and additional pages can be spawned from the same template each time the button or link action is invoked.

You can also use a different set of instructions to spawn pages from templates. The following code produces the same result as the one line of code used previously.

```
1. var a = this getTemplate("additionalEducation");
2. a.spawn ({
3.    nPage:this.numPages,
4.    bRename:true,
5.    bOverlay:false
6. })
```

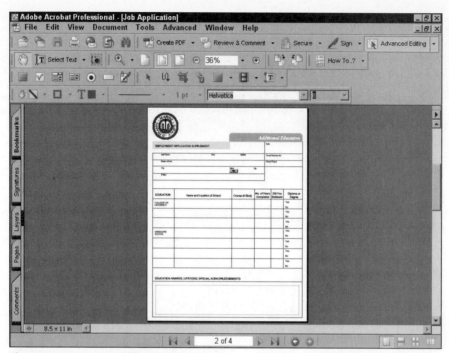

Figure 27-15: You can hide a page in the document that is not necessary for all users to fill in. To hide the page, create a page template.

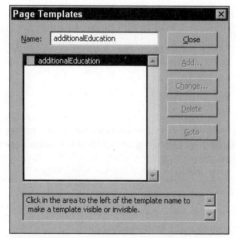

Figure 27-16: Hide page templates by clicking on the icon adjacent to the template name in the list window.

The template name is *additionalEducation* as defined in the first line of code. In the second line of code the instruction *a.spawn* spawns a page from a template. Lines 3 to 5 set the attributes for the spawned page. In line 3 the spawned page is placed after the last page in the template. You can change the value *this.numPages* to a page number and place the spawned page anywhere in the file. In line 5 any fields contained on the template page are renamed on the spawned page to provide unique field names, If the line is changed to: *bRename:false*, all fields are duplicated with duplicate field names. In line 5 the code instructs Acrobat to create a new page in the document. If you change the code to: *bOverlay:true*, the spawned page is superimposed over the last page in the file.

Lines 3 through 5 in the preceding script are default values. If you write the script as follows, Acrobat assumes using the defaults without specific notation for the attributes:

```
1. var a = this.getTemplate("additionalEducation");
2. a.spawn();
```

This two-line script works fine in Acrobat 6, however there are problems executing the script properly in earlier versions of Acrobat. Be certain to use the script with six lines of code and specify all attributes of the spawned page and you can be certain the script works in all versions of Acrobat.

You can also use an action type to instruct Acrobat to go to the newly created page. By default, spawned pages are created at the end of the PDF document. When pages are spawned, the page containing the button used to spawn a new page remains in view. To help a user navigate to the new spawned page, you can add another line of code to go to the new page. Add the following script after the last line of code used to spawn a page:

```
this.pageNum = this.numPages-1;
```

This line assesses the number of pages in the document, subtracts one from the number and opens the last page. JavaScript is zero based; therefore the –1 item subtracts one from the total number of pages. In JavaScript terms, page 1 is page 0.

Tip   If you have a document with many pages and need to spawn pages periodically as the user browses the document, use a Bookmark instead of adding buttons on all the pages. A single Bookmark takes up much less memory than button fields added to every page.

Creating Pop-up Menus

Application pop-up menus can be useful for nesting action items so you can save some space on a form. You might want to have a contents page where a user navigates via menu commands to many different files stored on a CD-ROM or network server. Rather than listing all files on a page or in Bookmarks you can categorize groups and nest them in submenus for a more economical use of space.

As an example, suppose you want to create links to other PDF documents. You have a small page and don't have enough room to display all the titles of the documents you want the user to access. By creating an application pop-up menu like the one shown in Figure 27-17, you can create categories, subcategories, and links to destinations that assist users in opening files in a relatively small section on a contents page.

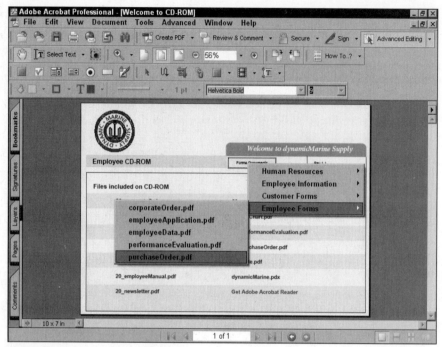

Figure 27-17: By adding application pop-up menus, you can create lists of destination documents in categorical groups.

Writing document-level JavaScripts

If you use JavaScript to open and close files, all destination files need to have a document-level JavaScript to make the open actions workable. In each file being addressed with a JavaScript, to open the file you need to add one line of code at the document level.

For each file you want to open from a pop-up menu, open each target document and choose Advanced ⇨ JavaScript ⇨ Document JavaScripts. In the JavaScript Functions dialog box type a name for the script in the field box at the top of the dialog box. Click on the Add button and the JavaScript Editor opens. Delete all the default text in the JavaScript Editor and type the following code:

```
this.disclosed = true;
```

Click OK in the JavaScript Editor to return to the JavaScript Functions dialog box as shown in Figure 27-18. Click Close and save the file. Repeat the steps for all files you want to open with a JavaScript.

If you don't add the aforementioned code to the document level, the files won't open with a JavaScript. Be certain to verify that all documents contain this one line of code at the document level.

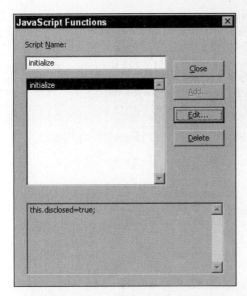

Figure 27-18: Opening secondary files with JavaScript requires you to add a Document JavaScript to each file. Type a name in the field box and click on the Add button. Write the necessary code in the JavaScript Editor and click OK to add the JavaScript function.

Creating a pop-up menu

After coding functions in the destination documents, create a button field on a form used as a contents page and add the following JavaScript:

```
1. var c = app.popUpMenu
2. (["Category 1", "1a.pdf", "1b.pdf"],
3. ["Category 2", "2a.pdf", "2b.pdf"],
4. ["Category 3", "3a.pdf", "3b.pdf"],
5. this.slave = app.openDoc (c), this);
```

The first line of code assigns the variable c to the `app.popUpMenu` method. In lines 2 to 4 are three categories. The category name is the first item in quote marks on each line. Following the category names are the filenames that open when the menu item is selected. Line 5 instructs Acrobat to open the selected file.

To create your own pop-up menus, change the category names to menu titles you want to use. Following each category, type the name of the respective document to open. Be certain to begin line 2 with an open parenthesis (and use a closed parenthesis) after the last line of code used to identify the category and filenames (line 4). Each line of code where the categories and filenames appear is contained within brackets.

Transposing Data

You may have a brochure or catalog in which a user can browse products and make decisions for placing orders. Typically the catalog is a larger file size and doesn't need to be sent back to a fulfillment department. The only item the fulfillment department needs is either the order data or an order page containing the specific items a user wants to order. In this scenario you have two different PDF documents. One document is used for the catalog and the other document is an order form.

As a user browses a catalog, he or she selects items to add to an order form or shopping cart document. When it comes time to place the order, the user needs to transfer data from the catalog to an order form. In Figure 27-19 a summary page within a catalog shows quantities and prices for an order.

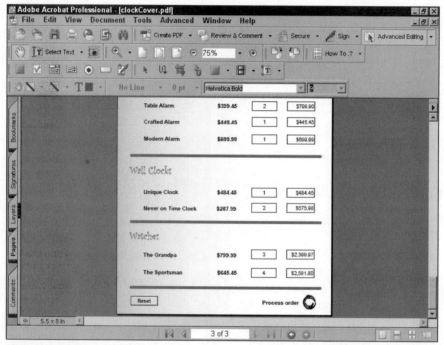

Figure 27-19: A summary page in a catalog contains order information. The data need to be transferred to an order form.

Figure 27-20 shows the lower half of an order form. The prices are fixed and the calculations are automatic as the quantity fields are completed. In this example the data that need to be transferred from the catalog are the Quantity fields. When an amount is added to a Quantity field, the respective total field in the same row has a math operation to multiply the Quantity times the Unit. The Unit fields all have default amounts defined in the Field Properties and the fields are marked as Read Only to protect the fields from being edited.

In this example I want to transpose the quantity data from the brochure document to the order form. From a button I need to instruct Acrobat to open the order form, loop through the data, and copy the data from the brochure to the order form. The following script performs the steps:

```
1. this.slave = app.openDoc("orderForm.pdf",this);
2.  this.bringToFront();
```

```
3. for (var i = 0; i < 7;i++) {
4.  var quantity = this.getField("qty."+i);
5.  var result = this.slave.getField("orderQty."+i);
6.  result.value = quantity.value;
7. }
8. slave.bringToFront();
```

Line 1 opens the order form. In line 2 the brochure document is brought to the front of the Document Pane. Lines 3 through 7 contain the loop, which gathers data from the `qty` fields and places the results in the destination (`slave`) document. After the loop halts, the slave document (order form) is brought to the front of the Document Pane.

As described earlier, you need the following document-level JavaScript in order to open the order form with JavaScript:

```
this.disclosed = true;
```

The scripts in this chapter are simplified to introduce you to writing JavaScript code. Try to practice by starting out with simple routines and then moving on to more complex scripts. Be certain to view the Acrobat JavaScript Scripting Reference contained in the Acrobat Help folder to learn more routines. JavaScript in Acrobat provides you with an infinite number of ways to help add automation and interactivity to all your PDF documents.

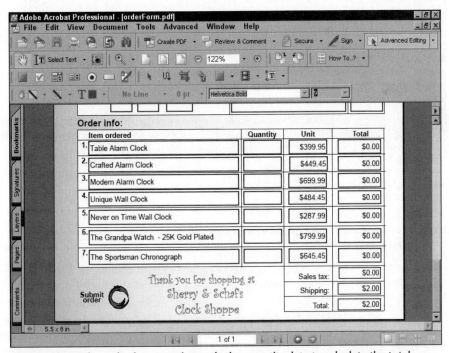

Figure 27-20: The order form requires only the quantity data to calculate the total invoice price.

Submitting E-mail Attachments

You may have a need to ask a user to fill out a form and return the populated form to you or another user. A user could fill out a form and attach it to an e-mail message like any other file. However, by using a little JavaScript you can help the user out by creating a button that automatically launches the default e-mail application and attaches the data to a message window when the user clicks on a button field. Depending on your need you can choose to send the complete PDF file or an FDF file. In order for a user to see the FDF data the PDF form is needed at the recipient end so the data can be imported. Conditions vary, so becoming familiar with both methods is a good idea.

The Submit a form action type enables you to submit documents and e-mail files, However, by using JavaScript you can also include as part of your script other items such as code that assesses fields for completion, response dialog boxes, and conditional statements.

Cross-Reference   The foregoing examples illustrate how to create e-mail attachments with JavaScripts for users of either the Acrobat Standard or Acrobat Professional product. To learn how to create submit buttons for Adobe Reader users, see Chapter 26.

Attaching PDF forms to e-mails

At the user end, the user can select the Send Mail tool in Acrobat or choose File ➪ Email and the current active PDF document is attached to an empty e-mail message ready for the user to type the message and send the e-mail. You can achieve the same effect by creating a button field and a JavaScript action on your form. By using a JavaScript you can check the form for empty fields before the button action is invoked. When you add a button, a user unfamiliar with the Acrobat tools or menu commands can easily send an e-mail attachment by clicking on the button you create on the form.

In this example I'll use a routine for assessing the viewer type and show you how to write a conditional statement. If the viewer type is not Adobe Reader, the routine executes a statement to attach a PDF document to an e-mail attachment.

```
1. if (typeof(app.viewerType)!="undefined")
2. if(app.viewerType == "Reader")
3. {
4.   var msg = "You must use Acrobat Standard or Acrobat Professional to
send the application back to us. To find out more information on
purchasing Adobe Acrobat Standard or Acrobat Professional visit:
http:www.adobe.com.";
5.   app.alert(msg);
   }
6. else
7.   {
8. this.mailDoc (true,{
9.   cTo: "management@company.com",
10.   cCc:"supervisor@company.com",
11.   bCc:"ceo@company.com",
12.   cSubject: "Employment Application Form"});

13.   }
```

In the preceding routine I start by examining the viewer version. If the user attempts to e-mail the file from Adobe Reader, an application alert dialog box opens, informing the user that Acrobat is needed to submit the form. The user is instructed where to acquire Acrobat Standard and Acrobat Professional to submit the form properly.

If the user's viewer is either Acrobat Standard or Acrobat Professional, the statement after else (line 7) executes. this.mailDoc instructs Acrobat to attach the active PDF document to an e-mail message. The three items in quotes begin with the recipient, the cc recipient, and the bcc recipient, respectively. The last item in quotes is the subject title for the e-mail message. If you want to eliminate a cc and a blind cc, the code in lines 10 and 11 would read as

```
8. this.mailDoc (true,{
9.   cTo: "management@company.com",
10:   cCc: "",
11:   bCc: "",
12. cSubject: "Employment Application Form"});
```

If you want to add multiple recipients, cc, or bcc recipients, just add a comma after the name of the recipient within the quote marks for the respective recipients.

When the user clicks on the button, the e-mail application launches with the active PDF file attached and the specified recipients placed in their respective locations, as shown in Figure 27-21.

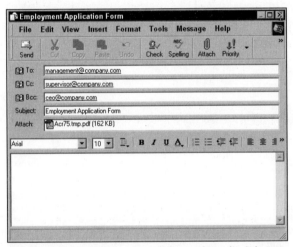

Figure 27-21: When the user clicks on the submit button, the default e-mail application is launched, the PDF file is attached, the recipients are designated, and the subject line is filled in.

Attaching FDF data to e-mails

In the example in the preceding section an e-mail attachment was used to submit an employee application form to several users. The entire PDF file was distributed to various parties. As a practical measure, submitting the entire form makes sense because some parties may not have the original PDF at hand. In other cases you may not need the original PDF document. For example, the employee application form is routed to the human resources department that screens all applications. The HR department certainly has the original PDF file and therefore only needs the data from the form that they import into an empty employment application form. In this regard, the company personnel need only receive the FDF data. Sending the data requires much less storage space and the file transfer is much faster, especially if the form is complex and contains many pages.

To send the data instead of the PDF file, you need to make one slight change in the JavaScript. Using the previous example, change the code in line 8 to:

```
8. this.mailForm {(true,
9.   cTo: "management@comany.com",
10.   cCc: "",
11.   bCc: "",
12. cSubject: "Employment Application Form"});
```

Suppose a user completes a form on a home computer or on the road on a laptop computer. Assume for a moment that the user has a different e-mail address for office and home or on the road. If you want to offer an option to enable the user to e-mail a copy of the FDF data to a second e-mail address you might want to ask for the address in a dialog box. The response from the dialog box can be placed in the cc line of the e-mail message. This way you can use a generic form suited for all users.

To send FDF data with a cc to an address specified from an application response dialog box, use a script as follows:

```
1. var cResponse = app.response({
2. cQuestion: "To copy yourself, enter your email address. Click cancel
to send data without sending a copy to yourself",
3. cTitle: "emailAddress", }); // title of the dialog box
4. {
5.   if ( cResponse == null)
6.   this.mailForm(true, "finance@company.com", "", "", "Purchase
Order");
7. else
8.   this.mailForm(true, "finance@company.com", cResponse, "", "Purchase
Order");
9. }
```

Note   The code in lines 6 and 7 are a simplified method for adding the To, CC, BCC, and Subject to the e-mail message. The results are the same as when using the code samples noted previously for sending a form or form data.

The beginning of the routine asks the question. Do you want to copy yourself? If not, the user clicks on the Cancel button in the response dialog box and the data are sent to the recipient (finance@company.com). If yes, the user types an address in a dialog box and clicks the OK button; the data from the response dialog box are posted in the cc line of the e-mail message.

Clicking on the OK button opens the dialog box shown in Figure 27-22.

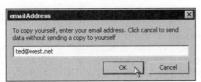

Figure 27-22: The e-mail address to send a copy of the FDF data to is supplied in a response dialog box.

After the user adds an e-mail address and clicks OK, the e-mail message window appears with the FDF data attached, and the cc line includes the address from the response dialog box as shown in Figure 27-23.

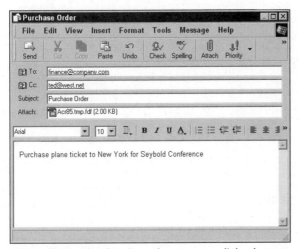

Figure 27-23: The data from the response dialog box are placed in the cc line of the e-mail message.

Summary

✦ One method for learning JavaScript is to examine forms with scripts. You can copy JavaScripts in the JavaScript Editor dialog box or copy form fields and links.

✦ JavaScripts are found in several places in PDF documents including fields, links, Bookmarks, Page Actions, document-level scripts, and Document Actions.

✦ The JavaScript Debugger lists all JavaScripts in a document. When learning how a form executes JavaScripts it's a good idea to examine all potential areas where scripts are written.

✦ Viewer types and viewer version alerts are used to inform users whether their Acrobat viewer is the correct version and type to complete a form.

✦ Sums of data in rows and columns are calculated with JavaScripts using loops to gather data through each pass in a loop.

✦ Document Actions are used to execute a JavaScript when a file opens, closes, or prints.

✦ Pages can be spawned in a document to create new pages from a template page. When pages are spawned, all fields, links, and JavaScripts on the new spawned pages are duplicated from the template page with new field names.

✦ Pop-up menus can save some space on a form where lists in nested menus are scripted to open documents.

✦ Data are transposed from one form to another with JavaScript. When opening secondary files with JavaScript, you need to add a script at the document level.

✦ Using JavaScripts to e-mail PDFs and data offers you more flexibility than using the Submit a form action type. With JavaScript you can open response dialog boxes, add conditional statements, and check a form for any blank fields.

✦   ✦   ✦

What's on the CD-ROM?

This appendix provides you with information on the contents of the CD that accompanies this book. For the latest and greatest information, please refer to the ReadMe file located at the root of the CD. Here is what you will find:

+ System Requirements

+ Using the CD with Windows

+ Using the CD with the Mac OS

+ What's on the CD-ROM

+ Troubleshooting

System Requirements

Make sure that your computer meets the minimum system requirements listed in this section. If your computer doesn't match up to most of these requirements, you may have a problem using the contents of the CD.

For Windows NT Workstation with Service Pak 6, Windows 2000 Professional with Service Pack 2, Windows XP Professional or Home edition, or Windows XP Tablet PC:

+ PC with a Pentium processor running at 100 MHz or faster

+ At least 128 MB of total RAM installed on your computer; for best performance, we recommend at least 256 MB

+ A CD-ROM drive

+ Acrobat 6 Standard or Professional

For Macintosh:

+ Mac OS computer with a G3 or faster processor running OS X (10.2.2 or greater).

+ At least 128 MB of total RAM installed on your computer; for best performance, we recommend at least 256 MB

+ Acrobat 6 Standard or Professional

Using the CD with Windows

To install the items from the CD to your hard drive, follow these steps:

1. Insert the CD into your computer's CD-ROM drive.

2. A window appears with the following options:

   Author: Opens a PDF document where you can navigate to pages describing the Acrobat PDF documents contained on the CD and those used in some of the chapter steps according to each chapter.

   Explore: Allows you to view the contents of the CD-ROM in its directory structure.

   eBook: Allows you to view an electronic version of the book (in PDF format).

   Links: Opens a hyperlinked page of Web sites.

   Exit: Closes the autorun window.

If you do not have autorun enabled or if the autorun window does not appear, perform the following steps to access the CD.

1. Click Start ⇨ Run.

2. In the dialog box that appears, type *d***:\setup.exe**, where *d* is the letter of your CD-ROM drive. This will bring up the autorun window described previously.

Choose the desired option from the menu. (See Step 2 in the preceding list for a description of these options.)

The folder titled *authorFiles* contains subfolders for some chapters where the PDF files are used in exercises respective to each chapter. Copy the entire folder with the subfolders to your hard drive or copy any Chapter subfolder when working on a respective chapter. Note: this step can bypass the preceding Install step if you want individual folders copied to your hard drive.

Using the CD with the Mac OS

To install the items from the CD to your hard drive, follow these steps:

1. Insert the CD into your CD-ROM drive.

2. Double-click the icon for the CD after it appears on the desktop.

Most programs come with installers; for those, simply open the program's folder on the CD and double-click the Install or Installer icon. If an installer decompresses a demo plug-in file, and the Acrobat plug-in is not installed in your Acrobat folder; copy the plug-in folder to the Adobe Acrobat Folder: Plug-ins folder.

Follow the same preceding steps for item 4 on Windows.

What's on the CD

The following sections provide a summary of the software and other materials you'll find on the CD.

Author-created materials

All author-created material from the book, including code listings and samples, are on the CD in the folder named *authorFiles*. Within this folder are files and folders related to many of the chapter steps and topics covered throughout the book. Most of the files in the folder are linked to a single PDF document. To ease your navigation through the files, open the *welcome. pdf* document contained in the *authorFiles* folder. Double click on the *welcome.pdf* document and the file opens in any Acrobat viewer. There are two pages in the document. The first page shown in Figure A-1 contains link buttons to the other PDF documents contained in the *authorFiles* folder.

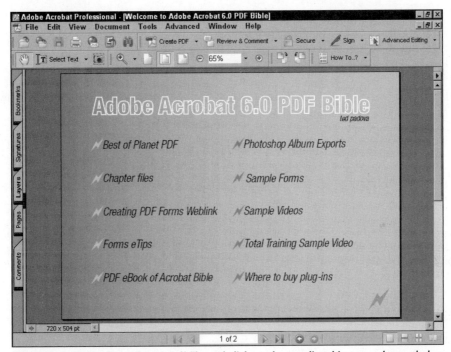

Figure A-1: Open the welcome.pdf file and click on the text listed in two columns below the title to open linked files.

Each of the text items listed in two columns below the page title is a link to either other documents or help information. The categories include:

✦ **Best of Planet PDF.** A PDF document developed by Planet PDF (www.planetpdf.com) covering milestone events over the past decade opens in full screen mode when you click on the text.

✦ **Chapter files.** Click on the text and a submenu opens where files are organized according to chapters. Many files you open from the submenu can be used to follow steps discussed in the respective chapter. Click on the *Chapter files* text and scroll through the chapters. The first submenu item is a description of what a file relates to and selecting the second submenu item opens a file. As shown in Figure A-2, Chapter 8 contains two topics. The topics include *Edit Text on Layers* and *Editing Rotated Text*. When you select the item listed in the third column, the respective fill opens. In Figure A-2, selecting *ttFlowchart.pdf* opens a file where you can edit text on different layers.

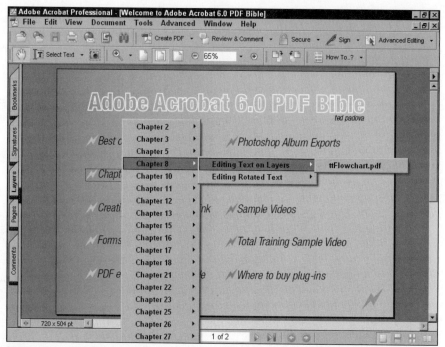

Figure A-2: Click on *Chapter files* and a submenu opens where a topic is listed. Select the item in the third column to open the respective PDF document.

✦ **Creating PDF Forms Weblink.** Click on this text to launch your Web browser and open a Web page on the John Wiley & Sons Web site, where my Creating Adobe Acrobat Forms book is listed.

✦ **Forms eTips.** An eBook containing many forms tips and JavaScripts is contained on the CD-ROM. Click on this text to open the eBook. For more information about this file, see the section "Bonus Material" later in this chapter.

✦ **PDF eBook of Acrobat Bible.** A PDF version of the book you are reading is available on the CD-ROM. Click on this text to open the electronic version of the Adobe Acrobat 6 PDF Bible. For more information on the eBook, see the section "eBook version of the Adobe Acrobat 6 PDF Bible" later in this chapter.

✦ **Photoshop Album Exports.** In Chapter 21 I cover multimedia and using Photoshop Album. Click on the text to open some sample files created in Photoshop Album.

✦ **Sample Forms.** Chapters 25 to 27 cover creating Acrobat PDF forms. For examining form samples and JavaScripts, look over the forms linked to the popup menu that opens when you click on the text.

✦ **Sample Videos.** When you roll over the text, a help message opens, informing you where sample video files are located. Use the sample videos to import in Acrobat PDFs as I discuss in Chapter 21.

✦ **Total Training Sample Video.** Roll over on the text to open another help message informing you where a sample video created by Total Training is located. The sample video is an excerpt from my new video series on Acrobat 6. For more information about this file, see the section "Total Training Video" later in this chapter.

✦ **Where to buy plug-ins.** Click on the text to open a URL link to the Planet PDF Store. From the Planet PDF Store Web page you can browse the catalog of available third party plug-ins that extend Acrobat features through the use of plug-ins.

The icon in the lower-right corner is a link to page two in the document. Click on the icon and page two opens, where you'll find Web links to sites offering information about Acrobat as shown in Figure A-3.

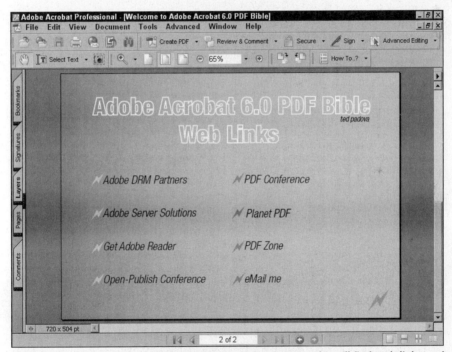

Figure A-3: Open page two in the welcome.pdf document and you'll find Web links to sites offering more information about Acrobat.

The links to Web sites found on page two of the welcome.pdf file include:

✦ **Adobe DRM Partners.** Click on the text to open Adobe's Web page where you can find links to third-party Web sites that offer signature handlers for securing PDF documents as I covered in Chapter 19.

- **Adobe Enterprise Solutions.** Click on the text to open Adobe's Web page where links to Adobe Server products are described. You'll find descriptions and information on server products as I discussed in Chapters 22 and 25.

- **Get Adobe Reader.** Click on the text to link to Adobe's Web site where Adobe Reader can be downloaded. Use this URL when adding buttons to your own Web site to help users find the Adobe Reader download page.

- **Open-Publish Conference.** Click on the text to open the Web site for Open-Publish Australia where an annual PDF conference is hosted.

- **PDF Conference.** The PDF Conference is held twice annually in the United States. Click on the text to find out more about the conference topics and locations.

- **Planet PDF.** Planet PDF hosts many interesting articles, forums, and distributes a wealth of information on Acrobat and PDFs. Click on the text to open the Planet PDF home page.

- **PDF Zone.** Another great site for Acrobat and PDF information, tips, techniques, and PDF usage is found at PDF Zone. Click on the link to open the PDF Zone Web site.

- **email me.** If you have questions or comments and want to get hold of me, click on the text and your default email application opens with my email address added to the message. Type a message and send it to me for any questions you may have regarding Acrobat or my book.

Total Training Video

Sample video files are located in the TotalTraining folder. You can view the sample videos and learn some techniques used in Acrobat 6. For a full set of video training materials, log on to www.totaltraining.com.

Bonus Material

An eBook sold at content provider Web sites during the Acrobat 5 life cycle is contained on the CD-ROM. In the authorFiles folder you'll find the eBook *acrobat_eTips.pdf*. The eBook was written for learning forms authoring and JavaScripting in Acrobat 5. However, most of the scripts contained in the eBook are applicable to Acrobat 6. All the fields and content in the eBook are *open* and accessible. You can examine and copy/paste JavaScript routines from the eBook into your own PDF files.

eBook version of Adobe Acrobat 6 PDF Bible

The complete text of this book is on the CD in Adobe's Portable Document Format (PDF). You can read and search through the file with the Adobe Acrobat Reader (also included on the CD). If you wish to perform the exercises and use the PDFs contained in the *Author* folder, you'll need either Acrobat Standard or Acrobat Professional.

The eBook version of the Adobe Acrobat 6 PDF Bible does not have an index file created from the eBook and copied to the CD-ROM. You can create your own index file by following the description for creating index files in Chapter 4. Note: Acrobat Professional is needed to create the index file.

Troubleshooting

If you have difficulty installing or using any of the materials on the companion CD, try the following solutions:

- ✦ **Turn off any anti-virus software that you may have running.** Installers sometimes mimic virus activity and can make your computer incorrectly believe that it is being infected by a virus. (Be sure to turn the anti-virus software back on later.)

- ✦ **Close all running programs.** The more programs you're running, the less memory is available to other programs. Installers also typically update files and programs; if you keep other programs running, installation may not work properly.

- ✦ **Reference the ReadMe:** Please refer to the ReadMe file located at the root of the CD-ROM for the latest product information at the time of publication.

If you still have trouble with the CD-ROM, please call the Wiley Product Technical Support phone number: (800) 762-2974. Outside the United States, call 1(317) 572-3994. You can also contact Wiley Product Technical Support through the internet at: `http://www.wiley.com/techsupport`. Wiley Publishing will provide technical support only for installation and other general quality control items; for technical support on the applications themselves, consult the program's vendor or author.

To place additional orders or to request information about other Wiley products, please call (800) 225-5945.

If all else fails, send me an email at ted@west.net.

✦   ✦   ✦

Keyboard Shortcuts

Keyboard shortcuts help you work quickly and efficiently in any Acrobat viewer. The number of keyboard shortcuts for Acrobat Standard and Acrobat Professional is extensive, as evidenced by the pages in this appendix. Committing all the shortcuts to memory is certainly not necessary, but learning the most frequently used keyboard shortcuts can help you speed through your editing sessions. Use this appendix as a reference when you work in Acrobat, and try to remember those shortcuts for editing tasks you use most often.

Basic Commands

Action	Windows	Macintosh
Close	Ctrl+W	⌘+W
Close all open documents	Ctrl+Alt+W	⌘+Option+W
Close dialog box (Cancel)	Esc	ESC or ⌘+. (period)
Compress PDF file size	Ctrl+Shift+C	⌘+Shift+C
Create PDF from file	Ctrl+N	⌘+N
Open	Ctrl+O	⌘+O
Open Context Menu	Right-click or Shift+F10	Control+click
Open Document properties dialog box	Ctrl+D	⌘+D
Open Help document	F1	F1
Open/Close How To menu	F4	F4
Open Preferences dialog box	Ctrl+K	⌘+K
Open Web page	Ctrl+Shift+O	⌘+Shift+O
Print Setup	Ctrl+Shift+P	⌘+Shift+P
Print	Ctrl+P	⌘+P
Print with comments	Ctrl+T	⌘+T
PrintMe Internet Printing	alt+Ctrl+P	⌘+Option+P
Quit	Ctrl+Q	⌘+Q
Save	Ctrl+S	⌘+S
Save As	Ctrl+Shift+S	⌘+Shift+S
Spell Checker	F7	F7
Undo	Ctrl+Z	⌘+Z

Accessing Tools

Action	Windows	Macintosh
Article tool	A	A
Attachment tool	J	J
Cycle through Attachment tools (when an Attachment tool is active)	Shift+J	Shift+J
Form tool	F	F
Cycle through Form tools	Shift+F	Shift+F
Graphics Markup tool	U	U
Cycle through Graphics Markup tools (when a Graphic Markup tool is active)	Shift+U	Shift+U
Snapshot tool	G	G
Hand tool	H	H
Hand tool temporary select (when another tool is active)	Spacebar	Spacebar
Link tool	L	L
Movie tool	M	M
Notes tool	S	S
Cycle through Note tools (when a Note tool is active)	Shift+S	Shift+S
Pencil tool	N	N
Cycle through Comment tools	Shift+N	Shift+N
Select Object tool	O	O
Sound tool	Shift+M	Shift+M
Highlight Text too	U	U
Cycle through Highlight tools		
Select Text tool	V	V
Cycle through Selection tools	Shift+V	Shift+V
TouchUp Text tool	T	T
Cycle through TouchUp tools	Shift+T	Shift+T
Zoom In tool	Z	Z
Zoom Out tool	Shift+Z	Shift+Z

Editing Tools

Action	Windows	Macintosh
Cut	Ctrl+X	⌘+X
Copy	Ctrl+C	⌘+C
Create Bookmark	Ctrl+B	⌘+B
Delete Pages	Ctrl+Shift+D	⌘+Shift+D
Deselect All	Ctrl+Shift+A	⌘+Shift+A
Insert Pages	Ctrl+Shift+I	⌘+Shift+I
JavaScript Debugger (Console)	Ctrl+J	⌘+J
Paste	Ctrl+V	⌘+V
Rotate Clockwise	Ctrl+Shift++ (plus)	⌘+Shift++ (plus)
Rotate Counterclockwise	Ctrl+Shift+− (minus)	⌘+Shift+− (minus)
Rotate Pages	Ctrl+Shift+R	⌘+R
Select All	Ctrl+A	⌘+A
Crop Pages	Ctrl+Shift+T	

Search Tools

Action	Windows	Macintosh
Find	Ctrl+F	⌘+F
Find Again	Ctrl+G or F3	⌘+G
Query (Search)	Ctrl+Shift+F	⌘+Shift+F
Find Again going Backwards	Ctrl+Shift+G	⌘+Shift+G
Select Indexes	Ctrl+Shift+X	⌘+Shift+X
Next Search Result (Document)	Ctrl+]	⌘+Shift+]
Previous Search Result (Document)	Ctrl+[	⌘+Shift+[
Word Assistant	Ctrl+Shift+W	⌘+Shift+W

Viewing and Navigation Tools

Action	Windows	Macintosh
Accessibility Quick Check	Ctrl+Alt+Q	⌘+Option+Q
Actual Size	Ctrl+1	⌘+1
Auto Scrolling	Ctrl+Alt+A	⌘+Option+A
Cascade Windows	Ctrl+Shift+J	⌘+Shift+J
Display Restrictions and Security	Ctrl+Alt+S	⌘+Option+S
Grid Show/Hide	Ctrl+U	⌘+U
Grid Snap To	Ctrl+Shift+U	⌘+Shift+U
First Page	Home or Ctrl+Shift+Page Up	Home or Ctrl+Shift+Page Up
Fit Page in Document Pane	Ctrl+0	⌘+0
Fit Width	Ctrl+2	⌘+2
Fit Visible	Ctrl+3	⌘+3
Full Screen Show	Ctrl+L	⌘+L
Full Screen Hide/Off	Esc or Ctrl+L	Esc or ⌘+L
Go to Page	Alt+Ctrl+N	⌘+N
Last Page	End or Ctrl+Shift+Page Down	End or Control+Shift+Page Down
Move Focus to Menus	F10, Arrow Keys	
Move Focus to Toolbar	Alt, Ctrl+Tab	
Navigation Pane/Document Pane Toggle View	F6 (just F6)	Shift+F6
Next Document	Alt+Shift+Right Arrow	⌘+Shift+Right Arrow
Next Document	Alt+Shift+Right Arrow	⌘+Shift+Right Arrow
Next Floating Window	Alt+F6	
Next Field	Tab	Tab
Next Page	Page Down or Right Arrow	Page Down or Right Arrow
Next Tab in Navigation Pane	Ctrl+Tab	⌘+Tab
Next View	Alt+Right Arrow	⌘+Right Arrow
Next Window	Ctrl+F6	
Overprint Preview	Ctrl+Alt+Shift+Y	⌘+Option+Shift+Y
Previous Document	Alt+Shift+Left Arrow	⌘+Shift+Left Arrow
Previous Field	Shift+Tab	Shift+Tab
Previous Page	Page Up or Left Arrow	Page Up or Left Arrow
Previous View	Alt+Left Arrow	⌘+Left Arrow

Action	*Windows*	*Macintosh*
Proof Colors	Ctrl+Y	⌘+Y
Reflow Text	Ctrl+4	⌘+4
Rulers Show/Hide	Ctrl+R	⌘+R
Scroll Up	Up Arrow	Up Arrow
Scroll Down	Down Arrow	Down Arrow
Show/Hide Pages Tab (when Pages tab is selected)	F6	F6
Show/Hide Bookmarks – by default	F6	F6
Show/Hide Toolbars	F8	F8
Show/Hide Menu Bar	F9	F9
Show/Hide Navigation Pane	F6	F6
Split Vertical	Shift+F12	Shift+F12
Split Off	Shift+F12	Shift+F12
Tile Horizontally	Ctrl+Shift+K	⌘+Shift+K
Tile Vertically	Ctrl+Shift+L	⌘+Shift+L
Toggle Toolbars	Ctrl+Tab	
Use Local Fonts	Ctrl+Shift+Y	⌘+Shift+Y
Zoom In	Ctrl++ (plus)	⌘++ (plus)
Zoom Out	Ctrl+− (minus)	⌘+− (minus)
Zoom To	Ctrl+M	⌘+M
Zoom In temporary access to Zoom In tool	Ctrl+Spacebar	⌘+Spacebar
Zoom Out temporary access to Zoom Out tool	Ctrl+Alt+Spacebar	⌘+Option+Spacebar

Index

Continued

Continued

It's everybody's PDF™

He might not know it yet, but it's his PDF too...

Finally, a software company that offers affordable yet flexible PDF solutions to meet every customer's needs. Using activePDF™ to automate the PDF creation process eliminates the need for end-user intervention so your employees can concentrate on what they do best. What's more, hundreds of documents can be converted in a fraction of the time it takes a user to manually generate one PDF!

Licensed per server, activePDF supports conversion to PDF from over 300 different file formats. Users can merge, stitch, stamp, secure, form-fill PDF and more, all at a fraction of the cost of comparable solutions. Download your free trial version today!

Mention the Acrobat PDF Bible and receive a 25% discount off your purchase of activePDF Toolkit Standard or Professional

activePDF
Leading the iPaper Revolution

http://www.activePDF.com - ☎ (866) GoTo PDF

Our Planet has
unlimited natural resources.

If you're a PDF user, and haven't yet visited us, what planet are you on? Planet PDF provides the perfect atmosphere for PDF Users from all walks of life. From developers and designers, to beginners, there's something here for you.

Planet PDF Store is our online software store, featuring an extensive range of the essential tools for creating, editing and delivering PDF files. All products are available for immediate purchase and download. Visit www.planetpdf.com and you'll discover a whole world of PDF.

Planet PDF

Wiley Publishing, Inc.
End-User License Agreement

5. Limited Warranty.

(a) WPI warrants that the Software and Software Media are free from defects in materials and workmanship under normal use for a period of sixty (60) days from the date of purchase of this Book. If WPI receives notification within the warranty period of defects in materials or workmanship, WPI will replace the defective Software Media.

(b) WPI AND THE AUTHOR OF THE BOOK DISCLAIM ALL OTHER WARRANTIES, EXPRESS OR IMPLIED, INCLUDING WITHOUT LIMITATION IMPLIED WARRANTIES OF MERCHANTABILITY AND FITNESS FOR A PARTICULAR PURPOSE, WITH RESPECT TO THE SOFTWARE, THE PROGRAMS, THE SOURCE CODE CONTAINED THEREIN, AND/OR THE TECHNIQUES DESCRIBED IN THIS BOOK. WPI DOES NOT WARRANT THAT THE FUNCTIONS CONTAINED IN THE SOFTWARE WILL MEET YOUR REQUIREMENTS OR THAT THE OPERATION OF THE SOFTWARE WILL BE ERROR FREE.

(c) This limited warranty gives you specific legal rights, and you may have other rights that vary from jurisdiction to jurisdiction.

6. Remedies.

(a) WPI's entire liability and your exclusive remedy for defects in materials and workmanship shall be limited to replacement of the Software Media, which may be returned to WPI with a copy of your receipt at the following address: Software Media Fulfillment Department, Attn.: Adobe Acrobat 6 PDF Bible, Wiley Publishing, Inc., 10475 Crosspoint Blvd., Indianapolis, IN 46256, or call 1-800-762-2974. Please allow four to six weeks for delivery. This Limited Warranty is void if failure of the Software Media has resulted from accident, abuse, or misapplication. Any replacement Software Media will be warranted for the remainder of the original warranty period or thirty (30) days, whichever is longer.

(b) In no event shall WPI or the author be liable for any damages whatsoever (including without limitation damages for loss of business profits, business interruption, loss of business information, or any other pecuniary loss) arising from the use of or inability to use the Book or the Software, even if WPI has been advised of the possibility of such damages.

(c) Because some jurisdictions do not allow the exclusion or limitation of liability for consequential or incidental damages, the above limitation or exclusion may not apply to you.

7. U.S. Government Restricted Rights.
Use, duplication, or disclosure of the Software for or on behalf of the United States of America, its agencies and/or instrumentalities "U.S. Government" is subject to restrictions as stated in paragraph (c)(1)(ii) of the Rights in Technical Data and Computer Software clause of DFARS 252.227-7013, or subparagraphs (c) (1) and (2) of the Commercial Computer Software - Restricted Rights clause at FAR 52.227-19, and in similar clauses in the NASA FAR supplement, as applicable.

8. General.
This Agreement constitutes the entire understanding of the parties and revokes and supersedes all prior agreements, oral or written, between them and may not be modified or amended except in a writing signed by both parties hereto that specifically refers to this Agreement. This Agreement shall take precedence over any other documents that may be in conflict herewith. If any one or more provisions contained in this Agreement are held by any court or tribunal to be invalid, illegal, or otherwise unenforceable, each and every other provision shall remain in full force and effect.